MOON

VANCOUVER & CANADIAN ROCKIES

Road Trip

CAROLYN B. HELLER

VANCOUVER AND CANADIAN ROCKIES ROAD TRIP

Quesnel

97

Williams Lake

20

97

93 Mile

24

Tête Jaune Cache

Valemount

16

Kamloops to the B.C. Rocki

Little Fort

5

BRITISH COLUMBIA

Shus L.

99

Cache Creek

Lillooet

KAMLOOPS

Canoe

12

97

Whistler and the Sea-to-Sky Highway

Mount Currie

WHISTLER

Lytton

Merritt

5

5A

Vernon

The Okanag

KELO

Saltery Bay

Egmont

99

Squamish

5

5A

97C

Naramat

Pencticto

Okanag Falls

97

Oliver

Horseshoe Bay

Nanaimo

Vancouver

VANCOUVER

Hope

Princeton

3

3

OSOYOOS

CANADA

UNITED STATES

Manning Park

Lake Cowichan

Bellingham

97

Port Renfrew

Mill Bay

Sidney

Victoria and Vancouver Island

VICTORIA

20

WASHINGTON

97

Beecher Bay

CONTENTS

DISCOVER
Vancouver & the Canadian Rockies

Snowy peaks, rushing rivers, and vineyard-lined valleys. Elaborate totem poles rising from the rainforest. Waterfront cities buzzing with outdoor cafés. Whales breaching and seals sunning just offshore. Clichés? Perhaps. But in Canada's most naturally spectacular region, these clichés are true. Stretching from Vancouver to the Rockies, western Canada is tailor-made for a road trip.

In Vancouver, an active city bordering the mountains and the sea, begin your trip by strolling or cycling through a 1,000-acre (400-ha) rainforest park and exploring diverse cultures, from the original indigenous inhabitants to modern-day communities that reflect the city's position on the Pacific Rim.

Across the Strait of Georgia on Vancouver Island, Victoria retains its British roots as it has morphed into a contemporary city. It's now known as much for its locally produced wine, beer, and spirits as for its tradition of afternoon tea. Beyond Victoria, opportunities abound for exploring Vancouver Island's forests, waterways, and dramatic coastal regions.

Back on the mainland, the Sea-to-Sky Highway is one of Canada's most beautiful short drives, winding along the coast between Vancouver and Whistler. North America's largest winter sports mecca, Whistler is busy in spring, summer, and fall, too, with hikers, cyclists, and other adventurers exploring the peaks and lakes.

Travel east from Vancouver to the sunny Okanagan Valley, with its string of freshwater lakes, orchards, and Canada's only desert—and more than 200 wineries lining its back roads.

From the Okanagan, head to the Rocky Mountains. The Trans-Canada Highway passes through several of British Columbia's mountain national parks, including Mount Revelstoke, Glacier, Yoho, and Kootenay, each more dramatic than the last.

Across the provincial border in Alberta are the marquee destinations of any western Canada road trip: Banff, Lake Louise, and Jasper. The region's best scenic drive

takes you along the Icefields Parkway, with its incredibly blue lakes and the largest area of glacial ice in the Canadian Rockies.

Once you've had your fill of hiking, rafting, and savoring the mountain vistas, continue on to the gateway city of Calgary, which not only hosts Canada's biggest annual cowboy party but also offers distinctive museums and a pretty riverfront promenade. Or follow the southern route back toward Vancouver, exploring the Kootenays' funky mountain towns and detouring along B.C.'s Hot Springs Highway.

From the ocean to the mountains, there's plenty to experience, taste, and enjoy. Let's hit the road.

PLANNING YOUR TRIP

Where to Go

Vancouver

The rainforest meets the city in Vancouver, where massive **Stanley Park** and forests of glass-and-steel skyscrapers populate the downtown peninsula. The North Shore mountains overlook the city skyline, while the sea hugs the city, with sandy beaches steps from urban hotels. Yet this outdoor-oriented metropolis has plenty of culture as well, reflecting its First Nations heritage (the totem poles at the **Museum of Anthropology** are a must-see) and its contemporary Pacific Rim society. **Granville Island, Gastown,** and **Kitsilano** draw food-lovers to their locally focused restaurants, while the suburb of **Richmond** has some of the best Chinese food outside China. With its well-connected international airport and location just north of the U.S. border, 145 miles (230 km) from Seattle, Vancouver is a convenient starting point for trips along the British Columbia coast and east to the Canadian Rockies.

Victoria and Vancouver Island

Across the Strait of Georgia at the southern tip of Vancouver Island, British Columbia's waterfront capital city of **Victoria** retains elements of its British heritage—visiting the world-class **Butchart Gardens** and taking afternoon tea at the grand **Fairmont Empress** are still beloved traditions for visitors—even as this increasingly cosmopolitan community booms with new restaurants, craft breweries, and cocktail bars. Elsewhere on the island, you can travel by boat to remote **hot springs,** take a **bear-watching tour,** or watch the waves crash along the Pacific coast.

Whistler and the Sea-to-Sky Highway

One of western Canada's most spectacular short drives, the **Sea-to-Sky Highway** connects Vancouver to the resort town of **Whistler.** Known for **winter sports,** Whistler has plenty to do in warmer weather, too, from riding the **gondolas** into the mountains, to **hiking, cycling,** and **canoeing,** to exploring the region's **indigenous heritage.**

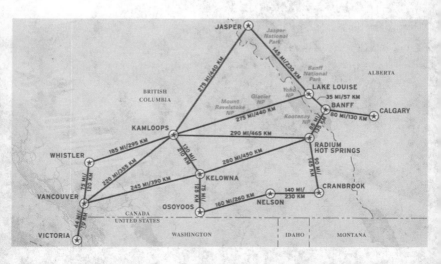

Clockwise from top left: hiking on Whistler Mountain; finding a quiet moment at Lake Louise; Victoria's Inner Harbour.

The Rockies by Train

This is a road-trip guide, of course, but western Canada, and particularly the Canadian Rockies region, is a fantastic destination to explore by train. So whether you combine road and rail travel, or simply head off on a rail-based holiday, here's where and how to explore the Rockies by train.

Two major rail carriers serve the Canadian Rockies region: **VIA Rail** (514/989-2626 or 888/842-7245, www.viarail.ca), which is Canada's national rail carrier, and the **Rocky Mountaineer** (604/606-7245 or 877/460-3200, www.rockymountaineer.com), a private rail tour company.

VIA Rail's flagship route, *The Canadian,* can take you 2,775 miles (4,466 km) across the western two-thirds of the country, traveling between Toronto and Vancouver, with stops in Winnipeg (Manitoba), Saskatoon (Saskatchewan), Edmonton and Jasper (Alberta), and Kamloops (British Columbia) on its way to the coast. Of course, you don't have to make this entire four-night, three-day journey; you can ride *The Canadian* between Vancouver and Jasper in the Canadian Rockies, which covers some of the rail route's most scenic terrain.

The Rocky Mountaineer offers several different Canadian Rockies rail trips, traveling between Vancouver, Banff, Lake Louise, Jasper, and Calgary. You can make a round-trip loop from the coast to the Rockies and back, or book a one-way journey through the Rockies between Vancouver and Calgary. Another route starts in Seattle and stops in Vancouver before continuing to the Rockies. You can book a Rocky Mountaineer holiday that covers rail fare and accommodations only or packages that include everything from gondola rides to helicopter tours, as well as all your transportation and accommodations. Check the website to review the tour options.

Kamloops to the B.C. Rockies

As you drive east from Vancouver and cross the Coast Mountains, you leave behind the green coastal rainforest and wind through the desert-like hills of British Columbia's interior. Here, the sunny city of **Kamloops** makes a convenient stopover point midway between Vancouver and the Rockies, with several small museums and an emerging wine industry. Continue east on the Trans-Canada Highway to a trio of national parks, **Mount Revelstoke, Glacier,** and **Yoho,** where you can hike, paddle the glacier-fed lakes, or enjoy the mountain scenery. Base yourself in towns like **Revelstoke** or **Golden** (only Yoho National Park has accommodations) and enjoy their cafés, restaurants, and comfortable lodgings.

Banff and Lake Louise

Banff National Park is a highlight of any Canadian Rockies road trip, with dramatic mountain peaks and natural mineral pools, the sparkling blue **Lake Louise,** and more than 1,000 miles (1,600 km) of hiking paths. Within the boundaries of Canada's first national park, the town of **Banff** bustles with restaurants, museums, and shops, and though its sidewalks can feel as jammed as New York City's during the busy summer season, there's plenty of space out on the trails.

Jasper

The **Icefields Parkway** between Lake Louise and **Jasper** is one of Canada's great drives, where you can stop at the **Columbia Icefield** to walk on a glacier or hike among the glacier-capped peaks. Without Banff's crowds, **Jasper National Park** is equally beautiful, and as the largest park in the Canadian Rockies, there's ample room to explore its lakes, canyons, and mountains.

The Kootenays

The Kootenays region extends across

southeastern British Columbia, between the Rocky Mountains and the Okanagan Valley. Here, you can explore the diverse landscape of **Kootenay National Park,** follow the **Hot Springs Highway** to several natural mineral pools, hang out in funky mountain towns like **Fernie, Nelson,** and **Rossland,** or learn more about the First Nations who've lived in the area for more than 10,000 years. Delve into the history of other communities, too, including the Japanese Canadians who were sent to **internment camps** across B.C. during World War II, and the Russian pacifists known as the **Doukhobors** who settled here in the early 20th century.

The Okanagan

More than 200 **wineries** hug the lakeshores and rocky hills of the sunny Okanagan Valley in central B.C., often called the "Napa of the North." This agricultural region stretches from **Osoyoos,** in the desert-like lands near the U.S. border, north to **Kelowna,** the area's largest city. If you love wine, or enjoy being outdoors along some of Canada's warmest **lakes,** stop in the Okanagan as you drive between Vancouver and the Rocky Mountains.

Calgary

Canada's fourth-largest city has the closest airport to the Canadian Rockies, so you can start or end your Rocky Mountain travels here. Known for the annual **Calgary Stampede,** Calgary has the excellent **Glenbow Museum** of western Canadian history, art, and culture; **Heritage Park Historical Village,** the country's largest living history village; and the excellent **National Music Centre.** The city's restaurants regularly rank among the country's top dining spots. A short drive from Calgary, the **Canadian Badlands** has a completely different geological profile, with its unusual hoodoo rock formations and deep rocky canyons.

Canadian Badlands

Before You Go

Seasons

High season in Vancouver and the Canadian Rockies runs May-October, when most attractions and roads are open and the weather is generally warm and sunny. **July and August** are the region's peak travel months, with the sunny, temperate conditions balancing out the big crowds and high prices.

Ask the locals about the best time to visit the Canadian Rockies, though, and everyone will say **September.** The summer crowds begin to abate, the weather is still mild, and the trees take on their fall colors. Temperatures can remain pleasant into October, though the nights get colder, and snow frequently begins in late October or early November.

While the long days and fewer tourists make **May and June** a reasonable alternative for a Rockies trip, prepare for more rain than in the summer. You might have occasional damp days on the coast, but the Rockies can be hit with a "June monsoon," when the rain turns heavy. These showers bring spring flowers, so pack a raincoat and get outdoors anyway.

Winter is mild in Vancouver and Victoria; rain is common November-March, but snow is unusual. As soon as you rise above coastal elevations, winter travelers should prepare for heavy snow. It snows *a lot* in the mountains of B.C. and in the Canadian Rockies, when severe weather can close highway mountain passes. Always check the forecast before you hit the road.

Reservations

If you're traveling in the summer, especially in July and August, book your **hotel reservations** in advance, particularly in Banff, Jasper, and Vancouver. Many of the national park campgrounds fill up early, so **reserving a campsite** for summer or holiday travel is also a smart idea. Car reservations are recommended on **B.C. Ferries** in the summer as well.

Visitors to **Yoho National Park** should note that two park activities require advance reservations and careful attention to the reservations procedure and deadlines: visiting **Lake O'Hara** and touring the **Burgess Shale** fossil beds. Refer to the Yoho National Park section for specifics.

HIT THE ROAD

The Classic 15-Day Vancouver-Rockies Loop

On a **two-week drive,** you can roadtrip from Vancouver to the Canadian Rockies and back, taking in many of western Canada's top attractions. See Vancouver's sights, then day-trip by ferry to Victoria, British Columbia's capital. Take another day to get outdoors in the mountains at Whistler. Get ready for the real mountains, though, as you head east, stopping in Mount Revelstoke, Glacier, and Yoho National Parks as you enter the Canadian Rockies. In Alberta, you'll visit Lake Louise, follow the scenic Icefields Parkway to Jasper, then return south for a couple of days outdoors in Banff National Park. From there, travel through B.C.'s Kootenays region, with stops in the fun towns of Fernie and Nelson, and go wine-tasting in the Okanagan Valley, on your way back to Vancouver and the coast.

You could also start and end the trip in Calgary, doing the loop in reverse.

Days 1-2
VANCOUVER
Begin your tour in Vancouver, circling the scenic Seawall in **Stanley Park,** snacking on **Granville Island,** and getting an introduction to indigenous culture at the **Museum of Anthropology.** Explore **Chinatown** in the peaceful **Dr. Sun Yat-Sen Classical Chinese Garden** and in the neighborhood's growing number of hip restaurants, or head to the North Shore to hike and enjoy the views from **Grouse Mountain.** With several beaches right downtown, wrap up your day with a sunset stroll along the sand.

Day 3
VICTORIA
Vancouver to Victoria (round-trip)
95 mi (150 km)
6 hrs, including ferries
Make a day trip to Vancouver Island today for a quick visit to **Victoria.** From Vancouver, drive south on **Highway 99** to catch an early-morning **B.C. Ferry** from **Tsawwassen;** it's a 90-minute trip to **Swartz Bay.** When you leave the ferry terminal, follow Highway 17A to the **Butchart Gardens** to wander among the floral displays.

From the gardens, take Keating Cross Road east to **Highway 17** toward downtown Victoria. Park your car, then tour the **Inner Harbour,** have afternoon tea at the stately **Fairmont Empress,** and visit the **Royal British Columbia Museum.** Have a drink in one of the city's **craft breweries** and dinner in a contemporary bistro, before returning to Swartz Bay for the ferry back to Vancouver.

Day 4
WHISTLER
Vancouver to Whistler
75 mi (120 km)
2 hrs
Head north from Vancouver to pick up the **Sea-to-Sky Highway** (Hwy. 99), a scenic route between the mountains and the ocean that leads to the resort town of **Whistler.** Consider stopping in **Squamish** for a ride up the **Sea-to-Sky Gondola;** either have lunch with a view from the gondola summit or continue on to Whistler. Visit the excellent **Audain Art Museum,** learn more about local First Nations communities at the **Squamish Lil'wat Cultural Centre,** then get outdoors, whether you choose to ride the **PEAK 2 PEAK Gondola,** climb the **Via Ferrata,** go **zip-lining,** or simply **take a hike.**

Best Scenic Drives

along the Icefields Parkway

Road-tripping in western Canada is one big scenic drive, so it's hard to pick just a few favorite routes. But here are some of the most spectacular sections of road in British Columbia and Alberta.

♦ **Sea-to-Sky Highway:** Highway 99 from Vancouver to Whistler winds between the mountains and the ocean, with views of offshore islands and snow-topped peaks around every bend. Stop at roadside kiosks to learn more about local First Nations communities (page 150).

♦ **Bow Valley Parkway, Banff National Park:** With numerous lookout points and stops for hikes, this 30-mile (48-km) drive is an ever-so-scenic alternative to Highway 1 between Banff and Lake Louise (page 239).

♦ **Icefields Parkway:** Take your time on this 143-mile (230-km) route between Lake Louise and Jasper, as you pass turquoise lakes, rushing waterfalls, and countless glacier-topped peaks. It's one of Canada's most spectacular drives (page 283).

♦ **Highway 3A along Kootenay Lake:** An alternate route between Nelson and the East Kootenays region, Highway 3A winds along the shores of Kootenay Lake and past one of B.C.'s quirkiest attractions: a house built from more than 500,000 empty bottles of embalming fluid (page 346).

Day 5
REVELSTOKE
Whistler to Revelstoke
315 mi (505 km)
6.5 hrs

Today is a long driving day as you set out for the mountains of eastern British Columbia. Leave Whistler on **Highway 99** north to **Highway 1** east; if you start early, you can reach **Kamloops** for lunch. Try to arrive at **Mount Revelstoke National Park** in time to zigzag up the **Meadows in the Sky Parkway** and take at least a short hike, before settling into the town of **Revelstoke** for dinner and a well-deserved rest.

Best Hikes

♦ **High Note Trail, Whistler:** Accessed from the top of the Peak Express chair, this trail follows the alpine ridges, with great views of the Black Tusk peak (page 159).

♦ **Eva Lake Trail, Mount Revelstoke National Park:** Starting from the summit of the Meadows in the Sky Parkway, this 8.5-mile (14-km) round-trip route takes you through wildflower meadows and boulder fields to a lovely alpine lake (page 195).

♦ **Iceline Trail, Yoho National Park:** If you're up for an all-day adventure, this challenging 13-mile (21-km) round-trip trail begins near Takakkaw Falls and rewards hikers with spectacular glacier vistas (page 220).

♦ **Johnston Canyon, Banff National Park:** This easy trail along the cantilevered walkways through this rock canyon is among Banff's most dramatic; get an early start to beat the crowds (page 239).

♦ **Plain of Six Glaciers Trail, Lake Louise:** This 6.6-mile (10.6-km) round-trip hike leads from the lakeshore up toward glacier-capped mountains en route to a historic teahouse, where you can stop for lunch or a sweet—or both (page 266).

♦ **Wilcox Pass, Jasper National Park:** What's the payoff for this moderate climb along the Icefields Parkway? Impressive views of the mountains and glaciers of the Columbia Icefield (page 284).

♦ **Maligne Canyon, Jasper National Park:** Hike the trails, over the bridges, and along the river through this deep limestone gorge, one of Jasper's most scenic spots (page 291).

Day 6
GOLDEN AND YOHO NATIONAL PARK
Revelstoke to Field
125 mi (200 km)
2.5 hrs

After breakfast, make a brief stop at the **Revelstoke Railway Museum** to learn about the railroad's importance to this region before continuing east on Highway 1 toward **Glacier National Park.** Stretch your legs on the **Skunk Cabbage Boardwalk Trail** or the **Giant Cedars Boardwalk Trail** (in Mount Revelstoke National Park) or on Glacier's **Hemlock Grove Trail** before stopping at the **Rogers Pass Discovery Centre.** After checking out the exhibits, drive on to **Golden** for lunch; you could ride the gondola at **Kicking Horse Mountain Resort** to eat at the **Eagle's Eye Restaurant,** Canada's highest restaurant. Don't forget to move

your clocks ahead; Golden is in the mountain time zone.

Keep going east on Highway 1 into **Yoho National Park.** Stop at the **Natural Bridge** and beautiful **Emerald Lake,** and if you have time, drive up to **Takakkaw Falls.** Have dinner and spend the night at one of the upscale lodges within the park.

Day 7
LAKE LOUISE AND THE
ICEFIELDS PARKWAY
Field to Jasper
160 mi (260 km)
4 hrs

Today will be another long one, but keep your camera handy. You'll pass through some of the most scenic terrain of the entire trip. It's just 20 minutes east on Highway 1 from Field in Yoho National Park to **Lake Louise,** where you can hike or paddle along its famous namesake lake.

From Lake Louise, turn north onto Highway 93, the **Icefields Parkway.** There are numerous places to ooh and aah along this route; highlights include **Peyto Lake, Wilcox Pass,** and the **Columbia Icefield,** where you can walk on the **Athabasca Glacier.** Continuing toward Jasper, another pretty place to pause is **Athabasca Falls.** Arrive in Jasper for dinner and a microbrew in the local pub.

Day 8
JASPER

Start your morning with a ride up the **Jasper Sky Tram.** Return to town to pick up a picnic lunch and take a look through the **Jasper-Yellowhead Museum.** Bring your picnic to **Maligne Canyon** to hike through this deep limestone gorge.

In the afternoon, drive to **Maligne Lake** for a leisurely 90-minute cruise. Have an early supper in town, then head for **Miette Hot Springs** to wrap up your day with a relaxing visit to these natural mineral pools.

Days 9-10
BANFF
Jasper to Banff
180 mi (290 km)
4.5 hrs

If you didn't make all the stops you wanted along the **Icefields Parkway,** you have another chance today, since you'll retrace your steps southbound on this picturesque parkway. When you get back to Lake Louise, detour to glacier-fed **Moraine Lake** for a short hike or canoe paddle. Then follow the **Bow Valley Parkway** south toward Banff, stopping to walk along **Johnston Canyon.** In **Banff,** have a leisurely dinner and a late-evening soak at **Banff Upper Hot Springs.**

Spend part of the next day at Banff's in-town attractions, including the **Cave and Basin National Historic Site, Banff Park Museum,** and **Whyte Museum of the Canadian Rockies,** and part of the day outdoors. Climb the **Mount Norquay Via Ferrata,** take a cruise on **Lake Minnewanka,** or ride the **Banff Gondola** and take a short hike at the top. In the evening, see a play, concert, or other event at the **Banff Centre.**

Days 11-12
KOOTENAY NATIONAL PARK AND FERNIE
Banff to Fernie
220 mi (355 km)
4.5 hrs

Pick up coffee and pastries at Banff's best bakeshop, **Wild Flour Artisan Bakery.** Then, leaving Banff, take Highway 1 west and turn south on **Highway 93** into **Kootenay National Park.** Stop at **Marble Canyon** and the **Paint Pots,** and keep your bathing suit handy for a dip in the **Radium Hot Springs.** Continue south on Highway 93/95, where the town of **Invermere** has several options for lunch.

If you're interested in history, stop at **Fort Steele Heritage Town,** a living history village. Keep following Highway 93/95 south and turn east on **Highway 3** to **Fernie,** where you'll spend the night. In the morning, check out the **Fernie Museum,** browse the downtown shops, and have lunch in one of the cafés. After you eat, head over to **Fernie Alpine Resort** to go for a mountaintop hike or to **Island Lake Lodge** to hike the lakeshore or explore the rainforest nearby.

Day 13
NELSON
Fernie to Nelson
200 mi (320 km)
4 hrs

Leave Fernie on Highway 3 west, stopping at **St. Eugene Resort** in Cranbrook to visit the First Nations-run **Ktunaxa Interpretive Centre** in this former mission and residential school for indigenous students; call first to be sure the center is open. Continue west on Highway 3, where you'll cross back into the Pacific time zone (set your

Clockwise from top left: Moraine Lake in Banff National Park; Banff Avenue; Emerald Lake Lodge in Yoho National Park.

Indigenous Culture

Aboriginal people have lived in western Canada for more than 10,000 years, and for many visitors, the opportunity to explore this traditional culture and its present-day manifestations is a highlight. Here are a few of the numerous places across the region where indigenous culture remains strong.

♦ **Bill Reid Gallery of Northwest Coast Art, Vancouver:** Dedicated to the work of Haida First Nations artist Bill Reid, this gallery showcases Reid's sculptures, carvings, and jewelry (page 38).

♦ **Museum of Anthropology, Vancouver:** This excellent museum illuminates the culture of British Columbia's indigenous peoples and traditional cultures from around the world (page 45).

♦ **Skwachàys Lodge, Vancouver:** Stay at Canada's first aboriginal arts and culture hotel, where works by First Nations artists adorn the guest rooms (page 79).

♦ **Meares Island:** Paddle by kayak or dugout canoe to this First Nations park across the harbor from Tofino, on Vancouver Island's Pacific coast (page 132).

♦ **Wya Point Resort, Ucluelet:** The Ucluelet First Nation runs this remote Vancouver Island waterfront lodging, where works by indigenous carvers decorate the upscale cabins (page 141).

♦ **Squamish Lil'wat Cultural Centre, Whistler:** Learn about the history and present-day culture of the region's First Nations communities at this modern gallery (page 160).

♦ **Kamloopa Powwow, Kamloops:** Most First Nations powwows welcome visitors, and this August celebration of First Nations culture, with dancers, drummers, and other performers, is one of western Canada's largest (page 186).

♦ **Cross River Wilderness Centre, near Kootenay National Park:** Choose outdoor adventures or aboriginal experiences that reflect both the owner's Métis heritage and the local First Nations culture at this unique wilderness lodge (page 324).

♦ **St. Eugene Resort, Cranbrook:** Set in a former mission that was once a residential school for indigenous children, this First Nations-run hotel with an on-site interpretive center mixes its historic past with contemporary amenities (page 340).

♦ **Nk'Mip Cellars, Osoyoos:** In the Okanagan Valley, the Osoyoos Indian Band runs Canada's first aboriginal-owned winery (page 385) and operates the adjacent **Nk'Mip Desert Cultural Centre** (page 390).

Most of western Canada's national parks, including Banff and Jasper in Alberta, and Mount Revelstoke, Glacier, Yoho, and Kootenay in B.C., offer interpretive programs focusing on First Nations culture. Another excellent source of information for visitors interested in aboriginal culture is the **Indigenous Tourism Association of British Columbia** (604/921-1070, www.indigenousbc.com).

watch back an hour), to the junction with **Highway 6,** where you go north to **Nelson.**

Visit **Touchstones Nelson: Museum of Art and History** and browse the shops along Baker Street. Stop at **Oso Negro Café** when you're ready for a coffee break. Another option is to tour the sobering **Nikkei Internment Memorial Centre** in New Denver, which is 60 miles (97 kilometers) north of Nelson on Highway 6. Nelson has lots of good restaurants, so take time to enjoy your evening meal.

Day 14
OKANAGAN VALLEY
Nelson to Osoyoos
165 mi (265 km)
3.5 hrs
From Nelson, follow Highway 6 west to Highway 3A south, and stop in **Castlegar** at the **Doukhobor Discovery Centre** to learn about the pacifist Russian community that settled in B.C. in the early 1900s. Then take **Highway 3** west toward the Okanagan Valley.

You should arrive in the **Osoyoos-Oliver** area early enough to spend the afternoon sampling local **wineries.** Plan a special dinner at **The Sonora Room** at Burrowing Owl Estate Winery or **Terrafina Restaurant** at Hester Creek Winery to celebrate the end of your holiday.

Day 15
RETURN TO VANCOUVER
Osoyoos to Vancouver
250 mi (405 km)
5 hrs
If you're not in a rush to return to Vancouver, pick up freshly baked cinnamon buns at **The Lake Village Bakery** in Osoyoos, then stop at the **Nk'Mip Desert Cultural Centre** or take a morning stroll along Lake Osoyoos. When you're ready to hit the road, follow **Highway 3** west to Hope, where you pick up **Highway 1** toward Vancouver.

Japanese garden at the Nikkei Internment Memorial Centre

Clockwise from top left: Athabasca Falls in Jasper National Park; grapes on the vine in the Okanagan Valley; Tofino sunset.

Options for Shorter Trips

FIVE DAYS ON THE B.C. COAST

If you have just five days, base yourself in **Vancouver** for three nights, which is enough time to see the sights and take a day trip along the **Sea-to-Sky Highway** to **Whistler.** On Day 4, catch the ferry to Vancouver Island to tour **Victoria;** you can stay the night there—the city has lots of good restaurants and lodgings—before returning to Vancouver.

Have a little more time? Extend your trip for two or three days by crossing Vancouver Island to **Tofino,** a laid-back beach town on the Pacific coast.

A WEEK IN THE ROCKIES

If you want to spend your time in the Canadian Rockies and you have just a week, start and end your trip in **Calgary.** Do a quick city tour, and then head for **Banff National Park,** 90 minutes to the west. Spend two days in Banff to hike, canoe, or take a lake cruise, and check out the museums and shops in town. Drive west on Highway 1 to explore the highlights of **Yoho National Park,** then turn back east to **Lake Louise,** where you can stay near the famous lake.

From Lake Louise, allow at least half a day to drive the **Icefields Parkway** to **Jasper;** there are enough lakes, glaciers, and hiking trails to fill many hours. Give yourself two nights and at least one full day in **Jasper National Park.** Returning south, you'll backtrack along the Icefields Parkway, but it will give you a chance to see any sights you missed. Spend one more night in Banff or stop off east of the park in **Canmore,** before returning to Calgary and heading for home.

VANCOUVER TO BANFF AND CALGARY

If you don't have time to make a full loop from Vancouver to the Canadian Rockies and back, consider starting in Vancouver and doing a one-way weeklong road trip to Calgary. To begin in Calgary and drive to Vancouver, just reverse the order of this itinerary.

After spending a couple of days in **Vancouver,** head east on the Trans-Canada Highway; at Hope, follow Highway 5 east, then take Highway 97A to **Kelowna,** where you can visit several Okanagan Valley wineries and stay the night.

The next day, continue east on Highway 1 to **Mount Revelstoke** and **Glacier National Parks,** and overnight in **Golden.** Explore **Yoho National Park** and cross into Alberta to stay at **Lake Louise.** Take the **Bow Valley Parkway** south to **Banff,** where you can easily spend two days in **Banff National Park.** From Banff, it's only 90 minutes east on Highway 1 to **Calgary.**

Vancouver

Vancouver

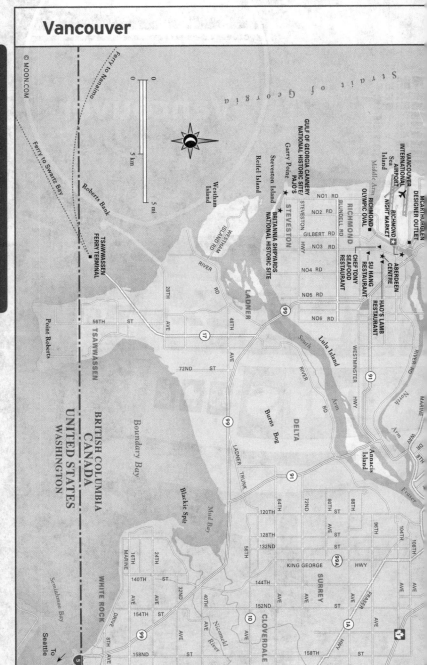

© MOON.COM

Ferry to Nanaimo

Ferry to Swartz Bay

0 — 5 km
0 — 5 mi

Strait of Georgia

Roberts Bank

TSAWWASSEN FERRY TERMINAL

Point Roberts

28TH AVE

56TH ST

TSAWWASSEN

BRITISH COLUMBIA
CANADA
UNITED STATES
WASHINGTON

Boundary Bay

Mud Bay

Blackie Spit

Semiahmoo Bay

To
Seattle

Westham
Island

GULF OF GEORGIA CANNERY
NATIONAL HISTORIC SITE/
PAJO'S
Garry Point

Steveston Island
Reifel Island

STEVESTON

WESTHAM
ISLAND RD

NO1 RD
NO2 RD
NO3 RD
NO4 RD
NO5 RD
NO6 RD

STEVESTON
HWY

BRITANNIA SHIPYARDS
NATIONAL HISTORIC SITE

RIVER RD

LADNER
48TH AVE

17

72ND ST

South
Arm

River

RD

DELTA

Burns Bog

99

LADNER TRUNK

91

64TH

72ND ST

80TH ST

88TH

120TH AVE

128TH ST

132ND ST

56TH

140TH ST

144TH AVE

152ND ST

158ND ST

16TH MARINE
24TH AVE

32ND AVE

8TH AVE

WHITE ROCK

99

5

Nicomekl River

154TH ST

40TH AVE

KING GEORGE HWY

99A

SURREY

96TH AVE

104TH AVE

108TH

FRASER AVE

CLOVERDALE

10

158TH ST

1A
HWY

Fraser

Middle Arm

VANCOUVER
INTERNATIONAL
AIRPORT
Sea
Island

RICHMOND
NIGHT MARKET

MCARTHURGLEN
DESIGNER OUTLET

RICHMOND
OLYMPIC OVAL

BLUNDELL RD
GILBERT RD

NO2 RD

RICHMOND

CHEF TONY
SEAFOOD
RESTAURANT

SU HANG
RESTAURANT

ABERDEEN
CENTRE

HAO'S LAMB
RESTAURANT

WESTMINSTER HWY

91

Lulu Island

North Arm

RIVER RD

MARINE
WAY

MARINE DR

Annacis
Island

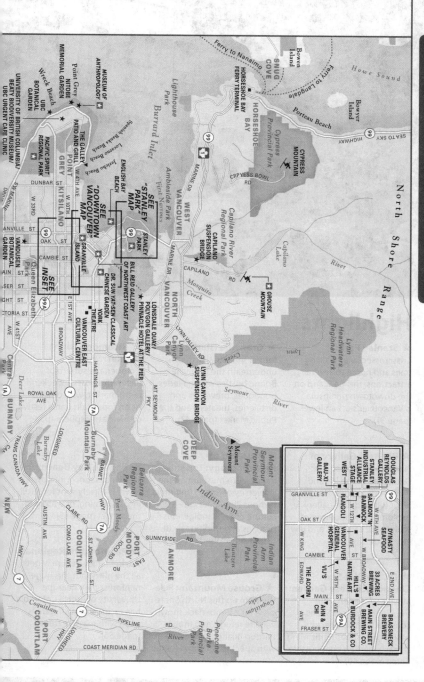

Highlights

★ **Stanley Park:** Crisscrossed with walking trails and home to several attractions, this parkland on the downtown peninsula is Vancouver's urban jewel (page 31).

★ **Bill Reid Gallery of Northwest Coast Art:** Dedicated to the life and work of Haida First Nations artist Bill Reid, this gallery explores his vast output of sculptures, carvings, and jewelry (page 38).

★ **Dr. Sun Yat-Sen Classical Chinese Garden:** Master craftsmen from the Chinese city of Suzhou constructed this peaceful oasis, the first authentic Ming Dynasty garden built outside China (page 40).

★ **Granville Island:** This former industrial district underneath the Granville Bridge bustles with galleries, boutiques, breweries and distilleries, theaters, and the Public Market (page 43).

★ **Museum of Anthropology:** This striking modern museum on the University of British Columbia campus illuminates the culture of B.C.'s indigenous peoples and traditional cultures from around the world (page 45).

★ **Grouse Mountain:** Ride the tram up this North Shore peak for a lumberjack show, wildlife refuge, and mountaintop hiking trails, along with spectacular views (page 50).

★ **Richmond Night Market:** Mid-May-mid-October, the suburb of Richmond hosts a weekend night market, with dozens of Asian food stalls and a festive carnival atmosphere (page 53).

★ **English Bay Beach:** This stretch of sand, right downtown, is a lively spot for strolling, swimming, or watching the sunset (page 55).

★ **Pacific Spirit Regional Park:** Stanley Park may get all the glory, but this huge rainforest park near the University of British Columbia has secluded walking trails lined with massive trees (page 56).

In a region of dramatic natural scenery, Vancouver cuts a dramatic urban figure.

Set on Pacific coastal inlets with forested mountains beyond, Vancouver mixes urban pleasures and outdoor adventures and is frequently named one of the world's most livable cities.

Downtown Vancouver is a vibrant mix of residential and commercial development, dotted with parks and green spaces. Tall glass-and-steel towers sprout along the downtown peninsula, with "view corridors" providing peeks of the peaks and waterfront. The city's active population takes full advantage of the cycling lanes, walking paths, beaches, and parks, particularly its 1,000-acre (400-ha) rainforest park right downtown.

Home to roughly two million people, the Vancouver region looks to the Pacific Rim. More than 40 percent of the metro area's population is of Asian descent, influencing the city in everything from urban design to art to food. Vancouver boasts, deservedly, of having the best Chinese cuisine outside China.

Another Vancouver influence to explore comes from its indigenous people, who've lived on this part of the continent for thousands of years. Vancouver has several museums, galleries, and other attractions where you can get acquainted with First Nations culture. If you land at Vancouver's international airport, you'll see its extensive collection of native art welcoming visitors to the region.

Just 35 miles (57 km) north of the U.S. border, Vancouver is a convenient starting point for trips along the British Columbia coast, east to the Okanagan Valley (a major wine-producing district), and on to the strikingly scenic Rocky Mountains. There's lots of gorgeous territory in this part of the world, and it all starts in the beautiful, livable city of Vancouver.

Getting to Vancouver

Driving from Seattle

It's a **145-mile (230-km)** drive from Seattle, Washington, to downtown Vancouver. **I-5** takes you north from Seattle to the U.S.-Canada border. The **Peace Arch Crossing** on I-5 is open 24 hours daily. When you pass through the border checks, you'll be on **Highway 99** in British Columbia.

If traffic is backed up at the Peace Arch crossing, consider the **alternate border crossing** at the **Pacific Highway/Highway 543** (Exit 275 from I-5), also open 24 hours. Once you're through the border here, you'll be on B.C.'s **Highway 15.** Follow Highway 15 north for 1.9 miles (3 km) and turn left (west) onto **8th Avenue.** In 1.2 miles (2 km), merge onto **Highway 99** north.

Continue north on Highway 99, passing through the **George Massey Tunnel** and crossing the **Oak Street Bridge** into Vancouver. To reach the city center, continue north on **Oak Street,** turn left onto **West 41st Avenue,** and then at the light, turn right onto **Granville Street.** Stay on Granville Street across the **Granville Bridge** into downtown. It's 35 miles (57 km) from the border to downtown Vancouver.

The **Washington State Department of Transportation** (www.wsdot.com) and the **British Columbia Ministry of Transportation** (www.th.gov.bc.ca/ATIS) provide information about border delays on their websites. Illuminated signs along I-5 and Highway 99 in B.C. also show border wait times.

Driving from Victoria (via Ferry)

B.C. Ferries (888/223-3779, www.bcferries.com) provides frequent service between the Vancouver metropolitan area on the mainland and Vancouver Island. Ferries transport foot passengers,

Best Accommodations

★ **Burrard Hotel:** Start your road trip at this old-time motor hotel that's been converted into a retro-chic lodging (page 76).

★ **Listel Hotel:** Original contemporary art distinguishes this low-rise lodging with a prime perch on Vancouver's main downtown shopping street (page 76).

★ **Fairmont Pacific Rim:** Vancouver's most elegant modern hotel is this luxurious Asian-influenced tower near the Coal Harbour waterfront (page 78).

★ **Rosewood Hotel Georgia:** Originally built in the 1920s, this classy restored hotel has upscale guest rooms, excellent eateries, and stylish lounges, all in a central downtown location (page 78).

★ **Skwachàys Lodge:** One-of-a-kind works by First Nations artists adorn the guest rooms at Canada's first aboriginal arts and culture hotel (page 79).

★ **Opus Hotel Vancouver:** At this cool Yaletown boutique lodging, the vibrantly hued rooms have windows into the baths. Don't be shy (page 80)!

★ **The Douglas:** Rooms are designed like upscale urban cabins in this boutique hotel, part of the large Parq Vancouver resort complex (page 80).

★ **Corkscrew Inn:** Handcrafted art deco-style stained glass and an unusual collection of antique corkscrews give this Kitsilano B&B its wine-themed charm (page 80).

bicycles, cars, trucks, and recreational vehicles. Reservations ($10 at least 7 days in advance, $17 1-6 days in advance, $21 same-day travel) are recommended for vehicles, particularly if you're traveling on summer weekends or during holiday periods. Reservations are not available for walk-on passengers or bicycles.

Ferries from the Victoria area depart from the **Swartz Bay Terminal** (Hwy. 17), 20 miles (32 km) north of Victoria via **Highway 17,** about a **30-minute** drive.

To travel between Victoria and Vancouver, take the **Swartz Bay-Tsawwassen Ferry** (one-way adults $17.20, ages 5-11 $8.60, cars $57.50, bikes $2). The ferry ride is **one hour and 35 minutes.**

On the mainland, the ferry docks at the **Tsawwassen Terminal** (1 Ferry Causeway, Delta), 24 miles (38 km) south of Vancouver. Leaving Tsawwassen Terminal, follow **Highway 17/17A** to **Highway 99** north. Continue north on Highway 99, passing through the **George Massey Tunnel** and crossing the **Oak Street Bridge** into Vancouver. To reach the city center, continue north on **Oak Street,** turn left onto **West 41st Avenue,** and then at the light, turn right onto **Granville Street.** Stay on Granville Street across the **Granville Bridge** into downtown. Plan about **45 minutes** to drive from Tsawwassen to downtown Vancouver, with extra time during the morning and evening rush hours.

Driving from Whistler

Allow about **two hours** to make the **75-mile (120-km)** drive between Whistler and Vancouver along the spectacular **Sea-to-Sky Highway.**

To get from Whistler to downtown Vancouver, follow **Highway 99** south to **Highway 1** east and take Exit 13, **Taylor Way,** toward Vancouver. At the foot of

Best Restaurants

★ **L'Abattoir:** On the site of Vancouver's first jail, this chic Gastown dining spot now detains diners with creative cocktails and ever-evolving west coast plates (page 69).

★ **Farmer's Apprentice:** Imaginative multicourse tasting menus inspired by local products bring adventurous diners to this petite South Granville dining room (page 72).

★ **West:** A wall of wine, inventive cuisine, and gracious service make any meal feel like an occasion at this upscale South Granville restaurant (page 72).

★ **Dynasty Seafood:** Love dim sum? This Chinese dining spot serves some of Vancouver's finest. There are great views, too (page 72).

★ **Burdock & Co:** On Main Street, this relaxed neighborhood bistro delivers a creative, hyper-local menu (page 73).

★ **Hao's Lamb Restaurant:** This always-busy Chinese eatery in Richmond specializes in lamb, which you'll find in dumplings, soups, chops, and other dishes from western China (page 75).

the hill, turn left onto **Marine Drive,** then bear right onto the **Lions Gate Bridge.** Many lanes merge onto the bridge here, so be prepared for delays. Once you've crossed the bridge, continue on **West Georgia Street** in downtown Vancouver.

Driving from Banff

The most direct route between Banff, in the Canadian Rockies, and Vancouver is to follow the **Trans-Canada Highway (Hwy. 1)** west. You'll pass through Yoho, Glacier, and Mount Revelstoke National Parks and the city of Kamloops.

From **Kamloops,** take **Highway 5 (Coquihalla Hwy.)** southbound, toward Merritt and Hope. Highway 5 meets **Highway 3,** which you take westbound to rejoin **Highway 1** at the town of Hope.

From **Hope,** continue west on Highway 1 toward Vancouver. After passing through the city of Burnaby, take Exit 25 for **McGill Street.** Follow McGill Street westbound and turn left onto **Nanaimo Street.** At the intersection with **Dundas Street,** turn right onto Dundas. Dundas

Street becomes **Powell Street,** which will take you into downtown Vancouver.

It's **530 miles (850 km)** from Banff to Vancouver. The drive takes **9-9.5 hours.** From **Kamloops** to Vancouver, it's **220 miles (355 km)** and takes **3.75-4 hours.**

Driving from Jasper

The **shortest route** between Jasper and Vancouver is to follow **Highway 16 (Yellowhead Hwy.)** west to **Highway 5 (Southern Yellowhead Hwy.),** where you turn south toward Kamloops. At **Kamloops,** continue south on Highway 5, following the Banff-to-Vancouver directions above. This Jasper-to-Vancouver route is **500 miles (805 km)** and takes about **8.5 hours.**

A **longer but scenic route** is to take the **Icefields Parkway (Hwy. 93)** south from Jasper to **Lake Louise,** where you turn west onto **Highway 1.** From there, follow the Banff-to-Vancouver directions above. From Jasper to Vancouver, this route is about **620 miles (1,000 km)** and takes about **11.5 hours.**

Getting There by Air, Train, and Bus

By Air

Vancouver International Airport (YVR, 3211 Grant McConachie Way, Richmond, 604/207-7077, www.yvr.ca) is a major international gateway with flights to Vancouver from across Canada, the United States, Mexico, Europe, Asia, and the Pacific, and connecting cities across the globe. The airport is south of the city center in the suburb of Richmond, about 20-25 minutes from downtown by public transit, car, or taxi.

Ground Transportation

The **Canada Line** (604/953-3333, www.translink.ca), part of Vancouver's SkyTrain rapid transit system, runs directly between the Vancouver International Airport and downtown. If you don't have a lot of baggage and you're not renting a car, it's the fastest and least expensive way to travel downtown from the airport. Trains operate from about 5am to 1am daily. When you purchase a transit ticket at YVR Airport station, you pay a $5 fee in addition to the regular transit fare.

Taxis wait outside the arrivals area of the domestic and international terminals. Fares between the airport and most Vancouver destinations are a **flat rate by zone.** To many destinations downtown or in Kitsilano, the flat-rate fare is $31. Other fares include Canada Place $35, Ballantyne Pier $36, Stanley Park $37, and the University of British Columbia $34. Gratuities are not included. Most cabs serving the airport accept credit cards. Note that returning to YVR by taxi, airport-bound cabs use their meters rather than the flat-rate system, so fares vary depending on your starting point and traffic conditions.

The major car rental companies all have offices at the Vancouver airport.

By Train
VIA Rail

Canada's national rail carrier, **VIA Rail** (514/989-2626 or 888/842-7245, www.viarail.ca), runs *The Canadian*, its flagship train, between Toronto and Vancouver. If you do the trip nonstop, Toronto-Vancouver takes four nights and three days. Major stops en route include Winnipeg, Saskatoon, Edmonton, Jasper, and Kamloops. *The Canadian* operates three times a week in each direction May-mid-October, and twice a week mid-October-April. The Vancouver rail depot is **Pacific Central Station** (1150 Station St.), a short walk from the Main Street SkyTrain station, where you can catch a train to other points downtown.

Amtrak

U.S. rail carrier **Amtrak** (800/872-7245, www.amtrak.com) operates two trains a day in each direction between Vancouver and Seattle; one of these trains continues to Portland, Oregon. In either Portland or Seattle, you can make connections to or from San Francisco, Los Angeles, and other California cities. Amtrak trains arrive and depart from Vancouver's **Pacific Central Station** (1150 Station St.).

Remember that when you arrive in Vancouver from the United States or travel from Vancouver to the United States, you're crossing an international border, and you need to allow time for customs and immigration procedures. Don't forget your passport!

The Rocky Mountaineer

The **Rocky Mountaineer** (1755 Cottrell St., at Terminal Ave., 604/606-7245 or 877/460-3200, www.rockymountaineer.com, mid-Apr.-mid-Oct.), a privately run luxury train, offers rail trips between Vancouver, Banff, Lake Louise, Jasper, and Calgary. You can travel round-trip from Vancouver to the Canadian Rockies and back, or book a one-way journey through the Rockies from Vancouver to Calgary (or vice versa).

Unlike a standard train trip, many Rocky Mountaineer packages include activities ranging from gondola rides to helicopter tours, with accommodations along the way. It's also possible to book a Rocky Mountaineer holiday that covers rail fare and accommodations only; for example, it offers two-day train trips between Vancouver and Lake Louise, Banff, or Jasper. Rail packages start at $1,579 per person and go up depending on the destinations, the number of days of travel, and the level of service and accommodations.

Rocky Mountaineer trains travel during the day and stop overnight in Kamloops en route to and from the Rockies. Note that in Vancouver, Rocky Mountaineer trains do not use Pacific Central Station, where VIA Rail and Amtrak trains depart; they have their own depot nearby.

By Bus

Pacific Central Station (1150 Station St.), the rail depot, is also the main Vancouver bus station.

Buses that travel between Seattle and Vancouver include **Bolt Bus** (877/265-8287, www.boltbus.com), which arrives and departs from Pacific Central Station, and **Quick Shuttle** (604/940-4428 or 800/665-2122, www.quickcoach.com), which stops at Canada Place and will also pick up or drop off passengers at a number of downtown hotels, with advance reservations. Bolt Bus takes four hours; Quick Shuttle takes 4-5 hours, depending on pickup and drop-off locations. Remember your passport if you're taking the bus between Seattle and Vancouver.

Sights

★ Stanley Park

Like New York's Central Park or London's Hyde Park, Vancouver's **Stanley Park** is the city's beating green heart.

Crisscrossed with walking trails, dense with trees, and home to several attractions, this 1,000-acre (400-ha) parkland sits on the downtown peninsula, a short walk from the city's skyscraping towers. The waters of English Bay and Burrard Inlet surround the park, making it even more scenic.

The Seawall, a 5.5-mile (9-km) walking and cycling path, circles the perimeter of Stanley Park and passes many of the park's attractions. You can also follow the park's perimeter by car along Park Drive. TransLink's **bus 19** travels through downtown along West Pender and West Georgia Streets into the park.

Totem Poles at Brockton Point

When you enter the park from West Georgia Street, one of the first attractions you reach illustrates the region's First Nations heritage. Nine colorful **totem poles** stand at Brockton Point.

The park board purchased four of these hard-carved poles in the 1920s from the northern Vancouver Island community of Alert Bay. Several more came from the islands of Haida Gwaii off the B.C. coast. Eventually, all of these poles were either returned to their original homes or sent to museums for preservation; the totems now standing in the park are replicas. A Squamish Nation artist, Robert Yelton, carved the newest pole, which was installed at Brockton Point in 2009.

Prospect Point

From **Prospect Point,** a lookout at the highest spot in Stanley Park, you have great views of the Burrard Inlet, North Shore mountains, and Lions Gate Bridge. Built in 1938 and spanning 1,553 feet (473 m), the **Lions Gate Bridge** is one of the world's longest suspension bridges.

You can stop for lunch at **Prospect Point Bar & Grill** (5601 Stanley Park Dr., 604/669-2737, www.prospectpoint.com, 11am-7pm daily, $15-24), which serves salads, fish-and-chips, burgers, and craft beer overlooking the water. At the same

Downtown Vancouver

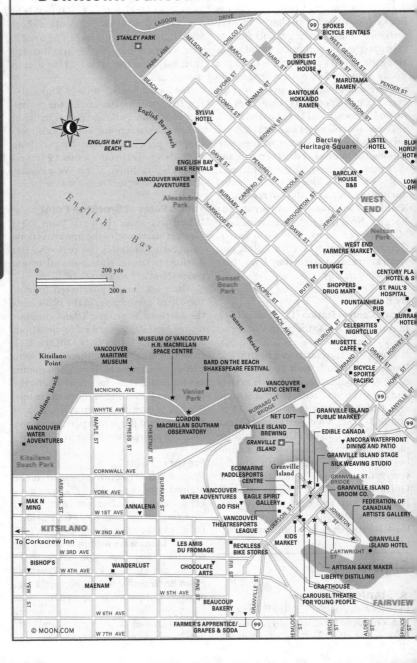

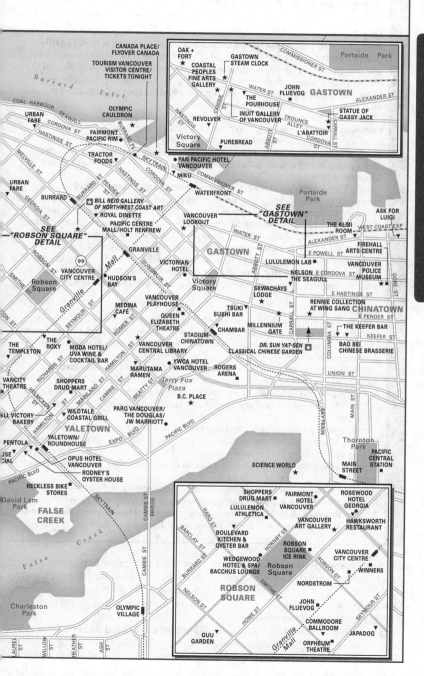

CANADA PLACE/
FLYOVER CANADA

TOURISM VANCOUVER
VISITOR CENTRE/
TICKETS TONIGHT

OAK +
FORT
COASTAL
PEOPLES
FINE ARTS
GALLERY

GASTOWN
STEAM CLOCK

Portside Park

COMMISSIONER ST

WATER ST

JOHN
FLUEVOG

GASTOWN

OLYMPIC
CAULDRON

SEAWALL

CORDOVA ST

THE
POURHOUSE

REVOLVER

INUIT GALLERY
OF VANCOUVER

TROUNCE
ALLEY

ALEXANDER ST

STATUE OF
GASSY JACK

URBAN
FARE

FAIRMONT
PACIFIC RIM

HASTINGS ST

TRACTOR
FOODS

SKYTRAIN

Victory
Square

PUREBREAD

L'ABATTOIR
CORDOVA
ST

Burrard

Inlet

COAL HARBOUR

URBAN
FARE

MELVILLE ST

HASTINGS ST

GEORGIA ST

BURRARD

PENDER ST

BILL REID GALLERY
OF NORTHWEST COAST ART

ROYAL DINETTE

PACIFIC CENTRE
MALL/HOLT RENFREW

CORDOVA ST

COMMISSIONER ST

PAN PACIFIC HOTEL
VANCOUVER

MIKU

WATERFRONT

VANCOUVER
LOOKOUT

Portside
Park

SEE
"GASTOWN"
DETAIL

ASK FOR
LUIGI

THE ALIBI
ROOM

WEST COAST EXP

SEE
"ROBSON SQUARE"
DETAIL

99

VANCOUVER
CITY CENTRE

Robson
Square

GRANVILLE

HUDSON'S
BAY

DUNSMUIR ST

VICTORIAN
HOTEL

WATER ST

GASTOWN

ALEXANDER ST

E POWELL ST

LULULEMON LAB

NELSON
THE SEAGULL

E CORDOVA ST

FIREHALL
ARTS CENTRE

VANCOUVER
POLICE
MUSEUM

GORE ST

E HASTINGS ST

SMITHE ST

MEDINA
CAFÉ

HOMER ST

VANCOUVER
PLAYHOUSE

QUEEN
ELIZABETH
THEATRE

Victory
Square

SKWACHÀYS
LODGE

TSUKI
SUSHI BAR

MILLENNIUM
GATE

RENNIE COLLECTION
AT WING SANG

CHINATOWN

E PENDER ST

THE KEEFER BAR

KEEFER ST

THE
TEMPLETON

THE
ROXY

RICHARDS ST

MODA HOTEL/
UVA WINE &
COCKTAIL BAR

HAMILTON ST

STADIUM-
CHINATOWN

CHAMBAR

DR. SUN YAT-SEN
CLASSICAL CHINESE GARDEN

COLUMBIA ST

BAO BEI
CHINESE BRASSERIE

UNION ST

MAIN ST

VANCITY
THEATRE

HELMCKEN ST

SHOPPERS
DRUG MART

MAINLAND ST

CAMBIE ST

VANCOUVER
CENTRAL LIBRARY

MARUTAMA
RAMEN

BEATTY ST

Terry Fox
Plaza

YWCA HOTEL
VANCOUVER

ROGERS
ARENA

ALL VICTORY
BAKERY

HAMILTON ST

WILDTALE
COASTAL GRILL

YALETOWN

EXPO BLVD

PARQ VANCOUVER/
THE DOUGLAS/
JW MARRIOTT

B.C. PLACE

PACIFIC BLVD

SKYTRAIN

Thornton
Park

PACIFIC
CENTRAL
STATION

PENTOLA

USE
CIAL

YALETOWN/
ROUNDHOUSE

OPUS HOTEL
VANCOUVER

RODNEY'S
OYSTER HOUSE

PACIFIC BLVD

RECKLESS BIKE
STORES

David Lam
Park

FALSE
CREEK

CAMBIE ST

SCIENCE WORLD

MAIN
STREET

False

Creek

Charleston
Park

OLYMPIC
VILLAGE

SKYTRAIN BRIDGE

SHOPPERS
DRUG MART

LULULEMON
ATHLETICA

FAIRMONT
HOTEL
VANCOUVER

ROSEWOOD
HOTEL
GEORGIA

HARO ST

BOULEVARD
KITCHEN &
OYSTER BAR

HORNBY ST

VANCOUVER
ART GALLERY

HAWKSWORTH
RESTAURANT

BARCLAY ST

WEDGEWOOD
HOTEL & SPA/
BACCHUS LOUNGE

BURRARD ST

ROBSON
SQUARE
ICE RINK

ROBSON
SQUARE

Robson
Square

ROBSON ST

VANCOUVER
CITY CENTRE

WINNERS

NORDSTROM

NELSON ST

HOWE ST

SMITHE ST

JOHN
FLUEVOG

SEYMOUR ST

COMMODORE
BALLROOM

JAPADOG

GUU
GARDEN

Granville Mall

ORPHEUM
THEATRE

LAUREL ST

WILLOW ST

HEATHER ST

ASH ST

Two Days in Vancouver

Day 1

Start your day on **Granville Island** with coffee and a water view in the **Granville Island Public Market.** Browse the market food stalls early, before the crowds arrive, and pick up snacks or picnic fixings to enjoy when you're done shopping, too. Wander the island to explore the craft shops and galleries. If you're feeling energetic, rent a kayak or a stand-up paddleboard at **Ecomarine Paddlesports Centre** and spend an hour on the water paddling around the island.

After lunch, head west to the University of British Columbia campus to visit the **Museum of Anthropology,** which has a particularly strong collection of First Nations art, including an awe-inspiring gallery of totem poles. On your way back downtown, stop along West 4th Avenue in **Kitsilano** to browse the boutiques or refresh with a pastry from **Beaucoup Bakery & Café** or a shot of rich drinking chocolate at **Chocolate Arts.**

Once you've returned to the city center, your next stop is **Stanley Park,** Vancouver's vast downtown green space. **Rent a bicycle** and circle the Seawall, stopping to see the **totem poles at Brockton Point,** or if you're visiting with kids, tour the **Vancouver Aquarium Marine Science Centre,** Canada's largest aquarium. Either way, make time for a late afternoon walk or a rest in the sand at **English Bay Beach,** which is also one of Vancouver's best spots to watch the sun set over the ocean.

Have dinner in Gastown or Chinatown at one of the deliciously fun contemporary restaurants, like **L'Abattoir, Chambar,** or **Bao Bei Chinese Brasserie.** Wrap up your evening with a nightcap nearby at the **Pourhouse** or **The Keefer Bar.**

Day 2

The next morning, choose between an urban or outdoor experience. If it's a fine day, cross the Burrard Inlet to the North Shore and explore **Grouse Mountain,** where you can laugh at the lumberjack show, see the wildlife refuge, go hiking, or simply take in the panoramic views.

Or stay in the city and tour the **Dr. Sun Yat-Sen Classical Chinese Garden,** the only authentic Ming Dynasty garden outside China; the **Bill Reid Gallery of Northwest Coast Art,** which showcases the work of a renowned First Nations artist; and the **Vancouver Art Gallery,** known for its collection of works by B.C. painter Emily Carr.

In the evening, hop on the Canada Line to have supper in Richmond's **Golden Village,** where you'll find some of the best Chinese cuisine outside China. Or if you're visiting on a weekend between mid-May and mid-October, head for the **Richmond Night Market,** an Asian-style festival of street foods from China, Taiwan, Japan, and more.

If you'd rather stay closer to downtown, sample the bounty of the seas at **Boulevard Kitchen & Oyster Bar,** get adventurous with dinner at **Farmer's Apprentice** or **Mak N Ming,** or indulge in a fine meal at **Hawksworth Restaurant** or **West** to wind up your two days in Vancouver with a delicious splurge.

location, **Prospect Point Cafe** (10am-7pm daily) sells java, pastries, and ice cream.

Siwash Rock

Another landmark is **Siwash Rock,** a towering pillar just offshore that you can see from the Seawall on the park's west side. Topped with a wind-buffeted Douglas fir tree, the rock figures in a Squamish First Nations legend, which tells of a young father who the gods turned to stone to honor his commitment to his family.

Second and Third Beaches

Stanley Park has two sandy beaches along the Seawall on the park's western side. **Third Beach,** which is farther into the park, is quieter, while family-friendly **Second Beach** is busier, with a seaside swimming pool and snack bar.

Vancouver Aquarium Marine Science Centre

Located in the center of Stanley Park and housing more than 50,000 marine creatures, the **Vancouver Aquarium** (845 Avison Way, 604/659-3474, www.vanaqua.org, 9:30am-6pm daily late June-early Sept., 10am-5pm daily early Sept.-late June, adults $38, seniors, students, and ages 13-18 $30, ages 4-12 $21) is Canada's largest aquarium. Exhibits highlight Canadian environments, but also explore marine life from the Amazon to Africa to the Arctic. Besides perusing the exhibit halls, you can watch live shows throughout the day, including popular beluga whale, dolphin, shark, and penguin programs, or immerse yourself in the films shown in the 4-D theater.

This popular attraction draws throngs of visitors, particularly in the busy summer months. Buy tickets online to avoid long waits at the door. In summer, visit before 11am or after 4pm when the crowds can be smaller; in winter, come in the mornings or after 2pm.

Stanley Park Nature House

An ecology center set on the park's Lost Lagoon, **Stanley Park Nature House** (nature house 604/257-8544, program information 604/718-6522, www.stanleyparkecology.ca, 10am-5pm Tues.-Sun. July-Aug., 10am-4pm Sat.-Sun. Sept.-June, free) has exhibits about the plants and animals that live in the park.

Nature House staff lead periodic two-hour **discovery walks** (check the website for schedules; generally adults $12.50, seniors and children $10) highlighting the park's plants, birds, and wildlife. To find the nature house, enter the park near the intersection of Alberni and Chilco Streets, and walk toward the lagoon.

Downtown and the West End
Canada Place

Among Vancouver's most famous landmarks is **Canada Place** (999 Canada Pl., 604/665-9000, www.canadaplace.ca), its billowing white sails recalling a ship ready to set off to sea. Canada Place does have a seafaring function; the building, with its five 90-foot (27-m) white sails made of Teflon-coated fiberglass, houses the city's cruise ship terminal. Also inside are the east wing of the Vancouver Convention Centre, the Pan Pacific Hotel Vancouver, and several attractions for visitors.

The coolest reason to visit Canada Place is **FlyOver Canada** (604/620-8455, www.flyovercanada.com, 10am-9pm daily, adults $33, seniors and students ages 13-21 $17, ages 12 and under $23), a multimedia simulated flight that has you swoop and soar across the country, flying over Arctic peaks, past Toronto's CN Tower, and across the Canadian Rockies. You even feel the spray as you hover above Niagara Falls, and at one point, the northern lights spread out around you. The FlyOver Canada experience lasts about 30 minutes; the flight itself is just eight minutes long. For a discount, buy your tickets online in advance.

While you're at Canada Place, follow the **Canadian Trail,** a walkway along the building's west promenade. Check out interpretive panels about Canada's ten provinces and three territories while enjoying the views of Stanley Park, Burrard Inlet, and the North Shore mountains. You'll frequently see massive cruise ships at the docks spring-fall.

Olympic Cauldron

When Vancouver hosted the 2010 Winter Olympic Games, the candelabra-like **Olympic Cauldron** (Jack Poole Plaza, foot of Thurlow St.) burned brightly. Although it's now lit only for special events, the 33-foot-tall (10-m) landmark

Stanley Park

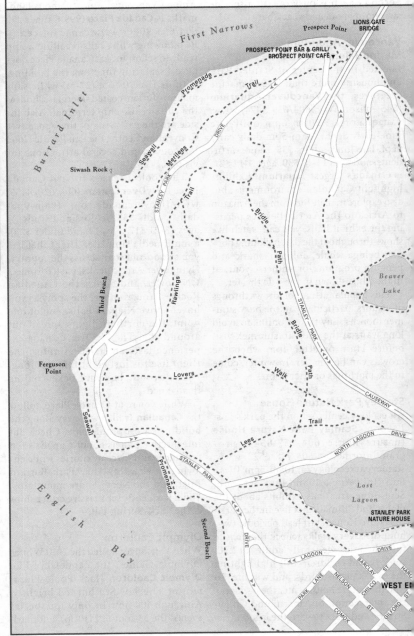

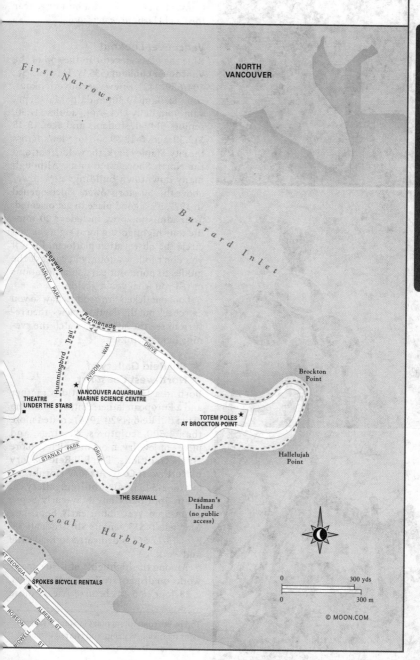

First Narrows

NORTH VANCOUVER

Burrard Inlet

Seawall

STANLEY PARK

Promenade

Hummingbird Trail

STANLEY PARK DRIVE

AVISON WAY

DRIVE

Brockton Point

★ **VANCOUVER AQUARIUM MARINE SCIENCE CENTRE**

■ **THEATRE UNDER THE STARS**

★ **TOTEM POLES AT BROCKTON POINT**

Hallelujah Point

THE SEAWALL

Deadman's Island (no public access)

Coal Harbour

ST GEORGIA ST

ST

■ **SPOKES BICYCLE RENTALS**

ROBSON ST

ALBERNI ST

BIDWELL ST

0   300 yds

0   300 m

© MOON.COM

still stands next to the Vancouver Convention Centre's west building, near the Coal Harbour waterfront.

Vancouver Lookout

Ride the glass elevator to the top of the **Vancouver Lookout** (555 W. Hastings St., 604/689-0421, www.vancouverlookout. com, 8:30am-10:30pm daily May-Sept., 9am-9pm daily Oct.-Apr., adults $17.50, seniors $14.50, students and ages 13-18 $12.50, ages 6-12 $9.50), for views across the city, Stanley Park, the waterfront, and the North Shore mountains. Although many downtown buildings now tower above this 30-story tower, which opened in 1977, it's a good place to get oriented. Your admission price includes a 20-minute tour highlighting local sights as you circle the observation platform. Even if you don't follow a tour, you can ask the guides to point out particular locations or tell you what you're seeing.

Lookout tickets are good all day, so you can check out the daytime views, then return to see the sunset or watch the evening lights twinkle.

★ Bill Reid Gallery of Northwest Coast Art

Born to a Haida First Nations mother and a European father, British Columbia artist Bill Reid (1920-1998) created more than 1,500 sculptures, carvings, and pieces of jewelry, most of which explore Haida traditions. The **Bill Reid Gallery of Northwest Coast Art** (639 Hornby St., 604/682-3455, www.billreidgallery.ca, 10am-5pm daily late May-early Sept., 11am-5pm Wed.-Sun. early Sept.-late May, adults $13, seniors $10, students $8, ages 13-17 $6) is dedicated to Reid's life and work.

Among the highlights of Reid's many works on display are *Mythic Messengers*, a 28-foot (8.5-m) bronze frieze; more

Top to bottom: totem poles in Stanley Park; signs for biking, walking, and craft beer along the Seawall; Gastown Steam Clock.

than 40 pieces of his gold and silver jewelry; and several of Reid's pieces that the Canadian government featured on Canada's $20 bill. The gallery showcases other First Nations art, including a full-size totem pole carved by James Hart of Haida Gwaii, and hosts changing exhibits of indigenous art of the northwest coastal region.

Vancouver Art Gallery

The permanent collection at the **Vancouver Art Gallery** (750 Hornby St., 604/662-4719, www.vanartgallery.bc.ca, 10am-5pm Wed.-Mon., 10am-9pm Tues., adults $24, seniors $20, students $18, ages 6-12 $6.50, 5pm-9pm Tues. by donation) includes more than 10,000 artworks, emphasizing artists from western Canada. The gallery has a particularly strong collection of works by British Columbia-born artist Emily Carr (1871-1945), one of Canada's most important early 20th-century artists. Carr is known for her paintings of B.C.'s landscapes and its indigenous people.

Hosting changing exhibitions throughout the year, the gallery is currently housed in the former 1906 court building designed by architect Francis M. Rattenbury (1867-1935), who also designed Victoria's Parliament Building. Noted B.C. modern architect Arthur Erikson (1924-2009) incorporated the courthouse into the expanded gallery that was completed in 1983. Built around a grand rotunda, the art gallery has exhibit spaces on four levels.

Need a break? The peaceful **Gallery Café** (604/688-2233, www.thegallerycafe.ca, 9am-9pm Mon.-Fri., 9:30am-6pm Sat.-Sun., $9-12) serves salads, paninis, quiche, and wine on a shaded patio.

The Vancouver Art Gallery has announced plans to relocate to a new building, designed by Herzog & de Meuron Architects, which will be constructed at West Georgia and Cambie Streets. Check the gallery website for updates.

Vancouver Central Library

Why go to the library when you're on holiday? The **Vancouver Central Library** (350 W. Georgia St., 604/331-3603, www.vpl.ca, 10am-9pm Mon.-Thurs., 10am-6pm Fri.-Sat., 11am-6pm Sun., free) is both an architectural landmark and a hub of information, art, and events.

Designed by Israeli Canadian architect Moshe Safdie and opened in 1995, the library building has a distinctive curved shape, modeled after Rome's Colosseum. Before you even get to the books, you can have coffee or a snack in one of several cafés in the library's light and airy interior atrium. Or go up to the 9th floor, where you can sit on the outdoor terrace to read or chat and enjoy views over downtown.

The library regularly hosts events, from lectures to author talks to movies. Most are free; check the calendar on the library website to see what's going on.

Gastown and Chinatown

Vancouver's historic **Gastown** district got its name from a fast-talking British sailor and riverboat pilot turned saloon-keeper. In 1867, Captain John Deighton, nicknamed "Gassy Jack" for his habit of telling tall tales, promised local mill-workers that he'd serve them drinks if they'd build him a saloon on the shores of Burrard Inlet. The motivated mill-workers constructed the bar in just one day, and the fledgling Gastown neighborhood took its title from Deighton's "Gassy" nickname.

Gastown, which centers along Water and Cordova Streets, between Richards and Main Streets, became part of the city of Vancouver in 1886. Many of its historic brick and stone buildings date to the early 1900s. There's a **statue of Gassy Jack** at Maple Tree Square, where Alexander, Carrall, Water, and Powell Streets converge.

Chinese immigrants began settling in Vancouver in the 1880s, and by the 1920s, Vancouver's **Chinatown** was thriving. However, in 1923, the Canadian government passed the Chinese Immigration Act, often called the Chinese Exclusion Act, which effectively stopped Chinese from immigrating to Canada. This lack of new residents, combined with the Great Depression of the 1930s, sent the neighborhood into decline. The Exclusion Act wasn't repealed until 1947.

Today, the ornate **Millennium Gate** (Pender St.), erected in 2002, marks the entrance to Chinatown. While the neighborhood still has Chinese markets, bakeries, and restaurants, hip galleries, shops, and eateries are moving in. Chinatown's busiest streets are East Pender, Keefer, and Georgia between Carrall Street and Gore Avenue.

Waterfront Station (Cordova St., between Granville St. and Seymour St.), a transit hub for the SkyTrain, buses, and SeaBus, borders Gastown; the **Stadium/Chinatown** SkyTrain station (Beatty St. at Dunsmuir St.) is also nearby. Many TransLink buses, including buses 4, 7, 14, 16, 20, and 22, travel between downtown and Gastown or Chinatown.

Like many North American cities, Vancouver has a significant homeless population, many of whom congregate on Gastown's and Chinatown's streets. While that isn't a reason to avoid the area, use caution as you would in any urban neighborhood.

Gastown Steam Clock

Sure, it's touristy, but you'll still find yourself in front of this local icon, waiting for it to toot its steam whistle every 15 minutes. The historic-looking **Gastown Steam Clock** (Water St., at Cambie St.) actually dates back only to 1977, when area businesses commissioned clockmaker Ray Saunders to create the clock as part of the neighborhood's revitalization. Saunders based his clock on an 1875 design; it draws power from the city's underground steam heating system (and from three electric motors).

Gastown Art Galleries

Several Gastown art galleries show and sell works by traditional or contemporary indigenous artists. Browsing is free at these commercial galleries.

On the main floor of Skwachàys Lodge, a boutique aboriginal art hotel, the **Urban Aboriginal Fair Trade Gallery** (29 W. Pender St., 604/558-3589, www.skwachays.com, 10am-4pm Mon.-Fri., 11am-5pm Sat.-Sun.) showcases works by Canadian aboriginal artists. The nonprofit Vancouver Native Housing Society owns the gallery, and gallery proceeds help support the society's mission to provide affordable urban housing for indigenous people.

Coastal Peoples Fine Arts Gallery (332 Water St., 604/684-9222, www.coastalpeoples.com, 10am-7pm daily May-Sept., 10am-6pm daily Oct.-Apr.) specializes in Northwest Coast and Inuit artwork in its spacious, modern gallery.

Another specialist in Canadian aboriginal art, the **Inuit Gallery of Vancouver** (206 Cambie St., 604/688-7323, www.inuit.com, 10am-6pm Mon.-Sat., 11am-5pm Sun.) exhibits works by First Nations and Inuit people.

★ Dr. Sun Yat-Sen Classical Chinese Garden

From the building tiles to the pathway pebbles, all the components of the **Dr. Sun Yat-Sen Classical Chinese Garden** (578 Carrall St., 604/662-3207, www.vancouverchinesegarden.com, 9:30am-7pm daily mid-June-Aug., 10am-6pm daily May-mid-June and Sept., 10am-4:30pm daily Oct.-Apr., adults $14, seniors $11, students and ages 6-17 $10, families $28) came from China, as did the 52 master craftsmen who arrived from Suzhou in 1985 to construct the first authentic Ming Dynasty garden outside China.

Take one of the informative **garden tours** (included with admission) to learn more about the peaceful garden's design and construction. Mid-June-August, tours start on the hour 10am-4pm with an additional tour at 5:30pm; check the garden website or phone for tour times during the rest of the year.

Adjacent to the garden is the free city-run **Dr. Sun Yat-Sen Park.** While built with Canadian materials and lacking the classical garden's Chinese pedigree, this smaller park is still a pretty spot to sit. Head for the shaded pagoda and watch the fish swim past.

Rennie Collection at Wing Sang

Vancouver real estate marketer Bob Rennie has assembled one of Canada's largest private collections of contemporary art. At the **Rennie Collection at Wing Sang** (51 E. Pender St., 604/682-2088, www.renniecollection.org, hours vary, free), a private museum in Chinatown's oldest structure, the 1889 Wing Sang Building, you can see changing exhibitions of these works by both established and emerging international artists. To visit an exhibit, you must reserve a spot on a free 50-minute guided tour, offered regularly; book in advance on the gallery website.

Even if you don't go inside, walk far enough away from the gallery building to see British artist Martin Creed's 2008 neon sculpture, *Work No. 851: EVERYTHING IS GOING TO BE ALRIGHT,* installed on the upper facade.

Vancouver Police Museum

If you're curious about some of shiny Vancouver's darker moments, visit the **Vancouver Police Museum** (240 E. Cordova St., 604/665-3346, www. vancouverpolicemuseum.ca, 9am-5pm Tues.-Sat., adults $12, seniors and students $10, ages 6-18 $8, families $30), where exhibits about policing, criminology, and various misdeeds are housed in the 1932 former city morgue and autopsy facility.

In the museum's Sins gallery, check out the collection of counterfeit money, illegal drugs, and confiscated weapons. The True Crime gallery exhibits photos and evidence from notorious regional crimes, many of which remain unsolved. You can also visit the autopsy suite, last used in 1980, which has a collection of preserved human organs.

The museum runs several 90-minute **Sins of the City Walking Tours** (www.sinsofthecity.ca, late Apr.-Oct., adults $18, seniors and students $14), where you can explore the underbelly of Gastown and Chinatown. The **Red Light Rendezvous Tour** (4pm Sat.) tells you about the neighborhoods' brothels and the women who ran them, while on the **Vice, Dice, and Opium Pipes Tour** (6pm Fri., 2pm Sat.), you walk the beat of a 1920s cop, on the lookout for gambling dens, bootlegging joints, and other nefarious activity. The **Soul Food and Shotguns Tour** (11am Sat.) highlights the cultural history of Vancouver's African Canadian and Italian communities, focusing on the city's multicultural heritage and social change movements. While kids are allowed in the police museum at their parents' discretion, the minimum age for these walking tours is 16.

The Police Museum is located east of Gastown, on the edge of Chinatown. **Buses 4 and 7** from downtown stop nearby.

Yaletown and False Creek

British naval officer and explorer George Henry Richards is credited with naming the waterway that separates downtown Vancouver from the rest of the city to the south. In 1859, Richards traveled up what he thought was a creek in search of coal deposits. However, Richards discovered that this waterway was actually an inlet of the Pacific Ocean. He named it **False Creek.**

Sawmills, rail yards, and other industrial developments once lined False Creek. On its northern shore, bounded by Nelson, Homer, Drake, and Pacific Streets, an eight-block warehouse district was built in 1900 in the neighborhood now known as **Yaletown.** Although the area grew derelict in the mid-1900s, its fortunes began to change when Vancouver hosted the Expo '86 World's Fair along False Creek's shores. These days, the renovated brick warehouses are home to a chic mix of condos, restaurants, boutiques, and drinking spots.

On the opposite side of False Creek, a new neighborhood developed, thanks to the 2010 Winter Olympic Games. The residential buildings where athletes lived during the Games have been transformed into the **Olympic Village,** also known as the Village at False Creek, comprising stylish condominiums, brewpubs, and cafés. Photographers: The Olympic Village provides a great vantage point for skyline photos.

To get to Yaletown's restaurants, shops, and pubs, you can take the Canada Line to **Yaletown/Roundhouse** station. From the Canada Line's **Olympic Village** station, across False Creek from downtown, you can walk east along the Seawall to the village itself. The **Main Street/Science World** station on the SkyTrain's Expo Line is closest to the city's science museum and to the rail and bus depot.

Science World

What's that dome thing? The kids may want to check out the distinctive geodesic dome (constructed for Expo '86) that houses Vancouver's cool science museum, even before they venture inside.

Officially called **Science World at Telus World of Science** (1455 Quebec St., 604/443-7440, www.scienceworld.ca, 10am-6pm Fri.-Wed., 10am-8pm Thurs. late June-early Sept., 10am-5pm Mon.-Fri., 10am-6pm Sat.-Sun. Apr.-late June and early Sept.-Mar., extended hours during Dec. winter break and Mar. spring break, adults $25, seniors, students, and ages 13-18 $20.25, ages 3-12 $17), the museum is full of hands-on exhibits about the human body, the natural world, light and sound, puzzles and illusions, and more. The littlest visitors have their own

Science World on Vancouver's False Creek

Kidspace, designed for children under age six. Live science shows and demonstrations take place throughout the day, and a rotating selection of films plays on the five-story-tall screen in the immersive OMNIMAX Theatre ($6 pp in addition to regular admission).

Outside in **Ken Spencer Science Park,** you can explore more interactive exhibits about the local environment and issues of sustainability. The park even has its own chicken coop.

The easiest way to get to Science World from other downtown points is on the SkyTrain to **Main Street/Science World** station. The **Aquabus** (604/689-5858, www.theaquabus.com) and **False Creek Ferries** (604/684-7781, www.granvilleislandferries.bc.ca) also stop nearby.

B.C. Place
The odd-looking structure along False Creek that resembles a giant space ship is **B.C. Place** (777 Pacific Blvd.,

604/669-2300, www.bcplacestadium.com, subway: Stadium/Chinatown), a sports and concert arena. The Vancouver Whitecaps Major League Soccer team plays here, as does the B.C. Lions football team.

Outside the arena, near the intersection of Robson and Beatty Streets, is the **Terry Fox Memorial,** a series of four progressively larger sculptures by Vancouver artist Douglas Coupland. The memorial honors Fox, the B.C. man who embarked on a cross-Canada run in 1980 to raise money for cancer research after losing his own leg to the disease. Fox unfortunately had to stop his "Marathon of Hope" after running 5,342 kilometers (3,339 mi), when his cancer returned. Although Fox raised more than $24 million, he died of cancer at age 22 on June 28, 1981.

★ Granville Island
This former industrial district underneath the Granville Bridge, across False Creek from downtown, is now one of Vancouver's most popular attractions. **Granville Island** (604/666-6655, www.granvilleisland.com) entertains visitors with art galleries, boutiques, breweries and distilleries, and the lively Granville Island Public Market. Granville Island also draws theatergoers to its several stages.

The best time to visit Granville Island is on a weekday morning. The island, particularly the Public Market, gets packed with visitors in the afternoons and on weekends, especially in summer.

From downtown, most TransLink buses that follow Granville Street over the Granville Bridge take you within walking distance of Granville Island. **Bus 50,** which stops at West 2nd Avenue and Anderson Street, is most convenient. You can also take **buses 4, 7, 10, 14, or 16** to Granville Street at 5th Avenue; from there, it's a 10-15 minute walk to the island.

The Island the Olympics Built

Before hosting the 2010 Winter Olympic Games, Vancouver embarked on numerous building projects: the Canada Line subway connecting downtown and the airport, the Olympic Cauldron on the Coal Harbour waterfront, and the Athletes Village on the shores of False Creek, which housed competitors during the Games and is now the fashionable Olympic Village district.

Yet one of the Olympics' most unusual legacies may be an artificial island. To build the Athletes Village, developers excavated a vast amount of rocks, sand, and gravel. More than 2 million cubic feet (60,000 cu m) of this excavated material was used to construct tiny **Habitat Island,** along Southeast False Creek.

Now city-owned parkland, Habitat Island has more than 200 native trees, shrubs, flowers, and grasses, and, as befits its name, it provides a habitat for birds, crabs, starfish, and other land and sea creatures.

Habitat Island is on the False Creek waterfront, near the foot of Columbia Street, east of the Cambie Bridge. Wander across the rock pathway leading onto the island from the Seawall path, and you can explore the island that the Olympics built.

The **Aquabus** (604/689-5858, www.theaquabus.com) and **False Creek Ferries** (604/684-7781, www.granvilleislandferries.bc.ca) can also take you across False Creek between downtown and Granville Island.

Granville Island Public Market

The island's main attraction is the year-round indoor **Granville Island Public Market** (1689 Johnston St., www.granvilleisland.com, 9am-7pm daily), where artistically arranged fruits garnish the produce stalls and you can nibble away the day on pastries, fudge, and other treats.

Start at **Blue Parrot Espresso Bar** (604/688-5127, www.blueparrotcoffee.com) for java with a water view. Sample the unexpectedly addictive **salmon candy** (cured, salty-sweet fish snacks) at any of the seafood counters, or line up with the locals for house-made charcuterie at **Oyama Sausage** (604/327-7407, www.oyamasausage.ca) or nut-studded grape loaves at **Terra Breads** (604/685-3102, www.terrabreads.com).

When you're looking for lunch, sample the soups at **The Stock Market** (604/687-2433, www.thestockmarket.ca), the well-prepared salmon burgers at the **Market Grill** (604/689-1918), or the Thai dishes

at **Sen Pad Thai** (604/428-7900, www.senpadthai.com). You might hope that the kids won't notice longtime favorite **Lee's Donuts** (604/685-4021), at least until it's time for dessert.

Net Loft

After you've explored the Public Market, browse the shops and galleries in the nearby **Net Loft** (1666 Johnston St., 10am-7pm daily).

Circle Craft Co-Operative (604/669-8021, www.circlecraft.net) sells ceramics, textiles, jewelry, and other work by B.C. craftspeople. **Wickaninnish Gallery** (604/681-1057, www.wickaninnishgallery.com) shows First Nations art. Other fun shops are **Little Dream** (604/683-6930, www.dreamvancouver.com), which carries locally made fashions; **Paper-Ya** (604/684-2531, www.paper-ya.com), for fine papers, notebooks, origami, and other paper goods; and **Granville Island Hat Shop** (604/683-4280, www.thehatshop.ca), where you can find almost anything to wear on your head.

Kids Market

On Granville Island, youngsters have their own marketplace. In the **Kids Market** (1496 Cartwright St., 604/689-8447, www.kidsmarket.ca, 10am-6pm daily), cute shops sell toys, games, and clothing. The kids can run around in the Adventure Zone, an indoor playground, or outside in the **splash park** (late May-early Sept.).

Art Galleries

Along the island's lanes are many artist studios and galleries. Wander around to see what you can discover, or look for some of these artisans.

Crafthouse (1386 Cartwright St., 604/687-6511, www.craftcouncilbc.ca, 10am-6pm daily May-Aug., 10:30am-5:30pm daily Sept.-Dec. and Feb.-Apr., 10:30am-5:30pm Tues.-Sun. Jan.) shows work by members of the Craft Council of B.C.

Federation of Canadian Artists Gallery (1241 Cartwright St., 604/681-2744, www.artists.ca, 10am-5pm daily May-Sept., 10am-4pm Tues.-Sun. Oct.-Apr.) exhibits work by its member artists from across Canada.

Harry Potter and his Quidditch team would covet the handmade sweepers from the **Granville Island Broom Co.** (1406 Old Bridge St., 604/629-1141, www.broomcompany.com, 10am-6pm daily).

At the **Silk Weaving Studio** (1531 Johnston St., 604/687-7455, www.silkweavingstudio.com, 10am-5pm daily), you'll find hand-woven scarves, shawls, and other garments.

The museum-like **Eagle Spirit Gallery** (1803 Maritime Mews, 604/801-5277 or 888/801-5277, www.eaglespiritgallery.com, 11am-5pm daily) specializes in original Northwest Coast native art, including sculptures, totem poles, woodcarvings, masks, and paintings by First Nations and Inuit artists.

Breweries and Distilleries

Thirsty? At Granville Island's breweries and distilleries, you can learn about the production process and sample the wares.

Granville Island Brewing (1441 Cartwright St., 604/687-2739, www.gib.ca, store 10am-8pm daily, taproom noon-8pm daily, tours noon, 2pm, and 4pm Mon.-Thurs., noon, 2pm, 4pm, and 5:30pm Fri.-Sun., adults $9.75) started producing craft beers back in 1984. Tour the brewery or try a sample in the taproom.

Liberty Distilling (1494 Old Bridge St., 604/558-1998, www.thelibertydistillery.com, 11am-9pm daily, tours 11:30am and 1:30pm Sat.-Sun., $10) brews small batches of vodka, gin, and whiskey in copper pot stills. Sample its handcrafted products in the cocktail lounge, or take a weekend distillery tour.

At the **Artisan Sake Maker** (1339 Railspur Alley, 604/685-7253, www.artisansakemaker.com, 11:30am-6pm daily, tastings $2), Vancouver's only local producer of Japanese rice wine, learn how sake is brewed, and taste it, too.

Kitsilano and the West Side

West of Granville Island, the Kitsilano neighborhood has a great beach, lots of shops and restaurants (mostly along West 4th Ave.), and several museums in waterfront Vanier Park.

On the city's far west side, the University of British Columbia campus is worth visiting for its stellar Museum of Anthropology, and for several gardens and smaller museums.

Two more of Vancouver's notable parks and gardens—VanDusen Botanical Garden and Queen Elizabeth Park—are located between Oak and Main Streets, near West 33rd Avenue.

★ Museum of Anthropology

If you're interested in exploring the culture of British Columbia's indigenous peoples, and traditional cultures from around the world, don't miss the striking **Museum of Anthropology** (6393 NW Marine Dr., 604/822-5087, www.moa.ubc.ca, 10am-5pm Wed.-Mon., 10am-9pm Tues. mid-May-mid-Oct., 10am-5pm Tues.-Sun. mid-Oct.-mid-May, adults $18, seniors, students, and children over age 6 $16, families $47, 5pm-9pm

Thurs. $10 pp) on the University of British Columbia campus.

Canadian architect Arthur Erickson (1924-2009), whose other work includes Toronto's Roy Thompson Hall, the Museum of Glass in Tacoma, Washington, and many other cultural and governmental buildings around the world, designed the museum, which opened in 1976. The window-lined Great Hall provides a dramatic backdrop for the immense totem poles, traditional canoes, and elaborate carvings. The museum also houses the world's largest collection of works by noted Haida First Nations artist Bill Reid, including his massive cedar sculpture, *The Raven and the First Men*.

To reach the museum by public transit, take any **UBC-bound bus** (including buses 4 and 14 from downtown, bus 84 from the Olympic Village SkyTrain station, or bus 99 from the Broadway/City Hall SkyTrain station) to the last stop at the UBC bus loop. From there, you can walk to the museum in 10-15 minutes, or transfer to **shuttle bus 68,** which stops near the museum.

By car, it's about 25 minutes from downtown to the museum. Cross either the Granville or Burrard Bridges, and go west on West 4th Avenue. West of Blanca Street, 4th Avenue becomes Chancellor Boulevard, which circles the campus and meets NW Marine Drive. There's a parking lot at the museum.

Nitobe Japanese Garden

You could be in Japan as you stroll among the flowers, waterfalls, and koi ponds at the serene **Nitobe Japanese Garden** (1895 Lower Mall, UBC, 604/822-6038, www.botanicalgarden.ubc.ca, 10am-4:30pm daily Apr.-Oct., adults $7, seniors and students $5.50, ages 6-12 $4, families $16, 10am-2pm Mon.-Fri. Nov.-Mar. by donation), one of the most authentic traditional Japanese gardens in North America. The garden is particularly scenic in April and May, when the cherry blossoms bloom.

The garden is named for Dr. Inazo Nitobe (1862-1933), a professor, author, and advocate for East-West relations who served as Japan's representative to the League of Nations in the 1920s.

You can participate in a traditional **Japanese tea ceremony** (May-Sept., $10 pp in addition to garden admission) in the garden's teahouse on the last Saturday of the month. Ceremonies are held on the hour 11am-3pm, and reservations are recommended; see the garden website for reservation details.

The garden is a short walk from the Museum of Anthropology. From the UBC bus loop, you can walk or take **shuttle bus 68.**

UBC Botanical Garden

A garden of native B.C. plants, a woodland garden, a traditional Asian garden: These are just a few groupings of the more than 10,000 trees and plants that thrive at the 70-acre (28-ha) **UBC Botanical Garden** (6804 SW Marine Dr., UBC, 604/822-4208, www.botanicalgarden.ubc.ca, 10am-4:30pm daily, adults $9, seniors $7, ages 6-12 $5), where walking paths wend through the woods and grounds.

A more adventurous way to explore the garden is on the **Greenheart TreeWalk** (10am-4pm daily Apr.-Oct., adults $20, seniors $15, ages 6-12 $10, including garden admission), a 1,000-foot (308-m) aerial trail system that takes you high into the rainforest canopy. You climb a series of swinging bridges to eight viewing platforms mounted in the trees.

Explore the walkway on your own or on a 45-minute **guided tour,** where your guide tells you about the surrounding second-growth forest. Though the area was once logged, many trees are more than a century old. You'll also learn how First Nations use various trees and plants, from carving canoes to traditional medicine.

The Botanical Garden is on the south side of the UBC campus. By public transit, the fastest way to reach the garden from downtown is to take the Canada Line south to the Langara-49th Avenue station and transfer to **bus 49 UBC,** which stops near the garden.

By car, it's about 25 minutes from downtown to the gardens. Cross the Granville or Burrard Bridges, and go west on West 4th Avenue. West of Blanca Street, 4th Avenue becomes Chancellor Boulevard, which circles the campus and meets NW Marine Drive, which becomes SW Marine. There's a parking lot at the garden.

Beaty Biodiversity Museum

An 85-foot (26-m) blue whale skeleton, the largest on display in Canada, greets visitors to the **Beaty Biodiversity Museum** (2212 Main Mall, UBC, 604/827-4955, www.beatymuseum.ubc. ca, 10am-5pm daily mid-May-mid-Oct., 10am-5pm Tues.-Sun. mid-Oct.-mid-May, adults $14, seniors, students, and ages 13-17 $12, ages 5-12 $10), a modern natural history gallery. This family-friendly museum has more than two million specimens of bugs, fish, plants, fossils, and more, many of which come from B.C. and the surrounding regions. Numerous items are set at kids' eye level for youngsters to check out.

The museum is near the center of the UBC campus, a short walk from the UBC bus loop.

Museum of Vancouver

Though its building resembles a flying saucer that might have landed in Kitsilano's Vanier Park, this city museum's unique structure, created by architect Gerald Hamilton, is actually designed to recall a traditional hat of the Haida First Nations people. Inside the **Museum of Vancouver** (1100 Chestnut St., 604/736-4431, www. museumofvancouver.ca, 10am-5pm Sun.-Wed., 10am-8pm Thurs., 10am-9pm Fri.-Sat., adults $20.50, seniors and students $17.25, ages 12-18 $13.75, ages 5-11 $9.75,

families $43), the exhibition spaces are no less distinctive.

The permanent galleries take you through Vancouver's past, from its indigenous heritage to early settlement days to the hippie era of the 1960s, while the sometimes controversial temporary exhibitions explore social phenomena from happiness to sex. Admission is by donation 5pm-8pm on the last Thursday of the month.

The museum hosts lectures, workshops, and social events that are as engaging as the exhibits themselves; check the calendar on the website for details.

The museum shares its building with the **H.R. MacMillan Space Centre** (1100 Chestnut St., 604/738-7827, www. spacecentre.ca, 10am-5pm daily late June-early Sept., 10am-3pm Mon.-Fri., 10am-5pm Sat., noon-5pm Sun. early Sept.-late June, adults $19.50, seniors and ages 12-18 $16.50, ages 5-11 $14, families $60.50), the city's planetarium, which has galleries of space exhibits to explore and astronomy shows throughout the day.

The Space Centre's **Gordon MacMillan Southam Observatory** (604/738-2855, Sat. year-round, Fri. early July-early Sept., evening show and stargazing adults $14, seniors and students $11, ages 5-11 $8.50, families $41) is also open for a planetarium show (7:30pm and 9pm) and guided stargazing (7pm-11pm) through the half-meter telescope. If you come only for stargazing, admission is by donation.

The **Dual Pass** (adults $31.50, seniors and students $26.50, ages 5-11 $18.50) covers admission to the Museum of Vancouver and the MacMillan Space Centre. The **Vanier Park Explore Pass** (adults $42.50, seniors and students $36.50) includes admission to the museum, the Space Centre, and the nearby Vancouver Maritime Museum.

Bus 2 travels from Burrard Street downtown into Kitsilano; get off at the corner of Cornwall Avenue and Cypress Street, where it's a short walk toward the water to the museum. Or take **False**

Creek Ferries (604/684-7781, www.granvilleislandferries.bc.ca) to Vanier Park from Granville Island or downtown.

Vancouver Maritime Museum

Built in B.C. in the 1920s, the historic Arctic-exploring schooner *St. Roch* recorded several firsts. The ship was the first to sail the Northwest Passage from west to east (1940-1942) and the first to circumnavigate North America, when it traveled from Vancouver to Halifax via the Panama Canal in 1950.

When the ship was retired, the *St. Roch* came to rest at the **Vancouver Maritime Museum** (1905 Ogden St., 604/257-8300, www.vancouvermaritimemuseum.com, 10am-5pm Fri.-Wed., 10am-8pm Thurs., adults $13.50, seniors and students $11, ages 6-18 $10, families $38), where it's now the centerpiece of the museum's exhibits about the high seas.

Climb aboard the *St. Roch* and learn more about its Arctic adventures. The museum has other hands-on exhibits designed for kids, as well as changing exhibitions about Pacific Northwest and Arctic maritime history.

To reach the museum, on the waterfront in Vanier Park, take **bus 2** from Burrard Street downtown to the corner of Cornwall Avenue and Cypress Street in Kitsilano. Or take **False Creek Ferries** (604/684-7781, www.granvilleislandferries.bc.ca) to Vanier Park from Granville Island or downtown.

South Granville Street

Granville Street, between West 5th and 15th Avenues, is worth browsing for its high-end boutiques and contemporary art galleries. Stop into **Douglas Reynolds Gallery** (2335 Granville St., 604/731-9292, www.douglasreynoldsgallery.com, 10am-6pm Mon.-Sat., noon-5pm Sun.) for the exhibits of historic and contemporary

Top to bottom: totem pole at the Museum of Anthropology; Beaty Biodiversity Museum; VanDusen Botanical Garden.

Northwest Coast First Nations art, or see what's on view at **Bau-Xi Gallery** (3045 Granville St., 604/733-7011, www.bau-xi. com, 10am-5:30pm Mon.-Sat., 11am-5:30pm Sun.), which features contemporary fine art.

Buses 10, 14, and 16 travel along Granville Street over the Granville Bridge from downtown. Get off at Broadway, and you'll be in the heart of the South Granville neighborhood.

VanDusen Botanical Garden

Wander the plant world without leaving Vancouver at the 55-acre (22-ha) **VanDusen Botanical Garden** (5251 Oak St., 604/257-8335, www.vandusengarden. org, 9am-8pm daily June-Aug., 10am-6pm daily Sept., 10am-5pm daily Oct., 10am-3pm daily Nov.-Feb., 10am-5pm daily Mar., 9am-6pm daily Apr., 9am-7pm daily May, extended hours during Dec. Festival of Lights; Apr.-Sept. adults $11.25, seniors and ages 13-18 $8.45, ages 4-12 $5.50, Oct.-Mar. adults $8, seniors and ages 13-18 $5.50, ages 4-12 $4.25).

With more than 250,000 plants from around the globe, the garden contains varieties native to the Pacific Northwest, to other parts of Canada, and to ecosystems in the Himalayas, the Mediterranean, and South America. A one-hour **guided tour** (1pm daily and 10:30am Wed. Apr.-Oct., 1pm Sun. Nov.-Mar.) helps you explore what's growing.

From downtown, **bus 17** for Oak Street stops at West 37th Avenue at the garden entrance.

Queen Elizabeth Park

At **Queen Elizabeth Park** (4600 Cambie St., www.vancouver.ca, dawn-dusk daily), at the highest point in Vancouver, you can explore several gardens, have a picnic on its manicured grounds, or take photos of the city skyline and mountains. Also in the park are tennis courts, a pitch-and-putt golf course, and a lawn bowling field.

In a geodesic dome near the park's center, **Bloedel Conservatory** (604/873-7000,

www.vancouver.ca, 10am-8pm daily May-Aug., 10am-6pm daily Sept.-Oct. and Apr., 10am-5pm daily Nov.-Mar., adults $6.50, seniors and ages 13-18 $4.35, ages 4-12 $3.15) houses three different ecosystems: a tropical rainforest, subtropical rainforest, and desert environment, with native plants and more than 200 free-flying birds. It's a warm destination for a cold or rainy day.

To get to the park by public transit, take the Canada Line to **King Edward** station. Then either transfer to **bus 15** southbound on Cambie Street to West 33rd Avenue, or walk south on Cambie Street to the park entrance. Follow the trails through the trees or walk along the park road to reach the conservatory; either way, it's a short but uphill climb.

Main Street and the East Side

Visit Vancouver's funky East Side for craft breweries, cafés, and local boutiques.

Breweries

The neighborhood around Main Street between 2nd and 8th Avenues has become a center of local craft beer production. Perfect for a brewery crawl, several breweries with tasting rooms are within walking distance of each other:

33 Acres Brewing (15 W. 8th Ave., 604/620-4589, www.33acresbrewing. com, 9am-11pm Mon.-Fri., 10am-11pm Sat.-Sun.) is known for beers like 33 Acres of Sunshine (a blond summer ale) and 33 Acres of Darkness (a malty dark beer). The sunny brewpub draws hordes for its weekend waffle brunches.

Brassneck Brewery (2148 Main St., 604/259-7686, www.brassneck.ca, 2pm-11pm Mon.-Fri., noon-11pm Sat.-Sun.) features frequently changing small-batch brews. Communal tables in the compact tasting room fill up fast, particularly on weekend evenings.

Main Street Brewing Company (261 E. 7th Ave., 604/336-7711, www.mainstreetbeer.ca, 2pm-11pm

Mon.-Thurs., noon-11pm Fri.-Sun.) is located in a 1913 heritage building with exposed brick walls. Choose from year-round staples like Main Street Pilsner or Naked Fox IPA, or opt for seasonal brews like a Barking Mad Plum Porter.

The North Shore

Across Burrard Inlet from downtown Vancouver, the North Shore mountains provide the backdrop for the waterfront cities of North Vancouver and West Vancouver. For visitors, exploring these peaks—on the hiking trails, suspension bridges, or ski runs—is the best reason to cross the bridges from downtown.

Two bridges connect Vancouver to the North Shore. The Lions Gate Bridge crosses from Stanley Park to West Vancouver, while the Ironworkers Memorial Second Narrows Bridge links Vancouver's east side to North Vancouver.

★ Grouse Mountain

Open for skiing and snowboarding in winter, and for hiking and lots of other activities spring-fall, a half-day (or longer) trip to **Grouse Mountain** (6400 Nancy Greene Way, North Vancouver, 604/980-9311, www.grousemountain. com, 9am-10pm daily) lets you experience the mountains less than 40 minutes from downtown.

Take the **Skyride** (8:45am-10pm daily), North America's largest tram system, to the **Peak Chalet,** where you can watch a film about the region's wildlife at the **Theatre in the Sky** or take in the entertaining 45-minute **Lumberjack Show** (11:15am, 2pm, and 4:30pm daily late May-mid-Oct.), complete with log rolling, tree climbing, and ax throwing. The **Birds in Motion demonstration** (1:30pm, 3:30pm, and 5:30pm daily late May-late Sept.) shows off the skills of eagles, falcons, and other birds of prey, while at the **Grouse Mountain Refuge for Endangered Wildlife,** you can learn more about bears, wolves, owls, and other creatures. Several

self-guided **walking trails** start near the Peak Chalet, or you can take a 45-minute **guided eco-walk** (late May-Sept.) that departs several times a day. The **Peak Chairlift** takes you to the top of the mountain.

Standard **Mountain Admission tickets** (adults $56, seniors $49, ages 5-16 $29, families $149) give you access to the Skyride, Theatre in the Sky, Lumberjack Show, Birds in Motion, wildlife refuge, the Peak Chairlift, and walking trails.

For extra fees, you can add activities such as **zip-lining** ($45-89), a **ropes course** ($39), **paragliding** (late June-Sept., $199), a visit to a mountaintop wind turbine called **The Eye of the Wind** ($15), and **breakfast with the bears** (8:30am daily late June-mid-Sept., 8:30am Sat.-Sun. late Mar.-late June and mid-Sept.-mid-Oct., adults $39, seniors $34, ages 5-16 $29, families $122) at the wildlife refuge. In summer, you even have the option to "surf" up the mountain on top of the tram on the **Skyride Surf Adventure** ($25).

Getting There

By car from downtown Vancouver, take West Georgia Street to the Lions Gate Bridge. Cross the bridge, turn right onto Marine Drive east, but move immediately into the left lane. Take the first left onto Capilano Road and follow it up the hill to the Grouse Mountain parking lot (3 hours $8, full day $10).

You don't need a car to get to Grouse Mountain, though. The mountain runs a **free shuttle** (May-Sept., call or check the website for schedule) from Canada Place.

By public transportation, take the **SeaBus** from Waterfront Station to Lonsdale Quay and change to **bus 236** for Grouse Mountain, which will drop you at the mountain's base.

Capilano Suspension Bridge

The **Capilano Suspension Bridge** (3735 Capilano Rd., North Vancouver, 604/985-7474, www.capbridge.com, 8am-8pm daily late May-early Sept., 9am-6pm daily early Sept.-mid-Oct., 9am-5pm daily mid-Oct.-late Nov., 11am-9pm daily late Nov.-late Jan., 9am-5pm daily late Jan.-mid-Mar., 9am-6pm daily mid-Mar.-late Apr., 9am-7pm daily late Apr.-late May, adults $46.95, seniors $42.95, students $34.95, ages 13-16 $27.95, ages 6-12 $14.95) draws daredevils who thrill to the swinging bridge, as well as others who want to explore this rainforest park.

Built in 1889, the 450-foot (137-m) **suspension bridge** is a highlight, swaying 230 feet (70 m) above the Capilano River. And yes, it does swing!

Before you cross the bridge, follow the **Cliffwalk,** a series of boardwalks and stairways cantilevered out over the river. If you're feeling brave, stand on the glass platform and look down (way down!) into the canyon where the river rushes below.

After you've made your way over the suspension bridge, explore the **Treetops Adventure,** a 700-foot (213-m) network of gently swaying wooden bridges linking eight treehouse platforms. Many of the surrounding Douglas firs are up to 300 feet (90 m) tall. Back on the ground, gentle **walking trails** lead through the rainforest.

Particularly in the summer high season, the least crowded times to visit the Capilano Suspension Bridge are before 10am or after 5pm.

Getting There
You can take a **free shuttle** to the suspension bridge from several locations downtown, including Canada Place, Hyatt Hotel (Melville St. at Burrard St.), Blue Horizon Hotel (1225 Robson St.), and Library Square (Homer St. at Robson St.). Check the website for seasonal schedules.

By car from downtown, cross the Lions Gate Bridge onto Marine Drive east, then take the first left onto Capilano Road, following it up the hill to the suspension bridge. **Parking** is $6 for up to four hours.

If you're also planning to visit Grouse Mountain, continue north on Capilano Road.

By public transportation, take the **SeaBus** from Waterfront Station to Lonsdale Quay and change to **bus 236** for Grouse Mountain. Get off at Ridgewood Avenue, a block from the suspension bridge.

Lynn Canyon Park
The 617-acre (250-ha) **Lynn Canyon Park** (Park Rd., North Vancouver, www.lynncanyon.ca, 7am-9pm daily summer, 7am-7pm daily spring and fall, 7am-6pm daily winter, free) is a little farther from downtown than the Capilano bridge, but it has its own **suspension bridge** built back in 1912—and it's free.

Hiking trails wend through the park, including the **30 Foot Pool trail** and the **Twin Falls trail** that both lead to popular swimming areas (bring your bathing suit); these easy trails are each 0.6 mile (1 km) long, starting from the suspension bridge. The **Ecology Centre** (3663 Park Rd., North Vancouver, 604/990-3755, www.lynncanyonecologycentre.ca, 10am-5pm daily June-Sept., 10am-5pm Mon.-Fri., noon-4pm Sat.-Sun. Oct.-May, donation $2) has kid-friendly exhibits about the region's plants and animals.

Getting There
To get to Lynn Canyon by car from downtown Vancouver, cross the Lions Gate Bridge, then turn right onto Marine Drive east. Take the first left onto Capilano Road and go up the hill to the Highway 1 entrance. Follow Highway 1 east to Exit 19. Take Lynn Valley Road northeast to Peters Road. Turn right (east) onto Peters, which will take you into the park.

By public transit from downtown, catch **bus 210** for Upper Lynn Valley on West Pender Street at Seymour Street, near Waterfront Station. Get off at Phibbs Exchange in North Vancouver and change to **bus 227,** Lynn Valley Center.

The Best Chinese Food Outside China

Do you love Chinese food? Then you've come to the right city.

Closely linked to the Pacific Rim, Vancouver has more direct flights to China than any other North American city, and more than 40 percent of the population in metropolitan Vancouver is of Asian descent. These strong Asian influences permeate the city, from business culture to food. In particular, the Vancouver region has hundreds of Chinese restaurants, many serving high-end cuisine that rivals the fare in Hong Kong, Taipei, and Beijing.

Chinatown, near the city center, was once a vibrant immigrant community. While it still has Chinese markets, bakeries, and restaurants, new hip shops and eateries have moved in, making the neighborhood fun to explore but not necessarily the best place for traditional Asian meals.

For that, hop on the Canada Line to **Richmond,** the region's new Chinatown, where dozens of restaurants serve cuisines from across China. It's a 25-minute ride from downtown.

Whether you're looking for spicy Sichuan fare, handmade noodles and dumplings like you'd see in Shanghai, delicately seasoned Cantonese seafood, or the hearty lamb dishes of China's western provinces, you'll find it in Richmond. Cafés serving bubble tea and Taiwanese shaved ice desserts draw a young crowd, while families pack the round tables of countless dim sum houses. Richmond's Alexandra Road, which runs for several blocks east from No. 3 Road, has so many restaurants that it's known locally as **"Food Street."** The city even has a **Dumpling Trail** (www.visitrichmondbc.com), which highlights where to eat pot stickers, *xiao long bao* (soup dumplings), and other delectable stuffed dough dishes.

The center of Richmond's Asian food scene is the **Golden Village,** along No. 3 Road from Cambie Road south toward Granville Avenue. From the Canada Line, get off at Aberdeen, Lansdowne, or Richmond-Brighouse stations, and you'll find plenty to eat.

The bus will stop at the corner of Peters and Duval Roads, about a 5-minute walk from the park entrance.

Lonsdale Quay

A food and shopping complex overlooking the water adjacent to the SeaBus terminal, **Lonsdale Quay** (123 Carrie Cates Ct., North Vancouver, 604/985-6261, www.lonsdalequay.com, 9am-7pm daily) is like a small-scale Granville Island Public Market. Vendors sell fruit, vegetables, seafood, sandwiches, and other prepared foods. **Green Leaf Brewing** (604/984-8409, www.greenleafbrew.com) makes craft beer; the **Artisan Wine Shop** (604/264-4008, www.artisanwineshop. ca) does complimentary wine-tastings.

The easiest way to get to Lonsdale Quay from downtown Vancouver is to take the **SeaBus** from Waterfront Station, a 12-minute ride.

Polygon Gallery

In a striking silver building on the North Vancouver waterfront, a short walk east of Lonsdale Quay, **Polygon Gallery** (101 Carrie Cates Ct., North Vancouver, 604/986-1351, www.thepolygon.ca, 10am-5pm Tues.-Sun, donation) exhibits contemporary art, specializing in photography and works by Canadian artists. The museum has a first-rate view of the downtown Vancouver skyline, too, from the 1st-floor glass atrium and from the 2nd-floor waterside terrace.

From downtown Vancouver, take the **SeaBus** from Waterfront Station to Lonsdale Quay and walk east.

Richmond

Vancouver is now considered the most Asian city outside Asia. Many of its Asian residents have settled in Richmond, a city of more than 200,000 on Vancouver's southern boundaries, where more than half the population is of Asian descent, with most people hailing from China, Taiwan, or Hong Kong.

Richmond has several attractions to explore and some of the best Chinese food in North America. The city's waterfront Steveston Village was important in the region's fishing history and still houses a bustling fish market and numerous seafood restaurants.

★ Richmond Night Market

Spring-autumn, the **Richmond Night Market** (8351 River Rd., 604/244-8448, www.richmondnightmarket.com, 7pm-midnight Fri.-Sat., 7pm-11pm Sun. mid-May-mid-Oct., adults $4.25, seniors and kids under 10 free) is packed with visitors enjoying Asian food stalls, quirky shopping opportunities, and a general carnival atmosphere. Go with an empty stomach since there's plenty to sample: grilled kebabs, squid on a stick, bubble waffles, handmade tofu pudding, and many other snacks; most dishes cost $5 or less. Vendors also sell cell phone cases, socks, electronic gadgets, and more.

To get to the night market, take the Canada Line from downtown to **Bridgeport Station.** From there, it's a 15-minute walk. Just follow the crowds.

Golden Village

The Richmond branch of the Canada Line follows No. 3 Road through the district known as the **Golden Village,** the region's new Chinatown. You'll know you've arrived when the Chinese-language signs outnumber those in English, and Asian restaurants, markets, and shops line the strip malls and surrounding streets.

A good place to start exploring is **Aberdeen Centre** (4151 Hazelbridge Way, 604/270-1234, www.aberdeencentre.

Top to bottom: Capilano Suspension Bridge; Richmond Night Market; Grouse Mountain Skyride.

com, 11am-7pm Sun.-Wed., 11am-9pm Thurs.-Sat.), a glitzy Hong Kong-style shopping mall, with shops selling tea, electronics, clothing, Asian-language books, and more. On the 3rd floor, stop for excellent Cantonese, Sichuanese, Taiwanese, Japanese, and Korean fare in the busy food court. The mall has several good sit-down restaurants, too, including **Fisherman's Terrace Seafood Restaurant** (604/303-9739, 10am-3pm and 5:30pm-10pm daily, dim sum $4-15, dinner $15-35) for dim sum and **Chef Hung Taiwanese Beef Noodle** (604/295-9357, www.chefhungnoodle.com, 11am-9pm Sun.-Thurs., 11am-9:30pm Fri.-Sat., $8-13) for Taiwanese noodle soup.

Aberdeen Centre is one block from **Aberdeen Station,** at the corner of Cambie Road and Hazelbridge Way.

Steveston

Where the Fraser River meets the Pacific Ocean, the village of Steveston has long been a launching point for fishing boats, and it remains among Canada's largest commercial fishing ports. Fish vendors sell their catch along the docks, and numerous eateries serve local seafood. Steveston is also a departure point for whale-watching tours.

In the late 1800s, Steveston was not only a fishing hub; it also became a major center for salmon canning. The largest of the more than 15 canneries that lined the waterfront is now the **Gulf of Georgia Cannery National Historic Site** (12138 4th Ave., 604/664-9009, www.gulfofgeorgiacannery.org, 10am-5pm daily, adults $11.70, seniors $10.05). Inside the 1894 cannery, you can see what it was like to work the canning line, alongside the Asian and European immigrant workers who were the main labor force. Other exhibits trace the history of the west coast fishing industry.

If you wonder how the multicultural community of fisherfolk, dockworkers, and cannery crews lived, visit the **Britannia Shipyards National Historic Site** (5180 Westwater Dr., 604/718-8050, www.britanniashipyard.ca, 10am-5pm daily May-Sept., noon-5pm daily Oct.-Apr., free), a collection of restored homes and shops, many dating back to the 1880s, that housed Chinese, Japanese, European, and First Nations people. Stop into the 1885 Murakami House, where a Japanese family of 12 lived and worked between 1929 and 1942, or explore the west coast's last surviving Chinese bunkhouse, which once accommodated 75 to 100 Chinese cannery workers. To walk to the shipyards from the Steveston waterfront, follow the harborside path 0.6 mile (1 km) east.

To reach Steveston by public transit, take the Canada Line south to **Richmond-Brighouse Station,** then change to any Steveston-bound bus, including **buses 402, 407, and 410.**

By car from downtown, follow Granville Street south toward the Vancouver airport. After crossing the Arthur Laing Bridge, stay in the right lane and exit toward Richmond. Continue south on Russ Baker Way, which becomes No. 2 Road. At Westminster Highway, turn right (west). At No. 1 Road, turn left (south) and continue south to Steveston.

Sports and Recreation

Whale-Watching

Several whale-watch companies run trips from Vancouver or from Steveston Harbour in Richmond.

Wild Whales Vancouver (1806 Mast Tower Rd., Vancouver, 604/699-2011, www.whalesvancouver.com, Apr.-Oct., adults $135, seniors and students $110, ages 3-12 $85) offers whale-watching trips leaving from Granville Island.

Steveston Seabreeze Adventures (12551 No. 1 Rd., Richmond, 604/272-7200, www.seabreezeadventures.ca, Apr.-Oct., adults $130, seniors and students $105, ages 3-12 $80) operates whale-watch trips from Steveston Village. It provides a **shuttle** (round-trip $10) from downtown Vancouver hotels. In the spring, it also offers 90-minute **sea lion tours** (Apr.-mid-May, adults $32, seniors and students $25, kids $20) to view migrating California sea lions.

Also departing from Steveston, **Vancouver Whale Watch** (210-12240 2nd Ave., Richmond, 604/274-9565, www. vancouverwhalewatch.com, Apr.-Oct., adults $130-140, seniors and students $110-140, ages 4-12 $75-140) offers whale-watching tours with a **shuttle** (round-trip $15) between Steveston and several downtown Vancouver hotels.

Beaches and Pools
Downtown and the West End
You don't have to leave downtown Vancouver to go to the beach. The city has several stretches of sand right downtown.

Along the Seawall on the west side of Stanley Park, you can swim or sun at quiet **Third Beach** or busier **Second Beach,** which has a seasonal snack bar as well as the kid-friendly seaside **Second Beach Pool** (Stanley Park Dr., 604/257-8371, www.vancouver.ca, May-Sept.).

As you'd expect from the name, **Sunset Beach** (Beach Ave. at Thurlow St.), along the Seawall near English Bay, is a west-facing beach with sunset views.

To swim year-round, head for the **Vancouver Aquatic Centre** (1050 Beach Ave., 604/665-3424, www.vancouver.ca, 6:30am-9:30pm Mon.-Fri., 8am-9:30pm Sat., 10am-9:30pm Sun., adults $6.15, seniors and ages 13-18 $4.40, ages 3-12 $3.10, families $3.10 pp), a public 50-meter indoor pool near Sunset Beach downtown.

★ English Bay Beach
English Bay Beach (Beach Ave. at Denman St.), in the West End, is the busiest of the downtown beaches, fun for people-watching, swimming, or watching the sunset. You can follow the Seawall path from here into Stanley Park or around to Yaletown. In summer, you can rent kayaks and stand-up paddleboards.

Kitsilano and the West Side
Popular **Kitsilano Beach** (aka "Kits Beach," Cornwall Ave. at Arbutus St.) is a good swimming spot. In summer, serious beach volleyball players flock here, and you can rent kayaks or stand-up paddleboards. From the beach, you can follow the Seawall path east around Vanier Park (popular with kite-flyers and home to the Museum of Vancouver and the Vancouver Maritime Museum) to Granville Island. Next to the beach, **Kitsilano Pool** (2305 Cornwall St., 604/731-0011, www.vancouver.ca, daily May-Sept., adults $6.15, seniors and ages 13-18 $4.40, ages 3-12 $3.10, families $3.10 pp) is a 450-foot-long (135-m) salt-water swimming pool with water slides to entertain the kids.

West of Kitsilano, three connected beaches, **Jericho Beach** (Point Grey Rd. west of Alma St.), **Locarno Beach** (NW Marine Dr. at Trimble St.), and **Spanish Banks Beach** (NW Marine Dr. at Tolmie St.), draw families with sandy swimming areas and grassy stretches for picnicking and playing.

Water Sports
One of the best ways to explore Vancouver is from the water, since sheltered seas surround the city. You can head out on the water in a **kayak** or **stand-up paddleboard** from English Bay, False Creek, Kitsilano Beach, and Jericho Beach.

Ecomarine Paddlesports Centre (604/689-7575 or 888/425-2925, www. ecomarine.com) rents kayaks and stand-up paddleboards and offers guided kayak and SUP tours. Find them year-round on **Granville Island** (1668 Duranleau St., 9am-9pm daily late May-July, 9am-8pm daily Aug.-early Sept., 10am-6pm daily early Sept.-late May) and in summer at **Jericho Beach** (Jericho Sailing Centre, 1300 Discovery St., 10am-dusk Mon.-Fri.,

9am-dusk Sat.-Sun. late May-early Sept.). The last rentals go out two hours before sunset at Jericho, three hours before sunset on Granville Island; call to confirm seasonal hours.

Vancouver Water Adventures (604/736-5155, www.vancouver wateradventures.com, May-Sept., call or check website for hours) rents kayaks and stand-up paddleboards, offers tours, rents Jet Skis, and teaches SUP yoga classes. It has branches on **Granville Island** (1812 Boatlift Ln.), **Kitsilano Beach,** and **English Bay Beach.**

Near the Olympic Village on False Creek, **Creekside Kayaks** (1 Athletes Way, 604/616-7453, www.creeksidekayaks.ca, 11am-dusk Mon.-Fri., 9am-5pm Sat.-Sun. late Apr.-mid-Oct.) rents kayaks and stand-up paddleboards.

Hiking
★ Pacific Spirit Regional Park
Although it's less well known than downtown's Stanley Park, **Pacific Spirit**

Regional Park (604/224-5739, www. metrovancouver.org, dawn-dusk daily, free), on Vancouver's West Side near the University of British Columbia campus, is actually larger, measuring more than 1,800 acres (760 ha). More than 40 miles (64 km) of hiking trails wend through this dense rainforest. Most are gentle forest strolls, although some steeper routes lead from the park to Spanish Banks Beach.

You can access several park trails off West 16th Avenue between Discovery Street and Acadia Road; several others start from Chancellor Boulevard west of Blanca Street. Another park entrance is on West 29th Avenue at Camosun Street. Maps are posted at the start of most trails. For an online map, see the website of the **Pacific Spirit Park Society** (www. pacificspiritparksociety.org).

Don't hike alone here. While you're close to the city, many trails quickly lead deep into the forest and feel quite remote.

paddleboarder and pet near Granville Island

The Grouse Grind

You can't call yourself a Vancouverite until you've hiked the Grind, or so say the many who've made the trek up Vancouver's best-known trail. Nicknamed "Mother Nature's Stairmaster," the **Grouse Grind** (6400 Nancy Greene Way, North Vancouver, 604-980-9311, www.grousemountain.com) is only 1.8 miles (2.9 km) long, but it's essentially a mountain staircase that you climb straight up, gaining an elevation of 2,800 feet (850 m). Along most of the trail, you're hiking in the forest. The reward comes at the top, with vistas across the city.

Average active hikers can generally complete the Grouse Grind, which has 2,830 steps, in about 90 minutes, but plenty of people need at least two hours. The very fit charge up the mountain in 30-60 minutes.

Hikers are allowed to walk uphill only. To return to the parking area, you ride down on the **Skyride** (one-way $15), the

Grouse Mountain tram. Check the trail status if you're planning a spring or fall hike; there can be snow on the trail even when it's warm in the city.

To get to the Grouse Grind trailhead by car from downtown Vancouver, take West Georgia Street to the Lions Gate Bridge. Cross the bridge, turn right onto Marine Drive east, but move immediately into the left lane. Take the first left onto Capilano Road and follow it up the hill to the Grouse Mountain parking lot (3 hours $8, full day $10). The mountain runs a **free shuttle** (May-Sept., call or check the website for schedule) from Canada Place. By public transportation, take the **SeaBus** from Waterfront Station to Lonsdale Quay and change to **bus 236** for Grouse Mountain, which will drop you at the mountain's base.

Cycling

Vancouver prides itself on being bicycle-friendly. The city has been adding off-street and dedicated cycling lanes throughout the area, and offers a bike-sharing program.

Vancouver's most popular cycling route runs along the **Seawall,** also signposted as the "Seaside Cycling Route." This paved path circles Stanley Park and follows False Creek through Yaletown and past Science World, the Olympic Village, Granville Island, and Kitsilano Beach. From Kits Beach, you can continue west on Point Grey Road, which becomes a bicycle-priority street west of MacDonald Street, then pedal the beachside paths along Jericho, Locarno, and Spanish Banks Beaches. You'll enjoy some of Vancouver's best views as you cycle this route.

Bike Rentals

Spokes Bicycle Rentals (1798 W. Georgia St., 604-688-5141, www.spokesbicyclerentals.com, 9am-7:30pm daily, 1 hour $9-11, full-day $45-69) and **English Bay Bike Rentals** (1754 Davie St., 604/568-8490, www.

englishbaybikerentals.com, 9am-6pm daily, 1 hour $9-14, full-day $35-54) are convenient to Stanley Park. **Bicycle Sports Pacific** (999 Pacific St., 604/682-4537, www.bspbikes.com, 10am-6pm Mon.-Sat., noon-5pm Sun., 2 hours $20, full-day $40-69) rents bikes from its location opposite the Burrard Bridge, where Yaletown meets the West End.

Reckless Bike Stores (www.reckless.ca, 1.5 hours $18.50, full-day $39.50) rents bicycles along the Seawall in **Yaletown** (110 Davie St., 604/648-2600, 10am-6:30pm Mon.-Fri., 10am-6pm Sat.-Sun.) and near **Granville Island** (1810 Fir St., 604/731-2420, 9:30am-6pm Mon.-Sat., 10am-5pm Sun.).

Bike Shares

Vancouver has a bike-sharing program that enables you to rent a bike at one location and return it at another. For visitors, the easiest way to use the **Mobi bike share system** (778/655-1800, www.mobibikes.ca) is to sign up online for a day pass. For $9.75 per day, you can take an unlimited number of 30-minute rides within a 24-hour period. If you keep the bike for more than a half hour during any ride, you'll pay an extra $5 for each additional 30 minutes, so it's more cost-effective to dock your bike when you stop to sightsee, shop, or eat. You can check out another bike after your stop.

After registering online, you'll receive a seven-digit user code that will unlock your bike. Bikes are stationed throughout the downtown area, in Kitsilano, and on the East Side; search the Mobi website for the bikes nearest you. Helmets, which local laws require cyclists to wear, are available at each rental station.

Winter Sports
Skiing, Snowboarding, and Snowshoeing

Vancouver has three local mountains that offer downhill skiing and snowboarding, weather permitting, December-March. It can often be snowing on the mountains

when it's raining in the city, so check the mountain weather forecast if you're hoping for a snow day.

Grouse Mountain (6400 Nancy Greene Way, North Vancouver, 604/980-9311, www.grousemountain.com) is closest to downtown and the only mountain that's easily accessible by public transportation. There are 26 runs for downhill skiing and snowboarding, and snowshoeing is offered.

The largest of the North Shore mountains, **Cypress Mountain** (6000 Cypress Bowl Rd., West Vancouver, 604/926-5612, www.cypressmountain.com) hosted several events during the 2010 Winter Olympics. You can ski and snowboard on the mountain's 53 downhill trails. Cypress has a separate Nordic area with trails for cross-country skiing and snowshoeing.

Family-friendly **Mount Seymour** (1700 Mt. Seymour Rd., North Vancouver, 604/986-2261, www.mountseymour.com), the area's smallest ski area, has five lifts serving 40 downhill runs. It's a good spot for snowshoeing.

Ice-Skating

You can ice-skate right downtown at **Robson Square Ice Rink** (800 Robson St., 604/209-8316, www.robsonsquare.com, 9am-9pm Sun.-Thurs., 9am-11pm Fri.-Sat. Dec.-Feb., free), underneath Robson Square, near the Vancouver Art Gallery. You can rent skates ($5) if you don't have your own.

During the 2010 Winter Olympic Games, the **Richmond Olympic Oval** (6111 River Rd., Richmond, 778/296-1400, www.richmondoval.ca) hosted the speed-skating events. You can practice your own skating moves during the Oval's public skating hours; rentals are available.

Spectator Sports

Vancouver is wild for hockey, particularly the city's National Hockey League team, the **Vancouver Canucks** (800/745-3000, www.nhl.com/canucks), whose regular season runs October-April. The Canucks take to the ice at **Rogers Arena** (800 Griffiths Way, 604/899-7400, www.rogersarena.com, subway: Stadium/Chinatown).

Vancouver's professional Major League Soccer team, the **Vancouver Whitecaps** (604/669-9283, www.whitecapsfc.com), plays March-October at **B.C. Place** (777 Pacific Blvd., 604/669-2300, www.bcplacestadium.com, subway: Stadium/Chinatown).

Curious as to how professional Canadian football differs from its American cousin? Watch the **B.C. Lions** (604/589-7627, www.bclions.com) run the field at **B.C. Place** (777 Pacific Blvd., 604/669-2300, www.bcplacestadium.com, subway: Stadium/Chinatown). The season runs July-November.

The city's minor league baseball team, the **Vancouver Canadians** (604/872-5232, www.canadiansbaseball.com), play June-September at family-friendly **Nat Bailey Stadium** (4601 Ontario St., subway: King Edward), near Queen Elizabeth Park.

Entertainment and Events

For local event listings, see the *Georgia Straight* (www.straight.com), the *Vancouver Theatre Guide* (www.gvpta.ca) from the Greater Vancouver Professional Theatre Association, or *Inside Vancouver* (www.insidevancouver.ca). The blog *Miss 604* (www.miss604.com) publishes monthly lists of upcoming events.

Nightlife
Downtown and the West End
First opened in 1930, the **Commodore Ballroom** (868 Granville St., 604/739-4550, www.commodoreballroom.com) hosts live concerts, featuring performers as diverse as the Tragically Hip, Lady Gaga, and Katy Perry.

Head to **The Roxy** (932 Granville St.,

604/331-7999, www.roxyvan.com) when you want to dance. Rockin' house bands play several nights a week. Sunday is country-western night.

Quiet enough for conversation, snug **Uva Wine & Cocktail Bar** (900 Seymour St., 604/632-9560, www.uvavancouver.com) serves creative cocktails, craft beer, and a long list of wines by the glass.

Secreted away on the 4th floor of the Rosewood Hotel Georgia, the outdoor **Reflections Lounge** (604/673-7043, www.rosewoodhotels.com, Apr.-Oct.), where you can sip your wine or classic cocktail on teak couches around a fire pit, brings Los Angeles glamour to Vancouver. The hotel's elegant **Prohibition Lounge** (604/673-7089) has a roaring twenties theme, with music or DJs several nights a week.

Polished **Bacchus Lounge** (845 Hornby St., 604/608-5319, www.wedgewoodhotel.com) at the Wedgewood Hotel is appropriate for cocktails with a colleague or a consort. There's live piano music every evening.

Davie Street, in the West End, is the center of Vancouver's LGBT community, where nightspots include **Celebrities Nightclub** (1022 Davie St., 604/681-6180, www.celebritiesnightclub.com), a party-hardy dance club; the easygoing **Fountainhead Pub** (1025 Davie St., 604/687-2222, www.thefountainheadpub.com); and **1181 Lounge** (1181 Davie St., 604/787-7130, www.1181.ca), an upscale lounge and music spot.

Gastown and Chinatown
With a name like the **Pourhouse** (162 Water St., 604/568-7022, www.pourhousevancouver.com), you'd expect a joint that serves great cocktails—and you'd be right. The resident mixologists at this upscale Gastown saloon concoct drinks like the Fire Drill (a blend of mezcal, passionfruit, lime, and amaro) and the Silver Tongue (Fernet-Branca, bourbon, cointreau, lemon, and honey).

Beer lovers need no excuse to visit the **Alibi Room** (157 Alexander St., 604/623-3383, www.alibi.ca), a low-key Gastown pub with 50 taps of local and imported craft beers.

The Keefer Bar (135 Keefer St., 604/688-1961, www.thekeeferbar.com), a hip Chinatown hideout, concocts aromatic cocktails using house-made bitters, teas, and syrups. Pair the Opium Sour (bourbon, grapefruit, tamarind, lemon, and poppy-seed tincture) or the Dragon Fly (dragonfruit-infused gin, sake, ginger, lemon, and magnolia bark tincture) with the Asian-inspired small plates.

Granville Island

For brews with water views, **Dockside Lounge** (Granville Island Hotel, 1253 Johnston St., 604/685-7070, www.docksidevancouver.com) looks out across False Creek, with a patio perfectly positioned for drinks on a sunny afternoon.

The Arts

Tickets Tonight (Tourism Vancouver Visitor Centre, 210-200 Burrard St., 604/684-2787, www.ticketstonight.ca, 9am-5pm daily) sells same-day, half-price theater tickets. Check the current day's availability by phone, on the website, or via the Twitter feed, @TicketsTonight. You have to buy tickets in person before 4pm for evening shows. Tickets Tonight also sells full-price advance tickets to many local productions.

Theater

Vancouver's top repertory theater and the largest theater company in western Canada, the **Arts Club Theatre Company** (604/687-1644, www.artsclub.com) performs on three stages. Its main stage shows are held at the 650-seat **Stanley Industrial Alliance Stage** (2750 Granville St.) in the South Granville district. The company also performs at the **Granville Island Stage** (1585 Johnston St.), next to the Public Market, and at the **Goldcorp**

Vancouver Folk Festival at Jericho Beach

Stage at the BMO Theatre Centre (162 W. 1st Ave.), in the Olympic Village.

The **Vancouver East Cultural Centre** (604/251-1363, www.thecultch.com), known locally as "The Cultch," hosts an eclectic season of theater, dance, and musical events. It has three performance spaces on the city's East Side: the 200-seat **Historic Theatre** (1895 Venables St.), the small black-box **Vancity Culture Lab** (also at 1895 Venables St.), and the nearby **York Theatre** (639 Commercial Dr.).

Another venue for diverse theatrical productions is the **Firehall Arts Centre** (280 E. Cordova St., 604/689-0926, www.firehallartscentre.ca), in a 1906 former city fire station on the edge of Chinatown.

June-September, the **Bard on the Beach Shakespeare Festival** (604/739-0559, www.bardonthebeach.org) performs Shakespeare's plays under billowing white tents in Kitsilano's Vanier Park.

With a mix of professional and aspiring actors, **Theatre Under the Stars**

(Malkin Bowl, 610 Pipeline Rd., information 604/734-1917, tickets 604/631-2877, www.tuts.ca) produces two summertime musicals outdoors in Stanley Park.

If you're traveling with kids, see what's on stage at Granville Island's **Carousel Theatre for Young People** (1411 Cartwright St., 604/669-3410, www.carouseltheatre.ca).

Comedy

The always-entertaining **Vancouver Theatre Sports League** (1502 Duranleau St., 604/738-7013, www.vtsl.com) performs regular improv shows at its waterside theater on Granville Island.

At **Yuk Yuk's Vancouver Comedy Club** (2837 Cambie St., 604/696-9857, www.yukyuks.com), you can see shows by local and visiting comedians.

Music

The **Vancouver Symphony Orchestra** (604/876-3434, www.vancouversymphony.ca) performs downtown in the historic **Orpheum Theatre** (601 Smithe St. at Granville St.).

Canada's second-largest opera company, the **Vancouver Opera** (604/683-0222, www.vancouveropera.ca) stages its productions in the 2,765-seat **Queen Elizabeth Theatre** (650 Hamilton St.) or at the adjacent **Vancouver Playhouse** (630 Hamilton St.).

On the University of British Columbia campus, the modern **Chan Centre for the Performing Arts** (6265 Crescent Rd., 604/822-2697, www.chancentre.com) hosts jazz, blues, and world music performers, as well as early music and chamber concerts.

Dance

Vancouver's professional contemporary ballet company, **Ballet BC** (855/985-2787, www.balletbc.com) presents several productions a year at the **Queen Elizabeth Theatre** (650 Hamilton St.).

DanceHouse (604/801-6225, www.dancehouse.ca) brings Canadian and

international dance companies to the **Vancouver Playhouse** (630 Hamilton St.) downtown.

Cinema

Vancity Theatre (1181 Seymour St., 604/683-3456, www.viff.org), a modern repertory cinema downtown, shows independent and art films from around the world and hosts the Vancouver International Film Festival every autumn.

Summer Cinema in Stanley Park (www.freshaircinema.ca/summercinema, July-Aug.) is a family-friendly series of free Tuesday-evening films shown outdoors at Ceperley Meadow off Stanley Park Drive, near Second Beach. Films begin at dusk. Bring a blanket or a lawn chair.

The **Vancouver Police Museum** (240 E. Cordova St., 604/665-3346, www. vancouverpolicemuseum.ca) presents a monthly film series, **Movies in the Morgue,** screening a mix of classics, comedies, and horror films on the second Tuesday of the month September-April. Tickets sell out, so book in advance on the museum website.

Festivals and Events
Spring
Close to 50,000 runners and walkers take to the streets for the **Vancouver Sun Run** (www.vancouversun.com/sunrun, Apr.), a fun-for-all 10K that starts and ends downtown.

Bring the kids to Kitsilano's Vanier Park when the **Vancouver International Children's Festival** (www. childrensfestival.ca, May-June) offers family-friendly concerts, circus performers, crafts, and other activities.

Summer
Vancouver celebrates Canada's birthday, **Canada Day** (www.canadaplace.ca, July 1), with a parade, outdoor concerts, and celebratory fireworks over Burrard Inlet. Canada Place is the center of the festivities.

It's not just folk music at the long-established **Vancouver Folk Festival** (www.thefestival.bc.ca, July), which draws world beat, roots, blues, and yes, folk musicians from across Canada and around the world to Jericho Beach for three days of always eclectic music on multiple outdoor stages. It's great fun for all ages.

Fireworks displays over English Bay bring thousands of Vancouverites and visitors out for the **Celebration of Light** (www.hondacelebrationoflight.com, July-Aug.) that takes place over several summer evenings. The best viewing spots are at English Bay Beach, but you can see them from Kitsilano Beach and other beaches around False Creek.

The **Vancouver Pride Festival** (www. vancouverpride.ca, July-Aug.) features more than 20 events celebrating the city's large gay, lesbian, bisexual, and transgender community, culminating in a festive parade through the downtown streets.

Fall
For two weeks, the **Vancouver Fringe Fest** (www.vancouverfringe.com, Sept.) takes over Granville Island and other stages around town with innovative, quirky, and often surprising theater, comedy, puppetry, and storytelling performances.

Movie lovers line up at the **Vancouver International Film Festival** (www.viff. org, Sept.) to see the latest releases from Canadian, American, and international filmmakers.

The **Vancouver Writers Fest** (www. writersfest.bc.ca, Oct.), a week of readings, lectures, and other literary events, features more than 100 authors from across Canada and abroad.

Dinners featuring chefs from across Canada, cooking workshops, a food expo, and lots of other delicious events draw foodies to the **EAT! Vancouver Food + Cooking Festival** (www.eat-vancouver. com, Nov.).

East Vancouver artists open their

studios to visitors during the popular **Eastside Culture Crawl** (www.culturecrawl.ca, Nov.). Whether you're in the market for artwork or just like to browse, most artists are interested in chatting with visitors.

Winter

The VanDusen Botanical Garden marks the holiday season with its annual **Festival of Lights** (www.vandusengarden.org, Dec.), illuminating its garden paths with thousands of sparkling lights.

More than 2,000 intrepid people welcome the year at the **Polar Bear Swim** (www.vancouver.ca, Jan. 1), an annual New Year's Day dip in the sea at English Bay. It's fun to watch, even if you don't dive in. And in case you're wondering, it's cold.

Dozens of restaurants offer special menus, and you can join in food events, from chef dinners to wine-tastings to food tours, during **Dine Out Vancouver** (www.dineoutvancouver.com, Jan.), the city's annual celebration of dining that has grown into one of Canada's largest food and drink festivals.

Vancouver's Chinatown, and many venues in Richmond, mark the **Lunar New Year** (Jan.-Feb.) with parades, lion dances, music, fireworks, and other special events.

Shopping

If you're coming from a major city in the United States, you may be disappointed with the shopping options in Vancouver, since selections are typically smaller and prices higher than at similar stores south of the border. Of course, if the exchange rate is in your favor, shopping here may be a better value.

Regardless of your home base, products to look for in Vancouver include Canadian-designed clothing, local art, B.C. wines and beer, and local food items. Vancouver has a number of well-stocked outdoor stores where you can find outdoor gear for your Canadian travels.

Shopping Districts
Downtown and the West End

Vancouver's main downtown shopping district is along **Robson Street,** between Jervis and Granville Streets. Department stores and boutiques line **Granville Street** as well. At **Pacific Centre Mall** (701 W. Georgia St., 604/688-7235, www.cfshops.com, 10am-7pm Mon.-Tues., 10am-9pm Wed.-Fri., 10am-8pm Sat., 11am-7pm Sun.), stores include Canadian and international brands such as Nordstrom, H&M, Banana Republic, Aritzia, and the Apple Store.

Gastown

Visit **Gastown** for smaller fashion boutiques and clothing by local designers. Several Gastown galleries carry high-quality First Nations art.

Kitsilano and the West Side

On Vancouver's West Side, the Kitsilano neighborhood mixes North American chains and local boutiques, centered along **West 4th Avenue** between Burrard and Vine Streets. There's a collection of ski and snowboard gear shops on 4th at Burrard.

Another street to browse is **South Granville** between West 5th and 15th Avenues, for high-end clothing and accessories and for contemporary art.

Main Street

Looking for clothes you won't find at the local mall? Several independent boutiques stocking clothing by local and Canadian designers are located on **Main Street,** between East 20th and 30th Avenues.

Richmond

The **McArthurGlen Designer Outlet-Vancouver Airport** (1000-7899 Templeton Station Rd., Richmond, 604/231-5525, www.mcarthurglen.com, 10am-9pm daily) has outlets and factory stores for brands such as Calvin Klein, Coach, Fossil, J.Crew, and Vans. Take the Canada Line (YVR branch) to Templeton Station.

Department Stores

The Vancouver flagship location of **Hudson's Bay** (674 Granville St., 604/681-6211, www.hbc.com, 9:30am-9pm Mon.-Sat., 11am-7pm Sun.), Canada's original department store, is in a 1914 building downtown, selling clothing and accessories for women, men, and kids, as well as housewares, luggage, and small appliances.

For high-fashion designer clothing, with prices to match, visit **Holt Renfrew** (737 Dunsmuir St., 604/681-3121, www.holtrenfrew.com, 10am-9pm Mon.-Sat., 11am-7pm Sun.) downtown.

High-end Seattle-based **Nordstrom** (799 Robson St., 604/699-2100, www.nordstrom.com, 9:30am-9pm Mon.-Sat., 11am-8pm Sun.) has a large store at Vancouver's Pacific Centre Mall downtown.

You can often find deals on designer apparel and other clothing at **Winners** (www.winners.ca), a discount department store with branches downtown (798 Granville St., 604/683-1058, 9am-9pm Mon.-Sat., 10am-8pm Sun.) and near Broadway and Cambie (491 W. 8th Ave., 604/879-3701, 9am-9pm Mon.-Sat., 10am-8pm Sun.).

Clothing and Accessories

The now-ubiquitous yoga- and workout-wear maker **Lululemon Athletica** (www.lululemon.com) got its start in Vancouver and still has its flagship stores downtown (970 Robson St., 604/681-3118, 10am-9pm Mon.-Sat., 10am-8pm Sun.), at Pacific Centre (701 W. Georgia St., 604/662-3880, 10am-7pm Mon.-Tues., 10am-9pm Wed.-Fri., 10am-8pm Sat., 11am-7pm Sun.), and in Kitsilano (2113 W. 4th Ave., 604/732-6111, 10am-8pm daily). To see what's new, check out **Lululemon Lab** (50 Powell St., 604/689-8013, www.lululemonlab.com, 11am-7pm Mon.-Sat., noon-6pm Sun.) in Gastown, a "concept store" offering prototypes and other clothing not carried at the other stores.

Launched in Vancouver, **Oak + Fort** (355 Water St., 604/566-9199, www.oakandfort.ca, 11am-7pm Mon.-Wed., 11am-8pm Thurs.-Fri., 10am-7pm Sat., 11am-6pm Sun.) has a spacious Gastown store purveying stylishly relaxed, moderately priced clothing for men and women, along with jewelry and accessories. Both the monochromatic designs and the high-ceilinged shop have a minimalist, almost Japanese aesthetic.

For clothing and accessories by emerging Canadian designers, check out **Two of Hearts** (1986 W. 4th Ave., 604/428-0998, www.twoofhearts.ca, 11am-6pm Mon.-Sat., noon-5pm Sun.) in Kitsilano.

The motto of **Barefoot Contessa** (3715 Main St., 604/879-8175, www.thebarefootcontessa.com, 11am-6pm Mon.-Sat., noon-5pm Sun.), which has no connection to cooking guru Ina Garten, is "all things lovely," and with its stock of frilly, flouncy, feminine styles, it's hard to dispute that claim. You can find the perfect dress to wear to a garden party or a flowery frock to brighten a rainy day. Check out the vintage-inspired jewelry and other sparkly baubles.

For vintage, designer consignment, and smart new clothing, the fashion-conscious frequent **Front and Company** (3772 Main St., 604/879-8431, www.frontandcompany.com, 11am-6:30pm daily).

Canadian shoemaker **John Fluevog** (837 Granville St., Downtown, 604/688-2828; 65 Water St., Gastown, 604/688-6228, www.fluevog.com, 10am-7pm Mon.-Wed. and Sat., 10am-8pm Thurs.-Fri., noon-6pm Sun.) launched his funky footwear line in Vancouver.

Kitsilano's **Gravity Pope** (2205 W. 4th Ave., 604/731-7673, www.gravitypope.com, 10am-9pm Mon.-Fri., 10am-7pm Sat., 11am-6pm Sun.) stocks style-conscious shoes for men and women, with brands like Camper, Vans, and its own in-house line.

Art

Just off Main Street, **Hill's Native Art** (120 E. Broadway, 604/685-4249, www.hills. ca, 10am-7pm daily) carries a large collection of First Nations arts and crafts, from souvenir-style items to high-quality prints, carvings, and more.

Books

Kidsbooks (2557 W. Broadway, 604/738-5335, www.kidsbooks.ca, 9:30am-6pm Mon.-Thurs. and Sat., 9:30am-9pm Fri., 11am-6pm Sun.) is Vancouver's best place to find reading matter for toddlers to teens. The Kitsilano shop stocks a large selection of titles by Canadian authors, plus games, crafts, and audio books.

Pulp Fiction Books (www. pulpfictionbooksvancouver.com) carries many new and used titles in Kitsilano (2754 W. Broadway, 604/873-4311, 11am-7pm daily) and in two East Side shops (2422 Main St., 604/876-4311, 10am-8pm Mon.-Wed., 10am-9pm Thurs.-Sat., 11am-7pm Sun.; and 1830 Commercial Dr., 604/251-4311, 11am-7pm daily).

Wander into **Wanderlust** (1929 W. 4th Ave., 604/739-2182, www.wanderlustore. com, 10am-7pm Mon.-Fri., 10am-6pm Sat., noon-5pm Sun.), a well-stocked travel store in Kitsilano, for guidebooks, maps, luggage, and other travel gear. Also in Kitsilano, **The Travel Bug** (2865 W. Broadway, 604/737-1122, www. thetravelbug.ca, 9:30am-6pm Mon.-Sat., 11am-5pm Sun.) has a cozy nook filled with travel books. This compact but well-stocked storefront carries luggage, bags, and travel supplies as well.

Gourmet Goodies

Looking for a souvenir for a foodie friend or an edible memory from your Vancouver visit? **Edible Canada** (1596 Johnston St., 604/682-6675, www. ediblecanada.com, 10am-5pm daily), opposite the Granville Island Public Market, stocks locally produced salts, jams, vinegars, and more from around British Columbia and across Canada.

The friendly cheesemongers at **Les Amis du Fromage** (www.buycheese. com) will help you pick the perfect wedge, whether you're looking for locally made Brie or a pungent Époisses from France. Sampling is encouraged. The Kitsilano shop (1752 W. 2nd Ave., 604/732-4218, 9am-6pm Sat.-Wed., 9am-6:30pm Thurs.-Fri.) is a short walk from Granville Island; there's a second location in East Vancouver (843 E. Hastings St., 604/253-4218, 10am-6pm daily).

British Columbia's largest privately owned liquor store, **Legacy Liquor Store** (1633 Manitoba St., 604/331-7900, www. legacyliquorstore.com, 10am-11pm daily), in the Olympic Village, has an excellent selection of B.C. wines. It holds complimentary wine-tastings and other special events; check the website or phone for a schedule.

Another source of wines from B.C. and elsewhere is **Liberty Wine Merchants** (1660 Johnston St., 604/602-1120, www. libertywinemerchants.com, 9:30am-8pm Mon.-Thurs., 9:30am-8:30pm Fri., 9am-8:30pm Sat., 9am-8pm Sun.), near the Granville Island Public Market.

Outdoor Gear

If you need outdoor clothing and equipment, camping supplies, or cycling gear, head for Broadway between Yukon and Main Streets, where you'll find a cluster of outdoor shops. The largest, **MEC** (130 W. Broadway, 604/872-7858, www. mec.ca, 10am-9pm Mon.-Fri., 9am-6pm Sat., 10am-6pm Sun.), as Mountain Equipment Co-op is known, is a Canadian chain stocking its own label and other brands of clothing, backpacks, and gear for hiking, bicycling, rock climbing, kayaking, and other sports.

Sports Junkies (102 W. Broadway, 604/879-6000, www.sportsjunkies. com, 10am-7pm Mon.-Wed., 10am-8pm Thurs.-Fri., 10am-6pm Sat., 10am-5pm

Sun.) has good deals on new and used sports equipment and clothing for both kids and adults.

Near West 4th Avenue at Burrard in Kitsilano, several shops sell gear for skiing, snowboarding, surfing, and cycling, including **Comor** (1787 W. 4th Ave., 604/736-7547, www.comorsports. com, 10am-6pm Mon.-Wed. and Sat., 10am-8pm Thurs.-Fri., 11am-5pm Sun.), **West Coast Sports** (1675 W. 4th Ave., 604/732-4810, www.westcoastsports. ca, 10am-6pm Mon.-Sat., 11am-5pm Sun. Mar.-Oct., 10am-6pm Mon.-Wed. and Sat., 10am-7pm Thurs.-Fri., 11am-5pm Sun. Nov.-Feb.), **Pacific Boarder** (1793 W. 4th Ave., 604/734-7245, www. pacificboarder.com, 10am-6pm Mon.-Wed. and Sat., 10am-8pm Thurs.-Fri., 11am-5pm Sun.), and **The Boardroom** (1755 W. 4th Ave., 604/734-7669, www. boardroomshop.com, 10am-6pm Mon.-Wed. and Sat., 10am-8pm Thurs.-Fri., 11am-5pm Sun.).

Food

What should you eat in Vancouver? Like any major North American city, Vancouver restaurants span the globe, serving meals that take cues from Italy, France, Spain, China, Japan, and more. But here's what Vancouver does best.

Vancouver is known for seafood, particularly salmon, halibut, oysters, and spot prawns, caught in regional waters. The city's restaurants have embraced the "eat local" movement, so look for seasonal produce and locally raised meats. With a large Asian population, Vancouver has some of the best Chinese food in North America, as well as good Japanese, Korean, and Vietnamese fare. Many restaurants also incorporate Pacific Rim influences in their dishes.

British Columbia wines, from the Okanagan Valley or Vancouver Island, are good accompaniments to most Vancouver meals, as are regionally brewed craft beers. Plenty of bartenders have adopted an "eat local" philosophy, too, incorporating locally grown herbs, house-made bitters, and other fresh ingredients into creative cocktails and alcohol-free drinks.

Downtown and the West End
Seafood

Sink into a cream-colored banquette at **Boulevard Kitchen & Oyster Bar** (845 Burrard St., 604/642-2900, www. boulevardvancouver.ca, 6:30am-11pm daily, breakfast $9-29, lunch $17-27, dinner $27-47), where the service is polished and dishes like wild side stripe shrimp served with chilled melon and fennel gazpacho, roasted sablefish with grilled mushrooms, or ling cod and pea shoots in a red curry cream highlight local seafood in refined Asian-accented preparations. You could stop in for a glass of bubbly and fresh oysters at the bar, too.

Contemporary

In a chandelier-bedecked space at the Rosewood Hotel Georgia, sophisticated **Hawksworth Restaurant** (801 W. Georgia St., 604/673-7000, www. hawksworthrestaurant.com, 6:30am-10:30am, 11:30am-2pm, and 5pm-10pm Mon.-Thurs., 6:30am-10:30am, 11:30am-2pm, and 5pm-11pm Fri., 7am-2pm and 5pm-11pm Sat., 7am-2pm and 5pm-10pm Sun., breakfast $12-26, lunch $23-42, dinner $42-60) attracts expense-account diners, couples celebrating occasions, and gourmets savoring a fine meal with solicitous service. From the foie gras parfait to wagyu steak to lobster with black truffle, it's all about the luxe ingredients in the regionally influenced contemporary fare. **TIP:** If the dinner prices are too rich, splurge on a leisurely lunch or light bites at the bar.

Styled like a Parisian brasserie, **Royal Dinette** (905 Dunsmuir St., 604/974-8077, www.royaldinette.ca, 11:30am-2pm and 4:30pm-10pm Mon.-Fri., 5pm-10pm

Vancouver's Food Trucks

Vancouver's growing number of **food trucks** park downtown, purveying a global gamut of meals to go. A cluster of trucks sets up shop around the Vancouver Art Gallery along Howe and Hornby Streets, while others locate closer to the waterfront along Burrard or Thurlow Streets. Most operate from 11am or 11:30am until 2:30pm or 3pm.

The best way to find what trucks are where is with the **Vancouver Street Food app** (http://streetfoodapp.com/vancouver), which also lists truck locations online. Some favorites include:

♦ **Mom's Grilled Cheese** (Howe St. at Robson St. and W. Cordova St. at Hornby St.) for, as you'd expect, grilled cheese sandwiches

♦ **Le Tigre Cuisine** (check website for locations, www.letigrecuisine.ca) for Asian fusion fare, including kick-ass fried rice

♦ **The Kaboom Box** (Granville St. at W. Georgia St., www.thekaboombox.com) for hot-smoked salmon sandwiches

♦ **Chickpea** (check website for locations, www.ilovechickpea.ca) for a vegan Middle Eastern menu of falafel, *sabich* (eggplant), and salads

♦ **Aussie Pie Guy** (check website for locations, www.aussiepieguy.com) for handheld Australian-style meat or vegetable pies

Sat., lunch $17-22, dinner $16-35) is a lively spot for inventive farm-to-table dining downtown. How do you choose among cucumbers with farm egg custard and salmon roe, B.C. rockfish with spiced tomato water, pasta made fresh daily, or short ribs glazed with angelica root? Find some willing dining companions and share. To drink, try a local craft beer or a fun cocktail.

Chinese

Watch the dumpling makers at work at **Dinesty Dumpling House** (1719 Robson St., 604/669-7769, www. dinesty.ca, 11am-3pm and 5pm-10pm Mon.-Fri., 11am-10pm Sat.-Sun., $7-23), and that's what you should order, too: Shanghai-style soup dumplings, pan-fried pork buns, and steamed vegetable and egg dumplings. Handmade noodles, fresh greens with garlic, and the unusual omelet with pickles are also tasty choices at this bustling West End eatery.

Japanese

Part of a local mini chain of *izakayas*, lively **Guu Garden** (888 Nelson St., 604/899-0855, www.guu-izakaya.com, 11:30am-2:30pm and 5:30pm-midnight Mon.-Thurs., 11:30am-2:30pm and 5:30pm-12:30am Fri., noon-3pm and 5:30pm-12:30am Sat., noon-3pm and 5:30pm-midnight Sun., $6-16) serves Japanese tapas designed to share, like grilled black cod cheeks, crispy cauliflower *karaage,* and sashimi-style tuna *tataki,* to pair with sake, *shochu,* or Japanese beer. Guu is on the top floor of a complex with a similarly named eatery on the main level, so be sure to go upstairs.

At **Santouka Hokkaido Ramen** (1690 Robson St., 604/681-8121, www.santouka. co.jp, 11am-11pm daily, $11-17), the local outpost of a Japan-based noodle shop chain, the signature dish is *tokusen toroniku* ramen, a rich, almost creamy soup made from pork cheek meat. This ramen revelation is worth the inevitable queue, but lingering in this tightly packed space is discouraged, so diners slurp and move on. There's another location on Broadway near Cambie.

Another Japanese import, **Marutama Ramen** (780 Bidwell St., at Robson St., 604/688-8837, www.marutama.ca, $9-18, 11:30am-10pm Mon.-Thurs., 11:30am-10:30pm Fri., 11am-10:30pm Sat., 11am-10pm Sun.) makes its noodle soup with a velvety chicken broth. The *tamago* ramen comes with roast pork and an egg, while the *tanmen* is full of fresh vegetables. In addition to this West End branch, you'll find a second location near the Vancouver Central Library downtown.

For sushi with a water view, visit **Miku** (200 Granville St., 604/568-3900, www.mikurestaurant.com, 11:30am-3pm and 5pm-10:30pm Sun.-Wed., 11:30am-3pm and 5pm-11pm Thurs.-Sat., $16-45), an upscale Japanese dining room opposite Canada Place. It's known for *aburi* sushi, fresh fish seared with a blowtorch.

A unique-to-Vancouver mash-up of hot dogs and Japanese flavors, **Japadog** concocts its signature sausages, like the *kurobuta* pork *terimayo,* sauced with teriyaki, mayonnaise, and seaweed, at a diminutive downtown counter-service restaurant (530 Robson St., 604/569-1158, www.japadog.com, 10am-10pm Mon.-Sat., 10am-9pm Sun., $4-8) and at two downtown food trucks.

Diners

Retro diner **The Templeton** (1087 Granville St., 604/685-4612, http://thetempleton.ca, 8:30am-10pm Sun.-Thurs., 8:30am-11pm Fri.-Sat., $8-16), complete with tabletop jukeboxes and soda-fountain stools, has morphed into a cool purveyor of comfort foods. Dig into hearty plates of pancakes, creative omelets, or burgers, which you can pair with coffee or "big people drinks" (craft beer, local wines, and cocktails). Save room for an ice cream sundae or old-fashioned banana split.

Cafés, Bakeries, and Light Bites

Cyclists congregate at bike-friendly **Musette Caffè** (1325 Burrard St., 778/379-4150, www.musettecaffe.com, 7am-8pm daily, $8-14), a spacious downtown coffeehouse with double-height windows and a sunny patio. You don't have to bring your bicycle, though, to enjoy an espresso, a beer, or a breakfast plate. To encourage patrons to be social, the café has a no-laptops-on-weekends policy.

Expect a queue at **Medina Café** (780 Richards St., 604/879-3114, www.medinacafe.com, 8am-3pm Mon.-Fri., 9am-3pm Sat.-Sun., $9-19), which is known for its sugar-studded Liège waffles and North African-influenced brunch fare. Try the tagine, a flavorful vegetable stew topped with poached eggs, merguez sausage, and preserved lemon.

For fresh salads, soups, rice bowls, and sandwiches near Canada Place, plow a path to cafeteria-style **Tractor Foods** (335 Burrard St., 604/979-0500, www.tractorfoods.com, 7am-9:30pm Mon.-Fri., 8am-9:30pm Sat.-Sun, $5-13). Other locations include Robson Street downtown, at the Olympic Village, in Kitsilano, and in the Broadway-Cambie neighborhood.

Groceries and Markets

The **West End Farmers Market** (Comox St. at Thurlow St., www.eatlocal.org, 9am-2pm Sat. late May-late Oct.) purveys produce, baked goods, and prepared foods; several food trucks park here, too.

Upscale **Urban Fare** (305 Bute St., 604/669-5831; 1133 Alberni St., 604/648-2053; www.urbanfare.com, 7am-11pm daily) sells groceries and meals to go from two downtown locations.

Gastown and Chinatown

Many of Vancouver's most innovative restaurants have opened in Gastown and Chinatown, so visit these districts when you're hungry for what's new and cool.

Contemporary

On the site of Vancouver's first jail, transformed into a multilevel space with exposed brick and polished woods, ★ **L'Abattoir** (217 Carrall St., 604/568-1701, www.labattoir.ca, 5:30pm-10pm Sun.-Thurs., 5:30pm-10:30pm Fri.-Sat., brunch 10am-2pm Sat.-Sun., dinner $29-35, brunch $15-23) detains diners with creative cocktails (how about an avocado gimlet with herb-infused gin, avocado, and lime?) and a changing menu of west coast plates. Meat eaters might bite into pan-fried sweetbreads, while fish fans might favor baked oysters, wild salmon confit with dashi butter, or braised octopus with smoked pork belly and charred eggplant. At brunch, order the oversize scone mounded with house-made jam and clotted cream.

Combining tastes of North Africa and Belgium with local ingredients, **Chambar** (568 Beatty St., 604/879-7119, www.chambar.com, 8am-3pm and 5pm-late daily, breakfast/brunch $9-21, lunch $16-29, dinner $25-36) pleases patrons all day in a window-lined rehabbed warehouse. Kick off your morning with a waffle studded with pearl sugar or breakfast cassoulet of sausage, beans, fried egg, and kale. Later, you might sup on roasted halibut with pea tips and savory oats or duck breast with gnocchi and goat cheese. *Moules frites* (mussels with french fries) are a specialty.

Chinese

At **Bao Bei Chinese Brasserie** (163 Keefer St., 604/688-0876, www.bao-bei.ca, 5:30pm-midnight Mon.-Sat., 5:30pm-11pm Sun., $6-23), many menu items, from *mantou* (steamed buns) to fried rice, would be at home in a traditional Chinatown kitchen, but this modern lounge and eatery isn't your grandmother's Chinese restaurant. The buns are stuffed with pork belly and peanut-chili jam, the fried rice is amped up with

smoked ham and fresh peas, and other dishes, like octopus salad with shaved kohlrabi, fermented radishes, and beet emulsion, start in Asia but wander the world. To drink? Clever cocktails, like Midnight Lucky, which blends sake, Aperol, ginger hibiscus tea, pink peppercorn, and shiso.

Japanese

Tsuki Sushi Bar (509 Abbott St., 604/558-3805, www.tsukisushibar.ca, 11:30am-2:30pm and 4pm-9:30pm Mon.-Fri., noon-9:30pm Sat., noon-9pm Sun., $11-22) does one thing and does it well: preparing fresh sushi and sashimi. See what's on special, or try the *chirashi* bowl, an assortment of raw fish on rice.

Italian

Why should you **Ask for Luigi** (305 Alexander St., 604/428-2544, www.askforluigi.com, 11:30am-2:30pm and 5:30pm-10:30pm Tues.-Thurs., 11:30am-2:30pm and 5:30pm-11pm Fri., 9:30am-2:30pm and 5:30pm-11pm Sat., 9:30am-2:30pm and 5:30pm-9:30pm Sun, lunch $17-21, dinner $25-28)? For first-rate handmade pastas, along with modern Italian small plates that might include fried cauliflower with chickpeas or bocconcini fritti, plus a good selection of wines by the glass. This tiny trattoria east of Gastown doesn't take reservations, so expect a line.

Cafés, Bakeries, and Light Bites

Gastown is Vancouver's coffee central. Sip your java among the designers, techies, and laptop-toting cool kids at **Revolver** (325 Cambie St., 604/558-4444, www.revolvercoffee.ca, 7:30am-6pm Mon.-Fri., 9am-6pm Sat.) or **Nelson the Seagull** (315 Carrall St., 604/681-5776, www.nelsontheseagull.com, 8am-5pm Mon.-Fri. 9am-5pm Sat.-Sun.).

Vancouverites used to have to drive to Whistler for the decadent pastries and wholesome breads at **Purebread** (159 W. Hastings St., 604/563-8060, www.purebread.ca, 8am-6pm daily). But Gastown has a Purebread of its own, with drool-inducing treats like fresh-baked scones, lemon chèvre brownies, and giant meringues. Additional locations bring goodies to Kitsilano and the Main Street neighborhood.

Yaletown and False Creek
Seafood

At chic **Ancora Waterfront Dining and Patio** (1600 Howe St., 604/681-1164, www.ancoradining.com, noon-2:30pm and 4pm-late Mon.-Fri., 5pm-late Sat., 11am-2:30pm and 5pm-late Sun., lunch $23-34, dinner $34-42), the terrace overlooking False Creek is among Vancouver's most scenic waterside dining destinations. Come at sunset or on a sunny day for the best views. On your plate, expect an innovative hybrid of Japanese and Peruvian flavors, crafted from west coast ingredients. The ceviche and sashimi are standouts.

Bring the gang, raise a glass, and start slurping—oysters, that is—at lively **Rodney's Oyster House** (1228 Hamilton St., 604/609-0080, www.rohvan.com, 11:30am-11pm daily). This nautical-themed pub-style Yaletown fish house, outfitted with buoys, model ships, and a pile of fresh oysters on ice at the bar, specializes in straight-up seafood dishes, from chowders and steamers to the namesake bivalve. To drink, choose from several beers on tap or wines from B.C. and farther afield.

Fresh seafood, simply prepared, is the lure at **Wildtale Coastal Grill** (1079 Mainland St., 604/428-9211, www.wildtale.ca, 11am-midnight Mon.-Sat., 11am-11pm Sun., lunch $17-26, dinner $25-38). Start with something from the raw bar, maybe oysters or ceviche, then order the day's fresh catch. Easy, right? On a sunny day, nab a patio seat to watch all of Yaletown go by. There's a second location in the Olympic Village.

Vietnamese

A modern Vietnamese eatery in a refurbished Yaletown warehouse, **House Special** (1269 Hamilton St., 778/379-2939, www.housespecial.ca, 11:30am-3pm and 5pm-10pm daily, $7-14) is named for the house special pho (noodle soup). From the menu of innovative sharing plates that pair well with cocktails and craft beers, try the spicy-sweet chicken wings, the soft-boiled "son-in-law egg" in a crispy panko crust, or the sautéed green beans with mushroom-based "XO" sauce. Many dishes can be adapted for vegetarians and vegans.

Cafés, Bakeries, and Light Bites

At times, it can seem like a small victory to get a seat at this Yaletown café that's filled with blond wood tables and lots of enticing aromas. At **Small Victory Bakery** (1088 Homer St., 604/899-8892, www.smallvictory.ca, 7:30am-6pm Mon.-Thurs., 7:30am-10pm Fri., 8am-10pm Sat., 8am-6pm Sun.), the coffee is excellent, and the short menu includes pastries, breads, and a few sandwiches. The almond croissants are a special treat.

Granville Island
Granville Island Public Market

The best place to eat on Granville Island, at least if you like to browse and graze, is inside the **Granville Island Public Market** (1689 Johnston St., www.granvilleisland.com, 9am-7pm daily), where vendors sell soups, sandwiches, sweets, and lots of goodies for a picnic.

Seafood

Like seafood? Then go fish—at **Go Fish** (1505 W. 1st Ave., 604/730-5040, 11:30am-7pm Tues.-Fri., noon-7pm Sat.-Sun., $8-20), an always busy take-out shack on the waterfront, a short walk from Granville Island. Choose fish-and-chips made from cod, salmon, or halibut, or go a little wild with a wild salmon sandwich, an oyster po'boy, or fish tacos. Expect lines on sunny days.

Contemporary

Edible Canada Bistro (1596 Johnston St., 604/682-6681, www.ediblecanada. com, 11am-9pm Mon.-Fri., 9am-9pm Sat.-Sun., brunch/lunch $14-26, dinner $18-31), opposite the Public Market, creates contemporary dishes with ingredients from around British Columbia and across Canada. At midday, you might try a grilled tuna bowl or eggs Benedict with Canadian bacon; for supper, find plates like crispy duck wings, seafood hot pot, and Dungeness crab risotto. It regularly partners with Canadian chefs to host special dinners; check the website for upcoming events.

Kitsilano and the West Side

The West Side neighborhoods with the most interesting dining options include West 4th Avenue in Kitsilano, South Granville Street, and the Broadway-Cambie district, near the Broadway/City Hall Canada Line station.

Contemporary

Though it's named for the chef's grandmothers, there's nothing old-fashioned about **AnnaLena** (1809 W. 1st Ave., 778/379-4052, www.annalena.ca, 5pm-9:45pm Tues.-Sun., shared plates $9-36), a smart Kitsilano bistro with white walls, black banquettes, and west coast wood trimmings. The changing menu, designed to share, might include tomato and green strawberry panzanella salad, buttermilk fried chicken with hot mustard sauce, and halibut with ricotta gnocchi and fava beans. To sip? Local microbrews, B.C. wines, and fun cocktails.

Chef-owner John Bishop helped pioneer Vancouver's farm-to-table movement long before the 100-mile diet was on the lips of every locavore. At his classy Kitsilano restaurant, **Bishop's** (2183 W. 4th Ave., 604/738-2025, www.

Top to bottom: latte art at Small Victory Bakery; dish at Mak N Ming; brunch at Farmer's Apprentice.

bishopsonline.com, 5:30pm-11pm Tues.-Sat., three-course menu $55), the polished staff can guide you to seasonal suppers that might start with grilled fennel salad with nectarine and fig or a tuna carpaccio with pomegranate vinaigrette before continuing with pan-fried sea bass with bacon mashed potatoes or organic beef tenderloin paired with baby artichokes. Finish with a blueberry mousse or "Death by Chocolate."

Imaginative multicourse tasting menus inspired by local products bring adventurous diners to ★ **Farmer's Apprentice** (1535 W. 6th Ave., 604/620-2070, www.farmersapprentice.ca, 5:30pm-10pm Mon., 11am-2pm and 5:30pm-10pm Tues.-Sun., lunch/brunch $14-19, dinner tasting menus $50-65), a petite South Granville dining room. Tomatoes with fermented carrots and dill? Lamb with figs and salsa verde? You won't find these creations on any other tables around town. The same team runs the more casual wine and tapas bar, **Grapes and Soda** (1541 W. 6th Ave., 604/336-2456, www.grapesandsoda.ca, 5pm-11pm Tues.-Sat., $12-15) next door.

Mak N Ming (1629 Yew St., 604/737-1155, www.maknming.com, 5pm-10pm Tues.-Sat., 10am-2pm Sun., brunch $14-18, dinner tasting menus $54 or $83) is the brainchild of Chef Makoto (Mak) Ono and pastry chef Amanda Cheng (her Chinese name is Ming). With fewer than 30 seats, in a spare space up the hill from Kitsilano Beach, the duo concocts two ambitious fixed-price menus each night, mixing Asian flavors and regional ingredients. Look for inventions like velvety sweet-pea *chawanmushi* (custard), wild salmon with morels and roe, and rice with azuki beans and summery greens. Even a simple corn bread served with honeycomb butter might hold a surprise (a shishito pepper hidden inside). Sunday brunch is less formal yet still creative.

A wall of wine sets the sumptuous scene at South Granville's ★ **West** (2881 Granville St., 604/738-8938, www.westrestaurant.com, 11:30am-2:30pm and 5:30pm-10:30pm Mon.-Fri., 10:30am-2:30pm and 5:30pm-10:30pm Sat.-Sun., lunch $20-29, dinner $29-42), where the gracious service and just-inventive-enough cuisine make any meal feel like an occasion. Wild salmon with fregola sarda and chorizo, pork chops with pickled mustard seeds, or Haida Gwaii sablefish with gailan are some of the locally sourced plates you might encounter. Sweets are special, too, with choices like shortcake with roasted B.C. strawberries and meringue crisps, or a chocolate soufflé.

First Nations

If you're keen to explore First Nations culture on your plate, visit **Salmon 'n' Bannock** (1128 W. Broadway, 604/568-8971, www.salmonandbannock.net, 5pm-10pm Mon.-Sat., $15-38). This modern aboriginal bistro uses traditional ingredients in the elk burgers, game sausages, and bison short ribs, and yes, there's plenty of salmon and bannock, a native bread, on the menu, too. Desserts include bannock bread pudding and homemade fruit pies.

Chinese

★ **Dynasty Seafood** (777 W. Broadway, 604/876-8388, www.dynasty-restaurant.ca, 10am-3pm and 5pm-10:30pm daily, dim sum $3-12) serves some of Vancouver's best dim sum, a sophisticated mix of traditional and creative dumplings, buns, and other small bites. Highlights include lemony baked barbecue pork buns, steamed black truffle dumplings, and sweet sago pudding, a tapioca dessert. The busy 2nd-floor dining room, with views of the downtown skyline and North Shore mountains, is a short walk west of the Broadway/City Hall Canada Line station.

Thai

Serving modern Thai cuisine in a minimalist Kitsilano space, **Maenam** (1938 W.

4th Ave., 604/730-5579, www.maenam. ca, 5pm-10pm Sun.-Mon., noon-2pm and 5pm-10pm Tues.-Sat., lunch $16-20, dinner $18-28) brightens Vancouver's dark nights with duck confit salad with taro, grilled fermented sausage with crispy rice, and flavorful curries. If you can't decide, go for the six-course chef's menu ($52-58).

Indian
Celebrated for its innovative riffs on Indian cuisine, **Vij's** (3106 Cambie St., 604/736-6664, www.vijsrestaurant. ca, 5:30pm-10:30pm daily, $26-32) became equally famous for its no-reservations lineups. Relocating the restaurant to a larger space, six blocks from the Broadway/City Hall Canada Line station, and introducing limited online reservations has helped tame the crowds who still come for dishes like jackfruit in black cardamom curry, rainbow trout in coconut-fenugreek masala, and the signature lamb "Popsicles." **TIP:** The same owners' **Rangoli** (1480 W. 11th Ave., 604/736-5711, www.vijsrangoli.ca, 11:30am-1am Sun.-Thurs., 11:30am-2am Fri.-Sat., $17-25) serves similarly interesting Indian dishes in a casual South Granville café.

Cafés, Bakeries, and Light Bites
With classic French pastries like croissants or buttery *kouign-amann,* and other baked treats like the kid-pleasing peanut butter sandwich cookies, petite **Beaucoup Bakery & Café** (2150 Fir St., 604/732-4222, www.beaucoupbakery. com, 7am-5pm Tues.-Fri., 8am-5pm Sat.-Sun.) makes a sweet stop for South Granville shoppers. It's a short walk from Granville Island, too.

If you like your chocolate rich, dark, and homemade, add **Chocolate Arts** (1620 W. 3rd Ave., 604/739-0475, www. chocolatearts.com, 10am-6pm Mon.-Sat.), near Granville Island, to your itinerary. Try a shot of drinking chocolate (think espresso but with chocolate) in the café or assemble a box of bonbons. The chocolate medallions with First Nations motifs make a unique gift.

Overlooking the sea from the 2nd floor of the Jericho Sailing Centre, **The Galley Patio and Grill** (1300 Discovery St., 604/222-1331, www.thegalley.ca, 9am-10pm daily summer, call for off-season hours, $15-18) cooks up simple, beach-friendly bites, including burgers, grilled salmon salads, and sweet potato fries, served on a deck with killer ocean views. Local beer is on tap. If you can't find a seat, take your food outside and picnic. Tip for morning beachcombers: In the summer, The Galley also serves breakfast.

Main Street and the East Side
Contemporary
Chef-owner Andrea Carlson runs the relaxed neighborhood bistro ★ **Burdock & Co** (2702 Main St., 604/879-0077, www. burdockandco.com, 5pm-10pm Mon.-Fri., 10:30am-2pm and 5pm-10pm Sat.-Sun., brunch $15-18, dinner $16-35), delivering a creative, hyper-local menu. Dishes like risotto with watercress and pickled garlic scapes, side stripe shrimp ceviche, or scallops with sea asparagus and smoked shoyu dashi butter change with the harvest. The crispy fried chicken with buttermilk mashed potatoes is a well-loved staple. Weekend brunch, which might bring avocado with cashew curd, tomato baked eggs with feta, and more of that fried chicken, will put you in the mood for some Main Street shopping.

Vietnamese
Fresh, updated Vietnamese dishes and a breezy outdoor patio bring steady lineups to **Anh & Chi** (3388 Main St., 604/874-0832, www.anhandchi.com, 11am-11pm daily, lunch $10-22, dinner $13-27). Among the menu standouts are *chả cá thăng long* (cod spiced with turmeric and dill), *cà tím tay cầm* (eggplant with okra and pickled radish), and *gỏi xoài* (a salad of fresh mango, roasted peanuts, and herbs). Ask the servers to recommend

favorite dishes, too. Even the restrooms have admirers; the smartly designed, gender-neutral facilities have been recognized as one of the top washrooms in Canada.

Vegetarian
At **The Acorn** (3995 Main St., 604/566-9001, www.theacornrestaurant.ca, 5:30pm-10pm Mon.-Thurs., 5:30pm-11pm Fri., 10am-2:30pm and 5:30pm-11pm Sat., 10am-2:30pm and 5:30pm-10pm Sun., brunch $12-18, dinner $20-22), plant food shakes off its crunchy-granola reputation with ambitious plates that would enhance any upscale table: kale salad with tempeh and smoked paprika croutons, beer-battered halloumi cheese with zucchini-potato pancakes, or a fermented summer squash tart. The dining space isn't much larger than the restaurant's name, and it doesn't take reservations (except for parties of 6-8), so you might chill at the bar with an Oma'sake (made from Granville Island sake, flowering currant, green strawberry bitters, and soda) or a craft cider.

Cafés, Bakeries, and Light Bites
The Pie Shoppe (1875 Powell St., 604/338-6646, www.thepieshoppe.ca, 11am-6pm Wed.-Sat., 11am-5pm Sun., slices $6-7, whole pies $22-35) turns out a seasonally changing array of sweet things in a crust. The proprietors of this East Side bakery-café, located down the street from several craft breweries, also run Panoramic Roasting Company, a small-batch coffee roaster, and pair the blueberry, nectarine-cardamom, chocolate pecan, or other slices with pour-overs, espressos, and cappuccinos from its own beans.

Airy coffeehouse **49th Parallel Coffee Roasters** (2902 Main St., 604/420-4900, www.49thcoffee.com, 7am-10pm Mon.-Sat., 7:30am-9pm Sun.) is perpetually packed with friends catching up over an espresso or freelancers tapping away at their laptops. The company sources its coffee beans from small producers and brews top-notch cups. Plus, it makes Lucky's Donuts fresh throughout the day, in flavors like classic old-fashioned, salted caramel, and white chocolate-matcha. In addition to this Main Street location, it has branches downtown and in Kitsilano.

Richmond
Why come to Richmond to eat? For some of the best Chinese food outside China. You might also find yourself in Richmond to explore the waterfront in Steveston or on your way to the Vancouver International Airport.

Chinese
Glitzy **Chef Tony Seafood Restaurant** (Empire Centre, 4600 No. 3 Rd., 604/279-0083, www.cheftonycanada.com, 10:30am-3pm and 5pm-10pm Mon.-Fri., 10am-3pm and 5pm-10pm Sat.-Sun., dim sum $8-20, subway: Aberdeen) is one of the area's best spots for dim sum, whether you're looking for classics like *har gow*

(shrimp dumplings) or more innovative creations, from pumpkin in black bean sauce to spicy clams. One specialty is the slightly sweet "salty egg bun," charcoal-hued dough that almost explodes with lava-like egg custard. Reservations are recommended.

Su Hang Restaurant (100-8291 Ackroyd Rd., 604/278-7787, www.suhang. ca, 11am-3pm and 5pm-10pm daily, $12-44, subway: Lansdowne) specializes in Shanghai dishes, from delicate *xiao long bao* (pork-filled soup dumplings) to fresh fish or crab to meaty pork ribs. To sample its signature dish, Hangzhou beggar chicken, order a day in advance. At lunchtime, it serves Shanghai-style dim sum. Make a reservation; the restaurant is small.

Sesame flatbread stuffed with sliced lamb, steamed lamb dumplings, creamy lamb soup with hand-pulled noodles, cumin-spiced lamb stir-fry—if you enjoy lamb dishes of many varieties, make

tracks to ★ **Hao's Lamb Restaurant** (1180-8788 McKim Way, 604/270-6632, 11am-9:30pm Fri.-Wed, subway: Aberdeen), which specializes in dishes from western China's Xi'an region. The kitchen uses every part of the sheep (yes, you can even order lamb penis). Accompany your meat with refreshing cold plates, including pickled radishes or garlicky cucumbers, from the display case at the counter or with vegetable options like the crisp and creamy fried eggplant. Reservations are recommended.

Seafood
A favorite among the seafood restaurants lining Steveston's waterfront, **Pajo's** (12351 3rd Ave., 604/272-1588, www. pajos.com, 11am-7pm daily Feb.-Oct., $8-21) is a simple picnic-on-the-pier spot known for its fish-and-chips, which you can order with cod, salmon, or halibut. Prepare to wait when the sun shines; it closes in foul weather.

Pajo's

Accommodations

Most Vancouver accommodations are on the downtown peninsula. Rates peak, and availability is limited, in July and August, so book early if you're planning a summer visit. At other times, especially during the slower winter season, hotel rates drop significantly from the high-season prices listed here.

Downtown and the West End
$150-300

Each of the six guest rooms at **Barclay House B&B** (1351 Barclay St., 604/605-1351 or 800/971-1351, www.barclayhouse.com, $170-270), in a yellow 1904 Victorian home in the midst of urban Vancouver, is decorated differently. The bay-windowed, turquoise-accented Beach room has a queen bed and a cozy sitting area, while the Peak room, under the eaves on the top floor, has skylights and a claw-foot tub. Guests can mingle in the lounge or game room, both furnished with a mix of contemporary and antique pieces. Rates at this West End inn include parking, Wi-Fi, and a full breakfast.

Built in the 1960s, the **Blue Horizon Hotel** (1225 Robson St., 604/688-1411 or 800/663-1333, www.bluehorizonhotel.com, $269-379, parking $19) was Vancouver's first high-rise. All 214 rooms in this skinny 31-story tower are corner units, with private balconies and city views, as well as flat-screen TVs, mini fridges, Keurig coffeemakers, air-conditioning, and free Wi-Fi. The family suites on the 29th floor have a separate living room with a queen bed and double sofa bed, as well as a king bedroom. Other amenities include an indoor lap pool, a hot tub, and a sauna. Prices rise as you get higher in the building.

What better spot to start a road trip than at an old-time motor hotel gone glam? Built in 1956, the four-story ★ **Burrard Hotel** (1100 Burrard St., 604/681-2331 or 800/663-0366, www.theburrard.com, $209-475, parking $28) emerged from a makeover as a retro-chic mid-century-modern lodging. The best feature is the courtyard garden, with palm trees and a fire pit, hidden from the surrounding city hum. The 72 guest rooms are small (baths are particularly petite), but they're well designed with espresso makers, mini fridges, and flat-screen TVs. Rates include Wi-Fi, North American phone calls, a pass to a nearby health club, and use of the hotel's bicycles. Off the lobby, **Elysian Coffee** serves pastries, coffee, and local beer.

The apartment-style **Century Plaza Hotel and Suites** (1015 Burrard St., 604/687-0575 or 800/663-1818, www.century-plaza.com, $260-449, parking $17) isn't fancy, but the studio and one-bedroom units have kitchen facilities and free Wi-Fi; outside the busy summer season, you can often find good deals here. The 240-room hotel has a fitness center, indoor pool, and a branch of the local Absolute Spa chain, and you're just a short stroll from most downtown attractions.

Original artworks adorn the lobby, corridors, and guest rooms at the low-rise 129-room ★ **Listel Hotel** (1300 Robson St., 604/684-8461 or 800/663-5491, www.thelistelhotel.com, $231-391, parking $37) on Vancouver's main downtown shopping street. The "museum" rooms feature works by First Nations artists, while staff from a local gallery decorated the eclectic "gallery" rooms. The retro 2nd-floor units are simpler but less expensive. Overall, the hotel is a comfortable and classy choice. **Forage** restaurant, which emphasizes B.C. ingredients, is a bonus. The Listel charges an additional 6 percent fee to cover Wi-Fi and North American phone calls.

In a restored 1908 building, the boutique **Moda Hotel** (900 Seymour St., 604/683-4251 or 877/683-5522, www.modahotel.ca, $219-404) has 67 cozy rooms. The smallest measure just 150 square feet (14 sq m), while standard doubles are 300-350 square feet (28-32 sq m), but they're smartly designed, with red accents, updated baths, air-conditioning, and free Wi-Fi and North American phone calls. You don't have to go far to eat and drink; **Uva Wine & Cocktail Bar, Red Card Sports Bar,** and **Cibo Trattoria** are all on the lobby level.

Sure, the ivy-covered **Sylvia Hotel** (1154 Gilford St., 604/681-9321 or 877/681-9321, www.sylviahotel.com, $179-369), constructed as an apartment building in 1912, is a little old-fashioned. But all units, from basic queens and kings to larger family suites, have free Wi-Fi and flat-screen TVs; some have kitchens, and the best rooms have million-dollar views of English Bay. Even if your room doesn't, you can walk out the front door to the beach, Stanley Park, and plenty of dining spots. Location, location, location.

Over $300

At the oldest of the Fairmont chain's downtown properties, the copper roof and stone gargoyles of the 1939 **Fairmont Hotel Vancouver** (900 W. Georgia St., 604/684-3131 or 866/540-4452, www.fairmont.com, $609-829, parking $62) make it a recognizable landmark amid the city's glass-and-steel towers. The least expensive of the 507 guest rooms are small, but all have been updated with a mix of traditional and more contemporary furnishings, air-conditioning, and flat-screen TVs, as well as the classic Fairmont service. For free Wi-Fi, sign up for the hotel's complimentary frequent-stay program. The indoor pool is in a window-lined greenhouse space, and on the lower level, **Absolute Spa at the Fairmont** (604/684-2772, www.absolutespa.com) caters to men, although women are welcome. Settle in for a drink or a bite at **Notch8 Restaurant & Bar,** which oozes modern-day elegance.

Top to bottom: the reception desk at The Douglas; the Victorian Hotel; Notch8 Restaurant & Bar at Fairmont Hotel Vancouver.

High-tech, Asian-inspired ★ **Fairmont Pacific Rim** (1038 Canada Pl., 604/695-5300 or 877/900-5350, www.fairmont.com, $814-1,329, parking $55) is one of the city's most luxurious lodgings. Stearns & Foster beds topped with Italian linens, plush robes, and marble baths with soaker tubs make the 367 contemporary guest rooms feel like urban oases. And that's before you open the electronically controlled drapes to check out the city and harbor views, or head for the rooftop to lounge around the secluded swimming pool. When you're ready to venture out, the hotel's bicycle butler can outfit you with two-wheeled transportation, or you can book the complimentary car service for downtown outings. As at all Fairmont properties, Wi-Fi is free to members of the hotel's frequent-stay program. Chic **Botanist** is equal parts cocktail "lab" (for its inventive drinks), garden eating space, and high-end dining room.

Located above the cruise ship terminal at Canada Place, the 21-story **Pan Pacific Hotel Vancouver** (999 Canada Pl., 604/662-8111 or 800/663-1515, www.panpacific.com, $379-849, parking $50-56) is convenient if you're starting or ending your Vancouver stay on a boat, though even landlubbers appreciate the panoramic views of the harbor and North Shore mountains. Enjoy the vistas from the heated saltwater pool and from many of the 503 nautical-style guest rooms, outfitted with padded leather headboards, white duvets trimmed with navy piping, and maple furniture. Have a drink in the **Coal Harbour Bar** or on the **Patio Terrace** for more sea-to-sky views.

Originally built in the 1920s and still channeling that era's glamour, the ★ **Rosewood Hotel Georgia** (801 W. Georgia St., 604/682-5566 or 888/767-3966, www.rosewoodhotels.com, $594-1,139, parking $55) has 156 classy guest rooms and suites done in blues, creams, and chocolate browns with Italian linens and luxe baths with heated floors. Make time to exercise in the indoor saltwater

Vancouver's Coal Harbour

---

lap pool or the 24-hour fitness center, since the hotel's **Hawksworth Restaurant** is among the city's top special-occasion dining spots, and **Bel Café** is an upscale place for a pastry or quick lunch. Room service is available around the clock, and when you need to go out, the hotel's car service can chauffeur you around town.

You don't hear much buzz about the **Wedgewood Hotel & Spa** (845 Hornby St., 604/689-7777 or 800/663-0666, www.wedgewoodhotel.com, $373-758, parking $35), but guests at this fashionable hideaway seem to like it that way. The 83 traditional rooms and suites feature deluxe amenities like plush robes and slippers, twice-daily housekeeping, and homemade bedtime cookies. You can work out in the up-to-date fitness facility and relax in the eucalyptus steam room; there's also a full-service spa. Elegant **Bacchus Restaurant and Lounge** serves French-accented cuisine with west coast ingredients.

Gastown
$150-300
At ★ **Skwachàys Lodge** (31 W. Pender St., 604/687-3589 or 888/998-0797, www.skwachays.com, $259-309, parking $20), Canada's first aboriginal arts and culture hotel, indigenous artists worked with hotel designers to craft 18 distinctive guest rooms in an early 20th-century brick Victorian. In the Poem Suite, poems and pencil drawings dance across walls; in the Moon Suite, artists painted a golden moon face on the ceiling watching over the bed below. An indigenous-owned company created the hotel's bath products; room rates cover Wi-Fi and North American phone calls. Guests can participate in sweat lodge or smudging ceremonies with an aboriginal elder, with advance reservations. An added benefit: Hotel profits help subsidize housing for First Nations artists.

The 47-room **Victorian Hotel** (514 Homer St., 604/681-6369, www.victorianhotel.ca, $94-324, parking $20) is a European-style boutique property in two brick buildings dating to 1898 and 1908. While the least expensive rooms are tiny and share hallway baths, others are more spacious and have private baths. All tastefully mix period pieces and modern furnishings, with pillow-top mattresses, robes, flat-screen TVs, and iPod docks. Rates include Wi-Fi and a continental breakfast.

Yaletown
Under $150
One of Vancouver's best options for travelers on a budget is the modern **YWCA Hotel Vancouver** (733 Beatty St., 604/895-5830 or 800/663-1424, www.ywcavan.org, $88-116 s, $99-215 d, parking $18). The 155 rooms range from basic singles with either a hall bath or a semi-private bath (shared between two rooms) or doubles with hall, semi-private, or private facilities to larger units that accommodate 3-5 people. All have air-conditioning, flat-screen TVs, mini fridges, and free Wi-Fi.

Guests can prep meals in one of the three common kitchens or grab a snack in the lobby café. The property is working on an expansion into 2020 but plans to remain open during construction; phone for details.

Over $300

A clear contender for the title of "Vancouver's coolest hotel," the boutique ★ **Opus Hotel Vancouver** (322 Davie St., 866/642-6787, http://vancouver.opushotel.com, $429-879, parking $45) outfitted its 96 guest rooms in eye-popping lime greens, magentas, purples, and vibrant oranges. Many of the spacious baths have a window into the bedroom, while in others, bath windows face outside (don't be shy!). Although rooms aren't huge, they come with high-tech toys like flat-screen TVs, Keurig coffeemakers, and iPads that you can use throughout your stay (with free Wi-Fi, of course). Staff greet guests with a complimentary glass of sparkling wine; to get around town, book the hotel's complimentary car service or borrow a gratis mountain bike. Fashionable **La Pentola** is known for its contemporary Italian dishes.

One block from the False Creek waterfront, adjacent to B.C. Place arena, copper-clad **Parq Vancouver** (39 Smithe St., 604/683-7277, www.parqvancouver.com, parking $40-45) houses a casino, eight food and drink outlets, and two upscale hotels. The lodgings share the window-lined fitness facilities and spa, as well as "The Park," the 6th-floor green space and outdoor lounge that gives the complex its name. ★ **The Douglas** (604/676-0889 or 888/236-2427, www.thedouglasvancouver.com, $439-949) is styled with a boutique ambience in its 188 rooms, designed like urban cabins with dark walnut furniture, concrete ceilings, plaid throws on the pillow-top beds, and quirky amenities like retro pencil sharpeners. In the larger **JW Marriott Parq Vancouver** (604/676-0888 or 888/236-2427, www.marriott.com, $439-999), 329 rooms in two towers feel light and airy if more corporate, though both business and leisure travelers will appreciate the floor-to-ceiling windows, colorful artwork, espresso makers, and marble baths.

Granville Island
Over $300

To stay right on Granville Island, book a room at the waterfront **Granville Island Hotel** (1253 Johnston St., 604/683-7373 or 800/663-1840, www.granvilleislandhotel.com, $369-619, parking $15). All the guest rooms are furnished differently; the nicest take advantage of the island location with balconies or water views. Wi-Fi is included, and the hotel has a small fitness room, though for a more scenic workout, you can walk or run along the Seawall just outside.

Kitsilano
$150-300

Glass artist Sal Robinson has outfitted ★ **Corkscrew Inn** (2735 W. 2nd Ave., 604/733-7276 or 877/737-7276, www.corkscrewinn.com, $185-310), the B&B that she co-owns with her husband, Wayne Meadows, in a 1912 Craftsman-style Kitsilano home, with her original art deco-inspired wine-themed stained glass. You'll see her work in the sitting areas, dining room, and the five guest rooms, which also have custom-designed baths; one features tiles that Robinson designed to depict the Empire State Building. The inn also takes its name from Meadows's collection of antique corkscrews, which he displays in a tiny "museum" on the lower level. Rates include a family-style hot breakfast, which might feature a wild salmon frittata or lemon ricotta pancakes.

The North Shore
Over $300

Convenient to mountain activities, eight-story **Pinnacle Hotel at the Pier** (138

Victory Ship Way, North Vancouver, 604/986-7437 or 877/986-7437, www.pinnaclepierhotel.com, $395-549, parking $22) has panoramic views across the water to the Vancouver skyline. Of the 106 modern guest rooms, with Wi-Fi included, those on the harbor side have small step-out balconies, and if you open the bath blinds, you can take in the vistas while you soak in the tub. City-side rooms glimpse the mountains. In the health club, you can enjoy the seascape from the cardio and weight machines, waterside sundeck, or indoor Olympic-size pool. The hotel is a five-minute walk from Lonsdale Quay and a 15-minute ride on the SeaBus to downtown Vancouver.

Information and Services

Visitor Information

Near Canada Place, the **Tourism Vancouver Visitor Centre** (200 Burrard St., plaza level, 604/683-2000, www.tourismvancouver.com, 9am-5pm daily) provides helpful information about the city. Inside the visitors center, **Tickets Tonight** (604/684-2787, www.ticketstonight.ca, 9am-5pm daily) sells half-price same-day theater and event tickets.

Tourism Vancouver's *Inside Vancouver* blog (www.insidevancouver.ca) details goings-on around town and provides event listings. **Destination BC** (www.hellobc.com), the provincial tourism agency, has a useful website with information about Vancouver and destinations across the province. The **City of Vancouver** website (http://vancouver.ca) provides details about city-run parks, theaters, and transportation. **TransLink** (www.translink.ca), the city's public transit system, has an online trip-planning function that can help you get around town.

Media and Communications

The city's local daily newspapers are the *Vancouver Sun* (www.vancouversun.com) and *Vancouver Province* (www.theprovince.com). The daily Toronto-based *Globe and Mail* (www.theglobeandmail.com) covers news across Canada, including Vancouver, as does the **CBC** (www.cbc.ca), Canada's public television and radio outlet.

The *Georgia Straight* (www.straight.com) provides arts and entertainment listings, restaurant reviews, and area news. Other community news outlets include the *Vancouver Courier* (www.vancourier.com) and the *Daily Hive* (www.dailyhive.com). *Vancouver Magazine* (www.vanmag.com), a glossy monthly also available online, covers city news, restaurants, and events.

The online *Scout Magazine* (www.scoutmagazine.ca) features Vancouver restaurant and food stories. *Miss 604* (www.miss604.com) and *Vancouver is Awesome* (www.vancouverisawesome.com) are established local blogs.

Medical Services

Call 911 for assistance in an emergency.

Vancouver General Hospital (920 W. 10th Ave., 604/875-4111, www.vch.ca) has a 24-hour emergency room, which will assist patients ages 17 and older. If children under 17 need emergency medical attention, take them to **B.C. Children's Hospital** (4480 Oak St., 604/875-2045, www.bcchildrens.ca).

Downtown, you can get 24-hour emergency care at **St. Paul's Hospital** (1081 Burrard St., 604/682-2344, www.providencehealthcare.org). On the University of British Columbia campus, the **UBC Urgent Care Clinic** (UBC Hospital, Koerner Pavilion, 2211 Wesbrook Mall, 604/822-7121, www.vch.ca, 8am-10pm daily) is a good choice for X-rays and nonemergency medical issues.

Several locations of **Shoppers Drug Mart** (www.shoppersdrugmart.ca) have

24-hour pharmacies, including branches in the **West End** (1125 Davie St., 604/669-2424), on **Broadway** near Vancouver General Hospital (885 W. Broadway, 604/708-1135), and **Kitsilano** (2302 W. 4th Ave., 604/738-3138). Other centrally located branches have extended hours, including **Robson and Burrard** downtown (748 Burrard St., 778/330-4711, 8am-midnight daily) and **Yaletown** (1006 Homer St., 604/669-0330, 8am-midnight Mon.-Sat., 9am-midnight Sun.).

London Drugs (www.londondrugs. com), another Canadian pharmacy chain, has several **downtown** locations that are open late, including 710 Granville Street (604/448-4802, 8am-10pm Mon.-Fri., 9am-10pm Sat., 10am-8pm Sun.) and 1187 Robson Street (604/448-4819, 9am-10pm Mon.-Sat., 10am-10pm Sun.).

Getting Around

You don't need a car to get around downtown Vancouver. The downtown peninsula is easy to navigate on foot, cabs are generally available, and the city has a good public transportation system with its SkyTrain subway and comprehensive bus network. It can be faster to go by car to some places outside downtown, like the University of British Columbia or the North Shore, but these destinations are not difficult to reach by transit.

TIP: If you're planning to rent a car in Vancouver for your Canadian road trip, you can save money by picking up that car when you're ready to leave the city, instead of when you arrive. And you won't have to pay for parking during your Vancouver stay.

By Subway and Bus

TransLink (604/953-3333, www. translink.ca) runs the city's public transportation system. Use the **Trip Planner** feature on the TransLink website to plot your route.

Transit Fares and Passes

Vancouver transit fares (one-zone/two-zone/three-zone adults $2.95/$4.20/$5.70, seniors, students, and ages 5-13 $1.90/$2.90/$3.90) are divided into **three zones,** based on the distance you travel. **Pay a basic one-zone fare** if:

- Your trip is entirely within the Vancouver city limits.

- You're traveling only by bus. All bus trips are one zone, regardless of distance.

- You're traveling anywhere after 6:30pm on weekdays or all day Saturday, Sunday, and holidays.

If you're taking the SkyTrain between downtown Vancouver and the airport Monday-Friday before 6:30pm, you need to pay a two-zone fare; during those hours, the SeaBus between Vancouver and North Vancouver is also a two-zone trip.

When you board the SkyTrain at the YVR Airport station, you pay a $5 surcharge in addition to the regular transit fare.

If you're going to be riding transit extensively, buy a **day pass** (adults $10.25, seniors, students, and ages 5-13 $8), which covers one day of unlimited travel on the SkyTrain, buses, and SeaBus across all zones.

How to Buy Tickets and Passes

At the SkyTrain or SeaBus stations, buy a ticket or day pass from the vending machine, which accepts cash, credit cards, and debit cards. Alternatively, without buying a ticket, you can "tap to pay," scanning your credit card or mobile device equipped with Apple Pay, Google Pay, or Samsung Pay directly at the fare gates. Each person tapping must have his or her own card, and you can tap to pay regular adult fares only (there are no youth or senior discounts). Tap your card when you enter the station and tap out when you exit; your fare, based on the zones you've traveled, will be charged to your credit card.

On the bus, you can pay your fare in cash with exact change or tap in with a credit card or mobile device; you don't have to tap out when you get off the bus, because all bus trips are a one-zone fare. If you've bought a ticket on the SkyTrain or SeaBus within the previous 90 minutes, you can use that same ticket on the bus.

For any mode of travel, you can also buy a **Compass Card,** an electronic stored-value card, which gives you a **discounted fare** (one-zone/two-zone/three-zone adults $2.30/$3.35/$4.40, seniors, students, and ages 5-13 $1.85/$2.85/$3.85). Buy Compass Cards at station vending machines, online (www.compasscard.ca), or at London Drugs stores around the city.

When you purchase a Compass Card, you're charged a $6 card deposit. You can get your deposit back when you no longer need the card, either by returning your card in person to the **Compass Customer Service Centre** (Stadium/Chinatown Station) or to the **West Coast Express Office** (Waterfront Station), or by emailing or mailing in a refund request. See the TransLink website for refund instructions.

How to Use a Compass Card
Before boarding the SkyTrain or SeaBus, tap your Compass Card at the fare gates. After your trip, tap out your card as you exit the station, so the system can calculate the correct fare and debit it from your card balance. **Remember to tap out,** or you'll be charged the maximum fare.

When you board a bus, tap your card on the card reader. You don't have to tap out when you get off the bus, since all bus trips are a one-zone fare.

SkyTrain
Vancouver's **SkyTrain** subway has three lines; two of the routes, the Canada and Expo Lines, converge downtown at Waterfront Station.

The **Canada Line** (4:45am-1:15am daily) has several downtown stops, and its two branches can take you between downtown and the airport (take the YVR branch) or other destinations in Richmond (the Richmond-Brighouse branch).

The **Expo Line** (5am-1:30am Mon.-Fri., 6am-1:30am Sat., 7am-12:30am Sun.) travels between downtown and Vancouver's eastern suburbs of Burnaby, New Westminster, and Surrey. Take this line to Chinatown, Main Street (near Science World), Commercial/Broadway, or points farther east.

The **Millennium Line** (5am-1:30am Mon.-Fri., 6am-1:30am Sat., 7am-12:30am Sun.), which starts at VCC-Clark Station and connects to the Expo Line at Commercial/Broadway, continues east through Burnaby to Port Moody and Coquitlam.

Bus
The main bus routes in downtown Vancouver run along Granville, Burrard, Robson, Georgia, Pender, Hastings, and Davie Streets. Useful routes outside downtown travel along West 4th Avenue, Broadway, Oak, Cambie, and Main Streets.

At any bus stop, text the posted stop number to 33333 and you'll receive a reply listing the next buses scheduled to arrive at that stop. For real-time bus arrival data, enter your stop number into the "Next Bus" page on the TransLink website (www.translink.ca).

Bus schedules vary by route, but regular service begins between 5am and 6am and runs until 1am or 2am. Vancouver also has 10 **Night Bus** routes that provide limited service into the wee hours; get schedules on the TransLink website (www.translink.ca).

By Ferry
Aquabus and False Creek Ferries
Two privately run ferry services shuttle passengers across False Creek

between downtown, Granville Island, Science World, and several other points. Schedules vary seasonally, but in summer, service starts around 6:45am-7am and continues until after 10pm. These ferries aren't part of the TransLink system and require separate tickets.

The colorful **Aquabus** (604/689-5858, www.theaquabus.com, adults $3.50-6, day pass $15, seniors and ages 4-12 $2-4, day pass $14) stops at the foot of Hornby Street, Granville Island, Yaletown's David Lam Park, Stamps Landing, Spyglass Place near the Cambie Bridge, the foot of Davie Street in Yaletown, Plaza of Nations, and Olympic Village. It operates 12-passenger mini-ferries, as well as 30-passenger boats that accommodate bicycles.

False Creek Ferries (604/684-7781, www.granvilleislandferries.bc.ca, adults $3.50-6, day pass $16, seniors and ages 4-12 $2.25-4, day pass $13) follow a similar route, stopping at the Vancouver Aquatic Centre in the West End, Granville Island, Vanier Park (near the Vancouver Maritime Museum and Museum of Vancouver), David Lam Park, Stamps Landing, Spyglass Place, the foot of Davie Street, Plaza of Nations, and Olympic Village.

SeaBus

The **SeaBus** (604/953-3333, www.translink.ca) ferry is the fastest route between downtown and North Vancouver's Lonsdale Quay, taking just 12 minutes to cross the Burrard Inlet. TransLink bus and SkyTrain tickets are valid on the SeaBus.

By Taxi

In downtown Vancouver, you can usually hail taxis on the street or find cabs waiting at hotels, restaurants, bars, and transit stations.

You can also phone for a cab or book one online. Local taxi companies include **Blacktop & Checker Cabs** (604/731-1111, www.btccabs.ca), **MacLure's Cabs**

a colorful Aquabus ferry

(604/831-1111, www.maclurescabs.ca), **Vancouver Taxi** (604/871-1111, www.avancouvertaxi.com), and **Yellow Cab** (604/681-1111, www.yellowcabonline.com).

Vancouver taxis are metered, with a base fare of $3.30 plus $1.89 per kilometer, except for trips starting at Vancouver International Airport. From the airport, you'll pay a **flat rate by zone** ($31-37) to most downtown Vancouver destinations. Cabs accept cash and credit cards.

As of 2019, the city of Vancouver is considering allowing Uber and other ride-sharing companies to offer services in Vancouver but has not yet approved these services.

By Car
Parking
Vancouver's on-street **parking meters** ($1-6 per hour) operate 9am-10pm daily, including holidays. Rates vary by location. You can park at most metered spaces for up to two hours. Pay for parking using

coins, credit cards, or the **Pay by Phone app** (604/909-7275, www.paybyphone.com).

You can also park at city-run parking garages and lots. Find these **EasyPark** (www.easypark.ca) locations and rates online, or look for the bright orange signs. EasyPark garages are usually less expensive than privately owned parking facilities.

Many residential neighborhoods, including the West End, Kitsilano, and Main Street, reserve some street parking for residents. Don't park in spaces marked "Parking by permit only," or you can be ticketed.

Car Rentals
The major car rental companies have offices at Vancouver International Airport, including **Alamo** (604/231-1400 or 888/826-6893, www.alamo.ca), **Avis** (604/606-2847 or 800/230-4898, www.avis.ca), **Budget** (604/668-7000 or 800/268-8900, www.budget.ca), **Discount** (604/207-8140 or 800/263-2355, www.discountcar.com), **Dollar** (604/606-1656 or 800/800-6000, www.dollar.com), **Enterprise** (604/303-1117 or 800/261-7331, www.enterprise.com), **Hertz** (604/606-3700 or 800/654-3001, www.hertz.ca), **National** (604/273-6572 or 888/826-6890, www.nationalcar.ca), and **Thrifty** (604/207-7077 or 800/847-4389, www.thrifty.com). Most also have downtown locations.

Victoria and Vancouver Island

Vancouver Island

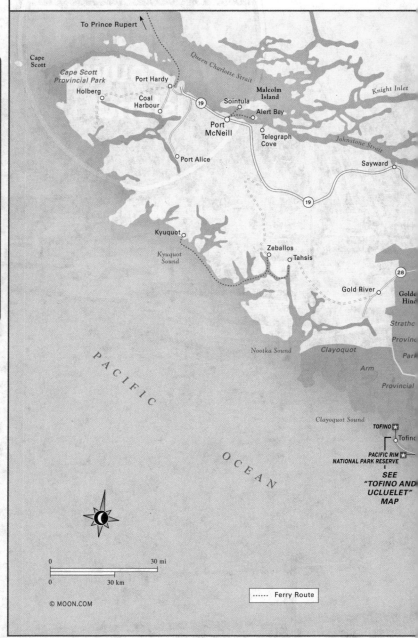

To Prince Rupert

Cape Scott

Cape Scott
Provincial Park

Holberg

Port Hardy

Coal
Harbour

Queen Charlotte Strait

Knight Inlet

Sointula

Malcolm
Island

Alert Bay

Port
McNeill

Telegraph
Cove

Johnstone Strait

Port Alice

Sayward

Kyuquot

Kyuquot
Sound

Zeballos

Tahsis

Gold River

Golde
Hind

Strathc

Provinc

Park

Nootka Sound

Clayoquot

Arm

Provincial

P A C I F I C

Clayoquot Sound

TOFINO

Tofino

PACIFIC RIM
NATIONAL PARK RESERVE

O C E A N

SEE
"TOFINO AND
UCLUELET"
MAP

0   30 mi

0   30 km

© MOON.COM

...... Ferry Route

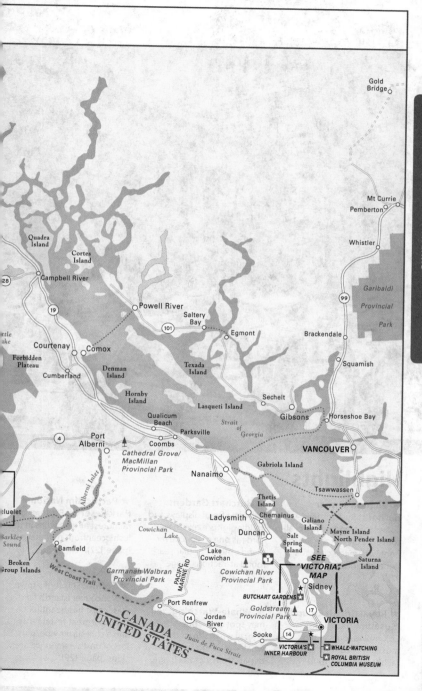

Highlights

★ **Victoria's Inner Harbour:** Buskers, ferries, floatplanes, and travelers all converge on Victoria's waterfront, where the city's major sights are located (page 97).

★ **Royal British Columbia Museum:** Trace British Columbia's roots at this museum of cultural and natural history (page 100).

★ **Butchart Gardens:** Elaborate floral displays and holiday lights make these gardens one of Vancouver Island's most popular year-round attractions (page 108).

★ **Whale-Watching:** You may spot orcas, humpbacks, or gray whales from the whale-watching boats that depart from Victoria (page 112).

★ **Pacific Rim National Park Reserve:** Explore the rainforest and beaches in this lush oceanfront national park (page 127).

★ **Tofino:** This funky town on Vancouver Island's far west coast has beautiful beaches, great restaurants, and a chill surfer vibe, plus lots of on-the-water excursions (page 129).

Vancouver Island offers lots of ways to relax, from enjoying a cup of tea or a glass of wine to watching whales and catching waves.

Situated at the southern tip of Vancouver Island, across the Strait of Georgia from the city of Vancouver, British Columbia's capital city of Victoria mixes historic and hip. You can easily spend a day or more taking in the sights along the Inner Harbour, venturing offshore for a whale watch, or enjoying traditional afternoon tea. A boom in contemporary restaurants, craft breweries, and cool cocktail bars means that you'll eat and drink well, too. Just outside Victoria, both the agricultural Cowichan Valley and the Saanich Peninsula are wine- and cider-making regions, where you can sample what's new in the tasting rooms.

North of Victoria, Nanaimo is an alternate ferry port between Vancouver and the island; it's the most convenient route between Vancouver and Tofino on the island's west coast. Besides an attractive waterfront and historical attractions, Nanaimo is worth a stop to sample a sweet Nanaimo bar, too.

Vancouver Island's striking west coast is the region's ocean playground. You can explore the beaches and rainforest trails in the Pacific Rim National Park Reserve, and unwind in the sand-and-surf communities of Tofino and Ucluelet. Day-trip to a remote hot springs, kayak to a First Nations island, or go on a whale- or bear-watching excursion. Oceanfront resorts and fine casual restaurants (seafood is a specialty) keep you comfortable when you come in from the sea.

Getting to Victoria and Vancouver Island

Driving from Vancouver (via Ferry)

B.C. Ferries (888/223-3779, www.bcferries.com) provides frequent service between the Vancouver metropolitan area on the mainland and Vancouver Island. Ferries transport foot passengers, bicycles, cars, trucks, and recreational vehicles. Reservations ($10 at least 7 days in advance, $17 1-6 days in advance, $21 same-day travel) are recommended for vehicles, particularly if you're traveling on summer weekends or during holiday periods. Reservations are not available for walk-on passengers or bicycles.

Metropolitan Vancouver's two ferry docks are both outside the city center. **Tsawwassen Terminal** (1 Ferry Causeway, Delta), the departure point for ferries to Victoria, is 24 miles (38 km) south of Vancouver. **Horseshoe Bay Terminal** (6750 Keith Rd., West Vancouver), where ferries leave for Nanaimo, is on the North Shore, 12 miles (20 km) northwest of downtown; if you're heading for Tofino or Ucluelet on the island's west coast, the most direct route is to take the ferry from Horseshoe Bay to Nanaimo and continue west from there.

Watch your speed approaching the ferry terminals on both the mainland and the island. Speed limits drop suddenly, and police frequently ticket unwary motorists.

To Victoria

Take the **Tsawwassen-Swartz Bay Ferry** (one-way adults $17.20, ages 5-11 $8.60, cars $57.50, bikes $2) to travel between Vancouver and Victoria. The ferry ride is **one hour and 35 minutes.**

Best Accommodations

★ **Inn at Laurel Point:** With rooms angled to take advantage of waterfront views, this contemporary Pacific Rim-style hotel has a Zen-like wing designed by noted Canadian architect Arthur Erikson (page 117).

★ **Fairmont Empress:** Victoria's grand hotel overlooking the Inner Harbour has been welcoming guests, and serving traditional afternoon tea, since the early 1900s (page 118).

★ **Magnolia Hotel & Spa:** Catering to both business and leisure travelers, this well-run boutique property is convenient to Victoria's harbor and downtown sights (page 118).

★ **Oak Bay Beach Hotel:** The lovely seaside swimming pool is reason enough to stay at this Victoria resort. The contemporary ocean-view rooms are a bonus (page 119).

★ **Pacific Sands Beach Resort:** This well-maintained complex of condo-style units on the beach at Tofino's Cox Bay accommodates families, groups of friends, and couples (page 139).

★ **Wickaninnish Inn:** Overlooking the surf in Tofino, this rustic yet elegant, art-filled inn is Vancouver Island's most deluxe beach getaway spot (page 139).

★ **Wya Point Resort:** The Ucluelet First Nation runs this unique west coast property where the wood-frame cottages, decorated with works by native carvers, sit on a remote ocean cove (page 141).

To drive from **Vancouver to Tsawwassen,** head south on **Oak Street,** following the signs for **Highway 99** south, and cross the **Oak Street Bridge** into Richmond. Stay on Highway 99 through the **George Massey Tunnel.** Exit onto **Highway 17** south toward the Tsawwassen Ferry Terminal. Allow about **45 minutes** to drive from downtown Vancouver to Tsawwassen, with extra time during the morning and evening rush hours.

Late June-early September, ferries between Tsawwassen and Swartz Bay generally run every hour between 7am and 9pm daily, and every two hours the rest of the year; because there are frequent variations, check the schedule on the B.C. Ferries website (www.bcferries.com) before you travel.

Swartz Bay Terminal (Highway 17) is 20 miles (32 km) north of Victoria at the end of **Highway 17,** about a **30-minute** drive. After you exit the ferry at Swartz Bay, follow Highway 17 south, which goes directly into downtown Victoria, where it becomes Blanshard Street.

To Nanaimo
Via Horseshoe Bay

The most direct route between Vancouver and Nanaimo is to take the **Horseshoe Bay-Departure Bay Ferry** (one-way adults $17.20, ages 5-11 $8.60, cars $57.50, bikes $2). The ferry ride is **one hour and 40 minutes.**

From downtown **Vancouver to Horseshoe Bay,** take **West Georgia Street** to the **Lions Gate Bridge.** Watch the signs carefully as you approach Stanley Park en route to the bridge to stay in the proper lane. The center lane on the three-lane bridge reverses its travel direction at different times of the day,

Best Restaurants

★ **OLO:** Local ingredients star on the always-changing menu at this stylish yet casual Chinatown restaurant, one of Victoria's most inventive eateries (page 114).

★ **Little Jumbo:** Victoria's cocktail connoisseurs find their way to this speakeasy-style joint hidden at the end of a hallway, where the kitchen is as creative as the bar (page 114).

★ **Brasserie L'Ecole:** A warm welcome and updated French bistro fare have made this edge-of-Chinatown eatery a long-standing Victoria favorite (page 115).

★ **Zambri's:** This sleek dining room serves modern Italian cuisine in Victoria's equally modern Atrium Building (page 115).

★ **The Wolf in the Fog:** Oysters in a potato web? The west coast's most imaginative dishes come from the open kitchen at this relaxed Tofino dining spot (page 135).

★ **The Pointe at the Wickaninnish Inn:** The crashing Pacific waves provide the backdrop for fresh seafood and an extensive wine list at Tofino's most romantic dining room (page 136).

GETTING TO VICTORIA AND VANCOUVER ISLAND

typically creating two travel lanes into the city in the morning and two travel lanes toward the North Shore during the afternoon rush hour.

After you cross the Lions Gate Bridge, bear left toward Marine Drive west/Highway 1/Highway 99. Enter **Marine Drive** and stay in the far right lane to take the first right onto **Taylor Way** (the sign says "Whistler"). Follow Taylor Way up the hill and exit left onto **Highway 1** west. Continue on Highway 1 to the ferry terminal. The drive from downtown to Horseshoe Bay generally takes about **30 minutes,** but allow extra time during the morning and afternoon commute times.

Late June-early September, ferries between Horseshoe Bay and Departure Bay generally make eight or nine trips daily, with six or seven daily runs the rest of the year; check the B.C. Ferries website (www.bcferries.com) for the seasonal schedule.

Departure Bay Terminal (680 Trans-Canada Hwy., Nanaimo) is 2 miles (3 km) north of downtown Nanaimo.

Via Tsawwassen

Another route between the mainland and Nanaimo is the **Tsawwassen-Duke Point Ferry** (one-way adults $17.20, ages 5-11 $8.60, cars $57.50, bikes $2). The ferry ride is **two hours.** Ferries run 6-8 times per day. Consider this route if you are traveling to the Nanaimo area from points south of Vancouver.

Duke Point Terminal (400 Duke Point Hwy., Nanaimo) is off Highway 1, 9 miles (15 km) south of downtown Nanaimo.

To Tofino and Ucluelet

A road trip from **Vancouver to Tofino** involves taking a ferry from the mainland to Nanaimo, and then driving west across the island; allow **six hours** to make the journey.

From Vancouver, drive northwest to the Horseshoe Bay Ferry Terminal and take the **Horseshoe Bay-Departure Bay Ferry** to Nanaimo.

Although the drive from **Nanaimo to Tofino** is just **130 miles (210 km),** it takes at least **three hours,** longer if you stop to sightsee en route. When you exit the

Departure Bay Ferry Terminal, follow the signs to **Highway 19/Parksville.** Just past Parksville, exit onto **Highway 4** westbound toward Port Alberni. **Check your gas;** there are no gas stations between Port Alberni and the Pacific coast.

Highway 4 winds its way across the island, over and around the mountains that form the island's spine. At several points, the road becomes quite narrow and curvy; don't be in a rush to make this trip. If you find that a line of impatient drivers is forming behind you, use one of the pullouts to move over and allow them to pass.

Highway 4 comes to a T at the **Tofino-Ucluelet junction.** Turn right (north) onto the Pacific Rim Highway toward Tofino; it's 20 miles (32 km) from the junction into town. Make a left if you're going to Ucluelet, which is 5 miles (8 km) south of the junction.

Driving from Whistler (via Ferry)
Via Horseshoe Bay
If you're traveling between Whistler and Vancouver Island, you don't have to go through the city of Vancouver. You can take the **B.C. Ferries** (888/223-3779, www.bcferries.com) service from Horseshoe Bay to Nanaimo's Departure Bay terminal.

To get from **Whistler to Horseshoe Bay,** follow **Highway 99** south **60 miles (97 km).** Allow about **75-90 minutes** for the drive.

The **ferry to Departure Bay** is **one hour and 40 minutes. Departure Bay Terminal** (680 Trans-Canada Hwy., Nanaimo) is 2 miles (3 km) north of downtown Nanaimo.

From Departure Bay, it's **75 miles (120 km)** south to **Victoria** via **Highway 1,** which takes **1.75 hours,** and **130 miles (210 km)** west to **Tofino,** via **Highways 19 and 4,** a **three-hour** drive.

Via Tsawwassen
If you want to go directly from Whistler to Victoria, another option is to drive through Vancouver to the Tsawwassen Terminal. You have to allow time to navigate Vancouver's traffic, but the overall travel time is similar to traveling from Horseshoe Bay.

From **Whistler to Tsawwassen,** follow **Highway 99** south to **Highway 1** east and take Exit 13, **Taylor Way,** toward Vancouver. At the foot of the hill, turn left onto **Marine Drive,** then bear right onto the **Lions Gate Bridge.** Many lanes merge onto the bridge here, so be prepared for delays. Once you've crossed the bridge, continue on **West Georgia Street** in downtown Vancouver and turn right onto **Howe Street,** following the signs for Highway 99. Howe Street will take you over the **Granville Bridge** and onto **Granville Street.** At West 59th Avenue, turn left onto **Park Drive** and then right onto **Oak Street.** Continue across the **Oak Street Bridge** into Richmond and onto **Highway 99.** After you pass through the **George Massey Tunnel,** exit onto **Highway 17** toward Tsawwassen. This route between Whistler and Tsawwassen is **105 miles (170 km)** and should take you **2.5 hours,** but allow extra time for traffic or for a stop downtown.

Getting There by Air
The fastest way to travel between Vancouver and Victoria or Nanaimo is by floatplane or helicopter. Both take off and land from the city centers, making this option convenient for a car-free day trip. It's more expensive than taking the ferry, but the scenery over the Gulf Islands and Strait of Georgia is impressive. Check the carriers' websites for schedules and occasional fare discounts. It's also possible to fly from Vancouver or Victoria to Tofino.

If you're coming from farther away, you can fly to Victoria's international airport from a number of U.S. and Canadian cities.

By Air to Victoria
Harbour Air (604/274-1277 or 800/665-0212, www.harbourair.com, 35 minutes, one-way adults $159-254) flies

frequently throughout the day between the **Vancouver Harbour Flight Centre** (1055 Canada Pl., behind the Vancouver Convention Centre, 604/274-1277) and the **Victoria Inner Harbour Centre** (1000 Wharf St., 250/384-2215).

Helijet (800/665-4354, www.helijet.com, 35 minutes, one-way adults $189-325) departs frequently throughout the day between **Vancouver Harbour Heliport** (455 Waterfront Rd., near Waterfront Station, 604/688-4646) and **Victoria Harbour Heliport** (79 Dallas Rd., 250/386-7676), between the Ogden Point Cruise Ship Terminal and Fisherman's Wharf. It offers passengers landing in Victoria a complimentary shuttle to downtown destinations. One child (ages 2-12) flies free with each adult; additional one-way children's fares are $99.

A number of airlines serve **Victoria International Airport** (YYJ, 1640 Electra Blvd., Sidney, 250/953-7533, www.victoriaairport.com), which is north of downtown. **Air Canada** (www.aircanada.com) flies between Victoria and Vancouver, Calgary, Montreal, Toronto, and San Francisco. **WestJet** (www.westjet.com) has flights between Victoria and Vancouver, Calgary, Edmonton, Kelowna (B.C.), and Toronto. Canadian discount carrier **Flair Air** (www.flairair.ca) connects Victoria and Edmonton. **Alaska Air** (www.alaskaair.com) makes the quick hop between Victoria and Seattle.

By Air to Nanaimo
Harbour Air (604/274-1277 or 800/665-0212, www.harbourair.com, 20 minutes, one-way adults $92-129) flies regularly between the **Vancouver Harbour Flight Centre** (1055 Canada Pl., 604/274-1277) and Nanaimo's **Pioneer Waterfront Plaza** (90 Front St., 250/714-0900).

Helijet (800/665-4354, www.helijet.com, 20 minutes, one-way adults $129-149) buzzes across the water several times a day between **Vancouver Harbour Heliport** (455 Waterfront Rd., near Waterfront Station, 604/688-4646)

and **Nanaimo Harbour Heliport** (Port of Nanaimo Welcome Centre, 100 Port Dr.). One child (ages 2-12) flies free with each adult; additional one-way children's fares are $99.

By Air to Tofino
Pacific Coastal Airlines (604/273-8666 or 800/663-2872, www.pacificcoastal.com) operates regular flights from the South Terminal at **Vancouver International Airport** (4440 Cowley Cres., Richmond, www.yvr.ca, year-round, 45 minutes, one-way adults $150-230) to **Tofino-Long Beach Airport** (YAZ, Pacific Rim Hwy., www.tofinoairport.com), which is 7 miles (11 km) southeast of the town and 18 miles (30 km) northeast of Ucluelet.

Harbour Air (604/274-1277 or 800/665-0212, www.harbourair.com, late May-mid-Oct., 1 hour, one-way adults $229-319) flies floatplanes seasonally between the **Vancouver Harbour Flight Centre** (1055 Canada Pl., behind the Vancouver Convention Centre) and **Tofino Harbour** (634 Campbell St.), landing near the Tofino Resort & Marina.

Getting There by Ferry
By Passenger Ferry
V2V Vacations (855/554-4679, www.v2vvacations.com, mid-Mar.-Oct., 3.5 hours, one-way adults $110-165) operates a 242-passenger catamaran, the *V2V Empress,* which takes you directly between downtown Vancouver and downtown Victoria's Inner Harbour spring-fall. The ship doesn't transport vehicles and travels once daily in each direction between the **Vancouver Harbour Flight Centre** (1055 Canada Pl.) and **Victoria's Steamship Terminal** (470 Belleville St.). If you want to day trip or don't need a car on the other side, this is an easy trip to make.

By Bus-and-Ferry Combo
A car-free way to travel between Vancouver and Victoria is to take a direct bus service that picks up passengers

at several points downtown, takes you onto the ferry at B.C. Ferries' Tsawwassen terminal, and continues to downtown Victoria.

It's also possible to reach the island ferries by public transportation in Vancouver, Victoria, and Nanaimo. Although you'll need to allow more time, you'll also save some cash.

To Tofino, a bus-ferry-bus combination can transport you from Vancouver, but it's not a fast route. Buses also run to Tofino from Nanaimo's Departure Bay Ferry Terminal, where the ferries from Vancouver arrive, and from downtown Victoria.

By Direct Bus to Victoria
BC Ferries Connector (604/428-9474 or 888/788-8840, www.bcfconnector.com, one-way bus adults $49.50, B.C. seniors $36, students $30, ages 5-11 $25), operated by Wilson's Transportation, transports passengers between downtown Vancouver and downtown Victoria. The bus takes you to the Tsawwassen Ferry Terminal and drives onto the ferry. At Swartz Bay, you reboard the bus and travel to downtown Victoria. Trips depart several times daily in each direction, and reservations are required; the entire trip takes about four hours.

In Vancouver, the BC Ferries Connector bus originates at **Pacific Central Station** (1150 Station St.). For a slightly higher fare (one-way bus adults $59.50, B.C. seniors $46, students $40, ages 5-11 $40), you can schedule a pickup from many downtown Vancouver hotels. In Victoria, the coach takes you to **Capital City Station** (721 Douglas St.), behind the Fairmont Empress Hotel, one block from the Inner Harbour.

The BC Ferries Connector fare does not include a ferry ticket (one-way adults $17.20, ages 5-11 $8.60), which you must purchase in addition to your bus ticket.

By Public Transit to Victoria
If you don't have a lot of luggage, it's possible to take public transit between downtown Vancouver and the Tsawwassen Ferry Terminal and from the Swartz Bay Ferry Terminal to downtown Victoria. It's much cheaper than the BC Ferries Connector, but it takes a little longer.

In Vancouver, take the **Canada Line** to Bridgeport Station, where you change to **bus 620 for Tsawwassen Ferry** (www.translink.ca, one-way adults $5.70, seniors, students, and ages 5-13 $3.90). The total trip takes about an hour.

After taking the **Tsawwassen-Swartz Bay Ferry** (www.bcferries.com, 1 hour and 35 minutes, one-way adults $17.20, ages 5-11 $8.60), catch **B.C. Transit bus 70 for Swartz Bay/Downtown Express** (www.bctransit.com/victoria, 50 minutes, one-way $2.50 pp) to downtown Victoria.

By Public Transit to Nanaimo
From downtown Vancouver, **bus 257 for Horseshoe Bay Express** (www.translink.ca, 45 minutes, one-way adults $4.20, seniors, students, and ages 5-13 $2.90) runs to the Horseshoe Bay Ferry Terminal from several stops along West Georgia Street. The slightly slower **bus 250 for Horseshoe Bay** (55 minutes, one-way adults $4.20, seniors, students, and ages 5-13 $2.90) follows a similar route.

After taking the **Horseshoe Bay-Departure Bay Ferry** (www.bcferries.com, 1 hour and 40 minutes, one-way adults $17.20, ages 5-11 $8.60), catch **B.C. Transit bus 2** (www.bctransit.com/nanaimo, 25 minutes, one-way $2.50) from the Departure Bay Ferry Terminal to downtown Nanaimo.

By Bus to Tofino
Tofino Bus (250/725-2871 or 866/986-3466, www.tofinobus.com) can take you to Tofino starting with bus service from Vancouver's **Pacific Central Station** (1150 Station St., adults $65, seniors and

students $59, ages 2-11 $33) to Horseshoe Bay, where you board the Horseshoe Bay-Departure Bay Ferry to Nanaimo. After arriving at the Nanaimo Ferry Terminal, you transfer to the Tofino Bus to the west coast. You must purchase a ferry ticket in addition to the bus fare. The total bus-ferry-bus trip takes 7.5 hours.

Tofino Bus can also take you to Tofino from **Nanaimo's Departure Bay Ferry Terminal** (4.25 hours, adults $54, seniors and students $49, ages 2-11 $27) and from downtown **Victoria** (6.5 hours, adults $69, seniors and students $62, ages 2-11 $36).

Victoria

The British Empire lived long and prospered in British Columbia's capital city, Victoria. British explorer James Cook became the first non-indigenous person to set foot in what is now British Columbia, when he landed on Vancouver Island's west coast in 1778. Sixty-five years later, the Hudson's Bay Company established a trading post on the island's southeastern corner, naming it Fort Victoria, after the British queen.

While Victoria is still known for its British traditions, particularly elegant afternoon tea, this increasingly modern community in Canada's warmest region is drawing entrepreneurs, passionate foodies, and other independent types, with cultural attractions, vibrant restaurants, and plenty to do in the mild outdoors.

Sights
Downtown
★ **Victoria's Inner Harbour**
Victoria's harbor is the center of activity downtown, with ferries and floatplanes coming and going, buskers busking, and plenty of tourists soaking up the scene. Many companies offering whale-watching tours and other excursions have their offices along the waterside promenade.

Destination Greater Victoria (812 Wharf St., 250/953-2033, www.tourismvictoria. com, 9am-5pm daily) runs a visitor information center here, with public restrooms.

Victoria Harbour Ferry (250/708-0201, www.victoriaharbourferry.com) operates a **water taxi** (11am-5pm daily Mar. and mid-Sept.-Oct., 11am-7pm daily Apr.-mid-May, 10am-9pm daily mid-May-mid-Sept.) around the Inner Harbour in cute colorful boats, with stops at Fisherman's Wharf, Delta Hotels by Marriott Victoria Ocean Pointe Resort, and many other waterside points. Fares vary by distance; a basic one-zone trip, which includes many Inner Harbour points, is $6 per person. It also offers 45-minute **harbor tours** (11am-5pm daily Mar. and mid-Sept.-Oct., 11am-7pm daily Apr.-mid-May, 10am-9pm daily mid-May-mid-Sept., adults $30, seniors and students $28, ages 1-11 $20, families $90), departing every 20 minutes from the Empress Dock in front of the Fairmont Empress Hotel.

Fairmont Empress Hotel
A landmark on the Inner Harbour, the **Fairmont Empress** (721 Government St., 250/384-8111, www.fairmont.com) has cast its grand visage across Victoria's waterfront since 1908. Architect Francis M. Rattenbury designed and built the hotel as one of the Canadian Pacific Railway's majestic château-style lodgings. British royals have slept here, including Prince Charles and Camilla in 2009, as have U.S. presidents and numerous celebrities, including Katharine Hepburn, Bob Hope, John Travolta, Harrison Ford, and Barbra Streisand.

Even if you're not staying at the Empress, you can walk through its public spaces, dine in its restaurants and lounges, or take afternoon tea (a Victoria tradition). On the front lawn, check out the beehives where Fairmont staff harvest honey to use in the property's kitchen.

Victoria

To Sooke

Sooke Hills Regional Wilderness Park Reserve

SOOKE

Malahat

VANCOUVER ISLAND HIGHWAY

Finlayson Arm

Luxton

Colwood

RD

14

METCHOSIN RD

Hatley Park National Historic Site

Esquimalt Lagoon

1A

Langford

View Royal

Thetis Lake

Theus Lake

1A

PROSPECT LAKE DR

17A

FORT RODD HILL AND FISGARD LIGHTHOUSE NATIONAL HISTORIC SITES

VICTORIA GENERAL HOSPITAL

Prospect Lake

WHALE-WATCHING

Macaulay Point

Esquimalt

Gorge Waterway

West Bay

Royal Oak

Elk Lake

PATRICIA BAY

17

HOTEL ZED

MOON UNDER WATER BREWERY AND PUB

HOYNE BREWING CO.

SHOPPERS DRUG MART

DOUGLAS ST

MCKENZIE AVE

QUADRA

Royal Oak

CORDOVA BAY RD

Cordova Bay

VICTORIA'S INNER HARBOUR

VANCOUVER ISLAND BREWING CO.

HIGHWAY

17

PART AND PARCEL

ST

Cordova Bay

SEE "DOWNTOWN VICTORIA" MAP

ROYAL BRITISH COLUMBIA MUSEUM

SHELBOURNE ST

ASH

Clover Point

ROYAL JUBILEE HOSPITAL

FOUL BAY RD

LANSDOWNE

HILL CROSS RD

SINCLAIR RD

Gordon Head

ABKHAZI GARDEN

WHITE HEATHER TEA ROOM

Oak Bay

Castle Point

Trial Islands

Gonzales Point

OAK BAY BEACH HOTEL

Cadboro Bay

0   2 km

0   2 mi

© MOON.COM

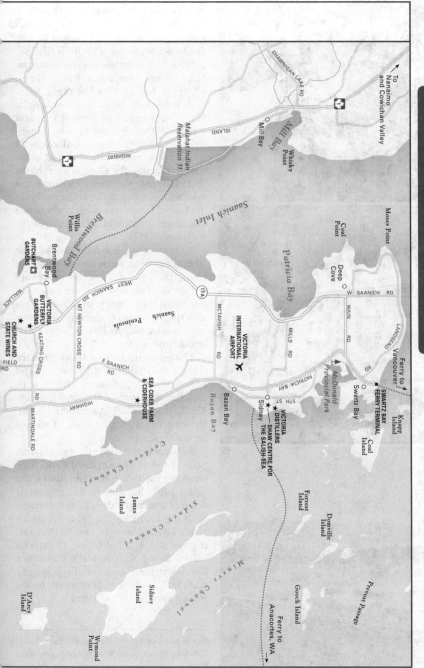

★ Royal British Columbia Museum

Tracing British Columbia's cultural and natural history, the **Royal British Columbia Museum** (675 Belleville St., 250/356-7226, http://royalbcmuseum.bc.ca, 10am-5pm Sun.-Thurs., 10am-10pm Fri.-Sat. late May-late Sept., 10am-5pm daily late Sept.-late May, adults $26.95, seniors and students $18.95, ages 6-18 $16.95) was founded in 1886. A highlight is the First Peoples Gallery, with totem poles, masks, regalia, and other indigenous objects, along with exhibits that illuminate the lives of Canada's first inhabitants. Also check out the multimedia Living Languages gallery, where you can listen to some of B.C.'s indigenous languages.

You can take a one-hour **guided tour** (included with museum admission); check the calendar on the museum's website or in the lobby for tour times and topics. To spread out your museum meanderings over two consecutive days, buy a discounted **two-day ticket** (adults $41, seniors and students $29, ages 6-18 $26).

The museum has an **IMAX Theatre** (IMAX only adults $11.95, seniors and ages 6-18 $9.75, students $10.75, with museum admission adults $36.90, seniors $28.70, students $29.70, ages 6-18 $26.70), showing a changing selection of movies on the big screen.

Adjacent to the museum, several totem poles stand in **Thunderbird Park.** Also outside is the 1852 **Helmcken House,** the oldest public building in B.C. still on its original site; the Hudson's Bay Company built the cabin for Dr. John Sebastian Helmcken and his wife, Cecilia Douglas. A physician and politician, Helmcken helped bring B.C. into the Canadian Confederation, though he allegedly once said that Canada would eventually be absorbed into the United States.

Top to bottom: totem pole at the Royal British Columbia Museum; Victoria's Fairmont Empress; ferry.

One Day in Victoria

Catch an early-morning ferry from Vancouver to Swartz Bay and head straight for the **Butchart Gardens** to wander the blossom-lined paths. When you've had your fill of flowers, drive to downtown Victoria and get oriented with a quick stroll around the **Inner Harbour.** Continue up Government Street to the narrow lanes of **Chinatown,** then browse the boutiques along Lower Johnson Street.

Wander into the grand **Fairmont Empress** for a glimpse of the city's Victorian past; for the full Empress experience, book **afternoon tea** in the hotel's elegant tea room. Or if you'd rather a more contemporary lunch, **Zambri's** serves fine Italian fare.

After lunch, visit the **Royal British Columbia Museum** to learn more about the region's cultural and natural history, take a short tour of the **Parliament Building,** or stop into the **Robert Bateman Centre** to explore the work of this noted B.C. artist. If you'd prefer an outdoor adventure, go **whale-watching;** plenty of tour boats depart from the Inner Harbour.

Unwind over drinks in one of Victoria's lounges, or do a beer crawl to sample the city's **craft breweries.** Then enjoy dinner at **Brasserie L'Ecole** if you're in the mood for a French bistro experience or **OLO** if you prefer more adventurous cuisine paired with creative cocktails.

After dinner, settle into your hotel or take the late ferry back to Vancouver, after your very full Victoria day.

B.C. Parliament Building

Although Vancouver, on the mainland, is a much larger city, Victoria has been the provincial capital since British Columbia joined the Canadian Confederation in 1871. The seat of the provincial government is the B.C. Legislative Assembly, which convenes in the stately 1897 **Parliament Building** (501 Belleville St., 250/387-8669, tour information 250/387-3046, www.leg.bc.ca, tours 9am-5pm daily mid-May-early Sept., 9am-5pm Mon.-Fri. early Sept.-mid-May, free), overlooking the Inner Harbour.

Thousands of twinkling white lights illuminate the Parliament Building, making the copper-roofed stone structure even more photogenic at night than it is during the day. British-born architect Francis M. Rattenbury (1867-1935) designed the building, winning a design competition and his first major commission less than a year after he arrived in B.C. from England at age 25.

On 30- to 45-minute tours of the grand building, you'll learn more about the province's history and governmental operations. In the legislative chambers, for example, desks are set two sword-lengths apart so that no one would get injured during the years when members of parliament carried swords.

Other notable features include a cedar canoe in the rotunda that Steven L. Point, the first indigenous lieutenant governor of British Columbia, carved in 2010, and stained-glass work commemorating Queen Victoria's diamond jubilee.

Tours are free, but **reservations are required.** Book your tour at the tour information kiosk, which is outside the building during the summer season and inside the main entrance fall-spring. On weekdays, visitors can also explore the building on their own (9am-5pm Mon.-Fri.).

Robert Bateman Centre

Artist and naturalist Robert Bateman is a notable Canadian wildlife painter. Born in Ontario in 1930, he made an epic round-the-world journey in a Land Rover before returning to Canada to teach and paint, eventually relocating to B.C.'s Salt Spring Island. View his paintings and learn more about his interesting life at the

VICTORIA AND VANCOUVER ISLAND

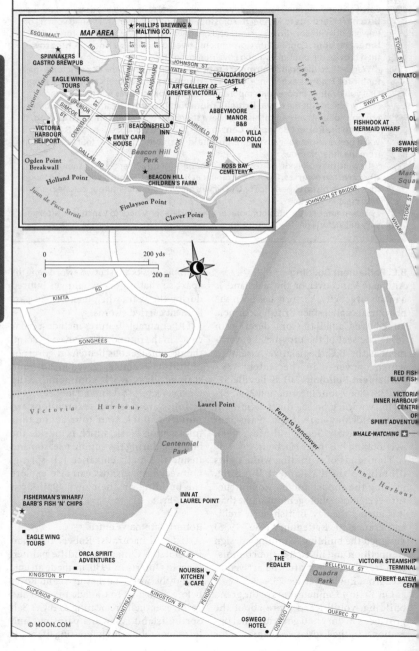

Downtown Victoria

MAP AREA

ESQUIMALT

★ PHILLIPS BREWING & MALTING CO.

★ SPINNAKERS GASTRO BREWPUB

EAGLE WINGS TOURS

JOHNSON ST
YATES ST

★ CRAIGDARROCH CASTLE

ART GALLERY OF GREATER VICTORIA

STORE ST

CHINATO

SWIFT ST

GOVERNMENT ST
DOUGLAS ST
BLANSHARD ST

Victoria Harbour

Upper Harbour

FISHHOOK AT MERMAID WHARF

OL

SUPERIOR ST
SIMCOE ST
OSWEGO ST

VICTORIA HARBOUR HELIPORT

EMILY CARR HOUSE

BEACONSFIELD INN

ST

COOK ST

FAIRFIELD RD

ABBEYMOORE MANOR B&B

VILLA MARCO POLO INN

SWANS BREWPUB

Beacon Hill Park

MOSS ST

Ogden Point Breakwall

DALLAS RD

ROSS BAY CEMETERY ★

Mark Squa

Holland Point

BEACON HILL CHILDREN'S FARM

JOHNSON ST BRIDGE

STORE ST

WHARF

Juan de Fuca Strait

Finlayson Point

Clover Point

0 — 200 yds
0 — 200 m

KIMTA RD

SONGHEES RD

RED FISH BLUE FISH

VICTORIA INNER HARBOUR CENTRE OF SPIRIT ADVENTUR

WHALE-WATCHING ◼

Victoria Harbour

Laurel Point

Ferry to Vancouver

Centennial Park

Inner Harbour

FISHERMAN'S WHARF/ BARB'S FISH 'N' CHIPS ★

INN AT LAUREL POINT

◼ EAGLE WING TOURS

ORCA SPIRIT ADVENTURES

QUEBEC ST

V2V F

KINGSTON ST

NOURISH KITCHEN & CAFÉ

THE PEDALER

BELLEVILLE ST

VICTORIA STEAMSHIP TERMINAL

SUPERIOR ST

KINGSTON ST

PENDRAY ST

MONTREAL ST

Quadra Park

ROBERT BATEM CENT

OSWEGO ST

QUEBEC ST

OSWEGO HOTEL

© MOON.COM

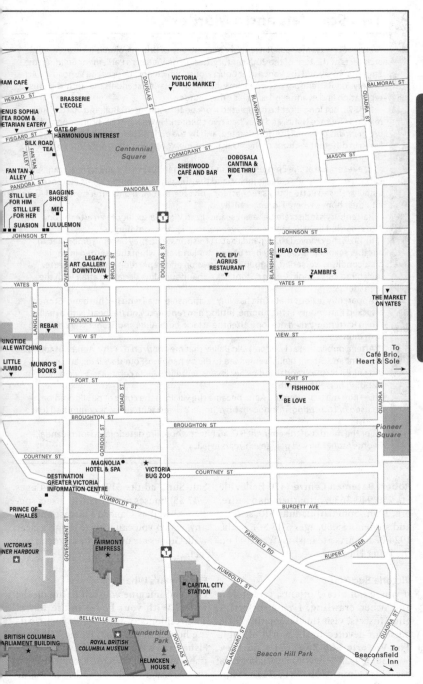

AM CAFÉ

HERALD ST

VENUS SOPHIA
TEA ROOM &
VEGETARIAN EATERY

FISGARD ST

BRASSERIE
L'ECOLE

GATE OF
HARMONIOUS INTEREST

SILK ROAD
TEA

FAN TAN
ALLEY

FAN TAN
ALLEY

PANDORA ST

STILL LIFE
FOR HIM

STILL LIFE
FOR HER

SUASION

BAGGINS
SHOES

MEC

LULULEMON

JOHNSON ST

GOVERNMENT ST

LEGACY
ART GALLERY
DOWNTOWN

BROAD ST

YATES ST

LANGLEY ST

REBAR

TROUNCE ALLEY

VIEW ST

RINGTIDE
WHALE WATCHING

LITTLE
JUMBO

MUNRO'S
BOOKS

FORT ST

BROAD ST

BROUGHTON ST

GORDON ST

COURTNEY ST

MAGNOLIA
HOTEL & SPA

VICTORIA
BUG ZOO

DESTINATION
GREATER VICTORIA
INFORMATION CENTRE

HUMBOLDT ST

PRINCE OF
WHALES

GOVERNMENT ST

VICTORIA'S
INNER HARBOUR

FAIRMONT
EMPRESS

BELLEVILLE ST

BRITISH COLUMBIA
PARLIAMENT BUILDING

ROYAL BRITISH
COLUMBIA MUSEUM

Thunderbird
Park

HELMCKEN
HOUSE

DOUGLAS ST

VICTORIA
PUBLIC MARKET

BLANSHARD ST

BALMORAL ST

QUADRA ST

CORMORANT ST

MASON ST

SHERWOOD
CAFÉ AND BAR

DOBOSALA
CANTINA &
RIDE THRU

Centennial
Square

PANDORA ST

JOHNSON ST

JOHNSON ST

BLANSHARD ST

HEAD OVER HEELS

FOL EPI/
AGRIUS
RESTAURANT

ZAMBRI'S

YATES ST

THE MARKET
ON YATES

VIEW ST

To
Café Brio,
Heart & Sole

FORT ST

FISHHOOK

BE LOVE

QUADRA ST

BROUGHTON ST

Pioneer
Square

COURTNEY ST

BURDETT AVE

FAIRFIELD RD

RUPERT TERR

HUMBOLDT ST

CAPITAL CITY
STATION

DOUGLAS ST

BLANSHARD ST

Beacon Hill Park

QUADRA ST

To
Beaconsfield
Inn

Two Scandals and a Murder

Architect Francis Mawson Rattenbury became one of British Columbia's most notable architects at the turn of the 20th century, designing Victoria's Parliament Building, the Empress Hotel, and the Vancouver Court House, which now houses the Vancouver Art Gallery. Yet Rattenbury became enmeshed in two marital scandals that tarnished his reputation and eventually led to his grisly murder.

In 1898, not long after he completed work on the Parliament Building, Rattenbury married Florence Nunn, and they had two children. However, as his professional stature grew, his personal life deteriorated, and by the early 1920s, he and Florence were living in different sections of their Oak Bay home, communicating only through their daughter.

At a reception at the Empress Hotel in 1923, Rattenbury met a young musician, Alma Pakenham, nearly 30 years his junior, and they began a very public affair. Florence initially refused Rattenbury's request for a divorce, agreeing only after he moved Alma into their home, where Florence still lived.

Rattenbury's indiscrete behavior scandalized Victoria society. Even after he and Alma married in 1925, they were never accepted in the community.

In 1929, they moved to England to start fresh. Instead, they became embroiled in another scandal. Rattenbury had begun drinking, and when they settled in England, his alcoholism worsened, triggering depression and, reportedly, impotence. After they hired 18-year-old George Stoner as a chauffeur, Alma began an affair with the teenager.

Apparently jealous that Alma had any relationship at all with her husband, Stoner attacked Rattenbury in their home, hitting him repeatedly on the head with a mallet. When Rattenbury died not long after the attack, both Alma and Stoner were charged with murder.

After a public trial at London's Old Bailey that mesmerized the city, Alma was found innocent and Stoner guilty, sentenced to die by hanging. Four days later, apparently distraught by the scandal and by her lover's sentence, Alma committed suicide by stabbing herself to death.

Despite the trial's verdict, Alma became the villain in the court of public opinion, accused of corrupting an innocent boy. Stoner's death sentence was commuted to life in prison.

For the murder of the eminent B.C. architect whose life deteriorated into scandal, George Stoner served only seven years in jail.

Robert Bateman Centre (470 Belleville St., 250/940-3630, http://batemancentre. org, 10am-5pm daily, adults $10, seniors and students $8.50, ages 6-18 $6), in the 1924 beaux arts Steamship Terminal on the Inner Harbour.

Victoria Bug Zoo

If you're not afraid of ants, tarantulas, and other crawling, flying, or wriggling insects, visit this fascinating little museum devoted to the world of bugs. The **Victoria Bug Zoo** (631 Courtney St., 250/384-2847, www.victoriabugzoo. ca, 11am-4pm Mon.-Fri., 11am-5pm Sat.-Sun., adults $12, seniors and ages 5-17 $8) houses more than 40 insect species, as well as Canada's largest ant colony, which you can view through a clear wall. Guides are on hand to share fun bug facts.

Fisherman's Wharf

Can you imagine yourself living on the water? With your house *in* the water? The residents of the 30 compact floating houses in the Float Home Village at **Fisherman's Wharf** (1 Dallas Rd., www. fishermanswharfvictoria.com) do just that. Wander the docks and envision life in this colorful waterfront community; these are private homes, though, so do respect residents' privacy.

Fisherman's Wharf has several outdoor eateries, including ever-popular Barb's Fish 'n' Chips, touristy shops, and kayak rentals. From the Inner Harbour, it's a lovely walk along the waterfront on the **David Foster Harbour Pathway,** or you can catch the **Victoria Harbour Ferry** (www.victoriaharbourferry.com).

Emily Carr House

Known for her paintings of British Columbia's landscape and its native people, artist Emily Carr (1871-1945) is considered one of Canada's most important early 20th-century painters. Unusual for a woman of her era, she made several solo trips to remote First Nations communities to document what she believed was the disappearing indigenous culture. She didn't begin seeing commercial success until late in her life, after a 1927 National Gallery of Canada exhibit featured some of her work; the now-famous artist managed a Victoria apartment building for 15 years to support herself.

Set in a Victorian home in Victoria's James Bay neighborhood where she was born and spent her childhood, **Emily Carr House** (207 Government St., 250/383-5843, www.emilycarr.com, 11am-4pm Tues.-Sat. May-Sept., adults $6.75, seniors and students $5.75, ages 6-18 $4.50, families $17) is a museum about her life and work, and about B.C. society during her era.

Beacon Hill Park

Established in 1882, the 200-acre (81-ha) **Beacon Hill Park** (bounded by Douglas, Southgate, and Cook Sts. and the Dallas Rd. waterfront, www.beaconhillpark.ca, free) is Victoria's urban green space, with flower gardens, walking paths, and several attractions, including one of the **world's tallest totem poles,** measuring nearly 128 feet (39 m) tall, and the **Mile 0 marker,** in the park's southwest corner, which denotes the start of the 5,000-mile (8,000-km) Trans-Canada Highway.

Near the center of the park, **Beacon Hill Children's Farm** (Circle Dr., 250/381-2532, www.beaconhillchildrensfarm.ca, 10am-5pm daily May-early Sept., 10am-4pm daily Mar.-Apr. and early Sept.-mid-Oct., free) has wandering peacocks, furry alpacas, and a petting zoo. A highlight is the daily **goat stampede** (10:10am and 5:10pm daily summer, 10:10am and 4:10pm daily spring and fall), when the farm's goats race between their sleeping barn and the petting area. It's one of those things you just have to see!

The **Cameron Bandshell,** near Arbutus and Bridge Ways, hosts summertime **Afternoon Concerts in the Park** (250/361-0500, www.victoria.ca, 1:30pm Fri.-Sun. mid-June-mid-Sept., free), with performances ranging from classical to swing to jazz and blues, as well as the once-a-week **Folk Music Evening Series** (6pm Tues. July-Aug.).

Chinatown

Settled in the 1850s, Victoria's **Chinatown** (Fisgard St. at Government St.) is the oldest in Canada. Although it has now shrunk to a couple of blocks around Fisgard Street, where the neighborhood's gateway, the **Gate of Harmonious Interest,** stands, the district was once Canada's largest Chinese settlement.

After B.C.'s gold rush drew the first Chinese immigrants, the community really began to grow as Chinese workers arrived in Victoria on their way to jobs on the Canadian Pacific Railway. More than 17,000 Chinese immigrants came to Canada between 1881 and 1884.

Today, you'll find a few Chinese-run shops and restaurants and many non-Asian boutiques and eateries. One remaining landmark is narrow **Fan Tan Alley** (between Fisgard St. and Pandora Ave.), a lane just 3-6 feet (1-2 m) wide, where, somehow, several shops have managed to squeeze in.

Breweries

Victoria's craft beer scene has bubbled up in recent years, with a cluster of breweries in an industrial district north of the downtown core, and other microbreweries and brewpubs scattered around the city. Here's where to find the suds:

Lively Victoria old-timer **Swans Brewpub** (506 Pandora Ave., 250/361-3310, http://swanshotel.com, 11am-1am Mon.-Sat., 11am-midnight Sun.) has a central location, pub fare, and even a hotel if you can't move on after a night of beer tasting.

At **Phillips Brewing & Malting Co.** (2010 Government St., 250/380-1912, www.phillipsbeer.com, tasting room noon-10pm daily, store 10am-7pm daily) you can sample its beers as well as handcrafted sodas in the tasting room overlooking its packaging facility.

Vancouver Island Brewing Co. (2330 Government St., 250/361-0007, www.vibrewing.com, 11am-6pm Sun.-Thurs., 11am-7pm Fri.-Sat., tours 3pm Fri.-Sat., $7, reserve online or by email) was the island's first craft brewery when it launched in 1984. It brews staples like the Victoria Lager and Faller Northwest Pale Ale.

Moon Under Water Brewery and Pub (350 Bay St., 250/380-0706, www.moonunderwater.ca, 11:30am-11pm Mon.-Sat., 11:30am-8pm Sun.) draws inspiration from European brewing traditions and crafts beers like Creepy Uncle Dunkel, a dark lager.

West of downtown is **Spinnakers Gastro Brewpub** (308 Catherine St., 250/386-2739, www.spinnakers.com, 11am-11pm daily). It has waterfront views and is known as much for its farm-to-table fare as for its craft brews, which includes a cask special every weekday afternoon.

Top to bottom: Chinatown's Gate of Harmonious Interest; Craigdarroch Castle; Swans Brewpub.

East of Downtown
Abkhazi Garden
The story of this manicured garden is a love story between a British woman born in Shanghai and an erstwhile prince from the Republic of Georgia. Marjorie Pemberton-Carter, known as Peggy, first met Prince Nicholas Abkhazi in Paris in the 1920s. Although they wrote to each other over the years, circumstances kept them apart; during World War II, each spent time in prisoner of war camps—Nicholas in Germany and Peggy in Shanghai.

En route from China to Britain in 1945, Peggy stopped to see friends in Victoria. Her visit turned more permanent when she purchased an overgrown lot and decided to build a summer home. Peggy had lost contact with Nicholas, but he wrote to her in early 1946; they met later that year in New York, and by November, they had returned to Victoria and married.

The home and garden that the newlyweds built on Peggy's property, and where they lived for more than 40 years, became the **Abkhazi Garden** (1964 Fairfield Rd., 778/265-6466, http://conservancy.bc.ca, 11am-5pm daily Apr.-Sept., 11am-5pm Wed.-Sun. Oct.-Mar., last admission 1 hour before closing, $10 donation). The compact garden, just over 1 acre (0.4 ha), features a rhododendron woodland with large Garry oak trees, a winding path known as the Yangtze River, and a variety of other plantings around the site's natural rock formations.

Peggy's 1947 summer home is now **The Teahouse at Abkhazi Garden** (778/265-6466, www.abkhaziteahouse.com, 11am-5pm daily May-Sept., 11am-5pm Wed.-Sun. Oct.-Apr., $13-22), which serves soups, salads, and light meals as well as traditional afternoon tea ($38-48).

From downtown Victoria, take B.C. Transit **bus 7** for UVIC (one-way $2.50) from Douglas and View Streets and get off on Fairfield Road at Foul Bay Road, opposite the garden.

Craigdarroch Castle
Like any good British-inspired city, Victoria has a castle, a grand stone Romanesque revival structure, complete with turrets, stained glass, and Victorian-era artifacts.

Robert Dunsmuir, a Scottish immigrant who made his fortune mining coal on Vancouver Island, built the 39-room mansion, known as **Craigdarroch Castle** (1050 Joan Cres., 250/592-5323, www.thecastle.ca, 9am-7pm daily mid-June-early Sept., 10am-4:30pm daily early Sept.-mid-June, adults $14.25, seniors $13.25, students $9.25, ages 6-12 $5, families $36), in the late 1880s. Sadly, Dunsmuir died before the castle was finished. His wife Joan lived here with three of her unmarried daughters (the Dunsmuirs had 10 children) from the castle's completion in 1890 until she died in 1908.

With more than 20,000 square feet (1,880 sq m) of floor space, the castle, now a National Historic Site, is decorated as it would have been in the Dunsmuirs' time, with lavish Victorian appointments, including sculptures, paintings, books, and period furnishings.

From downtown Victoria, any of the Fort Street buses (one-way $2.50), including B.C. Transit **buses 14 or 15** for UVIC, will drop you near the castle. On foot, allow 30-35 minutes from the Inner Harbour.

Art Gallery of Greater Victoria
Built around an 1899 Victorian mansion, the **Art Gallery of Greater Victoria** (1040 Moss St., 250/384-4171, www.aggv.ca) has a significant collection of work by Victoria-born painter Emily Carr and extensive Asian art holdings. The gallery's exhibitions typically showcase Canadian or Asian works.

The Art Gallery is slated to close in late 2019 for a multi-year renovation project but plans to organize events and exhibits at temporary locations during this construction period. Check the website for updates.

Ross Bay Cemetery

Many notable Victorians are buried in the historic **Ross Bay Cemetery** (Fairfield Rd. at Stannard Ave., dawn-dusk daily, free) that stretches between Fairfield Road and the Dallas Road waterfront. The Victorian-era cemetery's most visited grave is that of artist Emily Carr (1871-1945), near the intersection of Fairfield Road and Arnold Avenue. The cemetery is also the final resting place of Sir James Douglas, who served as British Columbia's first governor from 1858 to 1864, and Robert Dunsmuir, who built Craigdarroch Castle. The cemetery includes sections for different Christian denominations, with separate areas for First Nations and Chinese people, and a potter's field, where the poor were buried.

Get a cemetery map online from the **Old Cemeteries Society of Victoria** (250/598-8870, www.oldcem.bc.ca), which offers **tours** ($5) focusing on different aspects of the cemetery's history. In July and August, tours are offered every Sunday at 2pm, while September-June, tours generally run on the first and third Sundays; check the website for a schedule.

From Douglas Street in downtown Victoria, B.C. Transit **buses 3 or 7** (one-way $2.50) will take you along Fairfield Road to the cemetery. It's a 35- to 40-minute walk from the Inner Harbour.

The Saanich Peninsula

The Saanich Peninsula extends north of downtown Victoria to the communities of Saanich, North Saanich, Sidney, and Brentwood Bay. Partly suburban and partly a rural landscape of farms, forests, and fields, the peninsula is worth exploring for one major attraction—the popular Butchart Gardens—and for several smaller sights; it's also home to several wineries and distilleries. The Swartz Bay Ferry Terminal, with boats to Vancouver and several of the Gulf Islands, is at the northern tip of the Saanich Peninsula.

★ Butchart Gardens

How did a cement factory and limestone quarry become one of Vancouver Island's most popular garden attractions? Jennie Butchart and her husband, Robert, moved to the island from Ontario in the early 1900s, where Robert established a quarry and cement business, and Jennie became the company's chemist. The Butcharts built a large manor nearby and began planting flowers around it.

The Butcharts named their estate Benvenuto, Italian for "welcome," and by the 1920s, more than 50,000 people were visiting their gardens every year. Now, more than one million visitors annually come to ogle the floral displays at the 55-acre (22-ha) **Butchart Gardens** (800 Benvenuto Ave., Brentwood Bay, 250/652-5256, www.butchartgardens. com, 9am-10pm daily mid-June-early Sept., 9am-5pm daily early-late Sept., 9am-4pm daily Oct., 9am-3:30pm daily Nov., 9am-9pm daily Dec.-early Jan., 9am-3:30pm daily early Jan.-Feb., 9am-4pm daily Mar., 9am-5pm daily Apr.-mid.-June; mid-June-Sept. adults $33.10, ages 13-17 $16.55, ages 5-12 $3, reduced rates in other seasons).

When the company's limestone quarry was exhausted, Jennie had the former pit transformed into what is now known as the Sunken Garden. Other highlights include the Rose Garden, the Italian Garden, and the serene Japanese Garden. On summer Saturday nights (July-early Sept.), **fireworks shows** are choreographed to music. During the winter holidays, the pathways twinkle with thousands of lights.

The Butchart Gardens are located 14 miles (23 km) north of Victoria and 12.5 miles (20 km) south of the Swartz Bay Ferry Terminal. From downtown Victoria, B.C. Transit **bus 75** (one-way $2.50) can take you to the gardens in about 45 minutes during weekday rush hours and on the weekends. At other times, bus 75 doesn't start or end its route downtown; instead, take **bus 6** or **31** north to Royal Oak Exchange, where you can connect to bus 75.

Victoria Butterfly Gardens

Don't be surprised if a common Mormon or a blue morpho lands on your head inside this tropical greenhouse. More than 3,000 butterflies dart and flutter around the palm trees and exotic plants at the family-friendly **Victoria Butterfly Gardens** (1461 Benvenuto Ave., Brentwood Bay, 250/652-3822 or 877/722-0272, www.butterflygardens. com, 9:30am-6pm daily July-Aug., 10am-4pm daily early Mar.-June and Sept., 10am-3:30pm daily Oct.-early Mar., extended hours late Dec., last admission 1 hour before closing, adults $16.50, seniors and ages 13-17 $12, ages 5-12 $6), which houses about 75 different species from around the world.

The Butterfly Gardens are 12 miles (20 km) north of Victoria and 11 miles (18 km) south of the Swartz Bay Ferry Terminal, near the Butchart Gardens. B.C. Transit **bus 75** (one-way $2.50) can take you from downtown Victoria in about 40 minutes during weekday rush hours and on the weekends. At other times, when bus 75 doesn't start or end its route downtown, take **bus 6** or **31** north to Royal Oak Exchange, where you can connect to bus 75.

Shaw Centre for the Salish Sea

A small, modern aquarium on the waterfront in the town of Sidney, the **Shaw Centre for the Salish Sea** (9811 Seaport Pl., Sidney, 250/665-7511, www. salishseacentre.org, 10am-5pm daily mid-June-early Sept., 10am-4:30pm daily early Sept.-mid-June, last admission 30

Top to bottom: the Japanese Garden at Victoria's Butchart Gardens; checking out the fish at the Shaw Centre for the Salish Sea; Victoria Distillers' Empress 1908 Gin.

minutes before closing, adults $17.50, seniors $14, ages 13-18 $12, ages 4-12 $8) focuses on the marine life that thrives in the waters surrounding southern Vancouver Island. More than 3,500 creatures, representing 150 different species, are typically on view. On Saturday and Sunday, marine-themed games, crafts, and other special activities add to the fun for kids.

Along Highway 17, the aquarium is 17 miles (28 km) north of downtown Victoria and 4 miles (6.5 km) south of the Swartz Bay Ferry Terminal. B.C. Transit **buses 70 and 72** (one-way $2.50) stop in Sidney en route between Victoria and the ferry terminal. Get off at 5th Street and Beacon Avenue, and walk down Beacon to the aquarium.

Wineries and Distilleries

You don't have to go far from Victoria to go wine-tasting, with several wineries and distilleries across the Saanich Peninsula.

One of the region's more established wine makers, **Church and State Wines** (1445 Benvenuto Ave., Central Saanich, 250/652-2671, www. churchandstatewines.com, 11am-6pm Wed.-Sun., tastings $8) launched with just 10 acres (4 ha) on the island and now has a winery and vineyards in the Okanagan Valley as well. Try its wines at the tasting bar or with lunch in the **Bistro** (11am-3pm Wed.-Sun. May-Dec., $17-21).

On a 10-acre (4-ha) farm with more than 1,300 apple trees, **Sea Cider Farm & Ciderhouse** (2487 Mt. St. Michael Rd., Saanichton, 250/544-4824, www. seacider.ca, 11am-4pm daily May-Sept., 11am-4pm Wed.-Sun. Oct.-Apr., tastings $3-9) produces traditional fermented artisanal ciders, including special seasonal releases.

The master distillers at **Victoria Distillers** (9891 Seaport Pl., Sidney, distillery 250/544-8218, lounge and tour bookings 250/544-8217, www. victoriaspirits.com, lounge 2pm-7pm

Butchart Gardens

Sun.-Wed., 2pm-9pm Thurs.-Sat., reduced hours in winter, tours 1pm-4pm Thurs.-Sun., tastings $7) infuse their signature Victoria Gin with a custom blend of botanicals. They make an aged Oaken Gin and an unusual hemp vodka, too. In the lounge, order a gin and tonic with the deep-blue Empress 1908 Gin. It's infused with butterfly pea flowers and tea from the Fairmont Empress Hotel; when you add citrus or tonic, the drink turns a soft pinkish lavender. To take a 45-minute tour, which includes tastings, phone to book in advance.

West of Downtown

Wend your way through the suburbs west of the city center to reach a historic lighthouse and fort and another of Victoria's famous castles.

Fort Rodd Hill and Fisgard Lighthouse National Historic Sites

The **Fort Rodd Hill and Fisgard Lighthouse National Historic Sites**

(603 Fort Rodd Hill Rd., 250/478-5849, www.pc.gc.ca, 10am-5pm Wed.-Sun. Mar.-mid-May, 10am-5pm daily mid-May-mid-Oct., 10am-4pm Sat.-Sun. mid-Oct.-Feb., adults $3.90, seniors $3.40) combine two historic venues in one location.

Constructed in 1860 at the entrance to Victoria's Esquimalt Harbor, Fisgard Lighthouse was the first lighthouse on Canada's west coast. Inside, exhibits explain the light station's historic role and illustrate the lives of its light keepers, who manned the facility until 1929.

Fort Rodd Hill was built in the 1890s to protect the harbor and waterways around Victoria. Nearly all the fort's structures, from the stone fortifications, to the underground ammunition storage, to the soldiers' barracks, are original. Check the website for a calendar of special programs that help bring these sites to life.

These national historic sites are 7.5 miles (12 km) west of the Inner Harbour, easiest to reach by car.

Hatley Park National Historic Site

Given that his father, Robert, built Craigdarroch Castle, perhaps it's no surprise that James Dunsmuir (1851-1920) and his wife, Laura, wanted a castle of their own, particularly as the parents of 12 children. The 1908 Edwardian stone manor that they constructed, now known as **Hatley Castle** at the **Hatley Park National Historic Site** (2005 Sooke Rd., 250/391-2666, www.hatleypark.ca), has 40 rooms, including 22 bedrooms and eight baths. The only way to visit the castle, on the campus of Royal Roads University, is on a one-hour **guided tour** (10:30am, 11:45am, 1:30pm, and 2:45pm mid-May-early Sept., adults $18.50, seniors $15.75, ages 6-17 $10.75, families $51) that takes you through the grounds, gardens, and main-floor rooms while offering up details about the Dunsmuir family's history. The castle's upper floors, used as university offices, aren't part of the tour.

Alternatively, you can visit just the manicured **gardens** (10:15am-3pm daily, adults $9.75, seniors $8.75, ages 6-17 $6.75, families $30) or wander the 9 miles (15 km) of walking paths through the property.

Hatley Park is 7.5 miles (12 km) west of the Inner Harbour. While it's possible to get here by public transit, it's much faster to come by car.

Sports and Recreation
★ Whale-Watching

The waters off Vancouver Island, the Gulf Islands, and Washington's San Juan Islands are home to several pods of resident orcas (also known as killer whales), particularly during the summer. Pods of transient orcas, as well as Pacific gray whales, humpback whales, and minke whales, migrate through the region.

Numerous Victoria-based companies offer three- to five-hour whale-watching tours April-October; summer (July-Aug.) is peak season for both whales and tourists. Some operators use inflatable zodiac boats, which give you a rougher but more exhilarating ride. Others use larger boats for a calmer trip and more shelter from the weather, a better choice on rainy days or choppy seas. Victoria's whale-watching tour companies include:

- **Orca Spirit Adventures** (250/383-8411 or 888/672-6722, www.orcaspirit. com, adults $120, ages 13-17 $90, ages 3-12 $80), with departures from two Inner Harbour locations: 950 Wharf Street, at the Harbour Air Terminal, or 146 Kingston Street, at the Coast Harbourside Hotel

- **Prince of Whales** (812 Wharf St., 250/383-4884 or 888/383-4884, www. princeofwhales.com, adults $130, ages 13-17 $105, ages 5-12 $95)

- **Eagle Wing Tours** (Fisherman's Wharf, 12 Erie St., 250/384-8008 or 800/708-9488, www.eaglewingtours.com, adults $135, seniors $122, ages 13-17 $105, ages 3-12 $85)

- **SpringTide Whale Watching** (1119 Wharf St., 250/384-4444 or 800/470-3474, www.victoriawhalewatching. com, adults $119, seniors $109, ages 13-18 $99, ages 3-12 $89)

Festivals and Events

Honoring Victoria's namesake queen, the city's **Victoria Day** festivities (www. tourismvictoria.com, May) include a parade downtown.

Aboriginal dancers, singers, and musicians perform at Victoria's three-day **Indigenous Cultural Festival** (www. indigenousbc.com, June), which also showcases works by First Nations artists.

The annual **Victoria Symphony Splash** (www.victoriasymphony.ca, Aug.) includes a live performance by the Victoria Symphony from a floating stage moored in the Inner Harbour.

The **Victoria Fringe Fest** (www. victoriafringe.com, Aug.) is a 12-day festival of weird and often wonderful theater, comedy, and storytelling performances.

Shopping

Shops line Government Street, stretching north from the Inner Harbour, many selling T-shirts, Canadian flag patches, and other souvenirs. Lower Johnson Street in Chinatown and Fort Street east of downtown both have more distinctive local clothing, jewelry, and shoes.

Clothing and Accessories

In Chinatown, **Lower Johnson Street** between Government and Wharf is a mix of trend-conscious chains like yogawear maker **Lululemon** (584 Johnson St., 250/383-1313, www.lululemon.com, 9:30am-8pm Mon.-Sat., 10am-7pm Sun.) and locally run boutiques, including **Still Life for Her** (550 Johnson St., 250/386-5658, http://stilllifeboutique.com, 10:30am-6pm Mon.-Sat., 11am-5pm Sun.) and its companion store **Still Life for Him** (560 Johnson St., 250/386-5655, http:// stilllifeboutique.com, 10:30am-6pm

Mon.-Sat., 11am-5pm Sun.), and **Suasion** (552 Johnson St., 250/995-0133, http://shopsuasion.com, 10:30am-6pm Mon.-Sat., 11am-5pm Sun.).

Sneaker fans run into **Baggins Shoes** (580 Johnson St., 250/388-7022, http://bagginsshoes.com, 10am-6pm Mon.-Sat., 11am-5pm Sun.), which has one of the world's largest selections of Converse styles. In the Atrium Building, **Head Over Heels** (1323 Blanshard St., 250/590-5154, www.headoverheelsvictoria.ca, 10:30am-5:30pm Mon.-Sat., noon-4pm Sun.) sells fashion-forward footwear. The shoes, boots, and bags at **Heart & Sole** (1023 Fort St., 250/920-7653, www.heartandsoleshoes.ca, 10am-6pm Mon.-Sat., 11am-5pm Sun.) mix practicality and style.

Books

Nobel prize-winning author Alice Munro and her former husband Jim opened **Munro's Books** (1108 Government St., 250/382-2464, www.munrobooks.com, 9am-6pm Mon.-Wed., 9am-9:30pm Thurs.-Sat., 9:30am-6pm Sun.) in 1963. Although the writer is no longer involved in its management, this well-stocked old-school bookstore in a grand 1909 former bank carries titles by Canadian authors and other books of local interest.

Gourmet Goodies

Stocking a mind-boggling variety of teas, with helpful labels about the ingredients, flavors, and caffeine content, **Silk Road Tea** (1624 Government St., 250/382-0006, www.silkroadteastore.com, 10am-6pm Mon.-Sat., 11am-5pm Sun.) also carries tea-related products and cosmetics. Take a seat at the tea bar to rest your shopping-weary feet over a fresh-brewed cup, or book a massage in the on-site spa. It has a small branch in the Victoria Public Market.

Outdoor Gear

If you need clothing or supplies for outdoor adventures, head for the Victoria location of **MEC** (Mountain Equipment Co-op, 1450 Government St., 250/386-2667, www.mec.ca, 10am-7pm Mon.-Wed., 10am-9pm Thurs.-Fri., 9am-6pm Sat., 11am-5pm Sun.), Canada's largest retailer of outdoor wear and sports gear.

Food
Afternoon Tea

The **Fairmont Empress** (721 Government St., 250/384-8111, www.teaattheempress.com, 11am-5:45pm daily, reservations recommended, adults $78, ages 12 and under $39) has been offering afternoon tea since the hotel opened in 1908. Upholding that tradition, the regal tea room still serves an estimated 500,000 cups of tea every year, along with tiered trays of finger sandwiches, scones with jam and clotted cream, and assorted pastries.

The Dining Room at Butchart Gardens (800 Benvenuto Ave., Brentwood Bay, 250/652-8222, www.butchartgardens.com, 11am-4pm daily, $37.50) serves traditional afternoon tea, with a mix of sweet and savory items. A vegetarian version of afternoon tea is available.

In the traditionally British neighborhood of Oak Bay, the **White Heather Tea Room** (1885 Oak Bay Ave., 250/595-8020, www.whiteheather-tearoom.com, 11:30am-5pm Tues.-Sat., last seating 3:45pm) offers a traditionally British afternoon tea in several sizes, from the Wee Tea ($26 pp), to the Not-So-Wee Tea ($37), to the Big Muckle Giant Tea For Two ($80 for 2, each additional person $40).

For a less formal (and meat-free) tea, visit **Venus Sophia Tea Room & Vegetarian Eatery** (540 Fisgard St., 250/590-3953, www.venussophia.com, afternoon tea 11am-4:30pm daily, adults $39, kids $29), a pretty Chinatown storefront, where the tabletops are marble and the walls creamy beige. Choose among the signature teas to pair with a seasonally changing assortment of sandwiches, baked goods, and sweets.

Seafood

It's a little hard to find, but that hasn't stopped the hordes from lining up at the wharf-side shipping container housing **Red Fish Blue Fish** (1006 Wharf St., 250/298-6877, www.redfish-bluefish. com, 11am-9pm daily late May-early Sept., 11am-7pm daily Apr.-late May and early Sept.-early Oct., 11am-3pm daily Feb.-Mar. and early-late Oct., $6-26), a busy seafood takeaway at the foot of Broughton Street. Choose tempura-battered Pacific cod, wild salmon, B.C. halibut, or oysters for your fish-and-chips. The hand-rolled fish tacos and the salmon sandwich with pickled cucumbers are other popular picks.

Reel in a quick bite at **Fishhook** (805 Fort St., 250/477-0470, www.fishhookvic. com, 11am-9pm daily, $8-15), which specializes in seafood *tartines,* open-faced sandwiches topped with cured, broiled, or smoked fish. Try the smoked squid with shrimp and harissa or the tuna melt with cheddar and caramelized broccoli. This casual café also makes an array of fish curries. There's a newer branch on the waterfront at Mermaid Wharf, with a bigger menu of Indian-influenced seafood dishes.

A Victoria institution on Fisherman's Wharf, **Barb's Fish 'n' Chips** (1 Dallas Rd., 250/384-6515, www.barbsfishandchips. com, 11am-dark daily mid-Mar.-Oct., $6-23) has been serving up seafood since 1984. It's 1 mile (1.6 km) west of downtown; you can also get here on the Victoria Harbour Ferry (250/708-0201, www.victoriaharbourferry.com).

Contemporary

Taking its name from a Chinook word meaning "hungry," ★ **OLO** (509 Fisgard St., 250/590-8795, www.olorestaurant. com, 5pm-10pm Sun.-Thurs., 5pm-11pm Fri.-Sat., $20-36) doesn't just satisfy your hunger. This fashionably relaxed Chinatown restaurant, decorated with woven wooden light fixtures that dangle like outsized birds' nests, delights guests with its innovative seasonal fare, from shrimp toast with smelt roe and pickled seaweed, to spelt bucatini with lamb bacon, to poached halibut paired with octopus and dashi butter.

★ **Little Jumbo** (506 Fort St., 778/433-5535, www.littlejumbo.ca, 5pm-11pm Sun.-Thurs., 5pm-midnight Fri.-Sat., $16-35) feels like a secret speakeasy, set at the end of a narrow hallway. In the cozy narrow room with exposed brick walls and green lights illuminating the banquettes, the well-stocked bar and hard-working bartenders draw cocktail connoisseurs (they'll make you delicious "mocktails," too, if you're keeping with the Prohibition theme), but the kitchen is serious as well. Graze your way through plates like a summery tomato-burrata salad with ancho-honey purée or steamed clams with dill cream, or dig into the burger with smoked gouda and onion-bacon jam.

The owners of Fol Epi bakery expanded their operations into **Agrius Restaurant** (732 Yates St., 778/265-6312, www.agriusrestaurant.com, 9am-2pm Sun.-Mon., 9am-2pm and 5pm-10pm Tues.-Sat., brunch $9-18, dinner $15-21), where organic ingredients feature in creative daily brunches, like a fried cauliflower sandwich with crispy chickpeas and a salsa verde of mint and pumpkin seeds, or the ham hock hash with kale chimichurri. In the evenings, you might try beet salad with huckleberries and hazelnuts, wild ling cod with mussels, or pork belly with sauerkraut and golden turnips.

Café Brio (944 Fort St., 250/383-0009 or 866/270-5461, www.cafebrio.com, 5:30pm-9pm Tues.-Thurs., 5:30pm-9:30pm Fri.-Sat., $23-36) is an old favorite with a modern Mediterranean menu. Look for dishes like seared scallops with roasted pepper and fennel risotto, pan-roasted salmon in a broth of red wine and beets, or venison loin with chanterelles. Note to grazers or those with small appetites: You can order most dishes in full or half portions. The wine list is strong on B.C. labels.

An unassuming order-at-the-counter eatery, **Part and Parcel** (2656 Quadra St., 778/406-0888, www.partandparcel. ca, 11:30am-9pm Mon.-Sat., $10-16) surprises with the first-rate quality of its straightforward but innovative dishes. On the changing menu that leans heavily on salads and sandwiches, super-fresh greens might be topped with spring rhubarb, feta cheese and roasted broccoli might come sandwiched with pickled shallots, and pillowy gnocchi might be dressed with a cauliflower purée and pecans. In the Quadra Village neighborhood, not quite 2 miles (3 km) north of the Inner Harbour, this local joint is an easy pit stop on the way to or from the Swartz Bay ferry.

Asian

Dobosala Cantina & Ride Thru (760 Pandora Ave., 250/590-6068, www. dobosala.com, 11am-9pm Mon.-Thurs., 11am-10pm Fri., noon-10pm Sat., $7-17) has a take-out window just off a bike path, so as the name suggests, you could ride thru (or stroll by) to pick up your meal. Inside or out, this smart-casual dining spot creates fun plates like adobo-gochujang chicken thighs served with sticky rice balls, *pling pling* (duck and pork dumplings with tomatillo salsa verde), and tikka masala-braised brisket *tacones*—a mash-up of flavors from India, the Pacific Rim, and the Pacific Northwest. To drink, you might try a house-made limeade or a "GinGinger," a fizzy blend of Vancouver Island's Merridale gin and ginger syrup.

French

A long-standing French bistro on the edge of Chinatown, ★ **Brasserie L'Ecole** (1715 Government St., 250/475-6260, www.lecole.ca, 5:30pm-10pm Tues.-Thurs., 5:30pm-11pm Fri.-Sat., $20-40) continues to charm with its warm welcome and just-classic-enough menu.

You might find local trout paired with beets and a green tomato relish or a stew of duck confit, sausage, and cannellini beans. The restaurant stocks a long list of Belgian beers and French wines. Reservations aren't accepted.

Italian

The modern Italian fare at ★ **Zambri's** (820 Yates St., 250/360-1171, www. zambris.ca, 11:30am-3pm and 5pm-9pm Mon.-Thurs., 11:30am-3pm and 5pm-10pm Fri., 10:30pm-2pm and 5pm-10pm Sat., 10:30pm-2pm and 5pm-9pm Sun., lunch $9-18, dinner $17-34), in the equally modern Atrium Building, makes one of Victoria's best meals. The pastas, like penne with gorgonzola and peas or orecchiette with house-made sausages and rapini, are always good choices, as are the pizzas, or you can try more elaborate mains like crispy pork shoulder with greens, potatoes, grapes, and radishes or beef tenderloin paired with polenta. Save room for desserts like panna cotta or chocolate *budino*.

Vegetarian

You can order a local craft beer or a "superfood" cocktail (perhaps the Sombrio made with island gin, mead, algae, and kelp) at cool, laid-back **Be Love** (1019 Blanshard St., 778/433-7181, http://beloverestaurant.ca, 11am-9:30pm Sun.-Thurs., 11am-10pm Fri.-Sat., $9-23), a bright vegetarian café where veggie-friendly doesn't mean ascetic. Try a salad combining kale, avocado, cucumber, and cashew parmesan, or go for the Ganesha Bowl, a mix of curried chickpeas, spinach, and roasted squash served over quinoa with huckleberry chutney.

An old favorite among plant-eaters and their omnivorous dining companions, **Rebar** (50 Bastion Square, 250/361-9223, www.rebarmodernfood.com, 11am-9pm Mon.-Fri., 9:30am-9pm Sat., 9:30am-8pm Sun., $12-18) serves vegetarian comfort food like curries, enchiladas, and noodle bowls, along with a few seafood dishes.

Victoria's Chocolate Project

David Mincey is passionate about chocolate. The owner and resident chocolate obsessive at the **Chocolate Project** (Victoria Public Market, 1701 Douglas St., www.chocolateproject.ca) is on a mission to improve the chocolate that is produced around the world and that we eat closer to home.

the focus of the Chocolate Project

In his stall at the **Victoria Public Market,** Mincey carries single origin, sustainably produced chocolate from many different countries. If you stop to chat, he'll tell you about the horrors of conventional chocolate production; he says that most commercial chocolate comes from West African plantations where enslaved people provide the labor, which is how companies can produce chocolate bars selling for $3 or less. He can tell you about the small businesses and individual growers across the globe who produce the chocolate he sells, many of whom he has visited personally.

You can generally find Mincey at his stand during market hours, offering tastings and preaching the chocolate gospel. His chocolate bars start around $10 each, and he'll convince you that they're worth it.

The almond burger is a classic. Save room for a sweet, like a homey ginger molasses cookie or gooey carrot cake.

Diners

A favorite joint for breakfast or brunch is funky **Jam Café** (542 Herald St., 778/440-4489, www.jamcafes.com, 8am-3pm daily, $8-15), where the hip takes on diner classics include fried oatmeal, red velvet pancakes, and chicken and waffles. Come hungry, and be prepared to line up; it doesn't take reservations.

Cafés, Bakeries, and Light Bites

Pick up a croissant, *pain au chocolate,* or fruit danish from **Fol Epi** (732 Yates St., 778/265-6311, www.folepi.ca, 7am-6pm Mon.-Fri., 8am-6pm Sat.-Sun.), a petite patisserie that uses organic ingredients in its French-style baked goods.

The **Sherwood Café and Bar** (710 Pandora Ave., 250/590-3255, www.sherwoodvictoria.com, 7am-11pm

Mon.-Fri., 8am-11pm Sat., 8am-3pm Sun., $8-17) morphs from a breakfast café to a casual lunch spot to an after-work bar. Try the Dutch Baby, a puffy, sweet-savory pancake with berries and Swiss cheese, or graze your way through a breakfast board, with smoked trout, creamy ricotta, an egg, ham, and fruit. The same owners run the excellent coffee shop, **Habit** (www.habitcoffee.com), with nearby locations in Chinatown (552 Pandora Ave., 250/294-1127, 7am-6pm Mon.-Fri., 8am-6pm Sat.-Sun.) and the Atrium Building (808 Yates St., 250/590-5953, 7am-10pm Mon.-Fri., 8am-10pm Sat., 8am-6pm Sun.).

Homey **Nourish Kitchen & Café** (225 Quebec St., 250/590-3426, www.nourishkitchen.ca, 9am-3pm daily, $8-18), set in an 1888 Victorian house, has a full-service dining room on the main floor and an order-at-the-counter living room-style café upstairs. Throughout the space, there's local art on the walls and veggie-friendly breakfasts and lunches on the plates. A popular dish is "Benny Gone Nuts," a vegetarian eggs Benedict with turmeric-cashew hollandaise that will nourish you for a day of sightseeing.

Groceries and Markets

In a historic building that once housed the Hudson's Bay department store, the **Victoria Public Market** (1701 Douglas St., 778/433-2787, http:// victoriapublicmarket.com, 10am-6pm Mon.-Sat., 11am-5pm Sun.) draws foodies with stalls selling lunches-to-go, chocolate, tea, pie, and other goodies.

To buy groceries close to downtown, head for **The Market on Yates** (903 Yates St., 250/381-6000, www.themarketstores. com, 7am-11pm daily), a well-stocked local food store.

Accommodations and Camping

Victoria's hotels cluster around the Inner Harbour. In some surrounding neighborhoods, you'll find B&Bs and other good-value lodgings.

Under $150

An old motel given new life as a funky retro lodging, **Hotel Zed** (3110 Douglas St., 250/388-4345 or 800/997-6797, www. hotelzed.com, $109-269), decorated in vibrant oranges, turquoises, fuchsias, and purples, is Victoria's most fun place to stay. The 63 rooms have rotary phones (with free local calls), comic books in the baths, and complimentary Wi-Fi. The indoor-outdoor pool has a bubblegum-pink water slide. A hip diner-style restaurant, **The Ruby,** cooks big breakfasts and roasts free-range chicken; downstairs, there's a Ping-Pong lounge. It's 2 miles (3 km) north of the Inner Harbour, but the hotel runs a free shuttle downtown in its vintage VW bus.

$150-300

In a 1912 Victorian home in the residential Rockland neighborhood, **Abbeymore Manor B&B** (1470 Rockland Ave., 250/370-1470 or 888/801-1811, www.abbeymoore.com, $169-299) looks formal, with polished woodwork, oriental rugs, and period furnishings, but the owners keep things comfortable with help-yourself coffee, tea, soft drinks, and snacks, a book- and game-filled guest library, and hearty morning meals. The five guest rooms are all traditionally appointed, while the three suites (two on the garden level and one on the top floor) are more modern. Wi-Fi and local calls are included.

To capture Victoria's traditional ambience, stay at the **Beaconsfield Inn** (998 Humboldt St., 250/384-4044 or 888/884-4044, www.beaconsfieldinn. com, $169-279), a nine-room B&B in a 1905 Edwardian manor furnished with antiques, stained-glass windows, and chandeliers. Most guest rooms have fireplaces and whirlpool tubs; all have down comforters and Wi-Fi. Rates include full breakfast, afternoon tea and cookies, and evening sherry. No kids under 12 are allowed.

Over $300

Removed from the Inner Harbour's fray, but still an easy stroll from the sights, the condo-style **Oswego Hotel** (500 Oswego St., 250/940-7500 or 855/737-2685, www. oswegohotelvictoria.com, $209-499 d, 2-bedroom unit $359-759, parking $15) has 80 stylish, urban studio, one-bedroom, and two-bedroom units. All have kitchen facilities with granite counters, stainless-steel appliances, and French-press coffee-makers, as well as large baths with soaker tubs. The upper-floor suites have expansive city views. Wi-Fi is included.

Noted Canadian architect Arthur Erickson designed one wing of the art-filled ★ **Inn at Laurel Point** (680 Montreal St., 250/386-8721 or 800/663-7667, www.laurelpoint.com, $274-419, parking $17), where most of the Zen-like contemporary suites are angled to take advantage of the property's waterfront views. The Laurel Wing units are more

conventional, but the harbor vistas from these rooms aren't bad either. A short walk from the busy Inner Harbour, the Pacific Rim-style lodging has an indoor pool and a sundeck facing a Japanese garden. Wi-Fi is included. The well-regarded Asian-influenced **Aura Restaurant,** open for breakfast, lunch, and dinner, features lots of local produce and seafood.

A landmark on the Inner Harbour, the ★ **Fairmont Empress** (721 Government St., 250/384-8111 or 800/441-1414, www.fairmont.com, $339-869, parking $32) charms with its polished staff and stately public spaces. Blending classic and contemporary furnishings, the 464 guest rooms vary from petite to grand, but you're here for the heritage and gracious service as much as the physical space. An indoor pool and well-equipped health club keep you busy, while the Willow Stream Spa keeps you pampered. Join the hotel's complimentary frequent-stay program to get Wi-Fi access; otherwise, it's $15 per day. Decorated with royal portraits, **Q at the Empress** serves breakfast, lunch, and dinner, offering contemporary fare with produce from the rooftop garden and around the island, paired with classic cocktails and craft beers; the Empress is famous for its traditional **afternoon tea.**

★ **Magnolia Hotel & Spa** (623 Courtney St., 250/381-0999 or 877/624-6654, www.magnoliahotel.com, $229-529, parking $28), a well-managed boutique lodging two blocks from the Inner Harbour, caters to both business and leisure travelers. The 64 rooms are decorated in soothing grays and creams, with mini fridges, single-cup coffeemakers, complimentary Wi-Fi, and flat-screen TVs. The best rooms are on the 6th and 7th floors above the surrounding buildings; from the corner units, you can see the Parliament Building, illuminated

Top to bottom: Oak Bay Beach Hotel; afternoon tea at the Fairmont Empress; breakfast at the Inn at Laurel Point.

at night. Work out in the compact gym or borrow a complimentary bike to go touring. Staff are quick with a greeting or to offer assistance, from directions to restaurant recommendations. The hotel's restaurant, **The Courtney Room,** pairs regional products with French style from morning through evening.

A stay at the ★ **Oak Bay Beach Hotel** (1175 Beach Dr., 250/598-4556 or 800/668-7758, www.oakbaybeachhotel. com, $297-669) feels like an escape to a seaside resort, particularly when you swim or soak in the heated mineral pools fronting the ocean. The 100 generously sized suites have electric fireplaces, flat-screen TVs, kitchen facilities, and deluxe baths. The panoramic vistas from the water-facing rooms are spectacular. Rates include Wi-Fi, local calls, and parking. Open for breakfast, lunch, and dinner, the 34-seat main **Dining Room** overlooks the gardens and the ocean beyond. **The Snug,** a British-style pub, serves classics like fish-and-chips and bangers and mash with a cold pint; **Kate's Café** keeps guests and locals supplied with coffee and pastries. The hotel is in the residential Oak Bay district, east of downtown.

The five romantic guest suites at the deluxe **Villa Marco Polo Inn** (1524 Shasta Pl., 250/370-1524, www.villamarcopolo. com, $249-349), an upscale 1923 Italian Renaissance manor in the Rockland district, entice with European linens, Persian carpets, fireplaces, and a plush Silk Road style. Breakfasts feature homemade breads or muffins and organic produce from the region. Lounge in the garden or the wood-paneled library, checking your email if you must (Wi-Fi and local calls are included), but if you laze with your beloved in your double soaker tub instead, your messages can surely wait. No kids under 14 are allowed.

Camping

At the **Fort Rodd Hill and Fisgard Lighthouse National Historic Sites** (603 Fort Rodd Hill Rd., 250/478-5849, www. pc.gc.ca), west of the city center, you can camp in an **oTENTik** (mid-May-Sept., $120), a family-friendly canvas-walled platform tent that sleeps up to six. The five tents sit in a clearing in the middle of the fort grounds, a short walk from the lighthouse and a small rocky beach. A building with flush toilets and running water is nearby, although there are no showers on the grounds. Bring your own bedding and food; you can cook your meals on a propane barbecue. Book through **Parks Canada reservations** (877/737-3783, www.reservation. parkscanada.gc.ca).

Information and Services
Visitor Information
Destination Greater Victoria (812 Wharf St., 250/953-2033, www.tourismvictoria. com, 9am-5pm Sun.-Thurs., 8:30am-8:30pm Fri.-Sat.) runs a year-round information center on the Inner Harbour, with helpful staff who can assist you in booking tours and accommodations. The building has public restrooms, too.

Tourism Vancouver Island (www. vancouverisland.travel) publishes a guide to things to do across the island, available online and in print from area visitors centers.

Media and Communications
The **Victoria *Times Colonist*** (www. timescolonist.com) is the city's daily newspaper. *Monday Magazine* (www. mondaymag.com) reports on arts, entertainment, food, and recreation.

Medical Services
Victoria General Hospital (1 Hospital Way, 250/727-4212 or 877/370-8699, www.islandhealth.ca) and **Royal Jubilee Hospital** (1952 Bay St., 250/370-8000 or 877/370-8699, www.islandhealth.ca) provide emergency medical services. The pharmacy at **Shoppers Drug Mart** (3511 Blanshard St., 250/475-7572, www. shoppersdrugmart.ca) is open 24 hours daily.

Getting Around

Victoria's Inner Harbour is compact and walkable, easy to navigate without a car. It's possible to reach sights outside the city center on the region's public buses, although to explore farther afield on Vancouver Island, having your own vehicle is more convenient.

By Bus

B.C. Transit (250/382-6161, http://bctransit.com/victoria, one-way $2.50) runs buses around Victoria, to Butchart Gardens, and to the Swartz Bay Ferry Terminal. Hours vary by bus route, but major routes typically begin service between 6am and 7am and stop service between 11pm and midnight. Service to the Swartz Bay ferry begins at 5:30am Monday-Saturday and 6am Sunday.

By Ferry

Victoria Harbour Ferry (250/708-0201, www.victoriaharbourferry.com, 11am-5pm daily Mar. and mid-Sept.-Oct., 11am-7pm daily Apr.-mid-May, 10am-9pm daily mid-May-mid-Sept.) can take you around the Inner Harbour in its cute colorful boats, stopping at Fisherman's Wharf, Delta Hotels by Marriott Victoria Ocean Pointe Resort, and other waterside points. Fares vary by distance; a basic one-zone trip is $6 per person.

By Taxi

You can usually find taxis near the Inner Harbour and the Fairmont Empress Hotel. Victoria taxi rates start at $3.30, plus $1.93 per kilometer. Local cab companies include **Bluebird Cabs** (250/382-2222, www.taxicab.com) and **Yellow Cab of Victoria** (250/381-2222, www.yellowcabvictoria.com).

By Car

Victoria's downtown sights are clustered around the Inner Harbour, so if you've driven downtown, park your car and do your exploring on foot. Having a car is handy to visit attractions outside downtown, on the Saanich Peninsula, or in the Cowichan Valley.

Parking

Pay for downtown **on-street parking** (Mon.-Sat. 9am-6pm $1.50-3 per hour) at the nearby pay stations with coins, credit cards, or the ParkVictoria app. Parking is free in the evenings and on Sunday.

The city has five centrally located public parking garages (first hour free, second and third hours $2 per hour, fourth and subsequent hours $3 per hour, $16 per day), open 24 hours daily: **Bastion Square Parkade** (575 Yates St.), **Broughton Street Parkade** (745 Broughton St., below the Central Library), **Centennial Square Parkade** (645 Fisgard St.), **Johnson Street Parkade** (750 Johnson St.), and **View Street Parkade** (743 View St.). Rates are in effect 8am-6pm Monday-Saturday; parking is free in the evenings and on Sunday.

You can also park in these city-run surface lots ($2.50 per hour, $15 per day): **900 Wharf Street** (near the Harbour Air Terminal) and **820 Courtney Street.** There's no free parking in these lots; pay rates are in effect 24 hours daily.

Car Rentals

Avis (800/879-2847, www.avis.ca), **Budget** (250/953-5300 or 800/668-9833, www.budget.ca), **Hertz** (800/263-0600, www.hertz.ca), and **National** (250/656-2541 or 800/227-7368, www.nationalcar.ca) have rental desks at Victoria International Airport. **Enterprise** (250/655-7368, www.enterprise.com) has a nearby off-airport location. Both Budget and National also have rental offices downtown, near the Inner Harbour.

By Bike

Victoria is a bike-friendly city. Among the scenic routes for visitors on bikes are **Dallas Road,** which skirts the seashore on the city's southern edge, and **Fairfield Road,** which passes Ross Bay Cemetery.

Running along a former rail line, the 35-mile (56-km) **Galloping Goose Trail** takes you from Victoria west to the town of Sooke. The 18-mile (29-km) **Lochside Regional Trail,** another rail trail, connects Swartz Bay and Victoria.

The Pedaler (321 Belleville St., 778/265-7433, http://thepedaler.ca, 9am-6pm daily mid-Mar.-Oct., call for off-season hours) has a fleet of bikes (1 hour $12, 2 hours $16, full-day $30) and e-bikes (1 hour $40, full-day $90) for rent. It runs fun **guided cycling tours,** including the two-hour **Castles, Hoods & Legends** (adults $55, youth $50), a short tour of Victoria's major sights; the four-hour **Eat.Drink.Pedal.** ($110), which takes you through several Victoria neighborhoods with stops for coffee, pastries, ice cream, and lots of other snacks; and the three-hour **Hoppy Hour Ride** ($91), sampling Victoria's craft breweries.

◆ Pacific Marine Circle Route

Drive the Pacific Marine Circle Route to make a loop around the southern end of Vancouver Island and find British Columbia's gnarliest tree, hike to secluded beaches, and sample island-made wine, Canada's first locally grown tea, salt harvested from the Pacific, and gin flavored with ocean kelp.

Starting from Victoria, you'll wend your way north through the Cowichan Valley's wineries and small towns, head inland to skirt large Lake Cowichan, and loop south to the coast and the small seaside towns of Port Renfrew and Sooke before returning to the city. You could do this approximately 185-mile (300-km) drive in one very full day, traveling in either direction, though 2-3 days give you more leeway to enjoy the trip.

The Cowichan Valley

The agricultural Cowichan Valley, along Highway 1 and about 30 miles (48 km) from Victoria, an hour's drive north, is known for its wineries and cidermakers, and it has other artisan offerings as well. Wineries cluster around the small towns of Cobble Hill, Cowichan Bay, and Duncan.

Wineries

Start your Cowichan explorations with stops at some of these well-regarded winemakers; most charge a small fee for tastings, which they'll waive if you make a purchase. For more winery ideas, check out the **British Columbia Wine Institute** (www.winebc.com).

Unsworth Vineyards (2915 Cameron Taggart Rd., Mill Bay, 250/929-2292, www.unsworthvineyards.com, 11am-5pm Mon.-Tues., 11am-6pm Wed.-Sun. mid-May-mid-Oct., 11am-4pm Mon.-Tues., 11am-5pm Wed.-Sun. mid-Oct.-mid-May, tastings $5), a family-owned winery, has an upscale restaurant (11am-close Wed.-Sun., $15-39) in a restored 1907 farmhouse overlooking the vineyards.

Merridale Ciderworks (230 Merridale Rd., Cobble Hill, 250/743-4293, www.merridalecider.com, 11am-5pm daily, tastings $5) makes sparkling cider, brandies, fortified wines, and spirits. Its bistro (noon-3pm Mon.-Fri., 11am-3pm Sat.-Sun.) serves casual comfort food.

Venturi-Schulze Vineyards (4235 Vineyard Rd., Cobble Hill, 250/743-5630, www.venturischulze.com, 10am-4:30pm Wed.-Sun. Apr.-Aug., 10am-4pm Wed.-Sun. Sept.-Dec., tastings $5), another family-owned winemaker, produces organic wines from estate-grown grapes.

Blue Grouse Estate Winery (2182 Lakeside Rd., Duncan, 250/743-3834, www.bluegrouse.ca, 11am-5pm Fri.-Sun. Feb., 11am-5pm Wed.-Sun. Mar.-Apr., 11am-5pm daily May-Sept., 11am-5pm Wed.-Sun. Oct.-Dec., tastings $5), known for its sparkling wines and pinot gris, has a striking contemporary tasting room with a vineyard-view terrace and upper-level lounge.

Averill Creek Vineyard (6552 North Rd., Duncan, 250/709-9986, www.averillcreek.ca, 11am-5pm daily, tastings complimentary) has a patio where you can bring a picnic to enjoy with your wine.

Cowichan Bay

The scenic seaside town of Cowichan Bay is worth a stop between winery visits. Check out **Wild Coast Perfumery** (1721 Cowichan Rd., 250/701-2791, www.wildcoastperfumes.com, 10:30am-4:30pm Tues.-Sat., 11am-4pm Sun. mid-May-late Dec.), which crafts scents from natural botanicals, and pack a picnic with provisions from **Hilary's Cheese** (1725 Cowichan Rd., 250/748-5992, www.hilarycheese.ca, 10am-4pm Mon.-Fri., 9am-6pm Sat.-Sun.) and **True Grain Bread** (1725 Cowichan Rd., 250/746-7664, www.truegrain.ca, 8am-6pm daily).

Westholme Tea Farm

Canada's first tea growers, **Westholme Tea Farm** (8350 Richards Trail, Westholme, 250/748-3811, www.westholmetea.com, 10am-5pm Wed.-Sun. Feb.-Dec.), north of Duncan, sells several varieties of its own tea, along with others sourced from smaller farms and estates. Staff can tell you about the different types, and you can pair a pot with a selection of sweets in the tearoom or garden. Co-owner Margit Nellemann makes ceramics that she displays in the on-site gallery; your tea may be served in one of her creations.

Food and Accommodations

On a small family-run farm off Highway 18 between Duncan and Lake Cowichan, the **Farm Table Inn** (6755 Cowichan Lake Rd., Lake Cowichan, 250/932-3205, www.farmtableinn.ca, $19-32) is a relaxing spot for a meal or overnight stop. Locally raised meats and Pacific seafood might turn up in plates like braised lamb shank with barley risotto or halibut with dill-caper sauce, alongside fresh *yu choy* (a type of leafy green), roasted squash, and other produce from nearby farms. Two cozy rooms ($150-170), with private terraces and a shared kitchen, are in the farmhouse behind the restaurant. Call for restaurant reservations and to confirm seasonal hours.

Lake Cowichan to Port Renfrew

From Duncan in the Cowichan Valley, head west on Highway 18 and through the waterfront town of **Lake Cowichan,** where you can stretch your legs with a walk along the lakeshore. Follow South Shore Road west out of town and turn south on Pacific Marine Road toward Port Renfrew. Allow 1.75-2 hours for the 56-mile (90-km) drive.

Sights and Recreation

Pacific Marine Road is a remote winding route, with several one-lane bridges, and runs for just over 30 miles (50 km). At about the halfway point, look for signs for the **Harris Creek Spruce,** a giant Sitka spruce measuring 13 feet (4 m) wide. From the roadside pullout, it's about a five-minute walk along a wooded path to the big tree.

Just north of Port Renfrew, where Deering Road branches south toward town, bear right to stay on Pacific Marine Road, which will become the unpaved Gordon River Road; 4.5 miles (7 km) from the intersection of Deering and Pacific Marine Roads, you'll find an area highlight: **Avatar Grove,** a section of old-growth rainforest with some of Canada's largest Douglas firs and western red cedars. Hike the 1.25-mile (2-km) boardwalk loop—which includes a number of steps—in the Upper Grove to find Canada's "gnarliest tree," a massive red cedar with sections of its trunk contorted into fancifully bizarre twists and knobs. You can also walk a short loop trail through the flatter Lower Grove for more old-growth trees.

Food and Accommodations

The top-end option for an overnight in tiny Port Renfrew is **Wild Renfrew** (17310 Parkinson Rd., 844/647-5541, www.wildrenfrew.com, studios $199-299 d, 2-bedroom cottages $229-499), a collection of 11 oceanside cottages with stone fireplaces and water views, alongside the **Renfrew Pub** (250/647-5541, $13-20), a local hangout serving modern pub fare. The same owners run the **West Coast Trail Lodge** (6410 Cerantes Rd., $139-149), with 20 updated motel-style units across the street, up the hill from the shore.

Port Renfrew to Sooke

From Port Renfrew, drive southeast on Highway 14 through the rainforests along Vancouver Island's coast—offering glimpses of the ocean through the trees—for 70 scenic miles (112 km) to Sooke. Without stops, the drive takes about 1.25-1.5 hours.

Beaches

To get closer to the sea, stop for a walk at one of the remote beaches off Highway 14. With dense forests backing rocky coves, several beaches are part of the well-signposted **Juan de Fuca Provincial Park** (www.env.gov.bc.ca) along Vancouver Island's southern shore. Turn off 11.5 miles (19 km) east of Port Renfrew to find the trail to **Sombrio Beach;** it's a moderate 0.3-mile (0.5-km) walk through the forest from the parking area down to the shore. Further east, 23 miles (37 km) from Port Renfrew, is **China Beach,** where an easy 10-minute walk leads to a lookout over the water and stairs down to the sand. Note that bears are regularly spotted in this secluded region; even on these short beach trails, check for bear warnings posted at the trailheads before you set out.

Salt West

Salt West (7585 Lemare Cres., Sooke, 778/977-3994, www.saltwest.com,

noon-4pm Tues.-Sat. Apr.-Oct.) collects and distills seawater to produce fleur de sel and a variety of infused, smoked, and flavored salts. Drop in for a free tour of the production process.

Sheringham Distillery

Craft spirits maker **Sheringham Distillery** (6731 West Coast Rd., #252, Sooke, 778/528-1313, www.sheringhamdistillery. com, noon-5pm daily late May-mid-Oct., noon-5pm Fri.-Sat. mid-Oct.-late May) is best known for its Seaside Gin flavored with winged kelp, a local seaweed. Also look for seasonal specialties, like loganberry vodka, produced only in summer when the local berries are fresh.

Food and Accommodations

Sooke is an excellent stopping point to sit down and eat. The town's best-known dining destination is **Sooke Harbour House** (1528 Whiffen Spit Rd., 250/642-3421, www.sookeharbourhouse.com, 8am-11am and 5:30pm-9pm Mon.-Fri., 8am-3pm and 5:30pm-9pm Sat.-Sun., dinner prix fixe $75-95), a 28-room inn ($275-525) and elegant farm-to-fork restaurant overlooking the sea. The less formal **Wild Mountain Food & Drink** (1831 Maple Ave. S., 250/642-3596, www. wildmountaindinners.com, 5pm-9pm Wed.-Sun. mid-June-mid-Oct., 5pm-9pm Wed.-Sat. mid-Oct.-mid-June, $25-34), set in a little blue house with ocean views, highlights local ingredients in dishes like cider-steamed clams, roasted corn soup with grilled octopus, and seared ling cod in a carrot-verbena sauce. A meal at either spot would be a delicious way to wrap up your circle route experience.

You can also just pick up a coffee and pastries, or the popular "egg-a-majig" sandwich, at **Stick in the Mud Coffeehouse** (6715 Eustace Rd., 250/642-5635, www.stickinthemud.ca, 6am-5pm Mon.-Fri., 7:30am-5pm Sat.-Sun.), before returning the 25 miles (40km) to Victoria, about a 50-minute drive.

Nanaimo

This city of 90,000 on Vancouver Island's east coast, 70 miles (112 km) north of Victoria, is an alternate ferry port between the city of Vancouver and the island, convenient if you're traveling to Tofino on the island's west coast. British Columbia's third-oldest city, Nanaimo is worth a stop for its pretty waterfront, historic sites, and outdoor activities. Be sure to sample a Nanaimo bar, the local signature sweet.

Sights and Recreation
Nanaimo Museum
The modern **Nanaimo Museum** (100 Museum Way, 250/753-1821, www.nanaimomuseum.ca, 10am-5pm daily mid-May-early Sept., 10am-5pm Mon.-Sat. early Sept.-mid-May, adults $2, seniors and students $1.75, ages 5-12 $0.75) tells the stories of the city's development, from its First Nations communities to its days as a mining hub, when the Hudson's Bay Company established a coal mine nearby. Other exhibits focus on the city's quirkier traditions, like its annual summer bathtub race.

The Bastion
Built in 1853 by the Hudson's Bay Company, **The Bastion** (95 Front St.), on the Nanaimo waterfront, is the city's oldest structure and North America's only original wooden bastion (fortified tower). The 1st-floor exhibits (10am-3pm daily mid-May-early Sept., donation) talk about the Hudson's Bay Company and its trading activities; the upper floors illustrate the building's military uses.

Outside the Bastion, stop to watch the midday **cannon firing ceremony** (noon daily mid-May-early Sept.), with a local bagpiper and a really big bang.

Saysutshun (Newcastle Island Provincial Park)
The traditional home of the Snuneymuxw First Nation, **Saysutshun** (www.newcastleisland.ca), an island park known in English as Newcastle Island Provincial Park, is 15 minutes by ferry from downtown Nanaimo. Follow the 14 miles (22 km) of walking trails around the island or pack a picnic to enjoy on one of the pebbled beaches. The **ferry** (Maffeo Sutton Park, 100 Comox Rd., 250/802-0255, 9am-9pm daily June-mid-Sept., 10am-5pm daily Apr.-May and mid-Sept.-mid-Oct., 10:30am-3:30pm Thurs.-Sun. mid-Oct.-Mar., round-trip adults $8, ages 12 and under $5) normally runs every 30 minutes in each direction, but check the website to confirm.

Sailing Tours
Skipper Hans Bongarts, who runs **Island Marine Adventures** (250/714-5303, www.islandmarineadventures.com), offers morning, afternoon, and evening sailing tours of Nanaimo harbor and its surrounding beaches and coves on a comfortable cruising catamaran. You can bring food for a picnic or barbecue and arrange stops for swimming or crabbing. Tours for up to four people start at $65 per person for a 90-minute motoring cruise and $95 per person for three hours under sail; additional people can join in the fun for $10 per person or $25 per person, respectively.

Food
Start your day with pastries and coffee from **Mon Petit Choux** (120 Commercial St., 250/753-6002, www.monpetitchoux.ca, 8am-5pm Tues.-Sat., 9am-5pm Sun., $8-15), a sunny French-style café downtown. Beyond the sweets, it serves breakfasts, including scrambled eggs with smoked salmon or a *croque madame* on house-made brioche, and light lunches, from quiche to sandwiches on its own baguettes.

In a cheerful downtown space decorated with colorful artwork and lots of plants, **Gabriel's Gourmet Café** (39A Commercial St., 250/741-0271, www.

On the Nanaimo Bar Trail

The city of Nanaimo has its own namesake dessert: the **Nanaimo bar.** This sweet treat, which became popular in the 1950s, has three layers: a nutty base of coconut, cocoa, and graham cracker crumbs, with a custard filling and a thick dark chocolate coating on top. You can find Nanaimo bars at bakeries all around town.

You can get more adventurous with your Nanaimo bars, too, if you follow the city's **Nanaimo bar trail.** At more than 30 stops, you can sample numerous variations on the Nanaimo bar theme. There's a rich, creamy vegan version at **Powerhouse Living Foods** (200 Commercial St., 250/571-7873, www.powerhouseliving.ca) and a whipped cream-slathered deep-fried wonder at

deep-fried Nanaimo bars at Pirate Chips

Pirate Chips (1-75 Front St., 250/753-2447, www.pirate-chips.com). The **Modern Café** (page 125) even serves a Nanaimo bar martini.

Get a guide to the Nanaimo bar trail on the website of **Tourism Nanaimo** (www.tourismnanaimo.com), or pick up a copy at the **Nanaimo Visitor Centre.**

NANAIMO

gabrielscafe.ca, 8am-7pm daily, $7-15) uses locally sourced meats, eggs, and produce in its breakfasts (available till 3pm) and lunches. Coconut pancakes with roasted apples, omelets filled with oyster mushrooms and kale, or eggs with black bean corncakes kick off the morning; chicken curry wraps, lemongrass beef sandwiches with pickled vegetables, and rice bowls with tofu and peanut sauce round out the menu from midday on.

Despite its name, the **Modern Café** (221 Commercial St., 250/754-5022, www.moderncafebc.com, 8am-9pm Sun.-Mon., 8am-10pm Tues.-Thurs., 8am-midnight Fri.-Sat., breakfast $8-14, lunch $10-21, dinner $15-30) is one of Nanaimo's oldest restaurants, serving food and drinks in its pub-style space downtown since 1946. Burgers, sandwiches, salads, and macaroni and cheese are the lunchtime draws, while the dinner menu adds heartier plates like braised lamb shank or grilled steak. To drink? A Nanaimo bar martini!

Accommodations

If you're going to stay over in Nanaimo, the friendly **Buccaneer Inn** (1577 Stewart Ave., 250/753-1246 or 877/282-6337, www.buccaneerinn.com, $80-200) is the closest place to sleep near the Departure Bay Ferry Terminal. In this basic but well-maintained family-run motel, many of the nautical-themed rooms and suites have kitchens. Rates include parking, Wi-Fi, and local phone calls. The inn is on a busy road, although traffic typically quiets at night.

The modern 15-story **Coast Bastion Hotel** (11 Bastion St., 250/753-6601 or 800/716-6199, www.coasthotels.com, $179-354, parking $9) overlooks the harbor downtown, with water vistas from its upper floors; request a corner unit for prime views. White linens with colorful accents furnish the 179 rooms, where air-conditioning, coffeemakers, flat-screen TVs, safes, and included Wi-Fi and local calls are among the amenities. The hotel has a fitness room and spa.

The Island's Biggest Trees

Heading west from Nanaimo toward Vancouver Island's west coast, you'll pass through a section of old-growth rainforest, with massive trees that began their lives more than 800 years ago.

In **Cathedral Grove,** which is part of **MacMillan Provincial Park** (Hwy. 4, 250/474-1336, www.env.gov.bc.ca, dawn-dusk daily, free), you can follow two short trails through these forests of giants.

The biggest trees—colossal Douglas firs—are on the south side of the highway. The largest measures more than 30 feet (9 m) around. On the north side of the road, the trail passes through groves of ancient western red cedars and along the shore of Cameron Lake.

Cathedral Grove is 40 miles (65 km) west of Nanaimo and 10 miles (16 km) east of Port Alberni. Highway 4 runs directly through the park; there's a parking lot near the big trees.

Cathedral Grove

The waterside setting overlooking a peaceful mile-long pond elevates three-story **Inn on Long Lake** (4700 N. Island Hwy., 250/758-1144 or 800/565-1144, www.innonlonglake.com, $150-300) beyond an ordinary motel. In summer, you can rent kayaks, pedal boats, and stand-up paddleboards to cruise around the lake. The family-friendly rooms with lakeview patios or terraces come with fridges, microwaves, one-cup coffeemakers, and Wi-Fi. Rates include a simple continental breakfast, which you can eat on the lakeside terrace. The inn, which also has a guest laundry, is off the Island Highway (Hwy. 1), 5.5 miles (9 km) north of the city center.

Oh, the views! **MGM Seashore B&B** (4950 Fillinger Cres., 250/729-7249, www.mgmbandb.com, $229-325) has three guest rooms in a residential neighborhood north of town with panoramas stretching across the water, particularly on the mammoth deck where you can soak in the hot tub. Owners Marilyn and Glenn McKnight start guests' stays with a welcome Nanaimo bar, serve a full breakfast, and stock a guest lounge with espresso, tea, books, and movies. The Honeymoon Suite has a whirlpool tub positioned toward the ocean vistas, while the Sunset Room, with a round king bed, opens to the deck. The more basic King Room could accommodate a family, with a king bed and two singles.

Information and Services

Tourism Nanaimo (www.tourismnanaimo.com) runs the year-round **Nanaimo Visitor Centre** (2450 Northfield Rd., 250/751-1556 or 800/663-7337, 9am-4:30pm Mon.-Fri.), off Highway 19 northwest of the city center, providing information about the area.

The West Coast

Vancouver Island's west coast can feel like the edge of the world. After you climb the winding road up and over the spines of mountains in the center of the island, you finally reach the west shore, where the Pacific waves crash along the beach. Here are the ocean sands and coastal rainforests of the island's first national park, along with two easygoing coastal towns, larger Tofino to the north and Ucluelet to the south. These peninsula communities have whale-watching tours, First Nations canoe trips, and plenty of other outdoor adventures, as well as good restaurants and beachfront lodges.

The weather on the west coast can be cooler, damper, and more changeable than elsewhere on the island. Bring layers, rain gear, and shoes or boots that can get wet.

Whatever the weather, the west coast is a laid-back region where local surfers carry boards on their bikes, and cocktail hour can seem like a sacred ritual. And it's hugely popular with travelers: Tofino's population of 2,000 can swell to more than 20,000 on weekends in July and August.

Don't worry, though. Even in busy midsummer, it's still worth a visit to this edge of the world.

★ Pacific Rim National Park Reserve

With 14 miles (22 km) of sandy beaches and dunes backed by coastal rainforest, the reserve protects a wide swath of Vancouver Island's west coast. Established in 1970, it was the island's first national park.

Visiting the Park

Pacific Rim National Park Reserve has three geographically separate components. Most visitors head directly to the park's **Long Beach Unit** (Pacific Rim Hwy., 250/726-3500, www.pc.gc.ca), north of the Tofino-Ucluelet junction.

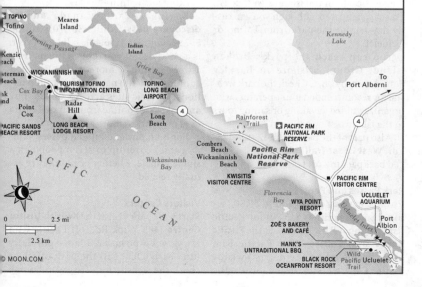

© MOON.COM

Rest Stop: Sproat Lake

Sproat Lake

When you're driving to or from Vancouver Island's west coast, there are few places to stop as you cross the mountains between Port Alberni and Tofino. For a break or some good food, stop at **Sproat Lake Landing** (10695 Lakeshore Rd., Port Alberni, 250/723-2722, www.sproatlakelanding.com), where **Drinkwaters Social House** (11am-11pm Mon.-Fri., 9am-11pm Sat.-Sun.; call for off-season hours) serves pub-style meals overlooking the 15-mile (24-km) lake. Book one of the seven modern guest rooms ($149-399) if you want a longer rest; the best have lake views.

The park visitors center is here, as is the longest beach on the island's west coast. You can camp, too, although you can easily day-trip to the park from Tofino or Ucluelet.

You can reach the park's **Broken Islands Group,** offshore in Barkley Sound, only by boat. Check the park website for recommended tour operators who organize guided kayaking or sailing tours to the islands.

Also part of the park is the 47-mile (75-km) **West Coast Trail** (May-Sept.), a rugged backpacking route.

Park Passes and Fees
Purchase a **day pass** (adults $7.80, seniors $6.80, families $15.70) for Pacific Rim National Park Reserve at the **Pacific Rim Visitor Centre** (2791 Pacific Rim Hwy., Ucluelet), at the park's **Kwisitis Visitor Centre** (Wick Beach, off Pacific

Rim Hwy.), or from vending machines at parking lots within the park.

Buying a Parks Canada **annual discovery pass** (adults $67.70, seniors $57.90, families $136.40), valid for a year, is a good deal if you're spending at least a week in one or more parks. It's good at more than 100 national parks and national historic sites across Canada. Buy annual passes online from Parks Canada or at any park visitors center.

For both day and annual passes, family passes cover up to seven people in a single vehicle, whether or not they're actually related.

Visitors Centers
Start your park visit at the **Kwisitis Visitor Centre** (485 Wick Rd., off Pacific Rim Hwy., www.pc.gc.ca, 10am-5pm daily June-early Oct., call the park office or check the website for off-season hours).

The park encompasses the traditional territory of the Nuu-chah-nulth First Nation, and you can get an introduction to its culture though the center's exhibits.

Sports and Recreation
Beaches
Confusingly, **Wickaninnish Beach** is not the beach where the deluxe Wickaninnish Inn is located; that hotel is on Chesterman Beach. Rather, the wide dune-backed Wick Beach is adjacent to the park visitors center.

North of Wick Beach and adjacent to old-growth forest, **Long Beach** creates the longest sand dune on Vancouver Island; it's more than 9 miles (15 km) long.

Hiking
Several gentle hiking trails start from the Kwisitis Visitor Centre. The 3-mile (5-km) **Nuu-chah-nulth Trail** is an easy loop with interpretive panels about First Nations culture. You can branch from this trail onto the 0.5-mile (0.8-km) **South Beach Trail** that leads to a pebble beach with often spectacular waves; don't swim here, though, due to the strong currents. The gentle **Shorepine Bog Trail,** a 0.5-mile (0.8-km) loop, takes you through an old-growth temperate rainforest.

Camping
Above the beach, 7.5 miles (12 km) north of the Tofino-Ucluelet junction, **Green Point Campground** (www.pc.gc.ca, May-mid-Oct., $27.40-32.30) has 94 drive-in sites with electricity, flush toilets, and showers. There are also 20 additional forested walk-in sites. In the walk-in area, you can also book an **oTENTik** ($120), a platform tent that sleeps up to six.

Make campsite **reservations** (877/737-3783, www.reservation.parkscanada.gc.ca) online or by phone, beginning in January for the upcoming season. Reservations are especially recommended for stays between mid-June and August.

★ Tofino
Like all of the west coast, the Tofino area was First Nations territory where generations of fishers and hunters lived and foraged, both on the mainland and on the islands offshore. Spanish explorers first ventured to the region in the late 1700s, followed quickly by British expeditions, but it wasn't until 1909 that the town of Tofino was officially established, when fishing, logging, and mining were the main occupations along the coast. Tofino's nickname comes from these hardscrabble jobs and the region's stormy winters: Tough City.

While surfers and other nature-seekers began arriving in the 1960s, the creation of the Pacific Rim National Park Reserve in 1970 and the paving of Highway 4 to the coast in 1972 launched the modern tourist era.

Today, laid-back, surfer-friendly Tofino has a small village around its scenic harbor, where fishing vessels set off to sea, whale-watching and other tour boats dock, and float planes come and go. The beaches and oceanfront lodges are on the peninsula, south of town.

Sights
The **Tofino Botanical Gardens** (1084 Pacific Rim Hwy., 250/725-1220, www.tbgf.org, 8am-dusk daily, adults $12, seniors $10, students ages 13 and over $8), 2 miles (3 km) south of town, offers a refuge from the wilderness of Vancouver Island's wild west coast, with cultivated plants, old-growth rainforest, and works by local artists. Many plants are local, including a tree that's roughly 800 years old, while others include Chilean rainforest vegetation, Himalayan lilies (the world's largest), and other varieties that grow in climates similar to that of British Columbia's coastal regions. Examine the traditional dugout canoe, handmade by First Nations carver Joe Martin, displayed with photos of his family and commentary from his children. Kids may appreciate the chickens and goats that

Tofino

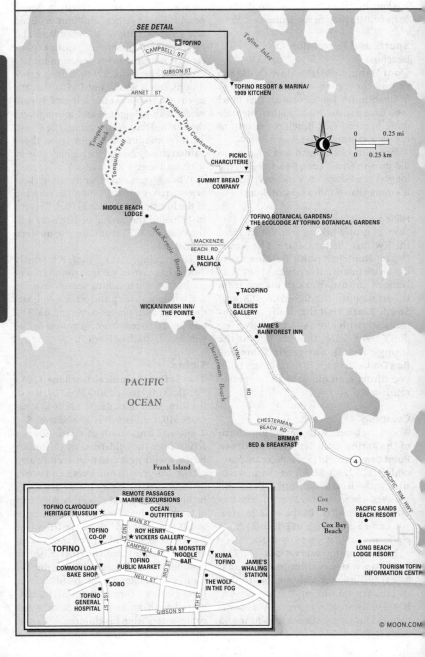

SEE DETAIL

★ TOFINO

CAMPBELL ST

GIBSON ST

Tofino Inlet

ARNET ST

Tonquin Trail

Tonquin Trail Connector

Tonquin Beach

▼ TOFINO RESORT & MARINA/ 1909 KITCHEN

PICNIC CHARCUTERIE ▼

SUMMIT BREAD COMPANY ▼

MIDDLE BEACH LODGE ■

MacKenzie Beach

MACKENZIE BEACH RD

BELLA PACIFICA

TOFINO BOTANICAL GARDENS/ THE ECOLODGE AT TOFINO BOTANICAL GARDENS ★

0   0.25 mi

0   0.25 km

▼ TACOFINO

■ BEACHES GALLERY

WICKANINNISH INN/ THE POINTE ▲

JAMIE'S RAINFOREST INN ■

Chesterman Beach

LYNN RD

PACIFIC OCEAN

CHESTERMAN BEACH RD

BRIMAR BED & BREAKFAST ●

Frank Island

4

PACIFIC RIM HWY

Cox Bay

Cox Bay Beach

PACIFIC SANDS BEACH RESORT ●

LONG BEACH LODGE RESORT ●

TOURISM TOFIN INFORMATION CENTR

REMOTE PASSAGES MARINE EXCURSIONS ■

TOFINO CLAYOQUOT HERITAGE MUSEUM ★

MAIN ST

OCEAN OUTFITTERS ■

TOFINO CO-OP ■

2ND ST

ROY HENRY ★ VICKERS GALLERY

TOFINO

CAMPBELL ST

SEA MONSTER NOODLE BAR ■

▼ KUMA TOFINO

COMMON LOAF BAKE SHOP ▼

TOFINO PUBLIC MARKET ▼

3RD ST

JAMIE'S WHALING STATION ■

NEILL ST

● THE WOLF IN THE FOG

▼ SOBO

TOFINO GENERAL HOSPITAL ■

1ST ST

4TH ST

GIBSON ST

© MOON.COM

wander the garden's grounds. Named for Charles Darwin and stocked with "books full of dangerous ideas," **Darwin's Café** (8am-5pm daily Mar.-Oct.) serves coffee and pastries.

Tiny **Tofino Clayoquot Heritage Museum** (331 Main St., no phone, www. tofinomuseum.com, 12:30pm-4pm Wed.-Sun. May-Aug., 12:30pm-4pm Sat.-Sun. Sept.-Apr., donation), on the lower level of the Royal Canadian Legion building, covers Tofino-area history from early days through the present. Exhibits highlight the region's First Nations culture, whaling and fishing industries, and environmental activism, along with stories of notable residents.

B.C. indigenous artist Roy Henry Vickers displays his original prints and paintings at **Roy Henry Vickers Gallery** (350 Campbell St., 250/725-3235, www. royhenryvickers.com, 10am-5pm daily). Accompanying each work is a short story about its inspiration, often from the artist's family or community.

Tours and Excursions

To really experience the west coast, get off-shore to explore the coastline and nearby islands and look for the wildlife that populates the region. Most tours operate March or April-October or November; trips can be postponed or cancelled if the seas get too rough.

The following companies are among those offering tours in the Tofino area:

- **Remote Passages Marine Excursions** (51 Wharf St., 250/725-3330 or 800/666-9833, www.remotepassages.com)

- **Ocean Outfitters** (368 Main St., 250/725-2866 or 877/906-2326, www.oceanoutfitters.bc.ca)

Top to bottom: Wickaninnish Beach in Pacific Rim National Park Reserve; Tofino Botanical Gardens; a whale-watching boat at Tofino Resort & Marina.

Two Days on Vancouver Island's West Coast

Day 1

Start with a morning stroll along the beach; **Chesterman Beach** is one of the area's most beautiful. Then wander through the **Tofino Botanical Gardens** to explore the old-growth rainforest, stopping at the garden's **Darwin's Café** when it's time for a coffee break.

Have lunch at the orange food truck, **Tacofino.** Then head for **Pacific Rim National Park Reserve** to check out the displays in the **Kwisitis Visitor Centre** and hike near the shore. Later, take a **surfing lesson,** go swimming, or book a **First Nations Dugout Canoe Tour** with the excellent guides at T'ashii Paddle School. Have dinner at **The Wolf in the Fog,** where the don't-miss appetizer is the potato-crusted oyster, and any local seafood is bound to be stellar.

Day 2

The next morning, pick up coffee and a ginger scone at **Common Loaf Bake Shop,** or a croissant from **Summit Bread Company,** before heading to the waterfront for an offshore excursion. Take a full-day trip to **Hot Springs Cove,** a kayak excursion to **Meares Island,** or a shorter **whale-watching** or **bear-watching tour.**

After your tour, clean up and drive to the **Wickaninnish Inn** for a cocktail in its window-lined lounge facing the sea. If your budget allows, stay for a special dinner at **The Pointe,** or if you'd prefer a more casual meal, go into town for a restorative bowl of ramen at **Kuma Tofino,** or graze on small plates in the window-lined dining room at **1909 Kitchen.** Either way, stop to take a few sunset photos over the harbor to remember your west coast adventures.

- **T'ashii Paddle School** (250/266-3787 or 855/883-3787, www.tofinopaddle.com)

- **The Adventure Centre at Tofino Resort & Marina** (778/841-0186, www.tofinoresortandmarina.com)

- **The Whale Centre** (411 Campbell St., 250/725-2132 or 888/474-2288, www.tofinowhalecentre.com)

Hot Springs Cove/Maquinna Marine Provincial Park

A full-day trip to these remote hot springs is a highlight for many Tofino visitors. Located 27 nautical miles (50 km) northwest of Tofino, **Hot Springs Cove,** in Maquinna Marine Provincial Park at the north end of Clayoquot Sound, is accessible only by boat (adults $109-139, under age 13 $89-109) or float plane (adults $224-229, under age 13 $204-209).

Traveling by boat (1.5-2 hours each way), you may spot whales, sea lions, and even bears or other wildlife, so you might consider this trip an alternative to a separate whale-watching tour. With the float plane option, you save a little time, traveling one way by boat, the other on a scenic 20-minute flight.

Once you arrive at the dock, it's a 1-mile (1.6-km) walk on a boardwalk through the rainforest to the natural hot springs. Climb down the rocks and take a natural hot shower in the gushing sulfur springs, then soak in the rock pools. The water temperature averages a soothing 110°F (43°C).

There's a rustic shelter with change rooms and a pit toilet above the springs and a restroom near the docks. Don't forget your bathing suit, towel, and water bottle. Sports sandals or water shoes will protect your feet from the rocks. Bring snacks or a picnic to enjoy before or after you soak.

Meares Island

Declared a park by the Tla-o-qui-aht and Ahousaht First Nations, **Meares Island**—its traditional name is

Wanachis-Hilthhoois—is across the harbor from the village of Tofino.

A popular way to get to the island is on a half-day **kayak excursion** ($84). Some companies run **water shuttles** (adults $25-30, under age 12 $15-20) to the island. Tour companies also collect a $5 park fee.

Once you arrive on Meares Island, you can hike through the rainforest on the moderate 1.9-mile (3-km) round-trip **Big Tree Trail,** which takes you into an old-growth forest, where some trees are more than 1,000 years old.

For experienced hikers, the island's steep, challenging **Lone Cone Trail** leads up to a 2,395-foot (730-m) peak with panoramic views across the island and the sound. It's only 0.6 mile (1 km) in each direction, but it's essentially a vertical trail.

Whale-Watching

On **whale-watching excursions** (adults $99-109, under age 13 $75-79) from Tofino, you'll likely spot Pacific gray whales. You might also see humpback whales, bald eagles, sea lions, harbor seals, and occasionally orcas or porpoises.

As on the trips that depart from Victoria, you can choose from a tour in an inflatable zodiac, which gives you a choppier but more thrilling ride, or on a larger, more sheltered boat, which would be more comfortable in inclement weather. On either type of craft, whale-watching tours typically last 2.5-3 hours.

Bear-Watching

From Tofino, you can take a boat through Clayoquot Sound to several spots where it's possible to observe the area's resident population of black bears. On these **bear-watching excursions** (adults $99-109, under age 13 $75-79), the tour boats dock offshore, where, if you're lucky, you'll spot bears foraging along the rocky beaches or in the tidal pools.

You stay on the boat throughout these 2- to 3-hour tours. Bring a camera with a telephoto lens for the best photos, since the boats must remain a safe distance away from the animals.

First Nations Dugout Canoe Tours

First Nations-owned **T'ashii Paddle School** (250/266-3787 or 855/883-3787, www.tofinopaddle.com) offers several excellent paddling tours in hand-carved dugout canoes, where you'll learn about local indigenous communities and their traditional culture.

Departing from **Jamie's Whaling Station** (606 Campbell St.), excursions include a two-hour **Coastal Canoe Tour** (late May-mid-Oct., $65 pp), which is especially lovely at sunset, and a **Meares Island Canoe Tour** (Mar.-mid-Oct., $89 pp), a four-hour paddling and hiking excursion.

Sports and Recreation
Beaches

Sandy beaches line the peninsula that stretches south from Tofino to Ucluelet. Except for Tonquin Beach, all are located off the Pacific Rim Highway, listed here from north to south.

Closest to town, **Tonquin Beach** still feels secluded, as you follow the walking trail through the rainforest and down the stairs to the beach.

Sheltered **MacKenzie Beach** has several resorts and campgrounds.

Beginning surfers hone their skills on the south end of 1.7-mile (2.7-km) **Chesterman Beach,** one of Tofino's most scenic and popular stretches of sand. Toward the beach's north side, you can explore the tide pools at low tide. The Wickaninnish Inn is on North Chesterman Beach.

Home to several resorts, including Pacific Sands and Long Beach Lodge, **Cox Bay Beach** has a popular surf break. At the bay's northern tip, you can explore several tidal caves, accessible only at low tide.

Continuing south, you'll reach the beaches in Pacific Rim National Park Reserve, including **Long Beach** and **Wickaninnish Beach.**

Surfing

Tofino is western Canada's **surfing** capital (yes, Canada really has a surfing capital), with plenty of places to take lessons or catch the waves. While you can surf year-round, hard-core surfers come in winter when the waves are biggest; if you're getting started, summertime is warmest, with the gentlest surf.

With a crew of women as instructors, **Surf Sister Surf School** (625 Campbell St., 250/725-4456, www.surfsister.com) specializes in teaching women to surf, although it offers lessons for both men and women. In addition to standard group lessons ($89 pp), it offers individual ($179), two-person ($119 pp), and three-person ($109 pp) private instruction.

The **Surf Club Adventure Centre** (250/725-2442, www.longbeachlodgeresort.com) at the Long Beach Lodge Resort is another highly regarded surf school, teaching group ($99 pp) and private lessons ($189 pp).

Stand-Up Paddleboarding

T'ashii Paddle School (250/266-3787 or 855/883-3787, www.tofinopaddle.com) offers stand-up paddleboard tours ($65-129), lessons ($80-140), and rentals (2 hours $29, full-day $39). You can also learn SUP surfing—surfing on a stand-up paddleboard ($89-140).

Hiking

The 1.9-mile (3-km) **Tonquin Trail** (www.tofino.ca/trails) is a moderate path through the rainforest that leads to several lookout points and to the scenic Tonquin, Third, and Middle Beaches, with dramatic rock formations along the shores. The trail starts in town behind the Tofino Community Hall (351 Arnet Rd.), where there's a parking lot.

The **Rainforest Education Society** (250/725-2560, www.raincoasteducation.org) offers free 90-minute interpretive walks in July and August that explore the tide pools and rainforest along Cox

surfers on Chesterman Beach

Bay. Check the website for the schedule and other details.

Guides from the First Nations-owned **T'ashii Paddle School** (250/266-3787 or 855/883-3787, www.tofinopaddle. com) lead winter **Cultural Walks on the Schooner Cove Trail** (10:30am daily mid-Dec.-Mar., $100 for 2 people, $20 each additional person) in Pacific Rim National Park Reserve that combine a gentle hike through the old-growth rainforest with information about local First Nations culture. Book in advance on the website.

Festivals and Events

In early spring, whales begin returning to the waters off Vancouver Island's west coast. During the weeklong **Pacific Rim Whale Festival** (www. pacificrimwhalefestival.com, Mar.), you can learn more about these creatures with presentations, documentary films, guided walks, whale-watching tours, and other events.

Feast Tofino (www.feasttofino.com, Apr.-May) celebrates the region's seafood and its "boat-to-table" food culture, organizing dinners and special events with local and visiting chefs.

Tofino Food and Wine Festival (www. tofinofoodandwinefestival.com, June) is a weekend of dining, sipping, and toe-tapping to live music on the grounds of the Tofino Botanical Gardens, with related events at other locations around town.

Food

For a small community, Tofino has a significant food culture, emphasizing innovative uses of local seafood and produce. Outside the summer months, many restaurants keep reduced or varying hours, so call before you set out. Except for The Pointe at the Wickaninnish Inn, Tofino's eating places are casual; patrons often look like they've wandered directly off a boat because, most likely, they have.

Contemporary

Oysters in a potato web? Fried cod cheeks with sea asparagus? Pacific octopus with black lentils and North African spices? Some of the west coast's most imaginative dishes come out of the open kitchen at ★ **The Wolf in the Fog** (150 4th St., 250/725-9653, www.wolfinthefog.com, 10am-2pm and 5pm-midnight daily, lunch/brunch $13-22, dinner $21-40), where the 2nd-floor dining room sparkles with polished wood and the big windows look toward the harbor. While there's some serious technique and respect for local ingredients here, the chefs don't take themselves too seriously; the menu suggests buying a six-pack for the kitchen. For your own drinks, try the signature Cedar Sour, with cedar-infused rye. Finish up with the intense dark chocolate blackout or a seasonal fruit creation. The bottom line? Good food, good drinks, good fun.

Overlooking the marina and offshore islands, with picture windows on two sides and portholes framing the views on the third, **1909 Kitchen** (634 Campbell St., 250/726-6122, www.tofinoresortandmarina.com, 7am-11am and 5pm-9:30pm daily, breakfast $6-16, dinner $12-36) at Tofino Resort and Marina shows off the waterfront panoramas. The chef's interest in foraging, fishing, and sourcing regional ingredients means that the menu of inspired sharing plates might encompass black rice with house-candied salmon, albacore "tacos" (with the fish served raw on radish "paper"), or the day's catch wood-roasted and paired with charred onion-ginger purée. For something simpler, try a pizza—perhaps the side stripe shrimp with chorizo and basil—from the wood-fueled oven. Sweets range from fruit cobblers to s'mores with salted caramel.

Though the name is short for "sophisticated bohemian," airy (and family-friendly) **SoBo** (311 Neil St., 250/725-2341, www.sobo.ca, 11:30am-9:30pm daily, lunch $10-16, dinner $15-30), with sunny yellow walls and floor-to-ceiling windows, is more refined than hippie, serving modern world-beat fare at lunch and dinner. Noon-hour dishes roam from a halloumi cheese and grain salad to huevos rancheros to pizza, while in the evening, you might try halibut with buttermilk mashed potatoes or whiskey-braised brisket. SoBo is justifiably famous for its smoked wild fish chowder.

Tofino's special-occasion restaurant, ★ **The Pointe at the Wickaninnish Inn** (500 Osprey Ln., 250/725-3106, www.wickinn.com, 7:30am-2pm and 5pm-10pm daily, dinner $30-46, brunch $16-34) emphasizes local seafood, foraged ingredients, and regional products. The polished staff and walls of curved windows wrapping the ocean panoramas around you don't hurt either. You might start with a foie gras tart or a Humboldt squid *sope* (a thick tortilla layered with squid, kohlrabi, and pickled sea asparagus) as a prelude to teriyaki-glazed steelhead with smoked salmon and squash agnolotti or scallops in a mussel and clam ragout. There are sweets, of course, from a platter of petit fours to unique creations like sea buckthorn mousse with espresso chocolate fudge. Can't decide (or ready to splurge)? Choose a multicourse tasting menu ($75-105), with optional wine pairings.

Asian

When you crave a restorative bowl of ramen or a rice bowl topped with miso-cured snapper, head for **Kuma Tofino** (101-120 4th St., 250/725-2215, www.kumatofino.com, 4pm-9:30pm daily, $10-14), a modern Japanese eatery. Sake and local craft beer stand up to sharing plates like crispy chicken *karaage,* fresh tuna *tataki,* and salmon croquettes.

For a quick bite in town, the order-at-the-counter **Sea Monster Noodle Bar** (421 Main St., 250/725-1280, www.seamonsternoodle.com, 11:30am-6:30pm daily, $12-15) offers several varieties of simple, tasty Asian-inspired noodle and rice bowls, from *dan dan* noodles to salmon poke. Try the Thai-style fish curry with fresh cilantro and basil.

Mexican

Before it became a Mexican mini chain with branches in Vancouver and Victoria, **Tacofino** (1184 Pacific Rim Hwy., 250/726-8288, www.tacofino.com, 11am-8pm daily summer, 11am-6pm daily off-season, $4-14) was a taco truck in Tofino ("Taco-fino," get it?). This orange truck parked behind a surf shop south of town channels a surfer vibe with tacos (try the tuna with seaweed and ginger), burritos, and slushie drinks like tangy lime-mint "freshies." Park at one of the long outdoor tables, or take yours to the beach.

Cafés, Bakeries, and Light Bites

From local hippies to texting teens to travelers, everyone stops into the red house that's home to long-standing **Common Loaf Bake Shop** (180 1st St.,

250/725-3915, 7am-6pm daily) for delectable cinnamon buns, ginger scones, breads, and muffins. The shop makes soup, sandwiches, and pizza, too.

It's not only bread at **Summit Bread Company** (681 Industrial Way, Units C&D, 250/726-6767, www.summitbreadco.com, 7am-4pm daily), where the aromatic baking may lure you to this shop in the south-of-town industrial district. It also turns out croissants, muffins, savory buns, and seasonally changing baked goods to take out. The salted dark chocolate cookie is becoming a local classic.

Groceries and Markets

The area's largest grocery store is **Tofino Co-op** (140 1st St., 250/725-3226, www.tofinocoop.com, 8:30am-9pm daily summer, 8:30am-8pm daily fall-spring). South of town, tiny but well-stocked **Beaches Grocery** (1184 Pacific Rim Hwy., 250/725-2237, 8:30am-10pm daily) carries fruits and vegetables, baked goods, and other food items, from chips to Asian chili sauce.

Picnic Charcuterie (700 Industrial Way, 250/889-5738, www.picniccharcuterie.com, 10am-7pm daily) sells its own cured and smoked meats, with a selection of local and imported cheeses.

Find local produce, prepared foods, and crafts at the **Tofino Public Market** (Tofino Village Green, 3rd St. and Campbell St., www.tofinomarket.com, 10am-2pm Sat. late May-early Oct.).

Accommodations

Many of Tofino's nicest accommodations are south of town, along the peninsula beaches. Book in advance for summer high season (mid-June-mid-Sept.). In winter, many lodgings offer **storm watching** packages, when the big winter surf and rain rolls in. For last-minute lodging, check the "current vacancies" page on the Tofino Tourism website (www.tourismtofino.com).

$150-300

Once a field station for research groups, **The Ecolodge at Tofino Botanical Gardens** (1084 Pacific Rim Hwy., 250/725-1220, www.tbgf.org, $159-239) is a simple, comfortable lodge in the midst of the gardens. Guests gather in the great room for continental breakfast or to relax; you can browse the lodge's nature library or use the kitchen to prep meals. Eight basic, colorfully decorated rooms share two large baths. Two additional suites, with private baths, have family-friendly nooks with bunk beds. There are no TVs, but Wi-Fi is included, as is garden admission.

At **Jamie's Rainforest Inn** (1258 Pacific Rim Hwy., 250/725-2323 or 855/433-2323, www.tofinorainforestinn.com, $209-249), a well-kept motel facing the woods on the inlet side of the highway, the 36 rooms have microwaves, mini fridges, coffeemakers, and included Wi-Fi. The king-bed rooms have gas fireplaces, and the larger units include kitchenettes with cooktops. Ask about discounts on whale-watching and other tours from its affiliated adventure company, **Jamie's Whaling Station** (www.jamies.com).

To stay close to the departure point for whale-watching trips and other tours as well as the town's cafés and restaurants, consider **Tofino Resort & Marina** (634 Campbell St., 844/680-4184, www.tofinoresortandmarina.com, $199-339). New owners revamped an old motel above a marina at the south end of Tofino into 62 simple, well-designed rooms in two buildings, all with coffeemakers, kettles, mini fridges, and Wi-Fi. The largest units, king or queen suites, have a small sitting area with a double sofa bed. Request a higher-floor unit for partial ocean views; the least expensive rooms face the parking areas. You can book whale-watching tours and other activities through the on-site adventure center. Have a beer or casual meal in **Hatch Waterfront Pub** or inventive

contemporary fare at **1909 Kitchen,** which both face the water.

Overlooking two beaches and the off-shore islands, **Middle Beach Lodge** (400 MacKenzie Beach Rd., 250/725-2900 or 866/725-2900, www.middlebeach.com, $165-475) offers a variety of accommodations. The original lodge has tiny, no-frills rooms with no TVs or closets, but the nicest of these economical units have ocean views. In the main lodge, rooms are slightly larger with wooden floors and flat-screen TVs; choose an end unit upstairs for the best water vistas. Also on the forested property are roomy cabins with kitchen facilities; some have sleeping lofts, fireplaces, or hot tubs. Your room almost doesn't matter when you take in the panoramic views from the overstuffed chairs in the wood-beamed great room, where a deluxe continental breakfast buffet (included in the rates) is served.

The three gold-and-burgundy guest rooms at the cedar-shingled **BriMar Bed & Breakfast** (1375 Thornberg Cres., 250/725-3410, www.brimarbb.com, $235-375) look right onto Chesterman Beach, close enough to hear the surf. On the 2nd floor, the spacious Moonrise Room has an equally spacious private bath, while the slightly smaller Sunset Room has a private bath across the hall. The secluded Loft Unit, under the eaves, runs the whole length of the top floor. Rates include Wi-Fi and an ample breakfast. Guests can help themselves to coffee and tea at all hours, and store snacks in the hallway fridge.

Over $300
Even if you're not staying at **Long Beach Lodge Resort** (1441 Pacific Rim Hwy., 250/725-2442, www.longbeachlodgeresort.com, $329-509 d, cottages $550-679), have a drink or a

Top to bottom: tacos and more at 1909 Kitchen; Pacific Sands Beach Resort overlooking Cox Bay; dessert at The Wolf in the Fog.

meal in the inviting **Great Room,** with walls of windows facing the ocean. The lodge has a well-regarded surf club, where both kids and adults can learn to ride the waves. When it's time to sleep, choose from 41 studio units in the main lodge, with sturdy Douglas fir furnishings, or from 20 two-bedroom cottages in the forest, set back from the beach. Solo travelers: In the off-season, the resort regularly offers discounts for individual guests.

Opened in 1972 on the beach at Cox Bay, family-friendly ★ **Pacific Sands Beach Resort** (1421 Pacific Rim Hwy, 250/725-3322, www.pacificsands.com, $255-449 d, 2-bedroom units $500-880) has grown to encompass 120 units, all with full kitchens, in several buildings. Most of the modern condo-style beach houses have two bedrooms and views across the lawn to the waterfront. In other buildings, the studio to two-bedroom units are smaller but still feel airy and beachy. The contemporary one-bedroom suites in the newest Oceanside Suites wing have patios or balconies with ocean vistas. The outdoor **Surfside Grill** cooks up fish-and-chips, seafood chowder, burgers, and tacos, and you can buy drinks, snacks, and quick meals in the lobby. Rent beach cruiser bikes to go cycling, or gather the gang in the gazebo to roast marshmallows.

The most deluxe lodging on Vancouver Island's west coast is the ★ **Wickaninnish Inn** (500 Osprey Ln., 250/725-3100 or 800/333-4604, www.wickinn.com, $360-1,020), which nestles into 100 acres (40 ha) of old-growth rainforest on Chesterman Beach. Behind the unassuming gray exteriors, the inn is filled with indigenous art and 75 rustic yet elegant accommodations with earth-tone furnishings, gas fireplaces, flat-screen TVs hidden in cabinets that open by remote control, soaker tubs, and heated bath floors. The **Ancient Cedars Spa** has six treatment rooms, including one set dramatically above the rocks; guests can join daily yoga classes. Local musicians perform at the **Driftwood Café** (named for its bar made of driftwood), which serves coffee, pastries, and light meals. **The Pointe,** the inn's premier restaurant, is among the region's finest.

Information and Services

The **Pacific Rim Visitor Centre** (2791 Pacific Rim Hwy., Ucluelet, 250/726-4600, www.pacificrimvisitor.ca, 9am-7pm daily July-Aug., 10am-5pm daily Sept.-June), at the Tofino-Ucluelet junction, where Highway 4 meets the Pacific Rim Highway, provides information about the region.

Tofino Tourism (www.tourismtofino.com) has a detailed website with useful trip-planning tips. It runs the **Tofino Information Centre** (1426 Pacific Rim Hwy., Tofino, 250/725-3414 or 888/720-3414, www.tourismtofino.com, 9am-5pm daily June-Sept., 10am-5pm daily Oct.-May), 4.5 miles (7 km) south of downtown Tofino and 15.5 miles (25 km) north of the Tofino-Ucluelet junction.

Small **Tofino General Hospital** (261 Neill St., 250/725-4010, www.islandhealth.ca) offers 24-hour emergency services.

Getting Around

Easy to explore on foot, the town of Tofino is just a few blocks square, with most shops and restaurants along Campbell or Main Streets, between 1st and 4th Streets. To travel between town and the beaches, it's easiest to have your own car, although it's possible to cycle or take a bus, a good idea in the busy summer season when the roads and parking areas can be congested.

By Car

From its junction with Highway 4, the Pacific Rim Highway runs 20 miles (32 km) up the peninsula to the town of Tofino, passing Pacific Rim National Park Reserve and beaches along the way. In town, the highway becomes Campbell Street.

If you arrive in Tofino without a car, rent one from **Budget** (1850 Pacific Rim Hwy., 250/725-2060, www.bcbudget. com) at the Tofino airport.

By Bus

The free **Tofino Shuttle** (www. tourismtofino.com, 7:30am-10:30pm daily late June-early Sept.) runs during the summer between town and Cox Bay, with stops near several beaches. Buses leave about once an hour in each direction, so check the schedule online before setting out.

By Bike

Cycling is a good way to travel between town and the beaches. Ride along the 3.75-mile (6-km) **Multi-Use Path,** locally known as the MUP, a fairly flat, paved trail that parallels Highway 4 from town to Cox Bay. Plans have been announced to extend the MUP south to the boundary of Pacific Rim National Park Reserve, where it will connect with the **ʔapsčiik t'ašii (ups-cheek-TA-shee) trail,** a 15-mile (24-km) pathway through the national park, which is planned for a 2020 opening; check with **Tofino Tourism** (www. tourismtofino.com) for updates.

TOF Cycles (660 Sharp Rd., 250/725-2453, www.tofcycles.com, 9am-6pm daily, 4 hours $30, full-day $35) or **Tofino Bikes** (1180 Pacific Rim Hwy., 250/725-2722, http://tofinobike.com, 10am-5pm daily, 4 hours $30, full-day $35), both located between MacKenzie and Chesterman Beaches, rent bikes.

Ucluelet

Once considered the workaday counterpart to more upscale Tofino, 25 miles (40 km) to the north, Ucluelet (population 1,700) is coming into its own as a holiday destination. It's close enough to Pacific Rim National Park Reserve to explore the trails and beaches, and you can also enjoy the sand and hiking routes around town.

Sights and Recreation

Ucluelet Aquarium (180 Main St., 250/726-2782, www.uclueletaquarium. org, 10am-5pm daily mid-Mar.-Nov., adults $14, seniors and students $10, ages 4-17 $7) has a rare "catch and release" philosophy. In the spring, staff bring in sealife from the local waters of Clayoquot and Barkley Sounds to populate the kids'-eye-level tanks, releasing them in the autumn back to the wild. The "please touch" displays are fun for youngsters and not-so-youngsters alike.

For hikers, the **Wild Pacific Trail** (www. wildpacifictrail.com) has several moderate options at the foot of the Ucluelet peninsula, with spectacular views of the Pacific coast. The 1.6-mile (2.6-km) **Lighthouse Loop** starts and ends on Coast Guard Road south of Terrace Beach, passing the 1915 Amphitrite Lighthouse. The hillier **Artist Loop** takes you 1.7 miles (2.8 km) along the cliffs starting from either Brown's Beach or Big Beach Park near Black Rock Oceanfront Resort. A short detour off the Artist Loop, the 0.6-mile (1-km) **Ancient Cedars Loop** leads through a forest of old-growth Sitka spruce, western hemlock, and giant red cedar trees. Get a map on the trail website or from the Pacific Rim Visitor Centre.

Food

Stop into **Zoë's Bakery and Café** (250 Main St., 250/726-2253, www. zoesbakeryandcafe.com, 7am-4pm daily, $5-10) for pastries, soups, quiche, sandwiches, and other baked goods. Try the Savory Breakfast Egg Bake Thingy, a delicious mash-up of sourdough bread cubes and bacon, topped with an egg. Zoë's is also known for its carrot cake.

Curing its own meats and sourcing ingredients locally may not make this barbecue joint in a little red house nontraditional, but at **Hank's Untraditional BBQ** (1576 Imperial Ln., 250/726-2225, www.hanksbbq.ca, 5pm-9:30pm daily, $24-27), it does make things good. Lead off with spicy hoisin duck wings or panko-crusted cod before muscling into the main event, whether it's coffee- and cocoa-rubbed beef brisket or barbecued pulled pork.

Accommodations and Camping

The Ucluelet First Nation runs the unique ★ **Wya Point Resort** (2695 Tofino-Ucluelet Hwy., 250/726-2625 or 844/352-6188, www.wyapoint.com), which has several lodging options on a remote section of coast. Nine wood-frame **lodges** ($349 one-bedroom, $559 two-bedroom), decorated with works by First Nations carvers, are upscale cabins, each sleeping 4-6, with solid hand-built bed frames, living rooms with sleep sofas, full kitchens, and spacious decks above Ucluth Beach. Fifteen heated **yurts** ($150-175) made of thick canvas offer more rustic accommodations. You can cook outside on the barbecue and sleep inside on the sofa bed; some yurts also have bunk beds for the kids. Shared washrooms are nearby. The third option is the **campground** (early Mar.-mid-Oct., $35-65), where some sites overlook the ocean and others sit in the forest near the beach.

Family-friendly 133-room **Black Rock Oceanfront Resort** (596 Marine Dr., 250/726-4800 or 877/762-5011, www.blackrockresort.com, $199-489) has everything you need for a beach getaway. Modern studios and one-bedroom suites in the main lodge, decorated in earthy greens and blacks, have kitchen facilities, spacious baths with heated floors and soaker tubs, and free Wi-Fi. Choose a 4th-floor room for the best views. Surrounded by trees in separate buildings, the Trail Suites range from studios to two-bedroom units. On the sea-facing deck is a plunge pool and two hot tubs; inside is a small fitness room and spa. When you get hungry, **Fetch Restaurant,** specializing in seafood, cooks up breakfast, lunch, and dinner; **Float Lounge** serves drinks and light meals.

Information and Services

Get local information at the **Pacific Rim Visitor Centre** (2791 Pacific Rim Hwy., Ucluelet, 250/726-4600, www.pacificrimvisitor.ca, 9am-7pm daily July-Aug., 10am-5pm daily Sept.-June), at the Tofino-Ucluelet junction.

Whistler and the Sea-to-Sky Highway

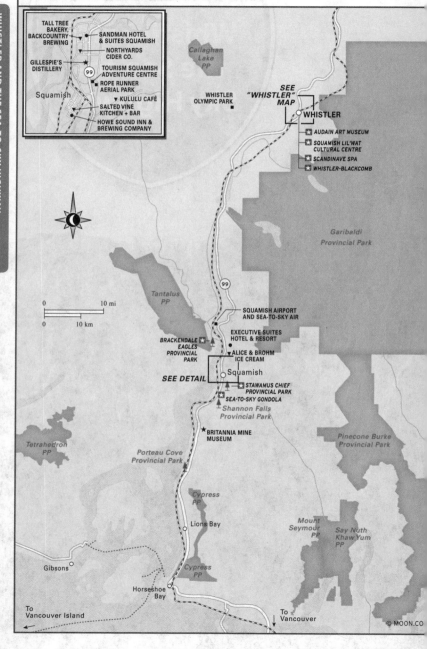

Sea-to-Sky Highway

Whistler

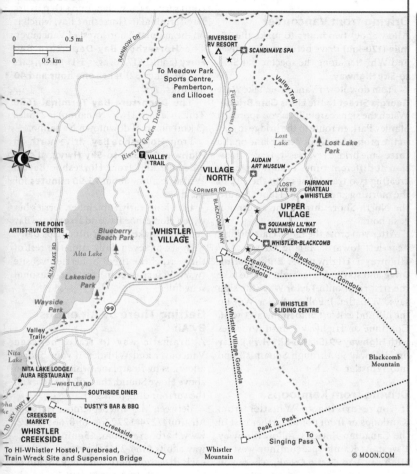

The stunning Sea-to-Sky Highway connects Vancouver to the year-round outdoor mecca of Whistler.

Just a two-hour drive, it's perfect for a day trip or as part of a longer exploration. Whistler offers not just North America's largest snow sports resort but plenty of opportunities for hiking, biking, paddling glacier-fed lakes, and exploring the region's First Nations heritage.

Between Whistler and Vancouver, the town of Squamish is a hot spot for outdoor activities, including excellent hiking and the region's best white-water rafting. For those looking for gentler adventures, Squamish's Sea-to-Sky Gondola delivers stellar views and access to mountaintop hiking trails.

Getting to Whistler

Driving from Vancouver

Allow about **two hours** to make the **75-mile (120-km)** drive between Vancouver and Whistler along the spectacular **Sea-to-Sky Highway.**

From downtown Vancouver, take **West Georgia Street** to the **Lions Gate Bridge.** Watch the signs carefully as you approach Stanley Park en route to the bridge to stay in the proper lane. The center lane on the three-lane bridge reverses its travel direction at different times of day, typically creating two travel lanes into the city in the morning and two travel lanes toward the North Shore during the afternoon rush hour.

After you cross the Lions Gate Bridge, bear left toward Marine Drive west/Highway 1/Highway 99. Enter **Marine Drive** and stay in the far right lane to take the first right onto **Taylor Way** (the sign says "Whistler"). Follow Taylor Way up the hill and exit left onto **Highway 1** west. Continue on Highway 1 until it merges with **Highway 99 (Sea-to-Sky Hwy.).** Stay on Highway 99 through Squamish and into Whistler.

Driving from Kamloops

If you're driving to Whistler from Kamloops or from points farther east in the Canadian Rockies, follow **Highway 1** west. At Kamloops, continue west on Highway 1 to **Cache Creek,** where you make a sharp right turn onto **Highway 97** north, following the signs for "BC-99/Prince George/Lillooet." When Highways 97 and 99 meet, take **Highway 99** west, which will take you through Lillooet, Pemberton, and on into Whistler. Kamloops to Whistler is **185 miles (300 km),** a **four-hour** drive.

Driving from Vancouver Island (via Ferry)

If you're traveling between Vancouver Island and Whistler, you don't have to go through the city of Vancouver. Take **B.C. Ferries** (888/223-3779, www.bcferries.com) service from Nanaimo's Departure Bay Terminal to Horseshoe Bay, which is on the mainland northwest of Vancouver. The **Horseshoe Bay-Departure Bay Ferry** (adults $17.20, ages 5-11 $8.60, cars $57.50, bikes $2) takes **one hour and 40 minutes.**

The **Departure Bay Terminal** (680 Trans-Canada Hwy., Nanaimo) is 2 miles (3 km) north of downtown Nanaimo.

From **Horseshoe Bay,** drive north on **Highway 99 (Sea-to-Sky Hwy.).** It's **60 miles (97 km)** from Horseshoe Bay to Whistler; allow about **75-90 minutes** for the drive.

Late June-early September, ferries between Horseshoe Bay and Departure Bay generally make eight or nine trips daily, with six or seven daily runs the rest of the year; check the B.C. Ferries website (www.bcferries.com) for the seasonal schedule.

Getting There by Air or Bus
By Air

A dramatic way to travel between Vancouver and Whistler, if your budget allows, is by floatplane, which takes you above Howe Sound, the Gulf Islands, and the surrounding peaks.

Between May and September, **Harbour Air** (604/274-1277 or 800/665-0212, www.harbourair.com, 45 minutes, one-way adults $164-236) flies twice daily in each direction between the **Vancouver Harbour Flight Centre** (1055 Canada Pl., behind the Vancouver Convention Centre, 604/274-1277) and **Green Lake** (8069 Nicklaus North Blvd.), 2 miles (3 km) north of Whistler Village. A free shuttle takes passengers between the Green Lake terminal and the village.

By Bus

Pacific Coach Lines (604/662-7575 or 800/661-1725, www.pacificcoach.com, 2 hours, one-way $20-27.50) runs buses several times daily between downtown

Highlights

★ **Sea-to-Sky Gondola:** A 10-minute ride up this Squamish peak gives you expansive views of Howe Sound and the surrounding mountains, as well as access to a suspension bridge, lots of hiking trails, and a great patio at the top (page 149).

★ **Brackendale Eagles Provincial Park:** One of North America's largest populations of bald eagles spends the winter months in this park near Squamish (page 152).

★ **Stawamus Chief Provincial Park:** A day hike up the rocky summit known as the Chief is a popular adventure (page 153).

★ **Whistler-Blackcomb:** From skiing and snowboarding to hiking, canoeing, rock climbing, and zip-lining, if it's an outdoor adventure, you can do it at this mountain resort (page 157).

★ **Squamish Lil'wat Cultural Centre:** Learn about the Whistler region's

First Nations communities at this modern museum and cultural facility (page 160).

★ **Audain Art Museum:** This beautifully designed museum highlights British Columbia artists from the earliest eras to the present day (page 161).

★ **Scandinave Spa:** After your adventures, ease your sore muscles in the hot and cold pools at this Scandinavian-style soaking spa (page 161).

Best Accommodations

★ **AAVA Whistler Hotel:** This modern, sociable hotel catering to active travelers is a good-value option, close to all the activities in Whistler Village (page 170).

★ **Four Seasons Whistler Hotel:** Solicitous staff and all sorts of amenities help make this grand lodging one of Whistler's top resort hotels (page 172).

★ **Fairmont Chateau Whistler:** Designed like an upscale mountain lodge, this classic Canadian hotel is convenient for hiking, skiing, or just cocooning in the comfortable rooms (page 173).

★ **Nita Lake Lodge:** Whistler's only lakeside accommodation, this contemporary hotel has large suites, rooftop hot tubs, a waterview dining room, and kayaks, canoes, and stand-up paddleboards for guests (page 173).

Vancouver and Whistler Village. The downtown stop is outside the Burrard SkyTrain Station (Melville and Burrard Sts.), adjacent to the Hyatt Vancouver. You can also take its **YVR Whistler SkyLynx bus** (2.5 hours, one-way adults $59-66.50, ages 5-11 $29.50-33.25) directly between Vancouver International Airport and Whistler.

Epic Rides (604/349-1234, www.epicrides.ca, 2 hours, one-way $24) operates several buses a day between Vancouver and Whistler. Late April-mid-November, buses stop downtown outside Burrard Station (Melville and Burrard Sts.). In winter (mid-Nov.-late Apr.), it adds early morning pickups on the UBC campus, at Granville and Broadway, and at Burrard and Comox Streets (at the Sheraton Wall Centre Hotel). Round-trip tickets are a good value at $35 per person.

Squamish

Midway between Vancouver and Whistler along the Sea-to-Sky Highway (Hwy. 99), the town of Squamish perches between the Coast Mountains and Howe Sound. Cafés, local eateries, and a few shops populate the town's sleepy downtown, while along Highway 99, strip malls and fast-food joints give Squamish

a mountain-suburban feel. The real action in Squamish, though, is outdoors.

It's a popular destination for all manner of adventures, including hiking, rock climbing, sailing, and white-water rafting. You can see the area's most famous peak, the Stawamus Chief, from the highway, or tackle the Chief on a day hike.

Squamish takes its name from the Squamish First Nation, whose traditional territory encompasses the modern-day town. In more recent times, mining was an important contributor to the local economy; a historic mine is now a visitor attraction. Another Squamish attraction, if you're passing through between December and February, are bald eagles; one of North America's largest populations of eagles spends the winter months near Squamish.

Squamish makes an easy day trip from Vancouver or a stopover between Vancouver and Whistler. It's 40 miles (65 km) from Vancouver to Squamish, a one-hour drive, and 37 miles (60 km) between Squamish and Whistler, which takes 45 minutes.

Sights and Activities
Britannia Mine Museum

For much of the 20th century, the Britannia Beach area south of Squamish was copper mining territory. During its heyday, the Britannia Mine produced

Best Restaurants

★ **Araxi:** Long considered one of Whistler's top dining spots, Araxi features regional ingredients, from fresh oysters to produce grown on area farms (page 167).

★ **Bearfoot Bistro:** Serving imaginative multicourse prix-fixe dinners, this stylish dining destination houses one of western Canada's largest wine cellars and features live jazz (page 167).

★ **Il Caminetto:** A classic Italian menu is enhanced with regional products in this elegant white-tablecloth Whistler dining room (page 168).

★ **Purebread:** Whistler's best bakery offers an irresistible array of sweet treats, homemade breads, and savory pastries (page 168).

more copper than any other mine in the British Empire. Workers from more than 50 countries settled here, living in barracks by the water or in a company town high in the surrounding hills.

While the Britannia Mine provided valuable resources and jobs for decades, it also created environmental havoc, particularly on the local water supply. After the mine closed in 1974, its environmental impacts took years to remediate.

The mine site is now the **Britannia Mine Museum** (1 Forbes Way, Britannia Beach, 604/896-2233 or 800/896-4044, www.britanniaminemuseum.ca, 9am-6pm daily, adults $29.95, seniors $26.95, ages 13-17 $23.95, ages 5-12 $18.95, families $110), where you can explore the mine's complicated history and get a glimpse of what it was like to work in the 130-mile (210-km) network of tunnels underground. Begin the 45-minute tour by donning a hard hat and riding a train into the mine. Guides demonstrate explosives, drilling tools, and how the "muck" (rocks sparkling with copper) was hauled out of the tunnels.

Aboveground, tours continue in the 1923 mill building that rises nearly 20 stories into the hill; inside, workers had to climb 375 steps to reach the building's highest level. The museum is also developing a multimedia exhibit inside the mill. Tours are offered throughout the day, but schedules vary seasonally; see the website or phone for tour times. The temperature in the mine (54°F/12°C) can feel chilly, so bring a sweater.

The Britannia Mine Museum is 32 miles (52 km) north of Vancouver and 7.5 miles (12 km) south of Squamish, along Highway 99.

Shannon Falls Provincial Park

Pull off the highway between Britannia Beach and Squamish for a short stroll to B.C.'s third-highest waterfall. At **Shannon Falls Provincial Park** (Hwy. 99, 604/986-9371, www.env.gov.bc.ca, dawn-dusk daily, free), the falls descend 1,100 feet (335 m) in a narrow, rushing gush. An easy 0.25-mile (400-m) walking trail leads through the forest to the falls.

Beyond the falls, up a short steep trail (there are stairs), you can hike to another viewpoint for a closer look at the cascading waters.

Shannon Falls is 36 miles (58 km) north of Vancouver and 1.25 miles (2 km) south of Squamish. The park has a snack bar and restrooms with flush toilets, open mid-May-mid-October.

★ Sea-to-Sky Gondola

For spectacular views of Howe Sound, the Chief, and the surrounding mountains, ride the **Sea-to-Sky Gondola** (36800 Hwy. 99, 604/892-2550, www.seatoskygondola.

Scenic Drive: The Sea-to-Sky Highway

Highway 99, the Sea-to-Sky Highway, is one of western Canada's most beautiful drives. And in a region full of beautiful drives, that's high praise.

At its southern end, the winding road that leads from West Vancouver to Whistler hugs the shores of Howe Sound, where the Gulf Islands rise from the water. You can stop at **Horseshoe Bay** (http://horseshoebayvillage.com), where the ferries depart for Vancouver Island and B.C.'s Sunshine Coast, to stroll the harbor and admire the vistas.

Another stopping point is **Porteau Cove Provincial Park** (www.env.gov.bc.ca), which has a small pebbly beach along a scenic stretch of coastline.

In **Squamish** (www.exploresquamish.com), you have views both of the water-

totem pole on the Sea-to-Sky Highway

front and the mountains, particularly the iconic Stawamus Chief that looms above the highway. As you continue toward **Whistler** (www.whistler.com), the road begins to climb, and both forests and peaks surround you.

Keep your camera handy, but pull off at one of the many turnouts to take in the views. At several viewpoints, informational kiosks explore the region's First Nations heritage, a "Cultural Journey" designed in partnership with Whistler's **Squamish Lil'Wat Cultural Centre.**

With rock faces plunging down to the roadway and forested islands just offshore, you can easily become distracted by the scenery, so drive carefully. Watch your speed, too, as the speed limit changes frequently, as do the number of travel lanes.

October-March, drivers are required to have winter tires or carry (and know how to use) chains, since sections of Highway 99 can become snow-covered and slippery.

Yet, whatever the season, this drive is a striking one, so pack up the car and hit the road from sea to sky.

com, 10am-6pm Sun.-Wed., 10am-8pm Thurs.-Sat. mid-May-mid-Sept., 10am-5pm daily mid-Sept.-Oct., 10am-4pm daily Nov.-mid-May, adults $43.95, seniors $39.95, ages 13-18 $25.95, ages 6-12 $15.95, families $107.95). A 10-minute trip in the eight-passenger gondola whisks you up to the 2,790-foot (850-m) summit, where you can enjoy the vistas, have lunch on the deck at the Summit Lodge, and access a network of hiking trails.

TIP: Purchase your gondola tickets online at least 24 hours before your visit to save a few dollars.

Once you've taken the gondola to the summit, a highlight is the **Sky Pilot Suspension Bridge,** a 330-foot (100-m) span that crosses from the Summit Lodge to a viewing platform with expansive views. If you're afraid of heights, don't worry; you don't have to cross the bridge to reach most of the hiking trails.

Another adventure that begins from the gondola summit is the **Via Ferrata** (604/892-2550, www.seatoskygondola.com, daily May-Oct., call for tour times, over age 7 $109). This "iron way" gives you the experience of rock climbing without needing any special climbing experience. With a guide, you take a short hike down from the Summit Lodge. From there, you clip into a safety cable, cross bridges and a catwalk, and climb a series of steel rungs up the rock face. You'll have beautiful views on this 1.5-hour tour, but skip this activity if you're acrophobic. You have to purchase a gondola ticket in addition to the Via Ferrata tour fee. Kids under 8 are not allowed on the Via Ferrata.

Hiking

A number of hiking trails start at the gondola summit. Two are easy walking paths: the 0.25-mile (400-m) **Spirit Trail,** a flat loop trail with interpretive panels about the region's First Nations, and the **Panorama Trail,** a 1-mile (1.6-km) loop that takes you to a lookout with excellent views of the Stawamus Chief.

Also starting from the summit is the moderate **Wonderland Trail.** This forested 1-mile (1.6-km) loop has a couple of slightly steeper segments, before flattening out as it circles small Wonderland Lake.

Experienced hikers can pick from several challenging trails that begin at the gondola summit, including the intermediate **Shannon Basin Loop Trail** (6 mi/9.7 km), and the more difficult **Al's Habrich Ridge Trail** (7.5 mi/12 km) and **Skyline Ridge Trail** (15 mi/24 km). Check with gondola staff for trail conditions before attempting these longer hikes, and be sure you have water, snacks, warm clothing, and a rain-resistant jacket, even if it's sunny and warm when you set out; mountain weather can change quickly.

Want a workout? You can hike *up* to the gondola summit on the **Sea-to-Summit Trail** and then ride the gondola (one-way $15) down. Average hikers should allow 3-5 hours for this steady 4.5-mile (7.2-km) climb.

Top to bottom: On the Squamish Via Ferrata; Sea-to-Sky Gondola; the Panorama Trail.

Winter Activities

The Sea-to-Sky Gondola is open year-round. December-April, weather permitting, trails are open for winter walking and snowshoeing, and kids can slide down a hill on inner tubes in the tube park. Before planning a winter visit, phone for trail conditions and current hours.

Food

The small **Basecamp Café** (9am-3pm daily) at the gondola base sells coffee, drinks, trail mix, pastries, and a few sandwiches, but it's worth waiting till you get to the **Summit Eatery and Edge Bar** (10am-5:30pm daily, $9-14), in the lodge at the top of the gondola, for a meal with a view. The kitchen cooks up burgers, sandwiches, salads, and baked goods, and serves beer from Squamish's Howe Sound Brewing Company. In summer, **Bodhi's Plaza BBQ** sells barbecue, ice cream, and drinks from an outdoor window. If you prefer to picnic, you can bring your own food.

Parking

Although you can park for free in the lot at the gondola base, stays in this lot are limited to three hours. If you're planning to do a longer hike or linger at the top (or if this parking area is full), park in the free lot at Darrell Bay, on Highway 99 opposite Shannon Falls Provincial Park, 0.3 mile (500 m) south of the gondola.

To walk from the Darrell Bay parking area to the gondola base, carefully cross Highway 99 toward Shannon Falls and follow the Shannon Falls Connector Trail, which has signs directing you to the Sea-to-Sky Gondola.

Flightseeing

For up-close views of Squamish's mountains and big-picture vistas over Howe Sound, take a flightseeing tour with **Sea-to-Sky Air** (Squamish Airport, 46041 Government Rd., 604/898-1975, www.seatoskyair.ca). Among the options are the Sea to Skypilot tour (adults $87), a 25-minute airborne introduction to the region, and the 35-minute Squamish Explorer (adults $155). Tours depart from the tiny Squamish airport on the town's north side.

★ Brackendale Eagles Provincial Park

Hundreds of bald eagles come to winter north of Squamish late November-mid-February in the now-protected 1,865-acre (755-ha) environs of **Brackendale Eagles Provincial Park** (www.env.gov.bc.ca). It's one of the most significant winter eagle populations in North America. In 1994, volunteers counted a record-setting 3,769 eagles in the vicinity.

You can't actually enter the park during eagle season; it's closed to visitors October-March to provide a protected habitat for the birds. However, you can watch the eagles from across the river. **Eagle Run Park** (Government Rd., dawn-dusk daily), along the municipal dyke, has several viewing points where you can spot the birds. Bring binoculars if you have them. On weekends late November-January, volunteer interpreters staff the Eagle Run viewing area (10am-3pm Sat.-Sun.) and can tell you more about the eagles and their migration patterns.

Coming from Vancouver or points south, follow Highway 99 past downtown Squamish, turn left (west) onto Mamquam Road, and then go right (north) on Government Road toward Brackendale.

Breweries and Distilleries

Squamish has embraced the craft beverage movement, with microbreweries, cidermakers, and distilleries setting up shop around town.

Howe Sound Inn & Brewing Company (37801 Cleveland Ave., 604/892-2603, www.howesound.com) is a brewery, restaurant, and place to stay. The **brewpub** (11am-midnight Sun.-Thurs., 11am-1am

Fri.-Sat., $11-26) serves pizzas, salads, burgers, and other pub fare to pair with the craft beer. Rates at the 20-room **inn** (www.howesoundinn.com, $129-165) include Wi-Fi and a brewery tour.

Pizza and beer? What's not to like, especially with quirkily named brews like "Bullet Holes the Size of Matzo Balls" (an IPA) or "Face Down Saaz Up" (a Czech-style pilsner)? Pair them with your pies in the pub-style tasting room at **Backcountry Brewing** (1201 Commercial Way, #405, 604/567-2739, www.backcountrybrewing.com, noon-10pm Mon.-Wed., noon-11pm Thurs., noon-midnight Fri., 11am-midnight Sat., 11am-10pm Sun.).

Northyards Cider Co. (38936 Queensway, #9, 604/815-2197, http://northyardscider.com, noon-10pm Sun.-Thurs., noon-11pm Fri.-Sat.) makes several varieties of cider from B.C. apples, which is served on tap and in cocktails, alongside charcuterie, cheeses, and other snacks, in a two-level tasting lounge.

In a space that recalls a basement rec room, **Gillespie's Distillery** (38918 Progress Way, Unit 8, 604/390-1122, www.gillespiesfinespirits.com, tasting room 1pm-6pm Wed.-Sun., cocktail lounge 6pm-11pm Wed.-Sat.) offers tastings of its products, which include vodka, gin, a raspberry gin, and limoncello. On weekends, the tasting room morphs into a casual cocktail lounge.

Sports and Recreation
Hiking
★ **Stawamus Chief Provincial Park**
Looming above Highway 99 just north of the Sea-to-Sky Gondola, the rocky cliff known as the Chief has long been a must-do climb for experienced hikers and rock-climbers. A challenging, but popular, day hike takes you from the Chief's base to the top of the cliffs in the **Stawamus Chief Provincial Park** (Hwy. 99, 604/986-9371, www.env.gov.bc.ca or http://seatoskyparks.com, dawn-dusk daily).

The Chief actually has three summits, and you can choose to hike one or all. **First Peak,** at 2,000 feet (610 m), draws the most hikers; from the summit, you have great views of Howe Sound. From the parking lot to the First Peak summit is just 2.5 miles (4 km) round-trip. However, because the trail is quite steep, most hikers allow 2-3 hours.

Second Peak, at 2,150 feet (655 m), has lots of viewpoints from its summit, looking across Howe Sound, the town of Squamish, and the mountains in nearby Garibaldi Provincial Park. From the parking lots, it's 3 miles (5 km) round-trip to the Second Peak. Allow 4-5 hours.

Third Peak is the tallest of the three summits, rising 2,300 feet (702 m). You can hike to Third Peak directly from the base or continue from the Second Peak trail. Either route is 4.5 miles (7 km) round-trip; allow 5-7 hours.

The hikes up The Chief are considered intermediate-level adventures. Note, though, that on the routes to First and Second Peaks, there are sections where you need to climb ladders or grab onto chains to help you reach the top. For all these hikes, bring water, snacks, a rain jacket, and warm layers. Get an early start, and especially in the summer, hike on a weekday to avoid congestion on these often-busy trails.

Garibaldi Provincial Park
The region's largest provincial park, the 750-square-mile (1,942-sq-km) **Garibaldi Provincial Park** (www.env.gov.bc.ca), extends from Squamish north to Whistler and beyond. Hikers have a lot of territory to explore in this vast park, with more than 55 miles (89 km) of hiking trails.

The park's southernmost section, **Diamond Head,** is closest to Squamish and includes the park's namesake, the 8,786-foot (2,678-m) Mount Garibaldi. For experienced day-hikers, a scenic trail in the Diamond Head area leads up to **Elfin Lakes** (7 mi/11 km each way); allow 3-5 hours one-way. To find the trailhead, turn east off Highway 99 onto Mamquam Road, 2.5 miles (4 km) north of Squamish. Follow the paved road past the Squamish Golf and Country Club, and take the gravel road just after the Mashiter Creek Bridge. In 3.7 miles (6 km), turn left onto the Garibaldi Park road, which will take you to the parking lot. It's 10 miles (16 km) from the highway to the parking area.

Farther north, you can do several day hikes in the park's **Black Tusk/Garibaldi Lake** sector. It's a 6-mile (9.7-km) climb to **Garibaldi Lake.** Allow 3-4 hours each way; the trail has an elevation change of nearly 2,800 feet (850 m). From the same starting point, you can hike to **Taylor Meadows.** This 4.75-mile (7.6-km) route follows the Garibaldi Lake trail for the first 3.75 miles (6 km) before heading up into the alpine meadows. Allow 3-4 hours each way; the trail also has an elevation change of about 2,800 feet (850 m). The Garibaldi Lake parking lot is 23 miles (37 km) north of Squamish or 12 miles (19 km) south of Whistler, along Highway 99.

At the park's higher elevations, snow is usually on the ground October-June or July. Check the trail conditions report on the park website before you set out.

Rafting

You can go white-water rafting on two Squamish-area rivers. Trips on the **Cheakamus River** are gentler, with Class I and II rapids, good for family excursions. The faster **Elaho-Squamish River,** with Class III and IV rapids, will give you more of a thrill. For the Elaho trips, kids generally need to be at least 12 years old and weigh at least 90 pounds (40 kg).

SunWolf Rafting (38145 2nd Ave., 604/898-4667 or 888/498-4667, www.sunwolf.net) offers full-day Elaho River trips (June-Sept., adults $169, ages 12-16 $155) that include a barbecue lunch. It also runs half-day Cheakamus River Family trips (June-Sept., adults $119, ages 5-12 $79). In winter, when hundreds of eagles nest at Brackendale

Eagles Provincial Park, SunWolf operates guided **Eagle Float Tours** (mid-Nov.-Feb., adults $119, ages 5-12 $79) that enable you to view the eagles from the river, closer than you can see them from the shore.

Canadian Outback Rafting (40900 Tantalus Rd., 866/565-8735, www.canadianoutbackrafting.com) runs Elaho River trips (May-Sept., adults $160, ages 13-16 $140) and Cheakamus River float trips (May-Sept., adults $110, ages 5-16 $75), as well as winter eagle float tours (mid-Nov.-Feb., adults $115, ages 5-16 $79). Whistler-based **Wedge Rafting** (211-4293 Mountain Square, Whistler, 604/932-7171 or 888/932-5899, http://wedgerafting.com) operates Elaho (May-Sept., adults $169, ages 12-16 $149) and Cheakamus (May-Sept., adults $119, ages 6-16 $79) trips as well.

Sailing

Squamish is located on Howe Sound, North America's southernmost fjord, which you can explore aboard a 40-foot

(64-m) sailing yacht with **Canadian Coastal** (www.canadiancoastal.com). Choose a three-hour afternoon sail ($129 pp) or a four-hour sunset dinner cruise (contact operator for details on options and prices), departing from Squamish Harbour (37778 Loggers Ln.) near downtown.

Rope Runner Aerial Park

While Squamish has plenty of natural adventures, you can challenge your balance and strength on this human-made one. Constructed in a parking lot near the Squamish Adventure Centre, **Rope Runner Aerial Park** (38400 Loggers Ln., 604/892-4623, www.roperunnerpark. com, 10am-3pm Wed.-Sun. mid-Apr.-June, 10am-4pm daily July-Aug., 11am-3pm Sept., 2-hour climbing session adults $45, ages 10-18 $40, ages 7-9 $35) tests you with 50 different elements, from vertical climbs to slack lines. As you venture higher on this ropes course, you'll look over the granite monolith of the Squamish Chief, before you swing back to earth with an (optional) free fall.

Festivals and Events

Wondering how lumberjacks get their jollies? At the **Squamish Days Loggers Sports Festival** (www.squamishdays.ca, July-Aug.), a weekend of family fun, you can watch competitions in ax-throwing, tree-climbing, birling (also known as log rolling), and other events, and enjoy pancake breakfasts, bed races, barbecues, and more.

Food and Accommodations

A modern lounge-style dining room in Squamish's oldest building (built in 1910), **Salted Vine Kitchen + Bar** (37991 2nd Ave., 604/390-1910, www. saltedvine.ca, 3pm-9pm Wed.-Sat., 10am-1:30pm and 3pm-9pm Sun., $17-29) serves creative cocktails (including interesting "designated driver" options) and plates to share. During afternoon happy hour, you might snack on a

sailing in Howe Sound

charcuterie platter or gochujang-sauced chicken wings. Later, look for dishes like beet and burrata salad, bucatini with grilled Humbolt squid, or soy-braised short ribs.

You'll have to hunt for tiny **Kululu Café** (38209 Westway Ave., 604/390-3933, 11:30am-3:30pm and 5pm-8pm Tues.-Sat., $5-13), a Japanese noodle shop and coffeehouse in a Squamish strip mall. It's worth the search for the carefully prepared bowls of tuna poke, spicy *tantan* noodles, organic chicken in a sesame-miso sauce, and other Japanese-style salads, rice, and noodle dishes. Organic coffees and teas, plus a selection of sweets, are also available.

Stop in early before the goodies sell out at **Tall Tree Bakery** (1201 Commercial Way, #404, 604/849-0951, www.talltreebakery.com, 8am-5pm Tues.-Fri., 9am-4pm Sat.-Sun.), a deliciously aromatic to-go bakeshop, whether you're looking for freshly baked scones, a seasonal fruit Danish, or a sandwich for the trail. The cookies, particularly the cranberry-pecan and double chocolate chip, are excellent, as is the coffee from local roaster Counterpart Coffee.

Located in the Squamish Town Hub, a collective of independent boutiques and eateries, **Alice & Brohm Ice Cream** (1861 Mamquam Rd., 250/571-9978, www.aliceandbrohm.com, 2pm-8pm Wed.-Mon.) makes creamy soft-serve ice cream from fresh blueberries, blackberries, and other fruit. It offers vegan alternatives, too.

If you want to stay overnight in Squamish, one of the nicest spots is the **Executive Suites Hotel and Resort** (40900 Tantalus Rd., Garibaldi Highlands, 604/815-0048 or 877/815-0048, www.executivesuitessquamish.com, $125-229), where many of the modern studio, one-, and two-bedroom suites with kitchen facilities overlook the mountains. Another mid-range option off Highway 99 is the **Sandman Hotel & Suites Squamish** (39400 Discovery Way, 604/848-6000 or 800/726-3626, www.sandmanhotels.ca, $149-199).

Information and Services

At the Squamish Adventure Centre, just off Highway 99, **Tourism Squamish** (38551 Loggers Ln., 604/815-4994 or 877/815-5084, www.tourismsquamish.com, 8am-5pm daily mid-May-mid-Sept., 8:30am-4:30pm daily mid-Sept.-mid-May) provides lots of information about the region, including details about hiking trails. The building has a café and restrooms, handy for a Sea-to-Sky pit stop.

Whistler

Nearly three million visitors every year make their way to this mountain town that has a permanent population of only 12,000. Restaurants, pubs, and shops line the walkways of the village's alpine-style pedestrian plaza, where all paths lead, sooner or later, to the ski lifts. Most people come to get outdoors—to ski or snowboard in winter, and to hike, cycle, canoe, kayak, rock-climb, or zip-line in the warmer months. Others simply want to stroll through the pedestrian village and perhaps ride the gondola to gaze across the mountains.

Just a two-hour drive from Vancouver, Whistler is close enough for a day trip. If you enjoy outdoor adventures, though, you might want to spend two days or more. There's plenty to do!

Whistler has several neighborhoods stretching along Highway 99, with the main **Whistler Village** about midway through the area. **Creekside,** where there's a separate base village with its own lifts, and **Function Junction,** a more industrial area with some of the town's services, are south of Whistler Village. The **Upper Village** and the **Blackcomb** base areas are just north of Whistler Village.

One Day in Whistler

If you've come to North America's largest winter sports resort during ⸺, you'll likely spend your day out on the snow. But if you're at Whistler before ⸺ falls, here's how to organize a great one-day trip.

Whistler is located on the traditional territory of two First Nations, so start your day with a visit to the modern **Squamish Lil'wat Cultural Centre,** where you can learn about the history and present-day culture of these two communities. There's also the excellent **Audain Art Museum,** which has noteworthy collections of Northwest Coast native masks, along with works by contemporary Vancouver photographers and paintings by B.C.'s Emily Carr. Or if you want to know more about how Whistler became the outdoor resort it is today, wander over to the informative **Whistler Museum,** which tells the stories of many area entrepreneurs.

Then get outdoors, whether you head up the mountain to ride the **PEAK 2 PEAK Gondola** that wings you between Whistler and Blackcomb Mountains, challenge yourself with a climb on the **Via Ferrata,** go **zip-lining** or **mountain biking,** or simply **take a hike.** The biggest challenge might be seeing how many activities you can fit into a single day.

When you've had your fill of outdoor adventure, relax at the forested **Scandinave Spa Whistler,** a Scandinavian-style bath experience where you alternate between hot soaks and cold plunges.

Then choose one of Whistler's top dining rooms, perhaps **Araxi** or the **Bearfoot Bistro,** for a leisurely evening meal. At Bearfoot Bistro, you can even have a nightcap in its **Ketel One Ice Room,** the coldest vodka tasting room in the world—a unique way to cap off your active Whistler day.

Sights and Activities
★ Whistler-Blackcomb

From more than 200 trails for skiing and snowboarding, to mountain biking, gondola rides, hiking, zip-lining, and much more, the two-mountain **Whistler-Blackcomb Resort** (604/967-8950 or 800/766-0449, www.whistlerblackcomb. com) has scads of outdoor things to do all year long.

PEAK 2 PEAK Gondola

Whistler's **PEAK 2 PEAK Gondola** (10:15am-5pm daily, adults $63, seniors $57, ages 13-18 $53, ages 7-12 $32) runs 2.73 miles (4.4 km) between Whistler and Blackcomb Mountains. It holds the world's record for the longest unsupported span (that is, the straight-line distance between two towers) at 1.88 miles (3,024 m) and for the highest lift of its kind, rising 1,427 feet (436 m) above the valley floor. It transports skiers and snowboarders between the two mountains in winter, and spring-fall, it's open to sightseers to enjoy the peaks' panoramas.

Allow about two hours for a sightseeing trip on the PEAK 2 PEAK Gondola. The PEAK 2 PEAK ride itself takes about 20 minutes, but to reach the gondola station, you need to take either the Whistler Village Gondola or Blackcomb mountain's gondola, which add another 25 minutes each way. If you plan to go hiking, budget additional time.

Gondola tickets are typically cheaper if you buy them online in advance, but check the weather forecast first. The views are obviously best on a sunny, clear day.

Cloudraker Skybridge

Installed in 2018, **Cloudraker Skybridge** (www.whistlerblackcomb.com, 10am-4pm Mon.-Thurs., 10am-5:30pm Fri.-Sun. July-early Sept., 11am-4pm daily early Sept.-mid-Sept) is a 425-foot (130-m) suspension bridge high above the Whistler Bowl, swinging from Whistler

Whistler Village

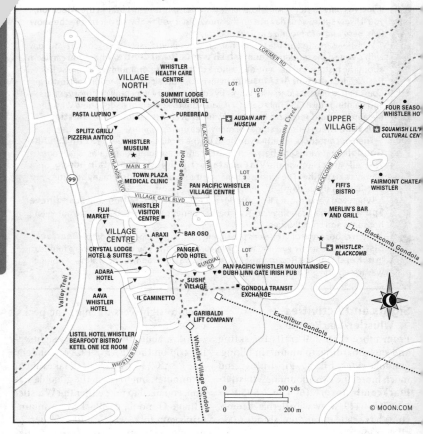

Labels on map:

LORIMER RD

VILLAGE NORTH

WHISTLER HEALTH CARE CENTRE

LOT 4

LOT 5

THE GREEN MOUSTACHE ▼

SUMMIT LODGE BOUTIQUE HOTEL

PASTA LUPINO ▼

PUREBREAD ▼

AUDAIN ART MUSEUM

Fitzsimmons Creek

UPPER VILLAGE

FOUR SEASO WHISTLER HO

SPLITZ GRILL/ PIZZERIA ANTICO

SQUAMISH LIL'W CULTURAL CEN

WHISTLER MUSEUM

Blackcomb Creek

NORTHLANDS BLVD

MAIN ST

Village Stroll

BLACKCOMB WAY

99

TOWN PLAZA MEDICAL CLINIC

VILLAGE GATE BLVD

PAN PACIFIC WHISTLER VILLAGE CENTRE

LOT 3

LOT 2

FIFI'S BISTRO ▼

FAIRMONT CHATEA WHISTLER

BLACKCOMB WAY

WHISTLER VISITOR CENTRE

MERLIN'S BAR AND GRILL ▼

FUJI MARKET ▼

VILLAGE CENTRE

ARAXI ▼

BAR OSO ▼

LOT 1

Blackcomb Gondola

WHISTLER-BLACKCOMB

Valley Trail

CRYSTAL LODGE HOTEL & SUITES

PANGEA POD HOTEL

SUNDIAL CR.

PAN PACIFIC WHISTLER MOUNTAINSIDE/ DUBH LINN GATE IRISH PUB ▼

ADARA HOTEL

SUSHI VILLAGE ▼

GONDOLA TRANSIT EXCHANGE

AAVA WHISTLER HOTEL

IL CAMINETTO

GARIBALDI LIFT COMPANY ▼

Excalibur Gondola

LISTEL HOTEL WHISTLER/ BEARFOOT BISTRO/ KETEL ONE ICE ROOM

WHISTLER WAY

Whistler Village Gondola

0   200 yds

0   200 m

© MOON.COM

Peak to the West Ridge. A viewing platform gives you 360-degree views of the surrounding mountains.

Access to the skybridge is included in the PEAK 2 PEAK Gondola sightseeing tickets. To reach the bridge, ride the Peak Express chair from the Roundhouse Lodge on Whistler Mountain.

Via Ferrata

Do you want to try rock climbing but don't have any training or experience? Consider Whistler's **Via Ferrata** (604/938-9242, www.mountainskillsacademy.com, 4 hours, adults $159, ages 12-18 $139), a guided climbing route that's open to anyone who's reasonably fit. The name comes from the Italian for "iron way," and the Via Ferrata route includes a series of iron rungs built into the mountain, which provide hand grips and footholds as you ascend the rock face. You clip onto a series of safety cables during your climb, which you do in small groups with a guide. Your guide will give you tips as you ascend and talk you through the more challenging sections.

The Via Ferrata route starts with a short hike up from the Whistler Roundhouse (at the top of the Whistler gondola) across a boulder field or a snowy slope or both, depending on the season, to the start of the climbing route. After your climb, you hike or take the chairlift back to your starting point. Wear sturdy hiking shoes, and bring a rain jacket and a small backpack with water and snacks.

You need to purchase a PEAK 2 PEAK Gondola or summer sightseeing ticket in addition to the Via Ferrata tour ticket. Via Ferrata tours are seasonal, generally beginning in late June or early July and continuing until early October; tours typically start at 9am or 1pm, but call or check the website to confirm.

Whistler Sky Walk

Easier than the Via Ferrata, the **Whistler Sky Walk** (604/938-9242, www.mountainskillsacademy.com, 2 hours, adults $109) is a guided hike along a series of narrow paths and ledges high on the mountain, with several stops to take in the views. As on the Via Ferrata, you clip onto a network of safety cables as you walk the route and over a short suspension bridge. While it could still be difficult for anyone with a fear of heights, the Sky Walk is primarily horizontal, rather than vertical, making it more of a moderately challenging hike than a rock-face climb.

You begin the Sky Walk experience with a hike up from the Whistler Roundhouse (at the top of the Whistler gondola)—the path can be snow-covered early in the season—and after you navigate the Sky Walk, you hike back down to the Roundhouse. Wear hiking shoes, and bring a small daypack with water, snacks, and a rain jacket.

You need to purchase a PEAK 2 PEAK Gondola or summer sightseeing ticket in addition to the Sky Walk tour ticket. The Sky Walk tours run spring-fall; call or check the website for specific schedules.

Lift-Accessed Hiking

Whistler-Blackcomb has lots of hiking trails, from short easy strolls to all-day

adventures, that you can access from the lifts or gondolas.

From the top of the Whistler gondola or the Whistler side of the PEAK 2 PEAK Gondola near the Roundhouse Lodge, you can access the moderate **Harmony Lake Trail and Loop,** a 1.6-mile (2.5-km) round-trip circuit through the forest to pretty Harmony Lake. You can extend this hike on the steeper 0.7-mile (1.1-km) **Harmony Meadows Trail,** which connects to the Harmony Lake route.

For a more challenging hike with panoramic views, take the Peak Express chair (a short walk from the Roundhouse Lodge) to the start of the 5.8-mile (9.4-km) **High Note Trail.** This trail follows the mountain ridges, with great views of the Black Tusk peak in Garibaldi Provincial Park and Cheakamus Lake far below. You can circle back on the trail and ride the lift down, or for an all-day adventure, hike back down to the village; the latter route is about 14 miles (22 km).

Pick up a trail map showing these and other hiking routes at the **Whistler Visitor Centre** (4230 Gateway Dr.), or get one online at the website of **Whistler-Blackcomb** (www.whistlerblackcomb.com).

Lift-Accessed Mountain Biking

Have you seen those cyclists, suited up in knee pads, elbow pads, helmets, and other protective gear, flying down the mountain trails? At Whistler-Blackcomb, you can join them, whether you're learning to mountain bike or whizzing down those trails yourself at North America's largest mountain bike park.

Mid-May-mid-October, more than 70 trails across four different areas are open to mountain bikers, who take their bikes up the lifts.

You can choose among several different ticket options, from a three-ride sampler to multiday passes to packages including lift tickets and lessons; check the Whistler-Blackcomb website to see the alternatives. Rent bikes through

Whistler on a Budget

Whistler is one of those destinations where there are more things to do than you could pack into a summer-long stay, but many of those activities can be budget-blowing adventures. If you're watching your loonies but still want to enjoy the best of what Whistler has to offer, follow these tips for organizing your Whistler stay.

♦ **Come off-season.** If you can schedule your Whistler visit for the spring (May-early June) or fall (Sept.-Oct.), you'll often find lower rates for accommodations and occasional deals for tours and activities.

♦ **Look for free or low-cost activities.** You can hike or cycle many trails around Whistler without purchasing a lift ticket to go up on the mountain. Go for a swim in area lakes or visit the Whistler Museum (by donation). Window-shopping in the village and walking the Valley Trail are both free, too.

♦ **Maximize your spending.** If you do buy a lift ticket for sightseeing or hiking, get an early start and spend as much time as you'd like up on the mountain. You can stay on the mountain all day on your single ticket.

♦ **Pack a lunch.** Look for accommodations with kitchen facilities, so you can prepare some of your own meals, even if it's just fruit and yogurt for breakfast or a sandwich for the trail. Another option is to have your big meal out at lunch when restaurant prices are a little lower than in the evenings.

♦ **Go easy on the booze.** Many of Whistler's bars and après-ski hangouts have free live music for the price of a drink.

Whistler-Blackcomb or at independent shops around the village.

Winter Sports

In winter, Whistler-Blackcomb has 37 lifts providing access to more than 200 trails across 8,171 acres (3,300 ha), so you can ski or snowboard here for days and still discover new terrain.

Whistler Village is at an elevation of 2,214 feet (675 m), while the highest lift takes you up to nearly 7,500 feet (2,284 m), so the weather can be very different at the base than it is in the alpine regions. Even when there's no snow in the village, the mountains are typically covered in the white stuff from late November into April.

Lift tickets (one-day adults $125-150) are most expensive when you walk up to the ticket window and purchase a single-day, same-day ticket. Discounts are available when you buy tickets online in advance, purchase multiday tickets or passes, or sometimes when you buy your tickets as part of a package with your lodging. Explore the pricing options at **Whistler-Blackcomb** (604/967-8950 or 800/766-0449, www.whistlerblackcomb. com).

★ Squamish Lil'wat Cultural Centre

For centuries before Whistler was an outdoor holiday destination, aboriginal communities called the region home. Discover this heritage at the **Squamish Lil'wat Cultural Centre** (4584 Blackcomb Way, 604/964-0999 or 866/441-7522, www.slcc.ca, 9:30am-5pm daily, adults $18, students $13.50, ages 6-18 $8, families $42), a fascinating multimedia exploration of the two First Nations whose traditional territory encompasses the Whistler region.

After rhythmic beats of a drum and a

traditional First Nations welcome song greet you, watch a short film about the history and present-day culture of these two communities. Then check out the exhibits, from hand-carved canoes to woven baskets to information about aboriginal languages. You can often try out a native craft or chat with "cultural ambassadors," museum staff from the Squamish or Lil'wat communities. The center's **Thunderbird Café** uses local ingredients in dishes like sockeye salmon chowder, venison chili, and bannock (a biscuit-like bread), and the gift shop sells locally made crafts.

★ Audain Art Museum

Whistler scored an art-world coup when Vancouver businessman and philanthropist Michael Audain decided to build a 56,000-square-foot (5,200-sq-m) gallery in this mountain town to house much of his extensive art collection. Focusing on British Columbia artists from the region's earliest eras to the present, the **Audain Art Museum** (4350 Blackcomb Way, www. audainartmuseum.com, 10am-5pm Sat.-Mon. and Wed., 10am-7pm Thurs.-Fri., adults and seniors $18, ages 18 and under free) has more than two dozen works by early 20th-century artist Emily Carr. Other highlights include 19th-century Northwest Coast masks, works by Canada's most important post-war modernists and contemporary artists, and Vancouver photography.

Whistler Museum

Like many ski "villages" with their alpine facades and purpose-built pedestrian strolls, Whistler can seem like a manufactured community. The **Whistler Museum** (4333 Main St., 604/932-2019, www.whistlermuseum.org, 11am-5pm Fri.-Wed., 11am-9pm Thurs., suggested donation $5) tells the history of how the present-day Whistler-Blackcomb resort came to be and the stories of the entrepreneurs and innovators who made it happen.

Another way to learn more about the town and its heritage is to take the museum's one-hour **Valley of Dreams Walking Tour** (11am daily June-Aug., donation), starting at the Whistler Visitor Centre (4230 Gateway Dr.). You'll hear tales of the community's entrepreneurial women, the year of the naked skiers, and much more.

Whistler Olympic Plaza

Whistler joined Vancouver in hosting the 2010 Winter Olympic Games. One legacy of the Games is now a popular photo stop: in front of the colorful Olympic rings that adorn **Whistler Olympic Plaza** in the village. Also in the plaza is an outdoor amphitheater, where concerts, festivals, and other special events take place.

Vallea Lumina

A dreamlike multimedia walk, **Vallea Lumina** (855/824-9955, www. vallealumina.com, daily late-May-mid-Oct., adults $29, ages 6-15 $24) incorporates lights, music, and special effects to bring an old-growth forest to life, enabling trees to talk, salmon to glow as they "swim" upstream, and a bear to "appear" in the smoke of a campfire.

Combining a light show and a self-guided forest walk, Vallea Lumina operates nightly at sundown spring-fall; check the website or phone for seasonal tour times. Tickets include a free shuttle from Whistler Village to the Vallea Lumina location north of town. The walk itself, along a 1-mile (1.6-km) wooded trail, takes about an hour. Although the trail can be dark in places, and there are a lot of stairs, the experience is family-friendly.

★ Scandinave Spa

To unwind after a day on the mountains, head for **Scandinave Spa Whistler** (8010 Mons Rd., 604/935-2424 or 888/935-2423, www.scandinave.com, 10am-9pm daily, adults $70-79, minimum age 19), a Scandinavian-style bath experience set among the trees. You alternate between

heat—in a series of hot pools, saunas, and steam baths—and brief cold plunges in a chilled pool or shower, following each sequence with a period of relaxation in the lounges or in a hammock in the forest. To make the experience more tranquil, the spa has a "silence" policy; you can't talk in the bath area.

Bring your own bathing suit. The spa provides towels and lockers. Several types of massage treatments are available for an additional fee.

Scandinave Spa is located 2 miles (3 km) north of Whistler Village, along Highway 99.

Train Wreck Site and Suspension Bridge

After a freight train derailed near Whistler in 1956, a logging company towed the mangled railcars into the woods nearby, where they were abandoned. Over the years, local graffiti artists began using the train cars as their canvas, and today, Whistler's **train wreck site** (off Jane Lakes Rd., www.whistler.ca, dawn-dusk, free), located south of town near Cheakamus Crossing, is an unusual outdoor art gallery, with the train cars tagged and retagged with vivid designs.

From Jane Lakes Road, you can follow a section of the Sea-to-Sky Trail that leads to a **suspension bridge** over the Cheakamus River that connects to the train site. It's about a 30-minute walk through the woods.

Sports and Recreation
Hiking and Biking

Winding 25 miles (40 km) through the Whistler area, the paved **Valley Trail** (www.whistler.ca) is open to both walkers and cyclists. You can follow short stretches of the trail, for example, between the Blackcomb base area and Whistler Village, or head north to Green

Top to bottom: on the Whistler Sky Walk; Squamish Lil'wat Cultural Centre; Whistler Museum.

Lake or south to the Creekside area and beyond.

Close to Whistler Village (you can follow the Valley Trail), **Lost Lake Park** has several easy hiking and cycling trails. Walkers can circle the lake on the Lost Lake Loop trail, while mountain bikers can follow several single-track routes through the park.

Whistler has several areas of old-growth forest with massive trees. A moderate 5-mile (8-km) loop hike takes you through one of these forests along the **Ancient Cedars Trail,** where the trees are up to 1,000 years old. The trailhead is north of the village; take Highway 99 north past Green Lake and turn left onto 16-Mile Forest Service Road. It's 3 miles (5 km) from the highway to the parking area. Bring mosquito repellent, since this area can be buggy.

Get trail maps showing these and other trails from the **Whistler Visitor Centre** (4230 Gateway Dr.) or online from the Whistler municipality website (www. whistler.ca).

Zip-Lining

Fancy a ride on the longest zip line in Canada or the United States? **Ziptrek Ecotours** (604/935-0001 or 866/935-0001, www.ziptrek.com) offers several different zip-line options, including **The Sasquatch** (daily May-mid-Oct., 2.5 hours, adults $129, seniors and ages 10-14 $109), which runs more than 7,000 feet (2 km), starting on Blackcomb Mountain and zipping down to the Whistler side.

Ziptrek also offers **The Eagle** (daily year-round, 2.5-3 hours, adults $149, seniors and ages 6-14 $129), which takes you down five zip lines and across four treetop bridges. If zip-lining is your passion, you can combine the Sasquatch and Eagle tours (4.5 hours, adults $219, seniors and ages 10-14 $199). Newcomers to zip-lining, or younger kids, may prefer **The Bear** (year-round, 2.5-3 hours, adults $119, seniors and ages 6-14 $99), a slightly gentler combination of zip lines

and bridges. Hours vary seasonally, so call or check the website for details.

Superfly Ziplines (211-4293 Mountain Square, 604/932-0647, www. superflyziplines.com, 9am-5pm daily, 3 hours, adults $149, ages 7-12 $109) has a zip-line tour that includes a 0.6-mile (1-km) line that's more than 500 feet (150 m) high.

Treetop Adventures

If you're looking for an activity that's gentler than zip-lining but still gets you high in the trees, consider a two-hour **TreeTrek Canopy Walk** (604/935-0001 or 866/935-0001, www.ziptrek.com, daily year-round, call or check the website for tour times, adults $49, seniors and ages 6-14 $39), which follows a series of bridges suspended among the old-growth forest on Blackcomb Mountain. The highest of the eight viewing platforms rises nearly 200 feet (60 m) above the forest floor; the oldest trees in the area are about 800 years old. On this excursion offered by Ziptrek Ecotours, your guide will introduce you to the local ecology as you explore the woods.

Want more of a challenge? Superfly's **Treetop Adventure Course** (211-4293 Mountain Square, 604/932-0647, www. superflyziplines.com, 9am-5pm daily, $69) takes you through the treetops on a ropes course, where you navigate swaying bridges, rope swings, tightropes, and zip lines. Kids not tall enough to reach 71 inches (180 cm) can try the **Kids Treetop Adventure Course** ($39), designed for youngsters ages 7-14 who can reach to 55 inches (140 cm).

Bobsled and Skeleton

During the 2010 Winter Olympic Games, the **Whistler Sliding Centre** (4910 Glacier Ln., 604/964-0040, www. whistlersportlegacies.com) hosted the bobsled, skeleton, and luge competitions. You can live out your almost-Olympic dreams with rides down the same slippery track that the Olympic athletes used.

Whiz down the track in the **Summer Bobsleigh** (daily late June-early Sept., adults $109), a bobsled on wheels. A pilot steers your sled, which holds up to four passengers and can reach speeds of 50 mph (80 km/h). Kids must be at least 12 to ride, but one youth (ages 12-18) rides free with each paying adult. Participants must be between 4 foot 6 and 6 foot 5 (137-196 cm) and weigh between 85 and 285 pounds (39-129 kg). Advance reservations recommended.

In winter, the **Bobsleigh Experience** (daily mid-Dec.-Mar., advance reservations required, adults $189) sends you down the ice at even faster speeds: up to 75 mph (120 km/h). The sled holds a pilot and one or two guests. For this experience, you must be between ages 14 and 75; youth ages 14-16 ride at a 50 discount when accompanied by a paying adult. All participants must be between 4 foot 6 and 6 foot 8 (137-207 cm) and weigh between 90 and 285 pounds (41-129 kg) with your winter clothing on.

If you're really adventurous, ride head-first down the icy track on the **Skeleton** (daily mid-Dec.-Mar., advance reservations required, adults $169). You get two solo runs, and you may find yourself hurtling down the track at close to 60 mph (100 km/h). Minimum age for the skeleton is 16, and the maximum is 75. All participants must be between 4 foot 6 and 6 foot 5 (137-196 cm) and weigh between 90 and 220 pounds (41-100 kg) with your winter clothing on.

To reach the Whistler Sliding Centre from Whistler Village, follow Blackcomb Way to Glacier Lane.

Water Sports

One of Whistler's most peaceful outdoor experiences is a kayak or canoe tour along the **River of Golden Dreams.** **Whistler Eco Tours** (604/935-4900 or 877/988-4900, www.whistlerecotours. com) offers three-hour guided (adults $135, under age 13 $126) or self-guided (adults $90, under age 13 $63) paddles that start on Alta Lake, travel through a scenic wetlands area, and wrap up at beautiful Green Lake. On the guided tour, your guide will tell you about the area's ecology and give you paddling tips. Both the self-guided and guided options are family-friendly and include transportation back to the village.

Whistler Eco Tours also rents single kayaks ($32 per hour) and canoes, double kayaks, stand-up paddleboards, and pedal boats (all $37 per hour) from its base in Wayside Park on Alta Lake, between the village and Creekside.

You can **swim** in several Whistler-area lakes, although the water can be chilly. You'll find beaches at **Alpha Lake** near Creekside, **Alta Lake** between Creekside and the village, **Lost Lake** near the village, and **Green Lake**, a large glacier-fed lake north of the village.

Prefer to swim indoors? Then visit **Meadow Park Sports Centre** (8625 Hwy.

99, 604/935-7529, www.whistler.ca, adults $8.75, ages 13-18 $5.25, ages 4-12 $4.50), a public recreational facility with a 25-meter lap pool as well as a kids pool with a lazy river. Located 2 miles (3 km) north of the village, the center and pool are generally open 6am-10pm daily, but call or check the website for seasonal variations.

Winter Sports

As an alternative to skiing and snow-boarding on Whistler-Blackcomb, go to the **Whistler Olympic Park** (5 Callaghan Valley Rd., 604/964-0060, www.whistlersportlegacies.com, late Nov.-early Apr., weather permitting) for **cross-country skiing** (adults $27.50, ages 7-18 $15.75), **snowshoeing** (adults $16.50, ages 7-18 $8.75), and **tobogganing** ($10 for first person in a vehicle, $5 each additional person). Gear rentals are available. The park is 15 miles (24 km) from the village; follow Highway 99 south to Callaghan Valley Road.

Entertainment and Events
Nightlife

One of Whistler's most popular pastimes is après (aka après-ski, literally "after ski-ing"), and what do you do after a day in the mountains but hit the pub? Here are several places where the party starts when the lifts close.

Merlin's Bar and Grill (4553 Blackcomb Way, 604/938-7700, 11am-1am daily), at the Blackcomb Mountain base, often has live music, as does the **Garibaldi Lift Company** (4165 Springs Ln., 604/905-2220, 11am-1am daily), at the base of the Whistler gondola. In the Creekside area, **Dusty's Bar & BBQ** (2040 London Ln., 604/905-2171, 11am-1am daily) has been pouring pints since the 1960s.

The laid-back **Dubh Linn Gate Irish Pub** (Pan Pacific Whistler Mountainside, 4320 Sundial Cres., 604/905-4047, www.dubhlinngate.com, 7am-1am daily), steps from the Whistler Village lifts, keeps 25 varieties of beer on tap and offers a long list of single-malt scotch.

skier on Blackcomb Mountain

Bearfoot Bistro (4121 Village Green, 604/932-3433, http://bearfootbistro.com, 6pm-10pm daily) is among Whistler's best restaurants, but it's also a destination for drinkers: Its **Ketel One Ice Room** is the coldest vodka tasting room in the world. Don a heavy parka (which the restaurant provides) and venture into the frosty tasting room, with its carved ice walls and year-round temperature of -25°F (-32°C). Choose a tasting flight ($48) from its selection of 50 different vodkas, made in destinations as diverse as Poland, the Ukraine, or Pemberton, B.C.

What about a private wine-tasting at your hotel or condo? **Taste Whistler** (604/902-9463 or 844/470-9463, www.tastewhistler.com, from $139 pp) creates customized wine-tastings for groups of friends, families, or corporate events, from a Wine 101 sampler to a B.C. wine or champagne tasting, and it comes to you.

The Arts

Arts Whistler (604/935-8410, www.artswhistler.com) hosts concerts, films, and other productions at Maury Young Arts Centre (4335 Blackcomb Way), where it also runs a small art gallery (www.thegallerywhistler.com).

See what's happening at **The Point Artist-Run Centre** (5678 Alta Lake Rd., 604/698-5482, www.thepointartists.com), which presents live music during July and August in the "Sundays at the Point" events, as well as occasional music, film, theater, and dance performances throughout the year. The facility is south of the village on the west side of Alta Lake.

Festivals and Events
Spring and Summer

Plenty of special events draw visitors to Whistler, particularly from late May through Canadian Thanksgiving in mid-October, when there's something on the calendar most weekends.

Bring the kids to the annual **Whistler Children's Festival** (www.whistlerchildrensfestival.com, July), a weekend of family-friendly arts, crafts, and entertainment ranging from African dancing to First Nations drumming.

A "celebration of mindful living," **Wanderlust Whistler** (www.wanderlust.com, July-Aug.) includes several days of yoga classes, meditation workshops, concerts, lectures, guided hikes, and local food.

Crankworx Freeride Mountain Bike Festival (www.crankworx.com, Aug.) draws wild and crazy mountain bikers for a week of downhill and cross-country cycling, stunt riding, and plenty more two-wheeled fun.

One of Whistler's top restaurants hosts the **Araxi Longtable Series** (www.araxi.com, Aug.), lavish alfresco dinners highlighting the region's late-summer bounty.

Fall and Winter

Whistler shows its artistic side during the annual **Whistler Writers Festival** (www.whistlerwritersfest.com, Oct.), when Canadian and international authors conduct readings, teach seminars, participate on panels, and mingle with guests to discuss their work.

Why come to Whistler in November, when it's chilly for hiking and cycling but too early to ski? Because that's when Whistler hosts a bang-up food and wine fest. The annual **Cornucopia Festival** (www.whistlercornucopia.com, Nov.) draws food and wine lovers from far and wide for two weeks of wine-tastings and seminars, guest chef events, special dinners, and extravagant parties.

Whistler Film Festival (www.whistlerfilmfestival.com, Dec.) screens up to 90 movies, including world premieres, features, documentaries, and shorts during this five-day international competition. At least 50 percent of the films are Canadian. You might even spot a celebrity or two.

Whistler hosts one of North America's largest gay and lesbian ski weeks, the **Whistler Pride and Ski Festival** (www.

gaywhistler.com, Jan.). It's eight days of LGBTQ-friendly snow sports, après-ski events, parties, concerts, and more.

Food
Like many resort towns, Whistler offers several splurge-worthy dining rooms. If you're watching your budget, you'll need to pick your dining spots carefully, but burgers, pizza, and diner-style meals can fill you up at moderate prices. Another money-saving option, when you're staying in a lodging with kitchen facilities, is to have one or more meals "at home" or pack a lunch for your outdoor adventures.

Contemporary
Long considered one of Whistler's top restaurants, ★ **Araxi** (4222 Village Square, 604/932-4540, www.araxi.com, 3pm-midnight daily, $30-50) emphasizes regional ingredients, whether it's fresh oysters or locally farmed produce. The menu might include line-caught tuna, grilled and paired with pearl couscous and minted cucumbers, or roasted duck breast with polenta and poached pears. Sate your sweet tooth with the warm Valrhona chocolate fondant or the refreshing lemon tart.

With more than 20,000 bottles, ★ **Bearfoot Bistro** (4121 Village Green, 604/932-3433, http://bearfootbistro. com, 6pm-10pm daily, prix fixe $76-178) has one of the largest wine cellars in western Canada, the better to pair with its modern Canadian cuisine. Accompanied by live jazz, dinners are multicourse prix-fixe affairs that might start with a salad of locally grown root vegetables with popped buckwheat and quince or cured steelhead trout with potato rosti and roe, and continue with pheasant dressed with chestnut brioche and mushroom stuffing, beef striploin with a truffle vinaigrette, or Moroccan spiced lamb shanks. Of course, there are sweets, including ice cream that's whipped up tableside, mixing cream

with liquid nitrogen. If you prefer a lighter meal, perhaps oysters and champagne, a game burger, or duck confit with a chili-honey glaze, take a seat in the less formal **champagne lounge** (from 4pm Mon.-Fri., from 3pm Sat.-Sun., $12-22), open from après-ski until late evening.

Aura Restaurant (2131 Lake Placid Rd., 604/966-5715, www.nitalakelodge. com, 6:30am-11am and 5:30pm-9:30pm daily, breakfast $12-23, dinner $29-44) at Creekside's Nita Lake Lodge is worth a visit even if you're not staying at this lakefront hotel, both for its fine contemporary fare and for the lovely lakeside setting. You might begin with a seasonal salad or pepper-crusted venison carpaccio. For your main course, you could try halibut with grilled pineapple salsa, steelhead salmon with fregola salad, or free-range chicken with savoy cabbage. On "Meatless Mondays," the restaurant offers a three-course vegan prix fixe option ($39).

Japanese
A longtime favorite for Japanese fare, upscale **Sushi Village** (11-4340 Sundial Cres., 604/932-3330, http://sushivillage. com, 5:30pm-10pm Mon.-Thurs., noon-2:30pm and 5:30pm-10pm Fri.-Sun., $11-48) has been keeping Whistler in *nigiri*, *maki*, teriyaki, and tempura since the 1980s. Another popular spot for Japanese meals is **Sachi Sushi** (106-4359 Main St., 604/935-5649, www.sachisushi.com, noon-2pm and 5:30pm-9pm Tues.-Fri., 5:30pm-9pm Sat.-Sun., $13-35) at the Summit Lodge.

Part grocery store and part quickserve Japanese eatery, **Fuji Market** (205-4000 Whistler Way, 604/962-6251, www.fujimarket.ca, 10am-9pm daily, $9-12), in a mini-mall near the Whistler Conference Centre, stocks ready-made sushi and cooks up ramen, tempura, and other inexpensive Japanese bites. You can pick up wasabi peas, jars of kimchi, and other Asian ingredients.

Italian and Pizza

A life raft of good value in a sea of expensive eateries, family-friendly **Pasta Lupino** (121-4368 Main St., 604/905-0400, www.pastalupino.com, 11am-9pm daily, lunch $8-14, dinner $14-18) serves a small menu of Italian classics, including spaghetti and meatballs, lasagna, and chicken parmigiana. In the evenings, pasta dinners come with soup or salad, plus homemade focaccia.

The wood-fired oven turns out traditional Neapolitan-style pizzas at **Pizzeria Antico** (101-4369 Main St., 604/962-9226, www.pizzeriaantico.ca, noon-11pm daily, lunch $9-20, dinner $14-20), like the Prosciutto con Ruccola, topped with arugula, prosciutto, tomato, and mozzarella, or the Funghi, sauced with porcini cream and layered with roasted mushrooms and onions. Several fresh salads, grilled paninis (at lunch), and pastas (at dinner) round out the menu.

In a white-tablecloth dining room with comfortably spaced tables, ★ **Il Caminetto** (4242 Village Stroll, 604/932-4442, www.ilcaminetto.ca, 5:30pm-11pm daily, $22-59) updates a classic Italian menu with regional products. You might kick off your meal with a nectarine and burrata salad or seared scallops paired with a taleggio cheese-stuffed squash blossom, then look for the handmade pasta of the day or the rich wild mushroom risotto. For the secondi, halibut with sea asparagus or grilled lamb with roasted cauliflower could be good options. The lengthy wine list highlights labels from B.C. and Italy. **TIP:** The kitchen periodically offers an excellent-value seasonal four-course weeknight menu ($35).

Spanish

Under the same ownership as Araxi, cozy **Bar Oso** (150-4222 Village Square, 604/962-4540, http://baroso.ca, 4:30pm-midnight Mon.-Fri., 11:30am-midnight Sat.-Sun., $9-35) serves Spanish-style tapas with a B.C. twist. You might nibble wild scallop *crudo* with olives and oranges, a salad of roasted beets with buffalo mozzarella, or a platter of house-made charcuterie. To sip, there are local beers, sangrias, and interesting cocktails.

Vegetarian

You might walk away with a green mustache after slurping down a fresh juice or smoothie at **The Green Moustache** (122-4340 Lorimer Rd., 604/962-3727, www.greenmoustache.com, 8am-5pm Sun.-Fri., 8am-6pm Sat., $9-15), a tiny juice bar and vegan eatery. In the morning, it serves Breakfast Bowls, like muesli or chia pudding topped with nuts, berries, and house-made almond or cashew milk. By midday, you might order a big salad or the Buddha Bowl, a blend of rice and quinoa piled high with fresh veggies.

Diners

For hearty meals served with friendly sass, head for the **Southside Diner** (2102 Lake Placid Rd., Creekside, 604/966-0668, www.southsidediner.ca, 7am-9pm Sun.-Thurs., 7am-10pm Fri.-Sat., breakfast $9-19, lunch and dinner $12-19), in the Creekside area. Morning menus get you going with breakfast poutine (home fries topped with poached eggs, sausage, cheese curds, and gravy), "big-ass pancakes" (yes, they're big), and the usual egg suspects. Later, you can stuff yourself with burgers, sandwiches, meatloaf, or macaroni and cheese.

Burgers

Like burgers? **Splitz Grill** (4369 Main St., 604/938-9300, www.splitzgrill.com, 11am-9pm daily, $6-14) has 'em, and they're not just traditional beef patties. You can get lamb, bison, lentil, even salmon. Line up at the counter, order your burger, and choose from a large selection of toppings. Poutine, fries, and beer are the favored accompaniments.

Cafés, Bakeries, and Light Bites

Whistler's best bakery, ★ **Purebread** (www.purebread.ca) offers an irresistible array of treats, from scones and croissants to lemon crumble bars, salted caramel bars, and oversized brownies. If you're packing for a picnic, try the Dysfunction Ale bread, a hearty loaf made with spent grains from the Whistler Brewing Company. Purebread has two Whistler branches: a convenient **Village location** (4388 Main St., Olympic Plaza, 604/962-1182, 8am-6pm daily) and its original **Function Junction shop** (1-1040 Millar Creek Rd., 604/938-3013, 8:30am-5pm daily) on the south side of town.

At the Blackcomb base, sunny **Fifi's Bistro** (4557 Blackcomb Way, 640/935-3263, www.fifisbistro.com, 8am-3pm daily, breakfast $9-24, lunch $12-21) serves creative twists on breakfast and lunch fare. Start your day with a fruit smoothie, eggs Benedict layered with house-smoked salmon, or smoked bacon hash with avocado and a fried duck egg. Lunchtime brings a range of salads and sandwiches, with a number of vegetarian and vegan options. If you're in a hurry, you can pick up coffee and pastries to go.

Groceries and Markets

The **Whistler Farmers Market** (4545 Blackcomb Way, www.whistlerfarmersmarket.org, 11am-4pm Sun. May-Oct., 2pm-7pm Wed. July-Aug.) brings locally grown produce and other goodies to the village every weekend spring-fall, with an additional midsummer weekday market.

Whistler Marketplace IGA (4330 Northlands Blvd., 604/938-2850, www.igastoresbc.com, 9am-9pm daily) is the largest and most centrally located grocery store in the village.

Handy to pick up a snack or the toothpaste you forgot, **Whistler Grocery Store** (4211 Village Square, 604/932-3628, www.whistlergrocery.com, 8am-11pm

Top to bottom: a smoothie bowl from The Green Moustache; Ketel One Ice Room at Bearfoot Bistro; halibut with sea asparagus at Il Caminetto.

daily) keeps long hours and is the closest market to the slopes. If you're staying in the Creekside area, your go-to grocery is **Whistler's Creekside Market** (305-2071 Lake Placid Rd., 604/938-9301, www. creeksidemarket.com, 7am-10pm daily).

Accommodations and Camping

Whistler accommodations include hotels and condominium buildings. Hotels provide more services, such as on-site restaurants, ski valets, and concierge staff; some, but not all, have kitchenettes or in-room fridges and microwaves. Renting a condo is often less expensive, particularly for a family, and you'll have a kitchen where you can prepare meals. Most Whistler accommodations charge for overnight parking, so factor that fee into your lodging budget.

Whistler has two "peak" seasons. The main high season is during the winter for skiing and snowboarding, which typically begins in late November and continues until April. There's also a "mini peak" during July and August, when visitors come for hiking, biking, and other summer activities. The most expensive time to stay at Whistler is during the Christmas-New Year holiday, when rates soar. The February-March school holiday weeks are also pricey. During the rest of the year, lodging rates are usually lowest midweek.

Check the **Tourism Whistler website** (www.whistler.com) for lodging deals, particularly if you're making last-minute plans. The **Whistler-Blackcomb website** (www.whistlerblackcomb.com) sometimes posts discounts on accommodations as well.

Under $150

Built to house athletes during the 2010 Winter Olympics, the **HI-Whistler Hostel** (1035 Legacy Way, 604/962-0025 or 866/762-4122, www.hihostels.ca, $45-51 dorm, $132-187 d), 5 miles (8 km) south of Whistler Village, offers dorm beds as well as good-value private rooms with flat-screen TVs and en suite baths. Dorms (female, male, or mixed) sleep four, each with bunk beds, reading lights, electrical outlets, lockers, and shared washrooms. Parking and Wi-Fi are free, and common areas include a café, TV room, lounge with a pool table, shared kitchen, and outdoor terrace. December-February, the hostel can have more of a ski-party atmosphere. Summer is typically quieter, when staff organize hikes, brewery tours, and other activities. B.C. Transit buses to the village stop out front.

$150-300

The accommodations at Canada's first pod hotel, **Pangea Pod Hotel** (4333 Sunrise Alley, 844/726-4329, www. pangeapod.com, $99-149 s, $170-285 d), are more private than a hostel but somewhat less expensive than a typical hotel room, all in a high-style, high-tech environment with a central location on the Village Stroll. Each of the 88 "pods," sleeping cabins clustered into eight suites, is outfitted with a double bed, lockable cabinet, hangers, charging ports, and a curtain in lieu of a door; in each suite, shared washrooms are separated into private shower, toilet, vanity, and changing rooms. Female-only suites are available. Guests can chill in the living room-like café and lounge, or up on the rooftop patio. Store your skis, bikes, or other equipment in a gear room dubbed "the toy box."

Catering to skiers and snowboarders in winter, and to cyclists and other active guests in summer, the ★ **AAVA Whistler Hotel** (4005 Whistler Way, 604/932-2522 or 800/663-5644, www.aavawhistlerhotel. com, $154-405, parking $20) will loan you a complimentary Go-Pro camera to record your day's adventures (neat, right?). While it's not upscale (hotel staff say, "We don't valet your car, but we do valet your bike"), this 192-room lodging feels sociable, with several lobby seating areas and a communal worktable with a charging station. There's space to

lounge on the outdoor deck, too, around the compact pool and hot tub. Outfitted with one king, two queens, or a queen plus a sofa bed, the guest rooms are crisp and modern, with mini fridges, safes, and Keurig coffeemakers; the prime top-floor units have vaulted ceilings. Wi-Fi and local calls are free. You can walk to the Whistler base in about 10 minutes.

Feeling funky? The boutique 41-room **Adara Hotel** (4122 Village Green, 604/905-4009 or 866/502-3272, www.adarahotel.com, $169-409, parking $25) goes beyond typical ski-lodge style, starting from its lobby, furnished with curvaceous orange banquettes, a massive stone fireplace, and stylized antler sculptures; you can grab coffee and a breakfast bar here in the morning. Out on the sundeck is a small hot tub and summer-only pool. Standard rooms have electric fireplaces, French-press coffeemakers, mini fridges, microwaves, and modern baths with rain showers, but the coolest units are the lofts, with a bedroom upstairs and a living area below. Wi-Fi is included.

The three-story **Listel Hotel Whistler** (4121 Village Green, 604/932-1133 or 800/663-5472, www.listelhotel.com, $152-459, parking $20) is simple but comfortable, with a quiet location off the Village Stroll yet close to the Whistler base lifts. Most of the 98 rooms are standard units with two queen beds, free Wi-Fi, coffeemakers, and mini fridges. There's a hot tub (but no pool) on the outdoor patio. Rates include continental breakfast. The excellent **Bearfoot Bistro** is on the property.

At **Summit Lodge Boutique Hotel** (4359 Main St., 604/932-2778 or 888/913-8811, www.summitlodge.com, $172-475, parking $20), the 81 studio and one-bedrooms suites, with colorful graphic-print walls, all have kitchenettes. Wi-Fi and local calls are included, and you can

Top to bottom: Crystal Lodge Hotel & Suites; pool at Fairmont Chateau Whistler; Nita Lake Lodge.

borrow a complimentary bike to cycle around town. The Asian-style **Taman Sari Royal Heritage Spa** (604/938-5982, www.tamansarispa.com) uses traditional Javanese herbs in many of its treatments. Other hotel amenities include a sauna, hot tub, and year-round outdoor pool. You're surrounded by lots of good restaurants, and it's a 10- to 15-minute walk to the lifts.

Location is the draw at the **Crystal Lodge Hotel & Suites** (4154 Village Green, 604/932-2221 or 800/667-3363, www.crystal-lodge.com, $235-589, parking $24), built in the 1980s, with 158 rooms in two sprawling wings directly on the Village Stroll. In the updated south wing, the hotel-style rooms and studios are decorated with turquoise headboards, gray accents, and original artwork; the larger north wing units, from studios to three bedrooms, are more traditionally furnished. All rooms have coffeemakers, kettles, fridges, and Wi-Fi. The hotel provides a complimentary bike valet in

summer, ski valet in winter. The narrow outdoor pool is open year-round, and the small fitness room is well stocked with cardio equipment.

Over $300

With a solicitous staff and all sorts of amenities, ★ **Four Seasons Whistler Hotel** (4591 Blackcomb Way, 604/935-3400, www.fourseasons.com, $300-634 d, $600-2,200 suites, parking $39-45) is among Whistler's top resort hotels. Decorated in ski-lodge earth tones, the 273 rooms and suites have gas fireplaces, big closets, mini fridges, and flat-screen TVs; ask for an upper-floor unit for slope-side views. If you haven't gotten enough exercise on the mountain, you can work out in the 24-hour fitness room or swim in the heated outdoor pool. The three hot tubs and eucalyptus steam room are popular après-ski, as is the library-style **Sidecut Bar.** Located in Whistler's Upper Village, the Four Seasons isn't a ski-in, ski-out property, but the hotel offers a

Four Seasons Whistler Hotel

free ski concierge, so you can leave your gear slope-side. A complimentary car service can take you around town.

Like a grand mountain lodge, the ★ **Fairmont Chateau Whistler** (4599 Chateau Blvd., off Blackcomb Way, 604/938-8000 or 800/606-8244, www. fairmont.com, $289-699, parking $35-39) keeps you comfortable, whether you're in your room, exploring the property, or out in the village. The 528 rooms and suites, some with views of the slopes, have down duvets, fluffy bathrobes, flat-screen TVs, and one-cup coffeemakers. The Fairmont charges a daily resort fee ($15 per room), which covers Internet access, use of the indoor and outdoor pools and the well-equipped health club, yoga classes, tennis, a shuttle to take you to various village destinations, and valet service for your skis, bikes, or golf clubs. The **Mallard Lounge** is busy for après-ski cocktails, and the several other dining outlets include **The Grill Room** for steak and seafood and the café-style **Portobello**

Market & Bakery, which spans the day from breakfast bowls and pastries to smoked meats and barbecue; it's known for its bacon-maple doughnuts.

You can't stay much closer to the lifts than at the 121-unit all-suite **Pan Pacific Whistler Mountainside** (4320 Sundial Cres., 604/905-2999 or 888/905-9995, www.panpacific.com, $279-689, parking $28-32), steps from the gondolas. Decorated with cherry-hued Craftsman-style furnishings, the studio, one-bedroom, and two-bedroom units all have full kitchens, gas fireplaces, flat-screen TVs, and DVD players. The studios nominally sleep four, with a queen-size Murphy bed and a sleep sofa, but the larger suites are more comfortable for families. Other amenities include a heated outdoor saltwater pool, two hot tubs, complimentary Wi-Fi, and free local phone calls. The **Dubh Linn Gate Irish Pub** is popular for its Irish breakfast and for drinks and pub fare, with more than 25 beers on tap and live music most nights.

Slightly farther from the gondolas than its sister property, the **Pan Pacific Whistler Village Centre** (4299 Blackcomb Way, 604/966-5500 or 888/966-5575, www.panpacific.com, $169-539, parking $28-32) has a more modern boutique feel, but similar amenities: suites ranging from studios to three bedrooms with full kitchens, a saltwater lap pool, two hot tubs, a sauna, and a fitness facility. Rates include breakfast, Wi-Fi, local calls, and a complimentary shuttle to get around the village. You can store your ski or snowboard gear at the Pan Pacific Mountainside.

Set on a lake in the Creekside area, ★ **Nita Lake Lodge** (2131 Lake Placid Rd., 604/966-5700, www.nitalakelodge. com, $249-579 d, 2-bedroom suites $529-869, parking $20-30) is a beautiful setting in any season. The 77 spacious contemporary studio, one-, and two-bedroom suites on four floors have fireplaces, compact kitchenettes hidden in an armoire, and modern baths with rain showers and soaker tubs; the best units have lake views. You can choose all kinds of activities, from lounging in the rooftop hot tubs or booking a massage in the spa to kayaking, canoeing, or stand-up paddleboarding on the lake, or riding the Valley Trail on the complimentary bicycles. Three restaurants, the more formal **Aura Restaurant** overlooking the lake, **Cure Lounge & Patio** for burgers, salads, and drinks, and casual **Fix Café**, which serves pastries, coffee, smoothies, and sandwiches, give you plenty of dining options. The hotel offers a free shuttle to the village or the Creekside gondola.

Camping and Cabins

The **Riverside Resort** (8018 Mons Rd., 604/905-5533, www.parkbridge.com), 2 miles (3 km) north of the village, has several lodgings options, including campsites for tents and RVs, yurts, and sturdy log cabins.

The 14 family-friendly **cabins** ($210-230), with solid wood furnishings, have a living room, small kitchen, bedroom with a queen bed, and bath on the main level, plus a sleeping loft with two twin beds. They're equipped with electricity and even a flat-screen TV. The **yurts** ($105-125) are more rustic, but they still have electricity and heat. Sleeping up to five, most have a bunk bed with a single over a double bed, and either a futon couch or a separate single with a trundle bed. Washrooms with showers are a short walk away. **Campsites for RVs** ($55-71) include both fully and partially serviced sites. There's a quiet wooded walk-in **tent campground** ($25-42) with sites along the river.

The campground's main building has a small market and café; bicycle rentals are available. Other amenities include a guest laundry, free Wi-Fi, a playground, a volleyball court, and a putting course. The Valley Trail crosses the campground property, so you can follow it into town.

Condo Rentals

You can book many condo accommodations through the **Tourism Whistler** (www.whistler.com) and **Whistler-Blackcomb** (www.whistlerblackcomb.com) websites, and through many of the standard online booking services for hotels. You can also find condos and houses to rent through **Airbnb** (www.airbnb.com).

TIP: Check locally based rental agencies, including **alluraDirect** (604/707-6700 or 866/425-5872, www.alluradirect.com), which sometimes offer deals that the larger booking services don't have.

Information and Services
Visitor Information

Tourism Whistler (www.whistler.com) should be your starting point for information about the Whistler region. The website has lots of details about the area, both on and off the mountain, and it runs the year-round **Whistler Visitor Centre** (4230 Gateway Dr., 604/935-3357 or 877/991-9988, www.whistler.com/whistler-visitor-centre), which supplies maps, answers questions, and books accommodations and activities. Hours vary seasonally, but the visitors center is open at least 8am-5pm daily, staying open until 9pm or 10pm on busy weekends and holiday periods.

Whistler-Blackcomb (604/967-8950 or 800/766-0449, www.whistlerblackcomb.com) books lift tickets, equipment rentals, ski and snowboard lessons, and accommodations (reservations 604/296-5316 or 888/403-4727), and can provide information about mountain activities in every season. Check the website for toll-free reservations numbers from many different countries.

Pique Newsmagazine (www.piquenewsmagazine.com) covers the Whistler area and provides events listings.

Medical Services

The **Whistler Health Care Centre** (4380 Lorimer Rd., 604/932-4911, www.vch.

ca, 8am-10pm daily) provides emergency medical services to both locals and visitors. Doctors are on-call after hours. **Town Plaza Medical Clinic** (40-4314 Main St., 604/905-7089, www.medicalclinicwhistler.com) will see visitors for minor issues.

Rexall (103-4360 Lorimer Rd., 604/932-2303, 9am-9pm daily; 4204 Village Square, 604/932-4251, www.rexall.ca, 9am-9pm daily, pharmacy 9am-7pm daily) has two Whistler pharmacies. **Shoppers Drug Mart** (121-4295 Blackcomb Way, 604/905-5666, www.shoppersdrugmart.ca, 9am-9pm daily) also provides pharmacy services.

Getting Around
By Car
Whistler Village is a pedestrian zone, so you have to leave your car outside the village proper. Whistler has several public **parking lots** where you can park all day.

Day lots 1-5, on Blackcomb Way near Lorimer Road, are closest to Whistler Village. Lots 1, 2, and 3, which are closest to the lifts, are paid lots ($2.50 per hour, $10 per day) until 5pm; they're free 5pm-8am. Lots 4 and 5 are free in the spring and fall but require payment the rest of the year ($2.50 per hour, $5 per day mid-June-mid-Sept. and mid-Dec.-mid-Apr., free mid-Apr.-mid-June and mid-Sept.-mid-Dec.). Closer to the Blackcomb base, off Glacier Lane, day lots 6, 7, and 8 are open in the winter only (free). November-March, you can't park overnight in any of the day lots; between April and October, you can park for up to 24 hours.

In the Creekside area, you can park free in the Creekside base underground garage. Follow London Lane off Highway 99.

Public paid parking is available at Whistler Conference Centre (4010 Whistler Way, $1 per hour, $15 per day, 24-hour maximum), Whistler Public Library (4329 Main St., $1 per hour, $15 per day, 24-hour maximum), and Whistler Municipal Hall (4325 Blackcomb Way, $1 per hour, 2-hour maximum).

By Bus
B.C. Transit (604/932-4020, http://bctransit.com/whistler, $2.50 pp) runs several bus routes through the Whistler area that are useful if you're staying outside of the central Whistler Village. The **Whistler Creekside** route travels between the village and Creekside. Other routes, such as the **Cheakamus** route to the HI-Whistler Hostel and Function Junction, or the **Alpine** route to Alpine Meadows and the Meadow Park Sports Centre, link Whistler's residential neighborhoods with the Whistler Gondola Exchange, where you can board the mountain gondola.

Two bus routes are free during the winter season, including the **Upper Village/Benchlands** route that can take you to the village from condos in those neighborhoods, and the **Marketplace Shuttle** between the Whistler Gondola Exchange and the Marketplace shopping center.

Bus schedules vary seasonally and by route; call or check the website for hours.

By Taxi
Whistler has two local taxi companies: **Whistler Resort Cabs** (604/938-1515, www.resortcabs.com) and **Whistler Taxi** (604/932-3333, www.whistlertaxi.com). Both operate 24 hours daily. Taxi fares average $5 within Whistler Village, $10 between the village and Creekside, and $15 between the village and other Whistler neighborhoods.

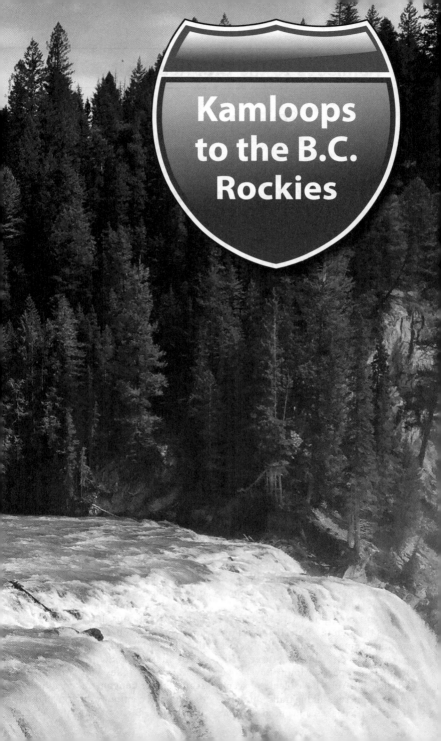

Kamloops
to the B.C.
Rockies

Kamloops to the B.C. Rockies

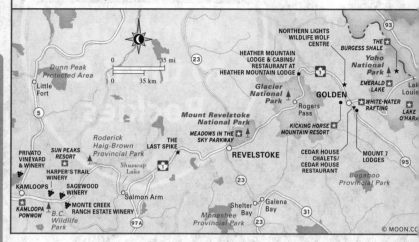

The Trans-Canada Highway takes you from the desert-like hills of British Columbia's interior to the evergreen forests and stark alpine peaks of the Rockies.

Midway between Vancouver and the Rockies, the city of Kamloops makes a logical road-trip stopping point, with several small museums, emerging wine and craft beer industries, and plenty of desert sunshine. Nearby, Sun Peaks Resort offers hiking and cycling along its rolling hills in summer and more than 130 trails for skiing and snowboarding once the snow starts to fall.

As you continue east, Highway 1 climbs through the Purcell and Selkirk mountain ranges en route to the Rockies, passing directly through three striking national parks. Mount Revelstoke, Glacier, and Yoho have plenty of scenic drives, numerous hiking trails, shimmering glacier-fed lakes, and one of Canada's highest waterfalls. Important in Canada's early development, particularly its transcontinental railroad, the mountain towns of Revelstoke and Golden are good bases for exploring the parks, with outdoor activities, cool restaurants, and comfortable places to spend the night.

Getting to Kamloops and the B.C. Rockies

Driving from Vancouver
To Kamloops

From Vancouver to Kamloops, the **most direct route** is to take the **Trans-Canada Highway (Hwy. 1)** east to Hope. Continue east at Hope onto **Highway 3,** then exit onto **Highway 5 (Coquihalla Hwy.)** north. Follow the Coquihalla over the mountains to Kamloops. It's **220 miles (355 km)** from Vancouver to Kamloops via this route, which takes **3.75-4 hours.**

An alternate route from Vancouver to Kamloops takes you through the **scenic Fraser Canyon.** Take **Highway 1** to Hope and continue north on Highway 1 through Boston Bar and Cache

Highlights

★ **Kamloopa Powwow:** One of western Canada's largest celebrations of First Nations culture brings dancers, drummers, and other performers to Kamloops every August (page 186).

★ **Sun Peaks Resort:** This ski resort near Kamloops has lots to do outdoors in the warmer months, especially mountain hiking and biking (page 188).

★ **Meadows in the Sky Parkway:** In Mount Revelstoke National Park, this winding road climbs to over 6,500 feet (2,000 m) above sea level, with great hiking at the top (page 193).

★ **White-Water Rafting:** The Kicking Horse River east of Golden is one of the region's top spots for white-water rafting (page 205).

★ **Kicking Horse Mountain Resort:** From getting up close with a grizzly bear to whizzing downhill in North America's highest bike park, this mountain getaway near Golden offers lots of warm-weather experiences—plus serious powder skiing in winter (page 209).

★ **Lake O'Hara:** Make your reservation early if you'd like to catch the shuttle bus to this Yoho National Park lake, so picturesque—and

popular—that Parks Canada limits visitor access (page 215).

★ **Emerald Lake:** As scenic as its name suggests, this green beauty in Yoho National Park is a lovely spot for canoeing, hiking, or enjoying the surrounding mountain landscape (page 216).

★ **The Burgess Shale:** Geologists have discovered some of the world's oldest fossils in these layers of rocks in Yoho National Park (page 218).

Best Accommodations

★ **The Cube Hotel:** For travelers on a budget, this Revelstoke lodging mixes the relaxed vibe of a guesthouse with the style of a boutique hotel (page 200).

★ **Explorers Society Hotel:** Sun on the rooftop deck, soak in the outdoor hot tub, and settle into well-designed guest rooms in this Revelstoke heritage building turned boutique hotel (page 201).

★ **Cedar House Chalets:** These modern wood-framed chalets near Golden are stocked with everything you need for a mountain getaway (page 209).

★ **Emerald Lake Lodge:** You can't ask for a prettier setting than that of these comfortable guest rooms overlooking one of Yoho National Park's most spectacular bodies of water (page 220).

★ **Cathedral Mountain Lodge:** In these upscale cabins in Yoho National Park, you don't have to rough it to live out your log-cabin dreams (page 220).

Creek, where the highway turns east to Kamloops. This Fraser Canyon route is **270 miles (430 km)** from Vancouver to Kamloops and it takes **five hours.**

To the B.C. Rockies

If you're heading on to the Rockies from Kamloops, pick up **Highway 1** in Kamloops, which continues east to Revelstoke, Golden, and Yoho National Park. The drive from Kamloops to **Revelstoke** is **135 miles (215 km)** and takes **2.5 hours;** from Kamloops to **Golden,** it's **225 miles (360 km)** and takes **four hours;** from Kamloops to Yoho, it's **260 miles (415 km)** and takes **4.75-5 hours.**

Driving from Whistler

If you want to stop off in Whistler between Vancouver and Kamloops, take the following route. After driving Highway 99 (Sea-to-Sky Hwy.) from Vancouver to Whistler, continue north on **Highway 99.** It will join **Highway 97,** and at **Cache Creek,** you'll meet up with the **Trans-Canada Highway (Hwy. 1)** east to Kamloops. This **Vancouver-Whistler-Kamloops** route is **260 miles (420 km)** and takes **5.75-6 hours;** the

Whistler-Kamloops leg is **185 miles (295 km)** and takes **four hours.**

Driving from Kelowna (Okanagan)
To Kamloops

Driving from Kelowna, in the Okanagan wine region, to Kamloops, you have two options: Follow **Highway 97C** west to **Merritt,** where you pick up **Highway 5** to Kamloops; this route is **130 miles (210 km)** and takes you through some beautifully remote ranchlands. Or take **Highway 97** north, which forks to the northwest and continues to Kamloops; this second option is **105 miles (170 km)** and follows some scenic stretches of lakeshore. The Merritt route is longer, but the roads are faster. Either option will take about **2.5 hours.**

To the B.C. Rockies

From Kelowna to Revelstoke, Golden, or Yoho, take **Highway 97** north, then continue north on **Highway 97A.** At **Sicamous,** turn east onto the **Trans-Canada Highway (Hwy. 1),** which leads east to these mountain destinations. The trip from Kelowna to **Revelstoke** is **125 miles (200 km)** and takes **2.5 hours.**

Best Restaurants

★ **Terra Restaurant:** This art-filled Kamloops bistro changes its menu monthly to take advantage of the season's freshest ingredients (page 186).

★ **Woolsey Creek Bistro:** Revelstoke's most accomplished restaurant cooks up a world-rambling menu in a sunny yellow house (page 200).

★ **La Baguette:** This sociable café is the place for coffee and pastries in Revelstoke (page 200).

★ **Eagle's Eye Restaurant:** With wraparound mountain views and an elevation of 7,700 feet (2,350 m), this contemporary eatery at Kicking Horse Mountain Resort is Canada's highest restaurant (page 211).

Driving from Banff

The **Trans-Canada Highway (Hwy. 1)** is the direct route from Banff to British Columbia. The road will take you west into B.C. to Yoho, Golden, Revelstoke, and Kamloops. The drive from Banff to **Yoho** is **55 miles (85 km)** and takes **one hour.** From Banff to **Kamloops**, it's **310 miles (495 km)** and takes **5.5-5.75 hours.**

Driving from Jasper

The **shortest route** between Jasper and Kamloops is to follow **Highway 16 (Yellowhead Hwy.)** west to **Highway 5,** where you turn south toward Kamloops. The trip from Jasper to **Kamloops** via this route is **275 miles (440 km)** and takes **five hours.**

A **longer but scenic route** is to take the **Icefields Parkway (Hwy. 93)** south from Jasper to **Lake Louise,** where you turn west onto **Highway 1.** You'll pass through Yoho, Glacier, and Mount Revelstoke National Parks and into the city of Kamloops. The drive from Jasper to **Yoho National Park** via this route is **160 miles (255 km)** and it takes **3.5-4 hours.** Driving this scenic route from Jasper to **Kamloops,** the trip is **415 miles (665 km)** and takes **8.25-8.75 hours.**

Getting There by Air, Train, or Bus

The most convenient way to get to Kamloops from most B.C. or Alberta destinations is with your own vehicle, although there are options to fly or take the train. To reach any of the B.C. national parks easily, you need a car.

By Air

Air Canada (888/247-2262, www.aircanada.ca) flies to the regional **Kamloops Airport** (YKA, 3035 Airport Rd., 250/376-3613, www.kamloopsairport.com) from Vancouver and Calgary. **WestJet** (888/937-8538, www.westjet.com) serves Kamloops from Calgary. **Central Mountain Air** (888/865-8585, www.flycma.com) flies to Kamloops from Edmonton and from several northern B.C. communities, including Fort St. John, Prince George, Smithers, and Terrace. The airport is 7 miles (11 km) west of downtown Kamloops.

Budget Car Rental (250/374-7368 or 888/368-7368, www.budget.ca), **Enterprise Rent-a-Car** (250/376-2883 or 888/305-8051, www.enterprise.com), and **National Car Rental** (250/376-4911, www.nationalcar.ca) have offices at the Kamloops Airport.

By Train

The Canadian, the **VIA Rail** (514/989-2626 or 888/842-7245, www.viarail.ca) Vancouver-Toronto train, stops in Kamloops. You can travel westbound to Vancouver or eastbound to Jasper and points farther east, including Edmonton, Saskatoon, Winnipeg, and Toronto. However, between Vancouver and Kamloops (9.5-13 hours) or between Kamloops and Jasper (9-10 hours), the train is significantly slower than driving. *The Canadian* operates three times a week in each direction May-mid-October, and twice a week mid-October-April.

Kamloops

Its name comes from *T'kemlups,* a Secwepemc First Nations' word meaning "the meeting of the rivers." Kamloops, a city of 90,000 at the confluence of the South Thompson and North Thompson Rivers and at the intersection of Highways 1, 5, and 97, is a convenient stopping point when you're traveling across the province. This dry region has a hot, almost desertlike climate in summer; it gets an average of 8.6 inches (218 mm) of rain every year, compared with more than 43 inches (1,100 mm) in coastal Vancouver. The city has several small museums, emerging wine and craft beer industries, and lots of sunshine.

Sights and Recreation
Secwepemc Museum and Heritage Park
A residential school for aboriginal children operated from the 1890s to 1978 on the grounds of what is now the **Secwepemc Museum and Heritage Park** (200-330 Chief Alex Thomas Way, 250/828-9749, www.secwepemcmuseum. com, 8am-4pm daily, adults $10.50, seniors and students $7.35, ages 7-17 $6.35, families $21), first in a wooden schoolhouse and later in the 1920s redbrick building that still stands on the site.

The museum details the history of the Shuswap First Nation (Shuswap is the English name for the Secwepemc people), whose traditional lands cover 56,000 square miles (145,000 sq km) between the Fraser River and the Rocky Mountains.

Take time to read the details in the exhibits that feature regalia and other clothing, dugout canoes, profiles of chiefs and other band members, facts about the Shuswap language and culture, and information about residential schools, both here and elsewhere in B.C.

Kamloops Heritage Railway
Ride back in time on the **Kamloops Heritage Railway** (250/374-2141, www. kamrail.com, July-Aug., call or check the website for schedules, adults $25, seniors $22, ages 3-17 $15, families $70), as a restored 1912 steam locomotive pulls rail cars through the desertlike hills outside the city on an hour-long, family-friendly tour. Don't be alarmed if horseback-riding "bandits" hold up your train in a simulated robbery.

You can buy tickets online or in person from the ticket office outside the former Canadian National Railway station (510 Lorne St.), where the rail tour starts and ends.

Museums and Galleries
Stop into the contemporary building in downtown Kamloops that houses the **Kamloops Art Gallery** (465 Victoria St., 250/377-2400, www.kag.bc.ca, 10am-5pm Mon.-Wed. and Fri.-Sat., 10am-9pm Thurs., adults $5, seniors $3, families $10) for exhibits of works by regional artists, including indigenous artists. Admission is free on Thursdays.

Kamloops Courthouse Gallery (7 W. Seymour St., 250/314-6600, www. kamloopscourthousegallery.ca, 10am-5pm Tues.-Fri., 10am-4pm Sat.), a local artists' cooperative, shows and sells work by its members in the stately former provincial court building that dates to the early 1900s.

Riverside Park
On the South Thompson River in downtown Kamloops, **Riverside Park** (Lorne St.) has a sandy riverside swimming beach with a splash park for the kids, as

Kamloops

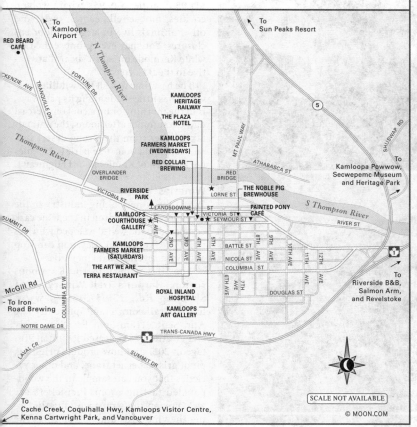

To Kamloops Airport

RED BEARD CAFÉ

MCKENZIE AVE

TRANQUILLE DR

FORTUNE DR

N Thompson River

Thompson River

OVERLANDER BRIDGE

VICTORIA ST

RIVERSIDE PARK

LANDSDOWNE ST

To Sun Peaks Resort

KAMLOOPS HERITAGE RAILWAY

THE PLAZA HOTEL

KAMLOOPS FARMERS MARKET (WEDNESDAYS)

RED COLLAR BREWING

MT PAUL WAY

ATHABASCA ST

RED BRIDGE

5

To Kamloopa Powwow, Secwepemc Museum and Heritage Park

SHUSWAP RD

S Thompson River

RIVER ST

LORNE ST

THE NOBLE PIG BREWHOUSE

KAMLOOPS COURTHOUSE GALLERY

VICTORIA ST

SEYMOUR ST

PAINTED PONY CAFÉ

1ST AVE

2ND AVE

3RD AVE

4TH AVE

5TH AVE

BATTLE ST

8TH AVE

9TH AVE

10TH AVE

11TH AVE

12TH AVE

SUMMIT DR

KAMLOOPS FARMERS MARKET (SATURDAYS)

THE ART WE ARE

TERRA RESTAURANT

NICOLA ST

COLUMBIA ST

6TH AVE

7TH AVE

DOUGLAS ST

To Riverside B&B, Salmon Arm, and Revelstoke

McGill Rd

To Iron Road Brewing

COLUMBIA ST W

ROYAL INLAND HOSPITAL

KAMLOOPS ART GALLERY

NOTRE DAME DR

LAVAL CR

TRANS-CANADA HWY

SUMMIT DR

To Cache Creek, Coquihalla Hwy, Kamloops Visitor Centre, Kenna Cartwright Park, and Vancouver

SCALE NOT AVAILABLE

© MOON.COM

well as changing rooms and restrooms. The park also has a rose garden and a riverfront walking trail. Every evening in July and August, at the park's Rotary Bandshell, there's **Music in the Park** (250/828-3611, www.tourismkamloops. com, 7pm daily July-Aug., free), a series of free 90-minute concerts.

Kenna Cartwright Park

To see more of Kamloops' desert surroundings, take a hike on the 25 miles (40 km) of trails in **Kenna Cartwright Park** (2000 Hillside Dr., www.kamloops. ca, dawn-dusk daily, free), which at 1,975

acres (800 ha) is the largest municipal park in British Columbia. For a moderate route up to a lookout over the city and the river, follow the Prickly Pear Cactus Trail to the Powerline Trail to the **Sunset Trail,** an out-and-back hike that totals about 3 miles (5 km).

B.C. Wildlife Park

If you're hoping to see Canadian wildlife as you journey across the region, start at the nonprofit **B.C. Wildlife Park** (9077 Dallas Dr., 250/573-3242, www. bcwildlife.org, 9:30am-4pm daily Mar.-Apr., 9:30am-5pm daily May-early Oct.,

9:30am-4pm Sat.-Sun. early Oct.-Feb., adults $15.95, seniors $13.95, ages 3-17 $11.95, families $49.95), where wolves, coyotes, moose, elk, eagles, owls, and other animals live in large outdoor enclosures. You may even glimpse the rare white Kermode or "spirit" bear that's native to the B.C. coast.

The best time to visit the wildlife park, which has little shade along its pathways, is in the morning or on a cool or overcast day. On summer afternoons, the animals take shelter from the strong desert sun, and so should you. The park is 12 miles (20 km) east of Kamloops, off Highway 1.

Wineries

While the wine-making industry in the Kamloops area is a drop in the wine cask compared to the well-developed wineries in B.C.'s Okanagan Valley, you can stop and sip at several local vineyards.

The first winery in the Kamloops region, **Harper's Trail Winery** (2761 Shuswap Rd., 250/573-5855, www.harperstrail.com, 11am-5pm daily late Apr.-Sept., 11am-5pm Fri.-Sun. early Oct., tastings $5) released its initial vintage in 2011 and now produces riesling, pinot gris, cabernet franc, and other varieties that you can sample in the wood-paneled tasting room. Picnickers are welcome on the wraparound patio facing the vineyards and desert hills. The winery is 12 miles (20 km) east of downtown Kamloops. Taking Highway 1 is a little faster, but the drive along Shuswap Road past the desert cliffs and hoodoos is more scenic.

Credited with coining the phrase, "Hands up!," notorious train robber Billy Miner held up his last Canadian train in 1906 on the ranchlands that now house **Monte Creek Ranch Estate Winery** (2420 Miner's Bluff Rd., Monte Creek, 250/573-5399 or 855/633-9463,

Top to bottom: church along the route of the Kamloops Heritage Railway; Kenna Cartwright Park; nachos and beer at Iron Road Brewing.

Rest Stop: Lillooet's First Winery

Highway 99 north of Whistler wends through the forests and mountains until it meets Highway 1 and continues toward Kamloops. If you're following this route between Whistler and eastern B.C., consider a stop about 80 miles (130 km) in, two hours from Whistler, to sample a winemaker's dream.

Rolf de Bruin and Heleen Pannekoek emigrated from the Netherlands to Canada with the goal of opening a winery and starting a new life for their family. They searched for suitable land throughout British Columbia and, in 2009, settled in the remote community of Lillooet, midway between Whistler and Kamloops, where they began growing grapes.

Fort Berens' wines

Why launch in Lillooet, an area that had never been a wine-producing region? As de Bruin tells it, the pair decided it was better to be the first winery in Lillooet than the 200th winery in the more popular Okanagan Valley.

Today, **Fort Berens Estate Winery** (1881 Hwy. 99 N., Lillooet, 250/256-7788 or 877/956-7768, www.fortberens.ca, 10am-6pm daily May-Oct., 10am-4pm Thurs.-Mon. Nov.-Apr.) produces a number of different wines, most from estate-grown grapes. It's particularly known for rieslings and cabernet francs. Complimentary tastings are available in a contemporary winery building, and you can enjoy lunch overlooking the vineyards in the patio restaurant, **The Kitchen** (noon-4pm daily mid-May-mid-Oct., $15-25), while you savor the fruits of one couple's winemaking dream.

www.montecreekranchwinery.com, 10am-6pm daily May-Oct., 11am-5pm daily Nov.-Apr., tastings $5). This Wild West history inspired the winery's Hands Up varieties, including a white blend of frontenac blanc, viognier, and la crescent grapes, and a red made primarily from merlot, marquette, and cabernet sauvignon. The tasting room, 20 miles (33 km) east of Kamloops along Highway 1, is in a striking, modern barn-inspired structure with a landmark bell tower, with views of the Lions Head rock face, desert headlands, and surrounding vines. On the Terrace, the winery's outdoor wine bar, you can sip wine while nibbling cheese or charcuterie.

Also east of town, **Sagewood Winery** (589 Meadow Lark Rd., 250/573-1921, www.sagewoodwinery.ca, 1pm-5pm Wed.-Sun. mid-June-Oct., call for off-season hours, tastings $5) makes riesling, gewürztraminer, pinot noir, and other wines.

At **Privato Vineyard & Winery** (5505 Westsyde Rd., 250/579-8739, www.privato.ca, 10am-5pm daily May-mid-Oct., 11am-4pm Wed.-Sun. mid-Oct.-late Oct., by appointment Nov.-Apr., tastings $7), an 80-acre (32-ha) family-run farm west of downtown that produces chardonnay, pinot noir, and rosé wines, you can purchase a picnic basket to enjoy with a glass of wine in the flower-filled garden.

Breweries

Try a tasting flight of house-brewed beers at **The Noble Pig Brewhouse** (650 Victoria St., 778/471-5999, www.thenoblepig.ca,

11:30am-11pm Mon.-Wed., 11:30am-midnight Thurs.-Sat., 3pm-10pm Sun.), a downtown brewpub and eatery where you might sample the Fascist Pig Pilsner, Wallonian Pig Belgian Peppered Ale, or the easy-drinking House Lager.

Another downtown craft beer maker with a laid-back pub-style tasting room, **Red Collar Brewing** (355 Lansdowne St., 778/471-0174, www.redcollar.ca, 5pm-10pm Tues.-Wed., 3pm-10pm Thurs.-Fri., 1pm-10pm Sat.) typically has 10 brews on tap, including a medium-bodied blonde, a dark Belgian-style dubbel, and seasonal beers like a Cherry Sour.

The co-owners of **Iron Road Brewing** (980 Camosun Cres., 778/765-8160, www.ironroadbrewing.ca, noon-10pm Mon.-Thurs., noon-midnight Fri.-Sat., noon-9pm Sun.) left their jobs as geologists, since as big beer drinkers they joked that "they couldn't afford not to open a brewery." Their production facility and brick-walled taproom is near the Thompson Rivers University campus, and they're known for the Locomotive Lager, Red Bridge Pale Ale, and Loop Line IPA, which you can pair with signature nachos and a rotating selection of tacos.

Festivals and Events
Kamloops International Buskers Festival

Professional street performers, including magicians, jugglers, acrobats, and more, show their stuff at the four-day **Kamloops International Buskers Festival** (www.kamloopsbuskers.com, July).

★ Kamloopa Powwow

One of western Canada's largest celebrations of First Nations culture, the annual **Kamloopa Powwow** (Secwepemc Powwow Grounds, Chief Alex Thomas Way, 250/828-9700, http://tkemlups.ca, Aug., $10 per day, $20 for the weekend) draws indigenous families and visitors from near and far for three days of traditional music, drumming, and dancing. Try to arrive for one of the Grand Entry

processions, where all the participating dancers assemble in the powwow arena. Vendors sell First Nations crafts, souvenirs, and snacks ranging from hot dogs to bannock to Indian tacos. You can bring your own food and drinks, but no alcohol is allowed on the powwow grounds.

Brewloops

Brewers from across the region bring their beers to the **Brewloops Festival** (www.brewloopsfest.ca, Sept.), a weekend of tastings, music, and more celebrating the region's craft beer scene.

Food

While many restaurants pay lip service to "local, seasonal food," ★ **Terra Restaurant** (326 Victoria St., 250/374-2913, www.terrakamloops.com, 5pm-9pm Tues.-Sat., $25-34), an art-filled bistro downtown, varies its menu every month to take advantage of the season's freshest ingredients. In summer, for example, you could work your way from an heirloom tomato tart with whipped ricotta, to roasted duck breast in a savory cherry jus, to a "berry fantasy" of fresh fruits and meringues. When fall arrives, the kitchen might concoct an autumn salad of hearty greens with warm veggies and a hazelnut vinaigrette, pan-roasted trout with beet and goat cheese risotto, and to finish, an apple fritter with salted caramel mousse. Most of the wines, beers, and ciders are hyper-local, too.

Launched by a First Nations family, the homey **Painted Pony Café** (705 Victoria St., 250/828-1131, www.paintedponycafe.com, 9am-9pm Mon.-Sat., 10am-2pm Sun., breakfast $8-14, lunch and dinner $8-24) uses indigenous ingredients and traditional recipes for breakfast, lunch, and dinner. Morning meals might include an egg sandwich on bannock, fried quail, salmon cakes topped with poached eggs, or a deer steak, while later in the day you can dig into buffalo burgers, elk stew, or cedar-planked salmon.

When you can't decide between coffee or a beer, head to the north side of the Thompson River to the **Red Beard Café** (449 Tranquille Rd., 250/376-0083, www.redbeardcafe.com, 8am-10pm Mon.-Thurs., 8am-11pm Fri.-Sat., 8am-5pm Sun., $4-16), which is part coffee shop and part beer garden. It's serious about both brews, roasting its own coffee and pouring B.C. craft beers from more than a dozen taps. The munchies range from breakfast toasts to international small plates like beet dip with za'atar or duck and bison wontons. For dinner, you might find pulled pork with kraut slaw or pan-fried trout.

For tea and coffee, sandwiches and salads, and—especially—sweets, pop into **The Art We Are** (246 Victoria St., 250/828-7998, www.theartweare.com, 9am-9pm Mon.-Sat., $7-9), a downtown café decorated with works by local artists. It hosts live music most Saturday evenings.

The **Kamloops Farmers Market** (250/682-7975, www. kamloopsfarmersmarket.com) has two downtown locations. On Saturday (8am-12:30pm Sat. late Apr.-Oct.) it's in the 200 block of St. Paul Street between 2nd and 3rd Avenues; on Wednesday (8am-2pm Wed. May-Oct.) it's in the 400 block of Victoria Street between 4th and 5th Avenues.

Accommodations
Under $150

From several decks, an outdoor hot tub, and a swimming dock, you can enjoy views of the Thompson River and the desert cliffs beyond when you stay at the **Riverside Bed & Breakfast** (2664 Thompson Dr., 250/374-1043 or 888/400-1043, www.riversidebnb.ca, $139-169), 5 miles (8 km) east of the city center. The three comfortable, air-conditioned guest rooms have private baths, mini fridges, microwaves, and coffeemakers; Wi-Fi, local phone calls, and parking are included. Owners Cynthia and Gordon James serve a full family-style breakfast in the dining room, which has more river views.

The orange stucco building doesn't look too stylish from the outside, but inside **The Plaza Hotel** (405 Victoria St., 250/377-8075 or 877/977-5292, www. theplazahotel.ca, $129-229, parking $8), built in 1928 on downtown Kamloops's main street, are 68 updated guest rooms in a range of sizes, all with flat-screen TVs, mini fridges, and air-conditioning. Rates include Wi-Fi, local and long-distance calls, a hot buffet breakfast, and access to the fitness facilities at the nearby YMCA.

$150-300

Like an estate in Kentucky's horse-racing country, the **South Thompson Inn and Conference Centre** (3438 Shuswap Rd. E., 250/573-3777 or 800/797-7713, www.souththompsonhotelkamloops. com, $159-249), east of downtown, has an equestrian theme, with a dark-paneled bourbon lounge and 57 guest rooms named for thoroughbreds. Rooms are traditionally furnished, with included Wi-Fi and balconies overlooking either the river or across the lawns to the desert hills. Also facing the river is an outdoor pool and hot tub. Guests can help themselves to complimentary morning coffee and tea in the lobby. The inn's restaurant, **Madisens,** serves traditional dishes like New York steak with blue cheese butter, pistachio-crusted rack of lamb, and local trout with lemon-caper sauce.

Information and Services

Tourism Kamloops (www. tourismkamloops.com) has a helpful website with detailed information about the region and things to do. It also runs the **Kamloops Visitor Centre** (1290 W. Trans-Canada Hwy., 250/374-3377 or 800/662-1994, 8:30am-6pm Mon.-Fri., 9am-5pm Sat.-Sun. spring-summer, 8:30am-4:30pm Mon.-Fri., 9am-3pm Sat.-Sun. fall-winter); take Exit 368 from Highway 1.

The main hospital facility for the Kamloops region, **Royal Inland Hospital** (311 Columbia St., 250/374-5111, www.interiorhealth.ca) has a 24-hour emergency room.

Getting Around

Downtown Kamloops is compact and walkable, although many accommodations and activities are outside the downtown core, most easily explored by car.

The **Kamloops Transit System** (250/376-1216, http://bctransit.com/Kamloops, one-way $2) runs buses across the city. Use the Trip Planner function on the website to figure out if you can get where you're going by bus.

Service hours vary by bus route and day of the week, so check the schedule online before you set out. Major routes begin service between 6am and 7am Monday-Friday (between 7am and 8:30am Saturday-Sunday) and run until between 11pm and midnight.

★ Sun Peaks Resort

When you turn off Highway 5 north of Kamloops, you quickly leave behind the desert-dry hills and begin to climb through the pines to Sun Peaks Resort.

Sun Peaks is 35 miles (56 km) from the city, less than an hour's drive, and offers summertime relief from Kamloops's heat with plenty of outdoor activities. In winter, it's B.C.'s second-largest ski and snowboard resort after Whistler-Blackcomb.

At the base of the mountain, Sun Peaks has a compact village with several hotels, restaurants, and shops. Compared to a large resort like Whistler, the village here is tiny, although it has everything you need for a mountain getaway.

Sports and Recreation
Hiking

In summer, you can take the **Sunburst Express Chair** (www.sunpeaksresort.com, 10am-5pm daily late June-early Sept., adults $21, seniors and ages 13-18 $18, ages 6-12 $12) up to an elevation of

hikers at Sun Peaks Resort

6,000 feet (1,850 m) to access a 22-mile (35-km) network of easy and intermediate hiking trails. Colorful wildflowers carpet the slopes, usually peaking in late July or early August.

If you'd rather not hike alone, or if you'd like to learn more about area flora and fauna while you walk, book a two-hour guided **alpine nature hiking tour** (10am and 1pm Thurs.-Sun. late June-early Sept., $27 pp).

Mountain Biking

Mountain bikers can tackle more than 35 lift-accessed trails in the **Sun Peaks Bike Park** (www.sunpeaksresort.com, 10am-5pm daily late June-early Sept., half-day adults $38, seniors and ages 13-18 $32, ages 6-12 $22, full-day adults $47, seniors and ages 13-18 $40, ages 6-12 $28).

Sun Peaks also has a network of **cross-country bicycle trails,** ranging from beginner to advanced, many of which you can access without purchasing a lift ticket. Get a trail map online to plan your routes. If you're new to mountain or cross-country biking, consider an **introduction to cross-country mountain biking** package (10am and 1pm daily late June-early Sept., $106.50 pp) that includes a bike rental, lift ticket, and two-hour lesson. Or book a **guided cross-country alpine tour** (10am and 1pm daily late June-early Sept., $31.50 pp) for an introduction to the mountain's trail network.

Elevation Bike Ski Board (Sun Peaks Grand Hotel, 250/578-5555, www.sunpeaksresort.com, 9am-8pm daily late June-early Sept.) rents bikes and related gear for downhill cycling (half-day $56-112, full-day $70-140) and cross-country cycling (1 hour $15-25, half-day $44-88, full-day $20-110).

Mountain Cross Carts

Imagine whizzing down the mountain in a grown-up go-kart. If that sounds like your thing, try out Sun Peaks' **mountain cross carts** (www.sunpeaksresort.com, 11am-8pm daily late June-early Sept., 11am-8pm Fri.-Sun. early-late June and early-late Sept., $25 pp). After you and your cart ride up a platter lift, you drive your vehicle back down a winding 1,680-foot (512-m) course, at speeds up to 35 mph (56 km/h). If that doesn't sound fast, remember you're in a go-kart. Your ticket lets you do four laps of the course; you must have a valid driver's license.

Segway Tours

Another way to tour the village and nearby trails is on a Segway. **Alpine Explorers** (3240 Village Way, 250/851-1905, www.alpine-explorers.com) offers **off-road Segway tours** (daily mid-May-Sept.) on a big-wheeled model of these self-balancing electric scooters. Among the tour options are a one-hour introductory experience ($60 pp), longer 1.5-hour ($75 pp) and two-hour adventures ($95 pp), and a three-hour tour that takes you out to McGillivray Lake ($150 pp). The minimum age is 14.

Rest Stop: Salmon Arm

If you need a break along Highway 1 as you're driving toward B.C.'s national parks, stop in Salmon Arm, a pleasant town on Shuswap Lake, 68 miles (110 km) east of Kamloops and 65 miles (105 km) west of Revelstoke.

Sights and Activities

Cheese-lovers should detour to **Grass Root Dairies** (1470 50th St. SW, 250/832-4274, www.grassrootdairies.com, 8:30am-5pm Mon.-Sat.), a family-run dairy just west of Salmon Arm that produces delicious gouda and several other varieties of cheese. You can watch the cheesemakers at work while the kids check out the cows in the barn or run around with the chickens. The dairy is about five minutes' drive from Highway 1. From the highway, bear right onto Salmon River Road. Take the first right onto 10th Avenue SW, which will turn left and become 50th Street SW.

Stretch your legs with a walk in **Marine Peace Park at Salmon Arm Wharf** (750 Marine Park Dr. NE, 250/832-4044, www.salmonarm.ca), which has trails along the lake and a boardwalk on the pier, where you might spot ospreys or blue herons. It's a nice spot for a picnic. If you're passing through on a summer evening, you might take in **WOW! Wednesday on the Wharf** (www.salmonarmartscentre.ca, 6:45pm Wed. mid-June-Aug.), a series of free concerts outdoors in the park.

For a more artistic break, see what's happening at the **Salmon Arm Arts Centre** (70 Hudson Ave. NE, 250/832-1170, www.salmonarmartscentre.ca, 11am-4pm Tues.-Sat., donation), which operates a small art gallery.

Food

What's a rest stop without pie? **Shuswap Pie Company** (331A Alexander St. NE, 250/832-7992, www.shuswappiecompany.ca, 7:30am-4:30pm Mon.-Fri., 8:30am-4pm Sat.), a café and bakery in downtown Salmon Arm, sates your baked goods cravings with a variety of savory and sweet pies. The coffee is good, too.

Stand-Up Paddleboarding

On Heffley Lake, off Tod Mountain Road on the way to Sun Peaks Resort, **Paddle Surfit** (2388 Heffley Lake Rd., Heffley Creek, 250/318-0722, www.paddlesurfit.com, 2 hours $50) rents stand-up paddleboards. The two-hour rentals include a lesson as well as all the paddling gear. Call or check the website for hours.

Voyageur Canoe Tours

Northwest Voyageur Canoe Tours (250/578-5268, www.voyageurbistro.ca, daily late-May-Sept.), under the same ownership as the Voyageur Bistro, offers guided paddles on McGillivray Lake in a 30-foot (9-m) replica voyageur canoe, similar to the boats used by Canada's early fur traders and explorers. Your guide will tell you about local history and point out wildlife along the way.

The standard tour is 90 minutes (adults $45, ages 10-16 $27.95, ages 6-9 $16.75). An entertaining add-on is a multi-course "fur trader's feast" (lunch $25 pp, dinner $45 pp), a traditional picnic served lakeside.

Make tour reservations at least 72 hours in advance. Because you need at least six people to paddle these substantial canoes, staff will try to match smaller parties with other groups.

Winter Sports

With a skiable area of 4,270 acres (1,728 ha) spread across three mountains, Sun Peaks Resort is the second-largest **winter sports resort** in Canada (www.sunpeaksresort.com, lift tickets adults $105, seniors and ages 13-18 $84, university students $95, ages 6-12 $53). The ski and snowboard season runs late

November-early April. Thirteen lifts serve 137 trails, rated 10 percent novice, 58 percent intermediate, and 32 percent expert.

Food

The **Voyageur Bistro** (Kookaburra Lodge, 3270 Village Way, 250/578-5268, www.voyageurbistro.ca, 4pm-9pm daily, $14-38) injects some Canadiana into its pub-fare-and-more menu. The soup of the day comes with bannock (a traditional aboriginal fried bread), the burger is made with bison, and the mains include venison with cranberry chutney and *tourtière* (French Canadian meat pie). There's poutine, too, of course. Frequent live music adds Canadian beats.

Specializing in both savory and sweet crepes, like spinach and feta or strawberries with Nutella, **Tod Mountain Café** (3170 Creekside Way, 250/571-0545, call for seasonal hours, $4-10) also serves breakfast all day, sandwiches, and smoothies.

Tiny **Bolacco Café** (Coast Sundance Lodge, 3160 Creekside Way, 250/578-7588, 8am-5pm daily, $4-7) squeezes a lot of good cheer, as well as espresso and fresh-baked pastries, into its pint-size space. Try the berry scones.

Bluebird Market (3250 Village Way, 250/578-2414, 9am-7pm daily) sells basic groceries, snacks, and essentials. Otherwise, the nearest full-service supermarket is in Kamloops, so stock up in advance if you want to prepare your own meals.

Accommodations

Most Sun Peaks accommodations are "ski-in, ski-out," or within walking distance of mountain activities. **Sun Peaks Resort Central Reservations** (250/578-5399, www.sunpeaksresort.com) assists with lodging bookings at the several slope-side hotels and nearby condo buildings. Summer rates are much lower than winter season prices.

Close to the lifts, the large **Sun Peaks**

Grand Hotel and Conference Centre (3240 Village Way, 250/578-6080 or 844/774-7263, www.sunpeaksgrand.com, $159-315, parking $15-20) has an upscale dark-wood lobby and 221 contemporary guest rooms. An outdoor heated pool and three outdoor hot tubs can soak away any adventure-induced aches and pains.

Another handy-to-the-lifts option with two outdoor hot tubs, the condo-style **Hearthstone Lodge** (3170 Creekside Way, 250/578-6969 or 800/811-4588, www.hearthstoneresorthotel.com, $169-255, parking $10-15) has 70 functionally furnished studios and loft studios. Efficiency kitchens come with a full-sized fridge, dishwasher, and cooktop.

Built by Canadian ski racer Nancy Greene, who won a gold medal in the 1968 Winter Olympics, **Nancy Greene's Cahilty Hotel & Suites** (3220 Village Way, 250/578-6969, www.cahiltyhotel.com, $135-304, parking $12) has 150 individually owned units, ranging from compact standard rooms with two queen beds, to two-level loft units, to studios and one- and two-bedroom suites. Many, but not all, have kitchen facilities. Greene and her husband, who live at the hotel, regularly greet guests at Sunday evening receptions.

Information and Services

Contact **Sun Peaks Resort** (1280 Alpine Rd., Sun Peaks, 250/578-5474, www.sunpeaksresort.com) for information about the mountain and various activities. For winter conditions, call the **Snow Report** (250/578-7232).

Tastefull Excursions (250/312-0707 or 844/314-4555, www.tastefullexcursions.ca, one-way adults $50, ages 6-12 $30) runs 50-minute shuttles between Kamloops Airport and Sun Peaks Resort several times a day year-round. Reservations are required at least 72 hours in advance.

To get to Sun Peaks for a day of skiing, you can take the **Mostly Mental Snow Shuttle** (250/828-2558, www.

sunpeaksresort.com, daily Dec.-Mar., one-way $20). The shuttle picks up passengers from locations in Kamloops and takes you to the mountain in the morning, then returns you to town in the afternoon.

Mount Revelstoke National Park

Mount Revelstoke National Park's main attraction is a great drive: the zigzagging Meadows in the Sky Parkway that climbs steeply to an elevation of more than 6,500 feet (2,000 m). From the top of the parkway, you can walk up the only mountain in Canada's national park system that you can summit by hiking just a short distance from your car. And lest you think that this snaking road to the summit is a modern innovation, the parkway was constructed between 1911 and 1927. Work on the road actually began before the region became a national park in 1914.

Located in the Selkirk range of B.C.'s Columbia Mountains, Mount Revelstoke National Park has longer hikes, too, including a number of great day hikes from the Meadows in the Sky summit. Another highlight at the summit area are the summer wildflowers that carpet the slopes with color, peaking in early-mid August.

The visitor season is short here, however; the parkway summit is typically open only July-September. The rest of the year, it's too snow-covered to travel.

Driving from the west along the Trans-Canada Highway (Hwy. 1), the turnoff for Revelstoke, the town closest to the park, is just before you get to the exit for the Meadows in the Sky Parkway. From the east, Highway 1 skirts, and in some cases crosses, the park's southern boundary after passing through Glacier National Park.

You can camp in Mount Revelstoke National Park. Nearby Revelstoke has accommodations, restaurants, and other services.

Visiting the Park
Entrances
The main entrance to Mount Revelstoke National Park is at the base of the Meadows in the Sky Parkway, off Highway 1 near Revelstoke. Highway 1 runs through parts of the park, and some hiking trails begin just off the highway.

Park Passes and Fees
A **day pass** (adults $7.80, seniors $6.80, families $15.70) for Mount Revelstoke National Park is valid until 4pm on the day after you purchase it. You can buy a park pass at the entrance to the Meadows in the Sky Parkway.

Purchasing a Parks Canada **annual discovery pass** (adults $67.70, seniors $57.90, families $136.40), which is valid for a year, is a good deal if you're spending at least a week in one or more parks. It's accepted at more than 100 national parks and national historic sites across Canada. You can buy an annual pass online from Parks Canada (www.pc.gc.ca) or at any park visitors center.

For both day and annual passes, family passes cover up to seven people arriving together in a single vehicle, whether or not they're actually related.

Visitors Centers
Park information is available in Revelstoke at the **Revelstoke Visitor Information Centre** (301 Victoria Rd. W., 250/837-5345 or 800/487-1493, www.seerevelstoke.com, 8:30am-7pm daily July-Aug., 8:30am-4:30pm daily Sept.-June) or the **Parks Canada information office** (301B 3rd St. W., 250/837-7500, www.pc.gc.ca, 8am-noon and 1pm-4:30pm Mon.-Fri.).

Getting Around
While Mount Revelstoke National Park is located just outside the town of Revelstoke, there are no public

Two Days in B.C.'s National Parks

You really need more than two days to take in even the highlights of B.C.'s national parks, but here's how to make the most of a short trip through the mountains, stopping in Mount Revelstoke, Glacier, and Yoho National Parks.

Day 1

Get an early start with a drive up Mount Revelstoke's **Meadows in the Sky Parkway.** The winding road that climbs to an elevation of more than 6,500 feet (2,000 m) opens at 8am daily in summer. From the parking area, catch the free shuttle to the summit, where you can hike one of the loop trails to capture the views across the mountains.

Head down the Parkway and stop in **Revelstoke** at the **Revelstoke Railway Museum** to learn about the railroad's importance in the development of this mountain region. After a quick lunch at **La Baguette,** start heading east along Highway 1.

Stretch your legs with a walk on the **Skunk Cabbage Boardwalk Trail** or the **Giant Cedars Boardwalk Trail,** short walkways that highlight different local ecosystems.

Continue east into **Glacier National Park,** enjoying the vistas of the mountains. Stop into the **Rogers Pass Discovery Centre** to explore the exhibits and watch one of the informative films about avalanche control, bear safety, or other eco-topics.

Your destination for dinner is the **Restaurant at Heather Mountain Lodge** for creative mountain fare. Remember if you're booking a dinner reservation that you've crossed into a new time zone—it's an hour later here than the B.C. coast. Spend the night at the lodge or continue into **Golden** for more lodging options.

Day 2

In the morning, if you're up for an adventure, go **rafting on the Kicking Horse River,** then drive east into **Yoho National Park.** If you have time, hike to **Wapta Falls** near the park's western entrance; it's the largest waterfall along the Kicking Horse River. Closer to the center of the park, stop to see the unusual **Natural Bridge** en route to gorgeous **Emerald Lake.** Hike the trail that loops around the lake, rent a canoe for a leisurely paddle, and take lots of photos.

Have dinner and stay in Yoho at one of the lodges: **Emerald Lake Lodge, Cathedral Mountain Lodge,** or, in the tiny town of Field, **Truffle Pigs.**

In the morning, try to take at least one more hike, perhaps to **Takakkaw Falls** or, if you've booked ahead, to **Lake O'Hara.** Then relax, knowing that you've seen the highlights of three of British Columbia's spectacular mountain national parks.

transportation options or shuttle services that operate to or within the park. You need a car to get around.

★ Meadows in the Sky Parkway

The park's 16-mile (26-km) **Meadows in the Sky Parkway** climbs steeply from an elevation of 1,315 feet (400 m) to over 6,500 feet (2,000 m). As the road rises and twists around the 16 switchbacks, snaking its way up the mountain, you can stop at several viewpoints; the Revelstoke Viewpoint looks down on the town in the valley below, while other lookouts offer vistas across the mountains.

It's not just about the drive, though. Once you reach the end of the parkway, you can access a number of hiking trails, ranging from easy to challenging.

You'll need to leave your car at the Balsam Lake parking lot, since the road is not open to private cars all the way to the mountain summit. From the parking area, it's a 0.6-mile (1-km) walk to the summit, either on the **Upper Summit Trail,** a gently climbing, wooded, dirt and gravel path, or along the road. Alternatively, take the free **summit shuttle bus** (10am-5:30pm daily July-early Sept., 10am-4:30pm early Sept.-early Oct., weather permitting), which runs every 15-20 minutes, up to the Heather Lake summit area. If you're heading up late in the day, confirm the time that the last shuttle returns. Before or after your time at the summit, take a few minutes to walk around tiny **Balsam Lake.**

Allow about three hours for your Meadows in the Sky excursion. It takes 35-45 minutes to drive each way, plus time to get from the parking lot to the summit area. Plan at least an hour to hike and enjoy the views at the summit; you could easily spend an entire day if you'd like to do one of the longer hikes.

The parkway is generally open May-October, but snow can remain at higher elevations until July or August, which means that the summit area is typically accessible only between mid-late July and late September. Confirm road conditions and open hours with park staff before you set out.

The **Meadows in the Sky Parkway Entrance Station** (8am-5pm daily mid-June-early Sept., 9am-5pm daily mid-May-mid-June and early Sept.-early Oct.) is 0.5 mile (0.8 km) northeast of Revelstoke off Highway 1.

The parkway closes to uphill drivers at 5:30pm, but you can return downhill until 8:30pm mid-June-early September, until 6:30pm mid-May-mid-June and September, and until 5:30pm in October.

Bring water and whatever food you might need; there are restrooms but no other services along the Meadows in the Sky Parkway and at the summit area. Bring extra layers of clothing, too, since it's always cooler up on the mountain than it is in town.

rest stop along the Meadows in the Sky Parkway

Hiking

Mount Revelstoke National Park has several trails from the summit area of the Meadows in the Sky Parkway. Other trails are off the parkway at lower elevations, and additional trails are to the east, off Highway 1.

From the Meadows in the Sky Summit

You get panoramic views across the mountains and down to the Columbia River from the **Firetower Trail,** a gentle 0.3-mile (480-m) climb to the 1927 Summit Firetower, a cabin with a cupola-style lookout on top. Park firefighters used the tower as a lookout until 1987, when satellite fire monitoring and aerial fire patrols replaced the human guards.

Another easy trail is the **First Footsteps Trail,** a 0.5-mile (0.8-km) loop, which has First Nations art, interpretive panels, and viewpoints along the way. You can also follow the 10-minute

Heather Lake Trail around the subalpine lake of the same name.

If you have more time, an excellent intermediate-level hike follows the **Eva Lake Trail** through wildflower meadows and boulder fields to a beautiful alpine lake, which is named for Eva Hobbs, a Revelstoke teacher and avid hiker who discovered the lake on a 1909 outing with the Revelstoke Mountaineering Club. The trail is 8.5 miles (14 km) round-trip. Along the way, you have the option to make a short detour to **Miller Lake.**

A more difficult hike climbs the **Jade Lakes Trail** (11 mi/18 km round-trip), crossing Jade Lake Pass into the alpine regions above the tree line. The Eva Lake, Miller Lake, and Jade Lakes Trails all start from the same point but divide along the way.

From the Meadows in the Sky Parkway

Nels Nelson (1894-1943) emigrated from his native Norway to Revelstoke, where he became known for his ski jumping prowess, making several record-setting jumps in the 1920s. You can follow in his footsteps—or stand in his (virtual) skis—with a hike on the **Nels' Knickers Trail.** At the trail's summit, you can lean into his "knickers," a metal sculpture outlining Nelson's body, crouched as if to jump, on a platform cantilevered out above the hill. It's a fun photo op. The easiest way to reach the Nels' Knickers platform is from the upper trailhead off the Meadows in the Sky Parkway at 0.8 mile (1.4 km); from there, you can follow a flat path for a 5- to 10-minute walk to the sculpture. Alternatively, you can park in the Nels Nelsen parking lot and hike up the short (less than 0.5 mi/0.8 km) but steep trail to the platform.

From Highway 1

As you travel Highway 1 between Revelstoke and Glacier National Park, you can stop off for several easy walks that illustrate different ecosystems within Mount Revelstoke National Park.

Have you ever seen a giant skunk cabbage? They look like, well, gigantic cabbages, and you can see them as you wander across the marshes and wetlands along the **Skunk Cabbage Boardwalk Trail,** an easy 0.75-mile (1.2-km) loop. If you visit in May when their yellow flowers bloom, you'll understand the "skunk" component of the name. The trail is 17 miles (27 km) east of Revelstoke, off Highway 1.

You typically find temperate rainforest climates along the British Columbia coast and in other coastal regions. B.C.'s Columbia Mountains, including sections of Mount Revelstoke National Park, house the world's only *inland* temperate rainforest, including plentiful old-growth forests where western red cedar and western hemlock predominate. Explore this old-growth forest on the **Giant Cedars Boardwalk Trail,** a 0.3-mile (480-m) boardwalk that loops past massive cedars, some of which are more than 500 years old. The trail starts 19 miles (30 km) east of Revelstoke.

Camping

A 50-site campground, accommodating tents and RVs, is slated to open in 2019 near the entry kiosk along the Meadows in the Sky Parkway at the base of Mount Revelstoke. Check the park website for updates and rates.

Revelstoke

Transportation, forestry, and tourism drive the economy of Revelstoke, a community of 7,500 in B.C.'s Selkirk and Monashee Mountains. Located on the Columbia River outside Mount Revelstoke National Park, the town is an outdoor-oriented place, drawing hikers and cyclists in summer, and skiers and snowboarders during the colder months. Revelstoke Mountain Resort is famous for its powder skiing; the area gets 40-60 feet (12-18 m) of snow in a typical winter season.

Sights and Recreation

Located in the town's former post office, the **Revelstoke Museum** (315 1st St. W., 250/837-3067, www.revelstokemuseum. ca, 10am-5pm Mon.-Sat., 11am-5pm Sun., adults $5, seniors $4, ages 13-18 $2, families $12) helps answer the question, "Why is Revelstoke here?" It's because of the railroad that the modern-day town developed, beginning in the 1880s as a construction base for workers building the transcontinental railroad. When the trains began to run—10 passenger trains every day once passed through town—the Canadian Pacific Railway was the region's major employer, drawing workers from across Canada and from China, Italy, and Scandinavia. Those Scandinavian settlers helped introduce Revelstoke to the sport that dominates today's tourism economy: skiing.

To learn more about Revelstoke's railroad history, including how the railroad was built and the people who built it, visit the **Revelstoke Railway Museum** (719 Track St. W., 250/837-6060, www. railwaymuseum.com, 9am-5pm daily May-mid-Oct., adults $10, seniors $8, ages 8-17 $5, ages 4-7 $2, families $22). Inside you can climb aboard a steam locomotive or imagine traveling in high style in the 1929 "Business Car No. 4," where the white tablecloths are set for dinner. Practice your skills as an engineer on the diesel locomotive simulator, or explore the stories of the Chinese railroad workers. Outside are more historic rail cars, including a coal car, a snowplow, and a caboose. You don't have to be a train buff to enjoy this well-designed museum.

North America's fourth-largest river, the Columbia, starts in British Columbia and flows through Washington and Oregon to the Pacific Ocean. The massive Revelstoke Dam, completed in 1984 after

Revelstoke

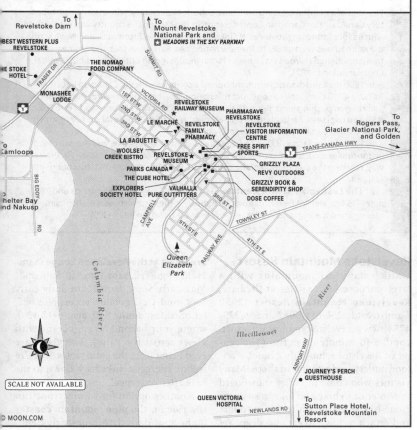

To
Revelstoke Dam

To
Mount Revelstoke
National Park and
★ MEADOWS IN THE SKY PARKWAY

BEST WESTERN PLUS
REVELSTOKE

HE STOKE
HOTEL

THE NOMAD
FOOD COMPANY

MONASHEE
LODGE

FRASER DR

SUMMIT RD

VICTORIA RD

1ST ST W

2ND ST W

3RD ST W

REVELSTOKE
RAILWAY MUSEUM ★

LE MARCHÉ

LA BAGUETTE

PHARMASAVE
REVELSTOKE

REVELSTOKE
FAMILY
PHARMACY

REVELSTOKE
VISITOR INFORMATION
CENTRE

FREE SPIRIT
SPORTS

To
Rogers Pass,
Glacier National Park,
and Golden

TRANS-CANADA HWY

WOOLSEY
CREEK BISTRO

REVELSTOKE
MUSEUM ★

PARKS CANADA

THE CUBE HOTEL

EXPLORERS
SOCIETY HOTEL

VALHALLA
PURE OUTFITTERS

GRIZZLY PLAZA

REVY OUTDOORS

GRIZZLY BOOK &
SERENDIPITY SHOP

DOSE COFFEE

CAMPBELL AVE

9TH ST E

RAILWAY AVE

3RD ST E

TOWNLEY ST

4TH ST E

To
Kamloops

BIG EDD
RD

o
helter Bay
nd Nakusp

Columbia River

Queen
Elizabeth
Park

Illecillewaet River

AIRPORT WAY

JOURNEY'S PERCH
GUESTHOUSE

SCALE NOT AVAILABLE

© MOON.COM

QUEEN VICTORIA
HOSPITAL

NEWLANDS RD

To
Sutton Place Hotel,
Revelstoke Mountain
Resort

eight years of construction, harnesses the Columbia to produce electricity, generating 25 percent of B.C.'s power. At the **Revelstoke Dam Visitor Centre** (Hwy. 23, 250/814-6697 or 800/224-9376, http://bchydro.com/revelstoke, 10am-4pm daily mid-May-early Sept., adults $6, seniors and ages 6-17 $5, families $15), 3 miles (5 km) north of Revelstoke via Highway 23, you can learn about the dam's construction and operation; take the elevator up to a viewing area at the top of the dam 30 stories above the river. B.C. Hydro, the provincial electric company, runs

the visitors center, so the exhibits have an industry perspective, but they're still interesting if you're curious about rivers, dams, and power generation.

For a short hike in town, follow the paved **Revelstoke Greenbelt Trails.** One route starts in Centennial Park, behind the Revelstoke Community Centre (600 Campbell Ave.), and meanders east along the Columbia and Illecillewaet Rivers. Another option is the Revelstoke Dyke Walk; cross the Big Eddy Bridge from Wilson Avenue at the west end of town and turn left onto the dyke.

The Last Spike

The idea of a railroad crossing the entire continent became an obsession in 19th-century Canada. After Canadian Confederation in 1867, when the country was established with its four founding provinces of Ontario, Quebec, New Brunswick, and Nova Scotia, the railroad was seen as key to the new nation's expansion. In fact, the promise of a transcontinental railroad was a major factor in convincing British Columbia to join the Confederation in 1871.

In 1880 the Canadian government signed a contract with the Canadian Pacific Railway (CPR) Company to construct this national rail line, and construction immediately began pushing west. Because the CPR couldn't recruit enough workers in B.C., it looked overseas, particularly to China. Roughly 15,000 Chinese laborers eventually helped build Canada's transcontinental railroad.

In 1885, Craigellachie, B.C, in the mountains west of Revelstoke, was the site of a historic milestone. It's where the last spike was driven along the Canadian Pacific Railway, marking the completion of the country's 3,100-mile (5,000-km) transcontinental railroad.

At **The Last Spike Visitor Centre,** 103 miles (165 km) east of Kamloops and 28 miles (45 km) west of Revelstoke along Highway 1, there's a historical marker commemorating the event, as well as restrooms and a gift shop (May-Oct.).

Revelstoke Mountain Resort

Unlike many ski mountains with a large purpose-built village at the base, **Revelstoke Mountain Resort** (2950 Camozzi Rd., 250/814-0087 or 866/373-4754, www.revelstokemountainresort.com), a 10-minute drive from the center of Revelstoke, has only a hotel, a few food outlets, and a couple of shops. Many visitors who come to ski or snowboard in winter or to hike and bike in summer come to the mountain to get outdoors and return to town to eat and sleep. Yet there's plenty to do at this 3,121-acre (1,263-ha) mountain resort, which, at 5,620 feet (1,713 m), has North America's greatest vertical drop.

Summer Activities

Although Revelstoke's peak season is winter, the resort offers some summer activities, too, including a network of lift-accessed **hiking trails,** ranging from beginner-friendly to expert-only routes. Most trails start at the top of the **upper gondola** (8:30am-5pm late June-early Sept., adults $30, ages 6-12 $15).

You can take the lower gondola partway up the mountain for a **buffet breakfast at the Revelation Lodge** (8am-11am Mon.-Fri., 8am-1pm Sat.-Sun. mid-May-early Sept., 8am-11am daily early Sept.-mid-Oct., gondola access plus buffet breakfast adults $40, ages 6-12 $20), where your bacon and eggs come with views across the valley. The vistas are even better from the patio tables. If you're feeling energetic, hike back down to the base after your meal.

Another option for summertime fun is a ride on the **pipe mountain coaster** (8am-8pm daily late June-early Sept., 9am-5pm daily mid-May-late June and early Sept.-mid-Oct., ages 8 and over $25 per ride), which whizzes 0.9 mile (1.4 km) through the forest between the Revelation Lodge and the mountain base.

Summer lift tickets are discounted if you buy them online in advance, and reduced-rate packages combining mountain activities are also available.

Winter Sports

Revelstoke Mountain is open for **skiing and snowboarding** (www.revelstokemountainresort.com, adults $109, seniors and ages 13-18 $89, ages 6-12 $44) late November or early

December-mid-April. The mountain's ski and snowboard terrain leans heavily toward the expert and intermediate categories. Only 7 percent of the 69 runs are classified as "beginner." Lift ticket prices vary with the season and the number of days purchased; you can usually save money buying your tickets online in advance.

Other winter activities include **snowshoe tours** (1.5-2.5 hours, adults $40-60, ages 11-16 $25-50, ages 8-10 free) and **dog-sled tours** (3 hours, $199 single, $279 double). Book online or through the resort's activity center.

Events
Every evening in late June-end of August, head downtown for **free live music** (6:30pm-9:30pm), outdoors at Grizzly Plaza (Mackenzie Ave. at Victoria Rd.), with bands from across the region.

Shopping
If you need clothing or gear for your outdoor adventures, look in downtown Revelstoke, where sport shops include **Free Spirit Sports** (203 1st St. W., 250/837-9453, www.freespiritsports. com, 9:30am-6pm Mon.-Thurs. and Sat., 9:30am-10pm Fri.), **Revy Outdoors** (201 Mackenzie Ave., 250/814-2575, 10am-6pm Mon.-Sat., 11am-5pm Sun.), and **Valhalla Pure Revelstoke** (213 Mackenzie Ave., 250/837-5517, www.vpo.ca, 9:30am-7pm Mon.-Sat., 10:30am-6pm Sun.).

You don't know what treasures you might find at the **Grizzly Book and Serendipity Shop** (208 Mackenzie Ave., 250/837-6185, www.grizzlybook.com, 9:30am-5:30pm Mon.-Sat.), part independent bookstore and part jewelry and gift shop. It's been supplying Revelstoke with things to read since 1989.

Top to bottom: historic rail cars at the Revelstoke Railway Museum; Woolsey Creek Bistro; The Cube Hotel.

Food

A sunny yellow house is home to the accomplished ★ **Woolsey Creek Bistro** (604 2nd St. W., 250/837-5500, www. woolseycreekbistro.ca, 5pm-9pm daily, $21-26), where you can enjoy world-rambling creations in a spacious casual dining room or on the outdoor patio. The simple house salad of greens and goat cheese is first-rate, while mains might range from confit duck leg with calendula risotto, to grilled salmon paired with cilantro-mint harissa and a grilled vegetable salad, to short ribs braised in local beer. Save room for a dessert like the dark-chocolate truffle cake or a fresh fruit sorbet.

You'd expect that an eatery named ★ **La Baguette** (607 Victoria Rd., Unit 103, 250/837-3755, 6:30am-5pm daily, $5-16) would make excellent breads and pastries, and you'd be right; the shop even bakes its own bagels. But this popular café doesn't stop there. First-rate coffee plus a changing assortment of sandwiches, pizzas, and pastas round out the menu. The same owners run **Le Marché** (607 Victoria Rd., Unit 101, 9am-8pm daily), a gourmet grocery around the corner, where you can pick up charcuterie, well-priced cheeses, organic produce, and some prepared foods—perfect for picnicking in the national parks.

Pull up a chair under the street art-style wall mural and stay awhile at **Dose Coffee** (101 2nd St. E., 250/837-6215, www.dosecoffee.ca, 6:30am-5pm daily, $7-12). This hip Revelstoke hangout can kick-start your morning with well-made espresso drinks, smoothie bowls, and breakfast sandwiches, or refresh you with soups, salads, and baked goods all day.

Nomads and locals alike stop into **The Nomad Food Company** (1601 Victoria St. W., 250/837-4211, 11am-9pm daily summer, 11am-8pm daily winter, $7-15) for cooked-to-order burgers, paninis, poutine, and other diner-style fare. With a few tables inside and picnic tables out in the parking lot, it's nothing fancy, but everything is hearty, fresh, and moderately priced.

Accommodations

Revelstoke has several chain motels along Highway 1, but it's much nicer to get off the highway and into town.

Under $150

Located downtown, ★ **The Cube Hotel** (311 Campbell Ave., 250/837-4086, www. cubehotel.ca, $72-140) pairs the relaxed vibe of a simple guesthouse with the style of a modern boutique hotel. Guests can hang out in the cool communal lounge space with lime-green walls and overstuffed couches, where a complimentary continental breakfast is served. You can prep meals in the shared kitchen. The 21 no-frills guest rooms provide a space to sleep, plus essentials like free Wi-Fi, flat-screen TVs, sinks, and toilets; seven individual shower rooms are down the hall.

An updated roadside motel on the west end of town, **The Stoke Hotel** (1911 Fraser Dr., 250/837-5221 or 877/837-5221, www.stokehotel.ca, $99-149) has simple rooms with a dose of quirky style. Outfitted with a mix of old wooden cabinets and newer pieces, like bright blue metal chairs, rooms all have interesting wall art, plus coffeemakers, microwaves, and mini fridges. Red plaid pillows and other Canadiana decorate the lobby, and you can head upstairs to the diner-style breakfast room for a basic continental spread.

Located in a former church, **Journey's Perch Guesthouse** (1502 Mountain View Dr., 250/683-8708, www.journeysperch. com, $45-53 dorms, $110-135 d) is friendly place to rest, with a contemporary hostel vibe. The three comfortable private rooms and the four-bed dorms share three modern baths. There's plenty of common space, from a communal kitchen to a sitting room with original stained-glass windows. Rates include continental breakfast, Wi-Fi, and free passes to the local aquatic center.

$150-300

It may be hard to get back on the road once you've settled into the rooftop hot tub at the ★ **Explorers Society Hotel** (111 1st St. W., 250/814-2565 or 855/814-2565, www.explorers-society.com, $199-259), a design-conscious boutique lodging in a 1911 heritage building downtown. The nine guest rooms—six standard units and three larger suites with sitting areas—mix historical features, like original brick walls, with geometric-patterned black-and-gray throws, exposed concrete, and other chic contemporary elements. French press coffee pots, minibars stocked with local craft beer and cider, Internet-connected TVs, and Wi-Fi are among the amenities. Staff set up a self-serve breakfast in the top-floor lounge with its mid-century modern furnishings and mountain-view terrace. The lobby-level **Quartermaster Eatery** takes you between North and South America with dishes like Peruvian-style chicken with smashed yams, mesquite-grilled wild salmon, and grass-fed steaks. Vegans (or veggie-lovers) should consider the house-made morel sausages paired with roasted vegetables.

Over $300

In the contemporary condo-style **Sutton Place Hotel Revelstoke Mountain Resort** (2950 Camozzi Rd., 250/814-5000 or 866/378-8866, www.suttonplace.com/revelstoke, $130-522 d, 2-bedroom suite $225-802, 3-bedroom suite $297-942), at the base of Revelstoke Mountain Resort, 205 suites, ranging from studios to three-bedroom units, all have fireplaces, fully equipped kitchens, and washer-dryers. Other amenities include an outdoor heated pool and hot tub, a spacious fitness room, a spa, and underground parking. In winter, you're steps from the lifts; in summer, you can go exploring with one of the complimentary mountain bikes.

Information and Services

Staff at the **Revelstoke Visitor Information Centre** (301 Victoria Rd. W., 250/837-5345 or 800/487-1493, www.seerevelstoke.com, 8:30am-7pm daily July-Aug., 8:30am-4:30pm daily Sept.-June) can assist with information about the Revelstoke region and other destinations across the province. If you're interested in hiking, staff can advise you about area trails and provide a hiking map. Pick up the free Tourism Revelstoke guide to the area here; it's also available online.

Parks Canada maintains a year-round information office (301B 3rd St. W., 250/837-7500, www.pc.gc.ca, 8am-noon and 1pm-4:30pm Mon.-Fri.) in the city's post office building.

The emergency room at Revelstoke's **Queen Victoria Hospital** (1200 Newlands Rd., 250/837-2131, www.interiorhealth.ca) is open 24 hours daily, seven days a week. Local pharmacies include **Pharmasave Revelstoke** (307 W. Victoria Rd., 250/837-2028, www.pharmasaverevelstoke.com, 9am-8pm Mon.-Thurs., 9am-9pm Fri., 9am-6pm Sat., 11am-5pm Sun.) and **Revelstoke Family Pharmacy** (555 Victoria Rd., 250/837-5191, www.pharmachoice.com, 9am-6pm Mon.-Sat., 11am-4pm Sun.).

Getting Around

Revelstoke's downtown area is compact and walkable. The community has limited bus service, run by **B.C. Transit** (250/837-3888, http://bctransit.com/revelstoke, 8am-6pm Mon.-Sat., adults $2, seniors and ages 5-17 $1.75). To explore the national parks outside town, you need a car.

When Revelstoke Mountain Resort is open for skiing and riding in winter, **Everything Revelstoke Resort Express** (250/837-5044, www.everythingrevelstoke.com, one-way $4) runs frequent shuttles between downtown and the mountain.

Glacier National Park

As you might guess from its name, Glacier National Park is known for the broad glaciers and jagged mountains that populate its 333,000-acre (135,000-ha) expanse. Established in 1886 along with Yoho National Park, not long after the completion of Canada's transcontinental railroad, it was British Columbia's first national park and the second national park in Canada, after Banff. It is not connected to the U.S. national park of the same name.

Most early visitors to Glacier National Park came by rail, after the transcontinental railroad opened the region to tourism. It wasn't until 1962 when the Rogers Pass section of the Trans-Canada Highway, which runs east-west across the park, was completed and visitors began road-tripping in and around the park.

A number of sights and short hiking trails are just off the Trans-Canada (Hwy. 1). If you're short on time, go directly to the **Rogers Pass Discovery Centre,** which has well-designed exhibits about the park and the surrounding areas.

Visiting the Park

The best months to visit Glacier National Park are July-early September. Much of the park's terrain is at high mountain elevations, and the region gets heavy snow during the winter months. While the park is technically open year-round, the weather makes many areas inaccessible between October and May. Park staff advise contacting them before visiting in spring (Apr.-June) or fall (Sept.-Oct.) for an update on road conditions and to confirm what's open.

TIP: Fill your gas tank in Revelstoke or Golden. There are no gas stations or other services between these two towns or anywhere in Glacier National Park.

Entrances

The Trans-Canada Highway (Hwy. 1) runs through Glacier National Park. Glacier's western boundary is 10 miles (16 km) east of Mount Revelstoke National Park. The east entrance is 35 miles (56 km) west of Golden.

Park Passes and Fees

There is no entrance gate when you approach Glacier National Park from the west, so purchase your park pass at the **Revelstoke Visitor Information Centre**. Similarly, if you're coming from the east, you can buy a park pass at the **Golden Visitor Centre.** If your first stop in Glacier National Park will be the visitors center at Rogers Pass, purchase your pass there.

A **day pass** (adults $7.80, seniors $6.80, families $19.60) for Glacier National Park is valid until 4pm on the day after you purchase it.

Buying a Parks Canada **annual discovery pass** (adults $67.70, seniors $57.90, families $136.40), which is valid for a year, is a good deal if you're spending at least a week in one or more parks. It's valid at more than 100 national parks and national historic sites across Canada. Buy your annual pass online from Parks Canada (www.pc.gc.ca) or at any park visitors center.

For both day and annual passes, the family passes cover up to seven people in a single vehicle, whether or not they're actually related.

If you're driving through the park along Highway 1 without stopping, a park pass isn't required. However, you need a pass if you get out of your car anywhere within the park boundaries.

Visitors Centers

The **Rogers Pass Discovery Centre,** which houses the **Glacier National Park Visitor Centre** (Hwy. 1, 250/837-7500, www.pc.gc.ca, 8am-7pm daily mid-June-early Sept., 9am-5pm daily May-mid-June and early Sept.-mid Nov., 7am-4pm daily mid-Nov.-Apr.), is at the Rogers Pass summit, 45 miles (72 km) east of Revelstoke and 50 miles (80 km) west of Golden.

Reservations
Glacier National Park's campgrounds are first-come, first-served; reservations are not possible.

Getting Around
There are no public transportation options or shuttle services that operate in Glacier National Park, so you need to have a car to get around.

Rogers Pass
The coast-to-coast Trans-Canada Highway is the longest highway in the world, running 4,849 miles (7,821 km) from Victoria, on British Columbia's Vancouver Island, to St. John's, Newfoundland. It was officially completed at **Rogers Pass,** in Glacier National Park, which helped open the region for tourism. Canadian prime minister John Diefenbaker led the opening ceremony at the pass in 1962.

You can learn more about the highway's history and construction, as well as the area's wildlife and weather, with the informative exhibits at the **Rogers Pass Discovery Centre** (Hwy. 1, 250/837-7500, www.pc.gc.ca, 8am-7pm daily mid-June-early Sept., 9am-5pm daily May-mid-June and early Sept.-mid-Nov., 7am-4pm daily mid-Nov.-Apr.), which is also the park's visitors center.

At an elevation of 4,364 feet (1,330 m), Rogers Pass is the third-highest point on the Trans-Canada Highway, and the pass is all too frequently closed in winter due to heavy snow or avalanche danger. If you have time, watch the film *The Snow Wars,* about managing avalanche risks. Although the film was made in the late 1970s, and communications technology (and hairstyles) have advanced, technicians still use the same processes

for testing the snow quality to predict avalanche risk and use blasts of the same military howitzers to trigger controlled avalanches around the region. You can see those howitzers on display in front of the Discovery Centre as well.

The Rogers Pass Discovery Centre is at the Rogers Pass summit, 45 miles (72 km) east of Revelstoke and 50 miles (80 km) west of Golden.

Hiking
Glacier National Park has 87 miles (140 km) of hiking trails. Some park trails are just off Highway 1, but they're not always well marked. Watch carefully for signs as you approach your stopping point.

Check the **Parks Canada Trail Conditions Report** (www.pc.gc.ca) online or ask about trail status at the **Glacier National Park Visitor Centre** before setting out on any long hikes.

Hemlock Grove
The **Hemlock Grove Trail** is a short 0.2-mile (350-m) boardwalk trail that loops through old-growth cedars and hemlocks. These trees are big! The trail is on the west side of the park, on the north side of Highway 1.

Rock Garden
For mountain views, follow the **Rock Garden Trail** up a series of rock staircases and stepping-stones. A 0.25-mile (400-m) loop, it's not long, but a few sections can be steep and slippery in wet weather. Like the Hemlock Grove Trail, the trailhead is on the west side of the park, on the north side of Highway 1.

Bear Creek Falls
The 0.6-mile (1-km) **Bear Creek Falls Trail** leads down a short, somewhat steep trail to a pretty waterfall. The turnoff from Highway 1 is sharp and not well marked, so watch carefully for the trailhead sign, 5.5 miles (9 km) east of the park visitors center.

Time Zones

While most of British Columbia is in the Pacific time zone and Alberta is in the mountain time zone, some B.C. national parks and communities close to the Alberta border are on mountain time. Here's how to set your clocks:

♦ **Revelstoke:** Pacific time

♦ **Mount Revelstoke National Park:** Pacific time

♦ **Glacier National Park:** Pacific time

♦ **Golden:** mountain time

♦ **Yoho National Park:** mountain time

♦ **Kootenay National Park:** mountain time

♦ **Fernie:** mountain time

♦ **Cranbrook:** mountain time

Avalanche Crest

For a longer day hike, the **Avalanche Crest Trail,** 5 miles (8 km) round-trip, climbs from the trailhead in the Illecillewaet Campground (1.9 mi/3 km west of the Rogers Pass summit) up into an alpine basin, where you have panoramic views over Rogers Pass. This steep trail has an elevation gain of 2,600 feet (800 m). Allow at least five hours for the hike.

Asulkan Valley

The **Asulkan Valley Trail** takes you to the tongue of the Illecillewaet Glacier. Another steep route, this trail starts gently as it leaves the trailhead in the Illecillewaet Campground, but after the 2.5-mile (4-km) mark, the pitch goes up much more sharply. The trail is 8.6 miles (13.8 km) round-trip, with an elevation gain of 2,850 feet (869 m). Plan 6-7 hours for this hike.

Food and Accommodations

Glacier National Park has three rustic drive-in campgrounds, but no other accommodations or food concessions. The park is close enough to the towns of Revelstoke and Golden that staying in either of these communities is an option.

If you don't want to camp, the best accommodations near the park are the **Heather Mountain Lodge & Cabins** (5400 Hwy. 1 W., Golden, 250/344-7490 or 866/344-7490, www.heathermountainlodge.com, mid-June-mid-Sept., $154-257 d, $300 cabin), 1.2 miles (2 km) outside the park's east gate. The 22 mountain-style guest rooms in a two-story motel block have been updated with light wood furnishings, modern baths, flat-screen TVs, free Wi-Fi, and Nespresso machines. Even nicer, and far more romantic, are the two private log cabins, with king beds, woodstoves, in-floor heating, rain showers, and deep soaker tubs. The lodge is 53 miles (85 km) east of Revelstoke and 33 miles (53 km) west of Golden. December-mid-April, the lodge is reserved for clients booked on heli-skiing trips with its sister company, **Great Canadian Heli-Skiing** (250/344-2326 or 866/424-4354, http://canadianheli-skiing.com).

Serving creative mountain fare, the **Restaurant at Heather Mountain Lodge**

(8am-10am and 6pm-9pm daily late June-mid-Sept., $24-42) is worth a stop, even if you're not staying at the lodge. Among the hearty mains, look for mustard-crusted rack of lamb or free-range Alberta beef tenderloin. The dining room, with a high wood-beamed ceiling and a stone fireplace, looks out to the nearby mountains. If you're making a reservation, note that the lodge is in mountain time zone, the same as Alberta but one hour later than Glacier National Park and the B.C. coast.

Camping

Glacier National Park's three campgrounds, all along Highway 1 near the center of the park, are open only during the summer months. Since reservations aren't accepted, plan to arrive before noon to make sure you get the site you want.

None of the campgrounds have showers, RV hookups, or laundry facilities. Most sites are designed to accommodate tents or small RVs, so if you're driving a big rig, you might need to look elsewhere.

The largest camping area, 60-site **Illecillewaet Campground** (late June-early Oct., $21.50), is 1.9 miles (3 km) west of the Rogers Pass summit. The **Loop Brook Campground** (July-Sept., $21.50), 3 miles (5 km) west of the summit, has 20 campsites. Both of these campgrounds have restrooms with flush toilets and drinking water.

The park also has a 15-site primitive campground, **Mount Sir Donald Campground,** with no facilities, 0.6 mile (1 km) west of the Loop Brook Campground. However, due to a spruce beetle infestation, this campground has been temporarily closed; check with the park office for updates.

Golden and Vicinity

One of the most centrally located towns in the B.C. Rockies, Golden makes a good base for visiting the region's national parks. It's set between Glacier to the west and Yoho to the east; Mount Revelstoke, Kootenay, Lake Louise, and Banff are all within a short drive.

Located at the confluence of the Columbia and Kicking Horse Rivers, the Golden region was an important travel route for indigenous people who lived in the area for millennia. Now its river location makes Golden a center for white-water rafting and river float trips. Just west of town is Kicking Horse Mountain Resort, which offers serious powder skiing in winter and a variety of outdoor experiences during the summer season.

When you're wandering through this town of 3,700, stop to see the **Kicking Horse Pedestrian Bridge** (8th Ave. N.), over the Kicking Horse River. You wouldn't think it's a record-breaker, but at 151 feet (46 m) across, it's the longest freestanding timber-frame pedestrian bridge in Canada.

Note that Golden is in the mountain time zone, the same as Alberta and one hour ahead of Vancouver and the B.C. coast.

Sights and Recreation
★ White-Water Rafting

Golden is a center for white-water rafting, with long stretches of Class III and IV rapids on the Kicking Horse River east of town. Several local outfitters offer half- and full-day **white-water rafting trips** ($99-269), as well as gentler family-oriented rafting tours ($59-89). Many trips have minimum age requirements, so check ahead if you're traveling with kids or teens.

Golden's rafting season typically runs May-September, with the highest river levels and fastest water in June and early July.

Glacier Raft Company (1509 Lafontaine Rd., 250/344-6521 or 877/344-7238, www.glacierraft.com) runs a variety of on-the-water adventures, from an introductory white-water experience to

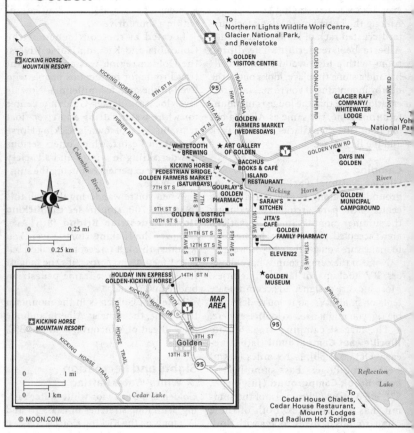

Golden

several wet-and-wild rafting trips; guides can even take you heli-rafting. It also offers a laid-back two-hour guided inflatable **kayak tour** (ages 10 and up $79) that begins on a gentle section of the Kicking Horse River and continues to the point where the Kicking Horse meets the Columbia.

Other Kicking Horse rafting outfitters include **Alpine Rafting** (101 Golden Donald Upper Rd., 250/344-6778 or 888/599-5299, www.alpinerafting.com), **Hydra River Guides** (2936 Kicking Horse Rd., 403/762-4554 or 800/644-8888, www.raftbanff.com), and **Wild**

Water Adventures (2750 Beaverfoot Rd., 403/522-2211 or 888/647-6444, http://wildwater.com).

Northern Lights Wildlife Wolf Centre

For a close-up look at Canada's gray wolves, visit **Northern Lights Wildlife Wolf Centre** (1745 Short Rd., 250/344-6798, www.northernlightswildlife.com, 10am-6pm daily May-June and Sept., 9am-7pm daily July-Aug., noon-5pm daily Oct.-Apr., adults $12, seniors and ages 12-16 $9, ages 4-11 $6, families $35). Housing several gray wolves in outdoor enclosures, this interpretive center offers 25-minute tours, explaining the wolves' habits, food preferences, and pack structure. Schedule your stop here for the morning, if you can, when the animals are typically most active.

The Wolf Centre is 11 miles (18 km) northwest of Golden, off Highway 1.

Museums and Galleries
The small but well-designed **Golden Museum** (1302 11th Ave. S., 250/344-5169, www.goldenbcmuseum.com, 10am-5pm Mon.-Fri., donation) tells the stories of the region's history, from its First Nations and Métis communities to its early explorers, to the importance of the railroad to the region. British explorer David Thompson was the first non-aboriginal person to settle in Golden, when he arrived in 1807 with his Métis wife, Charlotte Small, and their four children as part of a mapping expedition for the Northwest Company. Thompson and Small were married for 55 years and eventually had 14 children, although they remained in the Golden area for just a few years. Later, Golden had one of the earliest Sikh temples in Canada, when many Sikhs moved from the Vancouver region to work in the logging industry.

The **Art Gallery of Golden** (516 9th Ave. N., 250/344-6186, www.kickinghorseculture.ca, 10:30am-5:30pm Mon.-Sat., 11am-4pm Sun. July-Aug., 10:30am-5:30pm Mon.-Sat. Sept.-June) is part gallery and part craft boutique, showing and selling works by regional artists.

Breweries
Golden's first craft brewery, **Whitetooth Brewing** (623 8th Ave. N., 250/344-2838, www.whitetoothbrewing.com, 2pm-10pm daily) has a huge, sunny patio, where you can while away the afternoon with a beer or two, like the Whitetooth Session (a blond ale), the Belgian-style Icefields pale ale, or the malty Directissima Dubbel.

Events
In June, July, and August, **Kicking Horse Culture** (250/344-6186, www.kickinghorseculture.ca) organizes the Summer Kicks series of concerts and other arts events. Check the website or call for the schedule and details.

Food
Contemporary
In a log house on the river, **Island Restaurant** (101 10th Ave., 250/344-2400, www.islandrestaurant.ca, 9am-9pm daily, breakfast $9-17, lunch and dinner $15-33) serves a crowd-pleasing "Canadian mountain fusion" menu that includes sandwiches and salads, house-made pastas, and hearty plates like buffalo in mushroom-brandy sauce. Island is open for breakfast as well. On a warm day, ask for a patio table.

Cedar House Restaurant (735 Hefti Rd., 250/344-4679, www.cedarhousechalets.com, 5pm-10pm daily July-Aug., 5pm-10pm Wed.-Sun. Sept.-June, $28-37) serves contemporary Canadian fare using lots of local organic ingredients. After sipping a glass of B.C. wine or local craft beer, you might sup on a duck confit tart, arctic char in a lemon-ginger cream sauce, or balsamic-braised bison short ribs. In a wood-beamed house with a patio facing the mountains, Cedar House is located off Highway 95 south of town.

Ask Golden residents where to eat, and nearly everyone recommends **Eleven22** (1122 10th Ave. S., 250/344-2443, www.eleven22restaurant.com, 5pm-10pm daily, $16-26), a comfortably upscale bistro in a renovated house. Start with a shared plate like stilton fondue with marinated vegetables, bourbon- and maple-glazed lamb meatballs, or a mountain salad piled with greens, goat cheese, quinoa, yams, and cranberries. The menu crosses the globe with mains like sausage and cabbage, a miso noodle bowl with chicken, pork, and prawns, and duck breast served over couscous with sour

cherry compote, but the drink list leans local with plenty of B.C. beers and wines.

Korean

Sometimes you find interesting food in surprising places. With a few tables inside a local gas station, **Sarah's Kitchen** (818 10th Ave. S., 250/344-2222, www.sarahskitchen.ca, 11am-3pm and 4pm-8:30pm Wed.-Mon., $10-20) cooks up Korean dishes, including bibimbap and *bulgogi,* as well as Japanese-style rice bowls, noodles, and sushi.

Cafés, Bakeries, and Light Bites

Locals sip coffee on the couches at **Jita's Café** (1007 11th Ave. N., 250/344-3660, 7am-7pm daily, $8-11), a colorful hangout with Indian flavors and lots of veggie-friendly options. In addition to coffee drinks and baked goods, the café serves several breakfast dishes (eggs, burritos, bagels), curries (try the vegetarian "curry bliss" with sweet potatoes, white potatoes, lentils, kidney beans, and rice), and sandwiches. The house-made veggie burger is excellent.

Stocking new and used books, **Bacchus Books & Café** (409 9th Ave. N., 250/344-5600, www.bacchusbooks.ca, 9am-5:30pm Mon.-Sat., 10am-5:30pm Sun., $5-13) also has a 2nd-floor eatery. Stop for coffee and pastries or soup and a sandwich; there's a rack of magazines to peruse while you munch.

Groceries and Markets

Tiny **Golden Farmers Market** (www.goldenfarmersmarket.com, noon-5pm Wed., 10am-3pm Sat. mid-June-Sept.) has two downtown locations selling fresh fruits and vegetables, baked goods, and crafts. The Saturday market is in Spirit Square, next to the Kicking Horse Pedestrian Bridge (8th Ave. N.); on Wednesday, the market sets up in the

Top to bottom: beer at Whitetooth Brewing; a curry plate at Jita's Café; Grizzly Bear Interpretive Centre at Kicking Horse Mountain Resort.

parking lot next to the Kicking Horse Chamber of Commerce building (500 10th Ave. N.).

Accommodations and Camping

Most of Golden's chain motels are along or just off Highway 1. More accommodations are available at Kicking Horse Mountain Resort, a 15-minute drive from the town center.

The owners of Glacier Raft Company operate the 10-room **Whitewater Lodge** (1509 Lafontaine Rd., 877/344-7238, www.whitewaterlodge.com, $169-199), with log walls, a games room, and a comfortable lounge. Rates include Wi-Fi and a hearty hot breakfast. You don't have to book a rafting trip to stay here, but if you do want to get out on the water, ask about raft-and-stay packages. No kids under 14 are allowed.

High on a hill off Highway 95 south of town, the ★ **Cedar House Chalets** (735 Hefti Rd., 250/290-0001, www.cedarhousechalets.com, $220-350) are seven contemporary wood-frame cottages, ranging from one to three bedrooms, on 10 acres of forested land. All units have woodstoves, private hot tubs, and decks with barbecues, and they're stocked with board games, flat-screen TVs, and DVD players. The smallest unit, the romantic Adventure Chalet, has a loft bed; the high-ceilinged three-bedroom Mountain View Chalet has the best mountain vistas. Wi-Fi and phone calls (local, national, and even international) are included in the rates. You can have dinner on-site at the **Cedar House Restaurant.**

Jo-Anne and Dave Best came from the UK to ski western Canada's mountains. Their ski holiday turned permanent when they settled on a 68-acre (28-ha) property south of Golden, where they keep horses and rent out three upscale self-catering cottages. The secluded **Mount 7 Lodges** (891 Crandall Rd., 250/344-8973 or 888/344-8973, www.mount7lodges.com, $250-460 for 2-8

people), all built using local wood, include the two-bedroom Deer Lodge, the three-bedroom, two-bath Bear Lodge, and the four-bedroom, four-bath Eagle Lodge. All have open-plan living rooms, full kitchens, private hot tubs, and Wi-Fi included.

Located along the Kicking Horse River at the east end of town, **Golden Municipal Campground** (1411 9th St. S., 250/344-5412 or 866/538-6625, www.goldenmunicipalcampground.com, June-Oct., $35 tent sites, $38-42 electrical sites) has 72 campsites, including 32 with power. There are showers, laundry facilities, and included Wi-Fi.

Information and Services

Tourism Golden (www.tourismgolden.com) operates the seasonal **Golden Visitor Centre** (1000 Trans-Canada Hwy., 250/439-7290, 9am-7pm daily June-mid-Sept., 10am-5pm daily mid-late Sept.), where staff can answer your travel questions. The organization also provides regional information on its website, which has an online trip-planning tool.

The **Golden & District Hospital** (835 9th Ave. S., 250/344-5271, www.interiorhealth.ca) has a 24-hour emergency room. **Gourlay's Golden Pharmacy** (826B 9th Ave. S., 250/344-8600, www.pharmachoice.com, 9am-5pm Mon.-Fri.) and **Golden Family Pharmacy** (1104 10th Ave. S., 250/344-6821, www.pharmachoice.com, 9am-6pm Mon.-Sat., 10am-4pm Sun.) fill prescriptions and sell medical supplies.

★ Kicking Horse Mountain Resort

At **Kicking Horse Mountain Resort** (1500 Kicking Horse Trail, Golden, 250/439-5425 or 866/754-5425, www.kickinghorseresort.com), a mountain playground just outside Golden, there's plenty to do in both summer and winter. The resort is set in the Purcell Mountains, surrounded by the peaks of the Rocky and Selkirk Ranges.

To reach Kicking Horse Mountain, from Highway 95 (10th Ave. N.) in Golden, take 7th Street North toward the river, where it turns right and joins Kicking Horse Drive. Kicking Horse Drive crosses the river, becomes Kicking Horse Trail, and leads up the mountain to the resort, 9 miles (14 km) from Golden.

Summer Activities

For information about all the summer activities at the resort, contact the **Kicking Horse Mountain Activity Centre** (250/439-5425 or 866/754-5425, www.kickinghorseresort.com) at the mountain base.

In summer, you can ride the **Golden Eagle Express Gondola** (10am-2:30pm daily late May-late June, 10am-4:30pm daily late June-Aug., 10am-3pm Mon.-Thurs., 10am-4pm Fri.-Sun. Sept., adults $40.95, seniors and ages 13-17 $34.95, ages 6-12 $19.95, families $94.95) to the mountain summit for sightseeing, hiking, or a meal at the Eagle's Eye Restaurant.

Grizzly Bear Interpretive Centre

Even if you don't spot bears in the wild as you travel across western Canada, you can get close to a grizzly at Kicking Horse Mountain. At the **Grizzly Bear Interpretive Centre** (10am-2pm Mon.-Thurs., 10am-4pm Fri.-Sun. late May-Sept., adults $29.95, seniors and ages 13-17 $24.95, ages 6-12 $14.95, families $69.95), a mountainside bear sanctuary, Boo, an orphaned grizzly bear born in 2002 in B.C.'s northern Cariboo region, roams a 20-acre (8-ha) habitat. You can watch the omnivorous Boo digging, foraging, and munching on seeds, fruits, meat, or sometimes field mice that he hunts. He needs to chow down throughout the summer to reach his average hibernation weight of 750 pounds (340 kg).

Learn more about bears and their habits on one-hour interpretive tours, which run on the hour beginning at 10am (there's no 1pm tour). The best time to visit is in the morning, when Boo is likely to be most active.

To reach the bear reserve, take the Catamount Chairlift from the mountain base. You can purchase tickets for the bear reserve alone (which includes access via the chairlift), or buy an **Adventure Pass** (adults $45.95, seniors and ages 13-17 $38.95, ages 6-12 $22.95, families $106.95) that includes access to the reserve as well as a sightseeing gondola.

Hiking

From the top of the Golden Eagle Express Gondola, you can access several **hiking trails,** from the relatively easy 20- to 30-minute CPR Ridge Walk, which has several lookout points across the mountains, to the challenging Terminator Ridge Hike up to the T2 Summit. Get hiking information and trail maps online or from the resort's Activity Centre.

Via Ferrata

The Kicking Horse **Via Ferrata** (late June-Sept.) is a great adventure, an "iron way" route that enables nonclimbers to experience alpine climbing. The one-hour **Pioneer Route** (adults $85, ages 13-17 $75, families $285) is a good starting point if you've never experienced a Via Ferrata. For more of a challenge, try the two-hour **Discovery Route** (adults $135, ages 13-17 $125, families $419) or the longer **Ascension Route** (adults $175, ages 13-17 $165, families $570), which typically takes 3-4 hours.

Advance reservations are required; call or check the website for specific tour times. No rock-climbing experience is necessary for any of these routes, although you should be generally fit and comfortable with heights.

Mountain Biking

Kicking Horse Mountain's 31 **mountain biking trails** (full-day adults $54.95, seniors and ages 13-17 $40.95, ages 6-12 $26.95, families $127.95), accessed from the **Golden Eagle Express Gondola**

(10am-4:30pm daily late June-Aug., 10am-4:30pm Fri.-Sun. Sept.) or the **Catamount Chairlift** (10am-4pm daily late June-Aug., 10am-4pm Fri.-Sun. Sept.), make up the highest bike park in North America. The trails range from beginner to expert, and both equipment rentals and lessons are available.

Winter Sports

Kicking Horse Mountain Resort is known for the powder conditions on its 120-plus **skiing** and **snowboarding** runs (one-day adults $109.95, seniors $88.95, ages 13-17 $82.95, ages 6-12 $43.95). The mountain covers more than 3,400 acres (1,375 ha), with the fourth-highest vertical drop in North America (4,314 ft/1,314 m). Sixty percent of the terrain is rated "advanced" or "expert." The winter season typically runs mid-December-mid-April.

Food

It's Canada's highest restaurant: At the top of the gondola station on Kicking Horse Mountain, ★ **Eagle's Eye Restaurant** (250/439-5425 or 866/754-5425, www.kickinghorseresort.com, lunch $18-33) perches at 7,700 feet (2,347 m). Whether you ride up in summer to take in the sweeping mountain views (they're great from the picture windows inside and even better from the outdoor patio), or stop to refuel between ski runs in the winter, the creative plates aren't typical ski-café fare. Dig into dishes like grilled chicken panini with bacon jam, a meal-size salad of greens, fruits, candied nuts, and smoked salmon, or Alberta rib eye with peppercorn gravy. The restaurant is open for lunch during both the summer and winter seasons and for dinner ($26-48) on Friday and Saturday evenings December-March; call or check the website for hours. Note that you need to purchase a lift ticket to get to the

Top to bottom: Golden Eagle Express Gondola; views from the top of the Kicking Horse gondola; Golden Visitor Centre.

restaurant; gondola and meal packages are available.

At the gondola base, the **Double Black Café** (www.kickinghorseresort.com, 9am-5pm daily, $5-15) sustains you for your mountain adventures with breakfast sandwiches, hot soup, muffins, gelato, and coffee. Sit on the patio outside or at the window-facing counters indoors, which both look out to the slopes.

Accommodations

Rates at the resort's lodgings are highest during the winter months (Dec.-Mar.), so they can be a good value for a summer stay.

Kicking Horse Lodging (250/439-1160 or 877/754-5486, www.kickinghorselodging.com) manages several accommodations at the resort, including **Glacier Mountaineer Lodge** (1549 Kicking Horse Trail, $169-339 d, 2-bedroom suite $269-379), homey condos just steps from the gondola. In addition to standard hotel rooms, the building has one- and two-bedroom suites with full kitchens, washer-dryers, gas fireplaces, included Wi-Fi, and comfortable lodge-style furnishings. While you might prefer to overlook the ski runs, even the units facing away from the slopes have views to the more distant surrounding mountains. The outdoor hot tub, sauna, and steam room are popular après-ski.

The most surprising place to stay in the Golden area might be at the top of the Kicking Horse Mountain gondola station, where two private suites at the **Eagle's Eye** (250/439-5425 or 866/754-5425, www.kickinghorseresort.com, $900-1,500), above the restaurant of the same name, let you lodge in romantic seclusion at 7,700 feet (2,347 m) elevation. Yes, it's wildly expensive, but rates include a personal butler to pamper you and a private chef to prepare your meals. In winter, you have a private ski guide to show you the best runs, and since you're already at the top of the gondola when the lifts open, you can get into the powder before anyone else. The suites themselves are homey, rather than over-the-top upscale, with pine walls and modern baths, but their views of the mountain peaks are priceless.

Yoho National Park

As you drive through British Columbia's mountain regions, it's hard to imagine that each place you visit could be more stunning than the next. But when you reach Yoho National Park, hugging the provincial boundary between B.C. and Alberta, you have to conclude that the scenery is spectacular. How fitting that the park's name comes from a Cree expression for "wonder" and "awe."

Yoho National Park covers 507 square miles (1,310 sq km) on the western slopes of the Canadian Rockies, between Golden and Lake Louise. More than 30 mountains within the park rise to nearly 10,000 feet (3,000 m). Established in 1886, Yoho now protects stunning glacial lakes, some of Canada's highest waterfalls, and fossil beds that are among the world's oldest. A popular destination for hikers, Yoho also played an important role in Canada's railroad history.

Visiting the Park

Yoho National Park is open year-round, although many park services, including the visitors center and the park's campgrounds, are available only April or May-mid-October, and several destinations can remain snow-covered into June. Due to the risk of avalanches, Yoho Valley Road, which leads to Takakkaw Falls, is usually open only mid-June-mid-October.

The tiny town of **Field** is near the center of the park. The park visitors center is here, as are a couple of restaurants, a small grocery, a gas station, and an inn. Beyond Field, the park has limited services.

Yoho National Park and Vicinity

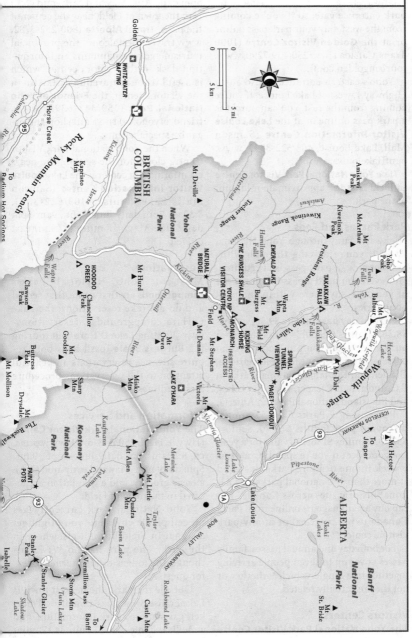

Entrances

Yoho's western entrance is along Highway 1, east of Golden. There's no park entrance gate, so if you're coming from the west, buy your park pass online or at the **Golden Visitor Centre** (1000 Trans-Canada Hwy., 250/439-7290, www.tourismgolden.com).

Yoho's eastern entrance is also along Highway 1, west of Lake Louise. If you're coming from the east, you can purchase a park pass online or at the **Lake Louise Visitor Information Centre** (Samson Mall, Lake Louise, 403/522-3833, www.banfflakelouise.com).

The **Yoho National Park Visitor Centre** in Field is at the approximate midpoint of the park.

Park Passes and Fees

Highway 1 runs through Yoho National Park. If you're driving through without stopping, a park pass isn't required. However, you need a pass if you get out of your car anywhere within the park boundaries.

A Yoho **day pass** (adults $9.80, seniors $8.30, families $19.60) is valid until 4pm on the day after you purchase it. Yoho passes can be used at Mount Revelstoke, Glacier, and Kootenay National Parks in B.C. and at Banff, Jasper, Waterton Lakes, and Elk Island National Parks in Alberta.

Purchasing a Parks Canada **annual discovery pass** (adults $67.70, seniors $57.90, families $136.40), valid for a year, is a good deal if you're spending at least a week in one or more parks. It's good at more than 100 national parks and national historic sites across Canada. You can buy an annual pass online from Parks Canada (www.pc.gc.ca) or at any park visitors center.

For both day and annual passes, family passes cover up to seven people arriving together in a single vehicle, whether or not they're actually related.

Visitors Centers

The **Yoho National Park Visitor Centre** (Hwy. 1, Field, 250/343-6783, www.pc.gc.ca, 8:30am-7pm daily June-Sept., 9am-5pm daily Apr.-May and early-mid Oct.) is in the town of Field, near the center of the park. **Travel Alberta** (800/252-3782, www.travelalberta.com), the provincial tourism agency, maintains an information desk in the visitors center, which is useful if you're traveling east. Also in the visitors center, the **Friends of Yoho National Park** (250/343-6393, www.friendsofyoho.ca) run a gift shop and organize special events.

When the Yoho National Park Visitor Centre closes for the season, the nearest information center is the **Lake Louise Visitor Information Centre** (Samson Mall, Lake Louise, 403/522-3833, 8:30am-7pm daily June-Sept., 9am-5pm daily Oct.-May), 17 miles (27 km) east of Field.

Reservations

Most of Yoho National Park's **campgrounds** are first-come, first-served and do not take reservations; the Lake O'Hara campground is reservations-only. Visiting **Lake O'Hara** and touring the **Burgess Shale** fossil beds both require advance reservations and careful attention to the reservations procedure and deadlines.

Information and Services

The **Yoho National Park Visitor Centre** (Hwy. 1, Field, 250/343-6783, www.pc.gc.ca, 8:30am-7pm daily June-Sept., 9am-5pm daily Apr.-May and early-mid Oct.), a basic grocery, and a gas station are located in the town of Field.

Yoho National Park currently has no cell phone coverage; you might get a signal in Field but not elsewhere in the park. The park has no Wi-Fi, although the lodges offer Internet access for guests.

Outside the park, the nearest town is Lake Louise, which has a small food market, gas stations, park information, and a medical clinic. Lake Louise is 17 miles

(27 km) east of Field via Highway 1. For more services, go to Golden, 35 miles (56 km) to the west, or Banff, 55 miles (85 km) to the east.

Getting Around

Except for the buses to Lake O'Hara, which are available only with required advance reservations, there is no public transportation within the park.

If you're planning to follow **Yoho Valley Road** toward Takakkaw Falls, note that RVs and trailers are not permitted on this road after the 6-kilometer mark. A short section of very steep, narrow switchbacks at this point make it impassable for large vehicles.

Sights and Activities

★ Lake O'Hara

One of the most beautiful areas of Yoho National Park is also one of the most challenging to reach—not because getting to **Lake O'Hara,** which is surrounded by meadows, mountain peaks, and dozens of smaller alpine lakes, requires an arduous journey, but because Parks Canada has limited visitor access to this wildly popular area. A visit requires careful advance planning.

Getting There

Private cars are not allowed on the Lake O'Hara road, so for day visitors, the only way to visit is on the Parks Canada shuttle bus or by hiking in 7 miles (11 km) from the Lake O'Hara parking lot, which is 8 miles (13 km) east of Field and 7.5 miles (12 km) west of Lake Louise.

To take the **Parks Canada shuttle bus** (mid-June-early Oct., round-trip adults $14.70, ages 6-16 $7.30), you must make **advance reservations** (519/826-5391 or 877/737-3783, www.reservations. parkscanada.gc.ca) online or by phone in early spring for the coming season. Typically, reservations for the entire season **sell out on the first day** they become available. Check the Parks Canada website (www.pc.gc.ca) for reservation

instructions, and be ready to make your booking as early as possible.

While reservations aren't required to return from the lake, pay attention to the bus schedule, as there are just a few departures per day, and you don't want to miss the last bus.

If you aren't able to reserve a shuttle spot, you can hike to the lake on the access road. You might be able to buy a one-way ticket (adults $9.75, ages 6-16 $4.75) to return from the lake on the bus, but only if space is available. If you choose to hike, be prepared to hike both ways.

Hiking

Once you've managed to get to the lake, it's a great destination for day hikes, from easy strolls to more adventurous mountain treks.

One of the easier routes is the scenic **Lake O'Hara Shoreline Trail,** a 1.7-mile (2.8-km) loop. The **Lake Oesa Trail,** 2 miles (3.2 km) each way, starts on the Lake O'Hara Shoreline Trail, before climbing to a cliff overlooking the lake; the elevation gain is 787 feet (240 m). The 3.7-mile (5.9-km) **Opabin Plateau Circuit** takes you to a hanging valley on top of a cliff above Lake O'Hara, with an elevation gain of 820 feet (250 m).

Get a more detailed description of these and all the Lake O'Hara trails on the Yoho National Park website (www. pc.gc.ca) or from the Yoho National Park Visitor Centre.

Lake O'Hara Campground

Unlike the rest of the Yoho campgrounds, where you can't make a reservation, you can stay overnight at the 30-site **Lake O'Hara Campground** (mid-June-Sept., $9.80) only by reservation. You'll have to be on the ball to book a campsite; all sites are usually reserved on the first morning that they become available, three months in advance.

To reserve a Lake O'Hara site, you must phone the **Yoho National Park reservation line** (250/343-6433,

8am-noon and 1pm-4pm mountain time Mon.-Fri. Apr.-late May, 8am-noon and 1pm-4pm daily late May-mid-June, 8am-noon and 1pm-4pm Mon.-Fri. mid-June-early Oct., reservation fee $11.70) **exactly three months** before your desired stay. You can book a site for up to three nights.

When you make your camping reservation, you also reserve a spot on the **Parks Canada shuttle bus** (adults $14.70, ages 6-16 $7.30). The amount of luggage you can bring is restricted, so check the details on the Yoho National Park website (www.pc.gc.ca).

Lake O'Hara Lodge

A stay at the remote **Lake O'Hara Lodge** (250/343-6418 or 403/678-4110, www.lakeohara.com, mid-June-early Oct. and late Jan.-early Apr., $705-795 d, cabins $995), built in 1926, takes you off the grid near the scenic lake. The eight rooms in the rustic main lodge each have two twin beds and share two large baths. In the summer or fall, you can stay in a log cabin with a private bath; some are on the lakeshore, while others (with a sofa bed and a Murphy bed to accommodate up to 4) are on a knoll above the lake.

Rates include three meals a day, afternoon tea, and transportation to the property on the lodge's private shuttle. Since no private cars are allowed on the Lake O'Hara road, guests catch the shuttle at the Lake O'Hara parking lot off Highway 1; it departs twice a day in each direction.

★ Emerald Lake

Emerald Lake is as beautiful as its name suggests, its waters shimmering light green, turquoise, and deep emerald as the sunlight bounces off the mountains and moves across the sky and behind the clouds. It's one of the park's most visited spots, with tour buses disgorging hordes of visitors who snap photos and hop back on their buses. But stay awhile. You can follow an easy trail around the lake and leave many of the other visitors behind,

Emerald Lake in Yoho National Park

or rent a canoe to go for a paddle and admire the surrounding cliffs.

The 3.25-mile (5.2-km) mostly flat **Emerald Lake trail** leads through the forest around the lake. Allow about two hours for a leisurely lake circuit.

From a lakeside boathouse, **Emerald Sports** (250/343-6000, www.khsc.ca) rents **canoes and rowboats** (10am-5pm daily May-June and Sept.-Oct., 9am-7pm daily July-Aug., $70 per hour) spring-fall. In winter it rents **snowshoes** (noon-4pm Mon.-Fri., 10am-4pm Sat.-Sun. Dec.-Mar., $10 per hour, $5 per additional hour, $20 per day) and **cross-country skis** ($15 per hour, $5 per additional hour, $25 per day).

Overlooking the lake, **Emerald Lake Lodge** (250/343-6321, www.crmr.com) has several restaurants that are open to nonguests. You can also picnic near the lake.

To reach Emerald Lake, follow Emerald Lake Road off Highway 1, west of Field. Try to visit early in the morning or late in the afternoon, when the crush of visitors may have lessened slightly.

Natural Bridge

On your way to Emerald Lake, stop to see the **Natural Bridge** (Emerald Lake Rd.), an unusual rock formation on the Kicking Horse River with a swirl of water rushing through it. Surrounded by mountain peaks and pines, the natural bridge is a scenic spot for photos. Several hiking and cycling trails start nearby, including the 2.3-mile (3.6-km) **Kicking Horse-Amiskwi Trail** and the 7.8-mile (12.6-km) **Kicking Horse-Otterhead Trail,** which both follow old fire roads.

Takakkaw Falls

One of the highest waterfalls in Canada, **Takakkaw Falls** (Yoho Valley Rd.) is 833 feet (254 m) tall. The falls, which cascade down a rock face in the Yoho Valley, are especially lovely late in the day when the afternoon or early evening sun illuminates the water. A short walking trail leads from the parking area to the base of the falls.

To reach the falls, follow Yoho Valley Road off Highway 1; the falls are 11 miles (18 km) northeast of Field. Because Yoho Valley Road has a short section of steep, narrow switchbacks, RVs and other large vehicles are not permitted to continue on this road beyond the switchbacks.

Spiral Tunnels

To complete the transcontinental railroad that would link Canada's Pacific coast with its eastern regions, Canadian Pacific Railway engineers needed to find a route across the Rocky Mountains. The route they chose, through the Kicking Horse Pass, required a precipitous descent—four times steeper than the average rail grade at the time—on what became known as the "Big Hill."

Unfortunately, climbing and descending the Big Hill, which is in present-day Yoho National Park, turned out to be complicated and dangerous. The first

train that tried to travel through the pass derailed, killing three workers. Engineer J. E. Schwitzer eventually came up with a solution: the **Spiral Tunnels,** two looping tracks that allowed trains to make a more gradual descent. Completed in 1909, these tunnels are still in use.

You can watch trains enter and leave these unusual tunnels from two viewpoints. From the **Lower Spiral Tunnel Viewpoint** (Hwy. 1, 4.7 mi/7.5 km east of Field), you can see trains pass through the tunnel on Mount Ogden. From the **Upper Spiral Tunnel Viewpoint** (Yoho Valley Rd., 1.5 mi/2.3 km from Hwy. 1), you can watch the tunnel through Cathedral Mountain.

While an average of 25 trains pass through the tunnels every day, the schedule is irregular, but if you're lucky, you'll get to see a train make its looping way through this engineering innovation.

★ The Burgess Shale

In 1909, American geologist Charles Walcott made a surprising discovery in the mountains near the town of Field. The well-preserved fossils that he unearthed were the remains of soft-bodied marine organisms that once lived in the Cambrian Sea in what is now Yoho National Park. Among the world's oldest fossils, they're estimated to be 505 million years old.

The area where Walcott discovered the fossils, known as the **Burgess Shale,** encompasses layers of fossil-filled rocks on Fossil Ridge between Wapta Mountain and Mount Field. To recognize the importance of its geological legacy, the Burgess Shale has been designated a UNESCO World Heritage Site.

The **Yoho National Park Visitor Centre** (Hwy. 1, Field) has an exhibit where you can learn more about the Burgess Shale fossils.

Burgess Shale Guided Hikes

Park visitors can tour the Burgess Shale fossil beds on a **full-day guided hike,** which you must reserve in advance. Make reservations with **Parks Canada** (877/737-3783, www.reservations.parkscanada. gc.ca, reservations fee $11 online, $13.50 by phone), beginning in early January for the coming season. Check the website to confirm when reservations will become available and book as early as possible. You can choose from two different guided Burgess Shale hikes in Yoho National Park. There's also a guided Burgess Shale hike in Kootenay National Park.

One of the guided hikes is to **Walcott Quarry** (daily early July-early Sept., Fri.-Sun. early-mid Sept., adults $70, seniors $59.50, ages 8-16 $35). You need to hike a challenging trail, a 13-mile (21-km) round-trip route with an elevation gain of 2,710 feet (825 m). Parks Canada staff caution that this elevation change is the equivalent of climbing up and down the stairs in a 234-story building. Along the way, as you traverse the striking mountain scenery, your guide will explain more about the Burgess Shale, the fossils and their importance, and local wildlife. Hikes depart from the Takakkaw Falls parking lot on Yoho Valley Road at 7am; expect to be on the trail for 10.5 hours.

An alternate guided hike takes you to the **Mount Stephen Fossil Bed** (Sat.-Mon. mid-June-early Sept., adults $55, seniors $46.75, ages 8-16 $27.50), where railroad workers found fossils even before Walcott made his groundbreaking discovery. This seven-hour hike is shorter but steeper than the Walcott Quarry hike, with an elevation gain of 2,610 feet (795 m) on a 5-mile (8-km) round-trip hike. This hike departs from the **Yoho National Park Visitor Centre,** off Highway 1 in Field, at 7am.

Field

The small town of **Field,** in the center of Yoho National Park, was settled in the 1880s when the Canadian Pacific Railway was built through Kicking Horse Pass. Originally a service center for the trains

How the Kicking Horse River Got Its Name

Beginning near the Alberta border, the Kicking Horse River runs through Yoho National Park before descending through a series of rapids as it approaches the town of Golden and joins the Columbia River. But who'd name a river Kicking Horse?

In 1858, the British exploring party known as the Palliser Expedition became the first non-aboriginal people to venture into the Yoho area. One day, while trying to recover a runaway horse near the river that fed Wapta Falls, James Hector, a member of the expedition, was kicked in the chest and presumed dead. The other members of his party began digging his grave. Fortunately, before they lowered Hector into the ground, one of his companions noticed Hector's eye blink.

Hector recovered enough to continue on the expedition. His fellow explorers named the river where he had nearly met his demise for the animal that would have sent him to the grave: the Kicking Horse.

climbing the Big Hill, the town began developing tourist infrastructure when the Mt. Stephen House hotel opened in 1886. In the early 1900s, up to 12 passenger trains passed through Field each day.

Though the Mt. Stephen House is no longer standing, another town landmark is: the **CPR Water Tower,** which was built in 1930 to supply the steam trains with water. The 70-foot (21-m) tower was retired in 1952 when diesel engines replaced their steam counterparts.

In summer, the Friends of Yoho National Park offer one-hour **historic walking tours of Field** (250/343-6393, www.friendsofyoho.ca, 8pm Tues. and Thurs. July-Aug., free) that depart from the Field Community Centre (315 Stephen Ave.), near the water tower. If you prefer to wander on your own, you can get a copy of the Friends' historic map of Field online or at the park visitors center.

Hiking

With more than 250 miles (400 km) of hiking trails, Yoho has plenty of options for hikers of all levels.

Wapta Falls

Near the park's western boundary, 16 miles (26 km) west of Field, the **Wapta Falls Trail** is a moderate hike with a big payoff: up-close views of the largest waterfall on the Kicking Horse River.

Most of the 2.9-mile (4.6-km) round-trip trail is fairly easy, with gentle ups and downs. Just above the first point where the falls come into view, the trail switchbacks down more sharply, but your reward from the next viewpoints is a full-on view of the falls with rocky peaks beyond. Then you can descend another short segment to the riverbank, where you'll be close enough to Wapta Falls, which is 98 feet (30 m) high and 490 feet (150 m) wide, to feel its spray.

Hoodoos

To see a series of hoodoos, pillar-like rock formations created from glacial debris, follow the steep **Hoodoos Trail,** which begins in the Hoodoo Creek Campground, 14 miles (23 km) west of Field off Highway 1. This 3.2-mile (5.2-km) round-trip trail climbs steeply, with an elevation gain of 1,066 feet (325 m), so take it slow and allow at least 2.5 hours for the hike.

Twin Falls

The mostly forested **Twin Falls Trail** (mid-June-mid-Oct.), leading to the 260-foot (80-m) waterfall of the same name, begins at the Takakkaw Falls parking lot on Yoho Valley Road, 10.5 miles (17 km) northeast of Field. This hike is 10.2 miles (16.4 km) round-trip, with an elevation gain of 985 feet (300 m); allow approximately six hours.

Iceline

One of the most popular all-day hikes in Yoho National Park, the challenging 13-mile (21-km) round-trip **Iceline Trail** rewards hikers with spectacular glacier views before climbing down through meadows in the Little Yoho Valley and past Laughing Falls. With a 2,329-foot (710-m) elevation gain, this trail takes most hikers about eight hours.

For a slightly shorter hike, follow an alternate Iceline route to **Celeste Lake,** a 10.9-mile (17.5-km) round-trip route with a 2,280-foot (695-m) elevation gain. This variation still takes about seven hours.

The trailhead for the Iceline Trail is near the Whiskey Jack Hostel. Park nearby at the Takakkaw Falls parking lot, on Yoho Valley Road, 10.5 miles (17 km) northeast of Field.

Food and Accommodations

Yoho National Park has two upscale lodges, both of which have dining rooms open to nonguests. The park also has a rustic hostel near Takakkaw Falls. In the town of Field, within the park boundaries, there's a small inn with a restaurant, and many homeowners rent rooms to guests. If you can't find accommodations in the park, or if you want other lodging options, consider staying in Golden or Lake Louise and making day trips to Yoho.

Around the Park

Why stay at the remote **HI-Yoho National Park Whiskey Jack Hostel** (Yoho Valley Rd., 778/328-2220 or 866/762-4122, www.hihostels.ca, late June-Sept., $30 dorm), a rustic cabin with no electricity? Because you can step onto the porch for views of nearby Takakkaw Falls or easily access several excellent hiking routes, including the Iceline Trail, which begins right at the hostel. Guests share three bunk rooms, each outfitted with nine beds and a small private bath with a flush toilet and hot shower. Propane powers the lamps and the appliances in the shared kitchen.

Bring food and a flashlight, and charge your batteries before you arrive. The hostel has no phone, cell service, or Wi-Fi.

You can't ask for a lovelier setting than that of ★ **Emerald Lake Lodge** (Emerald Lake Rd., 800/663-6336, www.crmr.com, $209-525), on the shores of the gorgeous green lake. The property has 85 comfortable, though not luxurious, guest rooms in 37 cabins; many cabins have two units on the main level and two upstairs. With standard rooms, studios, and one-bedroom suites, the accommodations all have fireplaces and balconies, with natural wood furnishings and fans but no air-conditioning. The Club House has a hot tub, a sauna, and a small gym, while the main lodge, constructed from handhewn wood, has a restaurant, a lounge, and a 2nd-floor games room with the second-oldest snooker table in Canada. Expect to disconnect while you're here: Wi-Fi is available in the main lodge only.

Emerald Lake Lodge has several dining options, open to both guests and nonguests. The more formal **Mount Burgess Dining Room** (250/343-6321, 7am-11am and 5:30pm-9:30pm daily, breakfast $15-23, dinner $32-45) overlooks the lake; it's known for game meats like elk or bison steak. In the casual **Kicking Horse Lounge** (11am-10pm Sun.-Thurs., 11am-11pm Fri.-Sat., $17-25), you can order from the dining room menu or from a lighter lounge selection, including a signature charcuterie plate for two. In summer, you can have drinks or lunch (salads, burgers, pizza, and sandwiches) at **Cilantro on the Lake** (11am-5pm daily June-Sept., $17-25), on the water near the bridge to the property. Cilantro's **take-out window** (10am-5pm daily June-Sept.) sells ice cream, coffee, and cold drinks.

What's more Canadian than a stay in a log cabin? At ★ **Cathedral Mountain Lodge** (Yoho Valley Rd., 250/343-6442 or 866/619-6442, www.cathedralmountainlodge.com, late May-early Oct., $366-855), which has 31 upscale cabins near the Kicking Horse

River, you don't have to rough it to live out your log-cabin dreams. Cabins are furnished with custom log beds, down duvets, soaker tubs, and porches with Adirondack chairs. Premier units have stone fireplaces and mini fridges. Five units can sleep up to four people; family cabins have a king bed on the main floor and a loft with two twins. Originally built in the 1930s to accommodate railroad workers and miners, the high-ceilinged, wood-framed main lodge building now houses the **Riverside Dining Room,** which serves a buffet breakfast (7am-10:30am daily, included in the room rates) and dinner (5:30pm-9:30pm daily, $29-46) to guests and nonguests. Guests can order a packed lunch ($36 for 2 people) to take on park adventures. The lodge is located 0.6 mile (1 km) from Highway 1. The only minor quibble with the otherwise serene setting is that you can sometimes hear the distant traffic hum.

In Field

A list of **rooms to rent** (www.field.ca, $140-450) in private homes in the town of Field is available online. Book early, especially if you're visiting in July and August, as availability is limited.

Truffle Pigs Bistro and Lodge (100 Center St., 250/343-6303, www.trufflepigs.com, Dec.-Oct.) runs a well-loved restaurant (11am-3pm and 5pm-9pm daily May-Sept., call for off-season hours, lunch $17-22, dinner $17-38) in a post-and-beam mountain lodge, where you can lunch on pulled pork *bao;* a veggie burger made of beets, millet, and sweet potato; or salads like "Got Rhubarb," with marinated rhubarb and fennel, arugula, and grilled

halloumi cheese. The inventive dinner mains could include pappardelle with pumpkin seed pesto, pork tenderloin with roasted pistachios, or salmon with bulgur tabbouleh and dill sour cream. If you want to crawl under the covers after your meal, the lodge ($145-285) has 13 guest rooms with queen beds, mini fridges, microwaves, private baths, and included Wi-Fi.

In a cozy yellow house, funky **Siding Café** (318 Stephen Ave., 250/343-6002, www.thesidingcafe.ca, 10am-5pm daily, longer hours in summer, $8-15) serves breakfast, burgers, sandwiches, and a tasty rice bowl with tofu, spinach, beets, and carrots sauced with a garlicky tahini dressing. It's also the town's liquor store.

Camping

At Yoho's four main campgrounds, sites are first-come, first-served, so arrive early in the day, especially in July and August. It's possible to camp mid-May-mid-October, although not all campgrounds remain open during the entire period.

The centrally located 88-site **Kicking Horse Campground** (Yoho Valley Rd., late May-mid-Oct., $27.40) is the park's largest camping area and the only one with flush toilets and showers. Nearby, **Monarch Campground** (May-early Sept., $17.60) has 44 sites.

Near the waterfalls of the same name, **Takakkaw Falls Campground** (Yoho Valley Rd., late June-mid-Oct., $17.60) has 35 walk-in sites.

The 30-site **Hoodoo Creek Campground** (mid-May-early Sept., $15.70) is off Highway 1 near the park's west entrance.

Banff
and Lake
Louise

Banff and Lake Louise

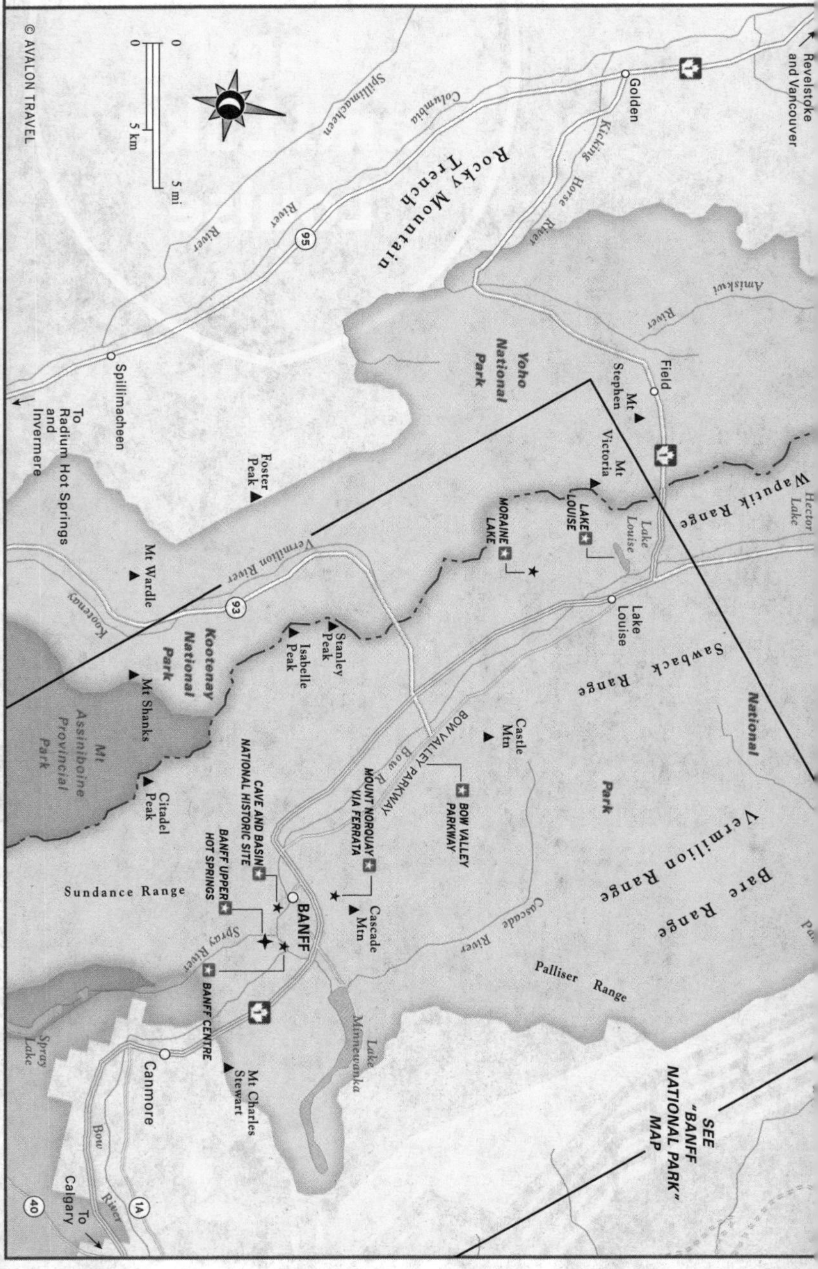

© AVALON TRAVEL

0
5 km
0
5 mi

Golden

To Revelstoke and Vancouver

Spillimacheen River

Columbia River

Rocky Mountain Trench

95

Kicking Horse River

Amiskwi River

Field

Mt Stephen

Spillimacheen

To Radium Hot Springs and Invermere

Yoho National Park

Wapik Range

Foster Peak

Mt Victoria

Lake O'Hara

Vermilion River

MORAINE LAKE

LAKE LOUISE

Lake Louise

Mt Wardle

93

Kootenay River

Kootenay National Park

Stanley Peak

Isabelle Peak

Lake Louise

Sawback Range

Mt Shanks

Castle Mtn

National

Mt Assiniboine Provincial Park

Citadel Peak

BOW VALLEY PARKWAY

MOUNT NORQUAY VIA FERRATA

BOW VALLEY PARKWAY

Bow River

Park

Vermilion Range

Bare Range

CAVE AND BASIN NATIONAL HISTORIC SITE

BANFF UPPER HOT SPRINGS

Sundance Range

BANFF

Cascade Mtn

Cascade River

Palliser Range

Spray River

BANFF CENTRE

Lake Minnewanka

Spray Lake

Mt Charles Stewart

Canmore

Bow River

40

1A

To Calgary

SEE "BANFF NATIONAL PARK" MAP

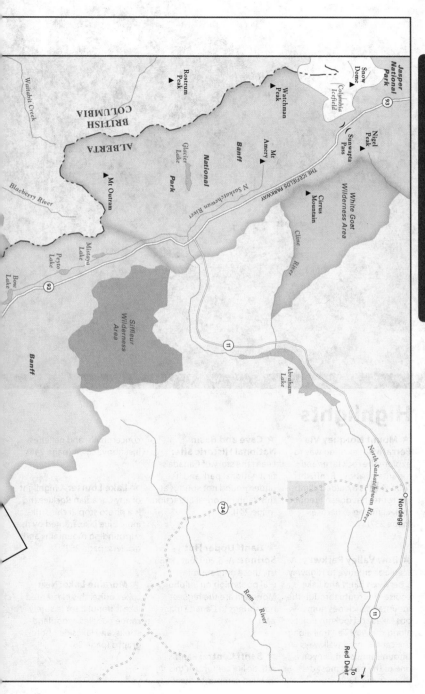

Highlights

★ **Mount Norquay Via Ferrata:** An exciting way to explore the rock faces and mountains above Banff, this "iron way" is a guided climbing route that doesn't require rock-climbing expertise (page 237).

★ **Bow Valley Parkway:** A scenic alternative to Highway 1 between Banff and Lake Louise, this route through the mountains includes numerous hikes and lookout points along the way. The trail along the cantilevered walkways through Johnston Canyon is one of the park's most dramatic (page 239).

★ **Cave and Basin National Historic Site:** Learn the story of Canada's first national park and its underground hot springs at this Banff historical attraction (page 241).

★ **Banff Upper Hot Springs:** At 5,200 feet (1,585 m), these outdoor mineral pools high on Sulphur Mountain are the highest hot springs in Canada (page 243).

★ **Banff Centre:** Banff's artistic life centers on this modern campus of theaters,

concert halls, and galleries just above town (page 248).

★ **Lake Louise:** A highlight of any Canadian Rockies trip is a photo stop at this strikingly blue lake, framed by the surrounding mountains and glaciers (page 262).

★ **Moraine Lake:** Near Lake Louise, this glacier-fed lake is popular for leisurely canoe paddles, woodland strolls, and lakeside photographs (page 267).

With dramatic mountain peaks, hot springs, and sparkling lakes, Banff National Park is one of western Canada's most spectacular destinations.

An underground hot spring led to the creation of Canada's first national park, now one of the country's most-visited destinations; more than four million visitors every year come to soak in the mineral-rich waters, hike the more than 1,000 miles (1,600 km) of trails, drive the scenic byways lined with craggy mountain peaks, or simply enjoy the glacier-fed lakes.

Start your Rocky Mountain adventures in the town of Banff, within the national park boundaries. This town of 9,000 people has museums, gardens, historic sites, and easy access to many of the park's hiking trails. It's home to the Banff Centre, where plays, concerts, lectures, and other artistic events draw world-class performers and add vibrancy to this small town's cultural life. You can eat a bison burger, fresh trout, or renowned Alberta beef, whether you dine in a classic mountain lodge, high in an alpine meadow, or around an evening campfire. Banff is even home to its own "castle in the Rockies"—the iconic Fairmont Banff Springs Hotel.

Another Canadian Rockies icon is 35 miles (57 km) northwest of the town of Banff: the impossibly beautiful Lake Louise. With sparkling blue water and glacier-capped peaks beyond, Lake Louise makes a stunning backdrop for photos. It's a starting point for several great hikes, too, including two trails to historic mountain teahouses. You can tour Lake Louise on a day trip from Banff, ideally including a drive up the scenic Bow Valley Parkway, or escape to one of its rustic yet elegant mountain lodges or the classic lakeside hotel.

With a famous trio of peaks called the Three Sisters, the town of Canmore, 20 minutes' drive southeast of Banff, is a quieter alternative to staying within Banff National Park. You're close enough to make day trips to all the park sights, and the town has good restaurants and several attractions of its own, particularly for outdoor enthusiasts.

Banff National Park can be your base for exploring elsewhere in the Canadian Rockies. Both Banff and Lake Louise are close enough to Yoho National Park and Kootenay National Park that you can stay in the Banff area and make day trips to these other mountain parks. The Icefields Parkway, one of the Rockies' best scenic drives, begins in Lake Louise and takes you north to Jasper.

Getting to Banff and Lake Louise

Driving from Vancouver

The most direct route from Vancouver to the Banff area is to take the **Trans-Canada Highway (Hwy. 1)** east to **Hope.** Continue east at Hope onto **Highway 3,** then exit onto **Highway 5 (Coquihalla Hwy.)** north. Follow the Coquihalla over the mountains to **Kamloops,** where you rejoin **Highway 1.** Stay on Highway 1 past Revelstoke, Golden, and Yoho National Park into Alberta, where you'll reach Lake Louise first and then Banff.

The drive from Vancouver to **Lake Louise** is **490 miles (790 km)** and takes **8.5-9 hours.**

To **Banff,** continue east from Lake Louise on **Highway 1.** The trip from Vancouver to Banff is **530 miles (850 km)** and takes **9-9.5 hours.**

Driving from Jasper

From Jasper to **Lake Louise,** follow the scenic **Icefields Parkway (Hwy. 93)** south; it's **145 miles (230 km)** and takes

Best Accommodations

★ **Juniper Hotel:** Staying at this fun mid-century-modern Banff lodging adds some style to your Rocky Mountain holiday (page 252).

★ **Mount Royal Hotel:** Rooms at this Banff boutique lodging have fashionable quilted headboards and Canadian-made furnishings, but the highlight is the rooftop lounge and hot tub (page 253).

★ **Fairmont Banff Springs Hotel:** Arguably the grandest hotel in the Canadian Rockies, this castle-like property blends history with mineral pools, mountain-view lounges, and other resort amenities (page 254).

★ **Grande Rockies Resort:** This comfortable condo-style lodging in Canmore is an alternative to the bustle of Banff—still just a short drive from the national park (page 261).

★ **Moraine Lake Lodge:** There's plenty to do at this rustic yet elegant, off-the-grid escape on the shores of Moraine Lake near Lake Louise, from canoeing to guided hikes to upscale dining (page 273).

★ **Fairmont Chateau Lake Louise:** You can't sleep closer to the famous lake than at this luxury lodging (page 273).

3.25-3.75 hours (but allow additional time for stops at the many scenic points along the way).

To **Banff**, continue east from Lake Louise on **Highway 1.**

Driving from the Kootenays
From Kootenay National Park

Follow **Highway 93** north through Kootenay National Park and into Alberta to the junction with Highway 1. Turn west on **Highway 1** to Lake Louise; turn east for Banff. It's **80 miles (130 km)** from the town of Radium Hot Springs at the park's southern boundary to **Lake Louise,** a **1.75- to 2-hour** drive. From Radium to **Banff,** it's 85 miles (140 km), also a **1.75- to 2-hour** drive.

From Fernie

Follow **Highway 3** west from Fernie to **Highway 93** north and continue through **Kootenay National Park.** At **Highway 1,** turn west for Lake Louise or east for Banff. It's **215 miles (345 km),** a **four-hour** drive, between Fernie and either Banff or Lake Louise.

From Nelson

If you're driving from Nelson to Banff or Lake Louise, you can choose from several different routes.

The most direct routing is to leave Nelson heading south on **Highway 6.** At **Highway 3,** turn east. When you reach **Cranbrook,** go north on **Highway 93** and continue through **Kootenay National Park.** Once you cross into Alberta and reach **Highway 1,** turn west to Lake Louise or east to Banff. Allow about **six hours** for this **310-mile (500-km)** drive to either Lake Louise or Banff.

For a scenic drive along the shore of **Kootenay Lake,** leave Nelson on **Highway 3A** toward **Balfour,** where you catch the free, 35-minute **Kootenay Lake Ferry** (250/229-4215, www2.gov. bc.ca, 6:30am-9:40pm daily) across the lake to **Kootenay Bay.** Take **Highway 3A** south, which winds along the lakeshore to **Creston,** where you can pick up **Highway 3** east. Follow the directions (above) to Cranbrook, Kootenay National Park, and Lake Louise or Banff. This Kootenay Lake alternative is also **310**

Best Restaurants

★ **The Sleeping Buffalo:** Yes, you can sample buffalo at this upscale dining room at Banff's Buffalo Mountain Lodge, where game meats, west coast seafood, and local produce are specialties (page 249).

★ **Juniper Bistro:** At this contemporary bistro, the spacious outdoor terrace overlooking Banff's mountains is a lovely setting for a leisurely breakfast or creative evening meal (page 249).

★ **Sky Bistro:** Dine above it all, especially at sunset, in this window-lined contemporary restaurant at the top of the Banff Gondola (page 249).

★ **Wild Flour Artisan Bakery:** Sweet and savory pastries, sandwiches, and fresh salads make this Banff bakery an excellent breakfast or lunch stop (page 252).

★ **PD3 by Blake:** Fasten your seat belts, diners! Canmore's coolest dining spot serves eclectic Asian-inspired plates in a silver double-decker bus (page 258).

★ **Crazyweed Kitchen:** Long considered Canmore's best restaurant, this modern kitchen still charms with its inventive world-beat menu and relaxed vibe (page 260).

★ **Plain of Six Glaciers Teahouse:** The only way to reach this historic Lake Louise teahouse is by hiking up from the lakeshore, but you'll appreciate your lunch (or rich chocolate cake) all the more (page 266).

★ **Mount Fairview Dining Room at Deer Lodge:** A short stroll from Lake Louise but miles from the tourist frenzy, this serene log-walled restaurant serves modern mountain meals (page 271).

miles **(500 km)** between Nelson and either Lake Louise or Banff, but budget an extra hour (about **seven hours** total) for the ferry and for the slower drive along Highway 3A.

Yet another scenic option takes you from Nelson through the **B.C. national parks** along Highway 1 en route to Lake Louise and Banff. Leave Nelson traveling north on **Highway 6** toward New Denver and Nakusp. At **Nakusp,** continue north on **Highway 23.** When you reach **Galena Bay,** take the free, 20-minute **Upper Arrow Lake Ferry** (250/265-2105, www2.gov.bc.ca, 5:30am-12:30am daily) across the lake to **Shelter Bay.** Continue on **Highway 23** north until you meet Highway 1 at **Revelstoke.** Turn east onto **Highway 1,** which takes you through

Mount Revelstoke, Glacier, and Yoho National Parks and into Alberta. This route is **295 miles (475 km),** or about **6.5 hours,** between Nelson and **Lake Louise,** and **335 miles (540 km),** or **seven hours,** from Nelson to **Banff,** although you may need to allow extra time for the ferry crossing.

Driving from Kelowna (Okanagan)

To travel from Kelowna, in the Okanagan Valley, to Banff, take **Highway 97** north, then continue north on **Highway 97A.** At **Sicamous,** turn east onto the **Trans-Canada Highway (Hwy. 1),** which will take you into Alberta. It's **300 miles (485 km)** from Kelowna to Banff, which takes **5.75-6 hours.**

Driving from Calgary

The **Trans-Canada Highway (Hwy. 1)** heads west from Calgary to **Banff.** The **80-mile (130-km)** drive takes about **90 minutes,** weather and traffic permitting.

To **Lake Louise,** continue west from Banff on **Highway 1;** Calgary to Lake Louise is **115 miles (185 km),** a **2.25-hour** drive.

Getting There by Air, Train, and Bus
By Air

Calgary International Airport (YYC, 2000 Airport Rd. NE, 403/735-1200, www.yyc.com) is the closest airport to Banff. The airport is on Calgary's northeast side, 90 miles (145 km) from Banff.

From the Calgary airport, you can take a scheduled shuttle directly to Banff. Both the **Banff Airporter** (403/762-3330 or 888/449-2901, www.banffairporter. com, one-way adults $67, seniors $61, ages 3-12 $34) and **Brewster Banff Airport Express** (403/762-6700 or 866/606-6700, www.banffjaspercollection.com, one-way adults $71, ages 6-15 $36) make the trip in about two hours and stop at most Banff hotels.

Brewster Banff Airport Express also runs buses from Calgary airport to Lake Louise (3.25-3.5 hours, one-way adults $98, ages 6-15 $49).

By Train

VIA Rail, Canada's national rail carrier, does not provide service to Banff. However, the **Rocky Mountaineer** (877/460-3200, www.rockymountaineer. com, mid-Apr.-mid-Oct.), a privately run luxury train, does, offering rail packages between Vancouver, Lake Louise, and Banff. You can travel round-trip from Vancouver to the Canadian Rockies and back, or book a one-way journey through the Rockies starting in either Vancouver or Calgary.

You can purchase a Rocky Mountaineer holiday with rail fare and accommodations only; the company offers a two-day train trip between Vancouver and Banff. Other packages add in a variety of activities and tours. All Rocky Mountaineer trains travel during the day and stop overnight in Kamloops en route to and from the Rockies.

Rail packages start at $1,579 per person and vary by the destination, number of days of travel, and level of service and accommodations.

By Bus

Brewster Banff Airport Express (403/762-6700 or 866/606-6700, www. banffjaspercollection.com), which provides bus service between Calgary airport and both Banff and Lake Louise, can also pick you up or drop you off in downtown Calgary (2.5 hours, one-way adults $71, ages 6-15 $36). Brewster buses can take you between Banff and Lake Louise (1 hour, one-way adults $33, ages 6-15 $16) year-round. The buses stop at several downtown Calgary hotels, most Banff hotels, and several locations in Lake Louise.

On-It Regional Transit (403/312-6139, www.onitregionaltransit.ca, mid-May-early Sept., one-way $10 pp) offers seasonal weekend bus service between Calgary, Canmore, and Banff. In Calgary, passengers can catch the bus downtown (1st St. SW at 8th Ave. SW, near the Hudson's Bay department store) or at the Crowfoot C-Train station northwest of the city center. In Canmore, the bus stop is located at the corner of Benchlands Trail and Bow Valley Trail. In Banff, buses drop passengers at the Banff Heritage Train Station (327 Railway Ave.) and Banff High School (330 Banff Ave.). Note that buses returning to Calgary pick up passengers at the high school only. Check the website for up-to-date schedules.

Banff National Park

Established in 1885, Canada's first national park is also one of its most popular, welcoming more than four million visitors a year. Banff National Park covers an area of 2,564 square miles (6,641 sq km) and has more than 1,000 miles (1,600 km) of hiking trails. You could hike in the park for years and never repeat the same route.

The towns of Banff and Lake Louise are both within the national park boundaries. Banff is larger, with a full complement of accommodations, restaurants, and in-town attractions, while Lake Louise is essentially a village with two famous lakes. Based in either community, though, you can easily reach most national park sites.

Visiting the Park
Entrances
The **Banff East Gate** is on Highway 1, west of Canmore. Coming from Calgary, Canmore, or anywhere east of Banff, you must stop here and purchase a park pass, if you haven't bought your pass in advance.

Traveling east on Highway 1 from British Columbia, you enter Banff National Park at the Alberta-B.C. provincial boundary.

If you're driving south on the Icefields Parkway (Hwy. 93) between Jasper and Lake Louise, you enter Banff National Park along the way. The northern section of the parkway is within Jasper National Park, while the southern sector is within Banff's boundary. You must have a valid park pass to travel anywhere on the Icefields Parkway.

TIP: Banff National Park's web page **Banff Now** (www.pc.gc.ca/banffnow) lists real-time availability of parking at different areas of the park and notes any seasonal closures.

Park Passes and Fees
A **day pass** (adults $9.80, seniors $8.30, families $19.60) for Banff National Park is valid at both Banff and Jasper and for travel along the Icefields Parkway; it's also good at Kootenay, Yoho, Mount Revelstoke, Glacier, Waterton Lakes, and Elk Island National Parks. Lake Louise is within the Banff National Park boundaries, so you must have a park pass to visit the lake area as well. A day pass is good until 4pm on the day after you purchase it. You can purchase your park pass online from **Banff-Lake Louise Tourism** (www.banfflakelouise.com) or at any park visitors center or entrance gate.

Purchasing a Parks Canada **annual discovery pass** (www.pc.gc.ca, adults $67.70, seniors $57.90, families $136.40), valid for a year, is a good deal if you're spending at least a week in one or more parks. It's good at more than 100 national parks and national historic sites across Canada. Buy an annual pass online from Parks Canada or at any of the parks' visitors centers.

For both day and annual passes, the family passes cover up to seven people in a single vehicle, whether or not they're actually related.

Visitors Centers
In the town of Banff, both **Parks Canada** (www.pc.gc.ca) and **Banff-Lake Louise Tourism** (www.banfflakelouise.com) staff the **Banff Visitor Information Centre** (224 Banff Ave., 403/762-8421, 8am-8pm daily mid-May-mid-Oct., 9am-5pm daily mid-Oct.-mid-May), providing information about the national park and surrounding area. You can purchase park passes and bear spray, pick up park maps, and get hiking tips here.

There's an additional **Banff Visitor Information Desk** (327 Railway Ave., 8am-8pm daily mid-May-mid-Oct., 9am-5pm daily mid-Oct.-mid-May) in the Banff Heritage Train Station.

Banff National Park

BRITISH COLUMBIA

Mitchell Range

Mt Assiniboine

Mount Assiniboine Provincial Park

Marvel Lake

Sunshine Meadows

SUNSHINE VILLAGE

Citadel Peak

Heald Creek

Sundance Range

Brewster Creek

CAVE AND BASIN NATIONAL HISTORIC SITE

Peter Lougheed Provincial Park

Spray Lake Reservoir

Spray River

Goat Range

Sulphur Mountain

BANFF UPPER HOT SPRINGS

Kananaskis Range

Goat Range

Tunnel Mtn

BANFF

Bow Valley Wildland Provincial Park

Three Sisters

Canmore Nordic Centre Provincial Park

Rundle Mountain

Kananaskis River

Mt Allan

CANMORE

BANFF CENTRE

Inglismaldie

TWO JACK LAKESIDE CAMPGROUND

MAIN CAMPGROUND

Elbow–Sheep Wildland Provincial Park

Mt Charles Stewart

Mt Girouard

Kananaskis Country

Exshaw

Bow Valley Wildland Provincial Park

Fairholme Range

Lake Minnewanka

40

Barrier Lake

Bow River

Bow Valley Wildland Provincial Park

68

Bow Valley Provincial Park

0   5 km

0   5 mi

1A

To Calgary

Black Rock Mountain

© MOON.COM

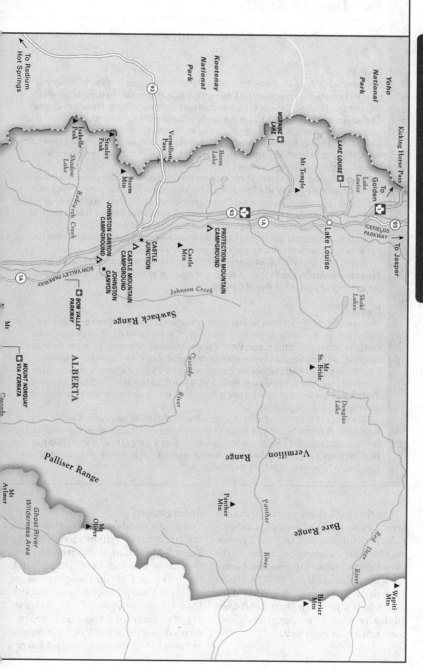

Two Days in Banff

Have two days to spend in Banff National Park? Here's how to make the most of your time.

Day 1

Get oriented with a walk around the town of Banff, with stops at some of its historic sites and museums, especially the **Cave and Basin National Historic Site,** which tells the story behind Canada's first national park; and the **Whyte Museum of the Canadian Rockies,** which traces the area's cultural and artistic roots.

When you're done at the museums, take a lunch break. Have soup, salad, or a sandwich at **Wild Flour Artisan Bakery,** but don't leave without a fresh-baked sweet. Or visit the grand **Fairmont Banff Springs Hotel** to dine in the restored **Vermillion Room;** on the weekends, it serves an elaborate brunch buffet.

If you're feeling adventurous in your quest for the best mountain views, book a tour on the **Mount Norquay Via Ferrata,** an exciting guided climbing experience that requires no previous rock-climbing expertise; the vistas from the top of the ridge are spectacular. Or go for a hike: The 3-mile (4.8-km) **Tunnel Mountain Trail** is close to town and climbs up to a lookout point with views across the Bow Valley.

Catch your breath at glacier-fed **Lake Minnewanka,** the largest lake in Banff National Park, where you can take a leisurely one-hour narrated cruise.

Have a cocktail at **Park Distillery** (it distills its own vodka) and dinner at **The Sleeping Buffalo,** which specializes in game meats. In the evening, see a concert, play, or other event at the **Banff Centre.**

Day 2

The next day, fortify yourself with an early breakfast at **Juniper Bistro,** where the views from the terrace help get your morning off to a good start. Then pack a picnic lunch and drive along the scenic **Bow Valley Parkway.** You want to get to **Johnston Canyon,** a dramatic rock canyon with cantilevered walkways through the gorge, to hike to the **Lower Falls** before the crowds descend on this extremely popular trail. Continue your hike to the **Upper Falls** and, if you have the time, keep going toward the **Ink Pots,** a series of colorful pools. Have your picnic along the trail or at another quiet spot along the parkway.

Back in town, drive up Sulphur Mountain for an afternoon ride in the **Banff Gondola.** Walk the boardwalk trail and make plenty of stops to take in the mountain panoramas. Stay for dinner in the window-lined **Sky Bistro.** Then, at **Banff Upper Hot Springs,** near the gondola base, have a relaxing evening soak in the mineral pools to wrap up your two busy days in Banff.

Another park visitors center is at Lake Louise. **Parks Canada** (www.pc.gc.ca) provides park information, sells park passes, and handles camping inquiries at the **Lake Louise Visitor Information Centre** (Samson Mall, 403/522-3833, 8:30am-7pm daily June-Sept., 9am-5pm daily Oct.-May), where staff from **Banff-Lake Louise Tourism** (www.banfflakelouise. com) assist visitors as well.

Reservations

The campgrounds in Banff National Park that accept reservations include all the Tunnel Mountain Campground sites, the sites at Two Jack Lake Campground, the Johnston Canyon Campground on the Bow Valley Parkway, and the two Lake Louise campgrounds. Reservations are also accepted—and highly recommended—for the **oTENTiks** (platform tents) at Tunnel Mountain and Two Jack Lake.

Town of Banff and Vicinity

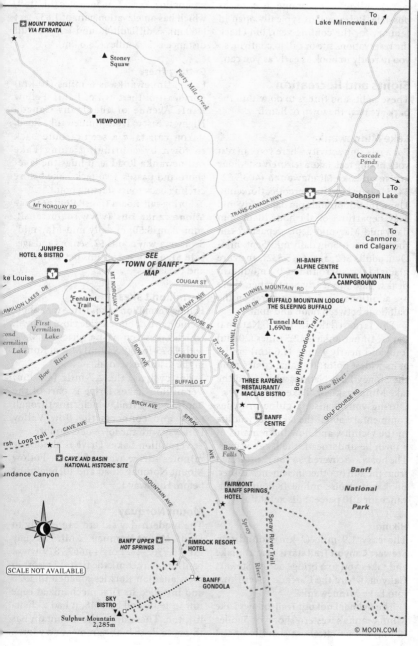

MOUNT NORQUAY VIA FERRATA

To Lake Minnewanka

Stoney Squaw

Forty Mile Creek

VIEWPOINT

Cascade Ponds

To Johnson Lake

TRANS-CANADA HWY

MT NORQUAY RD

To Canmore and Calgary

JUNIPER HOTEL & BISTRO

ke Louise

ERMILION LAKES DR

Fenland Trail

SEE "TOWN OF BANFF" MAP

MT NORQUAY RD

COUGAR ST

BANFF AVE

MOOSE ST

TUNNEL MOUNTAIN RD

TUNNEL MOUNTAIN DR

HI-BANFF ALPINE CENTRE

TUNNEL MOUNTAIN CAMPGROUND

BUFFALO MOUNTAIN LODGE/ THE SLEEPING BUFFALO

Tunnel Mtn 1,690m

First Vermilion Lake

cond ermilion Lake

Bow River

BOW AVE

CARIBOU ST

BUFFALO ST

ST JULIEN RD

Bow River/Hoodoos Trail

Bow River

THREE RAVENS RESTAURANT/ MACLAB BISTRO

BANFF CENTRE

GOLF COURSE RD

BIRCH AVE

rsh Loop Trail

CAVE AVE

SPRAY AVE

Bow Falls

CAVE AND BASIN NATIONAL HISTORIC SITE

undance Canyon

MOUNTAIN AVE

FAIRMONT BANFF SPRINGS HOTEL

Spray River Trail

Banff

National

Park

Spray River

SCALE NOT AVAILABLE

BANFF UPPER HOT SPRINGS

RIMROCK RESORT HOTEL

BANFF GONDOLA

SKY BISTRO

Sulphur Mountain 2,285m

© MOON.COM

Make **campsite reservations** (877/737-3783, www.reservation.parkscanada.gc.ca) online or by phone as soon as possible. Reservations typically open in January for the coming year, but check the reservations site or call to confirm, so you're ready to book as early as you can.

Sights and Recreation

These sights and things to do within the park are near the town of Banff.

Lake Minnewanka

For a relaxing activity where you can rest your hiking feet, take a leisurely one-hour **cruise on Lake Minnewanka** (403/762-3473, www.banffjaspercollection.com, 11am, 1pm, 3pm, and 5pm daily early-mid May, departures on the hour 10am-6pm daily mid-May-mid-Sept., departures on the hour noon-5pm daily mid-Sept.-mid-Oct., adults $62, ages 6-15 $32), an azure glacial lake surrounded by mountain peaks. Late July-early September, there are additional cruise departures on the half-hour between noon and 4pm.

The largest lake in Banff National Park, Minnewanka is 12.5 miles (20 km) long and nearly 1 mile (1.6 km) across at its widest point. Its name comes from the Stoney First Nation, who called the lake Minn-waki, or "Lake of the Spirits." During your cruise, a guide provides commentary about the lake, the wildlife in the vicinity, and how the remains of a town lie underneath the lake's waters. The boats are covered, so you're protected from the sun or other inclement weather. Book your cruise online 48 hours in advance for a 10 percent discount.

Hiking

The easy 1.9-mile (3-km) round-trip **Stewart Canyon Trail** starts near the lake and takes you to a bridge across Stewart Canyon, where the Cascade River flows into Lake Minnewanka.

The **Aylmer Lookout Trail** follows Lake Minnewanka's western shore for 5 miles (8 km) before climbing steadily up 2.4 miles (3.8 km) to a former fire lookout with views back to the lake and across the mountains. Parks Canada rates this trail, which has an elevation gain of 1,837 feet (560 m), as difficult. Round-trip, the full distance is 14.7 miles (23.6 km).

Getting There

Lake Minnewanka is 6 miles (10 km) northeast of the town of Banff. Follow Banff Avenue or the Trans-Canada Highway east to Lake Minnewanka Road.

You can take a scenic route back to town by continuing along Lake Minnewanka Road as it hugs the lakeshore and passes Two Jack Lake before circling back to its starting point.

Spring-fall, **Roam Transit Route 6: Lake Minnewanka bus** (www.roamtransit.com, 8am-8:50pm daily mid-May-mid-Sept., one-way adults $2, seniors and ages 6-18 $1, day pass $5) runs between town and the lake.

Vermilion Lakes

Follow **Vermillion Lakes Drive** for a short scenic drive or bicycle ride close to town, which takes you past a series of lakes, with 9,675-foot (2,949-m) Mount Rundle in the distance beyond.

For cyclists, the 2.7-mile (4.3-km) Vermillion Lakes Drive is part of the **Banff Legacy Trail,** which runs through town and connects the Bow Valley Parkway with the town of Canmore.

Vermillion Lakes Drive is about five minutes' drive west of town. Follow Mount Norquay Road and turn left just before Highway 1.

Mount Norquay

The modern-day ski era came early to Banff. **Mount Norquay** (2 Mt. Norquay Rd., 403/762-4421 or 844/667-7829, www.banffnorquay.com), the first ski resort in the Canadian Rockies, opened in 1926 and installed its first mechanized rope tow in 1938, and by 1948, it had a chairlift, too. These days, the mountain has things to do in both summer and winter.

A 10-minute ride on the **Sightseeing Chairlift** (9am-7pm daily mid-June-mid-Sept., 10am-6pm daily mid-Sept.-mid-Oct., adults $35, ages 6-15 $24) takes you up to a viewing platform with vistas across the town of Banff, the Bow River Valley, and the surrounding peaks.

At the top of the lift, you can have lunch with a view at the **Cliffhouse Bistro** (11am-6:30pm daily mid-June-mid-Sept., 11am-5:30pm daily mid-Sept.-mid-Oct., $16-18), built as a teahouse in the 1950s. These days, you can choose from meal-size salads, cheese and charcuterie platters, paninis, and bao-style sandwiches.

★ Mount Norquay Via Ferrata

A more adventurous way to explore the views and trails on Mount Norquay is to arrange a guided climb on the **Mount Norquay Via Ferrata** (daily mid-June-mid-Oct.). Designed to enable people with no rock-climbing experience to ascend a mountain climbing trail, Via Ferrata comes from the Italian for "iron way." Iron rungs and a system of fixed cables that you clip onto along the route assist in your ascent and descent. Your guide provides an orientation before you start and can talk you through the route's tougher sections. It's a good workout, though it's not the best activity for people who are afraid of heights.

Mount Norquay has four Via Ferrata routes. All include the Sightseeing Chairlift and finish at the top of the lift, where you can return to the base or have lunch or a snack at the Cliffhouse Bistro. All routes take you across at least one narrow **suspension bridge** high above a canyon. Dress in layers; it can be much cooler on the mountain than in town, but you'll get warm as you climb. Bring water, too.

For an introduction to the Via Ferrata, take the **2.5-hour Explorer**

Top to bottom: Lake Minnewanka; climbing the Mount Norquay Via Ferrata; Johnston Canyon hiking trails.

Winter Fun in the Canadian Rockies

Most road-trippers travel through the Canadian Rockies spring-fall, when the roads are usually snow-free and weather is temperate. But for adventurous travelers and snow-lovers, a winter holiday in the Canadian Rockies can be wondrous.

Downhill Skiing and Snowboarding

Banff has one of the longest ski seasons in North America, typically beginning in mid-November and extending until late May. Three ski areas are within the boundaries of Banff National Park: Mount Norquay, Sunshine Village, and Lake Louise. Farther north, you can ski at Marmot Basin in Jasper National Park.

The first ski area in the Canadian Rockies, family-friendly **Mount Norquay** (844/667-7829, www.banffnorquay.com) is closest to the town of Banff, just 15 minutes' drive up the winding Mount Norquay Road.

Much larger **Sunshine Village** (877/542-2633, www.skibanff.com), with 145 runs across more than 3,300 acres (1,335 ha) of skiable terrain, has one of Canada's longest ski seasons, lasting early November-late May. The ski area also has Canada's first heated chairlift. Sunshine Village is 11 miles (18 km) from town.

The **Lake Louise Ski Resort** (877/956-8473, www.skilouise.com), just 2 miles (3.2 km) from the Samson Mall, is the biggest of the Canadian Rockies winter sports resorts, with 145 runs and plenty of off-piste skiing across its 4,200 skiable acres (1,700 ha). The season generally runs early November-early May.

Jasper's **Marmot Basin** (866/952-3816, www.skimarmot.com) has the highest base elevation of all Canada's winter sports resorts, so you can usually ski or snowboard early November-early May. The 91 runs take you across 1,720 acres (696 ha) of terrain.

Other Winter Activities

Cross-country skiers have lots of terrain to explore in Banff and Lake Louise. The **Castle Junction** area along the Bow Valley Parkway has 5.4 miles (8.7 km) of easy groomed trails, while closer to town, the popular **Spray River Trail West** starts at the Fairmont Banff Springs Hotel and follows the rolling river valley. Beginning at the Lake Minnewanka parking lot, the **Cascade Valley Trail** is another local favorite. At **Lake Louise,** you can ski along the lakeshore and, when the lake itself has frozen solid, directly onto the lake.

You can usually go **snowshoeing** in the Canadian Rockies between late December and early April. When **Tunnel Mountain Drive** in the town of Banff closes to vehicles in the winter, it becomes a snowshoeing route, with views of Cascade Mountain. This trail also connects with the **Surprise Corner to Hoodoos Trail.**

Want to try **dogsledding?** Based in Canmore, both **Snowy Owl Sled Dog Tours** (403/678-4369, www.snowyowltours.com) and **Howling Dog Tours** (403/678-9588, www.howlingdogtours.com) offer several different dogsledding tours, including transportation from most Banff hotels. **Kingmik Dog Sled Tours** (403/763-7789, www.kingmikdogsledtours.com) runs excursions from Lake Louise.

Route (9am and 3:30pm daily mid-June-mid-Sept., 10am and 3:30pm daily mid-Sept.-mid-Oct., $149), which has plenty of challenges, but this shorter route doesn't take you all the way to the top of the ridge.

The **4-hour Ridgewalker Route** (8:30am, 10am, 1pm, and 2:30pm daily mid-June-mid-Sept., 10am, 1pm, and 2:30pm daily mid-Sept.-mid-Oct., $199) climbs up to spectacular views at the top of the Norquay ridge. This half-day excursion has a longer and steeper downhill section than the Explorer Route.

The newest of the four options, the **5-hour Skyline Route** (9:30am daily mid-June-mid-Sept., 10:30am Sat.-Sun. mid-Sept.-mid-Oct., $249) adds a high traverse on a sheer rock wall and crosses a 180-foot (55-m) suspension bridge.

The **6-hour Summiteer Route** (9am daily mid-June-mid-Sept., 10am Sat.-Sun. mid-Sept.-mid-Oct., $299) extends the Skyline Route with an additional traverse along the alpine ridge to Mount Norquay's 8,038-foot (2,450-m) East Summit. You also cross a **three-wire suspension bridge** (imagine a tightrope with two guide wires) over a deep chasm. This tour includes lunch and après-climb refreshments at the Cliffhouse Bistro.

Skiing and Snowboarding

In winter, compact, family-friendly **Mount Norquay** (9am-4pm daily Nov. and Mar.-Apr., 9am-4pm Sat.-Thurs., 9am-4pm and 5pm-9pm Fri. Dec., 9am-4pm and 5pm-9pm Fri.-Sat. Jan.-Feb., adults $89, seniors and ages 13-17 $68, ages 6-12 $35) has 74 runs spread over 190 acres (77 ha) for skiing and snowboarding, including night skiing. The terrain is rated 20 percent beginner, 36 percent intermediate, 28 percent advanced, and 16 percent expert. There's also a **tube park** (10am-4pm daily Nov. and Mar.-Apr., 10am-4pm Sat.-Thurs., 10am-4pm and 5pm-9pm Fri. Dec., 10am-4pm Sun.-Thurs., 10am-4pm and 5pm-9pm Fri.-Sat. Jan.-Feb., adults $35, seniors and ages 13-17 $30, ages 4-12 $25).

Getting There

From town, take Lynx Street to Mount Norquay Road, which will cross over Highway 1 and climb up the mountain to the ski area. It's a 15-minute drive.

In the summer, the **Banff-Mount Norquay shuttle** (7:55am-8:20pm daily June-Sept., free) can take you between downtown Banff hotels and the mountain, running about once an hour in each direction. See the Norquay website (www.banffnorquay.com) for schedules.

During the winter ski season, the **Banff Ski Shuttle** (daily Nov.-Apr., free) has three morning pickups in town and returns several times throughout the afternoon. Get schedules and details on the Norquay website (www.banffnorquay.com).

★ Bow Valley Parkway

The most direct route between Banff and Lake Louise is the Trans-Canada Highway (Hwy. 1), but a prettier alternative is the **Bow Valley Parkway** (Hwy. 1A), a 30-mile (48-km) secondary route. If you drove straight through, the Bow Valley route would add about 15 minutes of travel time. In fact, because you'll likely make numerous stops for hiking, picnicking, or simply enjoying the mountain views, plan on far more than 15 minutes extra for this scenic drive.

You must have a valid national park pass to travel on the Bow Valley Parkway, whether or not you plan to stop en route.

To protect wildlife in the area, Parks Canada restricts travel on the parkway in the spring (Mar.-late June); check the website (www.pc.gc.ca) for details on road closures.

Johnston Canyon

Thirteen miles (21 km) west of Banff, **Johnston Canyon** is the most popular stop on the Bow Valley Parkway. Though it can be packed with walkers, the trail through the woods and along the cantilevered walkways through this rock canyon rates among the park's most dramatic scenic stops. Come early in the morning for fewer crowds.

The busiest path is the **Johnston Canyon Lower Falls Trail,** a 1.5-mile (2.4-km) round-trip walk along a gentle path and several catwalks to the first set of waterfalls.

Continue past the Lower Falls on the **Johnston Canyon Upper Falls Trail,** which is slightly steeper, with an elevation gain of 394 feet (120 m). It's 3 miles (4.8 km) round-trip from the parking lot to the Upper Falls, which is nearly 100 feet (30 m) high.

If you have more time, you can keep hiking beyond the Upper Falls on the **Ink Pots Trail,** which leads to a series of brightly colored pools. This moderate trail, with an elevation gain of 705 feet (215 m), is 6.7 miles (10.8 km) round-trip from the parking area.

Spring-fall, Parks Canada operates **shuttle buses** (www.pc.gc.ca, 7:45am-7pm daily mid-May-mid-Oct., round-trip adults $5, under age 18 free) between Banff Heritage Train Station (327 Railway Ave.) and Johnston Canyon, a good way to avoid the growing traffic congestion in the canyon area. The ride takes 45 minutes.

Castle Junction

Highway 93, which travels south into Kootenay National Park, meets Highway 1 and the Bow Valley Parkway at **Castle Junction,** 19 miles (31 km) west of Banff. Nearby, you can spot the spiky limestone and granite cliffs of 9,076-foot (2,766-m) **Castle Mountain.**

A challenging full-day hike with a long steady climb takes you behind Castle Mountain to **Rockbound Lake.** With an elevation gain of 2,493 feet (760 m), this trail is 10.4 miles (16.8 km) round-trip. The trailhead is on the east side of Castle Junction.

The **Castle Lookout** was once a fire tower where fire spotters watched for blazes in the national park. Though the tower is gone, this 4.6-mile (7.4-km) round-trip hike with an elevation gain of 1,706 feet (520 m) leads up to a lookout point with views across the Bow Valley. The trailhead is 3 miles (5 km) west of Castle Junction.

Storm Mountain Viewpoint

Storm Mountain, 10,310 feet (3,155 m) tall, gets its name from its dramatic rain and snowstorms. You can see the mountain, along with several nearby peaks, from a pullout along the Bow Valley Parkway, west of Castle Junction. It's a pretty spot for photos or a picnic.

Castle Mountain Internment Camp

From 1915 to 1917, during World War I, **Castle Mountain Internment Camp** housed immigrants of Ukrainian, Austrian, Hungarian, and German descent who were considered enemy aliens. Though the camp is gone, you can pull off the parkway at a memorial plaque, with information about this and other wartime camps in Canada.

Camping

Banff National Park campsite **reservations** (877/737-3783, www.reservation.parkscanada.gc.ca) are accepted online or by phone for all the Tunnel Mountain, Two Jack Lake, and Johnston Canyon campsites, and they're highly recommended, especially if you'll be traveling June-September. The other areas are first-come, first-served. Only Tunnel Mountain has electrical service and RV hookups.

Tunnel Mountain

Close to town, **Tunnel Mountain Campground** (Tunnel Mountain Rd., tent sites $27.40, electrical sites $32.30-38.20) is the largest camping area in Banff National Park. It's divided into three sections: **Tunnel Mountain Village I** (mid-May-mid-Sept.) with 618 sites; **Tunnel Mountain Village II** (year-round) with 188 sites as well as 21 **oTENTiks** ($120), platform tents that can sleep up to six; and **Tunnel Mountain Trailer Court** (mid-May-early Oct.), which has 321 sites exclusively for trailers and large RVs up to 50 feet (15 m). All the Tunnel Mountain areas have washrooms with flush toilets and showers.

Two Jack Lake

Near Lake Minnewanka, 7.5 miles (12 km) northeast of the town of Banff, **Two Jack Lake Campground** (Lake Minnewanka Loop Rd.) accommodates tents and small RVs in two different areas: Main and Lakeside.

Located a five-minute drive from Two Jack Lake, **Two Jack Lake Main** (late June-early Sept., $21.50) has 380 sites. The restrooms have flush toilets but no showers.

If you don't have your own camping gear, consider one of the 32 **equipped camping sites** ($70) at Two Jack Lake Main, which come with a six-person tent, sleeping pads, a stove, and a lantern. You still need to bring sleeping bags or bedding, cooking supplies, food, flashlights, and other personal items.

Many camping spots are right on the lake at the 64-site **Two Jack Lake Lakeside** (mid-May-early Oct., $27.40), which includes 23 walk-in tent sites. This area has flush toilets and showers, as well as 10 **oTENTiks** ($120). These canvas-walled platform tents sleep up to six, with one double and two queen beds, heat, and electricity, as well as an outdoor barbecue and fire pit. You need to bring your own sleeping bags or bedding, as well as food, dishes, and cooking supplies.

Bactrax (225 Bear St., Banff, 403/762-8177, www.campingbanff.com, 8am-8pm daily) rents camping gear if you don't have your own.

Bow Valley Parkway

Three of the national park campgrounds are along the Bow Valley Parkway (Hwy. 1A) between Banff and Lake Louise.

Opposite the Johnston Canyon trailhead, 14 miles (22 km) from the town of Banff, **Johnston Canyon Campground** (Bow Valley Parkway, late May-late Sept., $27.40) has 132 sites for tents and small RVs. The campground has restrooms with flush toilets and hot showers.

The 43-site **Castle Mountain Campground** (Bow Valley Parkway, late May-mid-Sept., $21.50) accommodates tents and small RVs; there are flush toilets but no shower facilities. It's 21 miles (34 km) from Banff and 17 miles (28 km) from Lake Louise.

Small **Protection Mountain Campground** (Bow Valley Parkway, late June-early Sept., $21.50), 11 miles (18 km) from Lake Louise, has just 14 sites. The restrooms have flush toilets but no showers.

Town of Banff

On an August afternoon in the town of Banff, which has a population of just under 9,000, pedestrians stroll the sidewalks shoulder-to-shoulder, stopping for snacks or browsing the shops. Located entirely within the boundaries of Banff National Park, the town of Banff is the park's bustling heart.

Most of the park's accommodations, restaurants, and services are in town, as are some national park sights, along with numerous other privately run museums, gardens, and attractions. There's plenty to see and do.

The Bow River bisects the town. The town center, many of its restaurants and shops, the Banff Centre, and Tunnel Mountain are located between Highway 1 and the river. The Cave and Basin National Historic Site, Banff Upper Hot Springs, Banff Gondola, and the famous Fairmont Banff Springs Hotel are all south of the river.

Sights and Activities
★ Cave and Basin National Historic Site

How did Banff become Canada's first national park? The story begins with a bubbling mineral spring in an underground cave.

The **Cave and Basin National Historic Site** (311 Cave St., 403/762-1566, www.pc.gc.ca, 9am-5pm daily mid-May-mid-Oct., 11am-5pm Wed.-Sun. mid-Oct.-mid-May, adults $3.90, seniors $3.40) tells the park's story, beginning in 1883 when three railroad workers stumbled on a sulfurous spring in a grotto—the Cave that you can still walk into today, through a dimly lit rock-lined tunnel. Through exhibits at this historic site, you can learn more about the development of Canada's national park system and about the hot springs in the area. You can also check out the Basin hot springs pool (although you can no longer take a soak here). If

Town of Banff

To Trans-Canada Hwy

FOX ST

BADGER ST

ANTELOPE ST

BANFF AVE

To Lake Minnewanka and Trans-Canada Hwy

RABBIT ST

MOOSE ST

SQUIRREL ST

- BANFF RAILWAY STATION

BREWSTER TRANSPORTATION CENTRE

GOPHER ST

ELK ST

MOOSE HOTEL & SUITES ●

DEER ST

TUNNEL MOUNTAIN RD

BANFF MINERAL SPRINGS HOSPITAL ■

MARTEN ST

ELK + AVENUE HOTEL

IGA BANFF ■

BEAVER ST

MUSKRAT ST

RX DRUG MART BANFF ■

WOLF ST

Forty Mile Creek

BANFF CANOE CLUB ■

LYNX ST

BACTRAX ■

NOURISH BISTRO ▼

GOURLAY'S BANFF PHARMACY ■

BANFF VISITOR INFORMATION CENTRE ■

THE BISON/ BEAR STREET TAVERN ▼

ALPINE MEDICAL CLINIC ■

PARK DISTILLERY ▼

RAMEN ARASHI ▼

ST. JULIEN RD

WILD FLOUR BAKERY ■

BLOCK KITCHEN + BAR ▼

ULTIMATE SPORTS ■

CARIBOU ST

GRIZZLY ST

CANADA HOUSE GALLERY ■

BOW AVE

EDDIE BURGER + BAR ▼

BEAR ST

BANFF AVE

MOUNT ROYAL HOTEL ●

BEAVER ST

MUSKRAT ST

OTTER ST

To Banff Centre

Bow River

NESTERS MARKET ▼

MONOD SPORTS ▼

HUDSON'S BAY ■

THE NORTH FACE BANFF ■

WOLVERINE ST

LITTLE WILD COFFEE ▼

WHYTE MUSEUM OF THE CANADIAN ROCKIES ★

BANFF FARMERS MARKET ■

BUFFALO ST

Central Park ★

BANFF PARK MUSEUM NATIONAL HISTORIC SITE ★

Bow River

BOW RIVER PEDESTRIAN BRIDGE

CEMETERY ●

BUFFALO NATIONS LUXTON MUSEUM ★

BIRCH AVE

CAVE AVE

YWCA BANFF HOTEL ●

GLEN AVE

0   250 yds

0   250 m

CASCADE GARDENS ★

SPRAY AVE

© MOON.COM

you want to take the waters, visit Banff Upper Hot Springs; the **Thermal Waters Pass** (adults $11.35, seniors $9.95, families $30.05) covers admission to Banff Upper Hot Springs and the Cave and Basin NHS.

The Cave and Basin area also played a role during World War I, when the site housed a **wartime internment camp,** one of 24 camps in Canada for prisoners of war, most of whom were civilians of German or Eastern European heritage. Overall, Canada interned 8,579 people between 1914 and 1920. An on-site exhibit tells you more about this sobering history.

Getting There

The Cave and Basin National Historic Site is across the Bow River from the town center. Cross the Banff Avenue bridge, turn right onto Cave Avenue, and continue for 0.8 mile (1.3 km) to the museum.

Spring-fall, you can get to the site on **Roam Transit Route 4: Cave and Basin bus** (www.roamtransit.com, 9am-6:25pm Fri.-Sun. late May-mid.-June and daily mid-June-mid-Sept., one-way adults $2, seniors and ages 6-18 $1, day pass $5) from town.

Buffalo Nations Luxton Museum

Journalist, adventurer, and entrepreneur Norman Luxton (1876-1962), along with sea captain John Voss, attempted to sail around the world in a 100-year-old, 30-foot (9-m) red cedar dugout canoe, setting off from Victoria in 1901. After stops in Tahiti and Samoa, they reached Fiji, where Luxton, ill with fever, had to abandon the endeavor; Voss eventually reached England in 1904. Luxton made his way to Banff, hoping that the mountain climate would help him return to health.

Luxton took over the then-bankrupt *Crag and Canyon* newspaper, remaining as publisher from 1902 until 1951. In the 1950s he decided that he wanted to establish a museum.

This quirky, old-style gallery, in a fort-like structure now called the **Buffalo Nations Luxton Museum** (1 Birch Ave., 403/762-2388, www.buffalonationsmuseum.com, 10am-7pm daily May-Sept., 11am-5pm daily Oct.-Apr., adults $10, seniors $9, ages 7-17 $5), has exhibits about the First Nations people, primarily of the Rockies and plains regions. It showcases beadwork, drums, pipes, and taxidermy animals. Among the more unusual artifacts are a 6,000-year-old bison skull that was unearthed in downtown Banff and dioramas of the Sun Dance ritual, which involved piercing and other self-torture.

From the town center, cross the Banff Avenue bridge, turn right onto Cave Avenue, and make the first right onto Birch Avenue.

Cascade Gardens

You can (sometimes) escape from downtown Banff's crowds at **Cascade Gardens** (Cave Ave. at Banff Ave., dawn-dusk daily, free), peaceful flower gardens with fanciful burl log bridges and benches, terraced into the hill behind the 1936 park administration building. The gardens are open year-round, weather permitting; the flowers are most vibrant between June and September.

A classic Banff photo spot is in front of the administration building, looking across the gardens through town to Cascade Mountain beyond.

From town, follow Banff Avenue over the bridge across the Bow River, and the gardens are directly in front of you.

★ Banff Upper Hot Springs

You can't bathe at the Cave and Basin National Historic Site, where the discovery of an underground spring led to the creation of Banff National Park, but you can soak in the mineral pools high on Sulphur Mountain at **Banff Upper Hot Springs** (1 Mountain Ave., 403/762-1515 or 800/767-1611, www.hotsprings. ca, 9am-11pm daily mid-May-mid-Oct.,

10am-10pm Sun.-Thurs., 10am-11pm Fri.-Sat. Nov.-mid-May, last admission 30 minutes before closing, adults $8.30, seniors $7.30, ages 3-17 $6.30, families $24.50).

The first bathhouse here was built in 1886, though the current Queen Anne Revival stone bathhouse, which was constructed as a Depression-era unemployment relief project, dates to 1932. At 5,200 feet (1,585 m), surrounded by mountains, the Upper Hot Springs are at the highest elevation of any mineral springs in Canada.

The pool waters are kept between 98°F and 104°F (37-40°C). The minerals that give the waters their unique composition are a mix of sulfate, calcium, bicarbonate, magnesium, and sodium. You can rent towels ($1.90) and swimsuits ($1.90), including historical "bathing costumes." Lockers are available. The **Thermal Waters Pass** (adults $11.35, seniors $9.95, families $30.05) covers admission to both the hot springs and the Cave and Basin National Historic Site. Note: The hot springs are closed mid-late October for annual maintenance.

Getting There

Banff Upper Hot Springs is 2.5 miles (4 km) south of town. Follow Banff Avenue over the Bow River, turn left onto Spray Avenue, then turn right onto Mountain Avenue and follow the signs for 2.2 miles (3.5 km) to the hot springs parking lot.

You can also take the **Roam Transit Route 1: Sulphur Mountain bus** (www. roamtransit.com, 6:15am-11:30pm daily, one-way adults $2, seniors and ages 6-18 $1, day pass $5) between town and the springs.

Banff Gondola

The **Banff Gondola** (Mountain Ave., Sulphur Mountain, 403/762-2523, www. banffjaspercollection.com, 9am-8:30pm daily Apr.-mid-May, 8am-9:30pm daily mid-May-June and early-Sept.-mid-Oct., 8am-10:30pm daily July-early-Sept.,

views of Banff from Cascade Gardens

10am-4:30pm Mon.-Tues. and 10am-8:30pm Wed.-Sun. mid-Oct.-Mar., adults $64, ages 6-15 $32) whisks you to the top of Sulphur Mountain, an eight-minute ride to an elevation of 7,486 feet (2,281 m), where views of six surrounding mountain ranges spread out in all directions. The original gondola, which opened on this site in 1959, was the first in Canada.

When you reach the Summit Building at the top of the gondola, go up to the top (4th) floor observation deck for 360-degree views of the mountain peaks. You can stop for a meal at the cafeteria-style **Northern Lights** or in the window-lined **Sky Bistro** for a more elevated experience.

Outside the Summit Building, follow the **Sulphur Mountain Boardwalk,** a 0.6-mile (1-km) pathway that leads to several observation platforms and to the **Sanson Peak Weather Observatory,** a historic observatory station that opened in 1903. It's named for Norman Bethune Sanson (1862-1949), who hiked up to this station more than 1,000 times over a 30-year period to monitor the area weather. Sanson also served as the curator of the Banff Park Museum from 1896 to 1932.

If you'd like to follow in Sanson's footsteps and hike Sulphur Mountain yourself instead of riding up in the gondola, follow the 3.5-mile (5.6-km) **Sulphur Mountain Trail.** It starts from the Upper Hot Springs parking lot on Mountain Avenue and switchbacks up the mountain slopes, with an elevation gain of 2,149 feet (655 m). You can purchase a **one-way gondola ticket** (mid-May-mid-Oct. adults $32, ages 6-15 $16, mid-Oct.-mid-May free) to save your knees from the hike back down. Note that if you want to ride the gondola *up* and hike down, there's no discount; you have to buy a regular full-price gondola ticket.

In summer, when the gondola gets especially busy midday, visit before 10am or after 6pm to avoid long lines. Buy your tickets online 48 hours in advance for a 10 percent discount.

Getting There

The Banff Gondola is located 2.6 miles (4.2 km) south of town, beyond Banff Upper Hot Springs. Follow Banff Avenue over the Bow River, turn left onto Spray Avenue, then turn right onto Mountain Avenue, which leads up to the gondola parking area.

The **Roam Transit Route 1: Sulphur Mountain bus** (www.roamtransit.com, 6:15am-11:30pm daily, one-way adults $2, seniors and ages 6-18 $1, day pass $5) can take you between town and the gondola.

Fairmont Banff Springs Hotel

Built in 1888 as one of the original Canadian Pacific Railway hotels, the **Fairmont Banff Springs Hotel** (405 Spray Ave., 403/762-2211 or 866/540-4406, www.fairmont.com) is as much a landmark as it is a lodging. While fire destroyed the original wooden hotel building, the stately stone château that now stands on the site, with more

Taking the Waters

In 1883, three railroad workers stumbled on a sulfurous spring in an underground cave in what is now the town of Banff. Although indigenous people had known about the region's hot springs for centuries, Frank McCabe and brothers William and Tom McCardell recognized that the springs they had "found" were a new tourism opportunity, and potentially, a chance to make a lot of money. They wrote to the Canadian government, staking a claim to the springs.

However, after legal battles ensued, Canada's federal government, led by the country's first prime minister, John A. Macdonald, stepped in, creating the Hot Springs Reserve in 1885. That protected area was eventually expanded into Banff National Park, the first in Canada's national park system.

Banff Upper Hot Springs

As McCabe and the McCardell brothers predicted, the Canadian Rockies' hot springs became a draw for tourists, particularly after Canada's transcontinental railroad was completed. The general manager of the Canadian Pacific Railway, William Cornelius Van Horne, was keen to build traffic on the new railroad. He launched the construction of several mountain lodges to accommodate these rail travelers, including the Mount Stephen House in Field, B.C., now in Yoho National Park; the Glacier House at B.C.'s Rogers Pass; and a property that he hoped would create a new standard of Rocky Mountain luxury: the Banff Springs Hotel.

When the grand Banff Springs Hotel, now part of the Fairmont chain, opened in 1888, it helped put Banff on the tourist map. Trainloads of visitors came to "take the waters," soaking in the region's mineral pools.

Today, visitors to the Canadian Rockies still come for the mineral-rich waters at **Banff Upper Hot Springs** and in the mineral pools at the **Fairmont Banff Springs Hotel.** In Jasper National Park, you can soak in **Miette Hot Springs,** and in Kootenay National Park at **Radium Hot Springs.** Several more hot springs along B.C.'s Highway 93/95 have given that road the nickname "The Hot Springs Highway."

Even if more people travel to the Canadian Rockies these days by road than by rail, those 19th-century rail workers were right about one thing: Tourists will come from far and wide to "take the waters."

than 700 guest rooms, was constructed in 1928, and is designated a National Historic Site of Canada. Even if you're not staying at "The Castle in the Rockies," you might want to explore its grand public spaces, have a drink on its mountain-view terrace, or book **afternoon tea** in the Rundle Lounge (noon-3:30pm daily, $55, reservations recommended).

The hotel is on the south side of the Bow River. From town, cross the Banff Avenue bridge, turn left onto Spray Avenue, and follow it 1 mile (1.6 km) to the hotel.

TIP: To take those iconic photos of the Fairmont Banff Springs Hotel surrounded by forests and backed by the mountains, you need to get some distance away from the hotel. From town, follow Buffalo Street toward the Banff

Centre. The point where the road turns sharply uphill is known as **Surprise Corner.** Pull off here, walk up to the lookout platform above the Bow River, and you'll see the hotel standing regally amid the trees.

Banff Park Museum National Historic Site

Wandering into the **Banff Park Museum National Historic Site** (91 Banff Ave., 403/762-1558, www.pc.gc.ca, 10am-6pm daily mid-May-mid-Oct., 11am-5pm Sat.-Sun. mid-Oct.-mid-May, adults $3.90, seniors $3.40) is like stumbling into the home of a 19th-century mountain explorer.

Opened in 1903, the log building still has its original honey-hued wood paneling. Most of the collection, which includes taxidermy bears, bison, bighorned sheep, birds, and other animals native to the Banff area, was acquired between 1900 and the 1930s. The museum's oldest specimen, a red-breasted merganser, was mounted in 1860—before Canada had even become Canada.

Head upstairs to find the "cabinet of curiosities," housing various oddities that people donated to the museum.

Whyte Museum of the Canadian Rockies

Founded by local artists and philanthropists Peter Whyte and Catharine Robb Whyte, the **Whyte Museum of the Canadian Rockies** (111 Bear St., 403/762-2291, www.whyte.org, 10am-5pm daily, adults $10, seniors $9, students 12 and over $5) explores mountain history, art, and culture.

Exhibits showcase the Rocky Mountains' First Nations communities, early explorers, and mountain guides and skiers who helped develop the area for winter tourism. The museum also has an art gallery with a changing roster of exhibitions.

On summer weekends, the museum offers 60-minute **Banff Historic Walking Tours,** with stories about the people who helped build the town. Check the museum website for schedules.

Tours

Brewster Sightseeing (403/762-6700 or 866/360-8839, www.banffjaspercollection.com) offers several Banff tours (4.5-6 hours, adults $135-175, ages 6-15 $68-88), with options that include the Banff Gondola, a Lake Minnewanka cruise, or both. It also runs these day tours of Banff starting in Calgary or Canmore. From Banff, it operates tours to Lake Louise, the Columbia Icefield, and Jasper as well. Buy tickets online or at its **Explore Rockies Activity Centres** at the **Brewster Transportation Centre** (100 Gopher St., 800/760-6934, 7am-9pm daily), **Elk + Avenue Hotel** (333 Banff Ave., 403/760-3291, 7am-10pm daily), **Mount Royal Hotel** (138 Banff Ave., 403/760-8557, 7am-9pm daily), or **Cave and Basin** (311 Cave Ave., 403/760-3353, 11am-5pm Wed.-Sun.). The company also has an office at the **Banff Gondola** (Mountain Ave., 403/762-7475), open during the gondola's operating hours.

Discover Banff Tours (Sundance Mall, 215 Banff Ave., 403/760-5007 or 877/565-9372, www.banfftours.com, 8am-6pm daily) offers a **Discover Banff & Its Wildlife Tour** (Apr.-Nov., 3 hours, adults $68, ages 6-12 $35), with stops at Bow Falls, the Fairmont Banff Springs Hotel, Surprise Corner, and Lake Minnewanka. From Banff, the company also runs half-day and full-day tours for **Lake Louise, guided hiking tours, helicopter tours,** and **horseback riding tours.**

Sports and Recreation
Hiking

Starting right in town, a popular intermediate-level hike goes up the **Tunnel Mountain Trail** to a lookout point with views across the Bow Valley. The trail is 3 miles (4.8 km) round-trip, with a series of switchbacks to moderate the climb; the elevation gain is 850 feet (260 m). The trailhead is near the Banff Centre on St. Julien Road.

Another hike to take for its panoramic views is the **Sulphur Mountain Trail.** The trailhead starts from the Upper Hot Springs parking lot on Mountain Avenue and switchbacks up the mountain slopes, with an elevation gain of 2,149 feet (655 m). The trail is 3.5 miles (5.6 km) each way. If you don't want to walk back down, you can purchase a one-way ticket on the **Banff Gondola** (403/762-2523, www.banffjaspercollection.com, mid-May-mid-Oct. adults $32, ages 6-15 $16, mid-Oct.-mid-May free).

The **Surprise Corner to Hoodoos Trail** (3 mi/4.8 km each way) is an easy hike along the Bow River to a group of hoodoos, unusual limestone rock formations. The trail begins at Surprise Corner (Buffalo St.), which also has an overlook with views to the Fairmont Banff Springs Hotel. For a one-way walk, catch the **Roam Transit Route 2: Tunnel Mountain bus** (www.roamtransit.com, 6:15am-11:30pm daily, one-way adults $2, seniors and ages 6-18 $1, day pass $5) back to town from Tunnel Mountain Campground.

Canoeing and Kayaking

Take a laid-back paddle down the Bow River with a canoe or kayak rental from the **Banff Canoe Club** (403/762-5005, www.banffcanoeclub.com, 10am-6pm daily mid-May-mid-Oct., $40 per hour, $20 each additional hour). Its docks are on the riverbank at the corner of Wolf Street and Bow Avenue. It also offers 1.5-hour guided tours in 12-passenger voyageur canoes, including **River Explorer Big Canoe Tours** (11am, 1pm, and 3:30pm daily mid-May-mid-Oct., adults $54, ages 6-12 $25) and **Wildlife on the Bow Big Canoe Tours** (9am Sat.-Sun. and 6pm daily June, 9am and 6pm daily July-Aug., 6pm daily Sept., adults $54, ages 6-12 $25).

Cycling

The **Rocky Mountain Legacy Trail** (403/762-1556, www.pc.gc.ca) is a paved 17-mile (27-km) multiuse path that begins at the Bow Valley Parkway and travels through the town of Banff before running parallel to Highway 1 east to the town of Canmore. Nearly 14 miles (22 km) of the route are within the boundaries of Banff National Park, where it's known as the Banff Legacy Trail. Pick up a trail map at area visitors centers or online from the Banff National Park website.

Rent bikes from **Bactrax** (225 Bear St., 403/762-8177, www.snowtips-bactrax. com, 8am-8pm daily, 1 hour $10-16, full-day $35-60) or **Ultimate Sports** (206 Banff Ave., 403/762-0547, www. ultimatebanff.com, 8am-9pm daily, 1 hour $10-15, full-day $35-60). Bike rentals from **Banff Cycle** (403/985-4848, www.banffcycle.com, full-day $50-150) include free delivery and pick-up from any location in Banff.

Entertainment and Events
★ Banff Centre

The **Banff Centre** (107 Tunnel Mountain Dr., box office 403/762-6301 or 800/413-8368, www.banffcentre.ca) describes itself as "the largest arts and creativity incubator on the planet." Established in the 1930s as the Banff School of Drama, and quickly renamed the Banff School of Fine Arts, the Banff Centre provides professional development and training programs in a variety of artistic fields, including music, theater, dance, literature, painting, photography, sculpture, film, and new media. This campus-like complex of buildings on a hill overlooking the town presents a full calendar of performances, events, and exhibitions that are open to the public.

Festivals and Events

All summer long, the **Banff Summer Arts Festival** (www.banffcentre.ca, June-Aug.) presents more than 100 events, including concerts, dance, lectures, readings, and films on the Banff Centre campus.

The Banff Centre also hosts the **Banff Mountain Film and Book Festival** (www.banffcentre.ca, Oct.-Nov.), nine days of movies, book talks, lectures, and other events that incorporate a mountain theme.

Get started on your holiday shopping at the **Banff Christmas Market** (www.banffchristmasmarket.com, Nov.), or bring the family to the annual **Santa Claus Parade of Lights** (Nov.).

Shopping

Canada House Gallery (201 Bear St., 800/419-1298, www.canadahouse.com, 9:30am-6pm Sun.-Thurs., 9:30am-7pm Fri.-Sat.) shows work by Canadian artists, including Inuit art from Canada's Arctic regions.

Banff has several outdoor gear shops, including **Monod Sports** (129 Banff Ave., 403/762-4571 or 866/956-6663, www.monodsports.com, 10am-8pm daily) and **The North Face Banff** (124 Banff Ave., 403/762-0775, www.thenorthfacebanff.ca, 9am-10pm daily).

Ultimate Sports (206 Banff Ave., 403/762-0547, www.ultimatebanff.com, 7am-9pm daily) sells and rents gear for skiing, snowboarding, and cycling. **Bactrax** (225 Bear St. 403/762-8177, www.campingbanff.com, 8am-8pm daily) rents camping gear, including tents, sleeping bags, and cooking supplies.

There's a branch of the **Hudson's Bay** (125 Banff Ave., 403/762-5525, www.thebay.com, 10am-7pm Sun.-Thurs., 10am-9pm Fri.-Sat.) department store in the center of town.

Food
Contemporary
Yes, you can sample buffalo and other game at ★ **The Sleeping Buffalo** (700 Tunnel Mountain Rd., 403/760-4484, www.crmr.com, noon-5pm and 5:30pm-9pm daily, lunch $14-20, dinner $26-40), from a buffalo duo of grilled strip loin and braised short ribs to the house-made charcuterie platter, a sharing plate for two, with air-dried elk, smoked duck breast, and wild boar pâté. There are also west coast seafood options if meat isn't your thing. There's nothing sleepy about this upscale wood-beamed dining room at Buffalo Mountain Lodge, although you may need a nap after the warm chocolate molten cake, served with caramel sauce and Amaretto ice cream.

★ **Juniper Bistro** (Juniper Hotel, 1 Juniper Way, 403/763-6219, www.thejuniper.com, 7am-11am and 5pm-9pm Mon.-Thurs., 7am-11am and 5pm-10pm Fri., 7am-2pm and 5pm-10pm Sat., 7am-2pm and 5pm-9pm Sun., breakfast $10-15, dinner $17-35) starts with a lovely setting, with a wall of windows facing the mountains and a spacious outdoor terrace with even better views. It's an excellent choice for a leisurely breakfast, with creative plates like eggs Benedict smothered with braised rabbit over bannock, huevos rancheros topped with barbecue pork, or a breakfast salad with kale, greens, goat cheese, and poached eggs. In the evening, try a colorful vegetarian plate of yellow, pink, and red beets with roasted Brussels sprouts and yams, an Alberta wild boar chop with grilled fruit, or sea bass seasoned with olives, pine nuts, and anchovies. Nearly all the wines and beers are Canadian, so drink local, eh?

Ride the Banff Gondola to the ★ **Sky Bistro** (Sulphur Mountain, 403/762-7486, www.banffjaspercollection.com, 11am-4:30pm Mon.-Tues. and 11am-8:30pm Wed.-Sun. late Jan.-Mar., 11am-8:30pm daily Apr.-mid-May, 11am-9:30pm daily mid-May-June and early Sept.-mid-Oct., 11am-10:30pm daily July-early Sept., 11am-8:30pm Wed.-Sun. mid-Oct.-late Jan., lunch $17-22, dinner $28-39) for a contemporary meal with expansive vistas over the mountains, an especially atmospheric setting at sunset. Up here at 7,510 feet (2,290 m), you could share squash fritters or Alberta beef tartar with pickled egg yolk, then dig into locally raised lamb with toasted pumpkin seeds and sun-dried tomato pesto, a pork trio of local belly, pulled shoulder, and smoked hock stew, or a meal-sized citrus-dressed ancient grains salad with root vegetables, chard, and broccolini. Linger over the classic strawberry shortcake or the "gourmet PB&J bar," a childhood fantasy grown up, with layers of dark chocolate ganache, peanut butter mousse, and grape jelly. Packages including gondola tickets and meals are available; check the website or phone for details.

Brewing its own vodka, gin, and rye, and serving fun "campfire food," **Park Distillery** (219 Banff Ave., 403/762-5114, www.parkdistillery.com, 11am-10pm daily, lunch $15-25, dinner $20-48), a lively ski lodge-style pub, turns out plates like wild trout, rotisserie chicken, and Alberta sirloin from a wood-fired grill, and there's a long list of spirits and brews beyond its own. To get the scoop on the spirited scene, take a free 30-minute **distillery tour** (3:30pm daily, reservations recommended).

Where's the wildlife at **The Bison** (211 Bear St., 403/762-5550, www.thebison.ca, 5pm-10pm Mon.-Sat., 10am-2pm and 5pm-10pm Sun., brunch $15-18, dinner $23-56)? The chefs can get wild in the open kitchen at this bustling bistro, where the 2nd-floor dining room overlooks town and the mountains. And there's wildlife on the plates, too, when you graze on starters like escargots with bone marrow and bacon lardons or roasted scallops with chickpeas and crispy kale, before going where the signature bison roam: bison *tataki* (bison seasoned with a soy-citrus sauce and lightly seared), bison rib eye with chimichurri, or the classic bison short ribs, braised and served with baby potatoes.

When you're on the lookout for light bites and cocktails, there's **Block Kitchen + Bar** (5-201 Banff Ave., 403/985-2887, www.banffblock.com, 11:30am-10pm Sun.-Thurs, 11:30am-10:30pm Fri.-Sat., lunch $15-19, all-day small plates $8-36). From midday to late night, the Mediterranean-Asian sharing plates travel from vegetable samosas to Silk Road chicken skewers to smoked bison flatbread. At lunch, you can choose from a menu of world-roaming sandwiches, like a beef brisket "naanwich" or a black rice and falafel patty topped with smoked cheddar.

To dine before a show, or to enjoy fine modern fare with a valley view, head to the Banff Centre and its **Three Ravens Restaurant** (Sally Borden Bldg., 4th Fl., 107 Tunnel Mountain Dr., 403/762-6300, www.banffcentre.ca, 5pm-9pm daily, $30-41), where there's plenty to applaud on the imaginative menu. You might open with a salad of greens, quinoa, and coffee-braised carrots or braised Alberta lamb with ricotta gnocchi, before a second act of juniper-rubbed elk, steelhead trout with roasted peppers, or bison tenderloin paired with farro and candied yams. A more relaxed Banff Centre dining option is **MacLab Bistro** (Kinnear Centre, 1st Fl., 107 Tunnel Mountain Dr., 403/762-6141, www.banffcentre.ca, 7am-2am daily, food service till midnight, breakfast $4-16, lunch and dinner $15-28), serving salads, sandwiches, burgers, pizzas, and curries, as well as pre- or post-event drinks and snacks.

Japanese

Expect a line-up at **Ramen Arashi** (Sundance Mall, 215 Banff Ave., 403/760-0908, www.ramenarashi.com, 11am-9pm daily, $11-15), a Japanese noodle shop with fewer than 25 seats, tucked away on the 2nd floor of the Sundance Mall. The signature dish is *arashi tantan men,* noodles in a savory broth enriched with sesame paste and spiced with chili oil. Also popular is the flavorful *tonkatsu* ramen topped with barbecued pork. To drink, there's Japanese beer, sake, and plum wine.

Pizza

The choices are simple at the **Bear Street Tavern** (211 Bear St., 403/762-2021, www.bearstreettavern.ca, 11:30am-10pm daily, $16-22): pizza and craft beer. The pies build on the basics with options like the Tatanka (smoked bison, blue cheese, and caramelized onions) or the Wheeler Hut (wild mushrooms, pine nuts, truffle oil, and pesto). For the suds, Bear Street typically has eight local brews on tap and more microbrews in the bottle. If you're not into pizza, there's pork belly mac-and-cheese or smoked chicken wings with *piri piri* sauce. It's on the lower level of the same space that houses The Bison restaurant.

Vegetarian

Vegetarians, and anyone who's eaten their fill of Alberta beef, will appreciate the interesting plant-based fare at **Nourish Bistro** (110-211 Bear St., 403/760-3933, www.nourishbistro.com, 11:30am-10pm daily, $15-26). On the all-day menu of plates designed to share, you can start with the popular nachos or choose from veggie burgers, a grain and plant "nourishment bowl," or a vegan "mac and squeeze" made with quinoa noodles and coconut sauce. Several dishes come in either full or half portions.

Burgers

Deep-fried pickles, saucy chicken wings, hipster hot dogs, and classic poutine may grab your attention, but at **Eddie Burger + Bar** (6-137 Banff Ave., 403/762-2230, www.eddieburgerbar.ca, 11:30am-2am daily, $15-21), the name says it all. You want something on a bun, whether it's Alberta beef, bison, chicken, veggies, or even elk, and something from the bar. The milk shake bar has classics like vanilla or chocolate, newcomers like Nutella or chocolate raspberry,

Top to bottom: lunch at the Wild Flour Artisan Bakery; Sky Bistro at the top of the Banff Gondola; colorful vegetables at Juniper Bistro.

and "high-octane" concoctions like the Monkey's Lunch (vanilla ice cream, Kahlúa, and crème de banana) or the Burt Reynolds (vanilla ice cream, spiced rum, and butter ripple schnapps).

Cafés, Bakeries, and Light Bites

Cheerful ★ **Wild Flour Artisan Bakery** (101-211 Bear St., 403/760-5074, www. wildflourbakery.ca, 7am-4pm daily, breakfast $3.50-7, lunch $6-10) is always busy, and with good reason. From pastries, house-made granola, and frittata sandwiches to good-value lunchtime combos of soup, focaccia, sandwiches, or fresh salads, like kale with apples, cranberries, and pumpkin seeds, there's lots of deliciousness on your overflowing plate. Come at off-hours to snag a table or counter seat, or take your fresh-baked brownie, unusual fig-anise cookie, or other goodies for the trail. The same owners run **Little Wild Coffee** (119 Banff Ave., 403/762-0329, www.littlewildcoffee.ca, 8am-6pm daily), serving coffee and baked goods.

Groceries and Markets

At the **Banff Farmers Market** (Banff Central Park, Bear St. at Buffalo St., www. thebanfffarmersmarket.com, 10am-6pm Wed. late May-early Oct.), you can find fresh produce, bison jerky, baked goods, prepared foods, and crafts.

Banff has several grocery stores, including **Nesters Market** (122 Bear St., 403/762-3663, www.nestersmarket.com, 8am-11pm daily) and **IGA Banff** (318 Marten St., 403/762-5378, www.west.iga.ca, 8am-11pm daily).

Accommodations

Book early if you're visiting in July and August, as accommodations fill up months in advance. Staying south of Banff in the town of Canmore is a reasonable alternative if Banff is overly busy.

Under $150

Banff's best budget lodging is the **YWCA Banff Hotel** (102 Spray Ave., 403/762-3560, www.ywcabanff.ca), in a former hospital building overlooking the Bow River, opposite Cascade Gardens. Not only does it offer simple, moderately priced rooms, but revenue from the hotel funds a local domestic violence prevention program. Double rooms ($155-210) have a bed, desk, and fan; the more expensive ones have private baths. On the lower level, bunk-bedded dorms ($40-45 pp) sleep eight; most have their own washrooms with showers. None of the rooms has a TV, but you can catch your favorite show in the lounge. There's a shared kitchen and guest laundry; Wi-Fi, parking, and morning coffee in the lounge are free.

Banff has a busy year-round hostel, the **HI-Banff Alpine Centre** (801 Hidden Ridge Way, 778/328-2220 or 866/762-4122, www.hihostels.ca, $47-70 dorm, $149-235 d), off Tunnel Mountain Road. Sleeping options include four- to six-bed female, male, or mixed dorms, private doubles with a shared bath, private queens with en suite baths, and private standalone log cabins ($300-475) with two double beds, a sitting area with a sofa and TV, and a bath. All rates include Wi-Fi and a town bus pass (ask at the front desk). The hostel has a restaurant, pub, and shared kitchen; staff organize group hikes and nightlife excursions.

$150-300

At the 50-room ★ **Juniper Hotel** (1 Juniper Way, 403/762-2281 or 866/551-2281, www.thejuniper.com, $189-394), a redone 1950s lodge, there's plenty to see, inside and out, from the locally themed artwork and First Nations artifacts throughout the hallways, to the scenic vistas from the mountainside guest rooms. Rooms are mid-century-modern, with clean-lined cherry furnishings, earth-toned upholstery, and updated baths with stone counters and floors. There's no pool, but there is a small outdoor hot tub. Open for breakfast and dinner, **Juniper Bistro** has an expansive mountain-view terrace. The hotel is 1.2 miles (2 km) outside the town center, at the base of the road to the Mount Norquay Ski Area. Parking and Wi-Fi are included, and you can catch a shuttle into town or to the ski hill.

While it's best known for its arts programs, the **Banff Centre** (107 Tunnel Mountain Dr., 403/762-6148 or 800/884-7574, www.banffcentre.ca, $189-339) also offers hotel accommodations on its wooded campus above town. These aren't student dorms; rather, they're comfortable mid-range hotel rooms. The most modern units are in the Professional Development Centre, where standard rooms have dark woodsy furnishings and either one king or two queen beds; one-bedroom suites have a separate living room. A $15 facility fee covers Wi-Fi, parking, and access to the nearby Sally Borden Building, which houses a fitness center, a swimming pool, a climbing wall, and a running track, as well as several dining outlets.

Over $300

Up the hill from the town center, **Buffalo Mountain Lodge** (700 Tunnel Mountain Rd., 403/762-2400 or 800/661-1367, www.crmr.com, $269-429) has 108 lodge-style rooms, all with wood-burning fireplaces, TVs, DVD players, included Wi-Fi, and patios or balconies, in several different buildings. The top units are the "premier" rooms in log cabin-like lodges on the property's upper level, with pine ceilings and in-floor heating in the baths. Other accommodations are in townhouse units or standard hotel rooms. Parking is complimentary, as is ski and bike storage. You can soak in the large outdoor hot tub. The excellent **Sleeping Buffalo Restaurant** serves breakfast to guests and is open to the public for lunch and dinner.

Styled like an upscale mountain lodge, the **Moose Hotel & Suites** (345 Banff Ave., 403/760-8570, www.moosehotelandsuites.com, $249-779)

has 174 guest rooms, including standard doubles and both one- and two-bedroom suites. With balconies or patios and large windows, they feel open and airy; standard amenities include Wi-Fi, parking, in-room coffeemakers, fridges, and microwaves. Head to the top floor to swim in the indoor pool or soak in the two rooftop hot tubs. A unique feature in the middle of the hotel courtyard is a restored 1913 historic house, which originally stood on the lodging's current location.

Despite its traditional exterior, the **Elk + Avenue Hotel** (333 Banff Ave., 403/762-5666 or 877/442-2623, www.banffjaspercollection.com, $359-449) has 162 contemporary guest rooms, updated with gray faux-wood wallpaper, red desk chairs, coffeemakers, and modern baths. For more space, choose a junior suite with a sitting area or a loft unit with a bedroom upstairs and living space below. A whirlpool tub, sauna, and fitness facility, plus Wi-Fi and underground parking, are among the amenities. Tour operator Pursuit Collection runs the hotel, so its on-site activities office books excursions; ask about package rates for lodging and tours.

Part of the Pursuit Collection, the ★ **Mount Royal Hotel** (138 Banff Ave., 403/762-3331 or 877/442-2623, www.banffjaspercollection.com, $309-459), a sprawling boutique property in the center of town, was completely renovated in 2018. The 133 guest rooms range in size from compact heritage rooms to more spacious junior suites; all have fashionable quilted headboards, custom Canadian-made furnishings, one-cup coffeemakers, cozy robes, and sleek contemporary bathrooms. Rates include Wi-Fi and parking. Make time to chill in the hotel's highlight: the top-floor Cascade Lounge and rooftop hot tub, with views over town to the mountains.

On Sulphur Mountain, below Banff Upper Hot Springs and the Banff Gondola, the **Rimrock Resort Hotel** (300

Mountain Ave., 403/762-3356 or 888/746-7625, www.rimrockresort.com, $258-888) is a classic luxury hotel. The best of the 343 rooms and suites have up-close mountain vistas. Facilities include an indoor pool, a sauna, a hot tub, a 24-hour fitness center, and a spa. Two lounges (martinis are a specialty), a casual café, and two restaurants, including the upscale French-inspired **Eden,** ensure that you won't want for food or drink.

Known as "The Castle in the Rockies," the ★ **Fairmont Banff Springs Hotel** (405 Spray Ave., 403/762-2211 or 866/540-4406, www.fairmont.com, $619-1,504, resort fee $25 per day, parking $27-41) remains both a regional landmark and the town's most distinctive accommodations. Once you've settled into this stately stone manor, you might wish you had an appointment secretary to schedule all your activities, with its mountain-view indoor and outdoor pools, tennis courts, golf course, croquet lawn, bowling alley, large fitness center offering yoga and other exercise classes, and deluxe spa. Hotel guests can take a free one-hour **heritage tour** (1pm daily) of the property. The hotel's 757 guest rooms range from cozy 200-square-foot (19-sq-m) nooks to expansive suites fit for a queen (yes, more than one monarch has stayed here). A day pass to the hotel's lovely indoor **mineral pools** is $69 for hotel guests, $79 for nonguests; admission to the baths is complimentary with a massage, facial, or other spa treatment. The Fairmont's numerous dining outlets include the **1888 Chop House,** which focuses on wild game and Alberta beef; the Austrian-themed **Waldhaus;** the **Rundle Lounge,** which offers cocktails and light bites, as well as afternoon tea; and **The Vermillion Room** (www.vermillionroom.com, 7am-11am, noon-3pm, and 5pm-10pm Mon.-Fri.; 7am-3pm and 5pm-10pm Sat.-Sun., breakfast $14-34, lunch and dinner $16-65), a French-inspired all-day dining spot that serves a lavish weekend brunch (adults $55, kids $27).

Mountains surround the Fairmont Banff Springs Hotel.

Information and Services
Visitor Information
The **Banff Visitor Information Centre** (224 Banff Ave., 403/762-8421, www.banfflakelouise.com, 8am-8pm daily mid-May-mid-Oct., 9am-5pm daily mid-Oct.-mid-May) provides information about things to do in the area and keeps an updated list of available accommodations. **Parks Canada** (www.pc.gc.ca) staff are also on hand with park maps, brochures, and tips.

To learn more about Banff's historic buildings, or to plan your own walking tour, check out the town of Banff's online guide, **Walking Through Banff's History** (www.banff.ca).

Media and Communications
Banff's local newspapers include *The Crag and Canyon* (www.thecragandcanyon.ca) and the *Rocky Mountain Outlook* (www.rmoutlook.com).

The Canadian Rockies edition of *Where* **magazine** (www.where.ca) lists events and other things to do in Banff, Lake Louise, and surrounding mountain areas.

Medical Services
Banff Mineral Springs Hospital (305 Lynx St., 403/762-2222, www.covenanthealth.ca) provides 24-hour emergency services. **Alpine Medical Clinic** (Unit 201A, Bison Courtyard, 211 Bear St., 403/762-3155, www.alpinemedical.ca, 8:30am-7pm Mon.-Thurs., 8:30am-5pm Fri., 9am-5pm Sat.-Sun.) accepts visitors for minor health issues.

For pharmacy services, try **Gourlay's Banff Pharmacy** (220 Bear St., 403/762-2516, www.pharmachoice.com, 9am-7pm Mon.-Fri., 9am-6pm Sat., 10am-5pm Sun.) or **RX Drug Mart Banff** (317 Banff Ave., 403/762-2245, www.guardian-ida-pharmacies.ca, 9am-8pm Mon.-Thurs., 9am-9pm Fri.-Sat., 10am-6pm Sun.).

Getting Around
Highway 1, the Trans-Canada Highway, connects Banff with Lake Louise to the west and Canmore and Calgary to the east. The center of town is south of the highway and north of the Bow River. The town of Banff is compact and easy to get around on foot.

Several attractions and accommodations, including the Cave and Basin National Historic Site, Banff Upper Hot Springs, the Banff Gondola, and the Fairmont Banff Springs Hotel are on the south side of the Bow River. A bridge on Banff Avenue crosses the river.

If you're on foot, you can cross on the **Bow River Pedestrian Bridge.** Built in 2013, this graceful timber footbridge across the river is east of the Banff Avenue bridge. On the town side, you can access the footbridge along the river or via the Bow River Trail, near the corner of Buffalo and Muskrat Streets. On the south side, the footbridge takes you to Glen Avenue, behind the YWCA Banff Hotel.

By Car

Banff streets get very congested, particularly in summer and fall, so you may find it less frustrating to get around on foot or by public transit.

Parking

You can park for free on the street and in a number of lots and parkades around town. Time limits vary from 15 minutes to 12 hours, so check the signs before you leave your car. On residential streets without a posted time limit, you can park for up to 72 hours.

The easiest way to find parking is using the **Banff Parking app** (www.banffparking.ca), which indicates where you can park for how long and how busy each location typically is. You can search for spots for cars, RVs, and bicycles. The **Town of Banff** (www.banff.ca) also has a parking map on its website.

Car Rentals

Car rental companies with Banff locations include **Avis** (Cascade Plaza, Wolf St. at Banff Ave., 403/762-3222, www.avis.ca), **Budget** (202 Bear St., 403/226-1550, www.budgetcalgary.ca), **Enterprise** (Caribou Lodge, 521 Banff Ave., 403/762-2688, www.enterprise.ca), and **Hertz** (Fairmont Banff Springs Hotel, 405 Spray Ave., 403/762-2027, www.hertz.ca).

By Bus

Roam Transit (403/762-0606, www.roamtransit.com) operates several bus routes throughout the Banff area. If you can match your travel times with the bus schedule, taking the bus can be a viable way to get around town. Banff was the first municipality in Canada to run an all-hybrid electric transit fleet.

Route 1: Sulphur Mountain (6:15am-11:30pm daily) travels through town along Banff Avenue, then crosses the river and follows Mountain Avenue to Banff Upper Hot Springs and the Banff Gondola.

Route 2: Tunnel Mountain (6:15am-11:30pm daily) runs from the Tunnel Mountain Campground through town along Banff Avenue, across the river, and along Spray Avenue to the Fairmont Banff Springs Hotel.

Route 4: Cave and Basin (9am-6:25pm Fri.-Sun. late May-mid.-June and daily mid-June-mid-Sept.) is a seasonal route that can take you between town, the Cave and Basin National Historic Site, Banff Upper Hot Springs, and the Banff Gondola.

To travel between Banff and Canmore, you can ride **Route 3: Banff-Canmore Regional** (6am-10:50pm daily).

Use the **trip planner function** on the Roam Transit website (www.roamtransit.com) to figure out what bus to take. The system also has a real-time bus-tracking feature that lets you know when the next bus is arriving.

Transit Fares and Passes

Purchase **local fares** (one-way adults $2, seniors and ages 6-18 $1) or day passes ($5), good for multiple rides throughout the day,

on the bus. You can also buy **regional fares** (one-way adults $6, seniors and ages 6-18 $3) or day passes (adults $15, seniors and ages 6-18 $7.50) on the Canmore buses.

Pay for your bus fares with exact change if you can. The electronic fare boxes on the buses don't give change; if you don't have exact change, they issue you a **change voucher** that you can redeem at the **Bow Valley Regional Transit Customer Service Centre** (221 Beaver St.), **Banff Town Hall** (110 Bear St.), **Fairmont Banff Springs Hotel** (405 Spray Ave.), **Elk + Avenue Hotel** (333 Banff Ave.), and other locations around town.

Transfers are free between local routes (1, 2, and 4) and are valid for up to 30 minutes. You can also transfer from the regional Route 3 to one of the local routes. If you're starting your trip on a local route but plan to transfer to the Canmore bus, buy your regional ticket when you first board the local bus so you can transfer to the regional bus without paying an extra fare.

By Taxi
Banff Taxi and **Taxi Taxi,** both part of the **Banff Transportation Group** (403/762-0000, www.banfftransportation.com), provide 24-hour cab service. Taxis wait at stands around town; you can also hail them on the street or phone for a cab.

Canmore
Just 16 miles (26 km) southeast of the town of Banff and 65 miles (105 km) due west of Calgary, Canmore is a quieter alternative to staying within Banff National Park. You're close enough to make day trips to all the park sights, and the town, with a population of nearly 14,000, has attractions of its own, particularly for outdoor enthusiasts. With several good restaurants, it's worth a stop for a meal, even if you're only passing through.

Surrounded by mountains, Canmore is known for the Three Sisters, a triad of peaks named Faith, Charity, and Hope, also called the Big, Middle, and Little Sisters, that you can see from around the

Canmore

town. The Three Sisters Mountain is the highest in the Canmore area, with Big Sister rising to 9,632 feet (2,936 m).

Sights and Recreation

Downtown Canmore has several art galleries to browse, including **Carter-Ryan Gallery and Live Art Venue** (705 Main St., 403/621-1000, www.carter-ryan. com, 10am-6pm Thurs.-Tues.), which shows the colorful paintings and the soapstone carvings of aboriginal artist Jason Carter. Also on view is artwork from the children's book series, *Who Is Boo: The Terrific Tales of One Trickster Rabbit,* which Carter illustrated and author Bridget Ryan wrote. The gallery has a second location in **Banff** (229 Bear St., 403/985-5556, 10am-6pm Thurs.-Tues.).

Learn about the brewing process, and sample the suds, at Canmore's first microbrewery, **Grizzly Paw Brewing Company** (310 Old Canmore Rd., 403/678-2487, www.thegrizzlypaw. com, tasting room 11am-5pm Mon.-Wed., 11am-9pm Thurs.-Sun., tours 2pm Wed., 1pm, 2:30pm, and 4pm Fri.-Sun.). You can also quaff the brews along with flatbreads, salads, and sandwiches at **Tank 310** (noon-9pm Thurs.-Sun., $15-28), a window-lined dining spot at the brewery, or stop in for beer, burgers and other pub fare at its downtown **restaurant** (622 8th St., 403/678-9983, 11am-11pm Sun.-Thurs., 11am-midnight Fri.-Sat., $16-26).

Sweep over the Canmore region and get a close-up view of the Three Sisters peaks on an excursion with **Alpine Heli Tours** (91 Bow Valley Trail, 403/678-4802, www.alpinehelicopter.com). Tour options include the 12-minute **Three Sisters Peaks Tour** ($129); the 25-minute **Royal Canadian Tour** ($259), which starts with the Three Sisters tour route, before flying through the Goat Range Pass and along the Sundance Range in Banff National Park; and the 30-minute **Mount Assiniboine Glacier Tour** ($314), which adds views of the 11,870-foot

(3,611-m) peak dubbed the "Matterhorn of the Canadian Rockies."

Among Canmore's numerous hiking routes, a favorite is the **Grassi Lakes Trail,** which climbs up to two turquoise ponds. This 2.4-mile (3.8-km) round-trip trail, with an elevation gain of 820 feet (250 m), has two forks. The easier branch ascends gently along a gravel road, but the more difficult route, a forest trail with a short steep section near the top, has far better views. The trailhead is off Highway 742, west of town.

When you're ready to play indoors, head for **Elevation Place** (700 Railway Ave., 403/678-8920, www.elevationplace. ca, pool only adults $8, seniors and ages 18-25 $6, ages 12-17 $5, ages 3-11 $4, full facility adults $16, seniors and ages 18-25 $13, ages 12-17 $8, ages 3-11 $5), Canmore's modern public recreation center, which has a swimming pool, fitness equipment, and a climbing gym.

Festivals and Events

Alberta's longest-running folk fest, the **Canmore Folk Music Festival** (403/678-2524, www.canmorefolkfestival.com, Aug.) is a weekend-long showcase of folk, world, blues, and roots music that began back in 1978.

Food
Contemporary

Fasten your seat belts, diners. Canmore's coolest dining spot is ★ **PD3 by Blake** (806 Main St., 403/675-3663, www. blakecanmore.com, May-Oct.), in a silver 1960s double-decker bus parked in a courtyard off Main Street. It's actually two different restaurants. **PD3 Street** (11:30am-late Thurs.-Tues., $13-15), a take-out window with adjacent picnic tables, serves eclectic Asian-inspired street food, like the Backpacker, a tempura shrimp taco piled with Vietnamese slaw and dressed with peanut sauce, or the Crack Wrap, a cheese tortilla stuffed with chicken, ramen, pickles, mango, and chilies. A sit-down dining room upstairs

Canmore

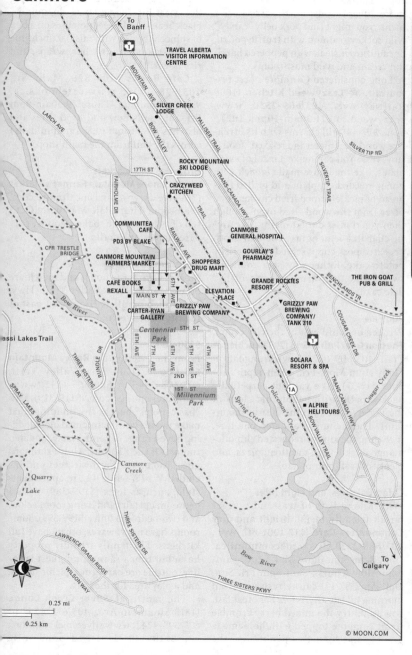

inside the bus, **PD3 Upper Saloon** (5pm-10pm Thurs.-Sat., prix-fixe $99) is even more adventurous; on the fixed-price menu, you might find pork belly "candy," wild sockeye salmon with truffle ponzu, or cauliflower steak with peppered hazelnut cream and wild mushrooms.

Long considered Canmore's best restaurant, ★ **Crazyweed Kitchen** (1600 Railway Ave., 403/609-2530, www.crazyweed.ca, 11:30am-10pm Tues.-Sun., $19-44) still charms with its inventive world-beat menu and relaxed "food is fun" vibe. You can make a meal of small plates, like the house-made *labneh* with honey-roasted eggplant and grilled flatbread or pickle-brined fried chicken, or a pizza from the wood-fired oven, though then you'd miss out on mains, like arctic char in a lemongrass-coconut broth or seared pork chops served with a crispy potato cake. Either way, save room for sweets, like the warm "swoon-worthy" date cake.

Pub Fare

Perched on a hill east of the city center, **The Iron Goat Pub & Grill** (703 Benchlands Trail, 403/609-0222, www.irongoat.ca, 11am-11pm Mon.-Fri., 10am-11pm Sat.-Sun., $17-37) has a vast but perpetually packed patio with panoramic views of the Three Sisters and other nearby mountains. The menu has updated pub fare, including the always-requested chipotle-mango duck wings, meatloaf, pizza, and plenty of craft beer on tap.

Cafés, Bakeries, and Light Bites

With a long lists of teas and a vegetarian-friendly menu, bright and airy **Communitea Café** (117-1001 6th Ave., 403/688-2233, www.thecommunitea.com, 8am-6pm daily May-Sept., 8am-5pm Mon.-Thurs., 8am-6pm Fri.-Sun. Oct.-Apr., $7-15) can refresh you from morning till late afternoon. For breakfast, you might try the mixed berry crumble (fruit compote topped with homemade granola and yogurt), a panini, like the Chinook (wild smoked salmon, eggs, avocado, and cream cheese), or the Big Breakfast Bowl (eggs, avocado, quinoa, black beans, and sweet potatoes on a bed of spinach topped with salsa). Lunchtime brings salads, sandwiches, wraps, and rice bowls.

Café Books (100-826 Main St., 403/678-0908, www.cafebooks.ca, 9:30am-7pm Sun.-Thurs., 9:30am-9pm Fri.-Sat.) sells new and used titles and also has a **tearoom** (9:30am-7pm daily) across the hall from the main shop.

Groceries and Markets

The **Canmore Mountain Farmer's Market** (7th Ave., www.tourismcanmore.com, 10am-6pm Thurs. late May-early Oct.) sells fresh produce, baked goods, prepared foods, and crafts.

Accommodations

Most of Canmore's hotels and motels are on or near the Bow Valley Trail (Hwy. 1A), which parallels Highway 1 east of the city's downtown.

$150-300

From the exterior, the **Rocky Mountain Ski Lodge** (1711 Bow Valley Trail, 403/678-5445 or 800/665-6111, www.canmoreskilodge.com, $119-319) says "basic motel," but the five buildings that make up this well-maintained older lodging have a range of comfortable, updated rooms. Of the 83 units, 41 are standard guest rooms with mini fridges and included Wi-Fi, while 42 are apartment-style, such as lofts ($199-389) with a bedroom upstairs and living room below, and two-bedroom units ($199-399). Some rooms have microwaves; others have full kitchens. The family-friendly property has a hot tub, a sauna, and guest laundry; outside are barbecues, picnic tables, and a play area for the kids.

The motto at **Silver Creek Lodge** (1818 Mountain Ave., 403/678-4242 or 877/598-4242, www.silvercreekcanmore.ca, $119-349 d, 2-bedroom suite

$159-549), which is far more upscale than the chain motels that surround it, is "Mountain Zen," and it feels like a quiet oasis with vaguely Asian decor. Most of the 70 condo units are one- or two-bedroom suites with dark wood furnishings, electric fireplaces, sleep sofas in the living rooms, full kitchens with stone floors, soaker tubs, Wi-Fi, and washer-dryers; a few are smaller studios with kitchenettes. A small interior fitness room has weights and two cardio machines; an outdoor hot tub, a steam room, and a day spa give you more pampering options. The **Wild Orchid Asian Bistro** serves sushi, rice bowls, and Asian-influenced small plates.

Over $300

The kids might dive right down the water slide at the ★ **Grande Rockies Resort** (901 Mountain St., 403/678-8880 or 877/223-3398, www.granderockies.com, $249-589 d, 2-bedroom suite $389-829), where the two indoor pools help make this urban-style property fun for families. Mom and Dad may head for the hot tub or compact fitness room. In the all-suite main building, the contemporary one- and two-bedroom units have full kitchens with granite countertops, stainless steel appliances, and washer-dryers. On the lobby level, **Grande Kitchen + Bar** serves breakfast with small plates, salads, burgers, and Alberta meats the rest of the day. If you don't need as much space, the adjacent annex has economical studios, more like standard hotel rooms, furnished in the same modern style but without kitchen facilities. Rates include Wi-Fi and parking.

At **Solara Resort & Spa** (187 Kananaskis Way, 403/609-3600 or 877/778-5617, www.solararesort.ca, $289-669 d, 2-bedroom suite $409-839, 3-bedroom suite $529-1,019), the one- to three-bedroom suites sprawl across three stone and wood buildings, with an outdoor courtyard in the center of the complex. The rustic-luxe suites have full modern kitchens with a wine fridge to chill your vino, fireplaces, and washer-dryers; the premium units on the top floor have vaulted ceilings. For your workout, visit the spacious and airy fitness center, with a sauna, steam room, hot tub, and cool "relaxation" pool, as well as a full-service spa; outdoors, you can go adventuring on the complimentary bikes. An on-site movie theater shows films nightly.

Information and Services

Tourism Canmore (www.tourismcanmore.com) provides lots of Canmore information on its website and publishes an annual visitor guide, also available online. Stop at the **Travel Alberta Visitor Information Centre** (2801 Bow Valley Trail, 403-678-5277, www.travelalberta.com, 9am-5pm daily) for other information about the region.

Medical Services

You can get 24-hour emergency medical attention at **Canmore General Hospital** (1100 Hospital Pl., 403/678-5536, www.albertahealthservices.ca).

If you need pharmacy services in Canmore, try **Gourlay's Pharmacy** (120-1151 Sidney St., 403/678-5288, www.gourlayscanmore.com, 9am-6pm Mon.-Fri., 10am-5pm Sat.), **Rexall** (901 8th St., 403/678-4301, www.rexall.ca, 9am-6pm Mon.-Sat.), or **Shoppers Drug Mart** (933 Railway Ave., 403/678-8750, www.shoppersdrugmart.ca, 9am-10pm daily).

Getting Around

Highway 1 runs through Canmore on its way between Calgary and Banff. In Canmore's compact and walkable downtown, numbered streets run east-west; 8th Street is the main street. Numbered avenues run north-south.

By Bus

Roam Transit (403/762-0606, www.roamtransit.com) runs regular buses between Canmore and Banff (6am-10:50pm daily, one-way adults $6, seniors and ages

6-18 $3, day pass adults $15, seniors and ages 6-18 $7.50).

By Bike

You can ride your bike between Canmore and Banff along the paved **Rocky Mountain Legacy Trail** (403/762-1556, www.pc.gc.ca). It's 14 miles (22 km) each way. If you don't want to ride both ways, you can put your bike on the Roam Transit bus for your return trip.

Lake Louise

Lake Louise is both a famous body of water and the name of the nearby village, located 45 minutes' drive from the town of Banff.

Like Banff, the village of Lake Louise, which has fewer than 1,200 residents, is within Banff National Park. However, the village isn't a quaint community that you can stroll and explore. The area's commercial center is the decidedly not quaint Samson Mall, a cluster of shops off Highway 1, including the visitors center, a grocery, a liquor store, and several cafés. Nearby, along Village Road, are a number of hotels.

Across the Bow River is where Lake Louise gets interesting. From here, Lake Louise Drive takes you to the famous lake, with a few lodgings and restaurants. Moraine Lake Road (open spring-fall only) leads to the area's other notable body of water: Moraine Lake.

★ Lake Louise

The main sight at **Lake Louise** is, of course, the lake, the brilliant blue glacier-fed body of water surrounded by mountain peaks. The ice-topped mountain that you see on the opposite side of the lake is the 11,365-foot (3,464-m) Mount Victoria, which sits on the Continental Divide between B.C. and Alberta, with the Victoria Glacier on its Lake Louise-facing side. Lake Louise is just 1.5 miles (2.4 km) long and 295 feet (90 m) deep.

The first non-aboriginal person to see the lake, Thomas Wilson, a Canadian Pacific Railway employee whose Stoney First Nation guides brought him to the lakeshore in 1882, named it Emerald Lake for the color of its water. It was later renamed to honor Queen Victoria's fourth daughter, Princess Louise Caroline Alberta. The blue-green lake

One Day in Lake Louise

Start your Lake Louise day not at the famous lake that gives the village its name but at another strikingly beautiful body of water: **Moraine Lake.** Located 8.7 miles (14 km) from Lake Louise Village, Moraine Lake can get so busy during the day that Parks Canada closes Moraine Lake Road, so you'll want to get there early, ahead of the crowds. Take a leisurely stroll along the lakeshore, then **rent a canoe** to go for a paddle.

When you leave Moraine Lake, **Lake Louise** should be your next stop. Take your lakeside photos, then if you're up for a long hike, follow the 6.6-mile (10.6-km) round-trip **Plain of Six Glaciers Trail** that takes you to the far side of Lake Louise and between several glacier-topped peaks. Have lunch and a pot of tea at the remote **Plain of Six Glaciers Teahouse.** Alternatively, it's a shorter hike up to the **Lake Agnes Teahouse,** another scenic setting for a sandwich or a snack.

After your hike, change clothes and have a cocktail in the Lakeside Lounge at the **Fairmont Chateau Lake Louise,** because you can't have enough opportunities to admire the lake. Then enjoy a leisurely dinner nearby at the **Mount Fairview Dining Room at Deer Lodge** for modern mountain fare, from house-made charcuterie to the triple chocolate mousse. You've earned it.

Lake Louise and Vicinity

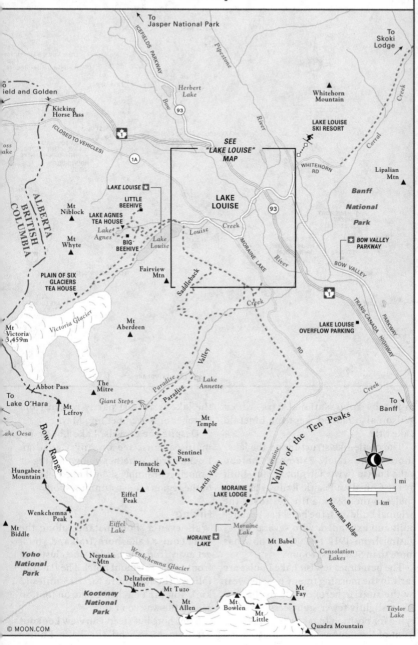

To Jasper National Park

To Skoki Lodge

ield and Golden

Kicking Horse Pass

ICEFIELDS PARKWAY

Herbert Lake

Bow

93

Pipestone

Whitehorn Mountain

Corral Creek

LAKE LOUISE SKI RESORT

(CLOSED TO VEHICLES)

1

SEE "LAKE LOUISE" MAP

WHITEHORN RD

Lipalian Mtn

1A

LAKE LOUISE

Banff

LAKE LOUISE

ALBERTA BRITISH COLUMBIA

Mt Niblock

LITTLE BEEHIVE

LAKE AGNES TEA HOUSE

Mt Whyte

Lake Agnes

BIG BEEHIVE

Lake Louise

Louise Creek

93

National

Park

oss ake

Fairview Mtn

Saddleback

Moraine Lake

River

BOW VALLEY PARKWAY

BOW VALLEY

PLAIN OF SIX GLACIERS TEA HOUSE

Victoria Glacier

Mt Victoria 3,459m

Mt Aberdeen

Creek

1

TRANS-CANADA HIGHWAY

PARKWAY

LAKE LOUISE OVERFLOW PARKING

Abbot Pass

The Mitre

Paradise

Valley

Lake Annette

Giant Steps

Creek

To Banff

To Lake O'Hara

Mt Lefroy

Paradise

RD

ake Oesa

Bow Range

Mt Temple

Valley of the Ten Peaks

Hungabee Mountain

Pinnacle Mtn

Sentinel Pass

Larch Valley

Moraine

0   1 mi

0   1 km

Wenkchemna Peak

Eiffel Peak

MORAINE LAKE LODGE

Mt Biddle

Eiffel Lake

Moraine Lake

Panorama Ridge

Yoho National Park

Neptuak Mtn

Wenkchemna Glacier

MORAINE LAKE

Mt Babel

Consolation Lakes

Deltaform Mtn

Mt Tuzo

Kootenay National Park

Mt Allen

Mt Bowlen

Mt Fay

Taylor Lake

Mt Little

Quadra Mountain

© MOON.COM

Lake Louise

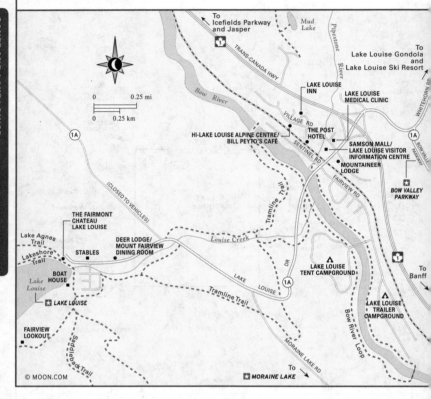

0   0.25 mi

0   0.25 km

To
Icefields Parkway
and Jasper

Mud
Lake

Pipestone

River

TRANS-CANADA HWY

Bow River

To
Lake Louise Gondola
and
Lake Louise Ski Resort

WHITEHORN

LAKE LOUISE
INN

LAKE LOUISE
MEDICAL CLINIC

VILLAGE RD

THE POST
HOTEL

HI-LAKE LOUISE ALPINE CENTRE/
BILL PEYTO'S CAFE

SAMSON MALL/
LAKE LOUISE VISITOR
INFORMATION CENTRE

SENTINEL RD

MOUNTAINEER
LODGE

FAIRVIEW RD

BOW VALLEY
PARKWAY

BOW RIVER

(CLOSED TO VEHICLES)

THE FAIRMONT
CHATEAU
LAKE LOUISE

Lake Agnes
Trail

Lakeshore
Trail

STABLES

DEER LODGE/
MOUNT FAIRVIEW
DINING ROOM

Louise Creek

Tramline Trail

LAKE LOUISE

DR

LAKE LOUISE
TENT CAMPGROUND

To
Banff

BOAT
HOUSE

Lake
Louise

LAKE LOUISE

Tramline Trail

LAKE LOUISE

LAKE LOUISE
TRAILER
CAMPGROUND

FAIRVIEW
LOOKOUT

Saddleback Trail

MORAINE LAKE RD

Bow River Loop

To
MORAINE LAKE

© MOON.COM

in nearby Yoho National Park, which Wilson also named, kept the Emerald Lake title.

The castle-like structure on the lakeshore is the stately **Fairmont Chateau Lake Louise** (www.fairmont.com). Built by the Canadian Pacific Railway as a log chalet in the 1890s (a fire destroyed the original building), the hotel has been rebuilt and expanded, with several wings dating from 1912 to 2004. It now has more than 500 guest rooms.

The best times to visit Lake Louise are early in the morning (many people swear by the sunrise here) or late in the day, when slightly fewer sightseers are jockeying for position to take their photos in front of the famous lake. In most years,

the lake is at least partly frozen from October or November into May.

Despite the crowds, Lake Louise remains a must-see on any Canadian Rockies trip. Whether you go hiking or canoeing, or simply sit by the lake, it's one of the region's most stunning spots.

Hiking

Walk even a short distance along the **Lake Louise Lakeshore Trail** and you'll get away from the hordes who cluster in front of the Fairmont hotel. The flat trail follows the lakeshore for 1.25 miles (2 km). You can't circle the lake on foot, so return the way you came.

The short but steep **Fairview Lookout Trail** starts behind the Lake Louise boathouse and climbs up to viewpoints over the lake. This trail is 1.25 miles (2 km) round trip, with an elevation gain of 328 feet (100 m).

Several other hiking trails start from the lakeshore, and they can also take you away from the crowds and offer different views of the lake and surrounding mountains. If you live close to sea level, you may notice the elevation when you're hiking near Lake Louise. The village is located at 5,033 feet (1,530 m), and many trails climb from the lakeshore into the mountains. Take it slow until you're acclimated.

Hike to the Lake Agnes Teahouse

One of the most popular hikes at Lake Louise is the **Lake Agnes Trail,** which takes you through the forests above the lakeshore and past small Mirror Lake. Your destination is the **Lake Agnes Teahouse** (www.lakeagnesteahouse. com, 8am-5pm daily early June-mid-Oct., $9-15 cash only), a rustic log cabin overlooking Lake Agnes, where you can have soup and a sandwich (the home-made bread is excellent) or a pastry with a pot of tea (the teahouse carries more than 100 varieties).

This moderate 4.2-mile (6.8-km) round-trip trail does climb steadily, gaining 1,263 feet (385 m) of elevation between the lakeshore and the teahouse.

Once you arrive at the teahouse, expect to wait a while for your lunch, even after you get a table; the kitchen is small and the crowds can be large.

Beyond Lake Agnes, you can climb the switchback trail to **Big Beehive,** a beehive-shaped crag. The trail gains 443 feet (135 m) of elevation in 1 mile (1.6 km) from Lake Agnes. Your reward for the climb is a panorama across Lake Louise.

Another side trip takes you to **Little Beehive,** once the site of a fire lookout,

Top to bottom: Big Beehive near Lake Agnes; Lake Agnes Teahouse; on the Plain of Six Glaciers Trail.

with views of the Bow Valley. This trail is 0.6 mile (1 km) each way, with a 355-foot (105-m) elevation gain from Lake Agnes.

From Lake Agnes, you can continue to the Plain of Six Glaciers Teahouse, following the **Highline Trail** between them. This route is 9 miles (14.5 km) total, starting and ending on the Lake Louise shore.

Hike to the Plain of Six Glaciers

The **Plain of Six Glaciers Trail** is an intermediate-level 6.6-mile (10.6-km) round-trip route that takes you to the far side of Lake Louise, then up and between mountain peaks that are topped with glaciers year-round. This trail has an elevation gain of 1,198 feet (365 m).

The trail goes to the ★ **Plain of Six Glaciers Teahouse** (9am-6pm daily July-Aug., 9am-5pm daily late June and Sept.-mid-Oct., $9-16), where you can enjoy tea, snacks, or a light lunch; the teahouse is known for its substantial slabs of rich chocolate cake. Swiss guides working for the Canadian Pacific Railway built the stone-and-wood teahouse in 1926.

If you want to go farther, take the 2-mile (3.2-km) round-trip trail, with an elevation gain of 165 feet (50 m), to the **Abbot Pass Viewpoint,** where you can look down onto the Lower Victoria Glacier and look up to Abbot Hut, one of the highest buildings in Canada.

For an excellent full-day hike, you can walk to both the Lake Agnes and Plain of Six Glaciers Teahouses, following the **Highline Trail** between them. This route is 9 miles (14.5 km) total.

Canoeing

A serene way to explore the lake is by canoe. You can rent a canoe at the **Fairmont Chateau Lake Louise Boathouse** (8:30am-8pm daily July-Aug., 11am-7pm daily June and Sept., 30 minutes $95, 1 hour $105) on the lakeshore.

Horseback Riding

With **Brewster Adventures** (403/762-5454, www.brewsteradventures.com),

you can visit Lake Louise's historic teahouses on horseback on either the three-hour **Lake Agnes Teahouse Half-Day Ride** (9am and 1pm daily late May-mid-Oct., $157.50) or the four-hour **Plain of Six Glaciers Teahouse Ride** (9am and 1pm daily late May-mid-Oct., $194.25).

Sightseeing Tours

Brewster Sightseeing (403/762-6700 or 866/360-8839, www.banffjaspercollection.com) offers a **Mountain Lakes and Waterfalls Tour** (daily May-mid-Oct.), with time at Lake Louise, Moraine Lake, and Takakkaw Falls in Yoho National Park, and a barbecue lunch at Emerald Lake. You can start this tour in Lake Louise (6.75 hours, adults $175, ages 6-15 $88), Banff (9.5 hours, adults $175, ages 6-15 $88), Canmore (12.5 hours, adults $175, ages 6-15 $88), or Calgary (14.75 hours, adults $280, ages 6-15 $140). Buy tickets online, at the **Explore Rockies Lake Louise office** (Fairmont Chateau Lake Louise, 403/522-1695, 7:30am-5:30pm daily May-mid-Oct.), or at Brewster Sightseeing's several Explore Rockies locations in Banff.

Discover Banff Tours (Sundance Mall, 215 Banff Ave., Banff, 403/760-5007 or 877/565-9372, www.banfftours.com, 8am-6pm daily) offers a half-day **Lake Louise & Moraine Lake Tour** (Apr.-Oct., 4.5 hours, adults $84, ages 6-12 $42), which begins and ends in Banff and takes you along the Bow Valley Parkway to both Lake Louise and Moraine Lake. Another option is the **Deluxe Lake Louise & Moraine Lake Tour** (May-Sept., 6 hours, adults $145, ages 6-12 $93), departing from Banff in the late afternoon, stopping for an early dinner at Baker Creek Bistro on the Bow Valley Parkway, and spending time at Lake Louise and Moraine Lake in the quieter evening hours, before returning to Banff.

Getting There

From Highway 1 or Lake Louise Village, follow Lake Louise Drive 2.6 miles (4.2

km) to the lake. Parking is available in several lots that are tiered above the lake.

Note, however, that the parking lots near the lake frequently fill up early in the morning, at which point no cars are allowed to drive to the lake. If you're driving to Lake Louise spring-fall, save yourself the hassle and park your car at the **free overflow parking lots** (mid-May-mid-Oct.) on Highway 1, outside of town. From there, you can ride the free **Parks Canada shuttle bus** (www.pc.gc.ca) to and from the lakeshore; confirm the seasonal shuttle schedules on the Parks Canada website.

If you're staying in Banff, another option is to take a **Parks Canada shuttle bus** (7am-6:15pm daily mid-May-mid-Sept., round-trip adults $10, under age 18 free) directly from Banff to Lake Louise. Buses operate spring-fall between the Banff Heritage Train Station (327 Railway Ave.) and the lakeshore. The ride takes about 70 minutes each way.

★ Moraine Lake

Glacier-fed **Moraine Lake,** in the Valley of the Ten Peaks, is another impossibly blue body of water surrounded by sharp mountain peaks and glaciers. It's a beautiful setting for a hike or a canoe paddle.

As at Lake Louise, the best times to visit Moraine Lake are in the early morning or early evening. Come at sunrise if you can, or at least before 9am; otherwise, you might consider waiting until after 5pm when the crowds thin, especially if you're visiting in the peak months of July and August. The road to the lake is typically open only mid-May-mid-October.

The **Snowshoe Café** (8am-4:30pm daily June-Sept.) at Moraine Lake Lodge is a quick-service café selling sandwiches, pastries, drinks, and ice cream. In the evenings, the lodge's lake-view **Walter Wilcox Dining Room** (5:30pm-9pm daily

Top to bottom: Moraine Lake; Plain of Six Glaciers Teahouse; Deer Lodge.

June-Sept., $34-58) accommodates hotel guests first, but nonguests can dine here if space is available.

Hiking

Several hiking trails begin in the Moraine Lake area. Follow the easy **Lakeshore Trail** for up to 1 mile (1.6 km) along the lake.

The **Consolation Lakes Trail,** 3.6 miles (5.8 km) round-trip with an elevation gain of 213 feet (65 m), takes you into alpine meadows with views of the Quadra Glacier.

On the **Larch Valley/Minnestimma Lakes Trail,** you hike into a larch forest above Moraine Lake, with great views of the Ten Peaks. Particularly popular in September when the larch trees turn autumn gold, it's a 5.3-mile (8.6-km) round-trip hike with a 1,755-foot (535-m) elevation gain.

Branching off from the Larch Valley Trail, the moderate **Eiffel Lake Trail,** which is 7 miles (11.3 km) round-trip with an elevation gain of 1,213 feet (370 m), leads up to an alpine lake with panoramas across the Valley of the Ten Peaks.

Note that Parks Canada issues seasonal **bear restrictions** for many of the Moraine Lake trails. During months when bears can be in the area, hikers must walk in groups of at least four and carry bear spray. Talk with park staff at the **Lake Louise Visitor Information Centre** (Samson Mall, 403/522-3833) or check the trail status on the **Parks Canada** website (www.pc.gc.ca).

Canoeing

One of the most peaceful ways to explore this scenic lake is by canoe. Moraine Lake Lodge rents **canoes** (9:30am-5pm daily mid-June-mid-Sept., $105 per hour) from a lakeside dock.

Getting There

From Highway 1 or Lake Louise Village, follow Lake Louise Drive to the Moraine Lake turnoff and continue onto Moraine Lake Road. It's 8.7 miles (14 km) from Lake Louise Village to Moraine Lake.

On busy days, the crowds at the lake can grow overwhelming. At that point, which happens regularly beginning early in the morning, Parks Canada restricts traffic on Moraine Lake Road, preventing cars from entering the road until other cars leave the area. **Mountain Park Transportation** (403/522-2525, www.morainelakeshuttle.ca, round-trip adults $25, ages 4-12 $15) runs a seasonal shuttle that can take you to Moraine Lake from the Samson Mall, Lake Louise Campground, or Deer Lodge. Call or check the website for the shuttle schedules.

Early September-mid-October, a free **Parks Canada shuttle bus** (www.pc.gc. ca) runs between the overflow parking lots on Highway 1, just outside of Lake Louise, to and from Moraine Lake; check the website for seasonal schedules.

Lake Louise Gondola

Spring-fall, you can ride the **Lake Louise Gondola** (Whitehorn Dr., 403/522-3555 or 877/956-8473, www.lakelouisegondola.com, 9am-4pm daily mid-May-mid-June, 8am-5:30pm daily mid-June-July, 8am-6pm daily Aug.-early Sept., 8am-5pm daily early Sept.-mid-Oct., adults $35.95, ages 6-15 $16.95) at the Lake Louise Ski Resort to take in the views over the mountains, go hiking, visit a wildlife center, or have a drink or a meal overlooking the peaks. You might even spot a grizzly bear.

Scan the meadows and woods for wildlife during the 14-minute ride up to an elevation of 6,850 feet (2,088 m). In summer, grizzly and black bears come to forage for dandelions, berries, and other edibles along the slopes near the lift. You might also spot cougars, mountain goats, deer, wolves, or bighorn sheep. Check the calendar in the gondola ticket office to find out what animals the staff or other guests have recently seen.

Wildlife Interpretive Centre

A short walk from the top of the gondola, the **Wildlife Interpretive Centre** (free with gondola ticket) has exhibits about bears and other creatures, including elk, moose, bighorn sheep, deer, gray wolves, and mountain goats, that live in the region. Staff offer **interpretive programs** (10am, noon, and 2pm daily) about the animals and also lead **guided walks,** including a daily 45-minute "Trail of the Great Bear" walk (on the hour 9am-5pm daily, adults and children over age 4 $15), about bear behavior and safety, plus tips on what to do if you see a bear.

In the same building, with a lovely mountain-view patio, **Whitehorn Bistro** (10am-3pm daily early June-late June, 10am-4:30pm daily late June-July, 10am-5pm daily Aug.-early Sept., 10:30am-3pm daily early Sept.-mid-Oct., $21-27) serves upscale plates from salads and burgers to pheasant or rabbit fricassee with tagliatelle, along with craft beer and creative cocktails.

wildflowers near the Lake Louise Gondola

Bears!

A highlight of a Canadian Rockies road trip is spotting local wildlife. Banff National Park is home to 53 species of mammals, and you'll likely see deer, bighorn sheep, and plenty of inquisitive squirrels as you explore the Banff and Lake Louise areas. If you're lucky, you might also catch a glimpse of larger mammals, like elk, cougars, or bears.

Two different bear species live in the Canadian Rockies: grizzlies and black bears. It's not the color that determines the bear type, though. While grizzlies are typically brown, their fur can range from almost blond to black, and black bears can be black, brown, blond, even nearly white.

One of the most noticeable differences between the two species is that grizzly bears have a prominent hump on their backs. It's a mass of muscle that looks like a large bump between their shoulders.

Approximately 20,000 grizzly bears currently live in western Canada, with roughly three-quarters in British Columbia and the remainder in western Alberta, Yukon, and the Northwest Territories. Parks Canada estimates that just 65 grizzlies reside within Banff National Park. Jasper National Park has a grizzly population of about 109, Yoho has 11-15, and Kootenay National Park has 9-16.

Black bears are much more common across North America, with an estimated Canadian population of more than 380,000, although they're somewhat less frequently seen in Banff National Park, where Parks Canada calculates that 20-40 black bears live. Among the other Rocky Mountain national parks, Jasper's black bear population is about 90, Yoho's is 20-50, and Kootenay's is 30-50.

Where to Learn More

At Lake Louise, ride the **Lake Louise Gondola** (403/522-3555 or 877/956-8473, www. lakelouisegondola.com) up to the mountainside **Wildlife Interpretive Centre** for exhibits, presentations, and guided hikes about bears and other wildlife.

Near Golden, B.C., the **Grizzly Bear Interpretive Centre at Kicking Horse Mountain Resort** (250/439-5425 or 866/754-5425, www.kickinghorseresort.com) houses an orphaned grizzly bear and offers regular interpretive tours where you can learn more about bears and their habits.

In Vancouver, bears live at the **Grouse Mountain Refuge for Endangered Wildlife** (604/980-9311, www.grousemountain.com), which offers wildlife education programs.

In central B.C., you can check out wolves, coyotes, moose, elk, eagles, owls, and even the rare white Kermode or "Spirit" bear, at the **B.C. Wildlife Park** (9077 Dallas Dr., Kamloops, 250/573-3242, www.bcwildlife.org).

Hiking

Several hiking trails begin at the top of the gondola. A 1.1-mile (1.7-km) round-trip loop takes you to the **Kicking Horse Viewpoint,** at an elevation of 7,497 feet (2,285 m). A 2.1-mile (3.4-km) round-trip trail leads to the **Ptarmigan Valley Viewpoint,** at 7,930 feet (2,417 m).

Since bears and other wildlife frequent the mountain's lower slopes, you aren't allowed to hike in this area, so you have to begin your hike at the upper gondola station. Even on the upper trails, gondola staff recommend that you don't hike alone and suggest traveling in groups of four.

Skiing and Snowboarding

In winter, **Lake Louise Ski Resort** (877/956-8473, www.skilouise.com, 9am-4pm daily early Nov.-early May, full-day adults $114, seniors and ages 13-17 $89, ages 6-12 $44, under age 6 free) is the largest in the Canadian Rockies, with 145 runs and additional off-piste skiing across its 4,200 skiable acres (1,700 ha).

Getting There

The gondola base is 2 miles (3.2 km) from Lake Louise Village, about a five-minute drive. Take Lake Louise Drive across Highway 1 toward the entrance to the Bow Valley Parkway. Follow the signs for the Lake Louise Ski Resort onto Whitehorn Drive.

You can catch a **free shuttle** to the gondola base from Lake Louise hotels or the Samson Mall. Call or check the gondola website for the shuttle pick-up schedule.

Food

Lake Louise does not have a tremendous range of food options, and nothing is inexpensive.

TIP: The major hotels all have high-end restaurants, but most also have pubs or casual dining spots that are more moderately priced.

Contemporary

Known for game meats, like bison and elk, the wood-beamed ★ **Mount Fairview Dining Room at Deer Lodge** (109 Lake Louise Dr., 403/522-4202, www.crmr. com, 7am-11am and 5:30pm-9pm daily, breakfast $14-18, dinner $32-45) pleases patrons with contemporary dishes using mountain-region ingredients. Lunch is served in the log-walled **Caribou Lounge** (11am-10pm daily, $15-24) or out on the patio (June-Sept.). An excellent plate to share, at lunch or dinner, is the Rocky Mountain charcuterie platter, with air-dried buffalo, elk salami, smoked duck, and wild boar pâté, along with a cranberry relish and a unique pickled "mustard melon." Other options include flatbread with duck confit and peppered pears, pan-seared salmon with citrus cucumber slaw, or elk steak with a bone marrow herb crust and pomegranate jus.

If you want to eat by the lakeshore, the **Fairmont Chateau Lake Louise** (111 Lake Louise Dr., dining reservations 403/522-1601, www.fairmont.com) has several dining options. For a quick bite, the cafeteria-style **Chateau Deli** (open 24 hours) sells sandwiches, salads, and pastries. You can try Swiss fondue, wiener schnitzel, and other European classics at **The Walliser Stube** (5:30pm-9pm daily, $38-55). The hotel's main dining room, **The Fairview** (5:30pm-9pm daily, $41-55, 3-course prix fixe $95), prepares contemporary dishes like octopus and blood orange salad, venison with squash and black garlic, or grass-fed beef tenderloin. Like many Fairmont properties, Chateau Lake Louise offers traditional **afternoon tea** (noon-2:30pm daily, $52). Several of the hotel's eateries reduce their hours in the off-season, so call or check online in advance.

Pub Fare

You don't have to be a hostel guest to eat at **Bill Peyto's Café** (203 Village Rd., 403/522-2200, www.hihostels.ca, 7am-10pm daily summer, 7:30am-9:30pm daily winter, breakfast $7-14, lunch and dinner $13-17), the family-friendly eatery at the HI-Lake Louise hostel. You just have to appreciate hearty pub grub, including burgers, wraps, and chili, at moderate (at least for a resort town) prices. Try the elk burger. In the morning, the café serves breakfast basics: eggs, pancakes, hot cereal.

Cafés, Bakeries, and Light Bites

Pick up coffee and breakfast-to-go or sandwiches for a lunchtime picnic at the tiny **Trailhead Café** (Samson Mall, 403/522-2006, 7am-6pm daily, $8-10).

Groceries and Markets

The **Village Market** (Samson Mall, 403/522-3894, 8:30am-8:30pm daily) sells basic groceries and picnic supplies.

Accommodations and Camping
Under $150

Lake Louise doesn't have any really cheap beds, but the least expensive accommodations are at the **HI-Lake Louise Alpine Centre** (203 Village Rd., 403/522-2201 or 866/762-4122, www.hihostels.ca, $37-52 dorm, $117-243 d) in a post-and-beam lodge on a wooded lot. The dorms sleep 4-6, in either female, male, or mixed rooms. The private rooms with shared baths come with either one double, two singles, or a bunk bed with a double and a single. You can also choose a private room with an en suite bath. Both Wi-Fi and parking are included. Two shared kitchens, a TV and games room, and a kids' playroom give you space to hang out. The hostel's **Bill Peyto's Café** serves breakfast, lunch, and dinner.

$150-300

A simple, comfortable motel, the **Mountaineer Lodge** (101 Village Rd., 403/522-3844 or 855/556-8473, www. mountaineerlodge.com, $200-427) has 80 rooms and suites in two buildings. In the main lodge, guests can soak in the indoor hot tub or have complimentary coffee in the sitting room; the second structure is a two-story drive-up motel block, where a complimentary breakfast buffet is served. Handy for road trippers: Rooms in both buildings include mini fridges, microwaves, coffeemakers, and Wi-Fi, and there's a guest laundry.

Spread over five buildings, the **Lake Louise Inn** (210 Village Rd., 403/522-3791 or 800/661-9237, www.lakelouiseinn. com, $139-589, resort fee $8) has 244 guest rooms, ranging from basic doubles to more upscale hotel rooms to condo-style units with full kitchens, all with flat-screen TVs and Wi-Fi. The main building, where the lobby and three restaurants are located, has an indoor pool, a hot tub, and a small gym with several cardio machines. Three buildings have guest laundries. Because the rooms are all so different, ask for details or photos when you book.

The wood and stone **Deer Lodge** (109 Lake Louise Dr., 403/522-3991 or 800/661-1595, www.crmr.com, $169-469) was built in the 1920s, complete with a turret, a massive stone fireplace, and heavy wood beams. The compact

Fairmont Chateau Lake Louise

guest rooms in the original building still have that rustic style; if you don't need frills, they're a good value. The newer wing's units are much larger and more contemporary, with cherry furnishings and modern baths. The lodge has Wi-Fi included in the rates and a guest laundry; none of the rooms have TVs. Common spaces include a games room with a pool table, a sauna, and best of all, a rooftop hot tub with glacier views. The 71-room lodge is just few minutes' walk from Lake Louise, so while you don't have lake vistas, you don't need your car to explore the lakeshore.

Over $300

Noted Canadian modernist architect Arthur Erikson (1924-2009) designed ★ **Moraine Lake Lodge** (Moraine Lake Rd., 403/522-3733 or 877/522-2777, www. morainelake.com, June-Sept., $508-1,129), which opened in 1991, with 33 guest rooms spread out between the main lodge and several townhouse-style blocks

of wood-frame cabins along the shore of the Lake Louise area's other notable lake. Rooms have handmade log beds with down duvets, rustic furnishings, and wood floors; some units have wood-burning fireplaces. At this adult-oriented property, room rates include breakfast, canoe rentals, guided hikes with a staff naturalist, and evening interpretive programs. Dinners in the lake-view **Walter Wilcox Dining Room** might feature arctic char with root vegetable bruschetta, Alberta beef tenderloin, or rack of venison with pickled cabbage. The lodge operates off the grid, generating its own electricity; there's no air-conditioning, TVs, or phones, although limited Wi-Fi is provided.

You can't stay closer to the famous lake than at the grand ★ **Fairmont Chateau Lake Louise** (111 Lake Louise Dr., 403/522-3511 or 866/540-4413, www. fairmont.com, $599-2,499, parking $30-35). It's hard to imagine that this lavish lakeside lodge started life as a log chalet in the 1890s (the original building was destroyed in a fire). With several wings dating from 1912 to 2004, the 550 traditional rooms vary from petite doubles overlooking the grounds or surrounding mountains to expansive suites with views across the lake. The hotel has an indoor heated pool, a fitness center, and a spa, and staff can arrange guided hikes (half-day adults $60, ages 8-12 $25, full-day adults $75, ages 8-12 $25), canoe rentals ($65 per hour), voyageur canoe tours (adults $55, ages 8-12 $30), and a variety of other activities. You can even take the hotel dog for a stroll along the lakeshore (free). Dining outlets range from a 24-hour deli to a Swiss fondue restaurant to a contemporary lake-view dining room. It's a splurge, yes, but it's the only lodging directly on Lake Louise. If you're traveling outside the peak summer months, check the website for off-season specials.

Originally built in 1942 and significantly expanded over the years, **The Post Hotel** (200 Pipestone Rd.,

403/522-3989 or 800/661-1586, www.
posthotel.com, $310-950) recalls an el-
egant ski lodge in the Alps, with an indoor saltwater pool, a hot tub, a fitness
room, a guest library, and a full-service
spa. Guests stay in 60 rooms, 29 suites,
or five cabins, outfitted with simple
traditional furnishings and complimentary Wi-Fi. For meals, choose from
the deluxe **main dining room,** a fondue
restaurant called **Fondue Stübli,** or the
more casual **Outpost Pub.**

Camping

Parks Canada runs two campgrounds
in the Lake Louise area, 0.6 mile (1 km)
from the village and 2.5 miles (4 km)
from the lake. Both have washrooms with
flush toilets and hot showers.

The seasonal **Lake Louise Tent
Campground** (late May-late Sept., $27.40)
has 206 sites for tent campers. At the **Lake
Louise Trailer Campground** ($32.30), the
187 fully serviced sites are open to campers year-round.

You can make campsite **reservations**
(877/737-3783, www.reservation.
parkscanada.gc.ca) online or by phone
for both Lake Louise campgrounds; reservations are strongly recommended,
particularly for summer and fall stays.

Information and Services
Visitor Information

Both **Parks Canada** (www.pc.gc.ca)
and **Banff-Lake Louise Tourism** (www.
banfflakelouise.com) staff the **Lake
Louise Visitor Information Centre**
(Samson Mall, 403/522-3833, 8:30am-
7pm daily June-Sept., 9am-5pm daily
Oct.-May). The visitors center has free
Wi-Fi as well as exhibits about the ge-
ology of the region, illustrating how its
lakes and mountains came to be, and
short films about the national park.

Even when the office is closed, you
can check out maps and other area details posted on the information boards
outside.

Medical Services

Lake Louise Medical Clinic (200 Hector
Rd., 403/522-2184, www.llmc.ca, 9am-
noon and 1pm-4pm Mon., Wed., and
Fri., 9am-1pm Tues. and Thurs.), opposite
the visitors center, can take care of minor
medical issues. It offers urgent care services, if necessary, outside regular office
hours. The closest hospital is in Banff.

Getting Around
By Car

Lake Louise is 35 miles (57 km) northwest of the town of Banff, a 45-minute
drive, and 17 miles (27 km), or a 20-min-
ute drive, east of Field, B.C., in the center
of Yoho National Park. Highway 1 runs
west from Lake Louise into B.C. or east
toward Banff. The scenic Bow Valley
Parkway is an alternate route between
Banff and Lake Louise; it's a 30-mile (48-
km) drive. From Lake Louise, you can go
north on the Icefields Parkway (Hwy. 93)
to Jasper.

Once you arrive in Lake Louise Village,
it's 2.6 miles (4.2 km) along Lake Louise
Drive to the lake itself. To Moraine Lake,
follow Lake Louise Drive to the Moraine
Lake turnoff and continue on Moraine
Lake Road. Moraine Lake Road is open
only mid-May-mid-October.

Note that both Lake Louise Drive and
Moraine Lake Road **close to traffic when
the parking lots are full.** Banff National
Park's webpage **Banff Now** (www.pc.gc.
ca/banffnow) lists real-time availability
of parking around the park.

Car Rentals

National (Samson Mall, 403/522-3870,
www.nationalcar.ca) rents cars in Lake
Louise. You'll have more car rental options in Banff or Calgary.

By Shuttle Bus

The road to Lake Louise closes to traffic when the parking lots near the lakeshore are full, which frequently happens
early in the morning spring-fall. At that

point, no cars are allowed to drive to the lake. Instead, park your car at the free overflow parking lots on Highway 1, just outside of town. From there, you can ride the free **Parks Canada shuttle bus** (www. pc.gc.ca) to and from the lakeshore; confirm the seasonal shuttle schedules on the website.

Mountain Park Transportation (403/522-2525, www.morainelakeshuttle. ca, round-trip adults $25, ages 4-12 $15) runs a seasonal shuttle among the Samson Mall, Lake Louise Campground, Deer Lodge, and Moraine Lake. Call or check the website for the shuttle schedules.

By Bike
If you're a fit cyclist, you can pedal from Lake Louise Village to Lake Louise (2.6 mi/4.2 km) or to Moraine Lake (8.7 mi/14 km). Use caution on these hilly, heavily traveled roads. **Wilson Mountain Sports** (Samson Mall, 201 Village Rd., 403/522-3636 or 866/929-3636, www.wmsll.com, full-day $39-69) rents bikes.

Jasper

Jasper and the Icefields Parkway

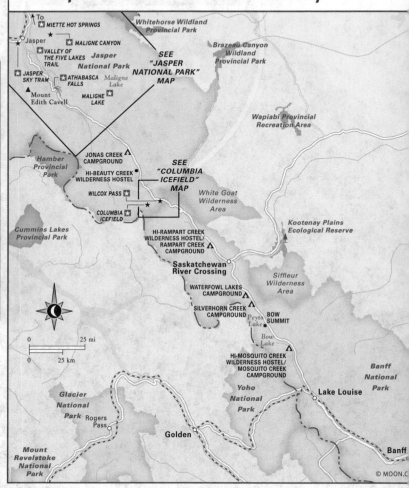

To ✚ MIETTE HOT SPRINGS
Whitehorse Wildland
Provincial Park
★ Jasper   ✚ MALIGNE CANYON   Brazeau Canyon
✚ VALLEY OF   Wildland
THE FIVE LAKES   Jasper   Provincial Park
TRAIL   National Park   SEE
✚ JASPER   "JASPER
SKY TRAM   ✚ ATHABASCA   Maligne   NATIONAL
FALLS   Lake   PARK"
▲ Mount   MAP
Edith Cavell   MALIGNE ✚
LAKE
Wapiabi Provincial
Recreation Area

JONAS CREEK ⌃
CAMPGROUND
Hamber   SEE
Provincial   HI-BEAUTY CREEK   "COLUMBIA
Park   WILDERNESS HOSTEL   ICEFIELD"
MAP
WILCOX PASS ✚   White Goat
Wilderness
COLUMBIA ✚   Area
Cummins Lakes   ICEFIELD   Kootenay Plains
Provincial Park   Ecological Reserve

HI-RAMPART CREEK
WILDERNESS HOSTEL/
RAMPART CREEK ⌃
CAMPGROUND
Saskatchewan
River Crossing   Siffleur
Wilderness
WATERFOWL LAKES   Area
CAMPGROUND ⌃
SILVERHORN CREEK
CAMPGROUND   Peyto BOW
Lake SUMMIT

Bow
Lake
HI-MOSQUITO CREEK
WILDERNESS HOSTEL/   Banff
MOSQUITO CREEK   National
CAMPGROUND   Park
Yoho
National
Glacier   Park   Lake Louise
National
Park   Rogers
Pass

Mount   Golden   Banff
Revelstoke
National
Park   © MOON.C

0   25 mi
0   25 km

J asper National Park offers glacial peaks, turquoise lakes, cascading waterfalls, and dramatic canyons that you can explore on trails, by boat, or simply from the highway.

Many people arrive in Jasper via the scenic Icefields Parkway (Hwy. 93), which runs between Lake Louise and Jasper. Along the way, you'll travel through the Columbia Icefield, the largest area of glacial ice in the Canadian Rockies, where you can walk on a section of the Athabasca Glacier, get a thrill on the Glacier Skywalk (a glass-floored bridge that arcs over a canyon), or hike up to a dramatic viewpoint looking across to the ice-topped mountains.

Highlights

★ **Wilcox Pass:** If you do one hike along the Icefields Parkway, make it this moderate climb that rewards you with impressive views of the surrounding glaciers (page 284).

★ **Columbia Icefield:** At the largest area of glacial ice in the Canadian Rockies, you can walk on a section of the Athabasca Glacier (page 284).

★ **Athabasca Falls:** Backed by mountain peaks, this powerful waterfall along the Icefields Parkway is an appealing photo opportunity (page 287).

★ **Maligne Canyon:** Hike on the trails and over the bridges through this deep limestone gorge that shows off how mountain rivers can carve through rocks (page 291).

★ **Maligne Lake:** Explore the turquoise waters of the largest natural lake in the Canadian Rockies and cruise to scenic Spirit Island (page 294).

★ **Miette Hot Springs:** Soak in Jasper's natural mineral-rich hot springs, the warmest in the Canadian Rockies (page 296).

★ **Jasper Sky Tram:** Ride this gondola for great views of the national park and the town of Jasper, then hike to the top of Whistlers Mountain for even better vistas (page 298).

★ **Valley of the Five Lakes Trail:** This moderate hike takes you along five bodies of water, shimmering with different photogenic shades of blue, turquoise, and green (page 300).

Best Accommodations

★ **Glacier View Lodge:** The name says it all: The best of the simply furnished rooms at the Columbia Icefield Glacier Discovery Centre have views of the Athabasca Glacier (page 289).

★ **Patricia Lake Bungalows:** This family-run and family-friendly lakeside property offers a range of well-kept accommodations, from standard hotel rooms to deluxe cabins (page 308).

★ **The Crimson:** For urban style in small-town Jasper, book a room in this 1950s lodge that has been converted into a boutique motel (page 308).

★ **Fairmont Jasper Park Lodge:** Jasper's most luxurious lodging is a full-service lakeside resort with a heated pool, an 18-hole golf course, a lake-view spa, and plenty of other amenities (page 308).

As the largest park in the Canadian Rockies, Jasper National Park has plenty to see, but even in the peak of summer, it doesn't normally have the crowds that clog the sidewalks in Banff. Oh, plenty of people come to Jasper; the park averages more than two million visitors every year. Yet, with more than 4,335 square miles (11,228 sq km) of protected land, Jasper has much more space.

The compact town of Jasper is located entirely within the boundaries of the national park. Most accommodations, restaurants, and other services are in or around town, although many park attractions are an hour's drive or more from the town site.

So take time to explore. It takes a little more effort to discover Jasper's attractions, but this incredible region is totally worth it.

Getting to Jasper

Driving from Banff

From Banff, go north on **Highway 1** to **Lake Louise,** where you take the scenic **Icefields Parkway (Hwy. 93)** to Jasper. The Icefields Parkway runs **143 miles (230 km)** from Lake Louise to Jasper, which takes **3.25-3.75 hours.**

The total trip from **Banff** to Jasper is **180 miles (290 km)** and takes **4-4.5 hours.**

Driving from Vancouver
Via Highway 5

The **shortest route** from Vancouver directly to Jasper is via **Highway 5 (Yellowhead Hwy.).**

Leave Vancouver, heading east on the **Trans-Canada Highway (Hwy. 1)** to Hope. Continue east at Hope onto **Highway 3,** then exit onto **Highway 5** north toward Kamloops. At **Kamloops,** continue north on Highway 5 until it intersects with **Highway 16** north of Valemount. Follow Highway 16 east to Jasper. This route takes you past **Wells Gray Provincial Park,** known for its three dozen waterfalls, and **Mount Robson Provincial Park,** where, on a clear day, you can catch a glimpse of the namesake mountain; at 12,900 feet (3,954 m), it's the highest peak in the Canadian Rockies.

This Vancouver-to-Jasper route is **500 miles (805 km)** and takes **8.5-9 hours.** From **Kamloops** to Jasper, the trip is **275 miles (445 km)** and takes **five hours.**

Via Highway 1

A **longer but scenic route** through the mountains of eastern B.C. is to take **Highway 1** east from Kamloops.

Best Restaurants

★ **Orso Trattoria:** The lake views alone are worth a visit to this modern Italian restaurant at the Fairmont Jasper Park Lodge (page 305).

★ **Bear's Paw Bakery:** At Jasper's favorite baked-goods purveyor, you can start your day with excellent scones or sticky buns (page 306).

★ **Patricia Street Deli:** It's nothing fancy, but this Jasper take-out spot makes excellent sandwiches, convenient for taking out on the trails (page 306).

From Vancouver, head east on the **Trans-Canada Highway (Hwy. 1)** to **Hope.** Continue east at Hope onto **Highway 3,** then exit onto **Highway 5** north toward Kamloops. From **Kamloops,** drive east on Highway 1. You'll travel through Mount Revelstoke, Glacier, and Yoho National Parks en route to Lake Louise. At **Lake Louise,** turn north on the **Icefields Parkway (Hwy. 93)** to Jasper.

From Vancouver, this route is about **620 miles (1,000 km)** and takes **11.5-12 hours.** From **Kamloops** to Jasper, the trip is **415 miles (670 km)** and takes **8.25-8.75 hours.**

Driving from Whistler

If you're traveling to Jasper from Whistler, follow **Highway 99** north until it joins **Highway 97,** and then meets up with the **Trans-Canada Highway (Hwy. 1).** Take Highway 1 east to Kamloops.

From **Kamloops,** either pick up **Highway 5** north to **Highway 16** east to Jasper, or continue east on **Highway 1** to **Lake Louise,** and then take the **Icefields Parkway (Hwy. 93)** to Jasper.

The trip from Whistler to Jasper via **Highways 5 and 16** is **465 miles (750 km)** and takes **9-9.5 hours.** The route via **Highways 1 and 93** is **600 miles (970 km)** and takes **12-12.5 hours.**

Driving from Edmonton

Edmonton to Jasper is **225 miles (360 km),** a straight **four-hour** drive west on **Highway 16.**

Getting There by Air, Train, and Bus
By Air

Edmonton International Airport (YEG, 1000 Airport Rd., 780/890-8900 or 800/268-7134, http://flyeia.com) is the closest major airport to Jasper. You can fly directly to Edmonton from many Canadian and several U.S. cities, and from Amsterdam and Reykjavik.

Car rental companies with offices at the Edmonton airport include **Alamo** (780/890-7345 or 877/222-9075, www.alamo.ca), **Avis** (780/890-7596 or 800/879-2847, www.avis.ca), **Budget** (780/890-4801 or 800/268-8900, www.budget.ca), **Enterprise** (780/980-2338 or 800/261-7331, www.enterprise.com), **Hertz** (780/890-4435 or 800/263-0600, www.hertz.ca), and **National** (780/890-7345 or 800/227-7368, www.nationalcar.ca).

SunDog Tours (780/852-4056 or 888/786-3641, www.sundogtours.com, one-way adults $99, kids $59) runs a shuttle between the Edmonton airport and Jasper. It operates once daily in each direction, offering pickups and drop-offs at several Jasper hotels. The trip takes approximately 5.5 hours.

By Train

Both VIA Rail, Canada's national passenger rail carrier, and the privately run Rocky Mountaineer train have service to the **Jasper Train Station** (607 Connaught Dr.), which is conveniently located in the center of town opposite

◈ Side Trip: Wells Gray Provincial Park

Off Highway 5 between Kamloops and Jasper is a beautiful and comparatively little-known outdoor destination: **Wells Gray Provincial Park** (250/587-2090, www.env.gov.bc.ca, daily, free). The main access point for Wells Gray Provincial Park is the town of **Clearwater** on Highway 5, 80 miles (129 km) north of Kamloops and 200 miles (320 km) southwest of Jasper

With a vast wilderness of 1.3 million acres (more than 525,000 ha), part of interior B.C.'s temperate rainforest, the park's highlights are its 39 waterfalls, several of which you can reach via short walks of 30 minutes or less—a great way to stretch your legs when passing through. **Spahats Creek Falls,** 8 miles (13 km) from the start of Clearwater Valley Road,

Helmcken Falls

the main north-south route through the park that begins at the town of Clearwater, plunges into a deep canyon of volcanic rock. **Dawson Falls,** 26 miles (42 km) down Clearwater Valley Road, is a wide waterfall, spanning 350 feet (107 m) across. The park's must-see attraction is **Helmcken Falls,** 30 miles (48 km) from the start of Clearwater Valley Road. At 460 feet (141 m) high, it's the fourth-highest cascades in Canada.

You could spend far more time exploring the park, which has 125 miles (200 km) of trails as well as several large lakes. In the park's Trophy Mountains, the peaks rise to more than 8,200 feet (2,500 m). Wells Gray encompasses 22 volcanoes, too, but don't worry; the last eruption was thousands of years ago.

For park information and maps, stop into the **Wells Grey Park Information Centre** (416 Eden Rd., Clearwater, 250/674-3334, www.wellsgraypark.info, 9am-5pm daily). **Tourism Wells Gray** (www.wellsgray.ca) publishes a useful visitor guide, available on its website and at the information center.

Parks Canada's **Jasper Information Centre** (500 Connaught Dr.).

VIA Rail

On its flagship route, *The Canadian,* **VIA Rail** (514/989-2626 or 888/842-7245, www.viarail.ca) trains arrive in Jasper from the west via Vancouver and Kamloops, and from the east from Edmonton, Saskatoon, Winnipeg, and Toronto. *The Canadian* operates three times a week in each direction May-mid-October, and twice a week mid-October-April.

Another VIA Rail route runs to Jasper three times a week from Prince Rupert and Prince George in northern British Columbia. The full Jasper-Prince Rupert trip is 720 miles (1,160 km) and takes two days. This train travels only during the daylight hours, so you stop overnight in Prince George. Prince Rupert is a starting point for trips to the islands of Haida Gwaii. From Prince Rupert, you can also travel aboard B.C. Ferries south to Vancouver Island.

The Rocky Mountaineer

The deluxe **Rocky Mountaineer** (877/460-3200, www.rockymountaineer.com, mid-Apr.-mid-Oct.) can take you to Jasper from Vancouver or Seattle. The classic Journey Through the Clouds runs from Vancouver to Jasper, with an overnight stop in Kamloops; it also offers a version of this trip that starts in Seattle. Another option is the three-day Rainforest to Gold Rush route, which takes you to Jasper from Vancouver with overnight stops in Whistler and in the northern B.C. city of Quesnel.

Unlike a standard train trip, many Rocky Mountaineer packages include activities ranging from gondola rides to helicopter tours, plus accommodations along the way. It's also possible to book a Rocky Mountaineer holiday that covers rail fare and accommodations only, such as a two-day train trip between Vancouver and Jasper. Rail packages start at $1,579 per person and go up depending on destinations, number of days of travel, and the level of service and accommodations.

By Bus

Between May and late October, **Brewster Airport Express** (403/762-6700 or 866/606-6700, www.banffjaspercollection.com) runs a daily bus in each direction between Jasper and Lake Louise (3.75 hours, one-way adults $77, ages 6-15 $38.50), Banff (4.75 hours, one-way adults $87, ages 6-15 $43.50), Calgary International Airport (7.25 hours, one-way adults $128, ages 6-15 $64), and downtown Calgary (8 hours, one-way adults $128, ages 6-15 $64). The bus also stops at the Columbia Icefield Centre.

The Icefields Parkway

The 143-mile (230-km) route between Lake Louise and Jasper is one of Canada's most spectacular drives. Highway 93, known as the Icefields Parkway, takes you past rushing waterfalls, turquoise lakes, and countless glacier-topped peaks. This scenic road helped open the Jasper region to tourism when the highway was completed in 1940.

Most people make the drive in anywhere from four hours to one day, with lots of stops en route. If you want to stay

longer, the parkway has a couple of lodgings, several campgrounds, and a network of rustic wilderness hostels.

The southern section of the Icefields Parkway is within the boundaries of Banff National Park, while the northern sector is part of Jasper National Park. You must have a valid **national park pass** (www.pc.gc.ca, adults $9.80, seniors $8.30, families $19.60) to drive anywhere on the parkway. If you don't already have a pass or need to purchase a pass for additional days, you can buy it at the **Lake Louise Visitor Information Centre** (Samson Mall, Lake Louise, 403/522-3833) before driving north or at the Parks Canada **Jasper Information Centre** (500 Connaught Dr., Jasper, 780/852-6176) if you're traveling south.

The Icefields Parkway is open year-round, although the road's limited services don't operate in winter, and heavy snows, primarily between December and March, can close the road for a day or more. Don't make this trip in winter, unless you have winter tires and you're comfortable in winter driving conditions.

At any time of year, be prepared for changeable weather. Since the parkway climbs through the mountains and crosses several mountain passes, the weather can vary significantly as you change elevation.

Note that there's currently no cell phone service along most of the Icefields Parkway.

Sights and Recreation

These highlights along the Icefields Parkway are listed from south to north, that is, from Lake Louise to Jasper. Parks Canada publishes **The Icefields Parkway Driving Guide,** available online (www.pc.gc.ca) and at park visitors centers, with more details about stopping points and hiking trails along this scenic route.

Bow Lake

At **Bow Lake,** a scenic stretch-your-legs and take-a-photo spot 23 miles (37 km) north of Lake Louise, the Wapta Icefield rises above the opposite lakeshore.

If you're ready for a picnic, follow the short road from the parking area (to your left as you face the lake) that leads to a quiet grove of lakeside picnic tables.

Bow Summit and Peyto Lake

Take time to stop at **Peyto Lake,** 25 miles (40 km) north of Lake Louise, where a paved trail climbs steeply up from the parking lot to a viewpoint overlooking this brilliant-turquoise glacier-fed lake. It's worth the 10-minute hike for this photogenic panorama.

For a longer hike, continue past the Peyto Lake lookout on the **Bow Summit Trail,** which follows an old fire road up to another scenic viewpoint. This route is 3.6 miles (5.8 km) round-trip, with an elevation gain of 804 feet (245 m).

★ Wilcox Pass

Have time for only one hike along the Icefields Parkway? Hike the **Wilcox Pass Trail,** a 5-mile (8-km) round-trip route that climbs up to a ridge and alpine meadows with spectacular views across the glaciers of the Columbia Icefield. This trail is an intermediate-level hike with an elevation gain of 1,100 feet (335 m).

Even if you don't hike the entire route, walk up 1.5 miles (2.4 km) to the first viewpoint, where the vistas spread out across glacier-topped peaks.

To reach the trailhead, turn off the Icefields Parkway at the Wilcox Campground, 79 miles (127 km) north of Lake Louise or 67 miles (108 km) south of the town of Jasper.

★ Columbia Icefield

If you want to explore glaciers, you'll want to visit the **Columbia Icefield,** the largest area of glacial ice in the Canadian Rockies. Measuring 77 square miles (200 sq km), the Icefield comprises several individual glaciers: the Saskatchewan, Columbia, Stutfield, Dome, and Athabasca. The Icefield region is unique

the Icefields Parkway in Jasper National Park

in North America for being a triple watershed, the only point on the continent where water flows to three oceans: the Pacific, the Atlantic, and the Arctic.

Columbia Icefield Glacier Discovery Centre

The starting point for exploring the Icefield is the **Columbia Icefield Glacier Discovery Centre** (Hwy. 93, www. banffjaspercollection.com, daily mid-Apr.-mid-Oct.), 81 miles (130 km) north of Lake Louise and 64 miles (103 km) south of Jasper, which has a small Parks Canada exhibit area and a theater. It's also the departure point for several Icefield tours. The center has a cafeteria (9am-6pm daily) and the more upscale Altitude Restaurant (7:30am-9:30am, 10:45am-2:45pm, and 6pm-9pm daily).

A tourist mecca, the Icefield Centre gets jammed, particularly on summer afternoons, when waiting times for tours can be lengthy. Get here before 11am if you can.

Athabasca Glacier

Resembling a frozen river extending down toward Highway 93, the **Athabasca Glacier** is visible from the road and from the Icefield Centre. It's not only the most accessible of the Columbia Icefield glaciers; it's the most visited glacier in North America.

Currently measuring 2.5 square miles (6 sq km), the Athabasca Glacier has been receding as the region's climate has warmed. It has lost close to 1 mile (1.6 km) of its length and nearly half its volume during the last century. Some experts think that the glacier may disappear completely in 50 years.

The most popular way to explore the glacier is on the **Columbia Icefield Glacier Adventure** (866/506-0515, www. banffjaspercollection.com, 3 hours, 10am-5pm daily mid-Apr.-mid Oct., adults $109, ages 6-15 $55); book online 48 hours in advance for a 10 percent discount. On these tours, you drive onto a section of the glacial ice in Ice Explorer buses, fat-tire snowcat coaches. When you get off the bus, you have about 15 minutes to walk directly on the glacier.

The Glacier Adventure tours depart from the Icefield Centre every 15-30 minutes. You board a bus that takes you across the road to a transfer point, where you climb onto the Ice Explorer vehicles. From there, you drive up through a rocky chasm of glacial moraine and into the alpine region above the tree line. As part of the short ride to the ice, the snowcats descend a nail-biting 32 percent grade down toward the glacier.

The Glacier Adventure tours also include a walk on the **Glacier Skywalk,** a steel bridge arcing 115 feet (35 m) out over the Sunwapta Valley. The most exciting (or terrifying, depending on your perspective) part of the Skywalk is a section with a glass floor, where you can look directly down into the canyon, 918 feet (280 m) below. A self-guided **audio tour** (included with the tour price) explores interpretive panels with details about

Columbia Icefield

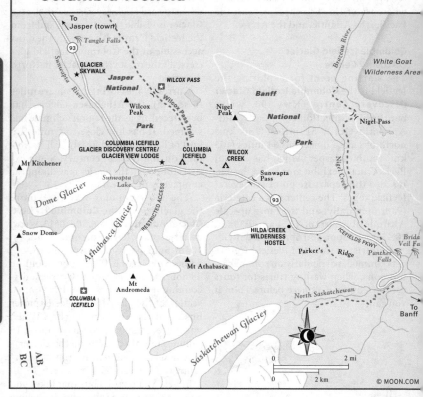

the icefield glaciers, geologic changes, and local wildlife and plants. Another interesting section of the exhibit details how the Skywalk was designed and built. If you don't want to do the full Glacier Adventure tour, sign up for a shorter tour to the Skywalk alone (10am-6pm daily mid-Apr.-mid-Oct., adults $35, ages 6-15 $18).

Without taking the Glacier Adventure tour, it's possible to walk the 1.1-mile (1.8-km) round-trip **Toe of the Athabasca Glacier Trail,** which starts across the road from the Icefield Centre and takes you to the glacier's base. However, since the Athabasca Glacier has more than 2,000 crevasses, Parks Canada staff caution that you shouldn't

wander on your own onto the glacier. The **Forefield Trail** (2.2 mi/3.5 km round-trip) also begins opposite the Icefield Centre and traverses the glacier's moraines and left-behind debris.

Tangle Falls

Four miles (6.4 km) north of the Icefield Centre, 114-foot (35-m) **Tangle Falls** streams down the rock face in several tiers, making the cascade especially photogenic. In winter, when the falls freeze, experienced ice climbers attempt to scale the frozen flow.

Tangle Falls is on the east side of the parkway, 85 miles (137 km) north of Lake Louise and 60 miles (97 km) south of Jasper.

Sunwapta Falls

Another waterfall viewpoint is at **Sunwapta Falls,** 111 miles (179 km) north of Lake Louise and 34 miles (54 km) south of Jasper. The main (upper) falls are closest to the parking area. You can also walk 0.6 mile (1 km) along the river to Lower Sunwapta Falls.

Thousands of years ago, receding glacial ice left behind U-shaped valleys. When larger valleys were carved more deeply into the rock than smaller valleys, these smaller valleys appeared to hang at a higher elevation where the valleys converged, leaving a path for waterfalls to form and flow. These hanging valleys created Sunwapta Falls and many of the other waterfalls in the Jasper region.

★ Athabasca Falls

At 955 miles (1,538 km), the Athabasca River is Alberta's longest. Along the river, near where Highway 93 meets Highway 93A, south of Jasper, a set of waterfalls along the river crash into the canyon below.

What makes **Athabasca Falls** worth a stop on your Icefields Parkway tour isn't its height; it's only 75 feet (23 m) high. But the strong rushing river causes the falls to cascade dramatically through the canyon. With a row of mountain peaks behind the falls, it's a photo-worthy spot.

A short paved path leads from the parking area to a viewpoint over the falls. Cross the bridge and walk around to the overlooks on the other side of the river for up-close falls views.

Athabasca Falls are close enough to Jasper, 19 miles (30 km) to the south, that you can visit them either from town or as you're traveling the Icefields Parkway. The falls are 126 miles (203 km) north of Lake Louise.

Top to bottom: Athabasca Falls; totem poles at Sunwapta Falls Resort; Athabasca Glacier.

Sightseeing Tours

Several companies offer day trips along the Icefields Parkway from Banff, Lake Louise, or Jasper.

Brewster Sightseeing (403/760-6934 or 800/760-6934, www.banffjaspercollection.com, May-mid.-Oct.), part of the Pursuit Collection, runs a one-day, one-way **Icefields Parkway Discovery Tour.** You can start in Calgary (12 hours, adults $292, ages 6-15 $143), Canmore (10.75 hours, adults $246, ages 6-15 $121), Banff (9.75 hours, adults $246, ages 6-15 $121), or Lake Louise (8.25 hours, adults $246, ages 6-15 $121) and travel north to the Columbia Icefields, where your tour ticket includes a buffet lunch, the Columbia Icefield Glacier Adventure, and the Glacier Skywalk. The tour concludes in Jasper. You can also do the tour southbound, starting in Jasper and ending in Lake Louise, Banff, Canmore, or Calgary.

Another Brewster Sightseeing option is the **Columbia Icefield Discovery Tour,** which provides round-trip transportation to the Columbia Icefield from Banff (10.25 hours, adults $250, ages 6-15 $127), Lake Louise (7.75 hours, adults $250, ages 6-15 $127), Jasper (8 hours, adults $206, ages 6-15 $105), Canmore (12.5 hours, adults $250, ages 6-15 $127), or Calgary (14.5 hours, adults $338, ages 6-15 $171). These tours also include a buffet lunch, the Glacier Adventure, and the Glacier Skywalk, and return to your starting point.

SunDog Tours (780/852-4056 or 888/786-3641, www.sundogtours.com, May-mid-Oct.) runs a **Columbia Icefields Tour** (5-6 hours, adults $205, ages 6-15 $105) that starts and ends in Jasper. It stops at Athabasca Falls and at the Columbia Icefield Centre, where your tour includes the Glacier Adventure and Glacier Skywalk. You can also do these SunDog tours one-way from Jasper to Lake Louise (9 hours, adults $239, ages 6-15 $120) or from Jasper to Banff (10 hours, adults $245, ages 6-15 $125), or

vice versa, starting in Lake Louise or Banff and ending in Jasper.

Alternatively, SunDog runs round-trip tours that start and end in either Lake Louise (9 hours, adults $250, ages 6-15 $127) or Banff (10 hours, adults $250, ages 6-15 $127) and travel to the Columbia Icefield. These tours include the Glacier Adventure and Glacier Skywalk, as well as a box lunch.

Food

Services are limited along the Icefields Parkway, so consider packing a picnic or at least bringing water and snacks.

Off Highway 93 at Saskatchewan Crossing, 50 miles (80 km) north of Lake Louise, **The Crossing Resort** (403/761-7000, www.thecrossingresort.com, mid-Apr.-mid-Oct.) has several food outlets, including **The Crossing Café,** a cafeteria serving lunch and snacks; **Mt. Wilson Restaurant,** open for breakfast, lunch, and dinner; and **The Parkway Pub,** a sports bar offering lunch, dinner, and drinks (if you're not the designated driver).

At the **Columbia Icefield Glacier Discovery Centre** (Hwy. 93, www.banffjaspercollection.com, daily mid-Apr.-mid-Oct.), you can have breakfast, lunch, or snacks in the **cafeteria** (9am-6pm); if the burgers, sandwiches, and other plates aren't special, the views across the road to the Athabasca Glacier are. Also in the Icefield Centre is the more upscale **Altitude Restaurant** (7:30am-9:30am, 10:45am-2:45pm, and 6pm-9pm daily).

Sunwapta Falls Resort (Hwy. 93, 780/852-4852 or 888/828-5777, www.sunwapta.com, mid-May-mid-Oct.), 111 miles (179 km) north of Lake Louise and 34 miles (54 km) south of Jasper, has a **deli** (7:30am-6pm daily, breakfast $7-13, lunch $10-17), serving eggs, french toast, and oatmeal in the morning, and soups, stews, and burgers midday, as well as premade sandwiches, muffins, yogurt, and fruit to go. In the evening, the window-lined white-tablecloth **Endless Chain Ridge Dining Room** ($26-40) is worth a stop for its candlelit setting and hearty mountain dishes: pan-seared wild sockeye salmon, game meat pot pie, and Alberta beef steaks. Reservations are recommended.

Accommodations and Camping
Many people travel the Icefields Parkway as a day trip from Banff, Lake Louise, or Jasper, but it's possible to stay overnight along the way.

Located on the 3rd floor of the Columbia Icefield Glacier Discovery Centre, the ★ **Glacier View Lodge** (888/770-6914, www.banffjaspercollection.com, June-mid-Oct., from $335 pp) has 32 large rooms, many with views across to the Athabasca Glacier. Stays here are available only as part of a package and include an evening tour on the Athabasca Glacier, complete with appetizers and cocktails, and a private guided excursion on the Glacier Skywalk, as well as dinner and breakfast. Book several months in advance for stays in July and August.

Wilderness Hostels
Hostelling International-Canada (778/328-2220 or 866/762-4122, www.hihostels.ca) runs several rustic wilderness hostels along Highway 93 between Lake Louise and Jasper. "Rustic" means no indoor plumbing, showers, electricity, or Wi-Fi, but you'll get a bunk in a cabin in the woods. From south to north:

- **HI-Mosquito Creek Wilderness Hostel** (May-mid-Oct. and mid-Nov.-mid-Apr., $32-37 dorm, $78-87 d) has both dorms and private rooms. It's located 18 miles (29 km) north of Lake Louise.

- **HI-Rampart Creek Wilderness Hostel** (May-mid-Oct. and mid-Nov.-early Apr., $32-37 dorm), 56 miles (90 km) north of Lake Louise and 88 miles (142 km) south of the town of Jasper, has dorm rooms only.

- **HI-Hilda Creek Wilderness Hostel** ($33-37 dorm) has just six dorm beds and no staff. It's 4.5 miles (7 km) south of the Icefield Centre, 75 miles (121 km) north of Lake Louise.

- **HI-Beauty Creek Wilderness Hostel** ($33-37 dorm) is open year-round but staffed only mid-May-mid-October. The hostel is 11 miles (18 km) north of the Icefield Centre, 55 miles (89 km) south of Jasper.

- **HI-Athabasca Falls Wilderness Hostel** ($32-37 dorm, $78-87 d) has both dorm beds and private rooms in five rustic cabins. It's 20 miles (32 km) south of Jasper.

Camping
Parks Canada operates a number of primitive campgrounds along the Icefields Parkway. Most have outhouses and no water or electricity, and none accept reservations. Mosquito Creek, Silverhorn Creek, Waterfowl Lakes, and Rampart Creek are in Banff National Park; Wilcox, Columbia Icefield, Jonas Creek, Honeymoon Lake, and Kerkeslin are within Jasper National Park's boundaries.

From south to north:

- **Mosquito Creek Campground** (June-mid-Oct., $17.60) is 15 miles (24 km) north of Lake Louise, with 32 unserviced sites for tents or RVs.

- **Silverhorn Creek Campground** (mid-July-early Sept., $15.70), with 45 sites, is 32 miles (52 km) north of Lake Louise. Silverhorn Creek has no running water; the nearest water is 3 miles (5 km) north at Waterfowl Lakes Campground.

- **Waterfowl Lakes Campground** (late June-early Sept., $21.50) has a washroom with flush toilets and hot and cold water (but no showers) for its 116 sites. This campground is 35 miles (56 km) north of Lake Louise.

- **Rampart Creek Campground** (June-mid-Oct., $17.60) has 50 sites, 55 miles (88 km) north of Lake Louise.

- **Wilcox Campground** (late May-mid-Sept., $15.70) has 46 sites that Parks Canada recommends for small motorhomes or trailers. It's just south of the Icefield Centre, near the trailhead for the Wilcox Pass Trail; it's 67 miles (108 km) south of the town of Jasper.

- **Columbia Icefield Campground** (mid-May-mid-Oct., $15.70) is the place to camp if you want to be close to the Athabasca Glacier. The 33 tent-only sites are convenient to the Icefield Centre, 66 miles (106 km) south of Jasper.

- **Jonas Creek Campground** (mid-May-early Sept., $15.70), 48 miles (77 km) south of Jasper, is a quiet area with 25 sites for tents or small RVs.

- **Honeymoon Lake Campground** (mid-May-early Sept., $15.70), 33 miles (53 km) south of Jasper, is a lakeside area not far from Sunwapta Falls. Its 35 sites accommodate tents and small motorhomes.

- **Kerkeslin Campground** (mid-June-early Sept., $15.70) has 42 sites for tents or small RVs, 22 miles (35 km) south of Jasper.

Information and Services

Parks Canada (780/852-6288, www.pc.gc.ca, 10:15am-5pm daily early May-Sept.) has a seasonal information desk in the Icefield Centre.

Check your fuel before you set out. **Gas** is available only at Lake Louise, Saskatchewan Crossing (50 mi/80 km, north of Lake Louise), and Jasper.

There is currently **no cell phone service** for most of the length of the Icefields Parkway, between Lake Louise and the Athabasca Falls area, 20 miles (32 km) south of Jasper.

Jasper National Park

Jasper National Park is the largest park in the Canadian Rockies, stretching across 4,335 square miles (11,228 sq km) in western Alberta. Initially created as a forest reserve in 1907, Jasper became a full-fledged national park in 1930.

Visiting the Park
Entrances
Coming from Lake Louise, Banff, or points south, you enter Jasper National Park along Highway 93, the Icefields Parkway.

Highway 16, the Yellowhead Highway, runs through the park. The park's west gate is on Highway 16 near the Continental Divide, at the B.C.-Alberta provincial border. The east gate is 19 miles (30 km) southwest of the town of Hinton, also along Highway 16.

Park Passes and Fees
A **day pass** (adults $9.80, seniors $8.30, families $19.60) for Jasper National Park is valid until 4pm on the day after you purchase it. Jasper day passes are also valid at Banff National Park. You need a park pass to travel the Icefields Parkway.

Purchasing a Parks Canada **annual discovery pass** (adults $67.70, seniors $57.90, families $136.40), valid for a year, is a good deal if you're spending at least a week in one or more parks. It's good at more than 100 national parks and national historic sites across Canada. Buy an annual pass online from Parks Canada or at any of the parks' visitors centers.

For both day and annual passes, the family passes cover up to seven people in a single vehicle, whether or not they're actually related.

Visitors Centers
Parks Canada runs the **Jasper Information Centre** (500 Connaught Dr., 780/852-6176, www.pc.gc.ca, 9am-7pm daily mid-May-mid-June, 8am-8pm

One Day in Jasper

If you have just one day, get an early start. Jasper National Park is a big area to explore.

Enjoy coffee and pastries at **Bear's Paw Bakery** before riding up the **Jasper Sky Tram** to get oriented with views across a wide swath of the park. Or if you'd rather begin the day with a hike, follow the 2.8-mile (4.5-km) **Valley of the Five Lakes Trail,** which takes you past five bodies of water of varying, dramatic shades of blue, turquoise, and green.

Stop at the **Jasper-Yellowhead Museum** to learn more about the history of the Jasper region, then walk over to **Patricia Street Deli** or **Coco's Café** to pick up a picnic lunch. Take your picnic to **Maligne Canyon,** where you can hike along the deep limestone gorge, past rushing springs and striking rock formations.

In the afternoon, drive to **Maligne Lake** for a 90-minute cruise on this impossibly scenic glacier-fed lake to tiny Spirit Island, one of the park's most photographed spots. Or rent a canoe or kayak from the historic boathouse and go for a leisurely lake paddle.

Have an early supper back in town, then head for **Miette Hot Springs** to wrap up your day with a relaxing soak in these natural mineral pools. If you're not ready to call it a night, stop for a microbrew at the **Jasper Brewing Company,** the local brewpub, where, over a pint, you can recap the highlights of your Jasper day.

daily mid-June-late Sept., 9am-7pm daily late Sept.-mid-Oct., 9am-5pm daily mid-Oct.-mid-May) in the town of Jasper, one block from the train station. The **Friends of Jasper National Park** (780/852-4767, www.friendsofjasper.com) operate a shop that sells books and souvenirs in the same location.

The Information Centre's rustic stone building is itself a National Historic Site. British Colonel Maynard Rogers, the park's first superintendent, built the stone structure as his home in 1913, using rocks excavated from the building site and from the nearby river. It was the first major building to be constructed at the Jasper town site after the government designated the surrounding region as Jasper Forest Park, a 5,000-square-mile (13,000-sq-km) protected area.

Reservations

You can normally make campsite **reservations** (877/737-3783, www.reservation.parkscanada.gc.ca) online or by phone for four of the campgrounds in Jasper National Park: Whistlers, Wapiti, Wabasso, and Pocahontas. Reservations are advised especially for July and August stays.

Sights and Recreation
★ Maligne Canyon

According to local legend, a 19th-century Belgian explorer tried to cross a river in the Jasper area. When the rough waters swept away all his belongings, he dubbed the river *maligne* (ma-LEEN), French for "evil" or "wicked." The name stuck to the river, the canyon, and the nearby lake that still bear the moniker. Fortunately, there's nothing especially wicked about scenic **Maligne Canyon,** a deep limestone gorge that showcases nature's carving power.

Several bridges cross the canyon, from First Bridge near the main canyon parking lot to Sixth Bridge, which is off Maligne Road to the west.

The **Maligne Canyon Trail** takes you through the gorge, past rushing springs and striking rock formations. An especially nice way to explore the canyon is to follow the trail from **Fifth Bridge;** from there, it's 1.4 miles (2.2 km) to First Bridge at the top of the canyon. The trail gains 325 feet (100 m) in elevation en route, with the steepest sections around the Second and Third Bridges. For a slightly longer hike, start at Sixth Bridge, which adds 1 mile (1.6 km) of gentle forest trail each way.

Jasper National Park

Caracombs Mountain
3,330m

Mount
Edith Cavell
3,363m

Glacier

Brussels Peak
3,161m

Mount Fryatt
3,361m

Geraldine
Lakes

WHIRLPOOL FIRE RD

Mount Lowell
3,150m

Moab
Lake

ATHABASCA FALLS

Mount Christie
3,103m

KERKESLIN
CAMPGROUND

GERALDINE
FIRE RD

260B

SUNWAPTA FALLS
RESORT

SUNWAPTA
FALLS

93

HI-ATHABASCA FALLS
WILDERNESS HOSTEL

93

Sunwapta River

Buck
Lake

Honeymoon
Lake

HONEYMOON LAKE
CAMPGROUND

Llysfran Peak
3,141m

Mount Unwin
3,268m

Mount Moffat
3,090m

Maligne
Lake

Medicine
Lake

Mount Charlton
3,217m

Samson
Narrows

MALIGNE LAKE

Beaver
Lake

Maligne Mountain
3,192m

Samson Peak
3,081m

Chivalry Peak
3,150m

0

0

5 km

5 mi

Mount Balinhard
3,130m

© MOON.COM

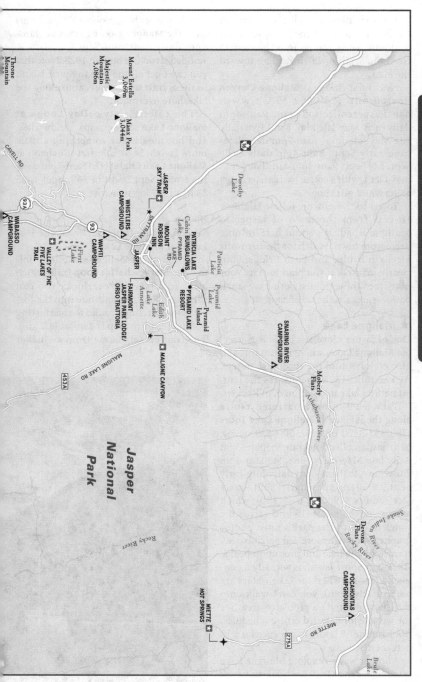

Throne Mountain

Mount Estella 3,069m

Majestic Mountain 3,086m

Manx Peak 3,044m

CAVELL RD

93A

93

WABASSO CAMPGROUND

WHISTLERS CAMPGROUND

WAPITI CAMPGROUND

JASPER

First Lake

VALLEY OF THE FIVE LAKES TRAIL

JASPER SKY TRAM

SKYTRAM RD

MOUNT ROBSON INN

Dorothy Lake

Cabin Bungalows

PATRICIA LAKE

Patricia Lake

PYRAMID LAKE RD

Pyramid Lake

Pyramid Island

PYRAMID LAKE RESORT

Annette Lake

Edith Lake

FAIRMONT JASPER PARK LODGE/ ORSO TRATTORIA

MALIGNE CANYON

MALIGNE LAKE RD

453A

SNARING RIVER CAMPGROUND

Moberly Flats

Athabasca River

Jasper National Park

Rocky River

Snake Indian River

Devona Flats

POCAHONTAS CAMPGROUND

MIETTE RD

275A

MIETTE HOT SPRINGS

Brule Lake

You can hike through the canyon in either direction, but the views are most dramatic when you go into the canyon from the Sixth or Fifth Bridges toward the First.

Near First Bridge is **Maligne Canyon Restaurant** (780/852-3583, www.banffjaspercollection.com, 9am-4pm daily early May-late May, 8am-4pm daily late May-late June, 8am-7pm daily late-June-early Sept., 8am-4pm daily early Sept.-late Sept., 9am-4pm daily late Sept.-mid-Oct.), with a coffee bar, cafeteria, art gallery, and gift shop.

To get to the canyon, follow Highway 16 east from the town of Jasper to Maligne Road. It's about a 15-minute drive from town. Watch for the turn-offs for Sixth Bridge and Fifth Bridge, both clearly marked, if you plan to start your hike from these points; both have small parking areas at the trailheads.

★ Maligne Lake

One of Jasper's loveliest lakes is glacier-fed **Maligne Lake,** where mountains and glaciers surround the turquoise waters. At 13.6 miles (22 km) long, it's the largest natural lake in the Canadian Rockies.

Take a 90-minute narrated **cruise** along the lake with **Maligne Lake Tours** (780/852-3370 or 866/360-8839, www.banffjaspercollection.com, 9:30am-3pm daily late May-early June, 9:30am-4pm daily June, 9:30am-6pm daily July-early Sept., 9:30am-4pm daily Sept.-early Oct., adults $79, ages 6-15 $40), which brings you 9.5 miles (15 km) across the water to one of the park's most photographed spots: tiny forested Spirit Island, framed by the lake and mountain peaks. Although Spirit Island is actually a peninsula (except when the lake waters are particularly high), you can't walk onto the island itself; it's a protected area. See the website for detailed cruise schedules. Book online 48 hours in advance for a 10 percent discount.

Another way to explore Maligne Lake is to rent a **canoe** ($60 per hour) or **kayak**

(single $60 per hour, double $75 per hour) from the **Maligne Lake Boathouse** (9am-4pm daily June-mid-Sept.), a historic wooden structure built in 1928. Note that you can't get all the way to Spirit Island in these craft unless you camp along the lakeshore overnight.

The cafeteria-style **Day Lodge at Maligne Lake** serves soups, sandwiches, and hot meals. For something a little more lavish, book a buffet luncheon at **Maligne Lake Chalet** (11:15am-2pm daily June-mid-Sept., adults $49, ages 6-15 $34), a 1927 log structure.

Hiking

Several hiking trails start near the Day Lodge at Maligne Lake.

To hike along Maligne's lakeshore, follow the **Mary Schaffer Loop** trail, which leads to a lakeside overlook. You can turn back here, or continue into the forest before circling around to the starting point; the entire loop is 2 miles (3.2 km). The trail gets its name from a Quaker

woman from Philadelphia who explored and wrote about the lake in 1907.

Leading through the woods, the 1.7-mile (2.7-km) **Moose Lake Loop** takes you through the site of a centuries-old landslide.

One of the steepest trails in the Maligne area, the **Opal Hills Loop,** a 5-mile (8-km) loop with an elevation gain of 1,510 feet (460 m), has great mountain vistas. Check with Parks Canada staff at the **Jasper Information Centre** before hiking here in July and early August, when bears often frequent the area.

Another steep route, the 6.5-mile (10.4-km) round-trip **Bald Hills Trail** rewards hikers with views of the lake and surrounding peaks. It has an elevation gain of 1,640 feet (500 m).

Getting There

Maligne Lake is 29 miles (47 km) east of town, about an hour's drive. From Highway 16, go east on Maligne Lake Road. Make sure you have enough fuel to get to the lake and back; there are no services en route.

To get to Maligne Lake without a car, book the **Explore Jasper Tour** (780/852-3370 or 866/360-8839, www. banffjaspercollection.com, late May-early Oct., 4 hours, adults $66, ages 6-15 $33), which provides bus transportation every morning from several stops in Jasper, returning to Jasper later in the day. You can also book this tour including transportation and the Maligne Lake cruise (6 hours, adults $133, ages 6-15 $66).

Maligne Adventures (780/852-3370 or 866/625-4463, www.maligneadventures. com) also provides service between town and Maligne Lake via its **Maligne Valley Hiker's Shuttle** (late May-early Oct., one-way adults $35, ages 5-15 $17.50); reservations are required.

Medicine Lake

En route to Maligne Lake, you'll pass **Medicine Lake** (Maligne Lake Rd.), an unusual "disappearing" lake.

Maligne Lake

The Maligne River feeds Medicine Lake, and in summer, waters from nearby melting glaciers cause the lake to fill. In fall and winter, when the snowmelt stops, the lake begins to disappear, draining out through sinkholes at the lake bottom. The water then flows through an underground cave system, before surfacing 10 miles (16 km) downstream in Maligne Canyon. The Maligne River is considered among the largest "sinking rivers" in the western hemisphere.

In 2015, triggered by a lightning strike, the Excelsior Wildfire decimated more than 2,300 acres (966 ha) of forest along Medicine Lake. You'll see the charred remains of this severe fire along the lakeshore.

★ Miette Hot Springs

Underground streams fuel hot springs throughout the Canadian Rockies, but the hottest of these mineral-rich waters flows into Jasper's **Miette Hot Springs** (Miette Rd., 780/866-3939, www.hotsprings.ca, 9am-11pm daily mid-June-early Sept., 10:30am-9pm daily May-mid-June and early Sept.-mid-Oct., adults $7.05, seniors $6.15, ages 3-17 $5.15, families $20.35). Its source is a steamy 129°F (54°C), though the waters are cooled to around 104°F (40°C) before they reach the large public soaking pools. The minerals concentrated in the Miette springs include sulfate, calcium, bicarbonate, magnesium, and sodium.

You can rent towels ($1.90) and swimsuits ($1.90), including early 20th-century bathing costumes (fun for those holiday photos!). Admission rates include a token for the lockers. You can't wear street shoes into the pool area, so bring water sandals or flip-flops if you'd rather not walk barefoot.

Before or after your soak in the pool, you can hike the **Source of the Springs Trail**, a moderate 1.9-mile (3-km) loop from the pool area, to see where the sulfurous waters come from. Along the way,

you pass the ruins of the original pool building, built in the 1930s.

The hot springs is an hour's drive from the town of Jasper. Take Highway 16 east for 27 miles (43 km) and turn right (south) onto Miette Road. From the Highway 16/Miette Road junction, it's 11 miles (18 km) to the springs.

Mount Edith Cavell

Edith Cavell was a British nurse who worked in German-occupied Belgium during World War I. In 1915, a German firing squad executed Cavell after she was caught helping Allied soldiers escape across the border from Belgium to the Netherlands. Jasper's 11,046-foot (3,367-m) **Mount Edith Cavell** bears her name.

You can drive up toward the mountain's north face on the snaking 8.7-mile (14-km) Cavell Road, which is located off Highway 93A south of town.

At the top of the road, follow the **Path of the Glacier Trail**, a short 1-mile (1.6-km) walk to a lookout opposite the Angel

Glacier, which perches on the mountain above Cavell Pond. Expect snow on the surrounding mountains (and sometimes on the trail) at any time of year.

Camping

You can make **reservations** (877/737-3783, www.reservation.parkscanada.gc.ca) online or by phone for four Jasper National Park campgrounds: Whistlers, Wapiti, Wabasso, and Pocahontas. Reservations are advised, particularly in July and August. You can make reservations starting in January for the upcoming year.

- **Whistlers Campground** (Hwy. 93, 2.2 mi/3.5 km south of Jasper, May-mid-Oct.) is Jasper's largest. However, this campground is closed for reconstruction at least through 2019. Check the Parks Canada website for updates.

- **Wapiti Campground** (Hwy. 93, 3.5 mi/5.6 km south of Jasper, $27.40 tent sites, $32.30 electrical sites)

accommodates both tents and RVs and has washrooms with hot showers. It has 362 sites available May-mid-October; 75 sites are open for winter camping (mid-Oct.-Apr.).

- **Wabasso Campground** (Hwy. 93A, 10 mi/16 km south of Jasper, mid-May-mid-Sept., $21.50-27.40), located off Highway 93A, which is quieter than the main Highway 93, has 231 sites for tents and small RVs. The washrooms have hot water but no showers.

- **Pocahontas Campground** (Hwy. 16, mid-May-early Sept., $21.50) is off Highway 16, near the Miette Hot Springs, 28 miles (45 km) east of the town of Jasper. Its 140 sites accommodate tents and small RVs. There is running water and flush toilets but no showers or electricity.

- **Snaring River Campground** (Hwy. 16, mid-May-mid-Sept., $15.70) is also off Highway 16, but it's closer to town, 8 miles (13 km) to the east. It has 63

Medicine Lake

sites, some along the river, for tents and small RVs; some tent sites are in a more private, walk-in-only area. It's a rustic campground without showers, electricity, or flush toilets—just outhouses.

Town of Jasper

Set along the Athabasca River entirely within the national park, the compact town of Jasper has a year-round population of about 5,000. In summer, that number can swell to over 20,000 as seasonal workers arrive to cater to the influx of high-season visitors.

A good way to get oriented, while learning something about Jasper's heritage, is on a 90-minute historical walking tour of the town: **Jasper: A Walk in the Past** (780/852-4767, www.friendsofjasper. com, 7:30pm daily late May-early Sept., free). Offered by the Friends of Jasper National Park, the tour is complimentary, but advance tickets are required; pick them up from the Friends store in the **Jasper Information Centre** (500 Connaught Dr.), which is also where the tour departs.

Sights and Activities
Jasper-Yellowhead Museum

How did Jasper get its name? Who are the Métis and what role did they play in Jasper's settlement? What's the story behind Jasper National Park?

If you're curious about these and other questions about the Jasper area, visit the **Jasper-Yellowhead Museum & Archives** (400 Bonhomme St., 780/852-3013, www. jaspermuseum.org, 10am-5pm daily June-Sept., 10am-5pm Thurs.-Sun. Oct.-May, adults $7, seniors, students, and over age 5 $6). The well-designed displays and artifacts trace the region's history from its aboriginal people to the early explorers and traders, the development of the railroad, the establishment of the national park, and the first days of tourism.

★ Jasper Sky Tram

For great views, ride the **Jasper Sky Tram** (Whistlers Rd., 780/852-3093 or 866/850-8726, www.jasperskytram.com, 10am-5pm daily late Mar.-mid-May and early Sept.-Oct., 9am-8pm daily mid-May-late June, 8am-9pm daily late-June-early Sept., adults $47, ages 6-15 $25, families $119), a seven-minute gondola trip that takes you 7,500 feet (2,300 m) above the national park and the town of Jasper. Book your tram ticket online to avoid the lines, especially in midsummer.

Want even better vistas of the surrounding snow-topped mountains? Then hike above the gondola station along the 0.75-mile (1.2-km) dirt and shale path to the summit of Whistlers Mountain, elevation 8,100 feet (2,500 m). On a clear day, you can see Mount Robson; at 12,972 feet (3,954 m), it's the highest peak in the Canadian Rockies. The hike to the summit is a moderate climb that should take 45-60 minutes round-trip, although in spring and fall, parts of the path can be snow-covered.

The Sky Tram is 5 miles (8 km) south of town; take Highway 93 south to Whistlers Road. **SunDog Tours** (780/852-4056 or 888/786-3641, www.sundogtours. com, adults $55, ages 5-12 $28) runs shuttles to the Sky Tram from town with pickups at several hotels; check the website or call for schedules. Prices include your tram ticket and transportation.

Sightseeing Tours

Maligne Adventures (780/852-3370 or 866/625-4463, www.maligneadventures. com) runs several Jasper sightseeing tours, including the **Maligne Valley Wildlife & Waterfalls Tour** (June-early Oct., 5-6 hours), with stops at Maligne Canyon, Medicine Lake, and Maligne Lake, where you can choose a lake cruise (adults $135, ages 5-15 $74) or a guided hike (adults $74, ages 5-15 $49), and an **Evening Wildlife Search** (May-early Oct., 3 hours, adults $69, ages 5-15 $49) that takes you to various Jasper locations

Town of Jasper

To Pyramid Lake

To Hwy 16

To
★ MALIGNE CANYON,
★ MALIGNE LAKE,
and
★ MIETTE HOT SPRINGS

JUNIPER ST

PYRAMID LAKE RD

16

YELLOWHEAD HWY

ASPEN AVE

BONHOMME ST

COLIN CRESCENT

GEIKIE ST

CONNAUGHT DR

PATRICIA ST

THE CRIMSON

ROBINSONS FOODS

Pyramid Benchland Trail

CEDAR AVE

BEAR'S PAW BAKERY

JASPER-YELLOWHEAD MUSEUM & ARCHIVES ★

To Mina Lakes

JASPER HERITAGE FIREHALL

ELM AVE

JASPER INFORMATION CENTRE

THE RAVEN BISTRO

WILDLIFE MUSEUM/ WHISTLER'S INN ★

MALIGNE AVE

SETON-JASPER HEALTHCARE CENTRE

RX DRUG MART JASPER

THE OTHER PAW

JASPER TRAIN STATION

COCO'S CAFÉ

PATRICIA STREET DELI

THE DOWNSTREAM

PHARMASAVE

JASPER BREWING COMPANY

MIETTE AVE

JASPER FARMERS MARKET

EVIL DAVE'S GRILL

PARK PLACE INN

PINE AVE

To
Icefields Parkway, Banff
(Banff National Park) and
Prince George, BC

To
Old Fort Point, HI-Jasper Hostel,
and Tekarra Restaurant

0   200 yds
0   200 m

© MOON.COM

where you might spot elk, bears, moose, sheep, or deer.

SunDog Tours (780/852-4056 or 888/786-3641, www.sundogtours.com) offers several tours in the Jasper region. The **Maligne Valley Sightseeing Tour** (June-mid-Oct., 5-6 hours) takes you to Maligne Canyon, Medicine Lake, and Maligne Lake, with options for a lake cruise (adults $129, under age 12 $65) or a guided hike on the Mary Schaffer Loop (adults $69, under age 12 $35). The family-friendly **Ultimate Jasper Interpretive Nature Walk** (May-Sept., 3 hours, adults $69, ages 6-12 $35) is a guided walk to explore the area's flora and fauna. SunDog can also take you to and from the **Jasper Sky Tram** (adults $55, ages 5-12 $28, including tram tickets).

Is riding a motorcycle on your bucket list? Then book a guided ride with **Jasper Motorcycle Tours** (610 Patricia St., 780/931-6100, www.jaspermotorcycletours.com, Apr.-Oct., adults $125-309), for a unique way to explore highlights of the Jasper region. You'll ride either on the bike behind your guide or in a sidecar attached to your guide's bike. Tours range 1-6 hours, taking you around town, out to Maligne Canyon, Maligne Lake, Miette Hot Springs, or all the way to the Columbia Icefield. Before you set out, staff will outfit you in a leather jacket, leather pants, gloves, goggles, and a helmet. Yes, you're encouraged to take photos.

Food Tours

To get the scoop on the local food scene with a sprinkling of area history and entertaining stories about Jasper residents past and present, book an eating-and-drinking walk with **Jasper Food Tours** (780/931-3297, www.jasperfoodtours.com). Owner Estelle Blanchette has lived in Jasper for two decades and shares lots of delicious details about the area. On the signature **Downtown Foodie Tour** (3 hours, $115 pp), you'll make four stops at local restaurants and pubs, grazing your way through dishes from elk burgers to churros with chocolate dipping sauce. You visit a local brewpub, and at every stop, there's plenty to drink, so if you don't have a designated driver, purchase a taxi voucher from your guide to get back to your lodging.

Sports and Recreation
Hiking
★ Valley of the Five Lakes Trail

You don't have to go far from town to find scenic hiking trails. A particularly striking route, the **Valley of the Five Lakes Trail** is a moderate 2.8-mile (4.5-km) loop that takes you through the woods and past five bodies of water, which are all different photogenic shades of blue, turquoise, and green. The differing lake depths account for the color variations. The trailhead is 5.6 miles (9 km) south of town, off Highway 93.

Other Trails

The **Jasper Discovery Trail** is a 5.2-mile (8.3-km) loop that circles the town. It's marked with a bear symbol and has informational signs and kiosks along the way.

For a short scenic stroll, visit **Pyramid Island,** near the north end of Pyramid Lake. A flat 0.3-mile (0.5-km) loop trail takes you around the island, with lake and mountain views. The parking area is 4.5 miles (7 km) from town, along Pyramid Lake Road.

Old Fort Point is a rocky hill that rises above the Athabasca River. From the top, you have panoramic views of the town and the entire Jasper valley. You can climb straight up to the top, starting with 80 wooden steps and continuing on a steep dirt-and-rock path, but the easier route is to follow the **Old Fort Point Trail** (2.4 mi/3.8 km), which begins as a gentle trail through the woods, then climbs steadily up to the lookout point; the elevation gain is 425 feet (130 m). From the top, you can either circle back the way you came, or go down the front face to the steps. To reach the trailhead, which is 1.25 miles (2 km) from town, follow Highway 93A to the Old Fort Point/ Lac Beauvert access road; there's a parking lot at the base of the trail.

Hiking Tours

Walks and Talks Jasper (780/852-4994 or 888/242-3343, www.walksntalks. com) meets in town and offers several guided interpretive hikes in the Jasper area, including a hike to **Mount Edith Cavell Meadows** (adults $90, kids $50) and a **Maligne Canyon Guided 5 Bridges Adventure** (adults $90, kids $50).

Rafting

You can go white-water rafting on several rivers in the Jasper area. The gentlest rides are on the Athabasca River, while rafting tours on the Sunwapta (a First Nations word meaning "turbulent water") and Fraser Rivers are more wet and wild.

along the Valley of the Five Lakes Trail

Marilyn Monroe's Adventures in Jasper

The Canadian Rockies are glamorous enough without celebrity visitors, but Jasper had its moment in the Hollywood sun when an American movie icon came to town.

In 1953, director Otto Preminger, who subsequently became recognized for films like *Anatomy of a Murder* and *Exodus,* arrived in Jasper to make a new movie. ***River of No Return*** would star Robert Mitchum and Rory Calhoun along with the actress formerly known as Norma Jeane Mortenson: **Marilyn Monroe.**

The blond bombshell had all sorts of now-legendary escapades in Jasper while making this Wild West epic. Most famously, staff at the Jasper Park Lodge (now the Fairmont) refused to allow her to enter the dining room because she was wearing inappropriate attire for a woman: blue jeans. (Decades later, designer Tommy Hilfiger bought a pair of jeans that Monroe wore in the film at auction for US$37,000.)

Monroe injured her leg while filming a rafting scene in Jasper, and according to rumors, she was also escorted out of the Athabasca Hotel—on the arms of two dashing Mounties—for causing some sort of drunken commotion.

Monroe and director Preminger had a stormy relationship during the film, too. The director reportedly sniped, "Directing Marilyn Monroe was like directing Lassie. You needed 14 takes to get each one of them right."

What remains of Monroe's Jasper visit, beyond these (perhaps apocryphal) stories and the film itself, are photos of the star in this mountain setting. Local photographer Ray O'Neill, who came to town in 1942 and lived in Jasper for the next 45 years, had his 15 minutes of fame when he photographed Monroe during the filming. The **Jasper-Yellowhead Museum** periodically exhibits some of his images. *Look* magazine staff photographer John Vachon also photographed the star during her time in Jasper; his photos are collected in the book *Marilyn, August 1953: The Lost Look Photos.*

While *River of No Return,* released in 1954, may be fading into history, it was still Jasper's Hollywood moment. After all, no matter how gorgeous your mountains are, it's not every day that Marilyn Monroe comes to town.

Jasper Raft Tours (780/852-2665 or 888/553-5628, www.jasperrafttours. com, mid-May-mid-Oct., adults $69, ages 6-17 $23, under age 6 $10) offers gentle 2.5-hour Athabasca River float tours, suitable for families and novice rafters.

Maligne Adventures (780/852-3370 or 866/625-4463, www.maligneadventures. com, May-Sept.) runs the family-friendly **Athabasca Falls Canyon Run** (3.5 hours, adults $94, ages 5-14 $47), which starts at the base of Athabasca Falls south of town and mixes Class II rapids with a gentle river float. The **Sunwapta River trip** (4 hours, $104 pp) has numerous Class III rapids; the water is highest and fastest mid-June-late July. For "big water," with Class III+ rapids, take the **Mighty Fraser River tour** (5 hours, $114 pp).

Water Sports

You can go canoeing, kayaking, and even swimming (if you can brave the chilly waters) on scenic Jasper lakes close to town.

Named for the wife of Colonel Maynard Rogers, Jasper National Park's first superintendent, **Lake Annette** (Lake Annette Rd.) has a sandy beach and turquoise water. The paved **Lake Annette Loop Trail** is a 1.5-mile (2.4-km) lakeside walking path. From town, take Highway 16 east to Maligne Road, then take the first right onto Old Lodge Road (toward the Fairmont Jasper Park Lodge). Turn left onto Lake Annette Road and follow it to the shore. Locals recommend swimming at **Lake Edith** (Lake Annette Rd.) in mid- to late summer when the lake level begins to drop and the water warms up slightly. The beach access is beyond Lake Annette on Lake Annette Road. Both lakes are about 4.5 miles (7 km) from the town center.

Ringed by mountains, **Pyramid Lake** (Pyramid Lake Rd.) is a scenic spot for canoeing or kayaking late spring-fall. Opposite the hotel of the same name, **Pyramid Lake Resort Boat Rentals** (780/852-4900 or 888/852-7737, www.mpljasper.com) rents out canoes ($40 per hour), kayaks (single $40 per hour, double $45 per hour), and rowboats ($40), as well as mountain bikes ($20 per hour). From town, follow Pyramid Lake Road (off Connaught Dr.) for 4 miles (6.4 km) to the lake.

Horseback Riding

Jasper Riding Stables (1 Pyramid Lake Rd., 780/852-7433, www.jasperstables.com, daily May-mid-Oct.) offers one-hour (ages 6 and over, $52), two-hour (ages 8 and over, $95), and three-hour (ages 9 and over, $135) trail rides, which take you to viewpoints above the surrounding lakes and mountains.

Winter Sports

At 5,570 feet (1,698 m), **Marmot Basin Ski Resort** (1 Marmot Rd., 780/852-3816 or 866/952-3816, www.skimarmot.com, 9am-4pm daily early Nov.-early May, lift ticket adults $102, seniors, students, and ages 13-17 $82, ages 6-12 $36.50) has the highest base elevation of all Canada's winter sports resorts, receiving an average of more than 160 inches (400 cm) of snow annually. The mountain's seven lifts serve 1,720 acres (696 ha) of terrain. The 91 runs are rated 30 percent novice, 30 percent intermediate, 20 percent advanced, and 20 percent expert.

Marmot Basin is 12.5 miles (20 km) south of Jasper, off Highway 93. You need a Jasper park pass to visit the ski area, which is within the national park

Top to bottom: canoeing in Jasper National Park; enjoying views of Pyramid Island; hikers in Jasper.

Jasper's Top-Secret Wartime Project

You might not think of Jasper as a place for a top-secret World War II mission or as a destination for scuba divers. But it was, and it is.

During the Second World War, the British government hatched a secret plan to build what it hoped would be an indestructible aircraft carrier out of a unique mixture of ice and wood pulp. The project team solicited Canada's participation, and after searching for a location that would be cold enough to build what essentially would be an ice boat, the designers began work at Jasper's Patricia Lake.

The clandestine project to construct this futuristic vessel took the code name "Habbakuk," based on the Old Testament's prophet Habakkuk, who wrote, "Regard and wonder marvelously. For I will work a work in your days which ye will not believe."

In 1943, working in secret at Patricia Lake, the team constructed a scale model of the boat, measuring 60 by 30 by 19.5 feet (18 by 9 by 6 m). At that point, however, the tide of the war turned, and despite the seemingly successful prototype, the project was quietly killed. The Canadian team members ordered that anything reusable be stripped off the boat and that the refrigeration units that kept the prototype afloat be turned off. As it began to melt, the Habbakuk project sank to the bottom of Patricia Lake, where its remains are today.

If you're a scuba diver, you can dive to the site of this abandoned wartime project. Based at the Patricia Lake Bungalows, **Jasper Dive Adventures** (780/852-3560, www.jasperdiveadventures.com) offers a **Guided Habbakuk Tour** (mid-May-Sept., $75, rental equipment not included) for experienced divers (with Open Water Certification and 15 logged dives), where you can learn more about this wartime project and dive to the Habbakuk's final resting place.

---

boundaries. The **Jasper-Marmot Shuttle** (one-way $7) can take you between in-town hotels and the mountain, running three trips a day in each direction during the ski season.

Festivals and Events

Jasper is one of the world's largest **dark sky preserves,** where illuminated signs and other outdoor lighting are limited to keep the skies clear and the stars visible. The town celebrates its status as a go-to stargazing destination during the annual **Dark Sky Festival** (www.jasperdarksky. travel, Oct.), with several days of lectures, workshops, storytelling, and star-spotting events.

Food
Contemporary

There's nothing sinister about **Evil Dave's Grill** (622 Patricia St., 780/852-3323, www. evildavesgrill.com, 5pm-10pm Mon.-Fri., 4pm-10pm Sat.-Sun., $20-40), a laid-back downtown eatery, except for the entertaining names of its dishes. Popular plates include Diabolical Tenderloin (Alberta beef paired with mashed potatoes and seasonal vegetables) and Malevolent Meatloaf, made with bison and wild boar bacon. The same owners run **Tekarra Restaurant** (Hwy 93A S., 780/852-4624, www.tekarrarestaurant. ca, 7:30am-10:30am and 5pm-9:30pm daily, $27-55), in an atmospheric heritage cabin above the Athabasca River south of town, known for mains like bison short ribs braised with Saskatoon berries or rainbow trout in a ginger cream sauce.

The Raven Bistro (504 Patricia St., 780/852-5151, www.theravenbistro.com, 11:30am-10pm Sun.-Thurs., 11:30am-11pm Fri.-Sat., lunch $16-27, dinner $18-36) takes you from Alberta to the Mediterranean with dishes like feta-stuffed falafel served with pickled cabbage and hummus, Moroccan-inspired kale and chickpea strudel topped with fresh arugula, and "the Three Pharaohs"—beef tenderloin with harissa, chicken with cilantro-mint yogurt, and lamb *chevapcici* with Israeli couscous. For something more mountain-inspired, order the fondue for two.

Italian

Starting with simple homemade pastas and moving on to grilled Alberta rib eye served with braised cipollini onions or a boar chop with smoked pepperonata, ★ **Orso Trattoria** (Old Lodge Rd., 780/852-3301, www.orsojasper.com, 7am-10am and 5:30pm-10pm Mon.-Fri., 7am-noon and 5:30pm-10pm Sat.-Sun. summer, breakfast $12-35, dinner $30-59), the classy main dining room at the Fairmont Jasper Park Lodge, with spectacular vistas across Lac Beauvert, channels Italy via the Rockies, using local produce and meats in its modern Italian meals.

Pub Fare

For a casual meal and a pint, head for the local brewpub, **Jasper Brewing Company** (624 Connaught Dr., 780/852-4111, www.jasperbrewingco.ca, 11:30am-1am daily, $15-34), the first brewery to open in a Canadian national park. It makes several beers, including Rockhopper IPA (a hoppy India pale ale) and Jasper the Bear Ale, brewed with honey from B.C.'s Okanagan Valley. The food menu begins with basic burgers but quickly progresses to more inventive salads and sandwiches, like the sweet potato and quinoa patty, plus heartier plates like Alberta beef or elk meatloaf.

The Downstream (620 Connaught Dr., 780/852-9449, www.downstreamjasper.ca, 5pm-2am daily, $18-34) takes good-value pub fare and amps it up with global flavors. You can nibble on miso-glazed steak bites or house-made falafel, travel the world with Moroccan chicken or sweet potato and goat cheese lasagna,

---

Top to bottom: Jasper Brewing Company; Tekarra Restaurant; The Raven Bistro's feta-stuffed falafel.

or come back to Canada for cabernet-glazed bison short ribs or a bacon-topped burger. Vegetarians and other tofu-lovers should try the Legendary Samba, a substantial sandwich piled with grilled tofu, peppers, onions, melted mozzarella, and hot sauce overflowing out of its pretzel bun. The Downstream is on the lower level below the Fiddle River Restaurant.

Cafés, Bakeries, and Light Bites

Start your day with a scone or sticky bun and coffee from Jasper's favorite baked goods purveyor, ★ **Bear's Paw Bakery** (4 Pyramid Rd., 780/852-3233, www.bearspawbakery.com, 6am-6pm daily). A second location, called **The Other Paw,** also makes sandwiches and salads.

For a sandwich to bring on the trails, find your way to the ★ **Patricia Street Deli** (606 Patricia St., 780/852-4814, 10am-5pm daily, sandwiches $10-12), a take-out spot hidden behind the escalator in a mini mall. Choose your meat (roast turkey, black forest ham, smoked beef, roast beef), cheese, and loads of veggies—lettuce, peppers, carrots, beets, pickles, and sprouts—and your sandwich will be made to order. It usually has homemade cookies, too.

A locally popular breakfast joint, **Coco's Café** (608-B Patricia St., 780/852-4550, www.cocoscafe.ca, 6am-6pm daily summer, 6am-4pm daily winter, $8-14) is known for its breakfast wrap, with eggs, ham, veggies, cheese, and "secret sauce" rolled into a curried tortilla (really, try them!). From overnight oats to tofu scrambles to sandwiches, you can choose from vegetarian, vegan, or carnivorous options.

Groceries and Markets

You can find local food at the summer **Jasper Farmers Market** (McCready Centre, 701 Turret St., 780/852-3599, 11am-3pm Wed. late June-mid-Sept.).

For groceries, Jasper's largest market is **Robinsons Foods** (218 Connaught Dr., 780/852-3195, www.robinsonfoods.com, 8am-10pm daily summer, 8am-8pm daily winter).

Accommodations
Under $150

As members of the **Jasper Home Accommodation Association** (www.stayinjasper.com, $75-190), many Jasper homeowners rent out a room or two to guests. Some offer breakfast, while others rent rooms only. Get a listing of available accommodations on the website or at the **Jasper Information Centre** (500 Connaught Dr.).

The **HI-Jasper Hostel** (708 Sleepy Hollow Rd., 778/328-2220 or 866/762-4122, www.hihostels.ca, $44-49 dorm, $150-210 d) replaced Jasper's aging hostel with this newly constructed accommodation. Walking distance to the town center, this three-story property houses four-bed dorms, plus private rooms—queens, quads, and family rooms—with en suite baths. Expect lots of room to hang out, with a café, lounge, media room, and common kitchen, as well as an outdoor fire pit.

$150-300

Among the nicest features of the alpine-style **Whistler's Inn** (105 Miette Ave., 780/852-3361 or 800/282-9919, www.whistlersinn.com, $175-335) are the two rooftop hot tubs where you can soak as you take in the mountain views. The 64 guest rooms, with cherry-toned furniture, white bedding, and plaid accents, have mini fridges, coffeemakers, and Wi-Fi included. The location opposite the Jasper train station couldn't be more central. On the inn's lower level, stop into the **Wildlife Museum** (7am-10pm daily, $3, families $6, hotel guests free), which was set up in the 1950s and exhibits 100 taxidermy animals native to Alberta's parks, including cougars, elk, and bears. To experience a different type of wildlife, hang with the locals at the hotel's **Whistle Stop Pub.**

Edmonton: Gateway to Jasper

If you're flying to Alberta, Edmonton has the closest international airport to Jasper National Park. If you're planning an Edmonton stopover, here are some things to do.

Sights and Activities

Alberta's provincial capital has several worthwhile museums, starting with the **Art Gallery of Alberta** (2 Sir Winston Churchill Square, 780/422-6223, www.youraga.ca, 11am-8pm Tues.-Wed., 11am-5pm Thurs.-Fri., 10am-5pm Sat.-Sun., adults $12.50, seniors and students $8.50, free 5pm-8pm Tues.-Wed.), which exhibits contemporary art in a downtown building designed by the late American architect Randall Stout. **Royal Alberta Museum** (9810 103A Ave. NW, 825/468-6000, www.royalalbertamuseum.ca, 10am-6pm Sat.-Wed., 10am-8pm Thurs.-Fri. mid-May-early Sept., 10am-5pm Fri.-Wed., 10am-8pm Thurs. early Sept.-mid-May, adults $19, seniors $14, ages 7-17 $10, families $48) traces Alberta's roots through exhibits on natural and human history, from a kid-friendly bug room to giant woolly mammoth skeletons.

Housed in four glass pyramids, **Muttart Conservatory** (626 96A St., 780/442-5311, www.edmonton.ca, 10am-5pm Fri.-Tues., 10am-9pm Wed.-Thurs., adults $12.50, seniors and students $10.50, ages 2-12 $6.50, families $37) is Edmonton's botanical garden, with plants and flowers from around the world and an excellent café.

North America's largest shopping center, the **West Edmonton Mall** (8882 170 St., 780/444-5313, www.wem.ca, 10am-9pm Mon.-Sat., 11am-6pm Sun.), has more than 800 stores, a waterpark, an aquarium, a casino, mini golf, a skating rink, and the world's biggest indoor amusement park. A great year-round showcase for local foods and crafts, **Old Strathcona Farmers Market** (10310 83 Ave. NW, 780/439-1844, www.osfm.ca, 8am-3pm Sat.) has more than 130 vendors.

If seeing bison is on your wish list, make a side trip to **Elk Island National Park** (Hwy 16 E., 780/922-5790, www.pc.gc.ca, 24 hours daily, adults $7.80, seniors $6.80), 30 miles (48 km) east of downtown Edmonton, where more than 1,000 bison roam.

Food

Squeeze into tiny trattoria **Corso 32** (10345 Jasper Ave., 780/421-4622, www.corso32.com, 5pm-10:30pm Sun.-Thurs., 5pm-11pm Fri.-Sat., $28-36) for fine handmade pastas and other imaginative Italian fare. On the same downtown block, **Uccellino** (10349 Jasper Ave., 780/426-0346, www.uccellino.ca, 5pm-10pm Sun.-Thurs., 5pm-11pm Fri.-Sat., $25-38), run by the same chef, is an even more stylish Italian choice.

Buzzing **Rostizado** (10359 104 St., #102, 780/761-0911, www.rostizado.com, 11am-2pm and 5pm-9pm Mon.-Thurs., 11am-2pm and 5pm-10pm Fri., 5pm-10pm Sat., lunch $15-24, dinner $19-48) serves modern Mexican dishes, from lunchtime tacos and burritos (the carnitas are top-notch) to steak served with charred avocado guacamole and signature platters of roast chicken, pork, and beef.

South of downtown, **Biera** (Ritchie Market, 9570 76 Ave. NW, 587/525-8589, www.biera.ca, 4pm-11pm Tues.-Fri., 1pm-11pm Sat., 1pm-5pm Sun., $12-29) takes brewpub fare beyond the ordinary with sharing plates like sourdough bread with buckwheat lardo, endives with preserved pear and pistachio crème, and chicken sautéed with Taiwanese cabbage, to pair with its own Blind Enthusiasm beer.

Information and Services

For more information about the region, contact **Explore Edmonton** (780/401-7696, www.exploreedmonton.com) or **Travel Alberta** (800/252-3782, www.travelalberta.com).

TOWN OF JASPER

Centrally located but quiet, the **Park Place Inn** (623 Patricia St., 780/852-9770 or 866/852-9770, www.parkplaceinn. com, $159-269) has 12 upscale rooms and two suites, decorated in earth tones with mini fridges and coffeemakers; some have whirlpool tubs or fireplaces. There's a common microwave that guests can use, and you're surrounded by the town's cafés and eateries. Underground parking and Wi-Fi are included.

Want a no-frills place to sleep? Friendly **Mount Robson Inn** (902 Connaught Dr., 780/852-3327 or 855/552-7737, www. mountrobsoninn.com, $211-449), a two-story motel a few blocks from the center of town, fills the bill. The basic guest rooms have microwaves, fridges, and coffeemakers; the larger units, including the recently updated deluxe rooms with two queens and several suites, can accommodate families. There's a laundry on-site and a hot tub facing the parking lot. Rates include continental breakfast, parking, and Wi-Fi. Staff are quick to help with tips on things to do.

Less than 15 minutes from town, the ★ **Patricia Lake Bungalows** (Pyramid Lake Rd., 780/852-3560 or 888/499-6848, www.patricialakebungalows.com, May-mid.-Oct., $115-410) feel like a world away. On a forested site by the lake, the 52 family-friendly units at this summer camp-style resort (the same family has run it for four generations) include everything from simple motel rooms to log cabins to deluxe suites. The newest units are in The Grove, where the modern one-bedroom cabins have barbecues and kitchens with cherry cabinets. Soak in the outdoor hot tub or rent kayaks, canoes, or rowboats to go exploring; the intrepid can swim in the chilly lake. There's a playground and games for the kids as well as a guest laundry. Internet access is available in the office; as in many Jasper locations, the included Wi-Fi can be erratic.

★ **The Crimson** (200 Connaught Dr., 780/852-3394 or 888/852-7737, www.

mpljasper.com, $228-428) brought urban style to small-town Jasper when the owners converted a 1950s lodge into a three-story boutique motel. In the 99 modern guest rooms, beige coverlets with red accents top the beds; all units have air-conditioning, microwaves, mini fridges, and Keurig coffeemakers, and many have kitchenettes. You can swim in the indoor pool (though it's in a windowless space) or soak in the hot tub. Rates include Wi-Fi and parking.

Across the road from a trout-filled lake 3.6 miles (5.8 km) from town, **Pyramid Lake Resort** (Pyramid Lake Rd., 780/852-4900 or 888/852-7737, www.mpljasper. com, $239-449) has 62 rooms, cabins, and chalets that vary from rustic to lodge-modern. All have updated baths as well as gas fireplaces, mini fridges, coffeemakers, teakettles, and flat-screen satellite TVs. There's Wi-Fi, too, although staff caution that the signal can be intermittent. Other amenities include an outdoor hot tub, a sauna, and a guest laundry. You can rent canoes, kayaks, rowboats, and bikes at the lakeshore.

Over $300

When Jasper Park Lodge opened in the 1920s overlooking Lac Beauvert, it was reportedly the largest single-story log building in the world. Sadly, a fire destroyed that original structure in the 1950s, but the hotel now on the site is Jasper's most luxurious lodging. ★ **Fairmont Jasper Park Lodge** (Old Lodge Rd., 780/852-3301 or 866/540-4454, www.fairmont.com, $575-1,299, self-parking free, valet parking $25), a 10-minute drive from town, has a range of accommodations, the best with lake views, including upscale hotel rooms, deluxe cabins, a one-bedroom cottage, and an eight-bedroom manor. Join Fairmont's complimentary frequent-stay program for free Wi-Fi. To explore the lake and surroundings, rent canoes ($50 per hour), kayaks (single $40 per hour, double $50 per hour), or mountain bikes ($30 per hour) at **The Boathouse** (780/852-3301, 10am-7pm May-Oct.). If you're not getting enough exercise in the mountains, you can work out in the fitness room or swim in the heated outdoor pool. The 18-hole golf course, opened in 1925, ranks among Canada's best. The lodge also has the lovely lakeview **Reflections Spa,** as well as several restaurants and lounges.

Information and Services
Visitor Information
Tourism Jasper (780/852-6236, www. jasper.travel) produces an annual Jasper visitor guide, available in print and online, and also provides information about things to do, places to stay, and area events on its website.

In town, get your questions answered at the Parks Canada **Jasper Information Centre** (500 Connaught Dr., 780/852-6176, www.pc.gc.ca, 9am-7pm daily mid-May-mid-June, 8am-8pm daily mid-June-late Sept., 9am-7pm daily late Sept.-mid-Oct., 9am-5pm daily mid-Oct.-mid-May).

Medical Services
The **Seton-Jasper Healthcare Centre** (518 Robson St., 780/852-3344, www. albertahealthservices.ca) provides 24-hour emergency medical services.

Local pharmacies include **Pharmasave** (610 Patricia St., 780/852-5903, www. pharmasavejasper.com, 9am-7pm daily) and **RX Drug Mart Jasper** (602 Patricia St., 780/852-4441, www.guardian-ida-pharmacies.ca, 9am-9pm Mon.-Sat., 9am-6pm Sun.).

Getting Around
The town of Jasper itself is small, and most accommodations, restaurants, shops, and in-town sights are within walking distance. However, many of the national park's attractions are spread out across a wide area. You either need to have your own vehicle, or book a tour with a local outfitter.

Parking
Jasper has three large **free public parking lots** on Connaught Drive; one is on the south side of the Jasper train station, while the other two are north of the station. You can park in these lots for up to 72 hours.

Street parking in Jasper is also free. Many town parking spots have a two-hour limit.

Car Rentals
Avis (414 Connaught Dr., 780/852-3970, www.avis.ca), **Budget** (414 Connaught Dr., 780/852-3222, www.budget.ca), and **National** (607 Connaught Dr., at the Jasper train station, 780/852-1117, www. nationalcar.ca) have car rental offices in Jasper.

The
Kootenays

The Kootenays

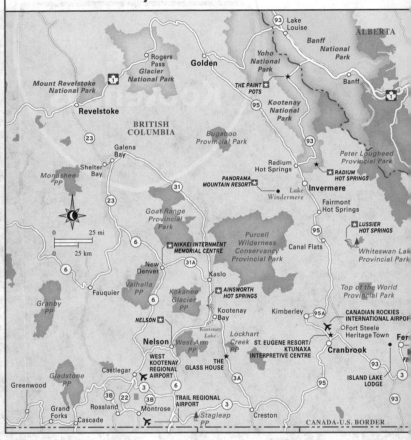

Rogers Pass Glacier National Park

Golden

Lake Louise

Banff National Park

ALBERTA

Yoho National Park

THE PAINT POTS

Mount Revelstoke National Park

Revelstoke

BRITISH COLUMBIA

Kootenay National Park

Banff

Galena Bay

Shelter Bay

Monashee PP

Bugaboo Provincial Park

Peter Lougheed Provincial Park

Radium Hot Springs

RADIUM HOT SPRINGS

PANORAMA MOUNTAIN RESORT

Lake Windermere

Invermere

Fairmont Hot Springs

Goat Range Provincial Park

NIKKEI INTERNMENT MEMORIAL CENTRE

Purcell Wilderness Conservancy Provincial Park

LUSSIER HOT SPRINGS

Canal Flats

Whiteswan Lake Provincial Park

New Denver

Kaslo

Fauquier

Valhalla PP

Kokanee Glacier PP

AINSWORTH HOT SPRINGS

Top of the World Provincial Park

Granby PP

NELSON

Kootenay Bay

Kimberley

CANADIAN ROCKIES INTERNATIONAL AIRPORT

Nelson

West Arm PP

Lockhart Creek PP

ST. EUGENE RESORT/ KTUNAXA INTERPRETIVE CENTRE

Fort Steele Heritage Town

Cranbrook

Fer

Gladstone PP

Castlegar

WEST KOOTENAY REGIONAL AIRPORT

THE GLASS HOUSE

ISLAND LAKE LODGE

Greenwood

Rossland

Montrose

TRAIL REGIONAL AIRPORT

Grand Forks

Cascade

Stagleap PP

Creston

CANADA–U.S. BORDER

0   25 mi
0   25 km

Rambling through the Kootenays in southeastern B.C., you can soak in natural hot springs, hang out in funky mountain towns, and explore the region's multicultural past.

The Kootenays' roads are made for meandering. Covering a wide swath, this region extends from the Rocky Mountain peaks along the Alberta border over several mountain ranges west toward the Okanagan Valley.

Two main highways cross the Kootenays region. The main east-west route across southern British Columbia, Highway 3, also known as the Crowsnest Highway, twists and climbs for 520 miles (840 km) between Alberta and the town of Hope, near Vancouver and the B.C. coast. Heading north-south through the Kootenay region, Highway 93/95 runs between Golden, Radium Hot Springs, Cranbrook, and the U.S. border; dubbed

Highlights

★ **The Paint Pots:** Among the distinctive geological features in Kootenay National Park are these mineral pools surrounded by orange ocher beds (page 320).

★ **Radium Hot Springs:** With a lap pool and a warm soaking pool, these natural springs in Kootenay National Park please everyone from kids to seniors (page 321).

★ **Panorama Mountain Resort:** Hikers and cyclists in summer and skiers and snowboarders in winter all come to get outdoors at this mountain playground near Invermere (page 328).

★ **Lussier Hot Springs:** Soak in a true natural hot spring, in an otherwise chilly river in remote Whiteswan Lake Provincial Park (page 330).

★ **Fernie:** With mountain peaks surrounding a historic downtown district, this charming East Kootenay community has lots to do, indoors and out (page 331).

★ **Nelson:** This funky town in the West Kootenays has everything you need for a road-trip stopover: excellent restaurants, independent shops, moderately priced accommodations, and plenty

of outdoor activities (page 342).

★ **Ainsworth Hot Springs:** At these hot pools near Nelson, you can soak and steam in a natural horseshoe-shaped cave (page 350).

★ **Nikkei Internment Memorial Centre:** Learn the dark heritage of Japanese Canadian wartime internment at this informative museum on the site of a World War II-era camp (page 352).

Best Accommodations

★ **Cross River Wilderness Centre:** At this unique log-cabin getaway, you can choose outdoor adventures, wilderness trips, or aboriginal experiences (page 324).

★ **Blackstone Bed & Breakfast:** This Fernie lodging feels more like a high-style boutique inn, with reclaimed wood furnishings, faux fur throws, and fireplaces in the three guest rooms (page 336).

★ **Fernie 901:** A former Fernie school has been transformed into striking modern condos, many available as short-term vacation rentals (page 336).

★ **St. Eugene Resort:** Once a residential school for aboriginal children, this Cranbrook hotel mixes its historic past with a casino, a golf course, and other modern amenities (page 340).

★ **Cloudside Hotel:** You can walk to the town's cafés, restaurants, and shops from this well-run eight-room hotel in a Nelson Victorian (page 349).

★ **The Sentinel:** Whether you're attending a wellness retreat or making your own Kootenays getaway, this lakeside lodging near Kaslo offers Zen-like rooms and a sunny yoga space (page 352).

the "Hot Springs Highway," this road passes several mountain mineral springs where you can stop for a soak.

Bordering Yoho and Banff National Parks, Kootenay National Park draws outdoor explorers to its varied landscape, encompassing mountain peaks, deep canyons, and arid grasslands. Throughout the Kootenays, down-to-earth mountain towns, like Fernie to the east and Rossland or Nelson farther west, make interesting stopovers, with heritage buildings housing restaurants and shops, and plenty to do outdoors.

Another reason to travel through the Kootenays is to delve into its multicultural past. Sites throughout the region illustrate the history of First Nations people, settlers drawn by the gold rush, and Russian pacifists known as the Doukhobors. You can also learn about a darker past as well, visiting an internment camp that housed Japanese Canadians during World War II.

But wherever you travel in the Kootenays, take your time. These roads are made for a leisurely road trip.

Getting to the Kootenays

Driving from Banff and Lake Louise

To Kootenay National Park

Kootenay National Park is an easy day trip from either Banff or Lake Louise. Take **Highway 1** west from Banff or east from Lake Louise to **Highway 93** south, which runs through the park. The town of **Radium Hot Springs** is at the park's southern boundary.

The trip from **Banff** to Radium Hot Springs is **85 miles (140 km)**. From **Lake Louise** to Radium Hot Springs, it's **80 miles (130 km).** Each of these routes takes **1.75-2 hours.**

To Fernie

After passing through Kootenay National Park, continue south on **Highway 93,** and at **Highway 3,** turn east. Highway 3 runs directly into Fernie. It's **215 miles (345 km)** to Fernie

Best Restaurants

★ **The Blue Toque Diner:** For the best breakfasts in Fernie, head to this inventive restaurant in the town's former rail station (page 334).

★ **Yum Son:** This stylish Nelson dining spot woos diners with modern takes on Vietnamese classics, prepared with local ingredients and coupled with well-crafted cocktails (page 347).

★ **Marzano:** Pizzeria classics updated with fresh, regional products are the draws at this bustling contemporary trattoria in Nelson (page 347).

★ **Oso Negro Café:** Nelson's own coffee roastery runs this popular café, where you can pair pastries or panini with your espresso or latté (page 347).

from either Banff or Lake Louise; the drive takes **four hours.**

To Nelson

If you're driving from Banff or Lake Louise to Nelson, you can choose several different routes.

One option is to take **Highway 93** south to **Highway 3** west. Then, to follow the **most scenic route,** turn north at **Creston** onto **Highway 3A,** which hugs the east shore of Kootenay Lake. At **Kootenay Bay,** take the free 35-minute **Kootenay Lake Ferry** (250/229-4215, www2.gov.bc.ca, 7:10am-10:20pm daily) across the lake to **Balfour.** Continue on **Highway 3A** to Nelson.

Alternatively, stay on **Highway 3** west beyond Creston to **Highway 6,** where you turn north to Nelson.

Both the Highway 3 and Highway 3A routes are **310 miles (500 km)** from Banff or Lake Louise. The **Highway 3** route takes **six hours.** The **Highway 3A** route adds about an hour of travel time, for a total of about **seven hours;** on this winding road, you'll need to take it slow—the better to scan the beautiful lake views—and allow time for the ferry crossing.

Another option from Banff or Lake Louise takes you along **Highway 1** westbound through B.C.'s Yoho, Glacier, and Mount Revelstoke **National Parks.** When you reach **Revelstoke,** turn south on **Highway 23.** Thirty miles (48 km)

south of Revelstoke, take the free 20-minute **Upper Arrow Lake Ferry** (250/265-2105, www2.gov.bc.ca, 5am-midnight daily) from **Shelter Bay** to **Galena Bay.** Continue south on **Highway 23,** then take **Highway 6** south into Nelson. At **295 miles (475 km),** this route is slightly shorter than the Highway 3 route from Lake Louise, but it takes an average of 30 minutes longer because of the ferry crossing.

Driving from the Okanagan
To Kootenay National Park

From **Kelowna,** the **most direct route** to Kootenay National Park is **Highway 1.** Follow **Highway 97** north to **Vernon,** where you continue north on **Highway 97A** to **Highway 1** east. Follow Highway 1 to **Golden,** then turn south on **Highway 95** to reach **Radium Hot Springs** and the park's south entrance. It's **280 miles (450 km)** from Kelowna to Radium; the drive takes **5.5 hours.**

From **Osoyoos** or the South Okanagan, you can either go north through the Okanagan Valley on **Highway 97** and north to **Vernon,** where you continue north on **Highway 97A** to **Highway 1** east, or take **Highway 3,** which runs east from Osoyoos into the Kootenays. To Kootenay National Park, stay on Highway 3 east to **Highway 93/95** north toward **Cranbrook, Invermere,** and **Radium Hot Springs.** From Osoyoos to Radium via **Highway**

1, it's **360 miles (580 km)** and the drive takes **7-7.5 hours;** via **Highway 3,** it's **365 miles (590 km)** and **7.5-8 hours.**

To Fernie

From **Kelowna** to Fernie, one option is to take **Highway 33** south to **Highway 3,** and continue east on Highway 3. This route is **390 miles (630 km)** and takes **eight hours.** A second option is to take **Highway 97 and 97A** north to **Highway 1,** follow Highway 1 to **Golden,** turn south on **Highway 95,** and then take **Highway 3** east. At **415 miles (670 km),** this alternative, which takes you through **B.C.'s national parks,** is slightly longer, but requires about the same amount of travel time.

From **Osoyoos** to Fernie, simply follow **Highway 3** east; it's **335 miles (540 km),** a **seven-hour** drive.

To Nelson

From **Kelowna** to Nelson, the **shortest route** is to follow **Highway 33** south to **Highway 3** east. At **Castlegar,** turn northeast on **Highway 3A** to Nelson. This route is **215 miles (345 km)** and takes **4.5-5 hours.**

Alternatively, go north from Kelowna on **Highway 97,** then at **Vernon,** follow **Highway 6** east. This **scenic** two-lane road takes you to **Needles,** where you board the five-minute **Needles Cable Ferry** (250/265-2105, www2.gov.bc.ca, 5:15am-9:45pm daily), a free shuttle across Lower Arrow Lake. Continue on **Highway 6** through Nakusp and New Denver to Nelson. The route is **240 miles (385 km)** and takes **5.5-6 hours.**

From **Osoyoos** to Nelson, take **Highway 3** to **Castlegar,** then follow **Highway 3A** northeast to Nelson. It's **160 miles (260 km),** a **3.75-hour** drive.

Driving from Vancouver
To Kootenay National Park

From Vancouver, follow **Highway 1** east to **Hope,** where you pick up **Highway 3** east, but exit immediately onto **Highway**

5 (Coquihalla Hwy.) north. Follow the Coquihalla over the mountains to **Kamloops,** where you rejoin **Highway 1** east and follow it to **Golden.** At Golden, turn south on **Highway 95,** toward **Radium Hot Springs** and the park's south entrance. This trip is **505 miles (810 km),** a **9.5-hour** drive.

To Fernie

You have two options to reach Fernie from Vancouver: **Highway 1** or **Highway 3.** Although the Highway 1 alternative is longer in distance, both take **11.5-12 hours.** For either route, leave Vancouver on Highway 1 and continue east to Hope.

For the **Highway 1** option, which goes through **B.C.'s national parks,** continue east at **Hope** onto **Highway 3,** then exit onto **Highway 5 (Coquihalla Hwy.)** north. Follow the Coquihalla to **Kamloops,** where you rejoin **Highway 1** east and continue to **Golden.** At Golden, turn south on **Highway 95** and then take **Highway 3** east to Fernie. This route is **645 miles (1,035 km)** from Vancouver.

The second option is to pick up **Highway 3** east at **Hope** and follow it all the way to Fernie. This route is **585 miles (940 km).**

To Nelson

From Vancouver to Nelson, go east on **Highway 1** to **Hope,** then continue east on **Highway 3** through **Osoyoos** and **Castlegar.** From there, follow **Highway 3A** northeast into Nelson. This trip is **410 miles (660 km)** and takes **8.5 hours.**

Getting There by Air

The city of Cranbrook's regional airport serves eastern British Columbia. From **Canadian Rockies International Airport** (YXC, 9370 Airport Access Rd., Cranbrook, 250/426-7913, www.flycanadianrockies.com), **Air Canada** (888/247-2262, www.aircanada.com) flies to Vancouver and Calgary. **Pacific Coastal Airlines** (800/663-2872, www.pacificcoastal.com) flies from Cranbrook to Vancouver, Victoria, or Kelowna. **WestJet** (888/937-8538, www.westjet.com) has service between Cranbrook and Calgary. **Budget** (250/426-5425 or 800/268-8900, www.budget.ca) and **Enterprise** (250/489-3689 or 800/261-7331, www.enterprise.com) have car rental offices in Cranbrook.

To reach Nelson by air, **Air Canada** (888/247-2262, www.aircanada.com) operates daily flights from Vancouver or Calgary to the small **West Kootenay Regional Airport** (YCG, Hwy. 3/3A, Castlegar, 250/365-5151, www.wkrairport.ca). **Budget** (250/365-5733 or 800/268-8900, www.budget.ca) rents cars from the airport. **Queen City Shuttles** (250/352-9829, www.kootenayshuttle.com, one-way adults $25) can take you into downtown Nelson, 25 miles (40 km) to the northeast.

To Rossland, you can fly **Pacific Coastal Airlines** (800/663-2872, www.pacificcoastal.com) from Vancouver to **Trail Regional Airport** (YZZ, 800/663-2872, www.trail.ca), 12.5 miles (20 km) to the east. **Mountain Shuttle** (250/362-0080, www.mountainshuttle.ca, one-way $62-73) takes passengers between the Trail airport and Rossland or RED Mountain.

Otherwise, the main international airport closest to the Kootenay region is **Calgary International Airport** (YYC, 2000 Airport Rd. NE, 403/735-1200, www.yyc.com).

Spokane International Airport (GEG, 9000 W. Airport Dr., Spokane, 509/455-6455, www.spokaneairports.net), across the U.S. border in Washington State, is another option, particularly if you're going to Nelson, Rossland, or other parts of the West Kootenays. It's 155 miles (250 km) from Nelson. Remember to add time for the international border crossing to what would otherwise be a three-hour drive.

Kootenay National Park

The 543-square-mile (1,406-sq-km) **Kootenay National Park** (250/347-9505 or 888/773-8888, www.pc.gc.ca) covers a diverse landscape, extending from the mountain peaks of Banff and Yoho National Parks to the north, through several deep canyons, and to arid grasslands regions at the park's southern end. Park staff describe its terrain as "from cactus to glacier."

Kootenay National Park owes its existence in part to a highway. In 1920, an agreement between the federal and provincial governments to build the first automobile route through the Canadian Rockies led to the creation of the park and the construction of the Banff-Windermere Highway. Now called Highway 93 or the Kootenay Parkway, this road runs 60 miles (97 km) through the park.

As you drive through the park, you can't help but notice rows and rows of burned trees. In 2003, a lightning strike set off a massive fire, which burned for 40 days and scorched more than 42,000 acres (17,000 ha) of forest in the northern half of the park, from the Stanley Glacier to Vermillion Crossing. While fires such as this one can be dangerous and appear devastating, the flames are an important element in the region's ecological restoration. New lodgepole pines, which actually need fire for their seeds to open, are sprouting, although it will take decades for the forest to regenerate. Wildflowers are growing throughout the burned area as well.

Kootenay National Park, particularly its northern side at the Alberta-British Columbia provincial border, is close enough to Lake Louise or Banff that you can visit on a day trip. If you're exploring the park's southern end, where the hot springs are located, it's more convenient to stay in the gateway towns of Radium Hot Springs or Invermere. Golden, B.C.,

Kootenay National Park and Vicinity

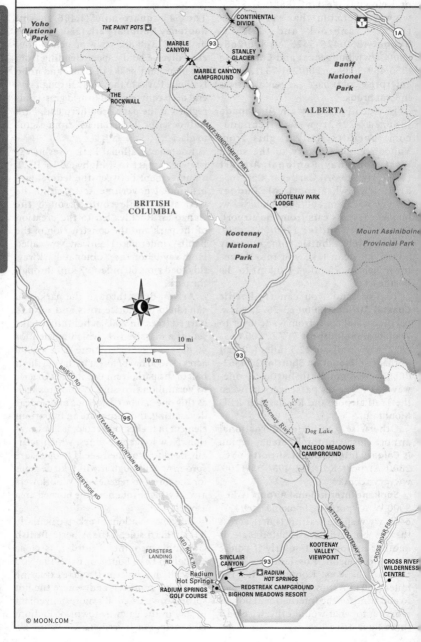

Yoho National Park

THE PAINT POTS

MARBLE CANYON

THE ROCKWALL

CONTINENTAL DIVIDE

93

STANLEY GLACIER

MARBLE CANYON CAMPGROUND

BANFF-WINDERMERE PKWY

Banff National Park

ALBERTA

BRITISH COLUMBIA

KOOTENAY PARK LODGE

Kootenay National Park

Mount Assiniboine Provincial Park

0   10 mi
0   10 km

93

Kootenay River

Dog Lake

MCLEOD MEADOWS CAMPGROUND

BRISCO RD

STEAMBOAT MOUNTAIN RD

95

WESTSIDE RD

RED ROCK RD

FORSTERS LANDING RD

SINCLAIR CANYON

Radium Hot Springs

RADIUM HOT SPRINGS

RADIUM SPRINGS GOLF COURSE

REDSTREAK CAMPGROUND

BIGHORN MEADOWS RESORT

93

KOOTENAY VALLEY VIEWPOINT

SETTLERS KOOTENAY FSR

CROSS RIVER FSR

CROSS RIVER WILDERNESS CENTRE

© MOON.COM

One Day in Kootenay National Park

Have just one day? Pack a picnic lunch and you can see the highlights of Kootenay National Park. This itinerary starts at the park's north end, coming from Lake Louise or Banff; alternatively, you can follow this route from south to north if you begin in the town of Radium Hot Springs.

As you enter the park from the north on Highway 93, stop for a photo at the **Continental Divide,** which marks the divide between the Pacific and Atlantic watersheds, the B.C.-Alberta provincial border, and the boundary between Kootenay and Banff National Parks.

Continue 4.5 miles (7 km) south to **Marble Canyon,** and follow the trail over several bridges across the deep, narrow gorge. You can hike from the canyon to the **Paint Pots,** or drive to the start of the short Paint Pots Trail; either way, don't miss the unusual orange ocher beds surrounding these small mineral pools.

Back on Highway 93, drive south to the **McLeod Meadows picnic area,** where you can enjoy the lunch you packed. If you're up for another hike, follow the **Dog Lake Trail** from here, or keep driving south, stopping at the **Kootenay Valley Viewpoint,** and then hike the **Juniper/Sinclair Canyon Trail,** near the park's south gate. End your Kootenay National Park day with a relaxing soak in the **Radium Hot Springs.**

---

is also within day-trip distance, 65 miles (105 km) northwest of Radium Hot Springs via Highway 95.

Visiting the Park
Entrances
The northern entrance to Kootenay National Park is 22 miles (35 km) south of Lake Louise and 25 miles (40 km) from Banff, on Highway 93. The park's southern entrance, where you can purchase a park pass, is on Highway 93, just north of Radium Hot Springs.

Park Passes and Fees
A **day pass** (adults $9.80, seniors $8.30, families $19.60) for Kootenay National Park is valid until 4pm on the day after you purchase it. Kootenay passes can be used at Mount Revelstoke, Glacier, and Yoho National Parks in B.C. and at Banff, Jasper, Waterton Lakes, and Elk Island National Parks in Alberta.

If you're driving through the park along Highway 93 without stopping, a park pass isn't required. However, you need a pass if you get out of your car anywhere within the park boundaries.

Purchasing a Parks Canada **annual discovery pass** (adults $67.70, seniors $57.90, families $136.40), valid for a year, is a good deal if you're spending at least a week in one or more parks. It's valid at more than 100 national parks and national historic sites across Canada. Buy an annual pass online from Parks Canada (www.pc.gc.ca) or at any of the parks' visitors centers.

For both day and annual passes, family passes cover up to seven people in a single vehicle, whether or not they're actually related.

Visitors Centers
In the village of Radium Hot Springs, just outside the national park, the **Radium Hot Springs Visitor Centre** (7556 Main St. E., 250/347-9331or 888/347-9331, www.radiumhotsprings. com, 9am-7pm daily mid-June-early Sept., 9am-5pm daily early Sept.-mid-June) has information about the region. Parks Canada staff are on hand April-mid-October to provide details about Kootenay National Park and the Rocky Mountain national parks in general. The visitors center also has a small exhibit area about local wildlife.

If you're coming from Alberta, the **Lake Louise Visitor Information Centre** (Samson Mall, 403/522-3833, www.pc.gc.ca or www.banfflakelouise.com, 8:30am-7pm daily June-Sept., 9am-5pm daily Oct.-May) or **Banff Visitor Information Centre** (224 Banff Ave., 403/762-8421, www.pc.gc.ca or www.banfflakelouise.com, 8am-8pm daily mid-May-mid-Oct., 9am-5pm daily mid-Oct.-mid-May) can assist with information about Kootenay National Park. You can purchase a Kootenay park pass at either of these locations.

Reservations

Reservations are accepted at the park's Redstreak Campground, and they're recommended for July and August stays. You can reserve campsites as well as **oTENTiks,** canvas-walled platform tents. To book, contact **Parks Canada reservations** (877/737-3783, www.reservation.parkscanada.gc.ca).

Marble Canyon and McLeod Meadows Campgrounds are first-come, first-served; reservations aren't accepted for these areas.

Information and Services

Kootenay National Park has no fuel or other services within the park boundaries, so get gas in Banff or Lake Louise if you're coming from the north or in Radium Hot Springs, south of the park. Radium has a grocery, a liquor store, and other basic services; you'll have more food and shopping options in the larger town of Invermere, 10 miles (16 km) south of the park's southern entrance.

There is cell phone service in Radium Hot Springs and in the park's Redstreak Campground, but no cell coverage or Wi-Fi elsewhere within Kootenay National Park.

Getting Around

The park's attractions are all located off Highway 93, which runs north-south through Kootenay National Park. The park has no shuttle service or public transportation, so you need a car to get around.

Sights and Activities

These things to see and do in Kootenay National Park are listed from north to south, along Highway 93.

The Continental Divide

Stop for a photo at the **Continental Divide,** which denotes the dividing line between the Pacific and Atlantic watersheds. It's also the provincial border between Alberta and British Columbia, as well as the boundary between Kootenay and Banff National Parks. It's along Highway 93, marked with a sign 22 miles (35 km) south of Lake Louise and 60 miles (97 km) northeast of the town of Radium Hot Springs.

Marble Canyon

The turquoise waters of Tokumm Creek have carved a deep, narrow gorge into the limestone and dolomite rock at **Marble Canyon.** The 1-mile (1.6-km) round-trip **Marble Canyon Trail** crosses the water on seven bridges with photogenic viewpoints above the canyon.

Marble Canyon is 4.5 miles (7 km) south of the Alberta-B.C. border and 54 miles (87 km) east of Radium Hot Springs, off Highway 93.

★ The Paint Pots

Among the most unusual geological features in Kootenay National Park are the **Paint Pots,** several small mineral pools surrounded by orange ocher beds. The Ktunaxa, Stoney, and Blackfoot First Nations used these natural pigments in ceremonies and later in trade, and aboriginal people still consider the ocher beds to be sacred. On the **Paint Pots Trail** (1.2 mi/2 km round-trip), a short path through the woods and along the ocher beds, you may find the unique colors of the land more noteworthy than the small pools themselves.

If you'd like to hike between Marble Canyon and the Paint Pots, take the gentle 4.2-mile (6.8-km) round-trip **Marble Canyon to Paint Pots Trail.** Part of the trail follows the Vermillion River.

The Paint Pots are off Highway 93, just south of Marble Canyon and 52 miles (84 km) east of Radium Hot Springs.

Kootenay Valley Viewpoint
As you're driving through the park along Highway 93, pull off at the **Kootenay Valley Viewpoint** for vistas of the surrounding Mitchell and Vermilion Mountains and down to the Kootenay River. The viewpoint is at the park's southern end, 10 miles (16 km) east of Radium Hot Springs.

★ Radium Hot Springs
A highlight of a Kootenay National Park visit is a soak in the **Radium Hot Springs** (5420 Hwy. 93, 250/347-9485 or 800/767-1611, www.hotsprings.ca, 9am-11pm daily mid-May-mid-Oct., 1pm-9pm Mon.-Fri., 10am-9pm Sat.-Sun. mid-Oct.-mid-May, adults $7.30, seniors $6.40, ages 3-17 $4.95, families $20.20), natural outdoor hot springs pools surrounded by the reddish rock walls of Sinclair Canyon.

The minerals in the hot pool, where the water temperature is kept at 102°F (39°C), include sulfate, calcium, bicarbonate, silica, and magnesium. A large "cool" pool, designed for swimming rather than soaking, is 84°F (27°C).

You can rent both towels ($1.90) and swimsuits ($1.90) at the springs. Lockers are available (included with your admission). Also on-site is the **Pleiades Spa Radium** (250/347-2288, www.pleiadesradiumspa.com, call for hours and rates), where you can add a massage, mud wrap, or other spa services to your soaking time.

Top to bottom: the Paint Pots; Radium Hot Springs; a historic cabin at Kootenay Park Lodge

Radium Hot Springs are located 1.9 miles (3 km) east of the town of Radium Hot Springs.

Sinclair Canyon

Near the park's south gate, less than 1 mile (1.6 km) east of the town of Radium Hot Springs, Highway 93 winds between **Sinclair Canyon** and the Redwall Fault Cliffs. You don't even have to get out of your car to take in the dramatic rock walls, but you can hike into the canyon on several different trails.

Hiking

Kootenay National Park has 143 miles (230 km) of hiking trails, including many short hikes. The best months for hiking are July-mid-September. Some passes and trails at higher elevations can remain covered with snow until late June, and snow can begin to fall again in October. In addition to the trails at Marble Canyon and the Paint Pots (above), the following are other popular park hikes.

Stanley Glacier and the Burgess Shale

In 1909, American geologist Charles Walcott unearthed surprisingly well-preserved fossils in the **Burgess Shale,** an area of what is now Yoho National Park. The fossils were the remains of soft-bodied marine organisms that lived in the Cambrian Sea. Estimated to be among the world's oldest fossils, they date back 505 million years.

In Kootenay National Park, visitors can tour a section of the Burgess Shale beds on a **full-day guided hike,** for which you must **book reservations in advance.** Make reservations with **Parks Canada** (877/737-3783, www.reservations. parkscanada.gc.ca, reservation fee online $11, phone $13.50), beginning in early January for the coming season. Check the website to confirm when reservations become available, and book as early as possible.

On this guided hike to the **Stanley Glacier** (mid-June-early Sept., adults

Kootenay National Park

$55, seniors $46.75, ages 8-16 $27.50, under age 8 free), guides will explain the Burgess Shale fossil beds and allow you to make fossil rubbings. You'll also get an up-close look at the glacier. Families are welcome, but make sure everyone is up to the challenge of this moderately difficult hike, a 7.5-hour, 6.3-mile (10.1-km) round-trip, with an elevation gain of 1,500 feet (450 m).

The Stanley Glacier hike departs at 8am from the Stanley Glacier parking lot on Highway 93, 9.3 miles (15 km) south of Castle Junction and 59 miles (95 km) north of Radium Hot Springs.

In addition to this Stanley Glacier hike, two other challenging guided Burgess Shale hikes are offered in Yoho National Park.

Juniper/Sinclair Canyon

The **Juniper/Sinclair Canyon Trail,** which starts near the hot springs, takes you high above the highway and deep into the canyon. It's a 3.7-mile (6-km) loop, with an elevation change of 850 feet (260 m). You can also hike a short section of the trail that switchbacks down into the canyon.

Redstreak Restoration

Starting near the Redstreak Campground, the 0.6-mile (1-km) **Redstreak Restoration Trail** loops through a sunny meadow where a prescribed fire destroyed many of the trees but where vegetation is now growing back. Interpretive panels explain the role fire plays in the local ecosystem. You may spot grazing bighorn sheep as you walk.

Dog Lake

The moderate **Dog Lake Trail,** 3.2 miles (5.2 km) round-trip, takes you through the forest and across two suspension bridges over the Kootenay River before reaching the lake. The trailhead is at the **McLeod Meadows picnic area,** 17 miles (27 km) north of Radium Hot Springs, off Highway 93.

Floe Lake

For a challenging all-day or overnight hike, the **Floe Lake Trail** leads through open meadows and sections of burned forest, with 25 switchbacks en route to a large lake, with glaciers and mountain peaks all around. The trail is 13 miles (21 km) round-trip, with an elevation gain of 2,345 feet (715 m).

The trailhead is at the Floe Lake parking lot in the northern half of the park, 45 miles (72 km) from Radium Hot Springs. If you don't want to go out and back in one day, you can camp at the Floe Lake backcountry campground.

Rockwall

Backpackers can tackle the 34-mile (55-km) **Rockwall Trail,** a three- to four-day adventure that takes you along a massive limestone cliff. At some points, this rock wall towers more than 2,950 feet (900 m) above the trail.

For this multiday hike, you need to purchase a **wilderness pass** ($9.80 per day) from any Parks Canada visitors center. You also need to **reserve campsites** in advance (reservation fee $11.70) by calling Parks Canada at the **Radium Hot Springs Visitor Centre** (7556 Main St. E., 250/347-9505, www.pc.gc.ca, mid-May-mid-Oct.) or the **Lake Louise Visitor Information Centre** (Samson Mall, 403/522-3833 or 403/522-1264, Apr.-mid-May). You can reserve backcountry sites up to three months in advance.

Accommodations and Camping

If you don't want to camp, there's one accommodation within the park and another unique lodge just outside the park boundary. Otherwise, to the south, you can find accommodations in Radium Hot Springs and Invermere. Another alternative is to stay in Lake Louise, Banff, or Golden and make a day trip to Kootenay National Park.

$150-300

The only accommodations inside Kootenay National Park are at **Kootenay Park Lodge** (Hwy. 93, Vermillion Crossing, 250/434-9648 or 844/566-8362, www.kootenayparklodge.com, late May-mid-Oct., $199-275), a collection of 12 rustic cabins dating to the first half of the 20th century. The older Heritage Cabins are more basic, with log walls and limited electrical outlets; the newer Vermillion Cabins have gas fireplaces and more modern baths. All units have mini fridges, microwaves, and coffeemakers. Rates include continental breakfast; the dining room (5pm-8pm daily mid-May-mid-Sept., $15-21) serves dinner. You can pick up a Wi-Fi signal in the on-site shop but not in the cottages.

The most uniquely Canadian place to stay in the Kootenay National Park area is outside the park boundary, 9 miles (14 km) down a gravel road. Owners Robert and Marilyn Patenaude have been running ★ **Cross River Wilderness Centre** (403/271-3296 or 877/659-7665, www.crossriver.ca, late May-early Oct.,

$230-256, meals $110 pp per day), a remote off-the-grid lodging, since 1996. They have modernized eight cozy log cabins, with country-style furnishings, solar-powered lighting, and wood-burning fireplaces, as well as private baths with propane-heated showers. Hearty meals are served family-style in the main lodge, where a wood stove heats an outdoor hot tub.

Robert is of Métis heritage and has three **tepees** ($124-138), sleeping up to six, where guests can also stay. With advance reservations, you can arrange a sweat lodge ceremony or cultural workshop with an indigenous elder. The center hosts yoga retreats and offers a variety of wilderness workshops, guided hiking excursions, and backpacking trips as well. There's no internet or cell service here, so plan to unplug. The owners provide directions to the lodge when you make your reservation.

Camping

Kootenay National Park has three campgrounds. The largest, **Redstreak Campground** (Redstreak Rd., 250/347-9505, www.pc.gc.ca, early May-mid-Oct., tent sites $27.40, electrical sites $32.30-38.20), is 1.6 miles (2.5 km) uphill from the town of Radium Hot Springs. On foot, you can follow the steep 0.75-mile (1.2-km) **Valleyview Trail** between the campground and the town; the 1.4-mile (2.3-km) **Redstreak Campground Trail** leads to the Radium Hot Springs pools.

This 242-site campground, which accommodates everything from tents to large RVs, has restrooms with flush toilets and showers.

In the Redstreak Campground, you can stay in an **oTENTik** (early May-mid-Oct., $120), canvas-walled platform tents sleeping up to six. Flush toilets and showers are nearby. Bring your own sleeping bags or bedding, food, dishes, and cooking supplies.

The 61-site **Marble Canyon Campground** (late June-early Sept.,

$21.50), near Marble Canyon in the north half of the park, and the 80-site **McLeod Meadows Campground** (mid-June-mid-Sept., $21.50), 17 miles (27 km) north of Radium Hot Springs, both have restrooms with flush toilets but no shower facilities.

Reserve campsites and oTENTiks in the Redstreak Campground by contacting **Parks Canada reservations** (877/737-3783, www.reservation.parkscanada. gc.ca). Reservations are recommended between late June and early September, and on any holiday weekend. Marble Canyon and McLeod Meadows Campgrounds are first-come, first-served.

The Town of Radium Hot Springs

Just outside the southwestern boundary of Kootenay National Park, at the intersection of Highways 93 and 95, the small town of **Radium Hot Springs** (www. radiumhotsprings.com) has lodgings, a few restaurants, a grocery store, gas stations, and other provisions, as well as the national park visitors center.

You may see **bighorn sheep,** with their distinctive curved horns, as you wander through town or around the Redstreak Campground, particularly in May and June and again from September into the winter. In midsummer, the Radium herd of well over 100 bighorns tends to graze at higher elevations, returning to town in the colder months. A popular sheep-spotting site is the **Radium Springs Golf Course** (4714 Springs Dr., www. radiumgolf.ca). In late autumn, during the rutting season, when male sheep butt heads to establish their dominance before mating, the town hosts the **Headbanger Festival** (www.radiumhotsprings.com, Nov.), with opportunities to see the bighorns, guided walks, and other interpretive programs.

Sports and Recreation

Another reason to stop in Radium Hot Springs is to go **white-water rafting.**

Kootenay River Runners (4987 Hwy. 93, 250/347-9210, www.raftingtherockies. com) offers rafting trips on several area rivers. On the **Kootenay River** (June-mid-Sept.), with Class I-III rapids, you can choose half-day (adults $87, ages 5-14 $68) and full-day (adults $123, ages 5-14 $98) rafting trips that depart from its Radium office. The two-hour **Toby Creek trip** (June-Aug., adults $67, ages 8-14 $57), good for first-timers, includes Class I-III rapids and starts at Panorama Mountain Resort near Invermere.

The more adventurous half-day **Kicking Horse River trips** (June-early Sept., adults $128-140) run Class I-IV rapids. These trips depart from its Kicking Horse River base, 15 miles (24 km) east of Golden on Highway 1; from Radium Hot Springs, it's 83 miles (134 km), about a 90-minute drive, on Highway 95 north to Highway 1 east.

Accommodations

Basic motels, from mom-and-pop places to major North American chains, line Radium's streets.

The town's nicest accommodations are the family-friendly condo units at **Bighorn Meadows Resort** (10 Bighorn Blvd., 250/347-2323 or 877/344-2323, www.bighornmeadows.com, $118-263 d, 2-bedroom $269-399), adjacent to the golf course. Choose from studio, one-, two-, or three-bedroom suites in eight different buildings, all with full kitchens and washer-dryers. Opt for a unit in the 700 or 800 buildings if you need access to an elevator. You can swim in the outdoor pool or soak in the hot tubs at the center of the complex; there's a basic fitness center inside the reception building, and the kids can romp on the small playground.

Information and Services

Radium Hot Springs Visitor Centre (7556 Main St. E., 250/347-9331 or 888/347-9331, www.radiumhotsprings.com, 9am-7pm Sat.-Thurs., 9am-9pm Fri. mid-June-early Sept., 9am-5pm daily early

Sept.-mid-June) has information about the area and about Kootenay National Park.

Next to the visitors center, **Radium Mountainside Market** (7546 Main St. E., 250/347-9600, 8am-10pm daily) sells basic groceries, along with sandwiches, salads, and barbecue chicken to go.

The East Kootenays

The **East Kootenays** region hugs the Alberta border and extends south to Canada's boundary with the United States. Cranbrook, with 20,000 people, is the region's commercial center.

Highway 3 meanders east-west through the East Kootenays and can take you toward the B.C. coast. Highway 93/95 is the East Kootenays' main north-south artery. Known as the **Hot Springs Highway,** Highway 93/95 runs south from Kootenay National Park and Radium Hot Springs through a region highly regarded for its mineral springs. Beyond these opportunities to soak, several scenic East Kootenays towns are worth a stop for outdoor activities, local history, and good food.

Invermere

Ten miles (16 km) south of Radium Hot Springs, **Invermere** (www.invermerepanorama.com) is another potential base for visiting Kootenay National Park. Art galleries and cute shops line its main street, and an in-town lake has a family-friendly sand beach.

Sights and Recreation

On Lake Windermere, **Kinsmen Park** (5th Ave. at 7A Ave.) draws families to its sandy beach, with a playground and splash pad for the kids, restrooms, picnic tables, and a snack bar. In winter, when the lake freezes, a local Nordic ski club creates the **Lake Windermere Whiteway** (www.tobycreeknordic.ca), a 21-mile (34-km) groomed track for ice skaters

and cross-country skiers; it's the longest skating path in the world.

Near the lake, craft distiller **Taynton Bay Spirits** (1701B 6th Ave., 778/526-5205, www.tayntonbayspirits.com, 9am-5pm daily) produces vodka and gin, and makes an unusual tea-infused vodka in flavors like ginger matcha or strawberry herbal. Samples at the tasting bar are complimentary.

Festivals and Events

Birders and others interested in the outdoors flock to the annual **Wings over the Rockies Festival** (www.wingsovertherockies.org, May) for birdwatching, guided hikes, environmental lectures, and other ecologically focused events held in Invermere, Kootenay National Park, and Golden.

Food
Cafés, Bakeries, and Light Bites
Canada's number-one organic fair-trade coffee comes from Invermere,

where **Kicking Horse Coffee** sources, imports, and roasts its beans. Adjacent to the factory, you can taste its brews at the **Kicking Horse Café** (491 Arrow Rd., 250/342-4489, www.kickinghorsecoffee. com, 7am-5pm Mon.-Fri., 7:30am-5pm Sat., 8am-4pm Sun.), which sells pastries (with lots of vegan versions) and serves all manner of coffee drinks.

Look for the giant pretzel on the roof to find the **Invermere Bakery** (1305 7th Ave., 250/342-9913, www.invermerebakery. com, 7:30am-6pm Mon.-Sat., 9am-4pm Sun. late June-early Sept., 7:30am-6pm Mon.-Sat. early Sept.-late June), which bakes flavorful pretzels, pastries, and other treats. It also makes tasty sandwiches served on chewy homemade pretzels.

A take-out spot with a few outdoor seats, **Fuze Food** (315 3rd Ave., 250/342-0209, www.fuzefood.com, 11am-8pm Tues.-Sat., $10-13) turns out quick, fresh food, from noodle bowls, wraps, and salads, to smoothies. The satay bowl (broccoli, carrots, cabbage, and peppers, topped with peanut sauce) and the veggie-filled green curry bowl are popular options. Pizzas are baked after 4pm.

Groceries and Markets
Invermere's several grocery stores include **Valley Foods** (906 7th Ave., 250/342-3330, www.agvalleyfoods.com, 7am-10pm daily), which carries some locally made and locally grown products.

Accommodations
Invermere's most upscale place to stay is **Copper Point Resort** (760 Cooper Rd., 250/341-4000 or 855/926-7737, www. copperpointresort.com, $139-425 d, two-bedroom suite $289-549), with 173 contemporary lodgings that range from standard rooms with a queen bed, mini fridge, and microwave to one- and two-bedroom suites with full kitchens with stainless-steel appliances and granite countertops. If you haven't soaked enough in the region's hot springs, you

Lake Windermere and Invermere

can swim in the indoor or outdoor pools or lounge in several hot tubs. A fitness facility, kids playground, and golf course keep you busy on the property; for skiers and snowboarders, Panorama Mountain Resort is 14 miles (22 km) from the hotel.

Information and Services
Pick up information about the area or get your questions answered at the **Invermere Visitor Centre** (651 Hwy. 93/95, 250/342-2844, www.cvchamber. ca, 9am-5pm daily July-Aug., 9am-5pm Mon.-Fri. Sept.-June). **Tourism Invermere Panorama** (www.invermerepanorama. com) has a helpful area website.

★ Panorama Mountain Resort
Summer or winter, **Panorama Mountain Resort** (2000 Panorama Dr., Panorama, 250/342-6941 or 800/663-2929, www. panoramaresort.com), 12.5 miles (20 km) west of Invermere in the Purcell Mountains, with views to the Rockies, has plenty of things to do, particularly for families who enjoy outdoor activities. Contact the resort's **Adventure Centre** (250/341-3044) to find out what's happening during the summer months.

Summer Activities
Hiking
In summer, you can ride the **Mile 1 Express Chairlift** (daily late June-early Sept., $12) to enjoy the mountain views or access several **hiking trails.** The family-friendly **Fort Hide 'n' Seek Trail** leads down from the top of the lift to a log playhouse with a slide. Just make sure the kids save some energy for the hike back up to the chair.

The short but steep **Lynx Loop** climbs through the woods above the lift for vistas across the mountains and down to the village. A challenging day hike, the **Panorama Summit Trail** takes you up to the mountaintop; riding the chairlift gives you a 1,246-foot (380-m) vertical head start on this 4,000-foot (1,220-m) climb.

Without riding the lift, you can walk the **Valley Trail,** a paved 2.1-mile (3.4-km) loop from the village to the golf course and the Cliffhanger Restaurant.

Mountain Biking
Mountain bikers can ride the chairlift (daily late June-early Sept., half-day adults $45, seniors and ages 13-18 $40, ages 6-12 $29, full-day adults $55, seniors and ages 13-18 $49, ages 6-12 $34) to access up to 19 miles (30 km) of mountain trails. Only 10 percent of the downhill routes are rated beginner; 40 percent are intermediate, and half are expert trails.

Yoga
Ride the Mile 1 Express for an outdoor **yoga class** (10:30am daily July-early Sept., $25) with mountain views. The one-hour class is designed for all levels. Reservations are required; book at the resort's **Adventure Centre** (250/341-3044).

Water Sports
The large **Panorama Springs Pool** (daily late June-early Sept.) entices families to swim and whoosh down the water slide. Several outdoor **hot tubs** are open year-round. You must be staying at one of the resort's accommodations to use the pools.

Winter Sports
For **skiing and snowboarding** (www. panoramaresort.com, daily mid-Dec.-mid-Apr., full-day adults $106, seniors and ages 13-18 $93, ages 6-12 $49), Panorama has 129 trails across 2,975 acres (1,204 ha) of mountain terrain. Trails are rated 20 percent beginner, 55 percent intermediate-advanced, and 25 percent expert. If you're staying on the mountain, you can purchase **discounted lift tickets** (full-day adults $79.50, seniors and ages 13-18 $69.75, ages 6-12 $36.75).

If you've wanted to try **heli-skiing** but haven't wanted to commit to a multiday trip, you can do a one-day adventure with **RK Heliski** (800/661-6060, www.rkheliski. com, adults $877-1,079 per day). Rates include a buffet breakfast, a helicopter flight up to untracked trails, lunch, and your choice of three or five runs through the powder.

Panorama Nordic Centre (250/341-4106, www.panoramaresort.com) has more than 12.5 miles (20 km) of trails for **cross-country skiing** (full-day adults $15, seniors and ages 13-18 $13, ages 7-12 $10), as well as 2.5 miles (4 km) of **snowshoeing** (full-day adults $10, seniors and ages 13-18 $8, ages 7-12 $6) trails.

Another winter sport option is **fat-tire biking** (adults 4 hours $30, full-day $50), where you ride specially equipped bicycles through the snow. Get details or reserve your bike from the Panorama Nordic Centre.

Food

The resort has the usual fuel-up cafés, pubs, and restaurants; hours vary seasonally. At the base of the Upper Village, get pastries and sandwiches at casual **Picnic Café** (250/342-6941) or coffee at skier-friendly **Lusti's Cappuchino Bar** (250/341-3084). On the Valley Trail overlooking the golf course, **Cliffhanger Restaurant** (1860 Greywolf Dr., 250/341-4102, www.cliffhangerrestaurant.ca, $13-38) serves salads, sandwiches, and burgers all day, adding steaks and other grilled items in the evening; the terrace is a beautiful spot on a sunny day.

Accommodations

At the base of the mountain, **Panorama Mountain Resort** (800/663-2929, www.panoramaresort.com) has accommodations in a number of modern condominium buildings, ranging from studios to three-bedroom units. All have kitchen facilities and are a short walk from the lifts.

Getting There

From Invermere, follow Panorama Drive, which becomes Toby Creek Road, to the mountain; it's a 25- to 30-minute drive.

During the winter season, the free **Mountain and Valley Shuttle** (www.panoramaresort.com, 9am-10pm daily) runs throughout the day between Invermere and Panorama Mountain. Service continues into the evening, so if you're staying on the mountain, you can take the shuttle into town for dinner and back to your mountain accommodations.

The **Panorama Mountain Resort Shuttle** (800/663-2929, www.panoramaresort.com, daily mid-Dec.-mid.-Apr., 4 hours, one-way adults $139, under age 13 $116) takes winter visitors between the mountain and Calgary International Airport, departing twice a day in each direction. Reservations are recommended, and guests staying on the mountain have priority for shuttle seats. The shuttle also provides daily service to Banff (one-way adults $106, under age 13 $82), by reservation only.

Fairmont Hot Springs

It may be the largest mineral pool in Canada, but that just means that more people can pack into the family-friendly **Fairmont Hot Springs** (5225 Fairmont Resort Rd., Fairmont Hot Springs, 250/345-6070 or 800/663-4979, www.fairmonthotsprings.com, 8am-9pm daily, adults $13, seniors $11, ages 13-17 $12, ages 4-12 $11, families $43) at the Fairmont Hot Springs Resort. There are actually three pools where you can swim and soak: the 102°F (39°C) hot pool, a large 89°F (32°C) swimming pool, and a diving pool, which is kept at 86°F (30°C).

The springs offers a discounted late-night swim ($8 pp) at the end of every day, although the exact time varies with the season; call for details.

In addition to the pools, Fairmont Hot Springs has accommodations in lodge buildings, cabins, cottages, and two campgrounds.

If you're staying in the Kootenay National Park area, you can easily stop for a soak at Fairmont Hot Springs. It's 24 miles (38 km) south of Radium Hot Springs and 17 miles (27 km) south of

Invermere, along Highway 95. Cranbrook is 67 miles (108 km) to the south.

★ Lussier Hot Springs

While the mineral pools run by Parks Canada and other commercial hot pools throughout the Kootenays-Rockies region are lovely, if you want a true natural hot springs experience, make your way to **Whiteswan Lake Provincial Park** (250/422-3003, www.env.gov.bc.ca), off Highway 93/95 between Invermere and Cranbrook.

At the remote park's **Lussier Hot Springs** (dawn-dusk daily, free), you can soak in several natural rock-lined hot pools in an otherwise chilly river.

Two outhouses in the parking lot above the springs serve as changing rooms, but there are no other facilities. Wear sturdy sports sandals or hiking shoes to walk up and down the short path to the springs. You'll also be more comfortable wearing sports sandals or water shoes into the

spring, since you have to clamber over some slippery rocks.

The park has several campgrounds down the road beyond the hot springs, and Whiteswan Lake begins at kilometer 25. The provincial park has no cell service or public phones.

Getting There

It takes some effort to get to Lussier Hot Springs. From Highway 93/95, turn east 3 miles (4.8 km) south of the town of Canal Flats onto the Whiteswan Forest Service Road. You don't need a 4WD or other special vehicle to follow this rutted gravel logging road; just watch your speed.

After you pass kilometer 14, Whiteswan Forest Service Road gets narrower as it winds along a ridge and through a canyon. Put your headlights on, take it slow, and use the pullouts if you meet a vehicle coming the other way. The hot springs are at kilometer 17.5.

Lussier Hot Springs in Whiteswan Lake Provincial Park

★ Fernie

If you're traveling between the Canadian Rockies and the Okanagan Valley, it's a short detour along Highway 3 to the town of Fernie. It's a detour worth taking, particularly if you're interested in regional history or in outdoor adventures, or if you'd like to chill in this down-to-earth mountain community. Victorian-era buildings line the downtown streets, home to cafés, restaurants, and eclectic shops, and the forested slopes and craggy peaks of the Rocky Mountains surround the town.

In 1919, Fernie's local newspaper wrote, "The scenery of Switzerland is no grander than our own." While it took some time before this southeastern B.C. district began drawing scenery-seeking visitors in any significant numbers, the area's first ski resort, which opened in the 1960s, became a major lure. Fernie now has a year-round population of 5,200, which almost doubles during the winter ski season.

Sights and Recreation

Fernie suffered two devastating fires in the early 20th century, in 1904 and again in 1908. After the second blaze, the town passed an ordinance decreeing that all downtown buildings must be made of brick. The result is that Fernie's downtown core is full of historic brick and stone buildings, most constructed between 1908 and 1912, including City Hall (1905), Fernie Heritage Library (1908), and Fernie Court House (1908). Many of the town's cafés, shops, restaurants, and pubs are in heritage structures as well.

Get the scoop on Fernie's history at the compact but well-designed **Fernie Museum** (491 2nd Ave., 250/423-7016, www.ferniemuseum.com, 10am-5:30pm daily, adults $5, seniors $4), which has a mix of permanent and changing exhibits. In summer, the museum offers entertaining guided 90-minute **walking tours** (11am and 2pm Sat.-Sun. July-Aug., adults $15) that highlight the town's past, from its coal-mining heritage to a legendary First Nations curse. Also in the museum is a **visitor information desk,** where staff can provide details about local attractions.

In the town's former train station, built in 1908, **The Arts Station** (601 1st Ave., 250/423-4842, www.theartsstation.com, 10am-3pm Mon.-Fri. and during events) is a community cultural hub, with two art galleries, a theater, a craft and painting studio, and the **Blue Toque Diner** (250/423-4637, 9am-2:30pm Thurs.-Mon., $10-17).

Local craft beer maker **Fernie Brewing Company** (26 Manitou Rd., 250/423-7797 or 855/777-2739, www.ferniebrewing.com, call or check website for seasonal hours) has a tasting room and shop at its brewery, off Highway 3 on the town's east side. You can sample the wares and do good, too, with its "Cheers to Charity Program"—$5 gets you a tasting flight of four beers, with profits going to local charities.

Led by one of a small number of female

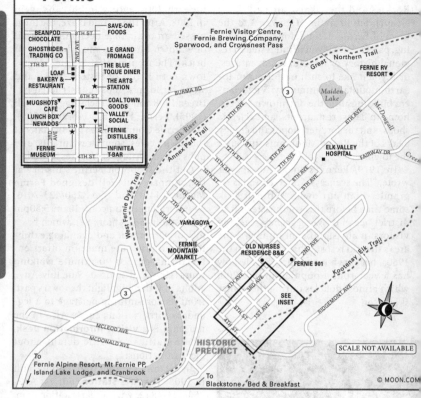

Fernie

distillers in Canada, **Fernie Distillers** (531 1st Ave., www.ferniedistillers.com, noon-10pm Wed.-Sat., noon-6pm Sun.) produces vodka made from Kootenay-ground wheat and an Earl Grey tea-infused liqueur dubbed "Fernie Fog." The tasting room and lounge, in a rehabbed section of the local legion hall, looks into the production facility.

One of Fernie's most photogenic spots hides behind a Canadian Tire store and a local strip mall on the east end of town. Take a stroll or pack a picnic to enjoy at **Maiden Lake** (19th St. at 9th Ave.), a small body of water ringed with mountains.

In winter, Fernie is a center for **catskiing,** where, instead of taking lifts up to groomed runs, you ride into the backcountry in a heated snowcat, which resembles a cross between a bulldozer and a limousine. On these excursions, your guide will direct you to the day's best terrain before you head off into the powder. **Island Lake Catskiing** (250/423-3700 or 877/423-6704, www.islandlakecatskiing. com) operates catskiing tours from its deluxe wilderness lodge. **Fernie Wilderness Adventures** (250/423-6704 or 877/423-6704, www.ferniewildernessadventures. com) offers one-day and multiday catskiing trips.

Fernie Alpine Resort

It's just 3 miles (5 km) from the town of Fernie to **Fernie Alpine Resort** (5339 Ski Area Rd., 250/423-4655 or 800/258-7669, www.skifernie.com), where you can play outdoors in both summer and winter. The mountain is off Highway 3 on the west side of town.

Summer Activities

Fernie Alpine Resort opens for summer activities from late June until at least mid-September. For more information or to book summer experiences, call or visit the **Resort Adventure Centre** (250/423-4655, www.skifernie.com) at the mountain's base.

Ride the **chairlifts** (10:30am-4:30pm daily, adults $25-27, seniors and ages 13-17 $21-23, ages 6-12 $12-13, families $58-63) up the mountain to take in the views or reach several **lift-accessed hiking trails** that start from the top of the Elk or Timber chairs. If you prefer to go with a guide, choose from several **guided hikes** (half-day adults $52, seniors and ages 13-17 $44, ages 6-12 $26, full-day adults $69, seniors and ages 13-17 $59, ages 6-12 $34), ranging from easy to challenging; prices include your lift ticket.

Fernie is known for **mountain biking** (10:30am-4:30pm daily, full-day adults $55, seniors and ages 13-17 $41, ages 6-12 $27, families $128), with 37 lift-accessed trails, from wide beginner routes to expert single-track through the trees and down steep slopes.

For more thrills, test your balance in the **Aerial Park** (10:30am, 11am, 2pm, and 2:30pm daily, adults $69, seniors and ages 13-17 $52, ages 6-12 $34, families $161), a high ropes course.

Winter Sports

With an average annual snowfall of 30 feet (9 m) and a skiable area of more than 2,500 acres (1,000 ha), encompassing 142 trails and five vast alpine bowls, Fernie Alpine Resort claims the most runs for **skiing and snowboarding** (9am-4pm daily early Dec.-mid-Apr., full-day adults

Top to bottom: Fernie welcome sign; craft spirits at Fernie Distillers; Fernie Museum.

$110, seniors $89, ages 13-17 $83, ages 6-12 $44) in the Canadian Rockies.

The resort has introduced winter **fat-tire biking** (250/423-2409, 2 hours $30, full-day $45), where you ride specially designed bicycles with low gears and fat tires on snow-covered trails.

Festivals and Events

The **Griz Days Winter Festival** (www.tourismfernie.com, Mar.) makes mid-winter merriment with scavenger hunts, a craft fair, a pancake-eating contest, a lumberjack show, a parade, dance parties, and fireworks.

Fernival (www.skifernie.com, Apr.), at Fernie Alpine Resort, wraps up the ski season with free concerts and other festivities.

Celebrating Canadian indie music, **Wapiti Music Festival** (www.wapitimusicfestival.com, Aug.) brings established and up-and-coming bands to town for a weekend of summer concerts.

Shopping

Sit on the purple and red couches and watch the chocolate makers at work at **Beanpod Chocolate** (691 2nd Ave., 778/519-5008, www.beanpod.ca, 10am-5pm Mon.-Sat., noon-4pm Sun.), a family-run chocolate and gelato shop. Among the goodies are handmade chocolates, ice cream, and coffee.

Le Grand Fromage (672E 2nd Ave., 250/531-0030, www.legrandfromage.ca, 10am-6pm Mon.-Sat., noon-4pm Sun.) sells cheese made locally and elsewhere, along with salami, jams, crackers, and other gourmet food items. Stop in for lunch, when the shop makes several varieties of grilled cheese sandwiches ($9).

In the Fernie General Store building, **Ghostrider Trading Co.** (661 2nd Ave., 250/423-5541, 10am-6pm Mon.-Sat., 11am-5pm Sun.) carries stylish casual clothing and shoes, as well as funky Fernie T-shirts.

For jewelry, leather goods, ceramics, and a curated selection of clothes,

most crafted by artisans from Fernie or around the region, check out **Coal Town Goods** (591B 2nd Ave., 778/519-5262, www.coaltowngoods.com, 11am-5:30pm Mon.-Sat., 11am-4pm Sun.). The entrance to this tiny boutique is on 6th Street, off Fernie's main downtown street.

Food
Contemporary

Located in the Arts Station, a cultural center in the town's former rail station, ★ **The Blue Toque Diner** (601 1st Ave., 250/423-4637, www.theartsstation.com, 9am-2:30pm Thurs.-Mon., $10-17) is *the* place for breakfast and brunch in Fernie. Try the Huevos del Karmalita, crispy corn tortillas piled with eggs, pulled turkey, and refried beans, or design your own omelet.

"Things you eat with bread" is the theme at the **Loaf Bakery & Restaurant** (641 2nd Ave., 250/423-7702, www.loafbakery.ca, 10am-10pm daily, brunch $10-17, dinner $16-19). It's a bakery by day, selling croissants, pastries, and fresh breads. It's a brunch spot and Italian restaurant, too, serving homemade pizzas, pastas, salads, and sandwiches.

Japanese

To satisfy your sushi cravings, visit long-popular **Yamagoya** (741 7th Ave., 250/430-0090, www.yamagoya.ca, 5pm-10pm daily, $14-30, sushi and sashimi $2-22) for traditional and funkier Japanese fare. The Fernie roll is made of tuna, kimchi, tempura, and green onion, while the fusion rolls include a curry version with prawns, mango, red pepper, and curry sauce. In addition to sushi, it serves tempura, salads, and teriyaki stir-fries.

Latin American

Tapas and tequilas are the specialties at **Nevados** (531 2nd Ave., 250/423-5566, www.nevados.ca, 5pm-10pm daily, $5-22), where the music and conversation can be lively, and the small plates draw inspiration from across Latin America.

Take a seat at a rustic wooden table or out on the patio for tacos, arepas, tortilla soup, and Argentine-style barbecue skewers, and choose from a long list of tequilas, mezcals, and cocktails.

Cafés, Bakeries, and Light Bites

Pop into laid-back **Mugshots Café** (592 3rd Ave., 250/423-8018, 7am-5pm Mon.-Fri., 8am-5pm Sat., $7-15) for your morning coffee and pastry, omelet, or breakfast skillet or for a panini and a cookie later in the day. The café has free Wi-Fi.

Whether you want a latte or a beer, you can hang out on the leather couches at **Valley Social** (562 2nd Ave., 778/519-5272, 8am-5pm daily), a hip café on the main downtown street.

It's not all coffee in Fernie. At **Infinitea T-Bar** (501 1st Ave., 778/519-5258, noon-11:30pm Wed.-Mon., $7-15), which feels like a homey living room inside, choose from an array of black, green, and herbal infusions, as well as veggie-friendly salads and sandwiches. It hosts live music some evenings.

Colorful walls and equally colorful fruit- and veggie-filled plates make the **Lunchbox** (561A 2nd Ave., 250/423-4500, www.fernielunchbox.ca, 10am-5pm Mon.-Sat., 11am-5pm Sun., $7-13), a smoothie and sandwich bar, a cheerful destination for freshly made soups, wraps, and blended drinks.

Groceries and Markets

The town's popular summer farmers market, **Fernie Mountain Market** (Rotary Park, 250/423-6674, www.mountainmarket.ca, 10am-2pm Sun. July-early Sept.) sells fresh produce, crafts, baked goods, and some prepared foods. The park is off Highway 3 at 5th Street.

Top to bottom: hikers at Fernie Alpine Resort; Blackstone Bed & Breakfast; hiking trail near Island Lake Lodge.

Accommodations and Camping

For accommodations on the mountain at **Fernie Alpine Resort**, contact **Resorts of the Canadian Rockies** (403/254-7669 or 800/258-7669, www.skicr.com or www.skifernie.com).

★ **Blackstone Bed & Breakfast** (30 Piedmont Dr., 250/531-0080, www.blackstonebandb.com, $124-200), a classy lodging in a newly developed residential neighborhood, feels more like a high-style boutique inn than a classic bed-and-breakfast. In the three guest rooms, the modern furnishings are crafted from reclaimed wood, accented with faux fur throws, and the spacious baths have walk-in rain showers. From the two main-floor rooms, you can walk out onto a patio with a burbling fountain, and the owners deliver a hot breakfast to your door. The third room, upstairs, has a separate entrance and is offered without breakfast. Melt away any adventure-induced aches in the small infrared sauna or outdoor hot tub.

A former 1908 brick school building, a short stroll from downtown Fernie's restaurants and shops, has been converted into ★ **Fernie 901** (901 2nd Ave., 2- and 3-bedroom $260-550), a condominium complex with upscale two- to five-bedroom suites available for short-term rentals. The units' spacious modern kitchens have granite countertops, stainless steel appliances, and everything you'd need to make meals for a crowd; the high ceilings, wood floors, and fireplaces give the apartments a mix of mountain and urban style. Units have washer-dryers, parking, and Wi-Fi. To book, contact **Fernie Central Reservations** (250/423-2077 or 800/622-5007, www.ferniecentralreservations.com).

Beginning in 1908, the Victorian manor that's now the **Old Nurses Residence B&B** (802 4th Ave., 250/423-3091, www.oldnurse.com, $149-259), a few blocks off Fernie's main downtown street, was a lodging house for unmarried local nurses. Its four guest rooms and comfortable guest lounge channel that Victorian era with antique furnishings, polished wood floors, and original stained glass. Rates include Wi-Fi. You can add a full breakfast for $25 per person.

As you snake your way up the washboard track toward **Island Lake Lodge** (250/423-3700 or 888/422-8754, www.islandlakecatskiing.com, mid-June-mid-Oct., $159-399), the road gets narrower and the trees get bigger; much of this area is an old-growth cedar forest. A get-away-from-it-all place on 7,000 acres (2,830 ha) of private land, the property has 26 rustic-luxe guest rooms in three timber lodges. A fourth lodge houses the restaurants: **Bear Lodge** and **Tamarack Dining Room.** The guest rooms have no TVs or phones, although there is cell service; rates include breakfast and Wi-Fi. Even if you're not staying at the lodge, you might come for a meal, go **canoeing** on the lake ($20 per hour), or explore its **hiking trails,** which are open to nonguests. From Highway 3, turn onto Mount Fernie Park Road, travel past Mount Fernie Provincial Park, and continue to the lodge. In winter, the lodge is open only to guests booked for **catskiing.**

Camping

Off Highway 3, 1.9 miles (3 km) southwest of Fernie, on the same road that leads to Island Lake Lodge, **Mount Fernie Provincial Park** (Mount Fernie Park Rd., 250/422-3003, www.env.gov.bc.ca, May-Sept., $28) has 43 forested campsites and restrooms with showers.

Close to town, privately owned **Fernie RV Resort** (2001 6th Ave., 844/343-2233, www.ferniervresort.com, tent sites $35-48, electrical sites $35-80) has 105 sites for recreational vehicles, space for 17 tents, and five yurts ($99-125) with electricity, heat, and wood floors, sleeping up to six. The RV sites at this newly developed property are not particularly shaded, although the yurts and tent sites border a forested area. Washrooms with

Once an Aboriginal Residential School, Now a Resort

St. Eugene Resort once housed an aboriginal residential school.

Beginning in the 1880s, the Canadian government began establishing residential schools for aboriginal children. Indigenous students were required to attend these church-run boarding schools, where children were removed from their families. The schools' objective was to assimilate aboriginal youth into mainstream Canadian culture.

While some students' experiences at the schools were positive, the vast majority suffered through poor education, inadequate food, isolation from their families and culture, and in some cases, physical or sexual abuse. The last residential schools closed, or were turned over to indigenous communities to operate, in the 1980s.

Outside the city of Cranbrook, **St. Eugene Mission** housed a residential school for most of the 1900s, opening to students in 1912 and remaining in operation until 1970. At its peak in the late 1950s and early 1960s, more than 200 students, both from local First Nations communities and from as far away as Port Hardy on Vancouver Island and Alberta, lived at the school.

The Roman Catholic Church had built the mission on aboriginal land, and in 1978, after the school was closed, the government stripped the building. In the process, workers found letters stuffed into the wall that students had written and hidden, attempting to send them home to their families.

The government returned the mission property to local First Nations bands, but it sat abandoned for many years. Eventually, several of the bands began redeveloping the former school, opening a golf course in 2000, a casino in 2002, and a hotel in 2003.

Today, the **St. Eugene Resort** is a resort hotel operated by the Ktunaxa First Nation, Chippewas of Rama First Nation, and Samson Cree Nation in the former mission building and adjacent new wings. Historic photos of the school, former students, and local First Nations residents line the hallways, where students' dormitories have been converted into guest rooms, and the former chapel is now a banquet hall.

showers, laundry facilities, and Wi-Fi are among the amenities.

Information and Services
Visitor Information

The **Fernie Visitor Centre** (102 Commerce Rd./Hwy. 3, 778/519-0748, www.tourismfernie.com, 9:30am-5:30pm daily mid-May-early Sept., 9:30am-5pm Mon.-Fri. early Sept.-Nov., 9:30am-5pm Tues.-Sat. Dec.-mid-Apr., 9:30am-5pm Mon.-Fri. mid-Apr.-mid-May) is on the east side of town. Out front is the last remaining **wooden oil derrick** (www.ferniederrick.com) still standing in B.C.

In downtown Fernie, there's a **visitor information desk** at the Fernie Museum (491 2nd Ave., 10am-5:30pm daily). Another excellent source of area information is the **Tourism Fernie** website (www.tourismfernie.com).

Medical Services

For emergency medical care, **Elk Valley Hospital** (1501 5th Ave., 250/423-4453, www.interiorhealth.ca) is open 24 hours daily.

Save-On-Foods (792 2nd Ave., 250/423-7704, www.saveonfoods.com, grocery 8am-9pm daily, pharmacy 8:30am-7pm Mon.-Fri., 9am-6pm Sat., 11am-5pm Sun.), the large grocery store downtown, has a pharmacy.

Getting There and Around

Fernie is located on Highway 3 in the southeastern corner of British Columbia, 43 miles (70 km) west of the Alberta border. It's 180 miles (290 km), a three-hour drive, southwest of Calgary, which has the closest major airport. From Calgary, the shortest route is to follow Highway 2 south to Nanton, where you pick up Highway 533 west, then turn south on Highway 22 and west on Highway 3 to Fernie. You can also reach Fernie from Alberta by taking Highway 93 south through Kootenay National Park and continuing south to Highway 3, where you turn east to Fernie.

Fernie is 42 miles (68 km) north of the U.S. border. Highway 93 leads north from Montana to Highway 3, which takes you east to Fernie. The closest U.S. airport, 115 miles (185 km) from Fernie, is **Glacier Park International Airport** (FCA, 4170 Hwy. 2 E., Kalispell, MT, 406/257-5994, www.iflyglacier.com).

Mid-December-March or early April, **Fernie Shuttle** (250/423-4023, www.thefernieshuttle.com, one-way adults $137.50) and **Mountain High Shuttle** (250/423-5008 or 877/423-4555, www.mountainhighshuttle.com, one-way adults $139, under age 15 $79) provide transportation between Calgary International Airport and Fernie. The trip averages four hours. Fernie Shuttle also runs a winter-season shuttle to and from Cranbrook's Canadian Rockies International Airport (one-way adults $104.50); it operates a summer weekend shuttle between Fernie and the Calgary airport as well.

Throughout the day during the winter ski season, **Fernie Ski Shuttle** (250/423-2435, www.skifernie.com, mid-Dec.-mid-Apr., one-way $4) takes skiers and boarders between downtown and Fernie Alpine Resort.

Cranbrook and Kimberley

The largest town in the East Kootenays, with a population of about 20,000, Cranbrook sits at the crossroads of two main roadways: Highways 3 and 95. Primarily a commercial hub, it's worth a stop for several historic sites.

Nearby, the small community of Kimberley highlights its European heritage on its Bavarian-themed pedestrian promenade, **The Platzl,** which has Canada's largest freestanding cuckoo clock, as well as a growing number of cool cafés and places to eat. Kimberley's main attraction is its natural setting, drawing outdoor enthusiasts for white-water rafting in summer and skiing or snowboarding in winter.

Sights and Activities
Ktunaxa Interpretive Centre
The people of the Ktunaxa First Nation, known in English as the Kootenay, have lived in western North America for more than 10,000 years. Their traditional territory extends through B.C.'s Kootenay region east to Alberta and south into Washington, Idaho, and Montana. A complicated chapter in the Ktunaxas' history unfolded at the former St. Eugene Mission, a red-roofed Spanish-style stone church outside of Cranbrook that served as a residential school for aboriginal children from 1912 until 1970.

Exhibits and artifacts tell the Ktunaxas' past and present-day story at the **Ktunaxa Interpretive Centre** (7777 Mission Rd., Cranbrook, 250/417-4001, www.steugene.ca, call for hours), which is on the lower level of the former mission, now **St. Eugene Resort,** a hotel and casino that several First Nations bands operate. Take time to watch a documentary film with interviews of former Ktunaxa students who were removed from their families and forced to attend the church-run school.

Fort Steele Heritage Town
In the 1860s, when gold was discovered near Fort Steele on Wild Horse Creek east of Cranbrook, more than 5,000 prospectors inundated the region, hoping to strike it rich. A living history village, **Fort Steele Heritage Town** (9851 Hwy. 93/95, Fort Steele, 250/417-6000, www.fortsteele.ca, 10am-4pm daily May-June and early Sept.-mid-Oct., 10am-5pm daily July-early Sept., adults $12-15, seniors $10-12, ages 6-17 $10, families $40-45) takes you back to the gold rush days, with more than 60 restored heritage buildings. Wander into the barbershop (which advertises hot and cold baths), the jail, or the dry goods store, and chat with costumed interpreters as they ply their

trades, from blacksmithing to dressmaking to panning for gold.

On the 30-minute **Gossip Tour** (included with admission), a costumed guide leads you through the village while sharing the local scuttlebutt about brothel owners, mail thieves, and other less-than-savory citizens. You can ride the **Fort Steele Steam Railway** (adults $12, ages 6-17 $7) or see a musical production at the **Wildhorse Theatre** (adults $10, ages 6-17 $5). The village itself and the museum building remain open through the winter (10am-4pm daily mid-Oct.-Apr., donation), but the heritage buildings are closed.

Sports and Recreation
Kootenay Raft Co. (220 Ross St., Kimberley, 250/427-3266 or 877/777-7238, www.kootenayrafting.ca) offers several water adventures from its Kimberley base, including the family-friendly half-day **St. Mary's Express Trip** (adults $81, ages 13-17 $66, under age 13 $53), a rafting excursion with Class I-III rapids; **Kayak Rafting** (adults $81, ages 13-17 $66), where you follow the St. Mary's route in an inflatable two-person kayak; and a full-day **Wilderness Whitewater Rafting Trip** (adults $135, ages 13-17 $110) with Class II-IV rapids on either the White, Bull, or Elk Rivers. It also runs half-day **stand-up paddleboard tours** (adults $75, under age 16 $65) on local lakes.

Kimberley Alpine Resort (301 North Star Blvd., Kimberley, 250/427-4881, www.skikimberley.com, early Dec.-mid-Apr., full-day adults $89.95, seniors $71.95, ages 13-17 $67.95, ages 6-12 $33.95) draws skiers and snowboarders to its 80 runs spread across 1,800 acres (729 ha).

Food
If you're vegetarian, vegan, dairy-free, or gluten-free, or just want something simple and wholesome to eat, **Soulfood** (1017 Baker St., Cranbrook, 778/517-5339,

www.kootenaysoulfood.com, 7:30am-9pm Mon.-Fri., 9am-9pm Sat., 9am-2pm Sun., $10-19) has your back. Smoothies, elixirs, eggs, coffees, and teas start the day in this local gathering place, then soups, salads, and sharing plates like naan pizza or a taco bowl, made from local and/or organic ingredients, come out of the kitchen later in the day. Organic wines and craft cocktails are available, and the eatery regularly hosts area musicians.

Pedal and Tap (215 Spokane St., Kimberley, 250/427-3325, www. pedalandtap.com, 4pm-9pm Sun.-Tues., 4pm-10pm Wed.-Sat., $14-26) cooks up fun twists on pub grub, like Meat & Spaghettiballs (fried balls of spaghetti and cheese on a tomato-meat sauce) and the Tuk-Tuk, a Vietnamese-style sandwich of pulled pork, carrots, and sweet curry mayonnaise. It's got substantial salads, craft beer, and a sunny patio, too.

For a quick bite to take on the road, head for a local gas station, where the organic grocery **Kimberley Centrex Market** (521 Wallinger Ave., Kimberley, 250/427-4944, www.kimberleycentexmarket.com, 6am-10pm daily) has a coffee, juice, and smoothie bar that also sells sandwiches and baked goods.

Accommodations

The former St. Eugene Mission, a residential school for indigenous children from 1912 until 1970, is now the ★ **St. Eugene Resort** (7777 Mission Rd., Cranbrook, 250/420-2000 or 866/290-2020, www. steugene.ca, $165-285), which three First Nations communities operate in partnership. Twenty-five of the 125 guest rooms are in the original ivy-colored, red-roofed mission building, where historic photos line the hallways; the remainder are in a newer lodge. All the units include Wi-Fi, flat-screen TVs, mini fridges, and coffee- and tea-making equipment. Also in the mission building are the **Ktunaxa Interpretive Centre,** which showcases local First Nations history, and **St. Eugene Dining Room.** Off Highway

horse-drawn wagon at Fort Steele Heritage Town

95A, 4 miles (6 km) north of downtown Cranbrook and 15 miles (24 km) south of Kimberley, St. Eugene Resort has a large outdoor swimming pool, 18-hole golf course, and casino.

Information and Services
The **Cranbrook Chamber of Commerce Visitor Centre** (2279 Cranbrook St. N., 250/426-5914 or 800/222-6174, www.cranbrookchamber.com, 8:30am-4:30pm daily June-early Sept., 8:30am-4:30pm Mon.-Fri. early Sept.-May) provides information about the area. For more local tips, see the **Cranbrook Tourism** website (www.cranbrooktourism.ca).

Tourism Kimberley Visitor Information Centre (270 Kimberley Ave., 778/481-1891, www.tourismkimberley.com, 10am-5pm daily July-early Sept., 10am-5pm Mon.-Sat. early Sept.-June) can assist with area details.

Based in Kimberley, **Kootenay-Rockies Tourism** (1905 Warren Ave., 250/427-4838, www.kootenayrockies.com) has a detailed website with lots of itinerary suggestions and ideas for planning a trip through B.C.'s Kootenay-Rockies region.

The West Kootenays

Hot springs, quirky mountain towns, and the history of several different communities give you plenty to explore in the West Kootenays, from the agricultural town of Creston in the east to funky Nelson between the Purcell and Selkirk Mountains, and along Highway 3 toward the Okanagan Valley.

Creston
Stop in this agricultural town along Highway 3 to stretch your legs, take a short hike, or explore the area's emerging wine industry.

Sights and Recreation
Follow the boardwalk trails through the marsh and along the river at the **Creston Valley Wildlife Management Area** (1760 West Creston Rd., West Creston, 250/402-6908, www.crestonwildlife.ca, trails dawn-dusk daily), a 17,000-acre (7,000-ha) nature preserve along the Kootenay River, off Highway 3, 7 miles (11 km) west of Creston. For bird-watching, climb the three-story wildlife-viewing tower on the March Trail loop. The **Kootenay-Columbia Discovery Centre** (9am-4pm Mon.-Sat. mid-May-June, 9am-4pm daily July-Aug., 9am-4pm Tues.-Sat. Sept.-mid-Oct., donation) has nature exhibits about the area, and staff offer guided canoe and walking tours; check the website for schedules and rates.

Creston has several wineries where you can stop and sip. **Baillie-Grohman Estate Winery** (1140 27 Ave. S., 250/428-8767, www.bailliegrohman.com, 11am-5pm Sat.-Sun. Apr.-mid-May, 11am-5pm daily mid-May-mid-Oct., tastings free) and **Skimmerhorn Winery & Vineyard** (1218 27 Ave. S., 250/428-4911, www.skimmerhorn.ca, 11am-5pm Fri.-Sun.

Apr. and mid-Oct.-late Dec., 11am-5pm daily May-mid-Oct., tastings free) are next door to each other on the south side of town. **Wynnwood Cellars** (5566 Hwy. 3A, 250/866-5155, www.wynnwoodcellars.com, 11am-6pm daily mid-May-mid-Oct.) is just north of town.

Food

To get off the road and take a break, stop for coffee or tea and something to read at **Black Bear Books & Coffee House** (1229B Canyon St., 250/428-2711, www.blackbearbooks.ca, 8am-5pm Mon.-Fri., 9am-5pm Sat.), a cozy bookstore-café with living room-style seating.

Real Food Café (223 10th Ave., 250/428-8882, www.realfoodcafe.ca, 11am-2pm and 4:30pm-8pm Mon.-Fri., 4:30pm-8pm Sat., lunch $12-15, dinner $12-18), a homey downstairs eatery, lives up to its name, serving straightforward meals using lots of local ingredients. Try the excellent peppery wild salmon chowder or the Grown-Up Grilled Cheese, with a locally produced organic cheese, apple chutney, and fresh greens. The café is also known for fish-and-chips and for homemade desserts, like carrot cake or sticky toffee pudding.

Information and Services

The **Creston Valley Visitor Centre** (121 Northwest Blvd., 250/428-4342, www.crestonvalleybc.com, 9am-5pm daily July-Aug., 9am-5pm Mon.-Fri. Sept.-June) can assist with area information and with travel details for elsewhere in B.C. and Alberta. The visitors center has free Wi-Fi.

★ Nelson

You may find yourself staying longer than you'd planned in this funky West Kootenays town of just over 10,000 inhabitants, located between the Canadian Rockies and the B.C. coast. Mountains surround Nelson, on the west arm of Kootenay Lake, with the Purcells to the east and the Selkirk range to the west.

In the late 1800s and early 1900s, most Nelson-area residents were miners, farmers, or loggers. The town has more than 350 heritage buildings, many dating to the Victorian era.

In the 1960s and 1970s, a new wave of migrants settled in Nelson and helped shape the town's present-day culture. During the Vietnam War, between 50,000 and 125,000 Americans who opposed the war or who wanted to avoid the draft came to Canada, and many settled in Nelson or the surrounding small towns of the West Kootenays.

Nelson still has that countercultural vibe, with alternative health providers, yoga studios, and vegetarian restaurants sharing the downtown streets with art galleries, book shops, and outdoor gear stores. Although the town had its moment in the Hollywood spotlight in the 1980s, when the movie *Roxanne,* starring Steve Martin, was filmed here, those 15 minutes of fame didn't go to its head. Slow down and stay awhile; Nelson is a friendly, laid-back place.

Sights and Recreation

Take time to explore **Touchstones Nelson: Museum of Art and History** (502 Vernon St., 250/352-9813, www.touchstonesnelson.ca, 10am-5pm Mon.-Wed. and Fri.-Sat., 10am-8pm Thurs., 10am-4pm Sun. June-mid-Sept., 10am-5pm Wed. and Fri.-Sat., 10am-8pm Thurs., 11am-4pm Tues. and Sun. mid-Sept.-May, adults $8, seniors and students $6, ages 7-18 $4, families $22, 5pm-8pm Thurs. by donation), a well-designed museum in a 1902 former courthouse. Touchstones traces the region's history, beginning with its First Nations heritage, and follows the explorers, miners, steamship captains, fisherfolk, skiers, and draft dodgers who've influenced the town's development. The museum also hosts changing art exhibitions. Listen to the recorded stories of past and current Nelson residents, and check out the gift shop, which sells locally made crafts,

Nelson

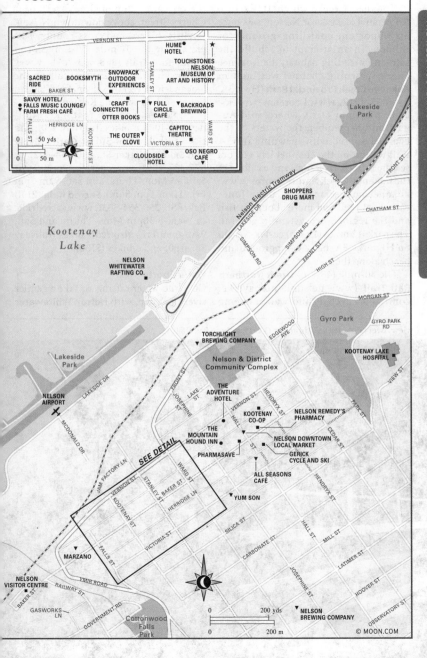

VERNON ST

HUME
HOTEL

TOUCHSTONES
NELSON:
MUSEUM OF
ART AND HISTORY

SNOWPACK
OUTDOOR
EXPERIENCES

STANLEY ST

SACRED
RIDE

BOOKSMYTH

BAKER ST

SAVOY HOTEL/
FALLS MUSIC LOUNGE/
FARM FRESH CAFÉ

CRAFT
CONNECTION
OTTER BOOKS

FULL
CIRCLE
CAFÉ

BACKROADS
BREWING

FALLS ST

HERRIDGE LN

KOOTENAY ST

THE OUTER
CLOVE

VICTORIA ST

CAPITOL
THEATRE

WARD ST

0   50 yds
0   50 m

CLOUDSIDE
HOTEL

OSO NEGRO
CAFÉ

Nelson Electric Tramway

LAKESIDE DR

POPLAR ST

FRONT ST

SHOPPERS
DRUG MART

CHATHAM ST

*Kootenay
Lake*

SIMPSON RD

SIMPSON RD

FRONT ST

HIGH ST

NELSON
WHITEWATER
RAFTING CO.

MORGAN ST

Gyro Park

GYRO PARK
RD

Lakeside
Park

LAKESIDE DR

TORCHLIGHT
BREWING COMPANY

EDGEWOOD
AVE

Nelson & District
Community Complex

KOOTENAY LAKE
HOSPITAL

VIEW ST

NELSON
AIRPORT

MCDONALD DR

FRONT ST

JOSEPHINE
ST

LAKE
ST

THE
ADVENTURE
HOTEL

VERNON ST

HENDRYX ST

HALL ST

PARK ST

SEE DETAIL

JAM FACTORY LN

VERNON ST

STANLEY S

WARD ST

BAKER ST

HERRIDGE LN

KOOTENAY ST

THE
MOUNTAIN
HOUND INN

PHARMASAVE

KOOTENAY
CO-OP

NELSON REMEDY'S
PHARMACY

ST

NELSON DOWNTOWN
LOCAL MARKET

GERICK
CYCLE AND SKI

CEDAR ST

HENDRYX ST

ALL SEASONS
CAFÉ

YUM SON

SILICA ST

VICTORIA ST

CARBONATE ST

HALL ST

MILL ST

FALLS ST

MARZANO

NELSON
VISITOR CENTRE

RAILWAY ST

YMIR ROAD

JOSEPHINE ST

LATIMER ST

HOOVER ST

GASWORKS
LN

GOVERNMENT RD

*Cottonwood
Falls
Park*

0   200 yds
0   200 m

NELSON
BREWING COMPANY

OBSERVATORY ST

© MOON.COM

jewelry, and gifts as well as books with local themes.

Kokanee Creek, which flows into Kootenay Lake east of Nelson, was once an important spawning ground for salmon. In an attempt to rebuild the salmon's breeding habitat, the Kokanee Creek spawning channel was built in **Kokanee Creek Provincial Park** (Hwy. 3A, 250/825-4212, www.kootenayswparks. com, May-mid-Oct.), where, mid-August-mid-September, the waters of the channel are red with spawning fish. A walkway along the channel lets visitors see the salmon in action, and exhibits in the **Kokanee Creek Nature Centre** (www. kokaneenaturecentre.org, daily June-early Sept.) tell you more about the fish and the region's ecosystem in general. The park, 12 miles (19 km) east of Nelson on Highway 3A, has a campground and beach along the lake.

The 30-mile (48-km) **Great Northern Rail Trail** (www.nelsonkootenaylake. com) takes cyclists and walkers along the lakeshores and through the forests between Nelson and Salmo; access the trail at the top of Gore Street, near Cherry Street, above downtown Nelson. Cyclists, hikers, and cross-country skiers all use the 31-mile (50-km) **Slocan Valley Rail Trail** (888/683-7878, www. slocanvalleyrailtrail.ca) that follows the Slocan River west of Nelson, from Slocan Lake south toward the Kootenay River.

In Nelson, you can rent bikes (full-day $50-100), e-bikes (full-day $70), and skis (full-day $20-30) at **Gerick Cycle and Ski** (702 Baker St., 250/354-4622 or 877/437-4251, www.gericks.com, 9am-5:30pm Mon.-Thurs. and Sat., 9am-7pm Fri., 11am-5pm Sun.). **Sacred Ride** (213B Baker St., 250/354-3831, www.sacredride. ca, 9am-5:30pm Mon.-Thurs. and Sat., 9am-6pm Fri.) also rents bikes (full-day $45-150) and e-bikes ($100).

Water Sports

Go white-water rafting, or take a gentler river float trip, with **Nelson Whitewater**

views over Kootenay Lake from the Great Northern Rail Trail

Rafting Co. (Prestige Marina, 701 Lakeside Dr., 877/808-7238, www. nelsonwhitewaterrafting.com). Among the trips offered are a leisurely all-ages 3.5- to 4-hour **Slocan River Scenic Float Tour** (June-Sept., adults $69, under age 16 $49) and the family-friendly **Slocan River Facchina Rapids White-Water Trip** (June-Sept., adults $79, ages 5-15 $49), a 3.5- to 4-hour tour through Class II-III rapids. The company also rents **stand-up paddleboards** (1 hour $20, full-day $60) and **kayaks** (1 hour $20, full-day $60) from its in-town marina.

Zip-Lining
At **Kokanee Mountain Zipline** (Kokanee Glacier Park Rd., 844/764-4484, www. zipkokanee.com, 9am-5pm daily May-mid-Oct., adults $94, under age 15 $84), off Highway 3A, north of Nelson, the six-line course takes you from a 90-foot (27 m) warm-up line to a 2,400-foot (730-m) zip across a canyon.

Winter Sports
Downhill skiers and snowboarders challenge the 82 runs at **Whitewater Ski Resort** (250/354-4944 or 800/666-9420, www.skiwhitewater.com, early Dec.-early Apr., adults $89, seniors and ages 13-18 $74, ages 7-12 $44), which gets an average annual snowfall of 40 feet (12 m). Although there are no accommodations on the slopes, Whitewater is just 14 miles (22 km) south of town, so it's easy to stay in Nelson and spend the day at the resort. The mountain operates a daily ski-season shuttle (one-way $7.50, round-trip $11) with pickups and drop-offs at area hotels.

Entertainment and Events
Nightlife
Like many B.C. towns, Nelson has a booming craft beer scene. Sample the suds at **Backroads Brewing** (460 Baker St., 778/463-3361, www.backroadsbrewing. com, noon-10pm Mon.-Thurs., noon-11pm Fri.-Sat., noon-8pm Sun.), a lively pub in the center of town; **Torchlight Brewing Company** (125 Hall St., 250/352-0094, www.torchlightbrewing.com, 11am-9pm Sun.-Tues., 11am-11pm Wed.-Sat.), known for its all-natural brews and sodas; **Savoy Brewery** inside the **Falls Music Lounge** (198 Baker St., 778/463-0700, www.savoyhotel.ca, 3pm-late daily), where the brews are accompanied by live music several nights a week; and **Nelson Brewing Company** (512 Latimer St., 250/352-3582, www.nelsonbrewing. com, noon-8pm Mon.-Sat.), which was the region's first microbrewery.

The Arts
A former 1920s movie house, the **Capitol Theatre** (421 Victoria St., 250/352-6363, www.capitoltheatre.ca) programs theatre, music, and dance events.

Festivals and Events
At the **Elephant Mountain Literary Festival** (www.emlfestival.com, July), a lineup of Canadian authors gives

Scenic Drive: Highway 3A Along Kootenay Lake

To travel between the East Kootenays and Nelson, you have two options. One is to follow Highway 3 east from Creston to the town of Salmo, where you pick up Highway 6 north. A scenic alternative, **Highway 3A,** takes you north from Creston along the eastern shore of Kootenay Lake.

The Glass House

Allow plenty of time to meander along this winding road to enjoy the views across the lake to the mountains. One of the largest lakes in B.C., Kootenay Lake is 67 miles (108 km) long, and at its widest point, it's 3 miles (5 km) across. From Creston north to Kootenay Bay, it's 50 miles (80 km), but even without stopping, the drive will take at least 90 minutes.

The most unusual sight along Highway 3A is a former funeral director's home. David H. Brown built **The Glass House** (11341 Hwy. 3A, Boswell, 250/223-8372, 9am-4pm daily May-June and Sept.-Oct., 8am-7pm daily July-Aug., adults $10, ages 13-17 $8, ages 6-12 $5) in the 1950s, constructing its walls from more than 500,000 empty embalming fluid bottles. Brown apparently felt there should be a practical use for this funeral industry byproduct; he collected discarded bottles from colleagues in the funeral business across western Canada. Guided tours of Brown's 1,200-square-foot (111-sq-m) home and the surrounding gardens overlooking Kootenay Lake 25 miles (40 km) north of Creston tell you about its construction and its unique story.

Another stop to make along Highway 3A is in the village of **Crawford Bay,** where you can visit studios and galleries of several artists and artisans, including a blacksmith, a broom maker, and a glassblower. Crawford Bay is 47 miles (76 km) north of Creston.

To cross Kootenay Lake and turn west toward Nelson, take the free **Kootenay Lake Ferry** (250/229-4215, www2.gov.bc.ca, 7:10am-10:20pm daily) from Kootenay Bay on the lake's eastern shore across to Balfour on the west. The 35-minute ferry bills itself as "the longest free ferry ride in the world"—who knew? Note, especially if you're coming from the east, that the ferry operates on Pacific time, one hour earlier than Alberta and the East Kootenays.

---

lectures, readings, and workshops on literary topics.

From Nelson to Fernie to Invermere, and in many towns in between, artists, galleries, and other cultural institutions open their doors to visitors during the weekend-long **Columbia Basin Culture Tour** (www.cbculturetour.com, Aug.).

The **Shambhala Music Festival** (www.shambhalamusicfestival.com, Aug.), an annual electronic music fest, draws music

fans and partiers to Salmo River Ranch, south of Nelson.

Shopping

Local shops line **Baker Street,** downtown Nelson's main shopping district, with more stores on the surrounding streets.

Among the many outdoor clothing and gear shops in Nelson, **Snowpack Outdoor Experiences** (333 Baker St., 250/352-6411 or 877/669-7225, www.snowpack.ca,

9:30am-5pm Mon.-Sat., 11am-4pm Sun.) is Canada's only Patagonia outlet store.

Craft Connection (378 Baker St., 250/352-3006, www.craftconnection.org, 9:30am-5:30pm Mon.-Sat.), a local artists' cooperative, sells high-quality jewelry, crafts, and gifts.

Nelson's independent bookstores include **Otter Books** (398 Baker St., 250/352-3434, www.otterbooksinc.ca, 9:30am-5:30pm Mon.-Sat., 11am-4pm Sun.) and **Booksmyth** (338 Baker St., 250/352-1225, www.booksmyth.ca, 11am-5pm Mon.-Sat., noon-4pm Sun.), which carries used books.

Food
Contemporary
If you don't like garlic, you might want to pass by the **Outer Clove** (536 Stanley St., 250/354-1667, www.outerclove.com, 11am-2:30pm and 5pm-9pm Mon.-Sat., lunch $10-12, dinner $15-24), an entertaining garlic-themed café. But if you do enjoy the stinking rose, try the garlic-spiked burgers, "40 Clove Fries" tossed in garlic and parsley, salads, pastas, or dishes like Chicken Cordon Clove (stuffed with brie and roasted garlic). Vegetarians have lots of options here. The signature dessert? Giant garlic chocolate chip cookies ($2) made with candied garlic. Yes, breath mints are provided.

One of Nelson's more upscale dining options, **All Seasons Café** (620 Herridge Ln., 250/352-0101, www.allseasonscafe.com, 5pm-10pm daily, $22-36) sits on a narrow lane half a block south of Baker Street. On the menu, which changes with the seasons, you might find mushroom risotto made with locally foraged varieties, duck glazed with black currants, or short ribs served with chive gnocchi. The wine list is strong on B.C. labels.

Vietnamese
Head for ★ **Yum Son** (522 Victoria St., 778/463-2234, www.yumson.ca, 11:30am-9pm Sun.-Thurs., 11:30am-10pm Fri.-Sat., $10-24) for modern riffs on Vietnamese fare in a smart-casual space. The kitchen prepares the broth for its pho from long-simmered grass-fed beef and organic chicken bones; try the "Pho Shizzle," with juicy and flavorful duck-pork meatballs, and add an order of tangy house-made pickles. Other options range from vegetarian pho to fresh salad rolls to rice noodle bowls layered with your choice of tofu, chicken and pork, or short ribs. Toast your Nelson adventures with a well-crafted cocktail, like the Tailor Made (bourbon, amaro, aperol, ardberg, and orange bitters) or the Silk Road (gin, soda, and the bar's own five-spice syrup).

Italian and Pizza
Big, bustling ★ **Marzano** (153 Baker St., 250/352-9205, www.marzanonelson.com, 6:30am-10pm Mon.-Thurs., 6:30am-11pm Fri., 7am-11pm Sat., 7am-10pm Sun.) channels the Neapolitan vibe with its traditional pizza oven, tile floors, and country-style wood tables, alongside a menu of pizzeria classics updated with fresh, local ingredients. Options range from traditional Margherita to chorizo with roasted peppers and pickled onions. In the evenings, the menu expands to pastas and steaks, while at breakfast, you might opt for poached egg and avocado served on a potato cake or a polenta bowl topped with arugula, chorizo, and eggs.

Cafés, Bakeries, and Light Bites
Nelson's own coffee roaster runs a bustling coffee-centric café, ★ **Oso Negro Café** (604 Ward St., 250/352-7661, www.osonegrocoffee.com, 7am-6pm Mon.-Sat., 8am-4pm Sun., $4-7), serving pastries, paninis, and, of course, coffee in a cozy house with a sunny garden.

With a checkerboard linoleum floor and mauve tables, cheery **Full Circle Café** (101-402 Baker St., 250/354-4458, 6:30am-2:30pm Mon.-Sat., 7am-2pm Sun., $7-17) serves breakfast till early afternoon. It's known for the hash, which comes in Veggie (topped with beet pesto and miso-almond gravy) and Kick Hash

versions, the latter mixing buffalo sausage with eggs, potatoes, peppers, and chipotle hollandaise. The grilled cinnamon buns and the burgers, from beef to buffalo to bean, have fans, too.

Groceries and Markets

For fresh produce, local cheeses, and other groceries, and to pick up that Nelson vibe, wander the aisles at the **Kootenay Co-op** (777 Baker St., 250/354-4077, http://kootenay.coop, 7:30am-9pm daily), the town's local grocery store. The co-op's café makes smoothies and sandwiches, and there's a salad bar, too.

Vendors at the **Nelson Downtown Local Market** (Hall St. at Baker St., 250/354-1909, www.ecosociety.ca, 9:30am-3pm Wed. mid-June-late Sept.) bring fresh produce, crafts, and prepared foods to the downtown streets. To be sold at the market, at least 80 percent of each vendor's wares must be made locally.

Accommodations

Nelson has several moderately priced inns and small hotels around downtown. Even if your lodging doesn't provide parking, you can park on most downtown streets for free between 5pm and 9am.

Under $150

In an older building on downtown's main street, the **Mountain Hound Inn** (621 Baker St., 250/352-6490, www.mountainhound.com, $89-114) has 19 no-frills but comfortable rooms, with private baths, air-conditioning, and flatscreen TVs. The vibe is friendly and hostel-like, although the only common space is the small lobby where a self-serve continental breakfast (muffins, fruit, and coffee or tea) is set up. Many rooms have windows that face an adjacent building, and if cinder block walls give you the

Top to bottom: Nelson Visitor Centre; pizza at Marzano; The Adventure Hotel.

creeps, look elsewhere. Wi-Fi and local calls are included.

Rest up from your adventures at **The Adventure Hotel** (616 Vernon St., 250/352-7211 or 888/722-2258, www. adventurehotel.ca), a vibrantly colored restoration of a historic downtown building. The least expensive of the 44 simple modern units, all with air-conditioning and Wi-Fi included, are the snug **budget rooms** ($95), with steel bunk beds (a double below and a twin above); the baths have a toilet and a sink, but you use the key-accessed shower down the hall. For a private bath, pick the **mid-priced rooms** ($145), with a queen bed or bunks, or the larger **deluxe rooms** ($165). All guests can relax in the 2nd-floor lounge and share the common kitchen, work out in the small gym, or take in the rooftop views on the private deck, which has a sauna. **Louie's Steakhouse, Uptown Sports Bar,** and **Empire Coffee** are all on-site.

$150-300

In a heritage building on a quiet street, the family-run ★ **Cloudside Hotel** (408 Victoria St., 250/352-3226 or 800/596-2337, www.cloudside.ca, $119-299) is both personal and stylish. The eight rooms, all with private baths, are individually furnished with a tasteful mix of modern and traditional pieces, with photos and art pieces from around the globe. One unit, a two-level family suite, has a kitchenette and separate entrance. Guests can hang out on the front porch or the rear sundeck. While there's no breakfast service, rooms have fridges, microwaves, and coffee/tea facilities, and you're a short walk from the town's many cafés.

The operator of Nelson's long-running Shambhala Music Festival rebuilt an aging property into a 12-room, music-filled boutique lodging, the **Savoy Hotel** (198 Baker St., 778/463-0050, www.savoyhotel.ca, $150-280). In addition to the small but smartly appointed guest rooms, with exposed brick walls, steam showers, robes and slippers, and

Nespresso machines, built around a 2nd-floor guest lounge, the property houses **The Falls Music Lounge,** where there's live music several nights a week as well as a tiny craft brewery, and on the lower level, **Bloom Nightclub,** where DJs take the stage Thursday-Saturday. The kid-friendly **Farm Fresh Café** serves breakfast and lunch, with many ingredients sourced from the owner's family farm. On the rooftop deck, soak in the hot tub as you take in views of the lake and surrounding mountains.

The most upscale of Nelson's downtown lodgings is the 45-room **Hume Hotel** (422 Vernon St., 250/352-5331 or 877/568-0888, www.humehotel.com, $139-299), an updated heritage property with a parlor-like lounge, a busy pub, and a small spa. Historic photos decorate the walls, and the classically furnished rooms, while all somewhat different in layout, have white linens, brown upholstery, and dark wood furniture, as well as Keurig coffeemakers and mini fridges. Rates include Wi-Fi, parking, and a hot breakfast in the **General Store Restaurant.**

Information and Services
Visitor Information

Nelson Kootenay Lake Tourism (250/352-7879, www.nelsonkootenaylake.com) produces an area visitors guide, with lots of information on its website.

For in-person assistance, stop into the **Nelson Visitor Centre** (91 Baker St., 250/352-3433 or 877/663-5706, www. discovernelson.com, 8:30am-5pm Mon.-Fri., 10am-4pm Sat.-Sun.), in the former rail station, where you can also pick up an espresso or latte from **Railtown Coffeehouse** (250/551-8965, 6:30am-5pm Mon.-Fri., 8am-2pm Sat.).

Medical Services

Serving the Nelson region, **Kootenay Lake Hospital** (3 View St., 250/352-3111, www.interiorhealth.ca) has 24-hour emergency services.

Vicinity of Nelson

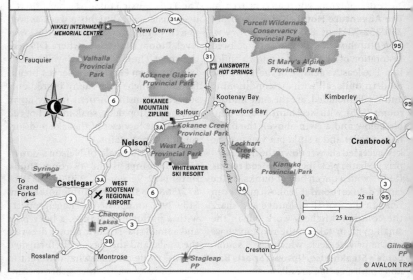

Nelson pharmacies include **Pharmasave** (685 Baker St., 250/352-2316, www.nelsonpharmasave.com, 9am-6pm Mon.-Fri., 9am-5:30pm Sat., 11am-3pm Sun.), **Shoppers Drug Mart** (Chahko Mika Mall, 1116 Lakeside Dr., 250/352-7268, www.shoppersdrugmart.ca, 8am-10pm daily), and **Nelson Remedy's Pharmacy** (737 Baker St., 250/352-6928, www.remedys.ca, 9am-5:30pm Mon.-Fri., 10am-4pm Sat.).

Vicinity of Nelson
★ Ainsworth Hot Springs
One of the best places to relax in the Nelson area is **Ainsworth Hot Springs** (3609 Hwy. 31, Balfour, 250/229-4212 or 800/668-1171, www.ainsworthhotsprings. com, 10am-9pm daily, adults $13, seniors and ages 13-17 $12, ages 3-12 $10, families $40), a natural mineral pool whose unique feature is a softly lit horseshoe-shaped cave where you can soak in secluded nooks. Immersing yourself in the steamy waters of the cave, which average 108°F (42°C), is especially romantic

in the evenings. The springs have a large hot pool as well, kept at a soothing 96°F (35°C). The brave can cool off with a dunk in a bracing plunge pool.

The changing rooms at the springs don't have individual lockers, but for 50 cents, staff provide guests with a large plastic bag for their belongings to check at the front desk. A hotel and restaurant are also on-site.

The hot springs are 30 miles (48 km) northeast of Nelson and 14 miles (22 km) south of Kaslo on Highway 31. If you're coming from eastern B.C., you can travel up the east shore of Kootenay Lake along Highway 3A and take the free ferry across the lake from Kootenay Bay to Balfour; from Creston, at the intersection of Highways 3 and 3A, to the hot springs is 65 miles (105 km).

Kaslo
The pretty village of Kaslo, on the shores of Kootenay Lake, was incorporated in 1893, and many of its buildings date to the Victorian era.

Sights and Recreation

Docked on Kootenay Lake, the **SS *Moyie* National Historic Site** (324 Front St., 250/353-2525, www.klhs.bc.ca, 10am-5pm daily mid-May-mid-Oct., adults $12, seniors and students $10, ages 6-14 $5, families $30) is the world's oldest intact passenger sternwheeler. Built in Nelson in 1898, the ship ferried passengers along Kootenay Lake until 1957. Watch a 10-minute video about the ship and then climb aboard to wander through the dining room, captain's quarters, and wheelhouse. The **Kaslo Visitor Centre** (10am-6pm daily mid-May-mid-Oct.) is near the ship's entrance.

To explore Kootenay Lake from the water, rent a stand-up paddleboard (2 hours $35) or kayak (half day $50) from **Kaslo Kayaking** (315 A Ave., 250/353-1925, www.kaslokayaking.com, 9:30am-6pm daily May-Oct.). It offers guided kayak tours, including a two-hour **sunset paddle** ($69 pp), a half-day **Kootenay Explorer tour** ($149 pp), and the full-day **Adventure Exploration tour** ($209 pp).

For a unique way to experience the outdoors near Kaslo, sign up for an adventure with **Between a Lake and a High Place** (250/353-3049, www.betweenlakeandhighplace.ca, adults $45-120). This experiential tour company offers imaginative guided activities, from an "acoustic walk," where you learn to tune into the sounds of the forest, to picking fruit to benefit a local food recovery program, to capturing the landscapes in a photographic storytelling session. Experiences vary with the seasons, so check the website to see what's happening.

When you're done adventuring, check out local craft beer maker **Angry Hen Brewing** (343 Front St., 250/353-3400, www.angryhenbrewing.com, noon-10pm daily), which has a tasting room and outdoor patio on Kaslo's main street.

Festivals and Events

The annual **Kaslo Jazz Festival** (www.kaslojazzfest.com, Aug.) brings blues, world music, folk, and of course, jazz performers to town for a weekend of outdoor concerts.

Food

With rose-colored walls and wooden tables, homey **BlueBelle Bistro & Beanery** (347 Front St., 250/353-7361, www.bluebellebistro.com, 8:30am-9pm Mon.-Fri., 9am-9pm Sat.-Sun., breakfast $9-15, lunch and dinner $8-19) dishes up simple wholesome meals, from coffee, baked goods, and eggs in the morning to soups, salads, sandwiches, and pizzas later in the day. Try the Bistro Bowl, brown rice mounded with chicken, greens, shredded beets, and other veggies, and save room for a homemade dessert. BlueBelle has live music some evenings.

Kaslo's breakfast destination is **The Treehouse** (419 Front St., 250/353-2955, www.kaslotreehouse.com, 6:30am-3pm Sat.-Thurs., 6:30am-7pm Fri., $5-17), a local diner serving morning meals all day. Eggs Benedict is a specialty, but it also cooks up pancakes, sandwiches, and other home-style dishes.

Accommodations

The **Kaslo Hotel** (430 Front St., 250/353-7714 or 866/823-1433, www.kaslohotel.com, $140-250) was originally built in 1896 when Kaslo was an active mining and logging community. As those industries declined, so, too, did the hotel, which closed in the 1920s. During World War II, the run-down structure housed Japanese Canadian internees who were relocated from the B.C. coast. After the war, the hotel was torn down. Rebuilt in 1958 and later extensively renovated, the Kaslo Hotel has 11 rooms, traditionally furnished, with free Wi-Fi, mini fridges, coffeemakers, and updated baths. Guest rooms on the building's back side, as well as the casual restaurant and pub, look out over Kootenay Lake.

Whether you're attending a wellness retreat or organizing your own Kootenays getaway, consider a stay at ★ **The Sentinel** (5278 Amundsen Rd., 250/353-2246, www.sentinelbc.ca, $165-200), a lodge and retreat center set above Kootenay Lake. Colorful pillows, white linens, and braided rugs furnish the 10 Zen-like rooms. The bathrooms, with lovely tile work, have rain showers and heated floors. Guests can refresh in the outdoor wood-fired sauna, soak in the hot tub on the waterview deck, use the window-lined studio for their own yoga practice, or borrow a kayak or stand-up paddleboard to explore the scenic lake. Rates include Wi-Fi and a generous breakfast with dishes like homemade granola served with thick Greek yogurt, a vegetable frittata paired with sautéed greens from the property's garden, and freshly baked coffee cake, along with espresso, cappuccino, or your choice of teas. This secluded property is off Highway 31, 5 miles (8 km) south of Kaslo and 38 miles (61 km) north of Nelson.

Getting There

Kaslo is on the west shore of Kootenay Lake, off Highway 31. It's 44 miles (70 km) northeast of Nelson and 14 miles (22 km) north of Ainsworth Hot Springs. Between Kaslo and New Denver, it's a scenic 29-mile (46-km) drive through the mountains on Highway 31A.

New Denver

★ **Nikkei Internment Memorial Centre**
During World War II, the Canadian government designated anyone of Japanese descent, whether they were Canadian citizens or not, an "enemy alien." The government created a 100-mile (160-km) exclusion zone on Canada's west coast between the Pacific Ocean and the Coast Mountains, extending south to the U.S.

Top to bottom: Angry Hen Brewing in Kaslo; Kootenay Lake; the outdoor sauna at The Sentinel.

border and north to the Yukon. Anyone of Japanese heritage was prohibited from remaining in this area.

In 1942, the government sent more than 22,000 Japanese Canadians, many of whom had lived in Vancouver or surrounding coastal communities, to internment camps in British Columbia's Kootenay and eastern mountain regions. One such camp, known as The Orchard, was set up in the tiny town of New Denver, north of Nelson along Slocan Lake.

When you walk through the gates of what is now the **Nikkei Internment Memorial Centre** (306 Josephine St., 250/358-7288, www.newdenver.ca/ nikkei, 10am-5pm daily May-Sept., adults $9, seniors and students $7, families $20), a National Historic Site of Canada, you're entering that former camp, which retains several original buildings. Walk into a 1940s-era 14- by 28-foot (4.25- by 8.5-m) shack that would have housed two families with up to six children each; The Orchard had roughly 200 of these rudimentary dwellings. Check out the outdoor latrine that would have served up to 50 people. Kyowakai Hall, built in 1943 as a bathhouse but used as a community hall for camp residents, is now a museum about Japanese Canadian history before, during, and after the internment period.

Also at the site is the **Heiwa Teien Peace Garden,** which Japanese Canadian master gardener Roy Tomomichi Sumi designed. Sumi, who was interned at the Rosebery camp north of New Denver, worked at Vancouver's Nitobe Japanese Garden at the University of British Columbia.

After the war, most interned Japanese Canadians were given the choice of moving east of the Rockies or returning to Japan; they were forbidden to return to the coast until 1949. Nearly all the internment camps were razed, but New Denver was an exception. Retained as a treatment facility for residents with tuberculosis, a number of the camp's buildings were preserved. In 1957, the B.C. government deeded the remaining shacks at The Orchard to their Japanese Canadian residents. One of these shacks, still on the property, was occupied until the 1980s.

Other Sights

On Slocan Lake, wander the peaceful paths of the **Kohan Reflection Garden** (1st Ave., www.newdenver.ca, dawn-dusk daily, donation), a small Japanese-style garden that local community members created in 1989 to honor Japanese Canadians who were forcibly relocated to New Denver during World War II.

You could spend hours reading interviews with local residents compiled in books at the **Silvery Slocan Museum** (202 6th Ave., 250/358-2201, www.newdenver. ca, 10am-2pm Sat.-Sun. late May-June, 9am-4pm daily July-early Sept., adults and over age 11 $4, families $8), New Denver's community history museum, which is packed with artifacts and details from the area's past. Old musical instruments, stained glass from a local church, even an iron lung that had belonged to the local hospital are on view, as are belongings from the local Japanese community. The museum is inside the 1887 former Bank of Montreal building, used as a bank until 1969; you can peek into the vault or peruse the old ledgers. The museum also houses the **New Denver Visitor Centre** (250/358-2719, www. slocanlake.com), open during museum hours.

Getting There

You can visit New Denver on a day trip from Nelson or as part of a Nelson-Kaslo-New Denver loop through the Kootenay Lakes region.

New Denver is 60 miles (97 km) north of Nelson via Highway 6. From Kaslo, follow Highway 31A west for 29 miles (46 km). From Revelstoke, which is 95 miles (150 km) north of New Denver, take Highway 23 south to Highway 6.

Who Are the Doukhobors?

Traveling along Highway 3 through southern British Columbia, you might not expect to find communities that trace their ancestry back to Russia's Caucasus Mountains. Pull over to learn more about the Doukhobors.

In the 1700s, a Christian sect split from the Russian Orthodox Church, seeking a simpler form of worship and a more personal connection to God. A Russian Orthodox archbishop dubbed these dissidents *doukhoborsti*, meaning "spirit wrestlers," which he intended as a derogatory term. However, the community adopted the Doukhobor name (pronounced DUKE-oh-bor), saying that they were wrestling both "with and for the spirit of God."

The Doukhobors became pacifists, and in a dramatic 1895 act, 7,000 Doukhobor soldiers burned all their weapons. Doukhobor men refused to join the army, and most of the community adopted a vegetarian diet, with bread and borscht (a vegetable soup) as their staple foods. Doukhobor borscht differs from its Russian counterpart, which is a meat-based beet soup; the Doukhobors make their version from cabbage, potatoes, onions, and tomatoes, with one beet to provide color.

Both the czarist government and the Russian Orthodox Church opposed the Doukhobors' beliefs, and many Doukhobors were persecuted, exiled from their communities, and tortured. Their plight attracted attention from the Quakers and from author Leo Tolstoy, who became a patron of the community, raising funds that enabled 7,500 Doukhobors to leave Russia and immigrate to Canada in 1899, where most settled in Saskatchewan and established communal villages.

Still seeking to live their motto of "toil and peaceful life," many Doukhobors began migrating again in 1908-1910, leaving Saskatchewan for British Columbia's Kootenay region, where most took up residence in and around the communities of Castlegar and Grand Forks. Descendants of these early settlers still live in southern B.C.

Castlegar

In the early 1900s, members of a pacifist religious community who had emigrated from Russia settled in B.C.'s West Kootenays. Known as the Doukhobors, from a Russian word meaning "spirit wrestlers," many made their home in the town of Castlegar, where you can learn more about the Doukhobors' legacy.

Located 28 miles (45 km) southwest of Nelson and 80 miles (130 km) west of Creston, at the intersection of Highways 3 and 6, Castlegar is an easy stop while traveling Highway 3 across southern B.C. It's 135 miles (220 km) east of Osoyoos.

Sights

Built in 1969 to preserve the Doukhobors' heritage in the Castlegar area, **Doukhobor Discovery Centre** (112 Heritage Way, 250/365-5327, www.doukhobor-museum. org, 10am-5pm Mon.-Sat., noon-5pm Sun. May-Sept., adults $10, seniors $8, students $5) illustrates how the community lived in the early 1900s. While most of the solid brick buildings aren't original, they represent the types of structures that the Doukhobors would have built. You can wander into the worship room stocked with bread, salt, and water (the three elements that the Doukhobors felt were necessary for survival), the communal kitchen, the *banya* (sauna and bathhouse), and the blacksmith shop, where craftsmen would have made spike-bottomed winter boots as well as rakes and other tools. Take time to chat with the guides who can explain more about Doukhobor history, life, and culture.

Another legacy of Castlegar's Doukhobor community is the **Brilliant Suspension Bridge** (Brilliant Rd.) that a group of roughly 100 Doukhobor men constructed over the Kootenay River in 1913, using traditional hand tools and construction methods. A wooden bridge supported by concrete towers, it's 331 feet (100 m) long. Designed by Vancouver engineer J. R. Grant, who later designed that city's Burrard Bridge (1932), the bridge, now a National Historic Site, is still standing, off Highway 3A at Robinson Road, and you can walk across it to take in the river views. It's no longer used as a transportation route, however; a new highway bridge replaced it in 1966.

Rossland

Surrounded by the Monashee and Selkirk Mountains, Rossland, with a population of 3,500, has been known primarily as a winter destination for skiing and snowboarding at its RED Mountain Resort. Yet hikers and mountain bikers are discovering this scenic setting in the warmer months, and a recently opened boutique hotel is luring road-trippers off the highway.

Rossland is a short detour off Highway 3, 22 miles (35 km) south of Castlegar and 137 miles (220 km) east of Osoyoos. If you're coming from the east, take Highway 3B toward Trail, then Highway 22 into Rossland. From the west, follow Highway 3B south into town.

Sports and Recreation

You don't have to go far from town to find forested hiking and mountain biking trails. Hike up the moderate **Kootenay-Columbia Trail** for views over Rossland, the nearby valley, and the surrounding mountains; the trailhead is off Kirkup Avenue just north of downtown. For more options, plus trail descriptions and maps, check the website for the nonprofit **Kootenay Columbia Trails Society** (www. kcts.ca), which manages more than 50 individual trails and 100 miles (160 km) of single-track mountain biking routes throughout the Rossland region.

Serious mountain bikers tackle the 22-mile (35-km) **Seven Summits Trail,** a challenging point-to-point route with 5,000 feet (1,525 m) of vertical ascent and 7,000 feet (2,100 m) of vertical descent

across the Rossland Range. The trail is typically snow-free July-September. **Kootenay Gateway** (2118 Columbia Ave., 250/362-0080, www.kootenaygateway. com, 10am-5:30pm Mon.-Fri., 9am-5pm Sat.) provides trail advice, guided rides, and shuttle services for cyclists. **Revolution Cycles** (1990A Columbia Ave., 250/362-5688, www.revolutioncycles.ca, 10am-5:30pm Mon.-Fri., 9am-5:30pm Sat., full-day $40-100) rents bikes and provides maps of local trails.

For downhill skiing and snowboarding, **RED Mountain Resort** (4300 Red Mountain Rd., 250/362-7384 or 800/663-0105, www.redresort.com, early Dec.-March, full-day adults $96, seniors $67, ages 13-18 $77, ages 7-12 $48) challenges winter sports enthusiasts with its network of 110 runs, 51 percent of which are rated advanced or expert. In summer, you can hike or mountain bike some of the resort's trails, although there's currently no lift access to the upper terrain. The resort's **Get Lost Adventure Centre** (778/457-5001) can help arrange outdoor activities, from hiking to fishing to cave tours, at the resort and around the region.

Food

In a former gas station, **Fuel Gastropub and Diner** (1890 Columbia Ave., 250/362-2254, 8am-10pm Mon.-Thurs., 8am-11pm Fri.-Sat., 8am-9pm Sun., breakfast and lunch $10-21, dinner $19-32) serves straight-up fresh fare all day. You can start the morning with a selection of egg dishes, vegetable hash, or breakfast sandwiches like the Anthony Bourdain (eggs, bacon, sausage, cheddar cheese, hash, and horseradish mayo all stuffed into a brioche bun). At lunch and dinner, look for souvlaki, burgers, and pastas. Try the Massaman red curry power bowl with crisp cauliflower or sautéed chicken and a colorful assortment of vegetables piled over miso-flavored barley.

Both locals and visitors hang out at **Alpine Grind Coffeehouse** (2104 Columbia Ave., 250/362-2280, www.

Rest Stop: Canada's Smallest City

Blink and you'll miss it: Highway 3 between the West Kootenays and the Okanagan runs directly through **Greenwood, B.C.,** Canada's smallest incorporated municipality.

Established in 1897, this hamlet of fewer than 700 people has some of the region's best-preserved heritage buildings. Stop into the **Greenwood Museum and Visitor Centre** (214 S. Copper Ave./Hwy. 3, 250/445-6355, www.greenwoodmuseum.com, 10am-4pm daily May-June, 9am-5pm daily July-Aug., 10am-4pm daily Sept.-Oct., by appointment Nov.-Apr., adults $5, ages 7-19 $2), with exhibits about local history, and ask for the free pamphlet outlining a short walking tour of the town's historic structures, including the 1903 city hall, 1915 post office, and 1899 saloon. You can also download walking tour details from the website.

For a coffee break, **Copper Eagle Cappuccino & Bakery** (325 S. Copper Ave./Hwy. 3, 250/445-6121, 6am-4pm daily), in an 1899 brick building along Greenwood's main street, makes a variety of java drinks, along with soups, sandwiches, and cinnamon buns and other sweets. The butter tarts have legions of fans.

alpinegrindcoffee.com, 7am-5pm Mon.-Fri., 8am-4pm Sat.-Sun., $6-12) for coffee, pastries, and light meals, from homemade soup to panini.

Accommodations

On the town's main street, **Prestige Mountain Resort** (1919 Columbia Ave., 250/362-7375 or 877/737-8443, www.prestigehotelsandresorts.com, $200-270) is a mid-range option with 67 rooms, complimentary cruiser bikes, and a hot tub. For condo rentals and other on-mountain accommodations, contact **RED Mountain Resort** (250/362-5553 or 877/969-7669, www.redresort.com).

Opened in 2018 at the base of RED Mountain, **The Josie Hotel** (4306 Red Mountain Rd., 250/362-5155 or 888/915-6743, www.thejosie.com, $175-440) is a boutique ski-in, ski-out lodging that's open year-round for luxury adventurers. A neutral palette of cream, brown, and gold makes the 106 guest rooms, studios, and one-bedroom suites feel like serene hideaways. The larger units have spacious baths with soaker tubs. The concierge team can take care of your ski gear or help you plan other experiences. In a window-lined space anchored by a central bar and a slopeside patio, **The Velvet Restaurant and Lounge** serves

contemporary cuisine for breakfast, lunch, après-ski, and dinner.

Also opened in 2018, and a short walk from the lifts, **HI-RED Mountain Nowhere Special** (4255 Red Mountain Rd., 250/362-5553 or 877/969-7669, www.nowherespecialhostel.com, $47-52 dorm, $140-175 d) is a modern year-round hostel, with four-bed dorms, private rooms with en suite baths, and quad or family rooms, also with private baths. A contemporary communal kitchen, included Wi-Fi, and laundry facilities are among the amenities.

Information and Services

For more information about the Rossland region, contact **Tourism Rossland** (250/921-4892, www.tourismrossland.com).

In winter, **Queen City Shuttles** (250/352-9829, www.kootenayshuttle.com, $115 pp) take skiers to RED Mountain Resort from Washington's **Spokane International Airport** (GEG, 9000 W. Airport Dr., Spokane, 509/455-6455, www.spokaneairports.net), which is 125 miles (200 km) south of Rossland. **Mountain Shuttle** (250/362-0080, www.mountainshuttle.ca, $69 pp) operates winter shuttles to Rossland from the small **Trail Regional Airport** (YZZ,

800/663-2872, www.trail.ca), 12.5 miles (20 km) to the east.

Grand Forks

Like Castlegar, the town of Grand Forks drew Doukhobor settlers, with most arriving between 1909 and 1913.

Grand Forks is just north of the Washington border, 60 miles (97 km) west of Castlegar and 80 miles (130 km) east of Osoyoos on Highway 3.

Sights

In a historic brick schoolhouse on the west side of Grand Forks, the **Boundary Museum and Interpretive Centre** (6145 Reservoir Rd., 250/442-3737, www.boundarymuseum.com, 10am-4pm Tues.-Sat. early May-early Sept., 10am-4pm Tues.-Fri. early Sept.-early May, adults $5, children $2) has exhibits and artifacts about local history, including its mining and forestry heritage, and about the Doukhobor community. The Doukhobors constructed the building, now called the Fructova Heritage Site, in 1929, and it served as a community school until the 1940s. June-early September, you can watch bread-baking demonstrations (11am Thurs.), where volunteers use locally milled Pride of the Valley Flour and traditional outdoor ovens.

That local flour comes from the **Grand Forks Doukhobor Heritage Mill** (3620 Mill Rd., 250/442-8252, www.usccdoukhobors.org, 10am-4pm Tues.-Sat. early May-Aug.), originally a steam-powered stone-grinding mill that operated between 1915 and 1945. Reconstructed in the 1960s by a cooperative milling society, the mill continues to produce unbleached white, whole wheat, rye, and other flours, which is sold throughout the West Kootenay region. You can normally tour the historic mill, although it closed for upgrades in 2018; call before visiting.

Near the mill is a **Doukhobor cemetery** (Cemetery Frontage Rd.), where graves date back to the early 1900s. The cemetery is still in use today.

Food

If you've been learning about Doukhobor culture, you may want to tuck into a hearty Doukhobor lunch. **The Borscht Bowl** (214 Market Ave., 250/442-5977, 10am-4pm Mon.-Sat., $4-14), in downtown Grand Forks, serves traditional Doukhobor dishes, including *pyrahi* (a savory baked turnover stuffed with potatoes, spinach, or cheese), *voreniki* (filled dumplings similar to pierogi), and *nalesniki* (crepes). The tasty borscht is Doukhobor-style, with cabbage, tomato, and a little beet for color.

The
Okanagan

The Okanagan

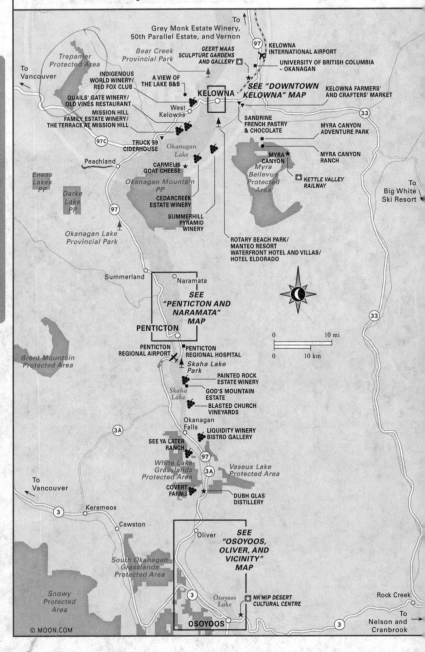

To Grey Monk Estate Winery, 50th Parallel Estate, and Vernon

97 KELOWNA INTERNATIONAL AIRPORT

UNIVERSITY OF BRITISH COLUMBIA – OKANAGAN

Trepanier Protected Area

Bear Creek Provincial Park

GEERT MAAS SCULPTURE GARDENS AND GALLERY

SEE "DOWNTOWN KELOWNA" MAP

KELOWNA FARMERS' AND CRAFTERS' MARKET

To Vancouver

INDIGENOUS WORLD WINERY/ RED FOX CLUB

A VIEW OF THE LAKE B&B

KELOWNA

QUAILS' GATE WINERY/ OLD VINES RESTAURANT

MISSION HILL FAMILY ESTATE WINERY/ THE TERRACE AT MISSION HILL

West Kelowna

SANDRINE FRENCH PASTRY & CHOCOLATE

33

MYRA CANYON ADVENTURE PARK

97C

TRUCK 59 CIDERHOUSE

Okanagan Lake

MYRA

MYRA CANYON RANCH

Peachland

CARMELIS GOAT CHEESE

Myra Bellevue Protected Area

KETTLE VALLEY RAILWAY

Eneas Lakes PP

Darke Lake PP

Okanagan Mountain PP

CEDARCREEK ESTATE WINERY

97

SUMMERHILL PYRAMID WINERY

Okanagan Lake Provincial Park

ROTARY BEACH PARK/ MANTEO RESORT WATERFRONT HOTEL AND VILLAS/ HOTEL ELDORADO

To Big White Ski Resort

Summerland

Naramata

SEE "PENTICTON AND NARAMATA" MAP

33

PENTICTON

0   10 mi
0   10 km

PENTICTON REGIONAL AIRPORT

PENTICTON REGIONAL HOSPITAL

Brent Mountain Protected Area

Skaha Lake Park

PAINTED ROCK ESTATE WINERY

Skaha Lake

GOD'S MOUNTAIN ESTATE

BLASTED CHURCH VINEYARDS

Okanagan Falls

3A

LIQUIDITY WINERY BISTRO GALLERY

SEE YA LATER RANCH

97

White Lake Grasslands Protected Area

3A

Vaseux Lake Protected Area

To Vancouver

COVERT FARMS

DUBH GLAS DISTILLERY

3

Keremeos

Cawston

South Okanagan Grasslands Protected Area

Oliver

SEE "OSOYOOS, OLIVER, AND VICINITY" MAP

Snowy Protected Area

3

Osoyoos Lake

NK'MIP DESERT CULTURAL CENTRE

Rock Creek

To Nelson and Cranbrook

OSOYOOS

3

© MOON.COM

Highlights

★ **Wineries:** You've got more than 200 wineries to sample in British Columbia's "Napa of the North," making wine-touring and tasting the centerpiece of an Okanagan stay (pages 366, 379, and 385).

★ **Geert Maas Sculpture Gardens and Gallery:** One of Kelowna's most unexpected attractions is this gallery and sculpture garden that the artist and his wife created at their rural home (page 370).

★ **Kettle Valley Railway:** This former rail line is now a cycling and walking path that stretches across the Okanagan and beyond. An especially scenic section near Kelowna crosses 18 historic trestle bridges high above Myra Canyon (page 371).

★ **Okanagan Wine Festivals:** Several times a year, the region celebrates its wine industry with tastings, dinners, and other special events (page 373).

★ **Nk'Mip Desert Cultural Centre:** The Okanagan includes Canada's only desert, which you can explore at this First Nations cultural center in Osoyoos (page 390).

Stop off for a wine tour or sunny lakeside detour in one of Canada's most popular wine-producing districts, often called the "Napa of the North."

Located in central B.C. along a chain of lakes, the Okanagan has become one of Canada's largest wine-producing districts. The weather changes dramatically when you approach the region, whether you're climbing over the Coast Mountains from Vancouver or crossing the Columbia Range from eastern British Columbia. Either way, you leave behind the rainforests and mountain passes as you descend into this sunny agricultural valley.

As wine regions go, the Okanagan is a youngster. It's been a fertile fruit-growing area for decades, producing peaches, apples, cherries, and more, but it wasn't until the 1980s that the modern wine industry took hold in earnest.

Now, more than 200 wineries hug the lakeshores and rocky hills between Osoyoos, in the desertlike lands near the U.S. border, and Kelowna, around the slightly cooler-climate growing areas to the north. The Okanagan makes a relaxing long-weekend getaway from Vancouver or road-trip stopover between the Rockies and the coast.

Getting to the Okanagan

Driving from Vancouver

From Vancouver to the Okanagan, the route you take will depend on which part of the wine region you're visiting. For all areas, leave the city via **Highway 1** and head east to **Hope.**

To Kelowna

To Kelowna, continue east at Hope onto **Highway 3,** then exit onto **Highway 5 (Coquihalla Hwy.)** north. Follow the Coquihalla over the mountains to **Merritt.** Exit onto **Highway 97C,** which becomes the Okanagan Connector. Stay on **Highway 97** north into Kelowna. Allow **4-4.5 hours** for this **245-mile (395-km)** drive.

To Penticton and Naramata

To the Penticton and Naramata area, the shortest route is to follow the **Coquihalla Highway** toward **Kelowna,** but when **Highway 97C** meets **Highway 97,** turn south and continue past Peachland and Summerland to Penticton. Because Naramata is on Okanagan Lake's eastern shore, you have to go into Penticton, skirt the lakeshore, and turn north on Naramata Road to reach Naramata. It's about **4.5 hours** from Vancouver to **Penticton (260 mi/420 km)** and another **20 minutes** to **Naramata.**

To Osoyoos

If you're traveling to Osoyoos, Oliver, and the South Okanagan, follow **Highway 3** east from Hope, which meanders over the mountains and through the Similkameen Valley to Osoyoos. This **250-mile (405-km)** drive from Vancouver takes **4.5-5 hours.** Oliver is 12.5 miles (20 km) north of Osoyoos along Highway 97.

Driving from Kamloops
To Kelowna

Driving from Kamloops to Kelowna, you have two options: Follow **Highway 5** south to **Merritt** and pick up **Highway 97C;** this route is **130 miles (210 km)** and takes you through some beautifully remote ranchlands. Or take **Highway 97** south; it's a **105-mile (169-km)** drive that follows some scenic stretches of lakeshore. The Merritt route is longer, but the roads are faster. Either option will take about **2.5 hours.**

To Osoyoos

To get from Kamloops to Osoyoos, follow the directions to **Kelowna** and

Best Accommodations

★ **A View of the Lake B&B:** This West Kelowna bed-and-breakfast lives up to its name, with great views over Okanagan Lake. The welcoming hosts (including a professional chef) are known for their morning meals (page 376).

★ **Hotel Zed:** Popping with color inside and out, this funky retro motel in downtown Kelowna offers entertaining amenities, from bikes and roller skates to a rooftop lounge (page 376).

★ **Delta Hotels by Marriott Grand Okanagan Resort:** Combining urban and holiday pleasures, this large lakefront property has an indoor-outdoor pool, lots of activities, and a range of accommodations, all just a short stroll from downtown Kelowna (page 377).

★ **Watermark Beach Resort:** On Lake Osoyoos, this condo-style resort has everything you need for a lakeside getaway, from comfortable condos to a lakeview dining room (page 395).

★ **The Guest House at Burrowing Owl Estate Winery:** This upscale winery inn with a solar-heated pool and excellent restaurant makes a romantic escape (page 395).

continue south to Penticton, Oliver, and Osoyoos on **Highway 97.** The drive from Kamloops to Osoyoos is **180 miles (290 km)** and takes **3.75-4 hours.**

If you're driving between Kamloops and Osoyoos and you don't want to meander through the Okanagan Valley, take **Highway 5** south to **Merritt,** then **Highway 5A** south to Princeton. At **Princeton,** follow **Highway 3** east to Osoyoos. This route is **180 miles (290 km)** and takes **3.5 hours.**

Driving from Banff

From Banff and the Canadian Rockies to the Okanagan, the best route depends on where in the Okanagan you're heading and what you'd like to see en route.

To Kelowna

The most direct route between Banff and Kelowna is **Highway 1,** which travels west from Banff through the B.C. Rockies to **Sicamous.** There, head south on **Highway 97A** and continue south on **Highway 97** into Kelowna. It's **300 miles (485 km),** a **5.5- to 6-hour** drive.

To Osoyoos

To get from Banff to Osoyoos, follow the directions to **Kelowna** and stay on **Highway 97** south to Penticton, Oliver, and Osoyoos. This Banff-Osoyoos route via Highway 1 and Highway 97 is a **375-mile (605-km)** drive that takes **7.5 hours.**

An alternate route between Banff and Osoyoos takes you **through the Kootenays** region. Leaving Banff on **Highway 1** west, turn south onto **Highway 93** toward **Radium Hot Springs.** Continue following **Highway 93/95** south from Radium Hot Springs beyond Cranbrook to **Highway 3.** Take Highway 3 west to Osoyoos. This Banff-Osoyoos route is a **450-mile (725-km)** trip; it takes **nine hours.**

Getting There by Air
By Air

The Okanagan's main commercial airport is **Kelowna International Airport** (YLW, 5533 Airport Way, Kelowna, 250/807-4300, http://ylw.kelowna.ca), which has regular flights from Vancouver, Victoria, Calgary, Edmonton, Toronto, Seattle, and

Best Restaurants

★ **The Terrace at Mission Hill:** At one of the Okanagan's grandest wineries, this contemporary West Kelowna restaurant on an outdoor patio is among the region's most scenic dining spots (page 373).

★ **Waterfront Wines Restaurant:** Long considered one of Kelowna's top dining destinations, this lively contemporary restaurant works its magic, whether you park at the bar for wine and small plates, or settle in for an inventive multicourse meal (page 374).

★ **Vice & Virtue Brewing Co.:** You might not expect a brewpub to serve particularly imaginative food, but this Kelowna craft brewery challenges that expectation—deliciously (page 374).

★ **RauDZ Regional Table:** This downtown Kelowna bistro sets a relaxed vibe with a long list of Okanagan wines and plates piled high with ingredients from around the region (page 375).

★ **The Bench Artisan Food Market:** You can get breakfast all day, espresso and pastries, or picnic fixings at this Penticton foodie destination that's part café and part gourmet grocery (page 383).

★ **The Sonora Room:** Excellent food, polished service, and a panoramic vista over the Black Sage Bench make this restaurant at Burrowing Owl Estate Winery a must-visit (page 393).

★ **Terrafina Restaurant:** At Oliver's Hester Creek Winery, this restaurant serves inventive Italian fare made from local products (page 393).

★ **Liquidity Bistro:** In an art-filled, window-lined space at Liquidity Wines in Okanagan Falls, the kitchen turns out some of the region's most inventive dishes (page 393).

Phoenix. **Air Canada** (www.aircanada. com) and **WestJet** (www.westjet.com) are the airport's main carriers; **Alaska Airlines** (www.alaskaair.com) operates the Kelowna-Seattle route. Canadian discount carrier **Flair Airlines** (204/888-2665, www.flairair.ca) connects Kelowna and Edmonton. The airport is 9 miles (14 km) north of the city center along Highway 97.

Car rental companies operating at the Kelowna airport include **Avis** (250/491-9500, www.avis.com), **Budget** (250/491-7368, www.bcbudget.com), **Enterprise** (250/491-9611, www.enterprise.com), and **Hertz** (250/491-8939, www.hertz.ca).

Once you've arrived at the Kelowna airport, it's possible on weekdays to get to the city center by public transit. **B.C.** **Transit bus 23** (250/860-8121, www. bctransit.com/kelowna, $2.50) stops at the airport 6am-6:30pm Monday-Friday; however, it doesn't go directly downtown. To travel between the airport and downtown Kelowna, take **bus 23** south to the UBCO Transit Exchange (at the University of British Columbia-Okanagan) and transfer to **bus 97.**

Another option for getting to the Okanagan by air is to fly to the small **Penticton Regional Airport** (YYF, 3000 Airport Rd., Penticton, 250/770-4422, www.cyyf.ca). **Air Canada** (www. aircanada.com) has daily flights to Penticton from Vancouver. **WestJet** (www.westjet.com) flies between Penticton and Calgary.

Planning an Okanagan Wine Tour

Do Some Research (or Just Explore)

The **British Columbia Wine Institute** (www.winebc.com) has an excellent website about wineries in the Okanagan and elsewhere in the province. If you're stopping in Penticton, the staff at the **B.C. VQA Wine Information Centre** (553 Vees Dr., 250/490-2006, www.pentictonwineinfo.com), which is also a wine shop, can tell you about local wineries. But there's no harm in stopping wherever a winery catches your fancy.

Focus Your Travels

Because the Okanagan covers a large region, 75 meandering miles (120 km) between Osoyoos and Kelowna, consider picking one or two areas to explore. You'll spend less time traveling around and get to know an area in depth.

In the South Okanagan, around **Osoyoos** and **Oliver,** the warmer, desertlike climate means longer-ripening grapes such as cabernet franc, cabernet sauvignon, merlot, and syrah grow well, as do chardonnay, gewürztraminer, and pinot gris. In the slightly cooler areas around **Penticton** and **Naramata,** chardonnay, pinot gris, and merlot are among the most popular grapes, while farther north, the **Kelowna** region—cooler still—has some of the Okanagan's oldest vineyards and is well-suited to growing pinot noir, as well as whites like riesling, pinot gris, chardonnay, and gewürztraminer.

While Kelowna is more urban, with a wider choice of restaurants and activities, the Penticton/Naramata and Oliver/Osoyoos areas offer more outdoor attractions.

Taste Large and Small

Visit a mix of larger producers and smaller family-run wineries. Larger facilities typically offer tours, while the smaller spots give you a more personal experience. Most wineries charge a small fee for tastings, which they'll typically refund if you make a purchase.

Include Beer or Spirits

While wine is the Okanagan Valley's major liquid asset, you'll find a growing number of craft distilleries, ciderhouses, and microbreweries as well. Consider balancing your wine-tasting with a beer-sampling, cider-tasting, or distillery tour.

Break It Up

Take time out for your wine-tasting for other activities. Go cycling, hiking, or swimming. Explore the desert, or stop at a fruit stand. Tour an art gallery, or visit a cheesemaker. Or simply enjoy the views across the lakes.

Designate a Driver

Limit your tasting, "sip and spit," or make sure one member of your party is the designated driver. Alternatively, book a wine tour that includes transportation. Local wine tour companies include **Discover Okanagan Wine Tours** (250/763-1161, www.discoverokanagantours.com, $80-125 pp), **Distinctly Kelowna Tours** (250/979-1211 or 866/979-1211, www.distinctlykelownatours.ca, $105-155 pp), **Roots & Vines Tour Co.** (250/868-0611 or 844/868-0611, www.rootsandvinestours.com, $105-155 pp), **Uncorked Okanagan Wine Tours** (250/769-3123, www.uncorkedokanagan.com, $99-199), and **Wine Away Tours** (604/316-8799, www.wineawaytours.ca, $60-80 pp).

Another enjoyable way to tour area wineries is by bicycle. Kelowna's **Monashee Adventure Tours** (250/878-3587, www.monasheeadventuretours.com) offers a number of different sip-and-cycle tours. In the South Okanagan, **Heatstroke Cycle and Sport** (778/437-2453, www.heatstrokecycle.comm $50-225 pp) runs cycling tours to the wineries along the Black Sage Bench and the Golden Mile.

For more recommended wine tour companies, see the **Tourism Kelowna** website (www.tourismkelowna.com) or talk to the staff at area visitors centers.

GETTING TO THE OKANAGAN

Kelowna and Vicinity

The largest city in the Okanagan, Kelowna has an enviable location directly on Okanagan Lake. The city's revitalized downtown district borders its beautiful park-lined waterfront, while orchards, wineries, and forests fill its surrounding rural districts. Alas, like many growing communities, Kelowna has plenty of not-so-bucolic suburban sprawl in between.

Because it's centrally located, Kelowna (population 129,500) makes a convenient stopover between Vancouver and the Canadian Rockies. You can tour numerous wineries, breweries, and distilleries, explore local cheesemakers, and go cycling along the lake or through the desert hills, before returning to the city for a first-rate meal. While some parts of Kelowna may not be as "resort pretty" as other areas of the Okanagan, you won't lack for things to do.

★ Wineries

Kelowna's wineries are concentrated in several different areas: south of the city's downtown on the east side of Okanagan Lake, on the lake's west shore, and north of Kelowna in the district known as Lake Country.

You don't have to leave central Kelowna for wine-tasting, though. **Sandhill Wines** (1125 Richter St., 250/762-9144 or 888/246-4472, www.sandhillwines.ca, 10am-6pm daily June-Oct., 10am-5pm Mon.-Sat., 10am-4pm Sun. Nov.-May, tastings $4-10) has a tasting room in the city's North End, 1 mile (1.6 km) from downtown.

Eastside Wineries

After releasing its first wines in 1987, long-established **CedarCreek Estate Winery** (5445 Lakeshore Rd., 778/738-1027, www.cedarcreek.bc.ca, 11am-7pm daily May-June, 10am-7pm daily July-Sept., 11am-5pm daily Oct.-Apr., tastings $8, tours 11am and 1pm daily May-mid.-Oct., $15-20) now produces a lengthy catalogue of wine, including riesling, gewürztraminer, ehrenfelser, chardonnay, pinot gris, merlot, meritage, syrah, and pinot noir, which you can sample year-round in the tasting room.

Summerhill Pyramid Winery (4870 Chute Lake Rd., 250/764-8000 or 800/667-3538, www.summerhill.bc.ca, 10am-6pm daily, tours 2pm Thurs.-Sun., tastings and tours free) produces organic wines that it ages in, yes, its own pyramid. On the complimentary 45-minute Pyramid Experience Tour, you'll learn about organic wine production and the history and significance of the unusual pyramid. The winery's **Sunset Organic Bistro** (11am-9pm daily) uses ingredients from its biodynamic gardens and local organic farms in the contemporary dishes.

Westside Wineries

Among the grandest of the Okanagan wineries, **Mission Hill Family Estate** (1730 Mission Hill Rd., West Kelowna, general information 250/768-6448, tours 250/768-6483, www.missionhillwinery.com, check the website or call for seasonal hours, tastings typically $5) welcomes guests through an imposing archway into a courtyard where a 12-story bell tower stands. From here, make your way to the wine shop where tastings are offered daily, or meet in the Wine Education Centre for one of several 45- to 60-minute **tours** ($20-35 pp). The winery hosts summer concerts in its outdoor amphitheater and offers culinary workshops and wine dinners throughout the year. **The Terrace** (11:30am-3pm and 5pm-8pm daily mid-May-mid-Oct.), with vistas across the vineyards, is among the region's most scenic dining destinations.

Most winery tours aren't geared for kids, but at **Quails' Gate Winery** (3303 Boucherie Rd., West Kelowna, 250/769-4451 or 800/420-9463, www.quailsgate.com, 9:30am-8pm daily late June-early Sept., 10am-7pm daily May-late June and

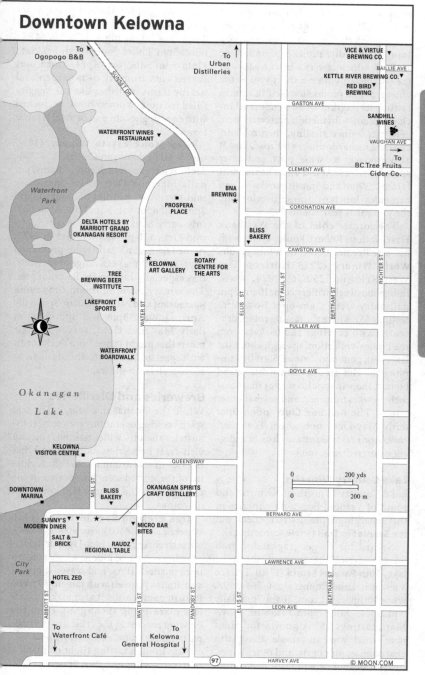

Downtown Kelowna

To Ogopogo B&B

SUNSET DR.

To Urban Distilleries

VICE & VIRTUE BREWING CO.

BAILLIE AVE

KETTLE RIVER BREWING CO.

RED BIRD BREWING

GASTON AVE

SANDHILL WINES

VAUGHAN AVE

To BC Tree Fruits Cider Co.

CLEMENT AVE

WATERFRONT WINES RESTAURANT

Waterfront Park

BNA BREWING

PROSPERA PLACE

CORONATION AVE

BLISS BAKERY

DELTA HOTELS BY MARRIOTT GRAND OKANAGAN RESORT

CAWSTON AVE

KELOWNA ART GALLERY

ROTARY CENTRE FOR THE ARTS

RICHTER ST.

TREE BREWING BEER INSTITUTE

LAKEFRONT SPORTS

WATER ST.

ELLIS ST.

ST. PAUL ST.

BERTRAM ST.

FULLER AVE

WATERFRONT BOARDWALK

DOYLE AVE

Okanagan Lake

KELOWNA VISITOR CENTRE

QUEENSWAY

0   200 yds

0   200 m

DOWNTOWN MARINA

MILL ST.

BLISS BAKERY

OKANAGAN SPIRITS CRAFT DISTILLERY

BERNARD AVE

SUNNY'S MODERN DINER

SALT & BRICK

RAUDZ REGIONAL TABLE

MICRO BAR BITES

LAWRENCE AVE

City Park

HOTEL ZED

ABBOTT ST.

WATER ST.

PANDOSY ST.

ELLIS ST.

BERTRAM ST.

LEON AVE

To Waterfront Café

To Kelowna General Hospital

97

HARVEY AVE

© MOON.COM

early Sept.-mid-Oct., 10am-6pm daily mid-Oct.-Apr., tastings $5), all ages are welcome on the one-hour **family winery tour** (11am daily, adults $15, under age 19 free), which covers a brief history of the Okanagan Valley, a short visit to the vineyards and production facilities, and a tasting. Its flagship Quails' Gate label includes pinot noir, merlot, marechal foch, gewürztraminer, riesling, chenin blanc, chasselas, chardonnay, and rosé, and it also produces ice wine, port, and other specialty wines. At **Old Vines Restaurant** (11am-2:30pm and 5pm-10pm daily), you can enjoy lunch or dinner overlooking the vineyards year-round.

The former chief of the Westbank First Nation, Robert Louie, along with his wife Bernice Louie, own **Indigenous World Winery** (2218 Horizon Dr., West Kelowna, 250/769-2824, www.indigenousworldwinery.com, 10am-8pm daily May-Oct., 11am-6pm Nov.-Apr., tastings $5), where the tasting room, decorated with carvings and baskets from the Louies' collection, sits high above the lake, with panoramic views. Start by sampling the Hee Hee Tel Kin white or red blends; the winery also makes marechal foch, gewürztraminer, and several other wines. The **Red Fox Club** (noon-9pm daily May-Oct., noon-8pm Tues.-Sat. Nov.-Apr.) restaurant uses lots of indigenous ingredients, too.

Lake Country Wineries

Lake Country is north of Kelowna and south of Vernon. For more wineries in this emerging wine district, check out the **Scenic Sip Trail** (www.scenicsip.ca).

Named for its geographic location on a 61-acre (25-ha) property above the lake, **50th Parallel Estate** (17101 Terrace View Rd., Lake Country, 250/766-3408, www.50thparallel.com, 10am-7pm daily Apr.-Oct., noon-5pm Fri.-Sun. Nov.-Mar., tastings $5) is known for pinot noir, which you can sample, along with chardonnay, pinot gris, and other wines, in an atmospheric window-lined tasting

room overlooking the water and vineyards. When you get hungry, sit down in **Block One** (11am-10pm daily May-Oct., noon-5pm Thurs., noon-8pm Fri.-Sat., 11am-8pm Sun. Nov.-Apr.), which uses ingredients from its own garden and nearby farms in dishes like the veggie-filled red quinoa power bowl, or chicken with squash gnocchi and Brussels sprout leaves.

Grey Monk Estate Winery (1055 Camp Rd., Okanagan Centre, 250/766-3168, www.graymonk.com, 10am-7pm daily May-mid-Oct., 10am-5pm daily mid-Oct.-Apr., tastings $5, tours 11am, 2pm, and 4pm Sat.-Sun. June, Mon.-Fri. July-early Sept., Sat.-Sun. early Sept.-mid-Oct., $20 pp) got its start in 1972, in the Okanagan's early wine-producing days. While it makes a range of varietals, it is especially known for its pinot gris. The winery's dining room, **Grapevine Restaurant and Patio** (11:30am-3pm daily Apr., 11:30am-3pm and 5pm-9:30pm daily May-mid-Oct.), serves upscale meals that might range from duck confit with spaetzle, to B.C. steelhead fillets, to Moroccan lamb sliders.

Breweries and Distilleries

While the Okanagan's beer, cider, and spirit brewing operations are younger industries than its wine-making, you can visit craft breweries, cideries, and distilleries in and around Kelowna. A cluster of these producers has located in the city's North End, 1 mile (1.6 km) from downtown.

Tree Brewing Beer Institute (1346 Water St., 778/484-0306 or 800/663-4847, www.treebeer.com, 11am-11pm daily) has a tasting room and lounge where you can taste pilsners, IPAs, and seasonal brews, and amuse yourself with tabletop Trivial Pursuit game cards. It also makes excellent **pizza** using spent grain from the brewing process in the crust; try the bratwurst, sauerkraut, and arugula pie.

Stop in for a tasting flight or snack—or to go bowling—at **BNA Brewing** (1250

Two Days in the Okanagan

You can follow this route from south to north, as it's described here, or begin at the northern end and head to the south.

tasting room at Joie Farm in Naramata

Day 1

Start your day in Osoyoos at the southern tip of the Okanagan Valley with an early morning stroll along Lake Osoyoos, ideally with a hot drink and a sourdough cinnamon bun from **The Lake Village Bakery.** Before it gets too hot, visit the **Nk'Mip Desert Cultural Centre** to learn about the region's ecology and First Nations culture. Stop into nearby **Nk'Mip Cellars** to sample the wares at Canada's first indigenous-owned winery.

Then it's time to begin **wine touring** in earnest. You can make several stops along the Black Sage Bench; **Burrowing Owl Estate Winery, Black Hills Estate Winery, Church and State Wines, Here's the Thing Vineyards,** and **Platinum Bench Estate Winery & Artisan Bread Co.** are all here. Another option is to follow Highway 97 north toward Oliver, visiting **Road 13 Vineyards, CheckMate Artisanal Winery, Tinhorn Creek, Maverick Estate Wines,** and **Hester Creek,** where you can enjoy lunch on the patio at **Terrafina Restaurant.**

In the late afternoon, check into your accommodations—**Watermark Beach Resort** in Osoyoos or **The Guest House at Burrowing Owl Estate Winery** are both excellent choices—to relax before dinner, maybe with a swim in the pool. Then have a leisurely evening meal at one of the winery restaurants, such as **The Sonora Room** at Burrowing Owl or **Liquidity Bistro.** Plan to arrive before the sun sets, so you can take in the views across the valley from their terraces.

Day 2

The next morning, check out of your hotel and drive north on Highway 97 toward Penticton, where you can explore the wineries in **Naramata,** including **Joie Farm, Therapy Vineyards,** and **Upper Bench Winery & Creamery.** Pick up a picnic lunch at **The Bench Artisan Food Market** or sit down at one of the winery restaurants, like **The Patio at Lake Breeze.**

When you're done exploring Naramata, get back on Highway 97, continuing north around Okanagan Lake to Kelowna. If you'd like to check out more wineries along the way, stop at **Mission Hill Family Estate, Quails' Gate Winery,** or **Indigenous World Winery** on Kelowna's west side. Then head for Myra Canyon for a late afternoon bike ride along the **Kettle Valley Railway,** where you can cross a series of reconstructed trestle bridges high above the canyon floor.

After settling into your Kelowna hotel, stop for a pre-dinner libation at one of the city's brewpubs, like the **Tree Brewing Beer Institute, BNA Brewing,** or **Vice & Virtue Brewing Co.** Then have dinner at **Waterfront Wines Restaurant** or **RauDZ Regional Table,** where you can compare notes on the best wines that you've tasted during your two days in the Okanagan.

Ellis St., 236/420-0025, www.bnabrewing. com, tasting room noon-6pm Sun.-Thurs., noon-7pm Fri.-Sat., food 4pm-midnight daily, bowling 1 hour $35-45), a microbrewery with its own bowling lanes.

In the lively warehouse-style tasting room at **Vice & Virtue Brewing Co.** (1033 Richter St., www.viceandvirtuebrewing. ca, 3pm-10pm Tues.-Thurs., noon-10pm Fri.-Sat., 10am-5pm Sun.), in Kelowna's North End, try a tasting flight of brews like The Homewrecker (a New England IPA) or the fizzy Brute champale. **TIP:** The creative small plates are a highlight here.

There's always something new on tap at **Kettle River Brewing Co.** (731 Baillie Ave., 250/862-5115, www.kettleriverbrewing. ca, 3pm-10pm Wed.-Sun.), a nanobrewery in a North End industrial space decorated with colorful local art, where the brewers are continually experimenting. A food truck regularly parks out front (spring-fall), and the Thursday open mic nights draw local musicians.

It's hard to miss **Red Bird Brewing** (1086 Richter St., 250/317-5468, www. redbirdbrewing.com, 2pm-10pm Wed.-Thurs., noon-midnight Fri.-Sat., noon-9pm Sun.), another North End craft brewer; vibrant red-and-white mountain scenes decorate the exterior. Inside the compact tasting room, communal wooden tables encourage conversation, and the names of the beers take you through Kelowna's history; the "Antipsipation IPA," for example, gets its moniker from a train that tipped over en route to Kelowna.

Owned by a regional fruit growers' cooperative, **BC Tree Fruits Cider Co.** (880 Vaughan Ave., 250/979-2629, www. bctreefruitscider.com, 11:30am-5:30pm Mon.-Sat., noon-4pm Sun.) produces apple, pear, and other ciders from surplus local fruit. They're on tap in this North End tasting room that shares space with the organization's produce market.

If you had a historic 1959 fire truck, wouldn't you name your cidery after it? The classic red vehicle that inspired **Truck 59 Ciderhouse** (3887 Brown Rd., West Kelowna, 778/754-1551, www. truck59cider.com, 10am-6pm daily May-Oct.) makes a great photo backdrop, outside the cidery on Kelowna's west side. In the tasting room overlooking the orchards and lake, try the classic dry apple cider, a slightly sweeter semi-dry variety, or a fermented blend infused with Okanagan cherry juice.

Okanagan Spirits Craft Distillery (5204 24th St., Vernon, 250/549-3120 or 888/292-5270, www.okanaganspirits. com, 10am-6pm Mon.-Sat., 11am-4pm Sun.) brews gin, vodka, fruit liqueurs, and Canada's first genuine absinthe. It offers "educationals"—complimentary introductions to craft distilling, along with tastings—at this main location north of Kelowna. It also has a tasting bar at a downtown Kelowna satellite.

Urban Distilleries (325 Bay Ave., #6, 778/478-0939, www.urbandistilleries.ca, 10am-6pm daily), in an industrial North End building, offers tours and tastings of gin, vodka, and B.C.'s first whiskey.

Sights and Activities

In downtown Kelowna, follow the 1.5-mile (2.4-km) paved **Waterfront Boardwalk** along the Okanagan Lake shore. Along the way, besides enjoying the lake views, look for the 2010 sculpture called *Bear* by Brower Hatcher, illuminated at night.

★ Geert Maas Sculpture Gardens and Gallery

One of Kelowna's most unexpected attractions might be the **Geert Maas Sculpture Gardens and Gallery** (250 Reynolds Rd., 250/860-7012, www. geertmaas.org, 10am-5pm daily, donation), which the artist Geert Maas and his wife created in their home northeast of the city. Inside the gallery are several rooms of the prolific Maas's bronze sculptures, stonework, and paintings, with many more pieces on the grounds outside. Born in the Netherlands in 1944, Maas immigrated to Canada in 1979. His works are included in public, private, and corporate art collections in more than 30 countries.

Kelowna Art Gallery
In a modern downtown building, the **Kelowna Art Gallery** (1315 Water St., 250/762-2226, www.kelownaartgallery. com, 10am-9pm Tues. and Thurs., 10am-5pm Wed. and Fri.-Sat., noon-4pm Sun. adults $5, seniors and students $4, families $10, free Thurs.) shows works by Canadian contemporary artists in changing exhibitions throughout the year.

★ Kettle Valley Railway
Opened in 1915, the **Kettle Valley Railway** provided the main rail link between the mines, mills, and farms of B.C.'s Kootenay region and the port of Vancouver. Following a meandering path between Midway, near the Canada-U.S. border east of Osoyoos, through the Okanagan Valley and over the mountains to the town of Hope, the railroad was the main transportation and communications connection between B.C.'s interior districts and the coast until 1949.

Passenger train service continued along the line until the 1960s, but by the 1980s, the entire line had been abandoned. Fortunately, after the railroad ceased operation and the tracks were removed, the former rail line was eventually converted into a 370-mile (595-km) cycling and hiking path across southern B.C.

The Myra Canyon Trestles
One of the most popular sections of the Kettle Valley Railway route is in the Kelowna area. The 7.5-mile (12-km) trail through **Myra Canyon** crosses 18 historic

Top to bottom: grapes ready to harvest at 50th Parallel Estate; bicycle on the Kettle Valley Railway; Kettle River Brewing Co.

wooden trestle bridges high above the deep canyon. It also passes through two tunnels in the rock cliffs. In 2003, a massive wildfire destroyed 16 of the 18 bridges; however, they've since been rebuilt and reopened.

Unless you're afraid of heights, cycling the Myra Canyon, high above the city of Kelowna, offers great views and a look back into the region's history. Interpretive panels along the way tell you more about the railroad and the trestle bridges.

Getting There

To reach Myra Canyon from downtown Kelowna, make your way south and turn left onto K.L.O. Road. At McCulloch Road, turn right and continue until you reach Myra Forest Service Road, where you turn right again. Follow Myra Forest Service Road 5 miles (8 km) to the parking lot. Allow 25-30 minutes for the drive.

Monashee Adventure Tours (250/878-3587, www.monasheeadventuretours.com) leads **guided rides** (4 hours, $120 pp) of the Myra Canyon Trestles that include commentary about the bridges, the railroad, and the region in general, plus pickup and drop-off at Kelowna hotels. You can also do a **self-guided ride** ($100 pp) at Myra Canyon, where staff will provide transportation, a rental bike, maps, and directions, then send you on your way.

Myra Canyon Rentals (Myra Station parking area, 250/878-8763, www.myracanyonrental.com, 9am-5:30pm daily mid-May-June and Sept.-mid-Oct., 9am-8pm daily July-Aug., half-day adults $39, children $30, full-day adults $69, children $45) rents bikes from a stand at the entrance to the Myra Canyon parking lot.

Carmelis Goat Cheese

At **Carmelis Goat Cheese** (170 Timberline Rd., 250/764-9033, www.carmelisgoatcheese.com, 11am-5pm Sat.-Sun., Mar., 11am-5pm daily Apr. and Oct., 10am-6pm daily May-Sept.), you can sample and purchase handcrafted goat cheeses, including soft chèvre, a firm gruyère-style cheese, and "goatgonzola," a distinctive blue. The goat's-milk gelato is a perfect afternoon refresher. Carmelis is located 7.5 miles (12 km) south of downtown Kelowna on the east side of Okanagan Lake.

Sports and Recreation
Beaches

Beaches line Okanagan Lake throughout the Kelowna area. Downtown, **City Park** (1600 Abbott St.) has a sandy beach, a kids' waterpark and playground, basketball courts, volleyball nets, and restrooms.

South of the city center, **Rotary Beach Park** (3726 Lakeshore Rd.) has a swimming beach, playground, and restrooms. Windsurfers and kiteboarders flock here for the winds.

Water Sports

The **Kelowna Paddle Trail** extends 17 miles (27 km) along Okanagan Lake, from McKinley Landing Park (2186 Bennett Rd.) in the north, past the downtown area, south to Bertram Creek Regional Park (5680 Lakeshore Rd.), with buoys marking the route along the way. From the downtown waterfront, you can go for a short paddle in either direction, or explore the lakeshore on a longer excursion. Rent kayaks or stand-up paddleboards at **Downtown Marina** (210 Bernard Ave., 778/760-1500, www.kelownadowntownmarina.com, May-mid-Oct., call for seasonal hours, 1 hour $25-30).

Adventure Park

The Von Andrian family, who operate Myra Canyon Ranch, also run the **Myra Canyon Adventure Park** (4429 June Springs Rd., 250/869-8494, www.myracanyon.com, 10am-7pm Sat.-Sun. mid-May-mid-June, 10am-6pm daily mid-June-early Sept., 10am-6pm Sat.-Sun. mid-Sept.-mid-Oct., adults $49-59, under age 18 $44-54), where you can challenge yourself on several ropes courses and zip lines. The adventure park is 9 miles (14 km) southeast of downtown Kelowna.

Winter Sports

Big White Ski Resort (5315 Big White Rd., 250/765-3101 or 800/663-2772, www. bigwhite.com, adults $105, seniors and ages 13-18 $89, ages 6-12 $64), Kelowna's local mountain, is one of Canada's largest fully ski-in, ski-out resorts. With 2,765 acres (1,147 ha) of patrolled terrain, Big White has 15 lifts serving 118 runs, rated 18 percent beginner, 54 percent intermediate, and 28 percent expert/extreme. This family-friendly mountain is typically open late November-mid-April.

Big White is 35 miles (56 km) southeast of Kelowna. From Highway 97, take Highway 33 southeast to Big White Road.

On weekends during the ski season, the resort operates an **Express Bus** (Fri.-Sun., one-way $20, round-trip $25) that can take you to the mountain from a number of Kelowna locations; check the Big White website for schedules.

The **Big White Airport Shuttle** (daily late Nov.-mid-Apr., 800/663-2772, one-way adults $53, ages 6-12 $37, ages 5 and under $23, round-trip adults $86, ages 6-12 $61, ages 5 and under $30) picks up passengers at Kelowna airport and brings them to the mountain. Reserve your shuttle at least 72 hours in advance.

Entertainment and Events
The Arts

The modern **Rotary Centre for the Arts** (421 Cawston Ave., 250/717-5304, www. rotarycentreforthearts.com) downtown presents theater, music, and visual arts events.

Prospera Place (1223 Water St., 250/979-0888, www.prosperaplace.com) is the city's sports arena and concert venue.

B.C.'s third-largest orchestra, the **Okanagan Symphony** (250/763-7544, www.okanagansymphony.com) performs in Kelowna, Penticton, and Vernon.

★ Okanagan Wine Festivals

The **Okanagan Wine Festivals** (www. thewinefestivals.com) are the largest celebrations of the region's wine industry, taking place several times a year, with wine-tastings, wine dinners, and other special events, from Kelowna to Osoyoos. The Spring Festival is held in late April or early May, the Fall Festival spans 10 days in late September or early October, and the Winter Festival is in January.

Other Festivals and Events

At its 1,000-seat outdoor amphitheater, **Mission Hill Family Estate** (1730 Mission Hill Rd., West Kelowna, 250/768-6483 or 800/957-9911, www.missionhillwinery. com) hosts a summer concert series, where Tony Bennett, the Gipsy Kings, Lyle Lovett, jazz trumpeter Chris Botti, and country singer Martina McBride have been among the past performers.

Parks Alive! (www.festivalskelowna. com, July-Aug.) is a summertime series of more than 50 concerts and other arts events in Kelowna's parks and outdoor spaces.

Food
Winery Restaurants

One of the Okanagan's most scenic dining spots is ★ **The Terrace at Mission Hill** (1730 Mission Hill Rd., West Kelowna, 250/768-6467, www.missionhillwinery. com, 11:30am-3pm and 5pm-8pm daily mid-May-mid-Oct., lunch $16-33, dinner $30-36), a patio restaurant with vistas across the vines all the way to Okanagan Lake. Catering to the changing seasons, the contemporary menu varies but always includes fresh salads, seafood, and other preparations using ingredients from the region. The gracious staff can assist you in pairing wine with your meal. Plan your visit for a sunny day; this outdoor restaurant closes when the weather turns inclement.

At Quails' Gate Winery, you can dine overlooking the vineyards year-round at **Old Vines Restaurant** (3303 Boucherie Rd., West Kelowna, 250/769-2500 or 800/420-9463, ext. 252, www.quailsgate. com, 11am-2:30pm and 5pm-10pm daily, lunch $18-33, dinner $24-48). Old Vines' seasonal menus incorporate regional products, from burrata with beets and pumpkin seed pesto, to Cornish game hen with herb gnocchi, to locally raised beef served with potato truffle pavé. Reservations are recommended in summer.

The **Red Fox Club** (2218 Horizon Dr. E., West Kelowna, 778/755-6360, www. redfoxclub.ca, noon-9pm daily May-Oct., noon-8pm Tues.-Sat. Nov.-Apr., lunch $16-29, dinner $20-35) at the Indigenous World Winery prepares an indigenous food-inspired menu, starting with house-made bannock or a local salad that might be topped with pears, apples, and dried grapes. For your main, try a wild rice bowl layered with an assortment of pickled and fermented vegetables, salmon with corn pancakes, or elk paired with foraged nettles and wheat dumplings. Sit in the snug dining room indoors for quiet conversation, or out on the patio to take in vistas high above the lake.

Contemporary

★ **Waterfront Wines Restaurant** (1180 Sunset Dr., #104, 250/979-1222, www. waterfrontrestaurant.ca, 5pm-10pm daily, $27-33) has long been one of Kelowna's top dining destinations, in a compact space with honey wood tables that feels both lively and cozy. Park yourself at the bar for a glass of Okanagan wine and small plates (perhaps the simple but excellent wild mushrooms on toast or an organic vegetable salad with pickled apricots and pecorino), or let executive chef Mark Filatow and his crew in the open kitchen work their magic on more elaborate dishes, like pan-roasted ling cod paired with prawn bisque, smoked ricotta *gnudi* with fennel and a carrot

marmalade, or local beef accompanied by squash beignets. Finish with a cheese plate or a sweet like the chocolate Kahlua cake with barley ice cream and toasted marshmallow.

Under the same ownership as Waterfront Wines, **Waterfront Café** (2245 Abbott St., #101, 236/361-4408, www. waterfrontcafe.ca) channels a similar respect for kitchen creativity and local ingredients into a more casual setting, across from the lakeshore south of downtown. The all-day **café** (7am-5pm daily) serves coffee, along with croissants, rich fudgy brownies, and other pastries, while the **bistro** (9am-2:30pm Mon.-Fri., 9am-3pm Sat.-Sun., $12-17), with bright green chairs and cheerful flowers on the tables, delivers an inventive brunch-lunch menu, from Swiss-style potato rosti with eggs to kale and chicken salad. If its take on falafel is on the menu, give it a try; it's a thick chickpea patty with crisp garbanzos on top, drizzled with yogurt sauce and paired with pickled vegetables.

You might not expect to find creative modern small plates in a brewpub, but then perhaps you haven't been to ★ **Vice & Virtue Brewing Co.** (1033 Richter St., www.viceandvirtuebrewing.ca, 3pm-10pm Tues.-Thurs., noon-10pm Fri.-Sat., 10am-5pm Sun., $13-19). The chef cures his own charcuterie, smokes his own meats, and sources produce from local farms, crafting dishes like an excellent cucumber salad with spicy miso, heirloom tomatoes and kale with smoked haloumi, and barbecued smoked brisket. A tasting flight of beers is a natural accompaniment.

The chef creates a daring new menu of sharing plates every night at **Salt & Brick** (243 Bernard Ave., 778/484-3234, www.saltandbrick.ca, 11:30am-10pm Mon.-Thurs., 11:30am-midnight Fri., 10:30am-midnight Sat., 10:30am-10pm Sun., $7-18), a snug bistro in a narrow brick-walled storefront. Brussels sprouts with beer cheese and cherries? Carrots with chili and milk chocolate? Pork with a warm apple-fennel slaw? Bring your appetite and sense of adventure.

The motto of this warm downtown bistro with exposed brick walls is "fresh, local, comfortable," and even though chef and co-owner Rod Butters is something of a local food celebrity, ★ **RauDZ Regional Table** (1560 Water St., 250/868-8805, www.raudz.com, 5pm-10pm daily, $17-36)—pronounced "Rod's"—keeps the vibe relaxed and fun. Sip a glass of Okanagan wine along with the crab cappuccino, a rich bisque swimming with Dungeness crab, or try the poutine, heaped with chicken confit. The oat-crusted arctic char comes with a big pile of local vegetables, while the signature dish, the RJB, is a decadent sandwich of beef tenderloin, butter-poached crab, bacon, and onion jam piled on a brioche bun. Fortunately, desserts like grilled olive oil carrot cake or chocolate caramel crunch (rich mousse topped with salted caramel ice cream and crispy caramel) are served in slightly less huge "taster" sizes.

The same owners run tiny **micro bar bites** (1500 Water St., 778/484-3500, www.microkelowna.com, 2pm-11pm Sun.-Thurs., 2pm-midnight Fri.-Sat., $6-20), down the street. Yes, it's petite (as the chef says, the space is so small, they don't even capitalize the *m*), but they find room to serve charcuterie, cheeses, oysters, and creative small plates.

Diners
Operated by the RauDZ team, **Sunny's Modern Diner** (235 Bernard Ave., 778/478-1170, www.sunnysmoderndiner. com, 7:30am-3:30pm Tues.-Sun., $8-18) is a sunny spot to start your day. Whether indoors or out on the streetside patio, you can dig into substantial all-day breakfast plates like chicken and waffles with chorizo crumble, or "chicks on a raft," a baguette piled with scrambled eggs, bacon,

Top to bottom: indigenous-inspired dish at the Red Fox Club; Salt & Brick in downtown Kelowna; a falafel plate at Waterfront Café.

and cheddar and slathered with peanut butter (it's surprisingly good). At lunchtime, look for sandwiches like the "ooey gooey grilled cheese" or "two-handed beef dip," along with old-timey milk shakes and root beer floats.

Cafés, Bakeries, and Light Bites

Convenient for breakfast or a light lunch downtown, sunny **Bliss Bakery** (109-1289 Ellis St., 778/484-5355, www.blissbakery. ca, 7:30am-5pm daily, $3-11) bakes excellent muffins (try the Kitchen Sink, with carrots, pineapple, and walnuts), scones, and other pastries, and prepares several daily varieties of sandwiches. It has a second downtown branch plus another location near the lakeshore south of Kelowna.

Sandrine French Pastry & Chocolate (1865 Dilworth Dr., 250/860-1202, www. sandrinepastry.com, 7:30am-6pm Mon.-Sat.) would look more at home on a Parisian boulevard than it does in a strip mall opposite Kelowna's Orchard Park shopping center, so perhaps it's no surprise that this jewel-box patisserie specializes in traditional French pastries and chocolates. Pick up a croissant (the chocolate almond is particularly decadent), a *pain raisin,* or a tart made with local fruits.

Groceries and Markets

More than 150 vendors hawk their wares at the **Kelowna Farmers and Crafters Market** (Dilworth Dr. and Springfield Rd., www.kelownafarmersandcraftersmarket. com, 8am-1pm Wed. and Sat. Apr.-mid-Nov.), featuring fresh fruits and vegetables, baked goods, jewelry, pottery, and other foods and crafts. In the colder months, the market moves into the Parkinson Recreation Center (1800 Parkinson Way, 9am-1pm Sat. mid-Nov.-Mar.).

Accommodations and Camping
Under $150

The **University of British Columbia Okanagan Campus** (1290 International Mews, 250/807-8050 or 888/318-8666, www.okanagan.ubcconferences.com) rents on-campus rooms to travelers May-late August. Options include singles with a private bath ($59-84 s), two single rooms rented together that share a bath ($96-104 d), or studio suites ($84-129 d) and one-bedroom units ($129-189 d), both with private baths and kitchens. Wi-Fi is included. Parking is $3.50 per day. These aren't plush accommodations (think basic dormitory decor), but they're a reasonable value. The campus is 9 miles (14 km) northeast of downtown Kelowna.

$150-300

★ **A View of the Lake B&B** (1877 Horizon Dr., West Kelowna, 250/769-7854, www. aviewofthelake.com, $150-195) lives up to its name, particularly from the expansive deck, where panoramic views extend across Okanagan Lake to downtown Kelowna. Gregarious owner Steve Marston, a former professional chef who runs the bed-and-breakfast with his wife, Chrissy, prepares three-course breakfasts, which guests can enjoy on this sunny east-facing terrace or in the window-lined living room with a fireplace. Three of the four guest rooms, with modern furnishings, contemporary art, and Wi-Fi, look out to the lake; the Grand View suite has a whirlpool tub with lake vistas. The B&B is in a residential neighborhood, a 15-minute drive to downtown Kelowna. No kids under 12 are allowed.

A sister property to the Victoria hotel of the same name, Kelowna's ★ **Hotel Zed** (1627 Abbott St., 250/763-7771 or 855/763-7771, www.hotelzed.com, $239-409) pops with color, from the pink, orange, and lime green exterior to the 55 compact guest rooms outfitted with retro rotary phones (and free Wi-Fi). At this fun and funky boutique motel, you can squeeze your friends into the "mini disco" for a karaoke session, challenge them to a match in the ping-pong lounge, borrow bikes or roller skates to cruise around, or lounge at the outdoor pool.

The spacious rooftop patio has a fire pit and barbecue, too, overlooking a leafy lakeside park. You can help yourself to free coffee and tea in the lobby, and you're just around the corner from downtown's cafés and restaurants.

Named for a mythical creature said to inhabit Okanagan Lake, **Ogopogo B&B** (845 Manhattan Dr., 250/762-7624, www.ogopogobedandbreakfast.ca, May-mid-Oct., $279-310) is an upscale two-bedroom inn, hidden in a residential neighborhood across the street from the lakeshore and a short walk from downtown. The spacious Manhattan suite upstairs has a king bed, a fireplace, and a view of the lake; the smaller Sunset suite, on the main floor, also has a king bed. Both units have mini fridges, coffeemakers, teakettles, and complimentary Wi-Fi. Borrow the kayak and beach chairs, and head for the lake. A full breakfast, alternating sweet and savory dishes like blintzes or frittatas, is served family-style in the open kitchen.

From the expansive deck at **Myra Canyon Ranch** (4675 June Springs Rd., 250/869-8494, www.myracanyonranch.com, $249-549), a four-suite guesthouse high in the hills above town, you have panoramic views across the valley to the city, the lake, and beyond. Owners Rolf and Kathrin von Andrian and their family relocated from Germany to open this modern wood-frame inn, where, inside, the clean-lined European-style furnishings and duvet-topped beds make the guest rooms simple but comfortable. It's a working ranch, too, with **stables** where you can arrange **trail rides** (1.5-2.5 hours, $99-119 pp) and introductory **kids rides** (ages 3-7, 30-60 minutes, $55-80). Myra Canyon Ranch is 9 miles (14 km) southeast of downtown Kelowna.

Over $300

The family-friendly **Manteo Resort Waterfront Hotel and Villas** (3762 Lakeshore Rd., 250/860-1031 or 800/445-5255, www.manteo.com, $289-449) has plenty for everyone to do, with a small private lakeside beach where you can rent canoes, kayaks, and stand-up paddleboards; three pools (two outdoors, one inside); several hot tubs; a gym; a games room, with ping-pong and pool tables; tennis and pickleball courts; a playground; and even a movie theater. When it's time to sleep, choose one of the 24 villas ($449-719), comfortable two- or three-bedroom townhouses with full kitchens and beds for 6-10, or the 78 hotel rooms and suites, with dark wood furniture and puffy duvets; the best rooms have lake views, but all are steps from the waterfront. Parking, local calls, and Wi-Fi are included in the room rates.

Right on Okanagan Lake near downtown, ★ **Delta Hotels by Marriott Grand Okanagan Resort** (1310 Water St., 250/763-4500 or 888/236-2427, www.marriott.com, $299-749, resort fee $20 per day, parking $24-32) combines urban and holiday pleasures. When you pull up a seat on the sunny patio overlooking the lakefront lagoon, lounge in the indoor-outdoor pool, or book a treatment in the spa, you definitely feel like you're on vacation. In the two guest towers, the 257 modern rooms have included Wi-Fi, flat-screen TVs, mini fridges, and coffeemakers. The 60 one-, two-, and three-bedroom suites feel more like vacation homes with full kitchens; some are traditionally appointed, while others have been updated with more contemporary finishes. A separate condo building, the Royal Private Residence Club, has large one- to four-bedroom apartments ($700-2,000), a private gym, and a gorgeous rooftop infinity pool above the lake. Like many of the region's eateries, **Oak + Cru Social Kitchen & Wine Bar** highlights local ingredients and wines.

An Austrian countess constructed the original **Hotel Eldorado** (500 Cook Rd., 250/763-7500 or 866/608-7500, www.eldoradokelowna.com, $289-549) in 1926, and the current lakeside property, decorated with old photos, has been rebuilt in a classic lake-villa style. Of the 49 guest rooms, those in the heritage wing are all different but have traditional furnishings and balconies overlooking the lake. In the newer four-story Arms wing, the cottage-style rooms are outfitted with white painted furniture and plaid comforters; eight one-bedroom suites have a small kitchenette and a living room with a pullout sofa and an electric fireplace. Popular for Sunday brunch, the window-lined **Lakeside** dining room resembles a cottage summer porch. You can swim in the indoor lap pool, or rent kayaks or stand-up paddleboards; there's a small gym, sauna, and hot tub. Parking is free.

Camping
Several provincial parks in the vicinity of Kelowna have lakeside campgrounds. To make reservations at any of these parks, contact **Discover Camping** (519/826-6850 or 800/689-9025, www.discovercamping.ca).

Bear Creek Provincial Park (Westside Rd., 250/548-0076, www.env.gov.bc.ca, Apr.-mid-Oct., $35), on the west shore of Okanagan Lake, northwest of Kelowna, has 122 campsites, flush toilets, and showers. Reservations are required between mid-May and early September. From Kelowna, take Highway 97 west to Westside Road; follow Westside Road north for 4.5 miles (7 km) to the park entrance.

Kekuli Bay Provincial Park (off Hwy. 97, 250/548-0076, www.env.gov.bc.ca, Apr.-late Oct., $32) is on the west side of Kalamalka Lake, between Kelowna and Vernon. The 69-site campground, with showers and flush toilets, is a short distance from the water, although with a rocky beach the area is more popular for boating than swimming. You can reserve sites between mid-May and early September. From Kelowna, take Highway 97 north toward Vernon and watch for the park signs; it's about a 45-minute drive.

South of Kelowna, **Okanagan Lake Provincial Park** (off Hwy. 97, 250/548-0076, www.env.gov.bc.ca, $35) has two different camping areas, both with showers and flush toilets. The North Campground (mid-May.-late Sept.) has 80 sites spaced out on three terraces overlooking the lake, while in the South Campground (mid-May-mid-Oct.), the 88 sites are closer together but closer to the lakeshore. You can make reservations for both campgrounds for stays between mid-May and early September; otherwise, sites are first-come, first-served. The park is on Okanagan Lake, 33 miles (53 km) south of Kelowna and 7 miles (11 km) north of Summerland.

Information and Services
Visitor Information
Tourism Kelowna (250/861-1515 or 800/663-4345, www.tourismkelowna.com) provides information about the city and surrounding region on its website and at the waterfront **Kelowna Visitor Centre** (238 Queensway, 8:30am-5pm daily). You can also tweet a travel question to @Tourism_Kelowna, using the hashtag #AskKelowna.

Media and Communications
Glossy *Okanagan Life* (www.okanaganlife.com) magazine reports on the region's restaurants, producing an annual restaurant guide, and on community, business, and real estate news.

Kelowna's *Daily Courier* (www.kelownadailycourier.ca) and *Capital News* (www.kelownacapnews.com) both cover local news.

Medical Services
The Okanagan's main hospital facility, **Kelowna General Hospital** (2268 Pandosy St., 250/862-4000 or 888/877-4442, www.interiorhealth.ca), provides emergency services around the clock.

The pharmacy at **Shoppers Drug Mart** (2271 Harvey Ave., Unit 1360, 250/860-3764, www.shoppersdrugmart.ca) in the

Orchard Park Shopping Centre is open 24 hours daily.

Getting Around

By Car

Kelowna is located off Highway 97 on the east side of Okanagan Lake. Highway 97 runs east-west through the city, where it's called Harvey Avenue. The main downtown shopping and restaurant street is Bernard Avenue, which is parallel to Harvey Avenue, three blocks to the north.

Street parking downtown is metered (9am-5pm Mon.-Sat., $1.25 per hour), with a two-hour maximum; purchase a parking ticket from the automated machines nearby. For longer stays, pull into one of the city-run parking structures ($1 per hour, $6 per day): **Library Plaza Parkade** (1360 Ellis St.), **Memorial Parkade** (1420 Ellis St.), or **Chapman Parkade** (345 Lawrence Ave.). Street parking is free in the evenings and on Sunday. The city parkades are free 6pm-6am Monday-Friday and all day Saturday and Sunday.

Most of the wineries are outside the city center, either in West Kelowna on the lake's west shore via Highway 97 south, or south of downtown, off Lakeshore Road.

By Bus

B.C. Transit (250/860-8121, www.bctransit.com/kelowna, $2.50) runs bus service around Kelowna.

By Bike

Kelowna has more than 185 miles (300 km) of on-street bicycle lanes and 25 miles (40 km) of paved multiuse cycling and walking paths. Download a **bike map** from the City of Kelowna website (www.kelowna.ca), or pick up a copy at the **Kelowna Visitor Centre** (238 Queensway).

You can rent bikes on the downtown waterfront, near the Delta Grand Okanagan Resort, at **Lakefront Sports** (1350B Water St., 250/862-2469, 10am-6pm daily, 2 hours $25, 4 hours, $39).

Penticton and Naramata

On the southern shore of Okanagan Lake, Penticton is the largest community in the Central Okanagan. The main reason to visit this city of 43,000 is to explore the wineries east of town, in the bucolic area above the lake known as the **Naramata Bench.**

★ Wineries

The wineries along the south end of Naramata Bench have Penticton addresses, while those to the north are in Naramata.

Harry McWatters is an icon in the Okanagan wine world. He established Sumac Ridge Estate Winery in 1980, one of the region's first modern wineries, and subsequently founded See Ya Later Ranch. His latest venture is **Time Winery** (361 Martin St., Penticton, 236/422-2556, www.timewinery.com, 10am-8pm daily, tastings free), crafting riesling, sauvignon blanc, merlot, cabernet franc, and several other varieties, in a former downtown Penticton movie theater.

Producing both wine and cheese, **Upper Bench Winery & Creamery** (170 Upper Bench Rd. S., Penticton, 250/770-1733, www.upperbench.ca, 10am-6pm daily Apr.-Oct., 10am-5pm daily Nov.-Mar., tastings $7) offers samples of both in its homey shop and tasting room. The U&Brie is especially flavorful. Under the arbor on the patio, you can sit down to a cheese platter and wine flight.

Another cheesemaker, **Poplar Grove Cheese** (1060 Poplar Grove Rd., Penticton, 250/492-4575, www.poplargrovecheese.ca, 11am-5pm Sat.-Sun. May, 11am-5pm daily June-mid-Oct.), makes several varieties, including a mild double-cream camembert and the full-flavored Tiger Blue. Sample them at the tasting bar, along with wines from **Lock and Worth** (www.lockandworth.com, tastings $5).

A small farm and winery, **Joie Farm** (2825 Naramata Rd., Naramata, 250/496-0092, www.joiefarm.com, 10am-5pm Thurs.-Mon. May-Oct., tastings $15) makes an excellent rosé as well as the Alsace-style Noble Blend, unoaked chardonnay, riesling, gewürztraminer, pinot blanc, gamay, and pinot noir, many of which sell out before they even reach the stores. The winery entrance is actually along Aikins Loop; turn off Naramata Road onto Old Main Road, then go left onto Aikins Loop to the winery.

Producing labels like Freudian Sip (a blend of pinot gris, riesling, sauvignon blanc, gewürztraminer, muscat, and viognier) and Pink Freud (a pinot noir-merlot rosé), cheeky **Therapy Vineyards** (940 Debeck Rd., Naramata, 250/496-5217, www.therapyvineyards. com, 10am-6pm daily Apr.-Sept., 11am-5pm daily Oct.-Nov., 11am-4pm daily Dec.-Mar, tastings $5) does make serious wine, too. Analyze it yourself in the tasting room.

Breweries and Distilleries

Doug and Dawn Lennie converted Naramata's former doctors' office into **Legend Distilling** (3005 Naramata Rd., Naramata, 778/514-1010, www. legenddistilling.com, 11am-6pm daily May-early Oct., noon-4pm Sat.-Sun. Nov.-Apr.), where they're producing gin, whiskey, amaro, vodka, and a vodka-spiked cold-brew coffee called Blasted Brew. You can enjoy cocktails and light meals on the patio at **Urtica Eatery** spring-fall.

Small-batch producer **Old Order Distilling Co.** (270 Martin St., Penticton, 778/476-2210, www.oldorderdistilling.ca, 1pm-8pm Thurs.-Sat.) is distilling vodka, gin, and whiskey from 100 percent B.C.-grown fruits and grains.

In downtown Penticton, microbrewer **Cannery Brewing** (198 Ellis St., Penticton, 250/493-2723, www.cannerybrewing. com, noon-9pm Mon.-Fri., 11am-9pm Sat.-Sun.) produces an amber ale, an IPA, and a pale ale, among others, along with seasonal brews. Sample them in the tasting room.

Sports and Recreation
Beaches

Right in town, **Okanagan Lake Beach** (Lakeshore Dr., Penticton) and small **Marina Way Park** (Marina Way, Penticton) have popular sandy stretches.

In Naramata, you can swim at **Three Mile Beach** (Three Mile Rd., off Naramata Rd.).

On Okanagan Lake between Penticton and Summerland, **Sun-Oka Beach Provincial Park** (off Hwy. 97, 250/548-0076, www.env.gov.bc.ca, mid-Apr.-mid-Oct.) has a large sandy beach on a bay that's good for swimming.

Another excellent swimming beach is in **Skaha Lake Park** (Skaha Lake Rd. at Parkview St., Penticton), on Skaha Lake south of downtown Penticton.

Water Sports

Want to combine water adventures with wine-tasting? **Hoodoo Adventures** (250/490-6084, www.hoodooadventures. ca) offers four-hour **wine tours by kayak** (mid-Apr.-Oct., adults $155). You start with a paddle along Okanagan Lake, then a shuttle brings you to a number of Naramata wineries. It offers other kayak tours as well, including **Paddle to the Pub** (adults $120), which pairs kayaking and a pub stop; a two-hour **sunset paddle** (adults $95); and a **kayak brunch tour** (adults $95). To go paddling on your own, rent **kayaks** (half-day $35, full-day $60) or **stand-up paddleboards** (2 hours $20, 4 hours $45).

Grab your inner tube for a gentle **river float** along the Okanagan River Channel that runs between Okanagan and Skaha Lakes. **Coyote Cruises** (215 Riverside Dr., 250/492-2115, www.coyotecruises.ca, 10am-5pm daily mid-June-Sept., inner tube rental and bus $12, bus only $6) rents inner tubes from its office near the

Penticton and Naramata

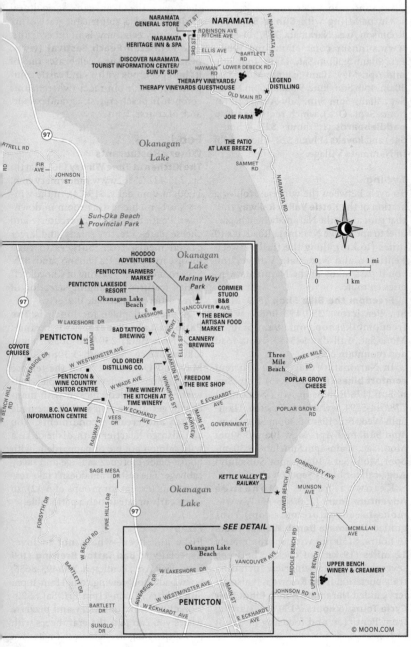

NARAMATA

NARAMATA GENERAL STORE

NARAMATA HERITAGE INN & SPA

DISCOVER NARAMATA TOURIST INFORMATION CENTER/ SUN N' SUP

THERAPY VINEYARDS/ THERAPY VINEYARDS GUESTHOUSE

ROBINSON AVE

RITCHIE AVE

ELLIS AVE

BARTLETT RD

HAYMAN RD

LOWER DEBECK RD

OLD MAIN RD

LEGEND DISTILLING

JOIE FARM

THE PATIO AT LAKE BREEZE

SAMMET RD

Okanagan Lake

1ST ST

3RD ST

N NARAMATA RD

NARAMATA RD

RTRELL RD

97

RD

FIR AVE

JOHNSON ST

Sun-Oka Beach Provincial Park

HOODOO ADVENTURES

PENTICTON FARMERS' MARKET

PENTICTON LAKESIDE RESORT

Okanagan Lake Beach

Okanagan Lake

Marina Way Park

CORMIER STUDIO B&B

VANCOUVER AVE

THE BENCH ARTISAN FOOD MARKET

CANNERY BREWING

W LAKESHORE DR

E LAKESHORE DR

FRONT ST

ELLIS ST

BAD TATTOO BREWING

PENTICTON

POWER ST

W WESTMINSTER AVE

COYOTE CRUISES

RIVERSIDE DR

W BENCH HILL RD

PENTICTON & WINE COUNTRY VISITOR CENTRE

B.C. VQA WINE INFORMATION CENTRE

OLD ORDER DISTILLING CO.

W WADE AVE

TIME WINERY/ THE KITCHEN AT TIME WINERY

W ECKHARDT AVE

VEES DR

RAILWAY ST

MARTIN ST

WINNIPEG ST

MAIN ST

FAIRVIEW

E ECKHARDT AVE

FREEDOM THE BIKE SHOP

GOVERNMENT ST

97

Three Mile Beach

THREE MILE RD

POPLAR GROVE CHEESE

POPLAR GROVE RD

SAGE MESA DR

FORSYTH DR

W BENCH DR

PINE HILLS DR

BARTLETT DR

97

Okanagan Lake

KETTLE VALLEY RAILWAY

CORBISHLEY AVE

LOWER BENCH RD

MUNSON AVE

MCMILLAN AVE

SEE DETAIL

Okanagan Lake Beach

W LAKESHORE DR

RIVERSIDE DR

VANCOUVER AVE

MIDDLE BENCH RD

S UPPER BENCH RD

UPPER BENCH RD

UPPER BENCH WINERY & CREAMERY

W WESTMINSTER AVE

W ECKHARDT AVE

PENTICTON

E ECKHARDT AVE

MAIN ST

JOHNSON RD

BARTLETT DR

SUNGLO DR

0   1 mi

0   1 km

© MOON.COM

starting point, and will pick you up when you get to the other end of the channel. Bring sunscreen, water, and snacks.

Go paddling with **Sun n' Sup** (176 Robinson Ave., Naramata, 778/514-5594, www.sunnsup.com, 11am-5pm Wed.-Fri., 10am-5:30pm Sat., 11am-4pm Sun. mid-Apr.-May, 10am-5:30pm Mon.-Sat., 10am-4pm Sun. June, 9:30am-6pm Mon.-Sat., 10am-5pm Sun. July-Aug., call for hours Sept.-Oct.), which rents **stand-up paddleboards** (1.5 hours $25, 4 hours $45) and **kayaks** (1 hour $20, 4 hours $30) in Naramata Village.

Cycling

To cycle between the wineries, follow a section of the **Kettle Valley Railway** trail that runs along the Naramata Bench, parallel to and above Naramata Road. It's 10 miles (16 km) along the trail between Penticton and Naramata Village, and you'll pass many of the Naramata wineries en route.

Freedom the Bike Shop (533 Main St., Penticton, 250/493-0686, www.freedombikeshop.com, 9am-5:30pm Mon.-Sat., full-day $45-80) rents road and mountain bikes.

In Naramata Village, you can rent **comfort bikes** (full-day $45) from **Sun n' Sup** (176 Robinson Ave., Naramata, 778/514-5594, www.sunnsup.com, 11am-5pm Wed.-Fri., 10am-5:30pm Sat., 11am-4pm Sun. mid-Apr.-May, 10am-5:30pm Mon.-Sat., 10am-4pm Sun. June, 9:30am-6pm Mon.-Sat., 10am-5pm Sun. July-Aug., call for hours Sept.-Oct.).

Kelowna-based **Monashee Adventure Tours** (250/878-3587, www.monasheeadventuretours.com) runs guided **Naramata Bench Winery Tours** (6 hours, $150 pp) with approximately 12 miles (19 km) of cycling between several Naramata wineries, including transportation from Kelowna. It also offers guided **Naramata Bench Pinot Noir Cycle Tours** (6 hours, $150 pp), starting from Penticton and focusing on pinot tastings.

Festivals and Events

While grapes may be getting the glory these days, the Okanagan's agricultural heritage, and a significant part of its present-day economy, is in other fruits. The **Penticton Peach Festival** (www.peachfest.com, Aug.) celebrates one of its bumper crops with a sand castle competition, peach-bin races (where teams compete in peach crates), a grand parade, and, of course, fruit.

Food

Winery Restaurants

The Kitchen at Time Winery (361 Martin St., 236/422-2556, www.timewinery.com, 11:30am-9pm daily, $15-24), in the winery's urban-chic tasting room in downtown Penticton, serves charcuterie and cheese plates, creative salads, and larger casual meals, from burgers to tuna niçoise to a porchetta cubano sandwich. Save room for the "Tasting of Chocolate," which features a changing selection of three different chocolate desserts.

A peaceful place for lunch is **The Patio at Lake Breeze** (930 Sammet Rd., Naramata, 250/496-5659, www.lakebreeze.ca, 11:30am-3:30pm daily May-mid-Oct., $17-29), on the terrace at Lake Breeze Vineyards. Simple sandwiches, like grilled chicken with manchego, get dressed up with homemade breads and creative condiments. You can also go heartier with dishes like a wild salmon pot pie or pappardelle with house-made merguez sausage and savoy cabbage. The restaurant doesn't take reservations (except for groups of 6-12), so come early or late to nab a patio table.

Pizza

Pizza and beer—what's not to love? Especially at **Bad Tattoo Brewing** (169 Estabrook Ave., Penticton, 250/493-8686, www.badtattoobrewing.com, 11am-10pm Sun.-Thurs., 11am-11pm Fri.-Sat., $22-29), a lively microbrewery and pizzeria where you can pair the craft beers with pizzas that range from basic to (in its own

Dinner on God's Mountain

A popular wine-country dinner takes place every week on God's Mountain. While some might consider the meals to be a religious experience, it has nothing to do with religion.

Joy Road Catering (250/493-8657, www.joyroadcatering.com), an Okanagan-based catering company, partnered with **God's Mountain Estate** (4898 Lakeside Rd., Penticton, 250/490-4800, www.godsmountain.ca), an inn outside Penticton, to present **Sunday Alfresco Vineyard Dining** (6:30pm Sun. mid-May-early Oct., $120 pp), a farm-to-table supper served outdoors at a long communal table on the inn's grounds. This four-course Sunday feast is paired with local wines and emphasizes seasonal ingredients.

The catering company also hosts a series of **Winemaker Dinners,** on location at different Okanagan wineries spring-fall. Check the Joy Road website for the schedule and prices of these multicourse meals.

Advance reservations are required for the dinners. Book online or call for details—and pray that there's space for you at these God's Mountain feasts.

words) "weird." The offbeat pies change, but among recent creations are the Okanagan barbecue, topped with smoky pulled pork, and the Cheeseburger, which has ground beef, cheddar cheese, and pickles piled on the crust. To drink, try the medium-dark Los Muertos Cerveza Negra or the Westcoast IPA.

Cafés, Bakeries, and Light Bites

Part café and part gourmet grocery, ★ **The Bench Artisan Food Market** (368 Vancouver Ave., Penticton, 250/492-2222, www.thebenchmarket.com, 7am-4pm Mon.-Fri., 8am-4pm Sat.-Sun., $5-16) serves breakfast all day, including a yummy salmon "eggwich" with smoked salmon, egg, and organic gouda grilled in an English muffin. Espresso and tea drinks go with the muffins, cookies, and other sweets, and lunches include paninis and salads. If you're planning a picnic, you can pick up locally made cheeses, gourmet crackers, and other treats.

Groceries and Markets

Shop for local produce and picnic fixings at the **Penticton Farmers Market** (100 block of Main St., 250/770-3276, www.pentictonfarmersmarket.org, 8:30am-1pm Sat. May-Oct.), one of the region's largest farm markets.

In Naramata, you can find food and snacks at the **Naramata General Store** (225 Robinson Ave., 250/496-5450, 7am-8pm Mon.-Thurs., 7am-10pm Fri., 8am-10pm Sat., 9am-8pm Sun.).

Accommodations

Owned by two artists who cater to independent art-loving travelers, **Cormier Studio B&B** (495 Vancouver Ave., Penticton, 250/493-3273, www.cormierstudio.com, $149-215) has three comfortable adult-oriented guest rooms on the lower level of a contemporary home set back from the street. Despite the "bed-and-breakfast" name, morning meals are not typically provided, but all units have kitchenettes with fridges, microwaves, and toasters, so you can prep your own, or head across the street to The Bench Artisan Food Market. More than a dozen wineries are within 3 miles (5 km) of the guest house.

Penticton Lakeside Resort (21 Lakeshore Dr. W., (250/493-8221 or 800/663-9400, www.pentictonlakesideresort.com, $188-400, parking $10) is two hotels in one. In the original building, directly on Okanagan Lake, rooms are more standard; the highlight is the balcony overlooking the water (in the lakeside units). The newer 70-room

West Wing is more boutique-chic, with contemporary blond wood furniture and spacious spa-like baths. In both buildings, rooms are equipped with coffee stations, mini fridges, and Wi-Fi. The property has a gym, indoor pool, and private beach, and you can rent kayaks, paddleboards, and other water toys to play on the lake.

Pack your sense of adventure for a stay at **God's Mountain Estate** (4898 Lakeside Rd., Penticton, 250/490-4800, www.godsmountain.ca, $215-299), an eclectic Mediterranean-style villa set on 115 secluded acres (47 ha) above Skaha Lake. The most unusual accommodations are in the Roofless Room, a romantic rooftop unit that's open to the sky. The other 13 guest rooms are an idiosyncratic mix of antiques and miscellanea, as you might envision in the home of an eccentric aunt. This adult-oriented property has no TV, radio, or phones, although Wi-Fi is included as is a full breakfast. The inn is located on the east side of Skaha Lake between Penticton and Okanagan Falls.

A stay at **Therapy Vineyards Guesthouse** (940 Debeck Rd., Naramata, 250/496-5217, www.therapyvineyards.com, $350-475), adjacent to the winery that produces wines like Pink Freud and Freudian Sip, may feel therapeutic, or at least supremely relaxing. Settle into one of the five deluxe rooms overlooking the vines, outfitted with contemporary cream and brown furnishings, spa-style baths, a large-screen TV, a fireplace, and a wine fridge. Rates include a complimentary wine-tasting as well as breakfast pastries, fruit, and tea or coffee served in the vineyard-view dining area.

There's a lot of history at the **Naramata Heritage Inn & Spa** (3625 1 St., Naramata, 778/514-5444, www.naramatainn.com, Apr.-Oct. $195-285), built in 1908

Top to bottom: produce for sale at Penticton Farmers Market; wines from Therapy Vineyards in Naramata; steak frites at The Kitchen at Time Winery.

in Naramata Village, on the shores of Okanagan Lake. Fruit baron John Moore Robinson constructed the property, which over the years has been a hotel, a private girls' school, and the Robinson family home. It still has its original woodwork and Mission-style furnishings; some of the 12 guest rooms, most of which are on the small side, have claw-foot tubs. Rates include continental breakfast and use of the inn's mountain bikes.

Information and Services

Tourism Penticton (www.visitpenticton. com) runs the **Penticton & Wine Country Visitor Centre** (888 Westminster Ave., 250/276-2170 or 800/663-5052, 9am-5pm Mon.-Fri.) and provides information about the area.

The **B.C. VQA Wine Information Centre** (553 Vees Dr., #101, Penticton, 250/490-2006, www.pentictonwineinfo.com, 9am-7pm daily spring-fall, 9am-6pm Mon.-Sat., 10am-5pm Sun. winter) is both a wine shop and an information office where staff can help you plan a wine tour, tell you about local wineries, and offer guidance on buying wines from its stock of more than 700 B.C. varieties.

For information about Naramata, stop into the **Discover Naramata Tourist Information Center** (176 Robinson Ave., 250/496-5450, www.discovernaramata. com, 10am-5pm Tues.-Sat., 11am-4pm Sun. May-June and Sept., 10am-5pm daily July-Aug.).

Penticton Regional Hospital (550 Carmi Ave., 250/492-4000, www. interiorhealth.ca) provides 24-hour emergency services.

Getting Around

Penticton is on the south end of Okanagan Lake, off Highway 97. Naramata borders Penticton to the east. Wineries line Naramata Road between Penticton and Naramata Village, which is on Okanagan Lake at the north end of Naramata Road.

OK Wine Shuttle (250/495-3278, www. okwineshuttle.ca) operates a **hop-on, hop-off shuttle** (11am-5pm daily Apr.-Oct., $85 pp), which picks up passengers at the Penticton Lakeside Resort and circles past the Naramata Bench wineries throughout the day; the driver normally returns to each stop every 30 minutes.

Osoyoos, Oliver, and Vicinity

When you think about Canada, does "desert" come to mind? Probably not—but the South Okanagan region along the U.S. border is a desert area. Situated at the northern end of the Sonoran Desert that extends south to Mexico, it's one of Canada's only deserts.

The warm, dry weather has long made the South Okanagan an agricultural area, growing fruits and vegetables years before the current grape boom took over. Orchards and farms are still abundant, but there are also plenty of wineries, from long-established producers to rising newcomers.

In addition to wine touring, the South Okanagan communities of Osoyoos, Oliver, and Okanagan Falls have other attractions, including several related to the desert environment and to the area's First Nations heritage. And when the warm, dry weather gets a little too warm, you can jump in the lake—Lake Osoyoos.

★ Wineries

For a directory of wineries in the South Okanagan, check the website for the **Oliver Osoyoos Winery Association** (www.oliverosoyoos.com), or pick up its brochure at area visitors centers. The following list includes some notable wineries to help you start planning your itinerary.

Osoyoos East Side

Canada's first indigenous-owned winery, **Nk'Mip Cellars** (1400 Rancher Creek

Rd., Osoyoos, 250/495-2985, www. nkmipcellars.com, 10am-8pm daily late June-Aug., 10am-7pm daily Apr.-late June and Sept.-Oct., 10am-5pm daily Nov.-Mar., tastings $5) is owned by the Osoyoos Indian Band, which manages the Spirit Ridge Resort and Nk'Mip Desert Cultural Centre on the same property. You can take a 90-minute winery tour (2pm daily Apr.-Oct., $15), where you learn how the band got into the wine business, tour the production facilities, and taste several wines. The winery currently produces chardonnay, pinot blanc, riesling, pinot noir, merlot, cabernet sauvignon, syrah, an ice wine, and several red blends. **TIP:** The name is pronounced "in-ka-meep."

Years ago, Osoyoos had a gold mine, and according to legend, American miners trying to smuggle gold across the border would curse at the bright moon that threatened to expose them. These tales gave rise to **Moon Curser Vineyards** (3628 Hwy. 3 E., Osoyoos, 250/495-5161, www.mooncurser.com, 10am-5pm daily Apr.-Dec., 10am-5pm Mon.-Fri. Jan.-Mar.), where the winemakers may not swear at the night sky but instead produce wines from less common varietals. In its tasting room, you might sample the smooth Dead of Night (a blend of tannat and syrah), arneis (an Italian grape similar to sauvignon blanc), or an unusual carménère.

Black Sage Road

One of the South Okanagan's most established wineries, **Burrowing Owl Estate Winery** (500 Burrowing Owl Pl., Oliver, 250/498-0620 or 877/498-0620, www. burrowingowlwine.ca, 10am-6pm daily Apr.-mid.-Oct., 10am-4pm Mon.-Wed., 10am-5pm Thurs.-Sun. mid-Oct.-mid-Dec., 10am-4pm Mon.-Fri. mid-Dec.-Feb., 10am-5pm daily Mar., tastings $5) donates proceeds from wine-tastings in its Tuscan-style shop to the Burrowing Owl conservation society, which is working to repopulate this endangered species; you can do your part for the local ecology as you sample chardonnay, pinot gris, pinot noir, merlot, and other varieties. Take a free **self-guided tour** by walking up the observation tower to scan the fermentation tanks, blending room, crush pad, and, at the top of the 103 steps, across the vineyards; informational panels tell you about the winery as you climb. Want to stay longer? Burrowing Owl has an excellent dining room and an upscale guest house.

Black Hills Estate Winery (4190 Black Sage Rd., Oliver, 250/498-6606, www. blackhillswinery.com, 11am-6pm daily, tastings $10-20) is something of a cult favorite among wine aficionados, particularly for its flagship Nota Bene, a Bordeaux-style blend of cabernet sauvignon, merlot, and cabernet franc. It's a "wow" wine, but the winery also makes the more affordable white Alibi (a sémillon-sauvignon blanc blend), viognier, or lush and peppery syrah. To go with your wine, have a meal-size salad or a creative pizza on the patio in the **Vineyard Kitchen Restaurant** (11:30am-5pm Thurs.-Sun. late May-mid-Oct.), overlooking the 40-acre (16-ha) property.

How do you pair wine with bread? Find out with a wine and bread tasting at **Platinum Bench Estate Winery & Artisan Bread Co.** (4120 Black Sage Rd., Oliver, 250/535-1165, www.platinumbench.com, 10am-5pm daily Apr.-Oct., noon-4pm Sat. Nov., by appointment Dec.-Mar., tastings $5), a winery with a bakeshop on its screened porch. Try Mur-Fi's White, a blend of chardonnay and viognier, named for husband-and-wife owners Murray Jones and Fiona Duncan, with the asiago cheese bread.

With cheeky labels suggesting "We Should Do This More Often" and "Tonight Is the Night," the Lost Inhibitions line at **Church and State Wines** (4516 Ryegrass Rd., Oliver, 250/498-2700, www.churchandstatewines.com, 11am-6pm Fri.-Sun. Apr., 11am-6pm daily May-Oct., by appointment Nov.-Mar.,

Osoyoos, Oliver, and Vicinity

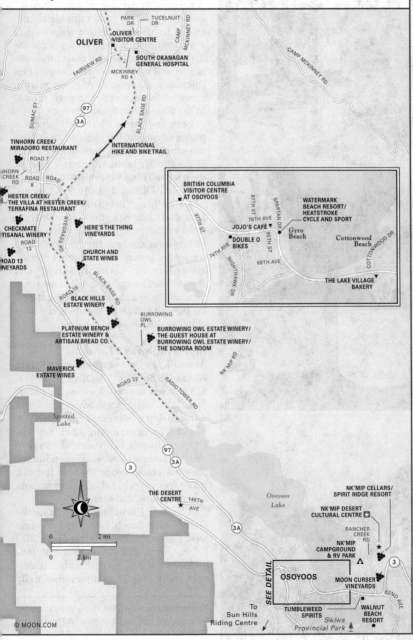

PARK DR
TUCELNUIT DR
CAMP McKINNEY RD

OLIVER
OLIVER VISITOR CENTRE
SOUTH OKANAGAN GENERAL HOSPITAL
CAMP McKINNEY RD
FAIRVIEW RD
McKINNEY RD
SUMAC ST
BLACK SAGE RD
97
3A

TINHORN CREEK/
MIRADORO RESTAURANT
ROAD 7
INTERNATIONAL HIKE AND BIKE TRAIL
TINHORN CREEK RD
ROAD 8
ROAD 9

HESTER CREEK/
THE VILLA AT HESTER CREEK/
TERRAFINA RESTAURANT

RYEGRASS RD

CHECKMATE TISANAL WINERY
ROAD 13
ROAD 13 VINEYARDS

HERE'S THE THING VINEYARDS

CHURCH AND STATE WINES

BLACK SAGE RD

ROAD 18
BLACK HILLS ESTATE WINERY

BURROWING OWL PL

PLATINUM BENCH ESTATE WINERY & ARTISAN BREAD CO.

BURROWING OWL ESTATE WINERY/
THE GUEST HOUSE AT BURROWING OWL ESTATE WINERY/
THE SONORA ROOM

NK'MIP RD

MAVERICK ESTATE WINES

ROAD 22
RADIO TOWER RD

Spotted Lake

97
3
3A

THE DESERT CENTRE
146TH AVE

Osoyoos Lake

3A

BRITISH COLUMBIA VISITOR CENTRE AT OSOYOOS
87TH ST
SPARTAN DR
78TH AVE
WATERMARK BEACH RESORT/
HEATSTROKE CYCLE AND SPORT
JOJO'S CAFÉ
97TH ST
85TH ST
Gyro Beach
Cottonwood Beach
COTTONWOOD DR
DOUBLE O BIKES
74TH AVE
68TH AVE
NIGHTHAWK DR
THE LAKE VILLAGE BAKERY

0   2 mi
0   2 km

NK'MIP CELLARS/
SPIRIT RIDGE RESORT

NK'MIP DESERT CULTURAL CENTRE

RANCHER CREEK RD

NK'MIP CAMPGROUND & RV PARK

SEE DETAIL

OSOYOOS

MOON CURSER VINEYARDS

62ND AVE
3

To Sun Hills Riding Centre

TUMBLEWEED SPIRITS

WALNUT BEACH RESORT

sẁiẁs Provincial Park

© MOON.COM

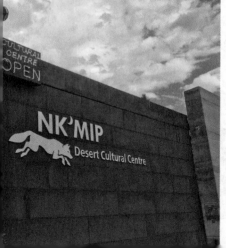

tastings $8) makes great gifts for a special someone—or someone not so special, since others bear less printable slogans. Either way, they're good-value blends, designed for drinkers with a sense of fun. For something more serious, sample the Trebella (a white blend of marsanne, rousanne, and viognier) or the Coup D'Etat (blending cabernet sauvignon, merlot, cabernet franc, syrah, and petit verdot) in the über-modern tasting room.

Leah and Jamie McDowell left their previous careers but decided they were too young to retire. After hatching a plan at the dinner table, the couple opened **Here's The Thing Vineyards** (4740 Black Sage Rd., Oliver, 250/498-9712, www.heresthethingvineyards.com, 11am-5pm daily late Apr.-mid-Oct., tastings free), a solar-powered winery in a sunny yellow house, where they're producing rousanne, gamay noir, cabernet merlot, a big-flavored "Seriously Syrah," and "Living the Dream" rosé. When you stop for a tasting or a glass on the patio, they'll happily tell you about the ups and downs of living this winemaking dream.

Along Highway 97
At small, family-owned **Maverick Estate Wines** (3974 Hwy. 97, Oliver, 778/437-3133, www.maverickwine.ca, 10am-5pm daily, tastings $3), where the South African-born winemaker previously worked for Burrowing Owl, try the Origin white (a full-flavored blend of gewürztraminer and sauvignon blanc), the spicy pinot gris, or the bold Rubeus, made from syrah, cabernet sauvignon, cabernet franc, and merlot.

A 95-acre (38-ha) property along the Golden Mile Bench, where its first vines were planted in 1968, **Hester Creek** (877 Rd. 8, Oliver, 250/498-4435 or 866/498-4435, www.hestercreek.com, 10am-6pm daily May-Oct., 10am-4pm daily

Top to bottom: Here's The Thing Vineyards; wine at Black Hills Estate Winery; Nk'Mip Desert Cultural Centre.

◈ Side Trip: Fruit and Wine in the Similkameen Valley

As the Okanagan's wine industry continues to mature, more wineries are opening in the agricultural **Similkameen Valley** (www.similkameenvalley.com), along Highway 3 west of Osoyoos. If you haven't had your fill of wines in the Okanagan, or you'd like to explore this up-and-coming destination, stop off when you're traveling between Osoyoos and Vancouver, or make a detour during your South Okanagan stay.

The Similkameen Valley has more than 15 wineries, a number of which offer complimentary tastings. Most are located around the communities of Keremeos and Cawston, where fruit stands selling peaches, apples, and other seasonal produce also line the roads. Many of the families who farm this area are of East Indian heritage, so at some markets, you'll find samosas, *pakoras,* and curries as well.

To start your Similkameen winery tour, consider stops at the following destinations:

♦ **Clos du Soleil Winery** (2568 Upper Bench Rd., Keremeos, 250/499-2831, www. closdusoleil.ca, 10am-5pm daily May-Oct.)

♦ **Crowsnest Vineyards** (2035 Surprise Dr., Cawston, 250/499-5129, www. crowsnestvineyards.com, 10am-5pm daily May-Oct.)

♦ **Forbidden Fruit Winery** (620 Sumac Rd., Cawston, 250/499-2649, www. forbiddenfruitwines.com, 10am-6pm daily Apr.-Oct.)

♦ **Orofino Winery** (2152 Barcelo Rd., Cawston, 250/499-0068, www. orofinovineyards.com, 10am-5pm Thurs.-Mon. May-June, 10am-5pm daily July-Oct.)

♦ **Seven Stones Winery** (1143 Hwy. 3, Cawston, 250/499-2144, www.sevenstones.ca, 10am-6pm daily May-Oct.)

And to keep up with what's new in the Similkameen region, check with the **Similkameen Wineries Association** (250/488-0878, www.similkameenwine.com).

Nov.-Apr., tastings $3-5) has a modern Mediterranean-style tasting room, where you can sample from its long list of wines. The winery hosts cooking classes, winemaker dinners, and other special events throughout the year. An Italian dining room and six-suite inn are also part of the business.

Have you ever sipped wine in a castle? The tasting room at family-owned **Road 13 Vineyards** (799 Ponderosa Rd., Oliver, 250/498-8330, www.road13vineyards. com, 10am-5:30pm daily mid-Apr.-mid-Oct., 1pm-4pm Mon.-Sat. mid-Oct.-mid-Apr., tastings $5) is designed like a Bavarian-style manor, complete with drawbridge. Here you can sample wines like a crisp marsanne or silky GSM (a red blend of grenache, syrah, and mourvedre). **Premium tastings** (11am-5pm daily mid-Apr.-mid-Oct., tastings $15) of the higher-end wines are available in a sleek lounge overlooking the vineyards. The winery also organizes a series of dinners May-October in partnership with a local farm; check the website for the schedule.

With a tasting room launched in a high-style window-lined pop-up shop, **CheckMate Artisanal Winery** (4799 Wild Rose St., Oliver, 250/707-2299, www.checkmatewinery.com, 11am-7pm daily May-Oct., 10am-4pm Mon.-Fri. Nov.-Apr., tastings $20-30) is producing high-end wines, including several chardonnays and merlots, and constructing a new winery building slated to open in 2019. Allow about an hour for the indepth guided tastings; appointments are recommended.

Tinhorn Creek (537 Tinhorn Creek Rd., Oliver, 250/498-3743 or 888/484-6467, www.tinhorn.com, 10am-6pm daily Mar.-Oct., 10am-4pm daily Nov.-Feb., tastings $5) produces whites (gewürztraminer, pinot gris, chardonnay, and the 2Bench White blend), rosé, and reds (cabernet franc, merlot, syrah, pinot noir, and the 2Bench Red blend). The hillside wine shop is open for tastings year-round, and in summer, the winery presents a **Canadian Concert Series** (May-Aug.) in an outdoor amphitheater.

You can start with a sampling in the rustic tasting room at **Covert Farms** (30 Covert Pl., Oliver, 250/498-9463, www.covertfarms.ca, 11am-5pm daily mid-Apr.-Oct., tastings $5), an organic winery and farm atop a steep hill north of Oliver that produces sauvignon blanc, sémillon, pinot blanc, rosé, and several proprietary red blends. It also offers a unique experience: a 1- to 1.5-hour **tour** (adults $59, ages 6-18 $20) of the farm and vineyards in a vintage 1952 truck. You can purchase organic produce from the farm stand (June-Oct.) or pick your own berries or other seasonal crops. The farm is also the starting point for a hike to **McIntyre Bluff,** a rocky cliff with views across the valley.

Okanagan Falls
North of Oliver, there's a cluster of wineries in the community of Okanagan Falls. Places to visit include **Blasted Church Vineyards** (378 Parsons Rd., Okanagan Falls, 250/497-1125 or 877/355-2686, www.blastedchurch.com, 10am-5pm daily May-mid-Nov., tastings $5) and **See Ya Later Ranch** (2575 Green Lake Rd., Okanagan Falls, 250/497-8267, www.sylranch.com, 10am-6pm daily July-early Sept., 10am-5pm daily Mar.-June and early Sept.-Oct., 11am-4pm Fri.-Sun.

Nov.-Dec., 11am-4pm Fri.-Mon. Feb., tastings $5).

Another distinctive property is **Liquidity Winery Bistro Gallery** (4720 Allendale Rd., Okanagan Falls, 778/515-5500, www.liquiditywines.com, 11am-6pm daily May-mid-Oct., noon-5pm daily mid-Oct.-mid-Dec. and Feb.-Apr., tastings $5), which, as the name suggests, makes wine, shows art from owner Ian MacDonald's contemporary collection, and serves excellent food in its **Bistro** (noon-8pm daily late-Mar.-mid-Oct.) in an art-filled dining room high above the valley.

Distilleries
Craft distiller **Tumbleweed Spirits** (6001 Lakeshore Dr., Osoyoos, 778/437-2221, www.tumbleweedspirits.com, 11am-6pm daily late May-mid-Oct., noon-5pm Thurs.-Sat. mid-Oct.-late May) is known for its rye, which it makes from 100 percent B.C.-grown grain. The distiller also produces vodka, gin, and Fireweed, a cinnamon- and chili-spiced whiskey.

Dubh Glas Distillery (8486 Gallagher Lake Frontage Rd., Oliver, 778/439-3580, www.thedubhglasdistillery.com, 11am-6pm Fri.-Sun.) brews its Noteworthy Gin from B.C.-grown barley. Try it at the distillery tasting room.

Sights
★ Nk'Mip Desert Cultural Centre
Have you ever touched a rattlesnake? Listened to the legend of the coyote? Wandered through the sagebrush on a desert trail? Explore the creatures and plants that live in the region's desert and learn more about Okanagan First Nations culture at the **Nk'Mip Desert Cultural Centre** (1000 Rancher Creek Rd., Osoyoos, 250/495-7901 or 888/495-8555, www.nkmipdesert.com, 9:30am-4:30pm daily, adults $14, seniors and students $13, ages 5-17 $11, families $38), a facility for natural and cultural education run by the Osoyoos Indian Band in an eco-friendly rammed earth structure. Visit

in July or August if you can, when interpreters introduce you to snakes and other desert inhabitants and lead daily guided trail walks; visits during the rest of the year are self-guided.

The Desert Centre
In the hills between Osoyoos and Oliver, **The Desert Centre** (14580 146th Ave., Osoyoos, 250/495-2470 or 877/899-0897, www.desert.org, 9:30am-4:30pm daily mid-May-mid-Sept., 10am-2pm daily late Apr.-mid-May and mid-Sept.-early Oct., adults $7, seniors and ages 6-17 $6, families $18) lets you explore the Okanagan's desert plants and animals. On this 67-acre (27-ha) protected site, a small exhibit area shows animal skulls, snakeskins, and displays about local wildlife. Outside, you can follow a 1-mile (1.6-km) boardwalk trail through the desert. Optional guided tours (10am, noon, and 2pm daily mid-May-mid-Sept.) are included with your admission, or you can explore on your own. The grounds are particularly vibrant in the spring, when the yellow antelope brush blooms.

Spotted Lake
The Okanagan First Nation considers it a sacred site, known for its healing properties. **Spotted Lake** (Hwy. 3), called *Kliluk* in the Okanagan language, is certainly an unusual geological feature. It's a mineral-rich lake whose waters evaporate over the summer months, leaving behind mineral deposits in circular spots, giving the lake its name and its distinctive appearance. The lake is located on private property, 6 miles (10 km) northwest of Osoyoos, but you can pull over and have a look from the side of the highway.

Sports and Recreation
Beaches
Osoyoos has an average summer temperature of 87°F (31°C), so a splash in the lake helps beat the heat. On Osoyoos Lake, **Gyro Beach** (off Main St.) is the area's largest, with sand, shade trees, and restrooms, right in town behind Watermark Beach Resort. **Cottonwood Beach** (Cottonwood Dr., off Main St.), on the town's east side, is another popular place to swim and sun.

On a skinny peninsula jutting into Osoyoos Lake, **Sẁiẁs Provincial Park** (off Hwy. 97, Osoyoos, 778/437-2295, www.env.gov.bc.ca), formerly known as Haynes Point before adopting its traditional Okanagan First Nations name, has a narrow swimming beach and a walking trail through the marsh. The park is 1.25 miles (2 km) south of downtown Osoyoos, off Highway 97; its name is pronounced "swee-yous."

Hiking and Cycling
The flat, 11.7-mile (19-km) **International Hike and Bike Trail** follows the Okanagan River in the Oliver area. More than half of the route is paved; the rest is gravel. A convenient access point for the trail is behind the **Oliver Visitor Centre** (6431 Station St.).

Cycling from winery to winery on the region's back roads is also a great way to explore, as long as you don't mind some hills and can moderate your wine consumption.

Double O Bikes (8905 Main St., Osoyoos, 250/495-3312, www.doubleobikes.com, 9:30am-5pm daily May-Sept., 9:30am-5pm Tues.-Sat. Oct.-Apr.) rents regular bikes (4 hours $15-30, full-day $30-80) and **electric bikes** (4 hours $45, full-day $90).

Heatstroke Cycle and Sport (15 Park Pl., Unit 225, Osoyoos, 250/689-5977, www.heatstrokecycle.com), based at the Watermark Beach Resort, rents road (1 hour $20, full-day $80), mountain (1 hour $10, full-day $40), hybrid (1 hour $8, full-day $30), and electric bikes (1 hour $25, full-day $99). It also offers a variety of **cycling tours,** including two where you travel by **electric bike:** the four- to five-hour **Golden Mile Wine**

Rest Stop: Hope

Most people end up in the small town of Hope when they're traveling between the Okanagan and Vancouver, since it's located near the junction of three major routes: Highway 1, Highway 3, and Highway 5. Take a break for gas and food here if you're heading east over the mountains or west toward the coast, or stretch your legs at the Othello Tunnels just east of the town center. For more area information, stop into the **Hope Visitor Centre** (919 Water Ave., 604/869-2021, www.hopebc.ca, 10am-4pm Mon.-Fri., 9am-5pm Sat.-Sun.).

The Othello Tunnels

On Hope's east side, about a 15-minute drive from town, stretch your legs with a short walk into history at the **Othello Tunnels** in **Coquihalla Canyon Provincial Park** (www.env.gov.bc.ca). Built in the early 1900s as part of the Kettle Valley Railway, which once provided the main rail link between B.C.'s interior and the coast, the Othello Tunnels enabled the railroad to pass through the Coquihalla Gorge, where the Coquihalla River carved a 300-foot-deep (91-m) channel of solid granite. And yes, the tunnels were named after Shakespeare's character. The Kettle Valley Railway was dismantled in the 1980s, and along the Othello Tunnels section, you can follow a flat walking path (2.1 mi/3.4 km round-trip) through these five impressive granite passages. Bring a flashlight; the tunnels are dark inside, and the path can be uneven and often wet.

To reach the tunnels coming from the west, take Exit 170 from Highway 1 at Hope and turn left at the end of the exit ramp. Turn right onto Old Hope-Princeton Highway, left at 6th Avenue, then right onto Kawkawa Lake Road. Take the second right onto Othello Road, and then stay right to continue on Othello Road to the parking area. It's 5 miles (8 km) east of Hope.

If you're traveling south on Highway 5 from Kamloops or Kelowna, take Exit 183 and follow Othello Road to the tunnels. Heading west on Highway 3, turn north onto Highway 5. Follow Exit 183 off Highway 5 and take Othello Road to the tunnels.

Food and Accommodations

Hope has 20 motels where you can rest for the night. Most are basic chains or local lodgings on Highway 1 (Water Ave.), the Old Hope-Princeton Highway, or Wallace Street.

Need a coffee break? Look for the **Blue Moose Coffeehouse** (322 Wallace St., 604/869-0729, www.bluemoose.coffee, 7am-9pm daily May-Sept., 7am-7pm daily Oct.-Apr., $5-10), where coffee is ground to order and you can choose from a wide selection of teas. Pastries and sandwiches can assuage most hunger pangs.

A time-honored stop for road-trippers, **Home Restaurant** (665 Old Hope-Princeton Hwy., 604/869-5558, www.homerestaurants.ca, breakfast $9-17, lunch and dinner $10-19) dishes up filling diner fare, including bacon and eggs, burgers, and roast turkey dinners. And yes, there's pie.

For something more interesting than ordinary roadside grub, try **293 Wallace** (293 Wallace St., 604/860-0822, www.293wallace.com, noon-3pm and 5pm-9pm Wed.-Mon., $13-34), a contemporary dining room with dark wood tables and parquet floors. The menu includes homemade soups, fresh salads, and sandwiches, like a veggie wrap stuffed with feta, eggplant, and peppers, or the well-loved beef dip.

Country Tour ($170), a guided ride to several South Okanagan wineries; or the **Black Sage Road Cycle Wine & Dine Tour** ($225), with wine and food samplings along the Black Sage Bench.

Horseback Riding

Sun Hills Riding Centre (3800 Golf Course Dr., Osoyoos, 250/408-9990, www.sunhillsriding.ca) rescues and rehabilitates horses. Once the animals regain their health, staff take visitors on guided **trail rides** (9am, 11am, and 6pm daily July-Aug., 1 hour $60, reservations required) around the Osoyoos property or into the surrounding hills. In addition to these scheduled rides, the center arranges custom 90-minute trail rides ($90) by reservation September-June. Riders must be at least eight years old.

Festivals and Events

What do running and wine-tasting have in common? You can do both at the annual **Half-Corked Marathon** (www.oliverosoyoos.com, May), an 11-mile (18-km) fun run with nearly a dozen stops for wine-tasting and food along the way. As the organizers advise, "If you're planning on setting a record, this might not be the race for you." Registration for this popular event is by lottery, which normally takes place in the fall; sign up online for the event newsletter to be notified of the lottery dates.

Oliver's annual **Festival of the Grape** (www.oliverfestivalofthegrape.ca, Oct.) includes music, wine-tastings, and a grape-stomping competition.

Food

Winery Restaurants

Top-notch food, polished service, and panoramic vistas over the Black Sage Bench make ★ **The Sonora Room** (500 Burrowing Owl Pl., Oliver, 250/498-0620 or 877/498-0620, www.burrowingowlwine.ca, noon-4:30pm and 5pm-8pm Thurs.-Mon. Apr., 11:30am-4:30pm and 5pm-9pm daily May-mid-Oct., 5pm-8pm Thurs. and noon-4:30pm and 5pm-8pm Fri.-Sun. mid-Oct.-mid-Dec. and mid-Feb.-Mar., lunch $20-32, dinner $26-46), at Burrowing Owl Estate Winery, a must-visit dining destination. You might kick off your meal with tuna and beef carpaccio served atop a black garlic emulsion or seared scallops with cauliflower and caper berries, and continue with local steelhead trout paired with heirloom beets and creamed greens,

honey-glazed pork belly with aubergine relish, or grilled beef tenderloin. The menu suggests a wine pairing for each dish, and staff can provide further assistance. A glass of the port-style Coruja and the sun setting over the vineyards wrap up an ideal evening.

The name is Italian, meaning "from the earth," so fittingly, ★ **Terrafina Restaurant** (887 Rd. 8, Oliver, 250/498-2229, www.terrafinabyraudz.com, 11:30am-9pm Wed.-Sat., 11am-3pm Sun. mid-Feb.-Apr., 11:30am-9pm daily May.-Oct., 11:30am-8pm Wed.-Sat., 11am-3pm Sun. Nov., brunch $14-21, lunch $15-26, dinner $20-34), at Hester Creek Winery, serves fine Italian-influenced fare made from local Okanagan ingredients. Pizzas come out of the wood-fired oven layered with potatoes and truffle aioli, or pears, smoked gorgonzola, and ham, and pastas might be topped with wild boar meatballs. The menu adds dishes like pillowy parmesan gnocchi with pesto, grilled Humboldt squid with pickled radicchio, and braised lamb shank in a tomato ragu. You can eat on the patio when the weather is fine.

At ★ **Liquidity Bistro** (4720 Allendale Rd., Okanagan Falls, 778/515-5500, www.liquiditywines.com, noon-8pm daily late Mar.-mid-Oct., lunch $19-26, dinner $23-34), an art-filled, window-lined dining room with views across the valley, even dishes with simple names are extremely inventive. "Veggies 'n' Dip" might give you fresh-from-the-farm vegetables with a creamy cucumber sauce, and "Lamb Meatballs and Eggs," might be served over heirloom greens with pickled peppers and arugula. Bring your explorer's spirit, particularly in the evening, when the kitchen might concoct pigeon with coffee kombucha, venison with bitter greens and black barley, or mushrooms steamed over kelp with salted plum. Celebrating something? Opt for the chef's multicourse tasting menu ($80) with optional wine pairings.

Perched on a hill at Tinhorn Creek

Winery, **Miradoro Restaurant** (537 Tinhorn Creek Rd., Oliver, 250/498-3742, www.tinhorn.com, 11:30am-9pm daily Mar.-Dec., $17-56) has a rustic elegance, whether you dine indoors in the window-lined dining room or out on the covered heated terrace. You can go simple with a Neapolitan-style pizza from the wood-fired oven, perhaps paired with a salad or a plate of house-cured charcuterie. The kitchen gets adventurous, though, with starters like grilled octopus with an olive salsa verde or a kale salad amped up with balsamic pickled egg, and mains like smoked sablefish with ramen risotto or duck paired with espresso-roasted beets. The gracious service and thoughtful wine pairings help make your meal more special.

Cafés, Bakeries, and Light Bites

It's worth waking up early for the sourdough cinnamon buns at **The Lake Village Bakery** (6511 Main St., Osoyoos, 250/495-3366, www.thelakevillagebakery.ca, generally 9am-4pm Wed.-Sat., call for seasonal hours), a family-owned strip-mall bakeshop that turns out all sorts of baked treats. It's also known for sourdough croissants, fresh-baked breads, and various cookies. Go early; it closes when the goodies sell out.

Everyone in town seems to pass through **Jojo's Café** (316 Main St., Osoyoos, 250/495-6652, ww.jojoscafe.ca, 7am-4pm daily, $4-10), a coffeehouse and community hub. Besides the java, it sells pastries and sandwiches and hosts periodic live music events. Wi-Fi is free.

Accommodations and Camping

Osoyoos has several upscale resort hotels overlooking Lake Osoyoos, as well as a strip of aging motels. In Oliver, you can stay amid the vineyards in posh winery guesthouses.

Top to bottom: plates to share at Liquidity Bistro; Watermark Beach Resort; lunch at Terrafina Restaurant.

You'd never know that stylish ★ **Watermark Beach Resort** (15 Park Pl., Osoyoos, 250/495-5500 or 888/755-3480, www.watermarkbeachresort.com, $159-858 d, 2-bedroom suite $279-1,098) was built on the site of a former fruit packinghouse. Today, this 153-suite resort has everything you need for a lakeside holiday. In the main building, the one-, two-, and three-bedroom suites, decorated in beachy terra-cotta or sage green, have full kitchens, washer-dryers, and balconies, many facing the sandy lakeshore or the large outdoor pool and patio. Families might also like the 30 townhouse-style beachfront villas. The resort can arrange cycling tours, wine experiences, and other activities; it's partnered with Covert Farms to offer a farm and winery tour. With a lakeview patio, **The Restaurant at Watermark** uses lots of local products in dishes like an unusual sockeye salmon falafel with pickled radish or roasted chicken thighs paired with heirloom tomatoes and handmade gnocchi.

Part of a complex of businesses owned by the Osoyoos Indian Band, **Spirit Ridge Resort** (1200 Rancher Creek Rd., Osoyoos, 250/495-5445 or 877/313-9463, www.spiritridge.ca, $199-499 d, 2-bedroom suite $249-609, 3-bedroom suite $359-719) is an upscale condo resort, now marketed through Hyatt's Unbound Collection. Backed by rolling hills, above the lake on Osoyoos's east side, with the vineyards of the Nk'mip Cellars winery all around, the Tuscan-style buildings house one-, two-, and three-bedroom suites, with full kitchens and balconies or patios. A restaurant, outdoor pool, hot tubs, fitness center, and golf course are among the amenities. The Nk'Mip Desert Cultural Centre is also on the property. Although the resort has a private beach, the accommodations aren't lakeside; a shuttle takes guests down to the lakeshore.

On the east side of Osoyoos Lake, condo-style **Walnut Beach Resort** (4200 Lakeshore Dr., Osoyoos, 250/495-5400 or 877/936-5400, www.walnutbeachresort.com, $189-449 d, 2-bedroom suite $309-679) has 112 straightforward earth-toned studio, one-, and two-bedroom suites, all with decks facing either the lake or the desert hills. The larger units have kitchens. The property has a small exercise room, a sauna, and a steam room, but the real action is outdoors, with a sandy lakeside beach, a year-round heated pool, two hot tubs, and a patio wine bar. You can rent kayaks, canoes, and Jet-Skis on the beach.

An intimate wine-country escape, ★ **The Guest House at Burrowing Owl Estate Winery** (500 Burrowing Owl Pl., Oliver, 250/498-0620 or 877/498-0620, www.burrowingowlwine.ca, mid-Feb.-mid.-Dec., $249-349) has 10 contemporary guest rooms, with fireplaces and decks that look over the winery's vineyards. Decorated with light woods, slate floors, and cream-and-beige soft goods, the upscale suites are air-conditioned with mini fridges, flat-screen TVs, and Wi-Fi. A full "wine country" breakfast is served daily. If you need more space, the inn has a grand two-bedroom penthouse with a gourmet kitchen. With walls decorated with local art, this deluxe inn's best features are the 25-meter seasonal solar-heated pool with vineyard views, the excellent **Sonora Room** restaurant, and the proximity to the wineries on the Black Sage Bench.

You may spend all your time on your patio at **The Villa at Hester Creek** (877 Rd. 8, Oliver, 250/498-4435 or 866/498-4435, www.hestercreek.com, mid-Feb.-Nov., $269-399), sipping wine overlooking the vineyards or enjoying your breakfast, but the six Mediterranean-style suites are pretty special inside, too. Five of the units have a duvet-topped king bed, a fireplace, a bar fridge, a microwave, and a large bath with granite countertops and both a soaker tub and a walk-in shower. In the larger La Sirena Executive Suite, the bed is a queen, but there's a separate living room. Wi-Fi is included in the rates.

◈ Side Trip: The Fraser Canyon

At the town of Hope, several hours' drive west of Osoyoos on the way to Vancouver, the Trans-Canada—Highway 1—turns north, where the Fraser River has shaped a deep canyon, creating a rocky gorge between the Cascades and Coast Mountains. Since the 1980s, when the faster Coquihalla Highway (Hwy. 5) replaced this section of the Trans-Canada as the most direct route between Vancouver and the Canadian Rockies, this scenic section of Highway 1 has often been overlooked. But for road-trippers who have time for a more leisurely drive, there's a lot to do along the Fraser Canyon.

Hell's Gate Airtram swings over the Fraser Canyon.

Explore Gold Rush History

The tiny hamlet of Yale, 15 miles (24 km) north of Hope, had two boom times in the late 1800s, when prospectors came north during British Columbia's brief gold rush, and again during the construction of Canada's transcontinental railroad. The town grew into the largest community west of Chicago and north of San Francisco. At **Yale Historic Site** (31187 Douglas St., 604/863-2324, www.historicyale.ca, 10am-5pm daily May-Sept., adults $10, seniors $9, ages 7-18 $8, families $30), you can trace this history as you peek into tents that served as the general store, doctor's office, and saloon. Visit St. John the Divine Church, where parishioners worshipped 1863-1976, or see what life was like in the Chinese boardinghouse where many railroad workers lived.

Swing Through Hell's Gate

For another perspective on the Fraser Canyon, ride the **Hell's Gate Airtram** (43111 Trans-Canada Hwy., 604/867-9277, www.hellsgateairtram.com, 10am-4pm daily mid-Apr.-May, 10am-5pm daily June-early Sept., adults $24, seniors and students $22, ages 6-18 18, families $84), which plunges (gently) into the gorge at the river's deepest and narrowest point. From the suspension bridge at the base, you can take in more river and canyon vistas. There's also an exhibit about the salmon that spawn in the river and another about the explorers who traveled the region. The airtram is on Highway 1, 43 miles (69 km) north of Hope.

Raft the Canyon

The Fraser Canyon is one of western Canada's hot spots for white-water rafting. Get on the water at the secluded **REO Rafting Resort** (Nahatlatch Rd., 604/941-9777 or 800/736-7238, www.reorafting.com, May-Sept.), which runs half- and full-day **rafting excursions** ($135-180 pp) on the Fraser and the nearby Nahatlatch and Thompson Rivers. If you want to stay longer, settle into one of the resort's riverview **"glamping" tents** ($275 pp including meals) for a stopover combining rafting, yoga, and relaxing by the river. To reach this remote property, which is about 52 miles (84 km) north of Hope, turn left off Highway 1 at the town of Boston Bar, following the signs for the resort along Chaumox and Nahatlatch Forest Service Roads; it's about 9.5 miles (15 km) from the main highway.

Camping

Run by the Osoyoos Indian Band, who operate the nearby Spirit Ridge Resort, the busy **Nk'mip Campground & RV Park** (8000 45th St., Osoyoos, 250/495-7279, www.campingosoyoos.com, tent sites $35-48, electrical sites $35-60, yurts $80-90) is located directly on Lake Osoyoos. The 400 sites accommodate everything from tents to big RVs. Campground amenities include washrooms with showers, laundry facilities, and an indoor pool and hot tub (Oct.-May).

At **Sẁiẁs Provincial Park** (off Hwy. 97, Osoyoos, 778/437-2295, www.env.gov. bc.ca, Apr.-mid-Oct., $32), on a narrow peninsula jutting into the lake, the 41 campsites are close together, although most are right on the lake. The park, which has flush toilets and cold-water taps, is 1.25 miles (2 km) south of downtown Osoyoos. You can reserve sites in advance mid-May-early September; **reservations** (519/826-6850 or 800/689-9025, www.discovercamping.ca) are recommended for all weekends during that period and anytime in July and August.

Information and Services
Visitor Information

The **British Columbia Visitor Centre at Osoyoos** (9912 Hwy. 3, at Hwy. 97, 250/495-5410, www.hellobc.com, 9am-6pm daily mid-June-mid-Sept., 9am-5pm daily early May-mid-June and mid-Sept.-mid-Oct., 9am-5pm Mon.-Fri.

mid-Oct.-early May) can assist with travel questions and information about the Okanagan region. The center has free public Wi-Fi.

Located in a former train station built in 1923, the **Oliver Visitor Centre** (6431 Station St., 778/439-2363 or 844/896-3300, www.winecapitalofcanada.com, 9am-5pm Mon.-Fri., longer hours July-Aug.) has details about local wineries and attractions.

Medical Services

South Okanagan General Hospital (911 McKinney Rd., Oliver, 250/498-5000, www.interiorhealth.ca) provides medical services for Osoyoos, Oliver, and the surrounding communities. The hospital has a 24-hour emergency room.

Getting Around

Osoyoos is at the intersection of Highways 3 and 97. Highway 3 runs east-west through town. Highway 97 will take you north from Osoyoos to Oliver and on to Penticton; heading south on Highway 97, you'll cross the U.S. border into Washington State.

OK Wine Shuttle (250/495-3278, www. okwineshuttle.ca) runs a **hop-on, hop-off shuttle** (11am-5pm daily Apr.-Oct., $85 pp), which picks up at several local hotels and then circles past the Oliver-Osoyoos wineries throughout the day; the driver normally returns to each stop every 30 minutes.

Calgary

Calgary

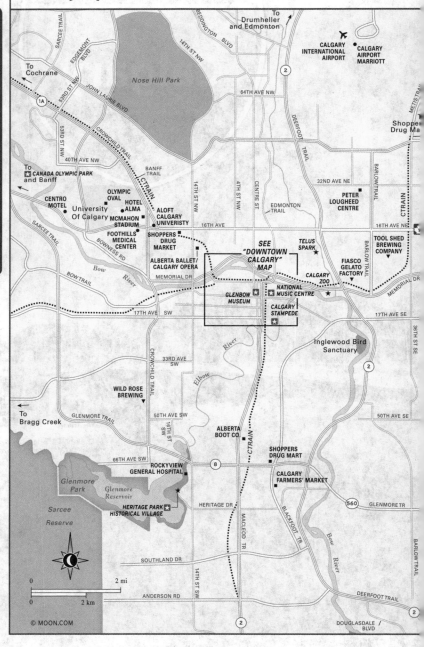

To Cochrane

Nose Hill Park

To Drumheller and Edmonton

CALGARY INTERNATIONAL AIRPORT

CALGARY AIRPORT MARRIOTT

SARCEE TRAIL

EDGEMONT BLVD

53RD ST NW

JOHN LAURIE BLVD

BEDDINGTON BLVD

14TH ST NW

64TH AVE NW

Shoppers Drug Ma

1A

53RD ST NW

40TH AVE NW

CROWCHILD TRAIL

BANFF TRAIL

CTRAIN

14TH ST NW

4TH ST NW

CENTRE ST

EDMONTON TRAIL

DEERFOOT TRAIL

32ND AVE NE

BARLOW TRAIL

CTRAIN

METIS TR

To CANADA OLYMPIC PARK and Banff

CENTRO MOTEL

University Of Calgary

OLYMPIC OVAL

HOTEL ALMA

MCMAHON STADIUM

ALOFT CALGARY UNIVERISTY

16TH AVE

PETER LOUGHEED CENTRE

16TH AVE NE

SARCEE TRAIL

FOOTHILLS MEDICAL CENTER

BOWNESS RD

SHOPPERS DRUG MARKET

Bow River

ALBERTA BALLET/ CALGARY OPERA

MEMORIAL DR

SEE "DOWNTOWN CALGARY" MAP

TELUS SPARK ★

CALGARY ZOO

NATIONAL MUSIC CENTRE ★

FIASCO GELATO FACTORY ▼

BARLOW TRAIL

TOOL SHED BREWING COMPANY ▼

MEMORIAL DR

BOW TRAIL

GLENBOW MUSEUM ✪

17TH AVE SW

CALGARY STAMPEDE ✪

17TH AVE SE

36TH ST SE

Elbow River

33RD AVE SW

CROWCHILD TRAIL

Inglewood Bird Sanctuary

2

To Bragg Creek

GLENMORE TRAIL

WILD ROSE BREWING ▼

50TH AVE SW

16TH ST SW

50TH AVE SE

66TH AVE SW

ROCKYVIEW GENERAL HOSPITAL

8

CTRAIN

ALBERTA BOOT CO.

SHOPPERS DRUG MART

CALGARY FARMERS' MARKET

560

GLENMORE TR

Glenmore Park

Glenmore Reservoir

★

HERITAGE PARK ✪ HISTORICAL VILLAGE

HERITAGE DR

MACLEOD TR

BLACKFOOT TR

Bow River

BARLOW TRAIL

Sarcee Reserve

0   2 mi

0   2 km

SOUTHLAND DR

14TH ST SW

DEERFOOT TRAIL

ANDERSON RD

2

DOUGLASDALE / BLVD

2

© MOON.COM

Highlights

★ **Glenbow Museum:** Part history museum, part art gallery, and part cultural curator, this excellent museum tells Calgary's stories from its earliest days to the present (page 406).

★ **National Music Centre:** With plenty of hands-on activities, this modern multimedia museum showcases Canadian music, performers, and composers past and present, and also presents concerts (page 406).

★ **Heritage Park Historical Village:** From rum running to fur trading to a "Little Synagogue on the Prairie," you can explore western Canada from the 1860s to 1950s at the country's largest living history village (page 407).

★ **Canada Olympic Park:** Whiz down the bobsled track, try out the luge, or go zip-lining, mountain biking, and more at Calgary's 1988 Winter Olympics venue, which also houses Canada's Sports Hall of Fame (page 411).

★ **Calgary Stampede:** One of western Canada's biggest festivals, this rodeo, county fair, and crazy party rolled into one takes over Calgary for 10 days every July (page 415).

Shop for a Stetson, graze on bison carpaccio, or head off to explore the mountains from this gateway to the Canadian Rockies.

With its trademark cowboy swagger, Calgary hosts one of Canada's biggest parties. The annual Calgary Stampede takes over the city every July, proclaiming itself "The Greatest Outdoor Show on Earth."

The rest of the year, this region of nearly 1.5 million wears its western heritage a little more quietly. Canada's fourth-largest metropolis is often compared to U.S. cities like Houston, as a headquarters for the energy business, or Denver, a gateway to the Rocky Mountains. And there's truth to these comparisons. Oil, gas, and related energy industries are major drivers of Calgary's economy, and with its location just 90 minutes from Banff, Calgary is the closest major city to Canada's Rocky Mountain national parks.

Yet beyond its cowboy roots, its company-town ethos, and its proximity to western Canada's best outdoor experiences, there's a lot more to Alberta's most populous city.

Calgary has an excellent museum of western Canadian history, art, and culture, as well as the country's largest living history village, where you can wander back to the 19th and early 20th centuries. The multimedia National Music Centre is the focus of a redeveloping downtown district that also includes a landmark New Central Library, along with urban condos, restaurants, and cafés. The city's food scene has taken off, with Calgary's restaurants regularly ranked among the country's top dining destinations.

Before you head for the mountains, you can get outdoors within the city limits. Cycle the scenic pathways along Calgary's riverfront, take a Segway tour, or follow in the footsteps (and bobsled tracks) of the Olympians at Canada Olympic Park, where the city hosted the 1988 Winter Olympic Games.

Then, when you're ready to road-trip, set off from Calgary to Banff, Lake Louise, and Jasper, or travel across British Columbia to the Pacific coast. Just take time to shop for your Stetson and cowboy boots before you hit the road.

Getting to Calgary

Driving from Vancouver
Via Highway 1
The **most direct route** from Vancouver to Calgary is via the **Trans-Canada Highway (Hwy. 1).**

From Vancouver, take **Highway 1** east to **Hope.** Continue east at Hope onto **Highway 3,** then exit onto **Highway 5 (Coquihalla Hwy.)** north. Follow the Coquihalla over the mountains to **Kamloops,** where you rejoin **Highway 1.** Stay on Highway 1 east into Alberta, where you'll reach Lake Louise, Banff, and then Calgary. This route from Vancouver to Calgary is **605 miles (975 km)** and takes **11 hours.**

Via Highway 3
You can also travel between Vancouver and Calgary via **scenic Highway 3.**

Through the Okanagan and Kootenays
Take the **Trans-Canada Highway (Hwy. 1)** from Vancouver east to **Hope,** where you pick up **Highway 3.** Highway 3 winds its way across southern British Columbia through the Okanagan and Kootenays regions. From here, the shortest route is to stay on Highway 3 into Alberta, then turn north on **Highway 22** and east on **Highway 533.** At **Nanton,** pick up **Highway 2** north, which will take you into Calgary. This Vancouver-Calgary trip is **745 miles (1,200 km)** and takes **14.5 hours.**

Best Accommodations

★ **Hotel Alma:** If you don't need to be right downtown, this up-to-date hotel on the University of Calgary campus is a good value (page 421).

★ **Hotel Arts:** Featuring works by Canadian artists throughout, this contemporary hotel lives up to its name. It has good restaurants, too (page 422).

★ **Hotel Le Germain Calgary:** From the illuminated marble check-in desk to the purple lounge chairs in the modern guest rooms, this downtown boutique hotel is one stylish lodging (page 423).

Through Radium Hot Springs and Kootenay National Park

Another alternative is to follow **Highway 3** east to **Cranbrook,** where you turn north on **Highway 95** through Invermere and Radium Hot Springs. From there, continue north on **Highway 93** through Kootenay National Park. North of the park, Highway 93 meets **Highway 1,** which will take you east through Banff and into Calgary. This scenic route from Vancouver to Calgary is **775 miles (1,250 km)** and takes **15 hours.**

Via Highway 5 and the Icefields Parkway

Yet another option is to go northeast from Vancouver to Jasper, then turn south along the scenic Icefields Parkway to Lake Louise, before continuing south through Banff and on to Calgary.

To follow this route, leave Vancouver on the **Trans-Canada Highway (Hwy. 1)** east to **Hope.** Continue east at Hope onto **Highway 3,** then exit onto **Highway 5** north toward Kamloops. At **Kamloops,** continue north on Highway 5 until it intersects with **Highway 16** north of Valemount. Follow Highway 16 east to Jasper.

From Jasper, follow the spectacular **Icefields Parkway (Hwy. 93)** south to Lake Louise, where you rejoin **Highway 1** and continue east to Calgary. Vancouver to Calgary via this Jasper route is **750 miles (1,200 km)** and takes **13.5-14.5 hours.**

Driving from Banff

The **Trans-Canada Highway (Hwy. 1)** runs east from Banff to Calgary, an **80-mile (130-km)** drive that normally takes about **90 minutes.**

Driving from the Okanagan
From Kelowna

To travel from Kelowna in the Okanagan Valley to Calgary, take **Highway 97** north, then continue north on **Highway 97A.** At **Sicamous,** turn east onto the **Trans-Canada Highway (Hwy. 1),** which will take you into Alberta and on to Calgary. It's **375 miles (605 km)** from Kelowna to Calgary; the drive takes **seven hours.**

From Osoyoos

From Osoyoos or other points in the South Okanagan, one option is to take **Highway 97** north to **Kelowna** and follow the directions from Kelowna. This route is **455 miles (730 km)** from Osoyoos to Calgary; the drive takes **8.5-9 hours.**

Alternatively, follow **Highway 3** east from Osoyoos. Continue on Highway 3 east past Cranbrook and Fernie and into Alberta, where you turn north on **Highway 22.** Stay on Highway 22 until you reach **Highway 533** east. Follow Highway 533 toward **Nanton,** where you'll pick up **Highway 2** north, which will take you into Calgary. This latter route is **515 miles (830 km)** from Osoyoos to Calgary; the drive takes **10 hours.**

Best Restaurants

★ **Ten Foot Henry:** This lively, plant-filled dining destination dishes out imaginative vegetable-forward plates, served family-style (page 418).

★ **Pigeonhole:** Difficult to pigeonhole, the ever-inventive small plates at this 17th Avenue hot spot are among Calgary's most exciting tastes (page 418).

★ **River Café:** Long considered one of Calgary's best restaurants, this eatery serving seasonal Canadian cuisine is still at the top of its game (page 418).

★ **Sidewalk Citizen Bakery:** Calgary's most delectable breads, pastries, and other baked goods come out of the ovens at this East Village bake shop, where you can also get Middle Eastern-influenced sandwiches and salads (page 420).

Getting There by Air, Train, and Bus
By Air
You can fly to **Calgary International Airport** (YYC, 2000 Airport Rd. NE, 403/735-1200, www.yyc.com) from across Canada and the United States and from Amsterdam, Frankfurt, London, Beijing, and Tokyo, among other cities. The airport is located on the city's northeast side, about 20 minutes' drive from downtown.

Ground Transportation
Calgary Transit's **bus 300** (403/262-1000, www.calgarytransit.com, 5am-midnight daily, one-way $10.50) runs between the airport and downtown Calgary every 20-30 minutes. The trip takes 40-50 minutes. Purchase a Calgary Transit pass from an automated machine at the airport bus stop or pay cash (exact change) on the bus.

Allied Airport Shuttle (403/299-9555 or 877/299-9555, www.airportshuttlecalgary.ca, 8am-midnight daily, one-way adults $15, ages 4-12 $10) is a scheduled van service that can take you between the airport and downtown Calgary hotels. Vans leave every 30 minutes. From the airport, reservations are not required; buy your ticket at the Allied desk on the arrivals level or on the shuttle. When you're going to the airport, however, you must make a reservation to be picked up at your hotel downtown.

Depending on your downtown destination, the trip takes between 30 and 60 minutes.

Taxis wait for passengers on the airport's arrivals level around the clock. Cabs are metered, and average fares between the airport and downtown are $40-45.

Uber (www.uber.com) operates in Calgary and can pick up passengers at the Calgary airport.

To go directly to **Banff** or **Lake Louise** from the Calgary airport without a car, you can take one of several shuttle services. **Brewster Banff Airport Express** (403/762-6700 or 866/606-6700, www.banffjaspercollection.com) provides bus service between the Calgary airport and both Banff (1.75 hours, one-way adults $71, ages 6-15 $36) and Lake Louise (3-3.25 hours, one-way adults $98, ages 6-15 $49). The **Banff Airporter** (403/762-3330 or 888/449-2901, www.banffairporter.com, one-way adults $67, seniors $61, ages 3-12 $33.50) can take you between Banff and the Calgary airport as well.

Numerous companies rent cars from the Calgary airport, including **Alamo** (403/543-3985 or 888/826-6893, www.alamo.ca), **Avis** (403/221-1700 or 800/230-4898, www.avis.ca), **Budget** (403/226-1550 or 800/268-8900, www.budget.ca), **Discount** (403/299-1203 or 800/263-2355, www.discountcar.com), **Dollar** (403/221-1806 or 800/800-6000, www.

One Day in Calgary

Get your Calgary day off to a delicious start in the East Village near downtown. In the restored Simmons Building, you can get excellent coffee at **Phil & Sebastian Coffee Roasters** to pair with the city's most delectable pastries at **Sidewalk Citizen Bakery.**

You're just a short walk from the modern multimedia **National Music Centre,** so begin your sightseeing with a tour through Canada's music scene, past and present. Stroll over to the **Calgary Tower** to get an overview of the city and what's where. Around the corner, the **Glenbow Museum** illustrates Calgary's history and culture and mounts changing art exhibitions.

When you're ready for lunch, wander a few blocks south of downtown for veggie-friendly plates at **Ten Foot Henry** or updated Asian fare at **Foreign Concept.**

In the afternoon, go back to Calgary's early days at the **Heritage Park Historical Village,** or if you'd prefer an active adventure, head west to **Canada Olympic Park** to test your mettle on the bobsled, luge, or zip line.

Back downtown, rent a bike to go **cycling** along Calgary's riverfront for an hour or so or try a riverside **Segway tour.**

For dinner, book a river-view table at the **River Café,** long considered one of Calgary's best restaurants, or head for 17th Avenue to try out one of the more contemporary eateries, like **Pigeonhole, Model Milk,** or **Anju.**

Later, if you're not ready to wrap up your Calgary day, have a nightcap at a **brewpub.**

---

dollar.com), **Enterprise** (403/233-8021 or 800/261-7331, www.enterprise.com), **Hertz** (403/221-1676 or 800/654-3001, www.hertz.ca), **National** (403/221-1690 or 888/826-6890, www.nationalcar.ca), **Routes** (403/398-3930, www.routes.ca), and **Thrifty** (403/221-1961 or 800/847-4389, www.thrifty.com).

By Train

The **Rocky Mountaineer** (604/606-7245 or 877/460-3200, www.rockymountaineer.com, late Apr.-mid-Oct.), a privately operated luxury train, travels between Vancouver, Banff, Lake Louise, and Jasper, with connections to Calgary. Another Rocky Mountaineer route starts in Seattle, stops in Vancouver, and continues to the Rockies. You can travel either route from west to east or east to west.

Neither **VIA Rail** nor **Amtrak** provide passenger service to Calgary.

By Bus

Brewster Banff Airport Express (403/762-6700 or 866/606-6700, www.banffjaspercollection.com) operates buses between Banff and downtown Calgary hotels (2.5 hours, one-way adults $71, ages 6-15 $36) or the Calgary International Airport (1.75 hours, one-way adults $71, ages 6-15 $36).

Red Arrow (403/531-0350 or 800/232-1958, www.redarrow.ca) runs buses to Calgary from Edmonton (3.5-4 hours, one-way adults $76) and other cities in Alberta.

Sights

Downtown Calgary has several sights to explore, including a first-rate museum of history and culture and the landmark Calgary Tower. In Calgary's rapidly developing East Village district just east of downtown, check out a cool multimedia museum dedicated to Canadian music. Other attractions, notably Canada's largest living history village and Canada Olympic Park, are outside the city center.

★ Glenbow Museum

Part history museum, part art gallery, and part cultural curator, the well-designed **Glenbow Museum** (130 9th Ave. SE, 403/268-4100, www.glenbow.org, 9am-5pm Mon.-Sat., noon-5pm Sun. July-Aug., 9am-5pm Tues.-Sat., noon-5pm Sun. Sept.-June, adults $16, seniors and students $11, ages 7-17 $10, families $40) tells Calgary's stories. The museum is downtown, one block from the Calgary Tower. In the permanent exhibits, you can explore the early days in Calgary, southern Alberta, and western Canada, from the indigenous communities to the entrepreneurs, adventurers, and even scoundrels who helped shape the region. Changing exhibitions have focused on everything from Canadian art to aboriginal residential schools to gun sculpture.

Calgary Tower

Standing 4,023 feet (1,228 m) above sea level, and 627 feet (191 m) above the downtown streets, the **Calgary Tower** (101 9th Ave. SW, 403/266-7171, www.calgarytower.com, 9am-10pm daily June-Aug., 9am-9pm daily Sept.-May, adults $18, seniors $16, ages 4-12 $9) has the highest 360-degree observation deck in the world. When it opened in 1968, it was originally called the Husky Tower, not because it was portly, but because Husky Oil and Marathon Realty constructed this downtown landmark as a joint venture. It was renamed in 1971.

As you walk around the observation deck, listen to the free **audio tour,** which gives you historical background about the city and points out highlights of what you're seeing, from City Hall to the Saddledome (where the Calgary Flames ice hockey team plays) to Stampede Park, which hosts the annual Calgary Stampede. On a clear day, you can see the Rocky Mountains.

A section of the observation area has a glass floor, so you can look down—way down—on the streets below.

★ National Music Centre

Listen to recordings by k. d. lang, Leonard Cohen, Joni Mitchell, Drake, Céline Dion, the Barenaked Ladies, and many more at the **National Music Centre** (850 4th St. SE, 403/543-5115 or 800/213-9750, www.nmc.ca, 10am-5pm daily mid-May-early Sept., 10am-5pm Wed.-Sun. early Sept.-mid-May, adults $18, seniors and students $14, ages 3-12 $11), a multimedia museum of music at **Studio Bell** in Calgary's East Village that showcases Canadian music, performers, and composers past and present. You can test your vocal skills in a recording booth or explore historic instruments including a 1679 harpsichord, a theremin, and Elton John's piano. Take the 45-minute guided tour, included with your admission, for an overview of the extensive collections.

The center also houses the Canadian Music Hall of Fame and the Canadian Country Music Hall of Fame, along with performance spaces and recording studios; check the website for schedules of concerts and other special events.

The National Music Centre is about 0.5 mile (0.8 km) due east of the Calgary Tower and a 10- to 15-minute walk from the C-Train's **City Hall station.**

Fort Calgary

Where the Bow and Elbow Rivers meet, the Northwest Mounted Police built an outpost in 1875 that eventually grew to become the city of Calgary.

At **Fort Calgary** (750 9th Ave. SE, 403/290-1875, www.fortcalgary.com, 9am-5pm daily, adults $12, seniors and students $11, ages 7-17 $7, ages 3-6 $5, parking $6), start by watching a short film about life in the late 19th century when the fort was first established. Then explore the exhibits that illustrate life at the fort, and in the fledgling city, in the late 1800s and early 1900s. The fort operated until 1914, when it was sold to the Grand Trunk Railroad.

Fort Calgary is 0.9 mile (1.5 km) directly east of the Calgary Tower, and a short walk from the East Village neighborhood. The C-Train's **City Hall station** is a 10- to 15-minute walk from the fort. Several buses that run along 9th Avenue from downtown, including **buses 1, 302, and 411,** stop near the fort.

★ Heritage Park Historical Village

Go back in time at the **Heritage Park Historical Village** (1900 Heritage Dr. SW, at 14th St. SW, 403/268-8500, www. heritagepark.ca, 10am-5pm daily mid-May-early Sept., 10am-5pm Sat.-Sun. early Sept.-mid-Oct., adults $26.50, seniors $20.70, ages 7-15 $18.95, ages 3-6 $13.65, parking $6), Canada's largest living history experience.

As you walk through the history of western Canada from the 1860s to 1950s, you can explore a 19th-century fur-trading fort and First Nations camp; wander the streets of a 1910 prairie railroad town, checking out the mounted police barracks, the snooker parlor, and the old-time bakery (which sells gooey butter tarts); and talk with the costumed interpreters who reenact life in these past eras. There's even a "Little Synagogue on the Prairie," an original 1916 house of worship from a Jewish farming community in eastern Alberta.

Top to bottom: National Music Centre; the landmark Calgary Tower; the snooker parlor at Heritage Park Historical Village.

CALGARY

Downtown Calgary

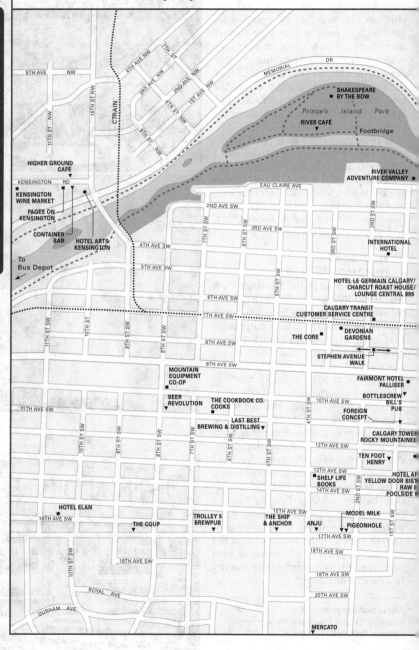

SHAKESPEARE BY THE BOW

Prince's Island Park

RIVER CAFÉ

Footbridge

5TH AVE NW

4TH AVE NW
7TH ST
3RD AVE NW
2ND AVE NW
1ST AVE NW

MEMORIAL DR

CTRAIN

10TH ST NW
8TH ST NW
9TH ST NW

11TH ST NW

HIGHER GROUND CAFÉ

RIVER VALLEY ADVENTURE COMPANY

KENSINGTON RD

KENSINGTON WINE MARKET

PAGES ON KENSINGTON

CONTAINER BAR

HOTEL ARTS KENSINGTON

To Bus Depot

EAU CLAIRE AVE

2ND AVE SW

3RD AVE SW

7TH ST SW
6TH ST SW
5TH ST SW
3RD ST SW
2ND ST SW

4TH AVE SW

5TH AVE SW

INTERNATIONAL HOTEL

HOTEL LE GERMAIN CALGARY/
CHARCUT ROAST HOUSE/
LOUNGE CENTRAL 899

6TH AVE SW

CALGARY TRANSIT
CUSTOMER SERVICE CENTRE

7TH AVE SW

THE CORE

DEVONIAN GARDENS

8TH AVE SW

STEPHEN AVENUE WALK

11TH ST SW
10TH ST SW
9TH ST SW
8TH ST SW

9TH AVE SW

MOUNTAIN EQUIPMENT CO-OP

FAIRMONT HOTEL PALLISER

BOTTLESCREW BILL'S PUB

BEER REVOLUTION

THE COOKBOOK CO. COOKS

10TH AVE SW

FOREIGN CONCEPT

11TH AVE SW

LAST BEST BREWING & DISTILLING

CALGARY TOWER
ROCKY MOUNTAINEE

12TH AVE SW

TEN FOOT HENRY

10TH ST SW
9TH ST SW
8TH ST SW
7TH ST SW
6TH ST SW
5TH ST SW
4TH ST SW

13TH AVE SW

SHELF LIFE BOOKS

HOTEL AP
YELLOW DOOR BIST
RAW B
POOLSIDE

14TH AVE SW

2ND ST SW

HOTEL ELAN

16TH AVE SW

THE COUP

TROLLEY 5 BREWPUB

15TH AVE SW

THE SHIP & ANCHOR

MODEL MILK

ANJU

PIGEONHOLE

1ST ST SW

17TH AVE SW

10TH ST SW

18TH AVE SW

19TH AVE SW

ROYAL AVE

20TH AVE SW

DURHAM AVE

MERCATO

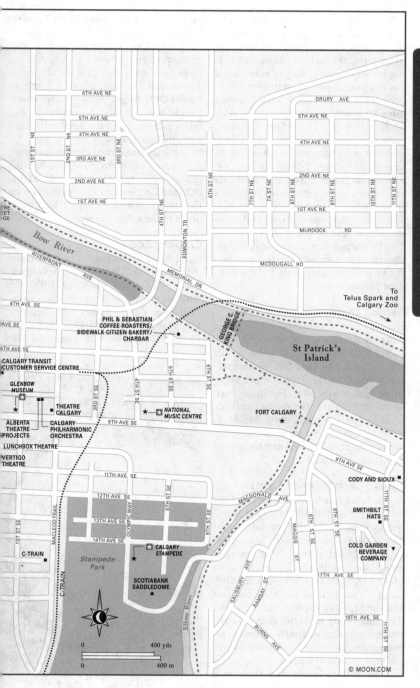

You can ride a passenger train, pulled by an antique steam locomotive, through the 127-acre (51-ha) park, and take part in activities throughout the day, including butter-making, wagon rides, First Nations games, and street theater.

Near the park entrance is the **Gasoline Alley Museum** (10am-5pm daily mid-May-early Sept., 10am-5pm Sat.-Sun. early Sept.-mid-Oct., 9:30am-4pm daily mid-Oct.-mid-May, winter adults $10.95, seniors $8.75, ages 7-15 $6.95, ages 3-6 $5.65), a car buff's fantasy of antique cars and trucks, along with North America's largest collection of restored gas pumps. The museum is open year-round, even when the rest of the park is closed. There's a separate museum-only admission fee in winter, while in summer, you can visit the museum as part of the standard park admission.

Getting There

Heritage Park is 6 miles (10 km) south of downtown Calgary, a 20-minute drive.

By public transit from downtown, take the C-Train **Red Line 201** (Somerset-Bridlewood) to Heritage Station. From there, catch **bus 502** (Heritage Park Shuttle) to the park. The shuttle runs only when the park is open, daily mid-May-early September and on weekends early September-mid-October, and for special events at other times of year.

Telus Spark Science Centre

At the **Telus Spark Science Centre** (220 St. George's Dr. NE, 403/817-6800, www.sparkscience.ca, 10am-5pm daily June-Aug., 10am-4pm Sun.-Fri., 10am-5pm Sat. Sept.-May, last entry 90 minutes before closing, adults $26, seniors $24, ages 13-17 $22, ages 3-12 $19, parking $10), Calgary's modern science museum, you and the kids can explore the earth and the human body, build things in the open studio workshop, watch live science demonstrations, and generally immerse yourself in the world of science.

Take in the planetarium show or a movie at the **HD Digital Dome Theatre** (entrance included with admission), or let the youngsters explore the Brainasium, an outdoor playground.

The museum isn't just for children. The second Thursday of every month is **Adults Only Night** (6pm-10pm), where people over age 18 can explore the exhibits and check out the demonstrations and other programs.

Telus Spark Science Centre is east of downtown, off Memorial Drive NE. By public transit, take the C-Train **Blue Line 202** (Saddletowne) to Zoo Station. From the station, it's a 0.6-mile (1-km) walk north to the science center.

Calgary Zoo

From bears to penguins to tigers, from the Canadian wilds to Africa, the **Calgary Zoo** (1300 Zoo Rd. NE, 403/232-9300 or 800/588-9993, www.calgaryzoo.com, 9am-5pm daily, adults $35, seniors $33, ages 3-15 $25 mid-Mar.-mid-Oct., adults $30, seniors $28, ages 3-15 $20

mid.-Oct.-mid-Mar., parking $10) shows off animals and their habitats. A current highlight is the "Panda Passage," where in 2018, four giant pandas settled in for a multiyear stay.

The zoo is east of downtown, off Memorial Drive NE, near the Telus Spark Science Centre. By public transit, take the C-Train **Blue Line 202** (Saddletowne) to Zoo Station.

Gelato Tours

Get behind the scenes at this Calgary ice cream maker, with an insider's tour of the **Fiasco Gelato Factory and Coffee Bar** (221 19 St. SE, 403/452-3150, www. fiascogelato.ca, 11am-7pm Tues.-Thurs., 11am-9pm Fri.-Sun., tours $15). The 45-minute tours (call for schedules) take you through the production facility, where you learn how the products are made. Of course, there are tastings; you can sample a flight of four varieties, choosing from flavors like salted caramel gelato or dairy-free dark chocolate

sorbetto, along with unique-to-the-factory seasonal creations.

True gelato aficionados might consider the **Gelato Academy** ($126 pp), a 2.5-hour experience where you tour the factory and then create your own gelato flavor, while enjoying drinks and snacking on charcuterie. You'll leave with four custom-made pints to savor at your leisure. The academy is typically offered Thursday evenings and Saturday afternoons; phone for details and reservations.

To reach the Fiasco Gelato Factory by public transit, take the C-Train **Blue Line 202** (Saddletowne) east to Barlow/Max Bell Station, then change to **bus 27** (Willowglen), which stops opposite the building.

★ Canada Olympic Park

Calgary hosted the Winter Olympics in 1988, the year that an unlikely team from Jamaica captured the world's attention when they competed in the bobsled event. Immortalized, at least in movie

an ice cream tasting flight at Fiasco Gelato Factory and Coffee Bar

fiction, in the 1993 film *Cool Runnings,* the Jamaican team sledded on the track at what is now WinSport's **Canada Olympic Park** (88 Canada Olympic Rd. SW, 403/247-5452, www.winsport.ca), where many events were held during the XV Olympic Winter Games, and where activities now draw both sports fans and the athletically inclined in winter and summer.

Year-round, you can visit **Canada's Sports Hall of Fame** (169 Canada Olympic Rd. SW, 403/776-1040, www.sportshall. ca, 10am-5pm daily July-Aug., 10am-5pm Wed.-Sun. Sept.-June, adults $12, seniors $10, ages 4-18 $8, families $35), with a dozen galleries featuring more than 60 sports, from swimming and wheelchair racing to curling, snowboarding, and, of course, ice hockey, with plenty of hands-on things to do and exhibits about Canada's athletic legends.

For other activities, hours vary throughout the year, so call or check the park website to see what's open when. In general, summer activities are open May-early October.

Summer Activities

Have Olympic dreams? In a wheeled sled driven by a professional pilot, you can reach speeds up to 50 mph (80 km/h) on the **summer bobsled** (over age 13, $75).

Whiz down the world's longest luge track at the park's **Skyline Luge Calgary** (403/776-0617, www.skylineluge.com, single ride $16). If one ride on the wheeled sled isn't enough, you can buy packages of tickets for multiple rides, as well as family tickets.

Another way down the mountain is on the park's **zip-line course** ($80), which comprises three lines: the Trainer; the Plaza Zip Line, where you might reach speeds of 50 mph (80 km/h); and the Monster Zip Line, where you start at the sky jump tower and zip 1,640 feet (500 m), with a vertical drop of more than 325 feet (100 m) and speeds up to 75 mph (120 km/h).

The park has a network of lift-accessed trails for **mountain biking** (full-day adults $28, seniors and ages 3-17 $23, families $75), as well as a skills park with dirt jumps and other obstacles. For something tamer, play the family-friendly 18-hole **mini golf** course (adults $12, seniors and ages 5-12 $10, preschoolers $7, families $25).

Winter Activities

In winter, whip down the Olympic **bobsled track** (over age 15, $170) at speeds up to 60 mph (100 km/h) in a four-person sled with a professional driver, or slide feet-first down the **luge** run (over age 7, $30). The park also has an **ice-skating rink** (adults $6, ages 13-17 $5, seniors and under age 13 $3, families $15).

You can **ski** or **snowboard** (full day adults $46, seniors $25, ages 6-18 $29, ages 3-5 $19, families $99) on the small ski hill, although serious powder hounds will want to go to Banff or Lake Louise. In addition to full-day passes, you can buy lift tickets for three hours (adults $36, seniors $17, ages 6-18 $23, ages 3-5 $15, families $79).

Getting There

Canada Olympic Park is on Calgary's west side, off Highway 1 (16th Ave. SW), 9 miles (15 km) from downtown, about a 25-minute drive. It's an easy stop on the way to or from Banff.

It's possible to reach Canada Olympic Park by public transit from downtown, but the trip will take about an hour. The most direct route is to take the C-Train **Red Line 201** (Tuscany) to Brentwood Station. Change to **bus 408** (Valleyridge), and get off at Canada Olympic Road.

Sports and Recreation

Cycling

Calgary has 525 miles (850 km) of pedestrian and cycling paths that you can follow throughout the region, one of the longest urban pathway networks in North America. A good introduction to cycling in the city is to ride along the **Bow River Pathway** that follows the river through downtown Calgary.

Rent bikes from **Eau Claire Rapid Rent** (200 Barclay Parade SW, 403/444-5845, 10am-6pm daily May-Sept., 1 hour $10-15, full-day $40-60) at the Eau Claire Market, near the Bow River Pathway, or from **Rath Bicycle** (439 8th Ave. SE, 403/617-5627, www.rathbicycle.com, noon-8pm Fri., 10am-6pm Sat.-Sun., by appointment Mon.-Thurs., 1 hour $15, full-day $50) in the East Village.

Winter Sports

Skate where the Olympians skated at the **Olympic Oval** (2500 University Dr. NW, 403/220-7954, http://oval.ucalgary.ca, adults $7, seniors and ages 6-17 $4.75, families $18.50), which was one of the venues for the 1988 Winter Olympic Games. It's on the University of Calgary campus northwest of downtown; you can take the C-Train **Red Line 201** (Tuscany) to University station.

At WinSport's **Canada Olympic Park** (88 Canada Olympic Rd. SW, 403/247-5452, www.winsport.ca), you can try out an Olympic bobsled, slide down the luge track, or go downhill skiing or ice-skating.

Segway Tours

An entertaining way to speed along Calgary's riverside pathway is on a Segway tour with **River Valley Adventure Company** (Riverfront Ave. at 1st St. SW, 403/970-7347, www.rivervalleyadventure.com, May-Oct.). If you've never ridden one of these self-balancing stand-up electric scooters, sign up for the one-hour Beginner Segway Adventure ($60 pp), with 30 minutes of instruction followed by a 30-minute guided ride; you can add on an extra half hour of cruising for $25. Check the website for tour times and availability; riders must be at least 14 years old. Experienced Segway riders should ask about the 60- or 90-minute Advanced Segway Adventures, which you must book in person or by phone. River Valley Adventure's "office," where tours start and end, is located in a shipping container in Sien Lok Park downtown.

Spectator Sports

Calgary's National Hockey League team is the **Calgary Flames** (403/777-4646 or 888/535-2637, www.nhl.com/flames), who play October-April at the **Scotiabank Saddledome** (555 Saddledome Rise SE). When they score a goal, watch for actual flames to shoot up toward the ceiling.

If you'd like to see what the professional Canadian Football League is about, go see the city's CFL team, the **Calgary Stampeders** (403/289-0258, www.stampeders.com) at McMahon Stadium (1817 Crowchild Trail NW), near the University of Calgary campus.

Entertainment and Events

Nightlife

As in many Canadian cities, the microbrewery industry is booming in Calgary. Fans of craft beer should head for **Last Best Brewing and Distilling** (607 11th Ave. SW, 587/353-7387, www. lastbestbrewing.com, 11:30am-midnight Mon.-Thurs., 11:30am-2am Fri.-Sat., 10am-midnight Sun.), which brews its own, as does **Wild Rose Brewing** (2-4580 Quesnay Wood Dr. SW, 403/727-5451, www.wildrosebrewery.com, 11am-11pm Sun.-Thurs., 11am-midnight Fri.-Sat.), which got its start in a former Air Force barracks.

Other Calgary craft breweries include **Cold Garden Beverage Company** (1100 11th St. SE, 403/764-2653, www. coldgarden.ca, noon-10pm Tues.-Thurs., noon-midnight Fri.-Sat., noon-8pm Sun.) in Inglewood, **Trolley 5 Brewpub** (728 17th Ave. SW, 403/454-3731, www. trolley5.com, 11am-1am Mon.-Wed., 11am-2am Thurs.-Fri., 10am-2am Sat., 10am-1am Sun.), and **Tool Shed Brewing Company** (801 30th St. NE, 403/775-1749, www.toolshedbrewing. com, 1pm-9pm Mon.-Wed., noon-10pm Thurs.-Sat., noon-6pm Sun.). Long-standing **Bottlescrew Bill's** (140 10th Ave. SW, 403/263-7900, www.bottlescrewbill. com, 11am-2am Mon.-Sat., 11am-1am Sun.) serves 300-plus beers, from local to international brewers.

To watch soccer or listen to local bands, join the diverse crowd at **The Ship & Anchor** (534 17th Ave. SW, 403/245-3333, www.shipandanchor.com, 11am-2am Mon.-Fri., 10am-2am Sat.-Sun.), a Calgary dive-bar landmark.

The Arts

Theater

Launched in the 1960s, the professional **Theatre Calgary** (Arts Commons, 220 9th Ave. SE, 403/294-7447, www. theatrecalgary.com) produces an annual season of contemporary and classical drama. It also presents the summertime **Shakespeare by the Bow,** a pay-what-you-can production performed outdoors at Prince's Island Park.

Focusing on contemporary Canadian and international works, the **Alberta Theatre Projects** (403/294-7402, www. atplive.com), a professional nonprofit company, presents several plays a year, performing in the **Martha Cohen Theatre** (215 8th Ave. SE) in the Arts Commons complex.

Canada's only professional mystery theater, **Vertigo Theatre** (115 9th Ave. SE, 403/221-3708, www.vertigotheatre. com) produces a season of thrillers and who-done-its. Its performance space is located at the base of the Calgary Tower.

Have an hour for lunch? Then you can see a play at the **Lunchbox Theatre** (115 9th Ave. SE, 403/265-4292, www. lunchboxtheatre.com), which presents a season of one-act noon-hour productions in the Calgary Tower complex. Bring your lunch or purchase food at the theater to eat during the show.

Music

The city's symphony orchestra, the **Calgary Philharmonic Orchestra** (403/571-0849, www.calgaryphil.com), performs at the Arts Commons downtown in the 1,700-seat **Jack Singer Concert Hall** (205 8th St. SE). It also plays at various venues around town, so check the details of any performance you plan to see.

The **Calgary Opera** (403/262-7286, www.calgaryopera.com) produces its mainstage season at the **Southern Alberta Jubilee Auditorium** (1415 14th Ave. NW); take the C-Train northwest to Jubilee Auditorium station. In August, the **Opera in the Village** festival features performances in ENMAX Park, across the Elbow River from downtown.

Bloody Caesar

Spend any time in a Canadian bar, and you'll likely spot someone drinking a "Caesar." Canada's version of a Bloody Mary, this spicy cocktail blends vodka, Worcestershire sauce, and hot sauce, with the uniquely Canadian addition of Clamato juice—tomato-clam juice substituting for standard tomato.

Though you'll find Caesars, often called bloody Caesars, at pubs and lounges across the country, credit for the first of these tomato-clam cocktails goes to a bartender in Calgary. In 1969, Walter Chell, a hotel bar manager, was asked to create a signature drink to celebrate the opening of the Calgary hotel's new Italian restaurant.

The flavors of spaghetti vongole (pasta with clams) reportedly inspired Chell's version of a Bloody Mary, which he concocted by mashing clams into tomato juice before adding vodka and spices. He garnished his creation with a stick of celery.

Around the same time, the California-based Mott's company began working on a clam-tomato juice and hired Chell as a consultant. Clamato juice was born. And with a premixed tomato-clam juice available, far easier than mashing clams by hand, Calgary, and Canada, had a new favorite drink.

Dance

With both classical and contemporary productions in its repertory, the **Alberta Ballet** (403/245-4549, www.albertaballet.com), Canada's second-largest professional ballet company, splits its time between Edmonton and Calgary, where dancers take the stage at the **Southern Alberta Jubilee Auditorium** (1415 14th Ave. NW).

Festivals and Events
★ Calgary Stampede

Alberta's biggest festival is the annual **Calgary Stampede** (www.calgarystampede.com, July), which has its roots in the region's cowboy culture. Taking over the city for 10 days every summer, the Stampede is a rodeo, county fair, and crazy party rolled into one.

The Stampede opens with a huge parade through downtown. Other attractions include chuck wagon races, calf roping, bull riding, horse shows, a carnival midway, concerts by big-name entertainers, and plenty of partying by cowboy hat-sporting locals and visitors. The Stampede draws more than a million people every year, so pull on your boots and come on down.

Other Festivals

Performers from more than a dozen countries take to the eight stages in Prince's Island Park for the annual **Calgary Folk Music Fest** (www.calgaryfolkfest.com, July).

Pride Calgary (www.pridecalgary.ca, Aug.-Sept.) hosts a week of events, including a big parade, celebrating the city's LGBTQ community.

What do you get when you mix art, science, and engineering into a weirdly fun five-day festival? That's quirky **Beakerhead** (www.beakerhead.com, Sept.), where the technical meets the creative in street performances, competitions, food labs, and other unexpected events.

Shopping

Shopping Districts

The main downtown shopping district, known as the **Stephen Avenue Walk,** is along Stephen Avenue, which is 8th Avenue SW, between 1st Street SE and 4th Street SW. It's a pedestrian-only street 6am-6pm daily.

At **The Core** (8th Ave. SW, between 2nd St. and 4th St., 403/441-4940, www. coreshopping.ca, 10am-6pm Mon.-Wed. and Sat., 10am-8pm Thurs.-Fri., noon-5pm Sun.), a shopping mall on Stephen Avenue, Holt Renfrew and Brooks Brothers share space with other Canadian and international chains. Make your way to the top floor for the secret-feeling **Devonian Gardens** (free), a sky-lit indoor park with benches, café tables, and lots of greenery, including more than 500 trees and a living wall.

Wander the **17th Avenue District** (www.17thave.ca), along 17th Avenue SW between 1st and 14th Streets, for funky independent clothing and specialty shops, but even more for its cool cafés and hip restaurants.

Across the Louise Bridge from downtown, the brick storefronts in **Kensington Village** (www.visitkensington.com) house an eclectic mix of bookstores, food businesses, and independent boutiques. The neighborhood's hub is near the intersection of Kensington Road and 10th Street NW. Another up-and-coming shopping district is **Inglewood** (www. inglewoodyyc.ca), along 9th Avenue SE, across the Elbow River east of the city center.

Western Wear

If you're in town for the Stampede, of course you need cowboy boots. Calgary's longstanding supplier of proper Western footwear is the **Alberta Boot Co.** (50 50th Ave. SE, 403/263-4623, www.albertaboot. com, 9am-6pm Mon.-Sat.). It stocks thousands of pairs, and also makes

Stephen Avenue Walk

custom boots to order. Prices start at around $375 a pair.

Another essential Stampede accessory is a cowboy hat. Known for creating the white hat that's become a symbol of the Calgary Stampede, **Smithbilt Hats** (1015 11th St. SE, 403/244-9131 or 800/661-1354, www.smithbilthats.com, 9am-5pm Mon.-Wed. and Fri., 9am-7pm Thurs., 10am-4pm Sat.) is a long-established vendor that can outfit your head in proper Calgary style.

For more contemporary Western styles for both men and women, check out **Cody and Sioux** (1226B 9th Ave. SE, 403/264-2489, www.codyandsioux.com, 11am-6pm Mon.-Wed. and Fri., 11am-7pm Thurs., 10am-6pm Sat., noon-5pm Sun.).

Books

In a building that once housed a branch of Calgary's library, **Pages on Kensington** (1135 Kensington Rd. NW, 403/283-6655, www.pageskensington.com, 11am-6pm Mon.-Wed. and Sat., 11am-7pm Thurs.-Fri., noon-5pm Sun.), a classic independent bookstore, sells thousands of titles and hosts readings and other literary events.

Another independent bookseller, **Shelf Life Books** (1302 4th St. SW, 403/265-1033, www.shelflifebooks.ca, 10am-6pm Mon., 10am-8pm Tues.-Fri., 11am-6pm Sat., noon-5pm Sun.) is in the Beltline neighborhood just south of downtown.

For food-related titles, visit **The Cookbook Co. Cooks** (722 11th Ave. SW, 403/265-6066, www.cookbookcooks.com, 10am-6pm Mon.-Fri., 10am-5:30pm Sat., noon-5pm Sun.), a bookstore that also offers **cooking classes.**

Gourmet Goodies

Besides selling wine, beer, and spirits from near and far, **Kensington Wine Market** (1257 Kensington Rd. NW, 403/283-8000 or 888/283-9004, www.kensingtonwinemarket.com, 10am-8pm Mon.-Wed. and Sat., 10am-9pm Thurs.-Fri., 11am-6pm Sun.) holds regular evening **tasting events.** Check the website or call for schedules and prices.

Outdoor Gear

Calgary's branch of **MEC** (Mountain Equipment Co-op, 830 10th Ave. SW, 403/269-2420, www.mec.ca, 9am-9pm Mon.-Fri., 9am-7pm Sat., 10am-6pm Sun.), the nationwide outdoor gear chain, can supply clothing and equipment for hiking, cycling, camping, and other active pursuits.

Food

Contemporary

Named for a 10-foot-tall replica of a 1930s cartoon character, ★ **Ten Foot Henry** (1209 1st St. SW, 403/475-5537, www.tenfoothenry.com, 11am-11pm daily, $9-25), a short walk south of the Calgary Tower, serves inventive vegetable-friendly dishes in family-style portions for sharing. Take a seat in the plant-filled dining room or at the chef's counter opposite the open kitchen and choose from dishes like spaghetti with pistachio pesto, jerk-spiced cauliflower, or adobo chicken with *aji verde*. Next door, **Little Henry** (8am-4pm daily, $3-12) does breakfast, light bites, and sweets to go, from interesting toasts (gravlax with pickles, fresh tomato with whipped feta and herbs), salads, and scones, to house-made granola bars.

Model Milk (308 17th Ave. SW, 403/265-7343, www.modelmilk.ca, 5pm-11pm daily, $26-43) occupies a former dairy, providing the exposed brick walls and heritage pedigree to back up the imaginative modern fare. The old dairymen would never have supped on wagyu beef tartare with beer cheese, roasted cauliflower with white miso and black truffle, local rainbow trout with tomatoes and kaffir lime, or any of the other imaginative dishes, though they might have appreciated the multicourse Sunday supper served family-style ($40).

Under the same ownership as Model Milk, ★ **Pigeonhole** (306 17th Ave. SW, 403/452-4694, www.pigeonholeyyc.ca, 5pm-midnight Mon.-Sat., $14-25), its newer sibling next door, is rather hard to pigeonhole, but the ever-inventive small plates, served on green marble tables in this buzzing room, are among Calgary's most exciting tastes. Prime your palate for summer peas with local greens and whipped feta, poached cod with smoked egg yolk, charred cabbage mounded with shredded mimolette cheese, or hand-rolled cavatelli with garlic scapes and burrata. Creative cocktails and wines from around the world keep things even livelier.

Long considered one of Calgary's best restaurants, ★ **River Café** (25 Prince's Island Park, 403/261-7670, www.rivercafe.com, 11am-10pm Mon.-Fri., 10am-10pm Sat.-Sun., brunch/lunch $14-27, dinner $34-52), overlooking the river on a downtown island, is still at the top of its game. The room is warm, almost rustic, and the gracious staff make you feel at home. The kitchen lives and breathes seasonal Canadian cuisine, so if you haven't sampled Alberta beef, try it here, where it might come with cheddar cauliflower, black lentils, and Okanagan grapes, or with caramelized parsley root and wild ramps. The trout with house-cured bacon and rhubarb, or eggplant with candied oyster mushrooms, might also tempt. To finish? Wild rice pudding with peaches, a maple-chocolate dome with tangerine-marigold shortbread, or a house-made popsicle. The wine list is strong on Canadian labels, along with selections from across the globe.

Take an alley, add a shipping container and a few picnic tables, then serve indulgent bar snacks like salted chicken skin and duck fat potato chips paired with fun cocktails and unusual beers, and you have the recipe for the hip **Container Bar** (1131 Kensington Rd. NW, 403/457-4148, www.containerbaryyc.com, 4pm-11pm Mon., 11:30am-11pm Tues.-Wed., 11:30am-midnight Thurs., 11:30am-1am Fri., 10am-1am Sat., 10am-11pm Sun., $12-20), in a lane next to Brasserie Kensington (a French bistro, which has the same owners). It's not just a crazy-munchies idea, though; excellent sandwiches like a chicken club, updated with juicy thigh meat, bacon, and gruyère, creative salads, and several variations on the poutine theme give it serious dining credentials, too. Outside of summer or in uncertain weather, call or check the Twitter feed @ContainerBarYYC to confirm that it's open.

For a hotel brunch that goes beyond the same-old thing, go behind the yellow door. The **Yellow Door Bistro** (119 12th Ave. SW, 403/206-9585, www.yellowdoorbistro.ca, 6:30am-10pm daily, breakfast $9-18, lunch $16-28, dinner $16-39), the comfortably trendy restaurant at the Hotel Arts, serves a weekend brunch that will kick-start your day with an omelet with house-smoked ham, a changing choice of pancakes, and salads like hibiscus-cured steelhead layered with butter lettuce, endive, and charred grapefruit. The rest of the day, the bistro fare is interesting enough for foodies but versatile enough for a business meal. The restaurant's enomatic wine system (that preserves open bottles) lets you sample wines in one-, three-, and five-ounce pours.

While a restaurant that butchers its own meats, cures charcuterie, and makes pickles and preserves could remind you of Grandmother's kitchen, **CHARCUT Roast House** (101-899 Centre St. SW, 403/984-2180, www.charcut.com, 11am-11pm Mon.-Tues., 11am-1am Wed.-Fri., 5pm-1am Sat., 5pm-10pm Sun., lunch $16-36, dinner $19-50) is anything but old-fashioned. Located at the Hotel Le Germain Calgary, this chic downtown dining spot handles its local ingredients with care and shakes off the apron strings with steak served with salsa verde, bison brisket with beech mushrooms and bacon, or the lunchtime rotisserie chicken sandwich with *piri piri* aioli. Homey desserts like preserved fruit in a jar with whipped cheesecake or salted caramel and milk chocolate pudding crunch would make Grandma proud.

A spin-off of CHARCUT Roast House, **Charbar** (Simmons Bldg., 618 Confluence Way SE, 403/452-3115, www.charbar.ca, 11:30am-10pm Mon.-Wed., 11:30am-midnight Thurs.-Fri., 10am-midnight

Top to bottom: colorful beet salad at Ten Foot Henry; a *bureka* plate at Sidewalk Citizen Bakery; a rice bowl at Foreign Concept.

Sat., 10am-10pm Sun., lunch $15-22, dinner $19-49, brunch $10-27), in the East Village, is built around an Argentine wood-fired grill that turns out deep-dish pizza and grilled meats to pair with ceviches, salads, and small plates to share. In mild weather, have your cocktails up on the rooftop bar.

Asian

Crispy tofu with pork belly and maple-sesame kimchi, gochujang-glazed chicken wings, and Brussels sprouts with bacon and rice sticks are just a few of the imaginative Korean tapas you can sample at hip **Anju** (344 17th Ave. SW, 403/460-3341, www.anju.ca, 11am-1am Mon.-Fri., 11am-3pm and 5pm-1am Sat.-Sun., $14-26), which serves what it describes as "Korean drinking food." Speaking of drinking, at this spirited spot for sipping and grazing, there's soju, beers from near and far, and unusual cocktails, like the Anju Flip, made with soju, green chartreuse, simple syrup, egg, and shiso powder.

In a chic window-lined space, with wall-sized photos and red banquettes, **Foreign Concept** (1011 1st St. SW, 403/719-7288, www.foreignconcept.ca, 11:30am-2pm and 5pm-10pm Mon.-Fri., 5pm-10pm Sat., lunch $16-25, dinner $25-35) creates modern riffs on Asian classics. At lunch, try a rice bowl with *char siu* pork and Korean chili sauce or ginger-scallion noodles with mushroom confit and roasted cauliflower. In the evenings, snack on soy-caramel Brussels sprouts or crispy preserved lemon chicken while you sip sake or a green tea martini, or share plates like Alberta trout done Vietnamese-style with turmeric and shrimp paste or beef tenderloin paired with fried forbidden rice, white kimchi, and an *onsen* egg.

Italian

Half gourmet market and half bustling Italian dining room, **Mercato** (2224 4th Ave. SW, 403/263-5535, www.

mercatogourmet.com, market 9:30am-7pm Mon.-Sat., 10am-6pm Sun., restaurant 11:30am-2pm and 5:30pm-10pm daily, $15-57), in the Mission district south of downtown, sells deli sandwiches, cheeses, and salads to go and serves updated Italian classics at long bars lining the upscale dining space. Specialties consist of traditional pastas, like *bucatini all'amatriciana* or handmade gnocchi with ricotta salata and pesto, and grilled dishes, including sea bream with a caper-berry-herb salsa verde or balsamic-glazed lamb. Dishes are sized and served family-style, designed to share.

Vegetarian

Alberta beef is ubiquitous on local menus, which may be why Calgary vegetarians considered it a coup when **The Coup** (924 17th Ave. SW, 403/541-1041, www.thecoup.ca, 11am-3pm and 5pm-10pm Mon.-Thurs., 11am-3pm and 5pm-11pm Fri., 10am-3pm and 5pm-11pm Sat., 10am-3pm and 5pm-9pm Sun., lunch/brunch $14-21, dinner $17-24) opened in the 17th Avenue district. Fresh juices, kombucha, and cocktails pair well with the world-roaming vegetarian menu of small plates, salads, and heartier dishes, including Vietnamese-style subs piled with cheese, eggplant, carrots, and kimchi, or falafel quesadillas, with falafel, hummus, tahini, feta cheese, pickles, and veggies grilled into a tortilla.

Cafés, Bakeries, and Light Bites

Calgary's most delectable breads, pastries, and other baked goods come out of the ovens at ★ **Sidewalk Citizen Bakery** (Simmons Bldg., 618 Confluence Way SE, 403/457-2245, www.sidewalkcitizenbakery.com, 8am-3pm Mon.-Thurs., 8am-4pm Fri.-Sun., $9-16) in the East Village. Try a *bureka*, an Israeli puff pastry baked with cheese, served with an egg, salad, and *harissa*. They make sandwiches on house-made sourdough, including roast chicken with pickled peppers and melted cheddar, and a daily stew and hummus combo. Naturally, there are sweets, too, including croissants, brownies, and single-serving cakes. They have another location in the Kensington neighborhood inside Sunnyside Natural Food market.

If you're serious about your coffee, head to **Phil & Sebastian Coffee Roasters** (Simmons Bldg., 618 Confluence Way SE, 587/353-2268, www.philsebastian. com, 6:30am-9pm Mon.-Fri., 7:30am-9pm Sat.-Sun.). The East Village location roasts its own beans and offers coffee tasting workshops (book online). Some additional branches are downtown and in the Mission neighborhood.

Since 1982, laid-back **Higher Ground Café** (1126 Kensington Rd., 403/270-3780, 7am-11pm Mon.-Thurs., 7am-midnight Fri., 8am-midnight Sat., 8am-11pm Sun.) has been giving the Kensington neighborhood its fair trade, organic caffeine fix from early morning to late at night.

Groceries and Markets

With more than 80 vendors, the year-round **Calgary Farmers Market** (510 77th Ave. SE, 403/240-9113, www. calgaryfarmersmarket.ca, 9am-5pm Thurs.-Sun.) sells Alberta products like bison jerky, gouda cheese, and locally grown produce, alongside prepared food and crafts.

Accommodations

Many Calgary accommodations cater to business travelers during the week, so except during holidays or the annual Calgary Stampede, lodging rates often drop on weekends when road warriors go home. Shop for deals on the hotels' websites directly, particularly if you can be flexible with your dates.

$150-300

Calling itself a "boutique motel," the **Centro Motel** (4540 16th Ave. NW, 403/288-6658, www.centromotel.com, $159-169 d) was built in the 1960s, but its 30 renovated rooms are much cooler than its roadside surroundings on the city's northwest side suggest. They all have white bedding, dark wood furnishings, and updated baths, along with flat-screen TVs, mini fridges, and Keurig coffeemakers. Rooms aren't large, so they're better suited to couples than families. Rates include Wi-Fi, North American phone calls, parking, and a light continental breakfast. The motel is about 20 minutes' drive from downtown.

On the University of Calgary campus northwest of downtown, ★ **Hotel Alma** (169 University Gate NW, 403/220-3203 or 877/498-3203, www.hotelalma.ca, $180-215, parking $10) is a modern seven-story hotel. The best rooms are the one-bedroom suites on the top floor, with king beds and separate living rooms with a pullout sofa. Most of the guest rooms are more compact, with one queen bed, a lounge chair, and a work desk. All units have mini fridges, microwaves, and coffeemakers. There's no air-conditioning, but the windows open. Wi-Fi and North American phone calls are included, as is a continental breakfast. Guests can use the nearby university fitness facility, with an Olympic-size pool; the Olympic Oval, also a short walk away, has public ice-skating. The hotel is a 10- to 15-minute walk from the C-Train's University station that can take you downtown in 15 minutes.

Much nicer than most of the chain motels that cluster in the Motel Village near the University of Calgary, **Aloft Calgary University** (2359 Banff Trail NW, 403/289-1973, www. aloftcalgaryuniversity.com, $159-223) is a sociable spot, with a pool table in the lobby and weekly live music in the WXYZ Bar. Lounge chairs and private cabanas surround the pool in an indoor courtyard. Other facilities include a 24-hour fitness room, spa, and guest laundry. Colorful Calgary-themed artwork and white linens accented with multicolored

pillows decorate the air-conditioned guest rooms, across three floors, which feature work desks, flat-screen TVs, coffeemakers, safes, and fridges. Rates include a hot buffet breakfast. The hotel is one block from the Banff Trail C-Train station. Parking in the hotel's outdoor lot is free; the indoor lot costs $10 per day.

A good-value downtown lodging, the 35-story all-suite **International Hotel** (220 4th Ave. SW, 403/265-9600 or 800/661-8627, www.internationalhotel.ca, $223-499, parking $31) opened in 1970, though it's since been updated with cherry-hued furnishings, white bedding, an indoor pool, and free Wi-Fi. The studio suites are comfortable, with separate sitting and sleeping areas, plus a wet bar with a fridge; the spacious two-bedroom units could easily accommodate a family or group of friends. Rates include a hot breakfast buffet. Popular with tour groups, the International can feel chaotic at times, but the central location makes up for it.

Over $300

Three blocks south of the Calgary Tower, in the Beltline neighborhood, ★ **Hotel Arts** (119 12th Ave. SW, 403/266-4611, www.hotelarts.ca, $229-450, parking weekday $21-30, weekend $7.50-20) lives up to its name. The 12-story property features works by Canadian artists throughout and is a popular place for musicians and other performers to stay. You can lounge around the courtyard pool, where a DJ spins tunes on summer weekends, or drop in for a poolside yoga class ($20). The 185 contemporary guest rooms have all the expected amenities, including triple-sheeted duvets and work desks with ergonomic chairs, included Wi-Fi, Keurig coffeemakers, and safes. Breakfast, lunch, and dinner are served in the **Yellow Door Bistro,** which also offers an excellent weekend brunch; the

Top to bottom: Aloft Calgary University; Calgary Farmers Market; Hotel Arts.

Raw Bar lounge whips up handcrafted cocktails and Vietnamese-influenced sharing plates.

The Hotel Arts team runs the intimate 19-room boutique lodging now known as **Hotel Arts Kensington** (1126 Memorial Dr. NW, 403/228-4442 or 877/313-3733, www.hotelartskensington.com, $229-450, parking $20), where you might feel like a guest at a stately manor house. The modern rooms (some with fireplaces) feel understated, with dark-gray upholstery and rich woods; the granite baths are luxurious, with robes and slippers waiting when you come out of the soaker tub or rain shower. Rates include Wi-Fi and a $20 per person food and beverage credit that you can use toward a meal or drinks at **Oxbow,** the petite contemporary dining room. You can stroll across the bridge to downtown or cruise off on one of the complimentary bikes.

From the illuminated marble check-in desk to the purple lounge chairs in the 143 modern guest rooms, ★ **Hotel Le Germain Calgary** (899 Centre St. SW, 403/264-8990 or 877/362-8990, www.legermainhotels.com, $210-519, parking weekday $42, weekend $20) is one stylish lodging. In a centrally located downtown tower, even the standard rooms are spacious, measuring 450 square feet (42 sq m), with honey-hued furniture, down comforters, rain showers, and Nespresso machines. Work out in the huge top-floor fitness center with windows overlooking downtown or relax in the **RnR Wellness Spa.** Rates include a generous breakfast buffet and Wi-Fi. The on-site restaurant is the well-regarded

CHARCUT Roast House, which also manages the sleek lobby lounge.

In a former 1980s apartment building that was completely gutted, soundproofed, and updated, the **Hotel Elan** (1122 16th Ave. SW, 403/229-2040 or 855/666-6612, www.hotelelan.ca, $214-327 d, $325-499 suites, parking $20) is one block from the 17th Avenue shopping and dining district. The standard rooms, at 250 square feet (23 sq m), are small but smart, with fun features like heated toilet seats and bath floors, as well as pillow-top mattresses, mini fridges, and Keurig coffeemakers. Larger one-bedroom units add a living room with a sleep sofa; the two-bedroom units are nearly 1,000 square feet (93 sq meters), and some have their own workout space with a recumbent bike and yoga mat. Rates include a deluxe continental breakfast, Wi-Fi, and international phone calls.

A traditional downtown luxury hotel, the **Fairmont Hotel Palliser** (133 9th Ave. SW, 403/262-1234 or 866/540-4477, www.fairmont.com, $299-549, parking weekday $45, weekend $35) opened in 1914, and in the lobby, the sparkling chandeliers and stone archways recall that bygone era. The indoor pool still has its traditional black-and-white tiles, though the health club is modern and there's an on-site spa. The 407 guest rooms on 12 stories feel classic; the baths are generally small, although most have natural light. Wi-Fi is included for members of Accor Hotels frequent-stay program, which is free to join, so there's no reason to pay the $14.95 per day connection charge.

Information and Services

Visitor Information

Tourism Calgary (800/661-1678, www. visitcalgary.com) provides visitor information on its website and answers questions through its Twitter and Facebook pages.

The provincial tourism agency, **Travel Alberta** (800/252-3782, www. travelalberta.com) has detailed information on its website about planning a trip to Calgary, the Canadian Rockies, and elsewhere in the region. They also publish provincial visitor guides, available online or at visitors centers throughout the area.

Media and Communications

Calgary's local daily newspapers include the *Calgary Sun* (www.calgarysun.com) and *Calgary Herald* (www.calgaryherald. com). The daily Toronto-based *Globe and Mail* (www.theglobeandmail.com) covers news across Canada, including Calgary, as does the **CBC** (www.cbc.ca), Canada's public television and radio outlet.

Avenue Calgary (www.avenuecalgary. com) is a monthly lifestyle magazine with extensive restaurant coverage and features about city neighborhoods, people, and activities.

Medical Services

The Calgary area has several hospitals (www.albertahealthservices.ca) that can provide emergency medical care to visitors, including **Peter Lougheed General Centre** (3500 26th Ave. NE, 403/943-4555, 24-hour emergency 403/943-4999), **Foothills Medical Centre** (1403 29th St. NW, 403/944-1110, 24-hour emergency 403/944-1315) on the University of Calgary campus, and **Rockyview General Hospital** (7007 14th St. SW, 403/943-3000, 24-hour emergency 403/943-7000).

For emergency services or other medical issues for children ages 18 and younger, contact the **Alberta Children's Hospital** (2888 Shaganappi Trail NW, 403/955-7211, 24-hour emergency 403/955-7070, www.albertahealthservices.ca), near the University of Calgary.

Several of Calgary's **Shoppers Drug Mart** (www.shoppersdrugmart.ca) locations have 24-hour pharmacies, including the **North Hill Shopping Centre** (1632 14th Ave. NW, 403/289-6761), the **Chinook Centre** (6455 Macleod Trail S., 403/253-2424), and **McKnight Village** (5500 Falsbridge Dr. NE, 403/293-2560).

Getting Around

Calgary is divided into four quadrants: northwest, northeast, southwest, and southeast. Numbered avenues run east-west, while numbered streets go north-south. Both begin downtown.

Two rivers also define Calgary's geography. The Bow River runs through the center of the city; downtown is on the Bow's south bank. The Elbow River meanders into the city center from the southwest and joins the Bow east of downtown.

In the downtown area, you can get around easily on foot or using the city's light rail system. Thanks in part to its extremely changeable weather, Calgary has built the world's largest indoor pedestrian pathway network. Calgary's **+15 Skywalk** (www.calgary.ca) runs 11 miles (18 km) through the downtown area, with weather-proof walkways between buildings 15 feet (5 m) above the street (hence, the +15 name). Signs on the sidewalk can direct you to a +15 entrance. The City of Calgary publishes a +15 map that's available on its website; you can also download it as a mobile app (www. calgaryplus15.com).

By Light Rail and Bus

Calgary Transit (403/262-1000, www. calgarytransit.com) runs the city's public transportation network, with two

⬧ Side Trip: A Day with the Dinosaurs

Drive east from Calgary and you're in the prairies, with farmland undulating along the gentle hills. Then as you turn slightly north and approach the small town of Drumheller, the terrain changes again. Suddenly, you're in the **Canadian Badlands.**

Known for its unusual hoodoo rock formations and rocky canyons, Canada's Badlands region also has some of the world's most extensive deposits of dinosaur fossils.

Survey the Badlands landscapes and discover their dinosaur legacy on a day trip from Calgary. Take Highway 2 north to Highway 567 east to Highway 9 east to Drumheller, which is 87 miles (140 km) northeast of Calgary. It's less than two hours' drive from the city to the dinosaurs.

Royal Tyrrell Museum

In 1884, Canadian geologist Joseph Burr Tyrrell put Alberta on the dinosaur map when he unearthed the 70-million-year-old skull of a carnivorous dinosaur near Drumheller. Tyrrell's discovery was christened *Albertosaurus sarcophagus,* the "flesh-eating lizard from Alberta."

Named for this geologist, the **Royal Tyrrell Museum** (Midland Provincial Park, Hwy. 838, Drumheller, 403/823-7707 or 888/440-4240, www.tyrrellmuseum.com, 9am-9pm daily mid-May-Aug., 10am-5pm daily Sept., 10am-5pm Tues.-Sun. Oct.-mid-May, adults $19, seniors $14, ages 7-17 $10, families $48) is Canada's only museum devoted to paleontology. Highlights include a gigantic *Tyrannosaurus rex* skeleton and the partial skull of an *Atrociraptor,* discovered nearby.

Outside the museum, follow the trails through the hoodoo-filled landscape in **Midland Provincial Park** (www.albertaparks.ca), or take a guided 1-mile (1.6-km) **Seven Wonders of the Badlands** walk (11:30am and 1:30pm Sat.-Sun. mid-May-late June, 11:30am, 1:30pm, and 3:30pm daily late June-Aug., 1:30pm daily Sept., $5) that museum staff lead through the desert-like terrain. The museum also offers fossil-collecting workshops and other kid-friendly programs.

The museum is 4 miles (6 km) northwest of Drumheller on Highway 838. As you come into town, follow the museum signs and turn left (west) onto Highway 838 (N. Dinosaur Trail).

The World's Largest T. Rex?

It's hard to pass through Drumheller without stopping for a photo with this kitschy attraction: the **World's Largest Dinosaur** (60 1st Ave. W., Drumheller, 403/823-8100 or 866/823-8100, www.worldslargestdinosaur.com, 9am-9pm daily, over age 5 $4, families $10.50).

This steel and fiberglass *Tyrannosaurus rex* stands 86 feet (26 m) high, more than four times bigger than an actual T. Rex would have been. You can climb up inside the dinosaur to its mouth; there are 106 stairs to the top.

The dino is located off Highway 56, next to the **Drumheller Visitor Information Centre** (60 1st Ave. W., Drumheller, 403/823-1331 or 866/823-8100, www. traveldrumheller.com).

Other Badlands Attractions

Continue along Highway 838 past the Royal Tyrrell Museum to **Horsethief Canyon,** with its multihued rock layers. On Highway 9, about 10 minutes' drive west of Drumheller, receding glaciers carved rock formations into a "U" shape, or horseshoe, in striking **Horseshoe Canyon.**

You can hike into both of these dramatic canyons or simply enjoy the views from above. Hikers should wear sturdy shoes, bring sunscreen, and carry water. Summer temperatures in the canyons can approach 104°F (40°C).

light rail transit lines, known as the C-Train, and more than 160 bus routes. Use the **trip planner** function on the Calgary Transit website to plot your transit trip.

C-Train and bus schedules vary by route, but regular service on major routes begins between 5am and 5:30am and runs until 12:30am or 1am daily.

Transit Fares and Passes

Fares (adults $3.30, ages 6-17 $2.30) for the C-Train and buses are valid for 90 minutes.

Buy your C-Train ticket from the vending machines in the station before you board the train; machines accept coins, credit cards, and debit cards. If you're transferring from the C-Train to the bus, show the driver your validated ticket from the light rail. You don't have to purchase an additional bus ticket.

When you board a bus, you can pay cash for your ticket, but you need to have exact change.

You can buy transit tickets in advance at the **Calgary Transit Customer Service Centres** (Centre Street Platform, 125 7th Ave. SE, and Bow Parkade, 234 7th Ave. SW, 10am-5:30pm Mon.-Fri.), and at many convenience stores and other shops around the city. Tickets are sold individually or in books of 10. Insert your ticket into the fare box when you board the bus, or validate it using the machines in the C-Train station before boarding the light rail.

If you're going to use transit extensively during a single day, purchase a **day pass** (adults $10.50, ages 6-17 $7.50).

By Light Rail

Calgary's **C-Train Light Rail System** (www.calgarytransit.com) has two lines: the **Red Line/Route 201** (Tuscany/Somerset-Bridlewood), which goes to the city's northwest and southeast neighborhoods, and the **Blue Line/Route 202** (69th Street/Saddletowne),

which crosses the city between west and northeast.

Both C-Train lines run through the city center along 7th Avenue, where you can ride **free downtown.** The free zone is between the Downtown West/Kerby (10th St. SW) and City Hall (Macleod Trail SE) stations.

By Bus

Calgary Transit's **bus 300** (403/262-1000, www.calgarytransit.com, 5am-midnight daily, one-way $10.50) can take you between the airport and downtown Calgary. These express buses, which have a different fare structure than the standard buses, run every 20-30 minutes; the trip takes 40-50 minutes.

For other routes, the **trip planner** on the Calgary Transit website (www.calgarytransit.com) can help you figure out how to get to your destination.

At any bus stop, text the posted stop number to 74000, and you'll receive a reply listing the next buses scheduled to arrive at that stop.

By Car

Highway 1, the Trans-Canada Highway, runs east-west across Calgary's north side, where it becomes 16th Avenue. Highway 2, also known as the Queen Elizabeth II Highway, is the main north-south route to the city, extending north to Edmonton and beyond, and south to the Montana border.

Other major roadways include the Crowchild Trail (Hwy. 1A), which crosses northwest Calgary and then turns south; Macleod Trail, which runs south from downtown; and Glenmore Trail (Hwy. 8), which can take you east-west through Calgary's southern suburbs.

Downtown Calgary is south of the Bow River, between 1st and 9th Avenues SW. A rail line crosses the city south of 9th Avenue SW, so some downtown streets stop at 9th Avenue, rather than continuing southbound.

Parking

Calgary's on-street **parking meters** ($1-5 per hour) generally operate 9am-6pm Monday-Saturday, with some downtown meters taking effect at 7am weekdays. Parking is free after 6pm and all day Sunday. Rates vary by location. You can park at most metered spaces for up to two hours.

You can look up meter rates and typical parking availability in different areas using the **Calgary Parking** website (www.calgaryparking.com). This site also shows the location and prices for parking garages and lots around the city.

By Taxi or Ride Share

Calgary taxis are metered, with a $3.80 base fare and 20 cents for each additional 120 meters. Most trips within the downtown area will cost less than $10. A cab between Calgary International Airport and downtown averages $40-45.

Local taxi companies include **Associated Cab** (403/299-1111, www.associatedcab.ca) and **Checker Yellow Cabs** (403/299-9999, www.thecheckergroup.com).

Uber (www.uber.com) also operates in Calgary.

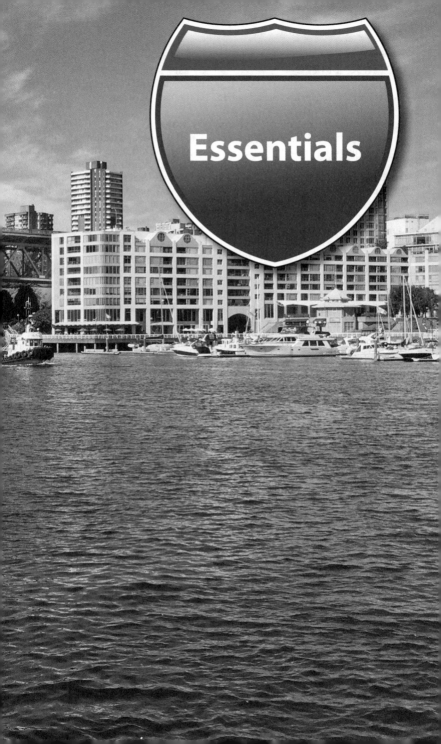

Essentials

Getting There

For a trip to Vancouver and the Canadian Rockies, the main gateway cities, particularly for international travelers, are Vancouver, British Columbia, and Calgary, Alberta.

Getting to Vancouver
By Car

Coming from the United States, **I-5** takes you north from Seattle to the U.S.-Canada border. When you pass through border control, you'll be on **Highway 99** in British Columbia, which leads to metropolitan Vancouver.

The main east-west route across Canada is **Highway 1,** the Trans-Canada Highway. It's possible to follow Highway 1 from eastern Canada, Calgary, and the Canadian Rockies all the way to Vancouver; however, it's not the fastest route.

If you're coming from Calgary or Banff to Vancouver, follow Highway 1 west into British Columbia and continue west to Kamloops. From Kamloops, take **Highway 5,** the Coquihalla Highway, southbound, toward Merritt and Hope. Highway 5 meets **Highway 3,** which you take westbound to rejoin **Highway 1** at the town of Hope and continue west to Vancouver.

From Jasper to Vancouver, the shortest route is to follow **Highway 16** west to **Highway 5,** where you turn south toward Kamloops. At Kamloops, continue south on **Highway 5,** to **Highway 3** west, to **Highway 1** west.

By Air

Vancouver International Airport (YVR, 3211 Grant McConachie Way, Richmond, 604/207-7077, www.yvr.ca) is a major international gateway with flights from across Canada, the United States, Mexico, Europe, Asia, and the Pacific. The airport is south of the city center in the suburb of Richmond, 25 minutes to downtown by public transit, taxi, or by car. All the major car rental companies have offices at the Vancouver airport.

By Train

Pacific Central Station (1150 Station St., Vancouver), near the intersection of Main and Terminal Streets on the edge of Chinatown, is Vancouver's main rail depot. It's also the city's long-distance bus station.

Amtrak

Amtrak (800/872-7245, www.amtrak.com), the U.S. passenger rail carrier, runs trains to Vancouver from Seattle, Washington, and Portland, Oregon. You can make connections in either Seattle or Portland to U.S. points farther south or east. Trains from Seattle (5.5 hours) operate twice a day; the direct Portland-Vancouver train (8 hours) runs once a day in each direction. These trains have electrical outlets and free Wi-Fi in both

standard economy and business classes; the latter seats give you additional legroom.

Tip for cyclists: You can walk your bike onto the Seattle or Portland trains for a fee of just US$5.

VIA Rail

Canada's national passenger rail carrier, **VIA Rail** (514/989-2626 or 888/842-7245, www.viarail.ca), runs cross-country trains to Vancouver from Toronto. The major stops along the Toronto-Vancouver route of *The Canadian,* VIA Rail's flagship train, are Winnipeg (Manitoba), Saskatoon (Saskatchewan), Edmonton and Jasper (Alberta), and Kamloops (British Columbia).

If you do the 2,775-mile (4,466-km) Toronto-Vancouver rail trip nonstop, it's a four-night, three-day journey. *The Canadian* operates three times a week in each direction May-mid-October, and twice a week mid-October-April. It's possible to get off en route and continue your

journey on a subsequent train. For example, you could take the train from Toronto to Jasper in the Canadian Rockies, get off the train for two or three days (depending on the schedule), and catch the next train onward to Vancouver.

VIA Rail offers several classes of service on *The Canadian.* In **Economy class,** the cheapest option, you have a seat that reclines and access to a washroom (but no shower). Meals aren't included, although you can buy meals and snacks on the train or outside the train during a few brief stopovers.

A more comfortable alternative is **Sleeper Plus** class, where you have several choices of accommodations. The least expensive is either an upper or lower **berth,** which is a seat by day that converts into a bunk, shielded by a heavy curtain, at night. Berth passengers have access to men's and women's restrooms and private shower rooms in the corridor.

Another Sleeper Plus option is a **cabin,** which can sleep one, two, three, or four

VIA Rail is Canada's national rail carrier.

people. Cabins have their own toilets and sinks, and passengers can use the shower rooms in the corridor. Note that in the one-person cabin, the bed folds down over the toilet, so if you need to use the facilities during the night, you have to fold up your bed or use the restroom in the hallway.

The top-end sleeper accommodations are in **Prestige Sleeper** class, which gives you a more modern cabin with a private bathroom and shower. These units have an L-shaped leather couch by day with a Murphy bed for two that folds down at night.

All Sleeper class fares include three meals a day in the dining car, nonalcoholic drinks, and access to both a window-lined viewing car and the bar-snack car, with complimentary coffee, tea, fruit, and cookies.

Outside of the busy summer travel season, VIA Rail frequently offers discounts of up to 50 percent off its standard fares. Check the website or sign up for its newsletter to find out about seat sales. Occasional last-minute travel deals also are posted on the VIA Rail website (www.viarail.ca).

The Rocky Mountaineer

The **Rocky Mountaineer** (1755 Cottrell St., at Terminal Ave., Vancouver, 604/606-7245 or 877/460-3200, www. rockymountaineer.com, mid-Apr.-mid-Oct.) is a privately run luxury train that offers rail trips between Vancouver, Banff, Lake Louise, Jasper, and Calgary. You can travel round-trip from Vancouver to the Canadian Rockies and back, or book a one-way journey through the Rockies from Vancouver to Calgary (or vice versa). Another route starts in Seattle and stops in Vancouver before continuing to the Rockies. Rocky Mountaineer trains travel during the day and stop overnight in Kamloops, where you stay in a hotel, en route to or from the Rockies.

Unlike a standard train trip, many

Rocky Mountaineer packages include gondola rides, helicopter tours, and other activities, as well as accommodations. It's also possible to book a Rocky Mountaineer holiday that covers rail fare and accommodations only; for example, it offers two-day train trips between Vancouver and Lake Louise, Banff, or Jasper. Rail packages start at $1,579 per person; pricing depends on the destinations, number of travel days, and the level of service and accommodations.

Rocky Mountaineer trains do not use Vancouver's Pacific Central Station, where VIA Rail and Amtrak trains depart; they have a separate depot nearby.

By Bus

Bolt Bus (877/265-8287, www.boltbus. com) provides bus service between Seattle and Vancouver, arriving at and departing from **Pacific Central Station** (1150 Station St., Vancouver). **Quick Shuttle** (604/940-4428 or 800/665-2122, www.quickcoach. com) runs buses between Seattle and Vancouver as well, stopping at Canada Place; it picks up or drops off passengers at a number of downtown hotels, with advance reservations.

Getting to Calgary
By Car

Highway 1, the Trans-Canada Highway, brings you to Calgary from Banff, Lake Louise, and points west in British Columbia. From the east, Highway 1 leads to Calgary from Medicine Hat (Alberta), Regina (Saskatchewan), Winnipeg (Manitoba), and eastern Canada.

Highway 2, also known as the Queen Elizabeth II Highway, is the main north-south route to Calgary. It extends north to Edmonton and beyond, and south to the U.S. border and the state of Montana.

By Air

You can fly to **Calgary International Airport** (YYC, 2000 Airport Rd. NE, 403/735-1200, www.yyc.com) from across Canada, from many U.S. cities, and from Amsterdam, Frankfurt, London, Beijing, and Tokyo, among other cities. The airport is located on the city's northeast side, about a 20-minute drive from downtown.

By Train

Neither VIA Rail nor Amtrak have passenger service to Calgary. The closet VIA Rail passenger station is in Edmonton, 185 miles (300 km) to the north.

The privately run **Rocky Mountaineer** (877/460-3200, www.rockymountaineer. com, mid-Apr.-mid-Oct.) offers luxury train trips that can start or end in Calgary and travel to Banff, Lake Louise, Jasper, and Vancouver. The Rocky Mountaineer also has a route that starts in Seattle, stops in Vancouver, and continues on to the Rockies and Calgary.

By Bus

Brewster Banff Airport Express (403/762-6700 or 866/606-6700, www. banffjaspercollection.com) runs buses from Banff to downtown Calgary hotels and to the Calgary International Airport. The **Banff Airporter** (403/762-3330 or 888/449-2901, www.banffairporter.com) can take you from Banff to the Calgary airport as well.

Red Arrow (403/531-0350 or 800/232-1958, www.redarrow.ca) runs buses to Calgary from Edmonton and other cities in Alberta.

Road Rules

Car Rental

The major North American car rental companies have outlets at Vancouver International Airport and Calgary International Airport. They also have offices in downtown Vancouver, downtown Calgary, and in many smaller cities across British Columbia and Alberta.

Many agencies provide discounts for weekly rentals and additional discounts for rentals of a month or more. Some offer discounts for members of the Canadian Automobile Association (CAA) or American Automobile Association (AAA).

If you're considering renting a car in the United States and driving it across the Canadian border, confirm with your car rental company in advance that you're allowed to drive out of the country. Make sure you have a copy of the rental contract handy at the border crossing.

RV Rental

Renting an RV is a popular way to travel across western Canada. Whether you rent a small van or a mega motor home, you're combining your transportation and lodging. The national and provincial parks, as well as privately run facilities across the west, have campgrounds where you can park for a night or more.

Some companies allow you to book one-way rentals. For example, you can pick up your RV in Vancouver, drive to the Canadian Rockies, and drop off the vehicle in Calgary, where you can depart from the international airport.

The following companies rent RVs or camper vans in western Canada: **CanaDream RV Rentals** (888/480-9726, www.canadream.com), **Cruise Canada** (800/671-8042, www.cruisecanada. com), **Fraserway RV Rentals** (800/661-2441, www.fraserway.com), **Traveland RV** (844/281-5251, www.travelandrvcanada. com), **Westcoast Mountain Campers** (888/608-8766, www.wcmcampers.com), and **Wicked Campers** (877/942-5380, www.wickedcampers.ca).

Driving Rules

In Canada, each province determines its rules of the road, so for a trip to the Canadian Rockies, you need to be aware of the laws in both British Columbia and Alberta. Differences between the provincial laws are typically minor but still worth knowing.

Winter Travel in the Canadian Rockies

When you're road-tripping in western Canada's mountain regions between October and March, your vehicle needs to be equipped with winter tires, since it can snow—a lot—at any time. Listen to the weather forecast regularly, and prepare to get off the road if you need to wait out a storm.

In January, the average daytime high temperature in Banff is 19°F (-7°C). In Jasper, it's 21°F (-6°C). For outdoor activities, make sure you have a warm water-repellent jacket, ideally with long underwear, fleece, and a vest that you can layer underneath, as well as gloves, a hat that covers your ears, and warm waterproof boots. Don't forget your sunscreen and sunglasses; even in winter, the sun can be strong, particularly when it's reflecting off the snow.

If you're not comfortable with winter driving conditions, or don't want the hassle of winter driving, you can make your winter trip without a car. Shuttles pick up passengers at Calgary International Airport, bringing you to Banff or Lake Louise, and you can take a shuttle from town to the ski areas.

Driver's Licenses

If you have a valid driver's license from your home country, that license will be valid in British Columbia for up to six months and in Alberta for a year.

If your license is not in English, you should either obtain an International Driving Permit (IDP) in your home country, which will be valid for six months in B.C. or one year in Alberta, or have your license translated into English. Always carry both your driver's license and the IDP (or translation of your license) when you're driving.

Even if your license is in English, Alberta recommends that you obtain an International Driving Permit and carry it along with your driver's license.

Insurance

If you're driving a rented car in B.C. or Alberta, make sure you always carry a copy of the rental contract and proof of insurance.

If you're driving over the border from the United States, bring the car's registration forms and proof of insurance. Either carry the insurance policy itself or get a free **Canadian Non-Resident Insurance Card** from your insurance agent.

In both B.C. and Alberta, you must have a minimum of $200,000 in third-party liability coverage. Check with your insurance provider in your home country to ensure that you have sufficient insurance.

Speed Limits

Canada uses the metric system, so speed limits are posted in kilometers per hour.

In British Columbia, the speed limit in urban areas is 50 km/h (31 mph) and outside metropolitan areas 80 km/h (50 mph), unless otherwise posted. On many B.C. highways, speed limits range from 90-120 km/h (56-74 mph).

In Alberta, speed limits on all roads in urban areas are 50 km/h (31 mph), on roadways outside the metropolitan areas are 80 km/h (50 mph), and on provincial highways are 100 km/h (62 mph), unless otherwise posted. On Alberta highways, the maximum speed limit is 110 km/h (68 mph).

Traffic Signals

You can make a **right turn at a red light** in British Columbia and in Alberta (as long as you stop and make sure it's clear), unless it's otherwise posted.

A **flashing red traffic signal** is equivalent to a stop sign. It means you must stop, allow any cross traffic to proceed, and then you can proceed when it's safe to do so. A **flashing yellow traffic signal** is a warning light, advising drivers to use caution in the area.

A **flashing green traffic signal** indicates that the traffic light is pedestrian-activated. That is, the signal remains flashing green and cars can proceed as you would on a standard green signal, until a pedestrian who wants to cross the street presses the "walk" button. The signal will turn yellow and then red, indicating that traffic must stop to allow the pedestrian to cross.

Even when there is no traffic signal, drivers must stop for pedestrians **in a crosswalk.**

Electronic Devices

In both B.C. and Alberta, it's against the law to drive while using a **handheld cell phone** or other electronic device. No texting or emailing while you're driving!

Drivers may use a hands-free cell phone if it is voice activated; the device must be attached to the vehicle or the driver's body (using an earpiece in one ear only). Similarly, you can't program a Global Positioning System (GPS) while you're driving; you can issue voice commands, but you can't touch it.

Seat Belts

By law, **you must wear a seat belt** when you're driving in B.C. or Alberta.

In both provinces, infants must ride in rear-facing car seats until they are at least one year old and weigh 20 pounds (9 kg). When children outgrow these infant seats, they're required to sit in forward-facing car seats until they weigh at least 40 pounds (18 kg).

In B.C., children who weigh more than 40 pounds must sit in a booster seat with a seat belt until they are nine years old or at least 4 feet 9 inches (145 cm) tall. Alberta law does not require booster seats, but they're still recommended.

Road Conditions

To check current road conditions in British Columbia, visit www.driveBC.ca online or phone 800/550-4997.

In Alberta, visit www.511Alberta.ca or call 511, which is a toll-free call within the province.

Keep your gas tank topped up as you're traveling across western Canada. In many areas, it can be 60 miles (97 km) or more between services.

Many of western Canada's highways pass through high mountain elevations, where it can snow at any time of year, even in the summer. Although heavy snow is uncommon outside the winter months, check the weather forecast regularly.

When you're traveling through the mountains between October and March, your vehicle must be equipped with **winter tires.** Among the roads on which winter tires are required are the Sea-to-Sky Highway between Vancouver and Whistler, and many sections of Highways 1, 3, and 5 throughout B.C., as well as Highway 1 and the Icefields Parkway in Alberta.

Maps and Tourist Information

Destination Canada (www.canada.travel) is the government of Canada's official guide to travel across the country.

British Columbia Visitors Centers

Destination B.C. (www.hellobc.com), British Columbia's provincial tourism agency, runs visitors centers across the province that provide maps and other travel information. The offices have public restrooms, and many offer free Wi-Fi.

If you're driving from the U.S. on I-5, you can get information from the visitors center at the **Peace Arch** (298 Hwy. 99, Surrey), as soon as you cross into Canada.

The **Vancouver Visitor Centre** (Plaza Level, 200 Burrard St.) is downtown, opposite Canada Place and the cruise ship terminal.

On Vancouver Island, look for visitors centers in **Victoria** (812 Wharf St.), **Nanaimo** (2450 Northfield Rd.), **Tofino** (1426 Pacific Rim Hwy.), and **Ucluelet** (2791 Pacific Rim Hwy.).

On the Sea-to-Sky Highway (Hwy. 99), get information at the visitors centers in **Squamish** (Squamish Adventure Centre, 38551 Loggers Ln.) and **Whistler** (4230 Gateway Dr.).

En route between Vancouver and Kamloops or the Okanagan, there is a B.C. visitors center in **Hope** (919 Water Ave.).

Along Highway 1, heading toward the B.C. Rockies, there are visitors centers in **Kamloops** (1290 W. Trans-Canada Hwy.), **Revelstoke** (301 Victoria Rd. W.), and **Golden** (1000 Trans-Canada Hwy.).

In the Kootenays, you'll find visitors centers in **Radium Hot Springs** (7556 Main St. E.), **Invermere** (651 Hwy. 93/95 Cross Roads), **Fernie** (102 Commerce Rd./Hwy. 3), **Kaslo** (324 Front St.), **Nelson** (91 Baker St.), and **Rossland** (1100 Hwy. 3B).

In the Okanagan, get your questions answered at visitors centers in **Kelowna** (238 Queensway), **Penticton** (888 Westminster Ave. W.), and **Osoyoos** (9912 Hwy. 3, at Hwy. 97).

Alberta Visitors Centers

In Alberta, you can pick up travel information at visitors centers operated by the provincial tourism agency, **Travel Alberta** (800/252-3782, www.travelalberta.com) and at local visitors centers around the province.

Alberta Visitor Centres are located at **Calgary International Airport** (arrivals level, May-Sept.), and in the Rocky Mountain region in **Canmore** (2801 Bow Valley Trail), **Field, B.C.** (Hwy. 1, May-Oct.) in Yoho National Park, and **Hinton** (309 Gregg Ave., May-Oct.), on Highway 16 northeast of Jasper National Park.

There's an Alberta Visitor Centre at **Crowsnest Pass** (Hwy. 3, Blairmore, May-Sept.) 3.7 miles (6 km) east of the B.C.-Alberta border, and another near the Canada-U.S. border near **West Glacier, Montana** (US 2 at Going-to-the-Sun Rd., May-mid-Sept.).

Canadian Automobile Association

The **Canadian Automobile Association** (CAA, www.caa.ca) provides road maps for its members through its provincial chapters. It has reciprocal agreements with the **American Automobile Association** (AAA, www.aaa.com), so that AAA members can get maps and assistance in Canada. Members can order maps by mail or pick them up at local CAA offices.

The CAA's British Columbia chapter, the **B.C. Automobile Association** (BCAA, www.bcaa.com), has offices in **Vancouver,** including its Yaletown location (289 Davie St., 604/801-7130, 9am-6pm Mon.-Fri., 9am-5pm Sat.), **Victoria** (1644 Hillside Ave., #115, 250/414-8320, 9:30am-5:30pm Mon.-Sat., 11am-5:30pm Sun.), **Kamloops** (500 Notre Dame Dr., #400, 250/852-4600, 9am-6pm Mon.-Fri., 9am-5pm Sat.), **Kelowna** (1470 Harvey Ave., #18, 250/870-4900, 9am-6pm Mon.-Fri., 9am-5pm Sat.), **Penticton** (2100 Main St., #100, 250/487-2450, 9am-6pm Mon.-Fri., 9am-5pm Sat.), and **Nelson** (596 Baker St., 250/505-1720, 9am-5pm Mon.-Sat.).

The **Alberta Motor Association** (AMA, http://ama.ab.ca), the CAA's Alberta chapter, has several offices in Calgary. The **Calgary Main Office** (4700 17th Ave. SW, 403/240-5300, 9am-6pm Mon.-Fri., 9am-5pm Sat.) is west of the city center.

Roadside Assistance

In an emergency, call **911** to reach police, fire, ambulance, or other emergency services. Never leave the scene of an accident without contacting the police.

The **Canadian Automobile Association** (CAA, www.caa.ca) provides roadside assistance for its members and for members of the **American Automobile Association** (AAA, www.aaa.com).

Visas and Officialdom

For the most up-to-date requirements for visitors coming to Canada, visit **Citizenship and Immigration Canada** (www.cic.gc.ca).

Important note: If you have a criminal record, including misdemeanors or driving while impaired (DWI), no matter how long ago, **you can be prohibited** from entering Canada unless you obtain a special waiver well in advance of your trip. Refer to the Citizenship and Immigration Canada website (www.cic.gc.ca) for additional information.

Passports and Visas
U.S. Citizens
The simple answer to the question of what documents U.S. citizens need to visit Canada is "a valid **passport**." It's always a good idea to travel with your passport, if you have one.

If you are driving over the border, you can use a **NEXUS** card, issued as part of the U.S. government's Trusted Travel Program, as your entry document. See the U.S. Customs and Border Protection website (www.cbp.gov) for NEXUS details.

If you're driving, a valid **U.S. Passport Card** can also be used instead of a passport. Get more information about U.S. Passport Cards, which cannot be used for air travel, from the U.S. State Department (www.travel.state.gov).

Citizens of the United States do not need a visa to visit Canada for stays of less than six months.

Citizens of Other Countries
All other foreign visitors to Canada must have a valid passport, and, depending on your nationality, you may also need either a visitor visa or an Electronic Travel Authorization (eTA). Check with Citizenship and Immigration Canada (www.cic.gc.ca) to confirm what documents you require.

British, Australian, and New Zealand citizens don't require a visa, nor do citizens of many European nations. However, in 2016, Canada introduced the **Electronic Travel Authorization (eTA)**, which is required for visa-exempt visitors who are traveling to Canada **by air.** For example, a British citizen who is driving into Canada from the U.S. would not require a visa or an eTA but would need the eTA to fly into Canada. If you need an eTA, apply for this document online on the **Citizenship and Immigration Canada** website (www.cic. gc.ca).

Embassies and Consulates
American citizens in western Canada can get assistance from the **U.S. Consulate General-Vancouver** (1075 W. Pender St., 604/685-4311, http://ca.usembassy.gov) or **U.S. Consulate General-Calgary** (615 Macleod Trail SE, 10th Fl., 403/266-8962, http://ca.usembassy.gov).

British nationals needing consular assistance can contact the **British Consulate General-Vancouver** (1111 Melville St., Ste. 800, 604/683-4421, www.gov.uk) or **British Consulate General-Calgary** (150 6th Ave. SW, #5100, main office 403/705-1755, emergencies 403/538-2181, www. gov.uk).

The **Australian Consulate and Trade Commission, Vancouver** (1075 W. Georgia St., Ste. 2050, 604/694-6160, www.canada.embassy.gov.au) provides consular assistance to Australian citizens in western Canada.

The **New Zealand Consulate General, Vancouver** (1050 W. Pender St., Ste. 2250, 604/684-7388, www.nzembassy. com/canada) can assist citizens of New Zealand in western Canada.

Customs
Visitors to Canada can bring a reasonable amount of personal baggage, including clothing, camping and sports equipment, cameras, and computers for personal use.

Travelers must declare all **food,** plants, or animals they bring into Canada. In general, you're allowed to bring food for personal use, although there are restrictions on fresh fruits, vegetables, meats, and dairy products. Get the latest information from the **Canadian Food Inspection Agency** (www.inspection. gc.ca).

As long as you're of legal drinking age (at least age 19 in B.C., age 18 in Alberta), you can bring a small amount of **alcoholic beverages** into Canada duty- and tax-free. You're allowed to bring *one* of the following: two bottles of wine (up to 53 fl oz/1.5 l), one standard bottle of other alcohol (40 oz/1.14 l), or 24 cans or bottles of beer or ale (up to a total of 287 oz/8.5 l). Visitors are also allowed to bring in up to 200 cigarettes or 50 cigars.

In general, visitors cannot bring weapons into Canada. You're specifically prohibited from bringing automatic weapons, sawed-off rifles or shotguns, most handguns, and semiautomatic weapons into Canada. There are some exceptions for hunters, and all visitors must declare any firearms in writing. Check the detailed requirements with the **Canada Border Services Agency** (www. cbsa.gc.ca).

Note that when you're flying to Canada from the United States or other international destinations, you clear immigration and customs at the Canadian airport after you land in Canada. However, if you're **flying to the United States** from Vancouver, Calgary, or other major Canadian cities, you clear U.S. immigration and customs at the Canadian airport *before* you board your flight. For example, if you were traveling from Vancouver to Los Angeles, you would clear U.S. immigration and customs at the Vancouver airport. **Allow extra time** for these immigration and customs procedures, in addition to the time it takes for standard airport passenger screening.

Travel Tips

In Canada, each province sets its own laws regulating activities such as drinking, smoking, and drug use. The **drinking age** in British Columbia is 19; in Alberta, it's 18.

Each province has its own laws about when and where you can **smoke,** and some cities have laws that are more restrictive than those at the provincial level. You must be 19 to smoke in B.C., 18 in Alberta. In both B.C. and Alberta, you can't smoke in any indoor public place, including restaurants, bars, shopping centers, and public transit, or in a car where anyone under age 16 is a passenger. Vancouver also prohibits smoking at any city parks or beaches and on restaurant patios. Similarly, in Calgary, you can't smoke in the +15 walkways or within 16 feet (5 m) of outdoor pools, skating rinks, playgrounds, or sports fields.

Cannabis in Canada

In 2018, recreational cannabis use became legal across Canada. In general, this means that, throughout the country, adults can possess up to 30 grams of legal cannabis and use or share up to 30 grams with other adults. You must be at least 19 in B.C. and 18 in Alberta to legally use marijuana, and you have to obey the same laws in each province and city about where you can smoke that apply to tobacco. Each jurisdiction can choose to further regulate use; for example, cannabis use is not permitted in public places, including streets, trails, and parks, within the town of Banff.

Marijuana is allowed in Parks Canada campgrounds, but only at your own campsite and not in cooking shelters, washrooms, or any other public areas. Parks Canada has other specific rules for cannabis use in the national parks, so refer to its website (www.pc.gc.ca) for up-to-date details.

Each province has its own rules about where you can legally buy cannabis products. In British Columbia, cannabis is sold at government-run stores, a limited number of licensed private retailers, and the B.C. government's online shop. In Alberta, it's available through authorized private stores and online through the provincial government.

Note that it is illegal to transport cannabis across international borders.

For more details, refer to the Government of Canada (www.canada.ca) and to each province's cannabis information site, such as British Columbia's (www.cannabis.gov.bc.ca) and Alberta's (www.alberta.ca).

Access for Travelers with Disabilities

Many of western Canada's attractions, hotels, restaurants, entertainment venues, and transportation options are accessible to travelers with disabilities. A useful general resource about accessible travel to and around Canada is the government's **Access to Travel** website (www.accesstotravel.gc.ca). It includes details about transportation between and around B.C. and Alberta cities and towns, as well as general tips and travel advice.

Most national and provincial parks offer accessible facilities. Many picnic areas, campsites, and park washrooms, as well as some trails, can accommodate wheelchairs and other mobility aids. Get details on facilities in specific parks from **Parks Canada** (www.pc.gc.ca), **B.C. Parks** (www.env.gov.bc.ca), and **Alberta Parks** (www.albertaparks.ca).

Traveling with Children

Western Canada is an extremely family-friendly destination. Not only are there tons of fun things for families to do, but plenty of resources also help support traveling families or make travel more affordable.

Many museums, attractions, and recreational facilities offer free admission for kids under a certain age (often 5 or 6, but sometimes 11 or 12). Many offer discounted family admission rates, which generally include two adults and at least two children. Ask about family discounts when you're buying tickets.

Kids stay free at many major hotels. Other good lodging options for traveling families, besides the typical chain motels, include suite hotels or apartments (in cities) and cabins or cottages (in more rural areas), which often provide more space for the money, as well as kitchen facilities where you can prepare your own food. Some bed-and-breakfasts don't accept kids, so always ask.

Many restaurants in Canada offer children's menus with a few kid-approved food selections. Encourage your kids to try new things, though, since they may surprise you with their newfound love for bison burgers, handmade noodles, or sushi.

When you're visiting a national park or national historic site with kids, ask for a free **Parks Canada Xplorer** booklet, which has child-friendly activities to help them explore that destination. At most parks, Parks Canada staff offer interpretive programs, from wildlife talks to guided hikes, that are designed for kids or suitable for families; ask at the park visitors center or check the Parks Canada website (www.pc.gc.ca) for details and schedules.

Note that if only one parent is traveling with his or her children, the Canadian government recommends that the parent carry a written letter of permission from the other parent. Divorced parents who share custody should also travel with a copy of their legal custody documents. If you are traveling with a child who isn't your own (or for whom you're not the legal guardian), you should carry written permission from the parents or guardians indicating that you're allowed to travel with the child. You may be asked to present these letters at the border when you enter Canada. For a sample letter of consent, see the **Travel and Tourism** section of the Government of Canada's website (www.travel.gc.ca).

Women Traveling Alone

Overall, western Canada is a relatively safe destination compared to many spots around the world, and women shouldn't hesitate to travel alone. However, exercise caution wherever you go, and avoid venturing out alone late at night or in the wee hours of the morning. If you are out late on your own, don't walk; take a cab. Take your cues from local women, too. If you don't see other women walking or waiting for the bus, that's a clue that maybe you shouldn't either.

Carry a cell phone with you, so you can phone for assistance if you need it. However, be aware that many parks and remote regions have limited or no cell phone coverage.

When hiking, many women suggest finding other groups of travelers that you might join, or hiking on busier trails where you won't be alone for long periods of time.

An excellent resource for women travelers is **Journeywoman** (www.journeywoman.com), a Toronto-based website where women travelers can share tips and ask for advice from local women around the world.

Senior Travelers

The good thing about getting older is that you can often get discounts. Many B.C. and Alberta attractions, lodgings, and transportation providers offer discounts for seniors. Normally, you need to be 65 to qualify for a senior discount, although occasionally these discounts are extended to travelers at age 60 or 62.

Parks Canada offers discounts at the country's national parks and national historic sites, with reduced rates for single-day admissions and annual passes.

Gay and Lesbian Travelers

Canada is far more welcoming to gay and lesbian travelers than many other destinations. Marriage equality is the law in Canada.

Western Canada's largest LGBTQ community is in Vancouver. The hub of the community is along Davie Street in the city's West End, with another popular area along Commercial Drive in East Vancouver, although accommodations, restaurants, and other facilities across the city (and indeed across B.C.) welcome gay travelers. **Tourism Vancouver** (www.tourismvancouver.com) publishes a quarterly LGBT newsletter, *Out in Vancouver*. **Gayvan Travel Marketing** (www.gayvan.com) can tell you more about the local community, events, and resources. *Gay Calgary Magazine* (www.gaycalgary.com) can tell you what's happening in that city.

Other resources for gay and lesbian travel to Canada include **Travel Gay Canada** (www.travelgaycanada.com), the country's gay and lesbian tourism association, and **TAG Approved** (www.tagapproved.com), which highlights gay-friendly hotels and attractions.

Traveling Without Reservations

You can travel without advance reservations across western Canada, leaving your itinerary flexible to explore intriguing areas that you discover en route or to alter your plans to accommodate the weather.

However, July and August are peak travel months across the region, and in the major cities and national parks, especially in Banff, Jasper, and Vancouver, you may have trouble finding last-minute accommodations. Holiday weekends, including **Victoria Day** (3rd Mon. in May), **Canada Day** (July 1), **August Civic Holiday** (1st Mon. in Aug.), **Labour Day** (1st Mon. in Sept.), and **Thanksgiving** (2nd Mon. in Oct.), are exceptionally busy travel times, as is the week of **Christmas** and **New Year's.** Note that Canada celebrates Thanksgiving in October, while the U.S. Thanksgiving holiday is in late November.

If you are looking for last-minute

lodgings, begin your search early in the day. You're far more likely to find a room before noon than you are at 5pm. Some area visitors centers keep lists of available accommodations or can provide suggestions for same-day places to stay. Similarly, if you're camping, claim your site early in the day.

When you're taking a car on the ferries between the mainland and Vancouver Island, you don't need to reserve a spot in advance. However, on weekends, holidays, and busy summer days, you may have a long wait if you don't. Making a reservation will ensure that you get your car on the boat you want.

Hotel and Motel Chains

Western Canada has many of the same roadside motels and urban chains that you find across the United States.

Best Western (www.bestwestern. com), **Choice Hotels** (www.choicehotels. ca, including Comfort Inn, Econo Lodge, Quality Inn, Rodeway Inn), **Hilton Hotels** (www.hilton.com, including Hampton Inn), **Holiday Inn** and **Holiday Inn Express** (www.ihg.com), **Hyatt Hotels** (www.hyatt.com), **Marriott Hotels** (www. marriott.com, including Courtyard, Fairfield Inn, Residence Inn, and Delta Hotels by Marriott), **Starwood Hotels** (www.starwoodhotels.com, including Sheraton, Westin, Aloft, Four Points), and **Wyndam Hotels** (www.wyndham. com, including Days Inn, Howard Johnson, Ramada, Super 8, Travelodge), as well as the upscale **Fairmont Hotels and Resorts** (www.fairmont.com), all have properties in British Columbia and Alberta.

Time Zones

Most of British Columbia is in the Pacific time zone, the same as the U.S. West Coast. Alberta is one hour later, in the mountain time zone.

However, some B.C. national parks and communities close to the Alberta border follow their neighbors to the east and use mountain time. Revelstoke, Mount Revelstoke National Park, and Glacier National Park are on Pacific time, but Golden, Yoho National Park, Kootenay National Park, Fernie, and Cranbrook are on mountain time.

Both B.C. and Alberta observe daylight saving time. Clocks move ahead one hour on the second Sunday in March and move back one hour on the first Sunday in November.

Health and Safety

Travelers should always carry a basic first-aid kit, including bandages, aspirin or other pain reliever, sunscreen, insect repellent, and an antiseptic or antibiotic ointment. You might want to include an ointment or other product to relieve the itching of mosquito bites; if you're prone to allergic reactions, consider packing an antihistamine, too. If you wear glasses, bring an extra pair. If you take prescription medication, carry a copy of your prescription.

Emergencies

In an emergency, call **911** to reach police, fire, ambulance, or other emergency services.

Nonemergency Medical Information

In **British Columbia,** to speak with a nurse for medical information 24 hours a day, call **811** to reach the **HealthLink BC** service (www.healthlinkbc.ca). You can also contact HealthLink BC at 604/215-8110.

In **Alberta,** call **811** or 866/408-5465 to reach that province's **Health Link** (www. albertahealthservices.ca) 24-hour medical information line.

Health Care and Insurance

If you become ill or injured while traveling in B.C. or Alberta, go to the nearest hospital emergency room or walk-in health clinic.

If you're a resident of another Canadian province, your provincial health plan may not provide health coverage while you're out of your home province. If the plan does provide coverage, it may pay only the amount it would pay for the service in your home province, not what you might be billed in B.C. or Alberta. Either way, before your trip, it's a good idea to purchase supplemental travel health insurance to cover unexpected medical costs while you're on the road.

If you live outside Canada, make sure that you have health insurance that will cover you and your family in Canada. You normally have to pay for any medical services provided in Canada and then file a claim with your health insurance provider after you return home.

Wilderness Safety
Poison Ivy

Touching the sap of the poison ivy plant can give you an intensely itchy skin rash. Found throughout western Canada, poison ivy often grows in wooded areas, beside hiking trails, and along the roadside. Its identifying characteristics are its leaves, which grow along a woody vine in clusters of three. The leaves can have a reddish cast, particularly in the spring and fall, although they may appear deep green during the summer.

A poison ivy rash usually appears within 24-48 hours after contact. The sap can also get on an animal's fur, and while your dogs won't get a rash, they can transfer the rash-inducing sap to you.

The best way to avoid getting a poison ivy rash is to avoid touching the plant. Wear closed-toe shoes, socks, and long pants when hiking or walking in the woods, and check for poison ivy before you sit down in a meadow or spread out your picnic blanket. If you think you may have come in contact with poison ivy, wash your skin with soap and cool water right away. Wash your clothing as soon as possible, too.

If you develop a poison ivy rash, applying calamine lotion or a hydrocortisone cream to the skin may help alleviate the itching. Go to a hospital emergency room right away if you have any trouble breathing or swallowing or if the rash causes swelling, particularly around your eyes. Seek medical attention as well if the rash appears on your face or if you develop a fever or any other signs of infection.

Ticks

Ticks are tiny bugs—a type of arachnid—that feed on the blood of animals or people. Most are harmless, although some varieties of ticks, primarily black-legged or deer ticks, can carry Lyme disease. Lyme disease is a bacterial infection that can cause flu-like symptoms, and if left untreated, more severe illnesses of the nervous system, joints, and heart. To date, Lyme-carrying ticks have infrequently been found in British Columbia or Alberta, except in certain parts of the Lower Mainland, parts of Vancouver Island, and some areas along the B.C. coast, where they are found more often.

It's still a good idea to reduce your exposure to ticks when you're hiking, camping, or exploring forested areas by wearing closed-toe shoes, socks, and long pants. Do a "tick check" whenever you finish any of these outdoor activities, examining your skin, and that of your kids or pets, to spot any ticks. You can generally avoid infection by removing a tick within 24-36 hours.

If you do find a tick attached to your skin, remove it by using clean tweezers to grab the head and pull it straight out. Then wash the skin with soap and water or disinfect it with alcohol or hand sanitizer.

Giardia

Crystal clear lakes and rushing rivers flow across western Canada, but that doesn't mean the water is safe to drink. While tap water in most parts of B.C. and Alberta is of excellent quality,

Stay Safe in Bear Country

It's important to know how to stay safe in wildlife country and how to protect bears and other animals from human encounters.

Wildlife on the Roads

If you spot animals by the roadside or along the trails, keep your distance. Parks Canada staff recommend staying at least 100 feet (30 m), or the equivalent of three bus lengths, from deer, sheep, goats, elk, and moose, and more than 300 feet (100 m), or 10 bus lengths, from bears, cougars, or wolves.

If you're in your car or RV and want to stop for wildlife along the road, pull over to avoid creating "wildlife jams," where traffic can't pass because cars are blocking the road. Use your warning lights to alert other vehicles. If you've stopped close to an animal, don't get out of your car! Snap a photo and move on.

Be extra careful when driving at dawn or dusk, when animals are most active. Scan the roadway and shoulders frequently for wildlife. And if you see one animal, others may be nearby.

Bear Safety on the Trails

If you're hiking or cycling, Parks Canada suggests three general steps to stay safe in bear country:

♦ **Prepare:** Carry bear spray and learn what to do if you encounter a bear.

♦ **Be aware:** Scan your surroundings and look for tracks, droppings, or diggings.

♦ **Let bears know you're there:** Make noise (consider singing), and ideally travel in a group of at least four.

During certain times of year, Parks Canada posts "bear warnings" on certain trails. Trails can be closed due to bear activity, or in some cases, park staff require that you hike in close groups of 4-6. These warnings are posted on the Parks Canada website (www.pc.gc.ca), in park visitors centers, and at trailheads. Always check for bear restrictions before you set out on a hike.

Be Careful with Garbage

Take care with food and garbage, too. Throughout western Canada, even in towns, you'll notice bear-proof garbage containers, where you have to reach under a covered metal handle to open the container; use them.

If you're camping, never leave food outside or in your tent. That includes food scraps, dirty dishes, empty bottles or cans, and toothpaste, soap, or other toiletries. These items need to be secured in your vehicle or in a bear-proof container. Coolers are not bear-proof.

Want to Learn More?

To learn more about Rocky Mountain wildlife and bear safety, talk to staff at any of the national park visitors centers. Interpretive programs held regularly in national park campgrounds often focus on bear safety.

Health Canada, the nation's public health agency, advises that you shouldn't drink any water in the great outdoors without treating it.

The main risk to backcountry travelers who drink untreated water is giardiasis, an intestinal illness caused by the *giardia* parasite that lives in streams, rivers, and lakes. Giardiasis symptoms, which include severe diarrhea, abdominal cramps, nausea, and sometimes vomiting or fever, typically begin between 6 and 16 days after you ingest the parasite.

If you must drink water from a backcountry source, boil it for 3-10 minutes or treat it with iodine. You can also use a water filter as long as it's small enough to block the *giardia*. Get more information about water treatment methods from **Health Canada** (www.hc-sc.gc.ca) or from staff at an outdoor equipment store like **MEC** (Mountain Equipment Co-op, www.mec.ca).

Heat Illnesses

When you're outdoors on especially hot days, wear loose-fitting, breathable clothing, sunglasses, and a hat with a brim to protect your face and head from the sun. Make sure to drink plenty of water, particularly when you're active. The higher elevations in the Canadian Rockies can make you more susceptible to **dehydration** or **heat exhaustion** than you might be at sea level.

Symptoms of heat-induced illness include dizziness or fainting, headache, decreased urination and/or unusually dark yellow urine, nausea or vomiting, and rapid breathing and heartbeat. Try to move to a cool place and drink water right away.

If someone has a high body temperature, becomes confused, stops sweating, or becomes unconscious, he or she may be suffering from **heat stroke.** Call 911 or seek medical attention immediately.

Winter Travel

Winter in the Canadian Rockies and in the mountainous regions of B.C. is cold, and it can snow at any time, particularly between October and March. For outdoor activities, dress in layers: a warm, water-repellent jacket, a fleece sweater, and long underwear, along with gloves or mittens and well-lined waterproof boots. Wearing a hat, ideally one that covers your ears, is especially important, since you lose a significant amount of heat through your head.

One risk of cold-weather travel is **frostbite,** which occurs primarily in the extremities: hands, feet, ears, and nose. To protect its core temperature, your body restricts blood flow to these outlying body parts when the temperature dips below freezing (32°F/0°C). In the early stages of frostbite, your skin can turn white or yellow. Once you get warm, the skin should regain its normal color; if it doesn't, or if the area remains numb, seek medical attention.

If your overall body temperature begins to drop due to extreme cold, you're at risk of **hypothermia,** a condition where your body is losing heat faster than it can retain it. You begin to shiver, and your hands or feet may turn numb.

To treat mild hypothermia, try to get to a warm place and keep your muscles moving. Remove wet clothing, wrap up in a blanket or sleeping bag, and drink warm sweet liquids. While drinking alcohol may make you think that you're warmer, it can actually prevent you from recognizing the degree to which your body is losing heat, increasing your risk of hypothermia.

Fatigue, nausea, or rapid shallow breathing can indicate that the hypothermia is becoming more severe. As it worsens, you may feel confused or uncoordinated. Call 911 or go to a hospital emergency room if these symptoms occur.

Internet Resources

Canada
Destination Canada
www.canada.travel
The government of Canada's official guide to travel across the country.

Parks Canada
www.pc.gc.ca
The federal government agency that manages national parks and national historic sites across Canada. The Parks Canada website has details about things to do, camping, hiking, and other activities in the parks in the West and throughout the country.

Parks Canada Reservation Service
www.reservation.pc.gc.ca
Reservations booking service for Canada's national park campgrounds.

Citizenship and Immigration Canada
www.cic.gc.ca
The federal government agency responsible for overseeing visitors and immigrants to Canada, including information about visitor visas, work permits, study permits, and applications for permanent residence.

Canada Border Services Agency
www.cbsa-asfc.gc.ca
The federal government agency that manages Canada's borders, including what items visitors can bring into Canada. The website also shows wait times at highway border crossings.

Environment Canada
www.weather.gc.ca
Provides weather forecasts and historical weather data for locations across Canada.

British Columbia
Destination British Columbia
www.hellobc.com
British Columbia's provincial tourism agency, which provides travel tips and information for the region and operates a network of visitors centers.

British Columbia Wine Institute
www.winebc.com
Has a detailed website with information about wineries and wine-touring tips in the Okanagan, Vancouver Island, and elsewhere in British Columbia.

Tourism Vancouver
www.tourismvancouver.com
Vancouver's tourism agency provides event schedules, tips for getting around, neighborhood profiles, and other information about the city's sights, hotels, restaurants, shops, and experiences.

Tourism Vancouver Island
www.vancouverisland.travel
Provides a free guide to things to do across Vancouver Island, available online and in print from area visitors centers.

Destination Greater Victoria
www.tourismvictoria.com
Promoting tourism in the city of Victoria, this organization runs a year-round information center on Victoria's Inner Harbour and provides information about attractions and activities, events, accommodations, and restaurants.

Tourism Whistler
www.whistler.com
Representing the Whistler region, this tourism agency has information to help you plan a mountain trip in any season.

Tourism Kamloops
www.tourismkamloops.com
Operates the Kamloops Visitor Centre and provides detailed information about the Kamloops region, including things to do and local events.

Tourism Kelowna
www.tourismkelowna.com
Provides information about the city of

Kelowna and the surrounding Okanagan region, including wineries, wine tours, outdoor activities, and events.

Tourism Revelstoke
www.seerevelstoke.com

This tourism organization publishes a free guide to the Revelstoke area that's available online and in print at the local visitors center.

Tourism Golden
www.tourismgolden.com

Golden's tourism agency provides information about the B.C. Rockies region, including the area's national parks, on its website, which also has an online trip-planning tool.

Kootenay Rockies Tourism
www.kootenayrockies.com

This regional tourism organization in eastern British Columbia has a detailed website with lots of itinerary suggestions and other ideas for planning a trip through the Kootenay-Rockies region.

Tourism Fernie
www.tourismfernie.com

Provides information about things to see and do, festivals, events, and other travel details for the town of Fernie and vicinity in southeastern B.C.

Nelson Kootenay Lake Tourism
www.nelsonkootenaylake.com

Provides travel information for Nelson, Kaslo, and the surrounding Kootenay Lake area in B.C.'s West Kootenays region.

Alberta
Travel Alberta
www.travelalberta.com

Tourism agency for the province of Alberta, providing travel tips and information about the region and operating a network of visitors centers.

Banff-Lake Louise Tourism
www.banfflakelouise.com

This area tourism organization has a detailed website with information about the towns of Banff and Lake Louise and about Banff National Park in the Canadian Rockies.

Tourism Jasper
www.jasper.travel

Produces an annual Jasper visitors guide, available in print and online, and also provides information on its website about things to do, places to stay, and events in and around Jasper National Park.

Tourism Calgary
www.visitcalgary.com

Calgary's tourism agency provides event schedules, tips for getting around, neighborhood profiles, and other information about the sights, hotels, restaurants, shops, and experiences in this city that's a gateway to the Canadian Rockies.

INDEX

QR

S

LIST OF MAPS

PHOTO CREDITS